McGRAW-HILL SERIES IN MARKETING AN

ROBERT D. BUZZELL, *Consulting Editor*

---

Baker—ADVERTISING LAYOUT AND ART DIRECTION
Baker—VISUAL PERSUASION
Barton—ADVERTISING AGENCY OPERATIONS AND MANAGEMENT
Barton—MEDIA IN ADVERTISING
Boyd, Fryburger, and Westfall—CASES IN ADVERTISING MANAGEMENT
Britt—THE SPENDERS
Britt and Boyd—MARKETING MANAGEMENT AND ADMINISTRATIVE ACTION
Brown, Cardozo, Cunningham, Salmon, and Sultan—PROBLEMS IN MARKETING
Buell—MARKETING MANAGEMENT IN ACTION
Crisp—MARKETING RESEARCH
Crisp—SALES PLANNING AND CONTROL
Dichter—HANDBOOK OF CONSUMER MOTIVATIONS
Dunn—ADVERTISING COPY AND COMMUNICATION
Haas—HOW TO DEVELOP SUCCESSFUL SALESMEN
Hattwick—THE NEW PSYCHOLOGY OF SELLING
Lazo and Corbin—MANAGEMENT IN MARKETING
Levitt—INNOVATION IN MARKETING
Lucas and Britt—MEASURING ADVERTISING EFFECTIVENESS
Martineau—MOTIVATION IN ADVERTISING
Mauser—MODERN MARKETING MANAGEMENT
Messner—INDUSTRIAL ADVERTISING
Norins—THE COMPLEAT COPYWRITER
Seehafer and Laemmar—SUCCESSFUL TELEVISION AND RADIO ADVERTISING
Stanton—FUNDAMENTALS OF MARKETING
Weir—TRUTH IN ADVERTISING
Weiss—MERCHANDISING FOR TOMORROW
Wolff—WHAT MAKES WOMEN BUY
Wright and Warner—ADVERTISING
Wright and Warner—SPEAKING OF ADVERTISING
Yeck and Maguire—PLANNING AND CREATING BETTER DIRECT MAIL

# MARKETING MANAGEMENT & ADMINISTRATIVE ACTION

*Completely Revised Edition*

STEUART HENDERSON BRITT, PH.D. IN PSYCHOLOGY
*Professor of Marketing, Graduate School of Business,*
*and Professor of Advertising, Medill School of Journalism*
*Northwestern University*

HARPER W. BOYD, JR., PH.D. IN MARKETING
*Sebastian S. Kresge Professor of Marketing*
*Director, International Center for the Advancement of*
*Management Education, Graduate School of Business*
*Stanford University*

McGRAW-HILL BOOK COMPANY
*New York St. Louis San Francisco Toronto London Sydney*

**MARKETING MANAGEMENT**
**AND ADMINISTRATIVE ACTION**
**Completely revised edition**



*Library of Congress Catalog Card Number 68-13089*

5 6 7 8 9 0 M A M M 7 5 4 3 2 1 0

To P.Y.E. and L.A.B.

# PREFACE

This is a completely revised edition of our 1963 book *Marketing Management and Administrative Action.*

Time has not eroded the significance of the materials in our original book. However, because marketing is an ever-changing and complex subject, 46 of the 70 selections in the first edition have been replaced, mainly with more recent materials.

Of the 62 selections in the present book 45, appeared in print during the 1960s, 16 during the 1950s, and 1 (by Veblen) in the 1890s. Only 24 of the 62 selections are from the earlier volume.

Yet the basic theme of the book, as for the previous one, is that marketing is not a collection of discrete marketing activities, but rather helps to unify a variety of activities of the business firm. As before, the purpose was to include those materials that make the greatest contribution in a broad context to understanding marketing management and administrative action. This has meant on our part careful consideration of all of the materials in our 1963 book, plus diligent reading and screening of countless articles and books on various phases of marketing.

Even though the readings in the present volume differ from those in the 1963 book, essentially the same basic topics as before constitute the framework of the book. The principal change has been to move the section on "Organizing the Marketing Function" from the next-to-last part of the book to Part II; and the order of the six major topics is now:

I. *The Scope* of Marketing Management
II. *Organizing* the Marketing Function
III. Establishing the Marketing *Objectives*
IV. Developing the Marketing *Plan*
V. Putting the Marketing Plan Into *Action*
VI. *Appraising and Controlling* the Marketing Program

For each selection in the book, *the author's affiliation is indicated as of the date the material was published.*

We appreciate the opportunity to reproduce materials from the following sources:

*Associations, Foundations, and Individuals:*

American Management Association, Inc.
American Marketing Association
Association of National Advertisers, Inc.
Foundation for Research on Human Behavior
The Paraffined Carton Research Council
Seymour Banks, Leo Burnett Company, Inc.

*Periodicals:*

*American Economic Review*
*American Sociological Review*
*Business Horizons*
*Business Topics*
*California Management Review*
*Cost and Profit Outlook*
*Harvard Business Review*
*Journal of Advertising Research*
*Journal of Marketing*
*The Management Review*

*Publishers:*

Appleton-Century-Crofts
Harcourt, Brace & World, Inc.
McGraw-Hill Book Company
University of Chicago Press
University of Illinois Press
The University of Michigan
The Viking Press, Inc.
Wadsworth Publishing Company
John Wiley & Sons, Inc.
Yale University Press

Special thanks go to Mrs. Dru Evarts, Mrs. Irene E. Peach, and to Mr. Robert E. Donath for assistance in the preparation of this book.

*January 1, 1968*

*Steuart Henderson Britt*

*and*

*Harper W. Boyd, Jr.*

# Contents

Page

# MARKETING MANAGEMENT & ADMINISTRATIVE ACTION

# I

# *The Scope of Marketing Management*

*Too frequently the study of marketing management is viewed along quite narrow lines. For example, the management of the sales operation or management of some other specific subject area is discussed without reference to the fact that the subjects–such as product planning, personal selling, advertising, channels of distribution, physical distribution, and inventory control–need to be "blended" together. Rarely in print has there been much emphasis on the impact of marketing on the totality of the management operation.*

*Accordingly, the selections included in this first section show the magnitude of the marketing task and how it relates to all aspects of the work of the business firm.*

*The materials demonstrate the increasing importance of marketing as a way of business life, the role that marketing plays in the administrative process, the origins and reasons for the development of the marketing concept, and the need and opportunities for more scientific management in marketing.*

*After all, marketing is not a specialized activity to be carried out* only *by personnel assigned to the Marketing Department without regard for how decisions are made elsewhere in the firm.*

*Although the materials in this section on "The Scope of Marketing Management" are concerned with the firm's point of view, they also present a view of marketing which can be related directly to the well-being of the total economy.*

# 1. WHAT IS A BUSINESS?

*Peter F. Drucker*

*Peter Drucker was one of the earliest management writers to define the purpose of a business as that of satisfying consumer needs. His statements on this purpose as well as those on the entrepreneurial functions have been widely quoted.*

*The following material is included because of its significance to all those interested in management.*

If we want to know what a business is we have to start with its *purpose.* And its purpose must lie outside of the business itself. In fact, it must lie in society since a business enterprise is an organ of society. There is only one valid definition of business purpose: *to create a customer.*

Markets are not created by God, nature or economic forces, but by businessmen. The want they satisfy may have been felt by the customer before he was offered the means of satisfying it. It may indeed, like the want for food in a famine, have dominated the customer's life and filled all his waking moments. But it was a theoretical want before; only when the action of businessmen makes it effective demand is there a customer, a market. It may have been an unfelt want. There may have been no want at all until business action created it—by advertising, by salesmanship, or by inventing something new. In every case it is business action that creates the customer.

It is the customer who determines what a business is. For it is the customer, and he alone, who through being willing to pay for a good or for a service, converts economic resources into wealth, things into goods. What the business thinks it produces is not

Source: From *The Practice of Management*, Harper & Row, Publishers, Incorporated, New York, 1954, pp. 37-41.  Peter F. Drucker: Professor of Management, Graduate School of Business, New York University.

of first importance—especially not to the future of the business and to its success. What the customer thinks he is buying, what he considers "value," is decisive—it determines what a business is, what it produces and whether it will prosper.

The customer is the foundation of a business and keeps it in existence. He alone gives employment. And it is to supply the consumer that society entrusts wealth-producing resources to the business enterprise.

## THE TWO ENTREPRENEURIAL FUNCTIONS

Because it is its purpose to create a customer, any business enterprise has two—and only these two—basic functions: marketing and innovation. They are the entrepreneurial functions.

Marketing is the distinguishing, the unique function of the business. A business is set apart from all other human organizations by the fact that it markets a product or a service. Neither Church, nor Army, nor School, nor State does that. Any organization that fulfills itself through marketing a product or a service, is a business. Any organization in which marketing is either absent or incidental is not a business and should never be run as if it were one.

The first man to see marketing clearly as the unique and central function of the business enterprise, and the creation of a customer as the specific job of management, was Cyrus McCormick. The history books mention only that he invented a mechanical harvester. But he also invented the basic tools of modern marketing: market research and market analysis, the concept of market standing, modern pricing policies, the modern service-salesman, parts and service supply to the customer and installment credit. He is truly the father of business management. And he had done all this by 1850. It was not until fifty years later, however, that he was widely imitated even in his own country.

The economic revolution of the American economy since 1900 has in large part been a marketing revolution caused by the assumption of responsibility for creative, aggressive, pioneering marketing by American management. Fifty years ago the typical attitude of the American businessman toward marketing was still: "The sales department will sell whatever the plant produces." Today it is increasingly: "It is our job to produce what the market needs." But our economists and government officials are just beginning to understand this: only now, for instance, is the U.S. Department of Commerce setting up an Office of Distribution.

In Europe there is still almost no understanding that marketing is the specific business function—a major reason for the stagnation of the European economies of today. For to reach full realization of the importance of marketing requires overcoming a deep-rooted social prejudice against "selling" as ignoble and parasitical, and in favor of "production" as gentlemanly, with its resultant theoretical fallacy of considering production as the main and determining function of a business.

A good example of this historical attitude toward marketing are those big Italian companies which have no domestic sales managers even though the home market accounts for 70 per cent of their business.

Actually marketing is so basic that it is not just enough to have a strong sales department and to entrust marketing to it. Marketing is not only much broader than selling, it is not a specialized activity at all. It encompasses the entire business. It is the whole business seen from the point of view of its final result, that is, from the customer's point of view. Concern and responsibility for marketing must therefore permeate all areas of the enterprise.

One illustration of this concept of marketing is the policy worked out by the General Electric Company over the last ten years, which attempts to build customer and market appeal into the product from the design stage on. It considers the actual act of selling but the last step in a sales effort that began before the first engineer put pencil to drawing paper. This, according to a statement in the company's 1952 annual report, "introduces the marketing man at the beginning rather than the end of the production cycle and would integrate marketing into each phase of the business. Thus marketing, through its studies and research, will establish for the engineer, the designer and the manufacturing man what the customer wants in a given product, what price he is willing to pay, and where and when it will be wanted. Marketing would have authority in product planning, production scheduling and inventory control, as well as in the sales distribution and servicing of the product."

## THE ENTERPRISE AS THE ORGAN OF ECONOMIC GROWTH

But marketing alone does not make a business enterprise. In a static economy there are no "business enterprises." There are not even "businessmen." For the "middleman" of a static society is simply a "broker" who receives his compensation in the form of a fee.

A business enterprise can exist only in an expanding economy, or at least in one which considers change both natural and desirable. And business is the specific organ of growth, expansion and change.

The second function of a business is therefore *innovation*, that is, the provision of better and more economic goods and services. It is not enough for the business to provide just any economic goods and services; it must provide better and more economic ones. It is not necessary for a business to grow bigger; but it is necessary that it constantly grow better.

Innovation may take the form of lower price—the form with which the economist has been most concerned, for the simple reason that it is the only one that can be handled by his quantitative tools. But it may also be a new and better product (even at a higher price), a new convenience or the creation of a new want. It may be finding new uses for old products. A salesman who succeeded in selling refrigerators to the Eskimos to prevent food from freezing would be an "innovator" quite as much as if he had developed brand-new processes or invented a new product. To sell the Eskimos a refrigerator to keep food cold is finding a new market; to sell a refrigerator to keep food from getting too cold is actually creating a new product. Technologically there is, of course, only the same old product; but economically there is innovation.

Innovation goes right through all phases of business. It may be innovation in design, in product, in marketing techniques. It may be innovation in price or in service to the customer. It may be innovation in management organization or in management methods. Or it may be a new insurance policy that makes it possible for a businessman to assume new risks. The most effective innovations in American industry in the last few years were probably not the much publicized new electronic or chemical products and processes but innovations in materials handling and in manager development.

Innovation extends through all forms of business. It is as important to a bank, an insurance company or a retail store as it is to a manufacturing or engineering business.

In the organization of business enterprise innovation can therefore no more be considered a separate function than marketing. It is not confined to engineering or research but extends across all parts of the business, all functions, all activities. It is not, to repeat, confined to manufacturing business alone. Innovation in distribution has been as important as innovation in manufacturing; and so has been innovation in an insurance company or in a bank.

The leadership in innovation with respect to product and service can normally be focused in one functional activity which is responsible for nothing else. This is always true in a business with a strong engineering or chemical flavor. In an insurance company, too, a special department charged with leadership responsibility for the development of new kinds of coverage is in order; and there might well be another such department charged with innovation in the organization of sales, the administration of policies and the settling of claims. For both together are the insurance company's business.

A large railroad company has organized two centers of innovation, both under a vice-president. One is concerned with systematic work on all physical aspects of transportation: locomotives and cars, tracks, signals, communications. The other is concerned with innovation in freight and passenger service, the development of new sources of traffic, new tariff policies, the opening of new markets, the development of new service, etc.

But every other managerial unit of the business should also have clear responsibility and definite goals for innovation. It should be responsible for its contribution to innovation in the company's product or service; and it should in addition strive consciously and with direction toward advancement of the art in the particular area in which it is engaged: selling or accounting, quality control or personnel management.

# 2. WHAT IS THE MARKETING MANAGEMENT CONCEPT?

*J. B. McKitterick*

*During the past decade the marketing management concept has received an ever-increasing amount of attention from business executives. Actually as a concept it is not new, since marketing textbooks have long advocated the need for the firm to be "market-oriented." What is new, however, is the amount of attention the marketing management concept is receiving, especially in regard to its impact on planning and organization.*

*This article traces the historical evaluation of the concept and does so within the framework of the total economic system. It also discusses the implications of the concept in decision-making.*

Anyone who gets a new idea bearing on business philosophy and who then takes the trouble to scan corresponding utterances of preceding generations will return to this thought with increased awareness of its apparent lack of originality. In an attempt to locate the historic significance of this marketing concept that we are going to discuss today, I started reading the 1930 and 1940 issues of the *Journal of Marketing* and the *Harvard Business Review.* To my surprise, I found that many of the viewpoints expressed and the stances advocated on business philosophy bear striking resemblance to current writings. Indeed, what really seems to have changed are the phenomena–the goings on–that the authors cite to validate the importance and rationale of their message. So we have here a not unfamiliar problem in the social sciences; namely that words change their meaning much more slowly than the things to which they refer.

Source: From Frank M. Bass (ed.), *The Frontiers of Marketing Thought and Science,* American Marketing Association, Chicago, 1957, pp. 71–82. J. B. McKitterick: Manager, Marketing Services Research Service, General Electric Company.

This is particularly true of concepts such as profit, overhead, productivity and marketing orientation—which deal not so much with things that happen as with ways of thinking about them.

In order to map changing meanings, it frequently is helpful to superimpose on a history of thought some crude scheme of classification which takes its definitions from the present. If we do this in the case of the marketing concept, we will notice that over the last thirty years the preoccupation of businessmen with the customer increasingly has been formulated in terms of an end rather than in terms of a means. Correspondingly, the conception of profit as the end objective in business seems to have declined, with a tendency to view it more as a basic condition that must be satisfied. To be sure, thirty years ago businessmen admonished each other to keep the customer's interests in mind, but they usually connected this focus merely with their own need to adjust prices and volume of production to what the market would accept. Indeed, if we read between the lines, we find that the customer used to be the chap that you sent the bill to—frequently a distributor, agent, or dealer, but very rarely the actual end user. And sales tactics were conceived in terms of exploiting some scheme that would permit dealing with these trade institutions on a semi-exclusive basis. There was almost no mention of the idea that the manufacturer should focus his attention on the end user, and base his competitive footing on some superiority of value that matched with the needs of a particular group of these users. And it was obvious that few manufacturers felt that they had ability to look at the trade structure as a group of institutions for hire, to be selected and employed to perform specific functions that this end user needed. On the contrary, the trade structure was regarded as an impenetrable barrier—it *was* the market, and this fellow we have been calling the end user was the exclusive problem of the dealer, and no concern of the manufacturer.

Occasionally someone like Oswald Knauth, who has always been a bit ahead of his time, would remind the manufacturer that packaging and product styling had better be customer oriented. But by comparison to these occasional warnings to the man at the helm to keep his eye on what the customer was doing, there were urgent exhortations to the man in the engine room to get more output with less input. Indeed, the problem of winning out over competition seemed to be conceived essentially in terms of subtracting from the costs of production, and delivering an equivalent product at a lower price. So it was quite fitting that in the 1930s manufacturers studied the economics of scale, economists explored marginal concepts for setting the volume of production, and the government tried to prevent the large and efficient firm from sinking its smaller adversaries with the torpedo of lower price. In a short body of remarks it is out of scale to put a generalization such as this to adequate test, yet I cannot entirely resist some elaboration, because the social implications of what we call the marketing concept in the end are going to be of much greater importance than its bearing on management theory.

If we examine the 1920-1940 period, we find that it witnessed great gains in productivity, but not all of these gains were distributed to the labor force. The installed horsepower per production worker almost doubled, and the output per worker more than doubled. However, the average hourly wage in these twenty years increased only from 50 cents to 66 cents—not quite a third, and the number of production workers stayed almost constant at around 8½ million members in a population that actually grew by over 20 per cent. So, with rising productivity only to a limited degree passed on to the static body of production workers in the form of wage increases, consumer prices fell steadily until in 1940 they were only 70 per cent of the 1920 level, and unemployment in a growing population was a serious and long continuing problem. During this same period, the design and manner of use of most products changed only slowly, and the gross national product increased a scant 14 per cent.

To sum it up, the business ideology of producing the same product for less cost scarcely turned out to be an adequate driving force for economic growth. While a great deal of criticism was directed at the imperfections of markets organized around administered prices, subsequent events suggest that the real trouble was that most consumers had inadequate income and inadequate reason to buy. In short, productivity gains unevenly accompanied by innovation of new products and broad distribution of purchasing power resulted in a condition of chronic underconsumption.

Starting around 1940, the threat of war and the sponsorship of government combined to introduce a basic transformation in the business process which has had far reaching consequences. In a nutshell, business discovered research. On the eve of this revolution the total research outlay of businessmen stood at perhaps 100 million dollars. Today, these outlays are somewhere around four billions, and for the first time over 50 per cent of all the research done in this country is being paid for by industry out of its own pocket. If we throw in the defense effort which the government pays for, the total research outlay rises to about 7.5 billions. However, our interest here is not so much in the growth of this new industry or the sheer size of its burden, which seems likely to surpass the total cost of all advertising; rather we are concerned to learn what research did to the growth of the economy and to the problems of designing and managing an enterprise.

Where the pre-1940 period was preoccupied with trying to make the same product cheaper, the postwar period saw a new dimension added to competition, in which the focus was to try and make the old product better, or even more bold, to try and launch a new product. And as the research-equipped manufacturer looked around for applications for his new-found creative power, he frequently discovered them in markets that he heretofore had not entered. The petroleum refinery began to turn out chemicals; the rubber plant, plastics; new alloys challenged older metals; electronics cast its shadows over hydraulics; and soon, everyone's research and competitive endeavor was attacking someone else's *status quo*. Established concepts of industry alignment began to obliterate, schemes narrowly conceived to defend market position in terms of price advantage proved inadequate; and managements began to contend with problems of uncertainty that had multiple dimensions. A labor plentiful economy overnight became a labor short economy, and even though the number of employees and production workers has grown 50 per cent since 1940, and their productivity probably another 50 per cent, still the demand for their services has grown even faster, and wages have gone up some 70 per cent in constant dollars. So here we had a reversal of the conditions of the preceding twenty years; worker income rose more rapidly than productivity, competition was focused on using research to obsolete old ways of doing things, a flood of new products poured forth to meet the rising discretionary spending power, and we became so impressed with the results of focusing on what would be better for the customer rather than merely cheaper that we invented a now familiar phrase—"the marketing concept"—to describe this triumph of innovation over productive capacity.

If we look back on these basic changes in the economy, we find clues to many of the problems which have concerned management science over the last ten years. I refer especially to the constant search for means of planning and control that can contend with these rapidly changing marketing conditions. For example, many businessmen have complained that the problem of predicting the customer's behavior has been greatly complicated both by his rapidly rising discretionary income and by his growing control over the use of leisure time. Mink coats and motor cars, buying things and buying experiences all have begun to interact, and the passing fad and the more slowly changing style of life of which it is a part have become very difficult to diagnose and distinguish. And as we already have noted, the industrial customer with his multiple raw material and process alternatives, and his possibilities of sub-contracting entire operations, swimming all the while in his own competitive sea of changing functions and market alignments, presents an equally fickle target for prediction.

At the same time both the need for and difficulty of business planning have been heightened by technological trends in the production and distribution process. The long term commitments required by automated plants, guaranteed wages, basic research, and multi-million dollar national promotions imply not only irreversible decisions, but also greater lead time, because the assumptions in planning have to hold good over a longer and longer period as the separation between decision and implementation grows apace. The annual budget in many companies has been supplemented with the five-year and even the twenty-year plan. The very considerable risks entailed in these large resource commitments, combined with the increasing hazards posed by the caprice of the customer and the research efforts of an undefined arena of prospective competitors, have resulted in a powerful urge for diversification. Few businesses today seem to be able to undertake the risk of staying in a single market with a single product. Indeed, observing the pell-mell flight to add new products and markets, one might say that the most characteristic response of modern corporations to uncertainty is to refuse to choose. As new product applications emerge, as new categories of customers come into the market, as new technologies compete to answer the old need, the corporation is inclined to embrace each in turn, forfeiting no opportunity, straddling all risks.

In due course, the organization structure begins to grow like a Christmas tree as the work of decision making is subdivided to take advantage of the specialized information and skills required. The sales executive is joined by the service manager, the product development manager, the advertising manager, the distribution planning manager, the market research director, and the whole team is duplicated anew as further lines are added. Many decisions become difficult to deal with in such a structure because they straddle the responsibilities of individuals. And when it comes to prepare purposive plans, the business is troubled by its inability to bring its own identity into view—to see entirely its unique resources, skills and commitments, and the whole market environment of which they are a part.

Finally, in analyzing this planning problem and its bearing on the marketing concept, something probably should be said about the decline of the owner-manager. The great size of modern enterprise, the progressive tax structures, and the new-found affluence of even the most lowly worker all have combined to lessen the inclination and ability of individuals to undertake an entrepreneurial role in many markets. Fortunately, the very economic growth which rules out individual enterprise in one area opens up an opportunity for it somewhere else—as in the service industries. But it is my impression that the passing of the entrepreneur, where it has occurred, has removed an important element in the planning process, because he supplied the reason for planning in the sense that he specified the objectives to be attained. Indeed, this entrepreneur made planning easy—if at the same time fickle—by telling people what he wanted to accomplish, and the whole matter was scarcely less personal or more complicated than his choice of a necktie for the day. In the modern corporation we have replaced the owner-manager with a hired management accountable in concept to a diffuse and rapidly changing body of shareholders, but actually in performance quite sensitive to the appraisal of multiple audiences among customers, suppliers, labor, financial institutions, government and the public at large. By degrees, therefore, the decline of perfect competition and the decline of the entrepreneur with his simple conception of objectives are not unrelated events. Today's complex markets with many dimensions of competition have been accompanied by a corresponding multiplication of the values to be reconciled in the policies of modern enterprises.

So to summarize, business management has very difficult planning decisions to make, requiring that it foresee and analyze many alternate developments relating to its customers, competitors, and its own resources, and management must get these decisions made by people who are organized in an enormously complex structure, in which they are aware of the interrelationships of their part and the business, but unable to adequately see the whole business and its environment, and the ends to be served by all these forecasts and decisions are becoming increasingly diffuse and uncertain. It is in this sort of setting that the marketing concept was born, and it is my belief, after reflecting both on the background of the movement and the many statements of the case which businessmen have set forth, that what this really represents is a search for a management philosophy—a primacy of decision values—that can restore order and manageability out of what threatens to seem like chaos. Indeed, at the risk of introducing controversy, I would speculate that looking back on this development twenty years hence, the marketing concept belatedly will be recognized as an appropriate voicing of the basic purpose of corporate institutions grown too large to be adequately guided by the profit interests of a single compact group of owners. Certainly, anyone who carefully subtracts out of the total expenses of a modern business all of the sums expended on preparation for the future—ranging from research and advertising to new plant and training of personnel—is bound to discover that profit is a feeble measure of the current day's battle with competition, and is certainly meaningless if not considered with reference to accompanying changes in market position. With many companies today operating in conditions of oligopoly, it is small wonder that enlargement of the market and competitive share held in that market have become matters of management concern at least equal if not prerequisite to profit.

Now I want to turn from the general economic conditions and management problems which accompanied the emergency of the marketing concept to a discussion of its implications for business practices. Necessarily, this will be a highly personal statement because it is next to impossible to synthesize into a single theme what others have already set forth on this subject. It does seem to me, however, that the real distinction of the marketing concept which leads to the conclusion "this company has it" or "this one doesn't," is not so much a matter of organization structure or day-to-day tactics as it is a matter of what the management is trying to accomplish.

A moment ago I referred to the shifting focus of objectives that has characterized the evolution of modern business enterprise—first, from a focus on profit for the owner to a striving for market position and success against competition, and most recently to a focus on growth in which there is a continuing planned effort to enlarge the size of the market. It seems to me that the crux of the marketing concept is expressed in the latter not by depriving its historic competitors of the market position which they already have captured, but by the application of research and insight to the task of creating new markets—indeed, new businesses—then we know that we are dealing with a management that has fully embraced the marketing concept. To be sure, as already has been brought out rather fully, any such endeavor is not without its economic repercussions in other markets and industries, but the very extent of these effects, reaching as they do to far and foreign places, confirms that something more than a minor improvement in the lot of the customer must have occurred. So to say it precisely, a company committed to the marketing concept focuses its major innovative effort on enlarging the size of the market in which it participates by introducing new generic products and services, by promoting new applications for existing products, and by seeking out new classes of customers who heretofore have not used the existing products.

In all cases the word "new" means more than just new to the company in question. It means "new," period. This is a somewhat more rigorous definition than to merely say that the business must constantly think of the customers' best interests or put supremacy in marketing functions foremost. And I might add that the rigor is deliberate, because only thinking of the customer and mere technical proficiency in marketing both turn out to be inferior hands when played against the company that couples its thoughts with action and actually comes to market with a successful innovation. To be sure, the business that seeks to apply its research and mass production and national promotion prowess to such ambitious notions as doing really new things is going to have to be knowledgeably benign with respect to the customer, and it certainly will reduce its risk to the degree that it is experienced and skillful in its marketing organization. But if the product and the service and the way they are sold are fundamentally in the customer's best interests, a great deal of amateurism in marketing tactics can be tolerated without serious consequences. Turning the issue around, if business enterprises are to compete successfully in the quicksilver of modern markets, something more than sophistication in means of doing marketing work is going to be required. Indeed, to plan at all, and think adequately of what competition might do and its possible effects before committing multi-million dollar resources, requires knowledge of the customer which penetrates to the level of theory. *So the principal task of the marketing function in a management concept is not so much to be skillful in making the customer do what suits the interests of the business as to be skillful in conceiving and then making the business do what suits the interests of the customer.* As Frank Knight observed some years ago, in conditions of real uncertainty, the outcome of a venture will be controlled much more by the entrepreneurial decision on what major course of action to undertake than by expert practice in implementation.[1] Thus, the central meaning of the marketing concept to the decision structure of a business is that the major purpose of the venture is taken from the need to solve some problem in the outer environment–some betterment for the customer–and all subsidiary decisions dealing with the acquisition and allocation of resources within the business are bent to that objective. In this light, certain tests can be applied to our daily business practices which sharpen the distinction between the marketing concept and the mere awareness in management that superiority in the marketing function is beginning to be of greater strategic importance than superiority in the production function.

For example, we might ask, is the service of customers or defense against competition the main focus of the creative search for better courses of action? Is the business in the habit of undertaking tactics which pay their way in added sales volume, but which in prompt imitation by competition fail to add to profit? If so, is the overall marketing effort really adding consumable value for the customer, or only adding cost–as for instance, advertising expenditures which seek to make like products seem unlike, and product redesign which attempts to produce obsolescence without adding to the functions performed by the product? Is the business constantly exhausting itself, trying to hold back changes introduced by its competitors–as when it refuses to recognize a new product technology, a new service, or a new sales channel which the customer seems to prefer? Is foolish pride–as the songwriter puts it–causing the management to reject the verdict of the marketplace? Is the business trying to be all things to all customers when their requirements and interests in the product are so fragmenting that some forfeiture of clientele and specialization of customer alignment obviously are needed? Is what the business considers a good salesman essentially a customer oriented man or is he a loyal "company" man, intent on making the customer understand his employer's policies? And finally, is the business using its resources and ability to innovate on tasks that smaller competitors with less overhead can handle better, or is it taxing its capacities to the fullest in undertakings that really challenge it?

These are fairly direct questions, but the answers turn on rather subtle differences in the marketing posture of a company. By and large, it is my observation that concerns

[1] Frank H. Knight, *Risk, Uncertainty, and Profit,* Houghton Mifflin Company, Boston, 1921.

which are in an active growth phase will pass this sort of test; those that have slowed down and see themselves as digging in for a defense against younger, more vigorous competitors in time will fail the test. Certainly, anyone who examines the turnover in rankings of the hundred largest corporations, or the turnover in the leadership position in even the smallest markets, cannot fail to see that the graveyards of business are full of those who conceived their obligations to the customer too narrowly.

Now, one might ask, how can the active growth phase of a company be infinitely prolonged? In the end, will not the constant adding of new products, new applications and new users lead to a loss of identity and a nomadlike wandering over the entire market terrain? And how does a company so oriented—or disoriented—respond to the attack of competition? Must every action pass the test of what is truly in the customer's interests? To be sure, these are important questions. But much of the difficulty is removed if we remember that it often is in the interests of both the customer and the company that it abandon a market, that it forego an existing product line and forfeit some present clientele to competition.

Where two groups of product users have different requirements in either the product or the services that go with it, the constant temptation is to suppress these differences, to force homogenization of the requirements, and we all are familiar with examples of the skillful use of price policy, engineering standards, advertising, and product design to such ends. Yet when such an unnatural marriage is challenged by a competitor who selects only one of the two user groups as his intended clientele, a competitor who aligns all his decisions in the interests of that single group and who brings to it a specially designed product, then the profit position of the company that is straddling the issue is likely to become quite untenable. In the same way, a company may choose to deal with two unrelated markets in a manner that is dictated by the desire to apply some common technology or shared resource of production or distribution. The endeavor in each market being limited by the requirements of the opposite market, this company, too, is vulnerable to a competitor that specializes in only one of these undertakings. So I submit, it is no prescription of dogma but the hard facts of competition that argue for coupling a program of innovation and growth with a sharp pruning knife to cut out the commitments that threaten to compromise the marketing concept. If we all freely admitted our mistakes and were prompt in forfeiting a losing battle to competition, a great deal of pointless advertising could be turned into profit, and a substantial improvement could be worked in sales to other markets where efforts have been less than customer oriented due to the conflicts that have been baked in. Indeed, it is precisely because of this constant need for pruning that companies which were guided by pre-war notions of production efficiency, and which grew along lines of by-product diversification and vertical integration are in the gravest sort of difficulty today. Hence the most cogent argument for designing an industrial enterprise from the customer backward into the factory, rather than from the production process forward, so to speak, is that the success of the venture is becoming much less dependent on its production efficiency and much more dependent on its flexibility in adjusting to the risks posed by the changing requirements of its customers.

In closing now I want to briefly refer to the implications of this marketing concept to the society at large. Recently several provocative viewpoints have been set forth on the threat of underconsumption in our economy. David Riesman has raised the question as to whether business enthusiasm for the defense effort is entirely explained by patriotic and profit considerations. Melman in his recent book has theorized that a substantial part of the productive output of our economy is burned up in the form of administrative overhead—useless labor that we enjoy doing—but which does not lead to further gains in productivity.[2] Several recent books have looked askance at trends in advertising which attempt to subversively guide buying behavior. All in all, there is considerable evidence of a somewhat latent but chronic concern among businessmen with the possibility that we are able to produce more than people will consume. Hence, perhaps we do welcome the creation of markets by the government as a source of stability, and perhaps we are elaborating a style of management and distribution functions that is sort of subconsciously wasteful and antithetical to the interests of the consumer. There are two reasons why even in the presence of scant evidence such trends deserve sober consideration.

In the first place, if, as we all pray, this armed preparedness leads to peace rather than to war, then we will be thrown into an economic contest with Russia in which their political system, through lower labor costs and near equal technology, will battle for our foreign markets. If it turns out that we have built a style of competition and type of business venture in this country that burdens our native genius for manufacturing efficiency with a staggering load of nonproductive overhead and distribution costs, we then may find ourselves a country-island of democracy in a sea of communism. More hopefully, if we conceive of marketing as the work of finding out what the customer would consider a better product and a better way to sell it, and use motivation and all these other new research and communication techniques to help the customer to advise the business on such questions, and if we then apply all of our war-born technology to problems of human betterment, guiding the effort with a marketing concept that insists upon constant innovation—then the heat of competition in our economy will be made to yield up consumable value and real economic growth, and our concern with under-consumption and fear for the outcome of a contest with a state-directed economic system will be pointless in the extreme.

In the second place, there has been a long continuing harangue in Washington over the state of competition in American markets. Administered prices and conditions of oligopoly are deplored as a counterfeit type of competition which resists true economic progress. Ironically, the very same postwar period that heightened these concerns has witnessed the development of an intensive form of competition that has ranged far and wide across the traditional market and industry boundaries. As I see it, the greatest asset of our present industrial structure is that the declining number of companies in each market has been accompanied by an increasing number of markets for each company, so that today, more than ever before, hundreds of American businesses are sufficiently diversified to undertake the great risks of real innovation.

[2] Seymour Melman, *Dynamic Factors in Industrial Productivity,* John Wiley & Sons, Inc., New York, 1956.

In the final analysis, it is the basic purpose of the marketing concept to exploit this risk-taking and product developing capacity, reckoning with all the uncertainties and making a positive virtue out of an economic system that offers the customer a choice, and at that, a choice that is not confined to price alone, but one that explores the full dimensions of the consumption experience.

# 3. MANAGEMENT MYOPIA

*Theodore Levitt*

*The author elaborates on the Peter Drucker concept that the primary objective of a firm is to "create a customer." He does so by stating the premise that the failure of a firm to develop is not because the industry has stopped growing or is in decline, but rather because management has failed to think in terms of market requirements as well as product requirements.*

*The author also discusses the timely subject of R&D expenditures and notes that all too often too much is spent on R&D instead of finding out first what customers want and need.*

## SHADOW OF OBSOLESCENCE

It is impossible to mention a single major industry that did not at one time qualify for the magic appellation of "growth industry." In each case its assumed strength lay in the apparently unchallenged superiority of its product. There appeared to be no effective substitute for it. It was itself a runaway substitute for the product it so triumphantly replaced. Yet one after another of these celebrated industries has come under a shadow. Let us look briefly at a few more of them, this time taking examples that have so far received a little less attention:

*Dry Cleaning.* This was once a growth industry with lavish prospects. In an age of wool garments, imagine finally being able to get them safely and easily cleaned. The boom was on.

Source: From *Innovation in Marketing: New Perspectives for Profit and Growth,* McGraw-Hill Book Company, New York, © 1962, pp. 43–50, 54–71. Used by permission of McGraw-Hill Book Company.
Theodore Levitt: Lecturer on Business Administration, Harvard University Graduate School of Business Administration.

Yet here we are thirty years after the boom started, and the industry is in trouble. Where has the competition come from? From a better way of cleaning? No. It has come from synthetic fibers and chemical additives that have cut the need for dry cleaning. But this is only the beginning. Lurking in the wings and ready to make chemical dry cleaning totally obsolescent is that powerful magician, ultrasonics.

*Electrical Utilities.* This is another one of those supposedly "no-substitute" products which has been enthroned on a pedestal of invincible growth. When the incandescent lamp came along, kerosene lights were finished. Later the water wheel and the steam engine were cut to ribbons by the flexibility, reliability, simplicity, and just plain easy availability of electric motors. The prosperity of electrical utilities continues to wax extravagant as the home is converted into a museum of electrical gadgetry. How can anybody miss by investing in utilities, with no competition, nothing but growth ahead?

But a second look is not quite so comforting. A score of nonutility companies are well advanced toward developing a powerful chemical fuel cell which could sit in some hidden closet of every home silently ticking off electric power. The electric lines that vulgarize so many neighborhoods will be eliminated—so will the endless demolition of streets and service interruptions during storms. Also on the horizon is solar energy, again pioneered by nonutility companies.

Who says that the utilities have no competition? They may be natural monopolies now, but tomorrow they may die natural deaths. To avoid this, they too will have to develop fuel cells, solar energy, and other power sources. To survive, they themselves will have to plot the obsolescence of what now produces their livelihood.

*Grocery Stores.* Many people find it hard to realize that there ever was a thriving establishment known as the "corner grocery store." The supermarket has taken over with a powerful effectiveness. Yet the big food chains of the 1930s narrowly escaped being completely wiped out by the aggressive expansion of independent supermarkets. The first genuine supermarket was opened in 1930, in Jamaica, Long Island. By 1933 supermarkets were thriving in California, Ohio, Pennsylvania, and elsewhere. Yet the established chains pompously ignored them. When they chose to notice them, it was with such derisive descriptions as "cheapy," "horse and buggy," "cracker-barrel storekeeping," and "unethical opportunists."

An executive of one big chain announced at the time that he found it "hard to believe that people will drive for miles to shop for foods and sacrifice the personal service chains have perfected and to which Mrs. Consumer is accustomed."[1] As late as 1936, the National Wholesale Grocers convention and the New Jersey Retail Grocers Association said there was nothing to fear. They said that the supers' narrow appeal to the price buyer limited the size of their market. They had to draw from miles around. When imitators came, there would be wholesale liquidations as volume fell. The current

[1] For more details see M. M. Zimmerman, *The Supermarket: A Revolution in Distribution,* McGraw-Hill Book Company, New York, 1955, p. 48.

high sales of the supers was said to be partly due to their novelty. Basically people wanted convenient neighborhood grocers. If the neighborhood stores "cooperate with their suppliers, pay attention to their costs, and improve their services," they would be able to weather the competition until it blew over.[2]

It never blew over. The chains discovered that survival required going into the supermarket business. This meant the wholesale destruction of their huge investments in corner-store sites and in established distribution and merchandising methods. The companies with "the courage of their convictions" resolutely stuck to the corner-store philosophy. They kept their pride but lost their shirts.

## SELF-DECEIVING CYCLE

But memories are short. For example, it is hard for people who today confidently hail the twin messiahs of electronics and chemicals to see how things could possibly go wrong with these galloping industries. They probably also cannot see how a reasonably sensible businessman could have been as myopic as the famous Boston millionaire who fifty years ago unintentionally sentenced his heirs to poverty by stipulating that his entire estate be forever invested exclusively in electric-streetcar securities. His posthumous declaration, "There will always be a big demand for efficient urban transportation," is no consolation to his heirs who sustain life by pumping gasoline at automobile filling stations.

Yet, in a casual survey I took among a group of intelligent business executives, nearly half agreed that it would be hard to hurt their heirs by tying their estates forever to the electronics industry. When I then confronted them with the Boston streetcar example, they chorused unanimously, "That's different!" But is it? Is not the basic situation identical?

In truth, I believe, there is no such thing as a growth industry. There are only companies organized and operated to create and capitalize on growth opportunities. Industries that assume themselves to be riding some automatic growth escalator invariably descend into stagnation. The history of every dead and dying "growth" industry shows a self-deceiving cycle of bountiful expansion and undetected decay. There are four conditions which usually guarantee this cycle:

1. The belief that growth is assured by an expanding and more affluent population,
2. The belief that there is no competitive substitute for the industry's major product,
3. Too much faith in mass production and in the advantages of rapidly declining unit costs as output rises,
4. Preoccupation with a product that lends itself to carefully controlled scientific experimentation, improvement, and manufacturing cost reduction.

[2] *Ibid.*, pp. 45–47.

I should like now to begin examining each of these conditions in some detail. To build my case as boldly as possible, I shall illustrate the points with reference to three industries—petroleum, automotive, and electronics—particularly petroleum, because it spans more years and more vicissitudes. Not only do these three have excellent reputations with the general public and also enjoy the confidence of sophisticated investors, but their managements have become known for progressive thinking in areas like financial control, product research, and management training. If obsolescence can cripple even these industries, it can happen anywhere.

## POPULATION MYTH

The belief that profits are assured by an expanding and more affluent population is dear to the heart of every industry. It takes the edge off the apprehensions everybody understandably feels about the future. If consumers are multiplying and also buying more of your product or service, you can face the future with considerably more comfort than if the market were shrinking. An expanding market keeps the manufacturer from having to think very hard or imaginatively. If thinking is an intellectual response to a problem, then the absence of a problem leads to the absence of thinking. If your product has an automatically expanding market, then you will not give much thought to how to expand it.

One of the most interesting examples of this philosophy is provided by the petroleum industry. Probably our oldest "growth" industry, it has an enviable record. While there are some current apprehensions about its growth rate, the industry itself tends to be optimistic. But I believe it can be demonstrated that it is undergoing a fundamental yet typical change. It is not only ceasing to be a growth industry but may actually be a declining one, relative to other business. Although there is widespread unawareness of this fact, I believe that, unless it changes drastically, within twenty-five years the oil industry may find itself in much the same position of retrospective glory that the railroads are now in. Despite its pioneering work in developing and applying the present-value method of investment evaluation, in employee relations, and in working with backward countries, the petroleum business is at times a distressing example of how complacency and wrongheadedness can stubbornly convert opportunity into near disaster. Only in the last two years does it seem to have been aroused out of its heavy slumber.

One of the characteristics of this and other industries that have believed very strongly in the beneficial consequences of an expanding population, while at the same time being industries with a generic product for which there has appeared to be no competitive substitute, is that the individual companies have sought to outdo their competitors by improving on what they are already doing. This makes sense, of course, if one assumes that sales are tied to the country's population strings because the customer can compare products only on a feature-by-feature basis. Hence I believe it is very significant that not since John D. Rockefeller sent free kerosene lamps to China has the oil industry done anything really outstanding to create a demand for its product. Not even in product improvement has it showered itself with eminence. The greatest single improvement, namely, the development of tetraethyl lead, came from outside the industry, specifically from General Motors and Du Pont. The big contributions made by the industry itself are confined to the technology of oil exploration, production, and refining.

## ASKING FOR TROUBLE

In other words, the industry's efforts have focused not nearly so much on improving the generic product or its marketing as on improving the efficiency of getting and making its product. Moreover, its chief product has, until quite recently, continuously been defined in the narrowest possible terms, namely, gasoline, and not energy, fuel, or transportation. This attitude has helped assure that:

1. Major improvements in gasoline quality in the past have tended not to originate in the oil industry itself. Also, the development of superior alternative fuels comes from outside the oil industry, as will be shown later.
2. Major innovations in automobile fuel marketing have been originated by small new oil companies that are not primarily preoccupied with production or refining. These are the companies that have been responsible for the rapidly expanding multipump gasoline stations, with their successful emphasis on large and clean layouts, rapid and efficient driveway service, and quality gasoline at low prices.

Thus the oil industry has asked for trouble from outsiders. Sooner or later, in this land of hungry inventors and entrepreneurs, a threat is sure to come. The possibilities of this will become more apparent when we turn to the next dangerous belief of many managements. For the sake of continuity, because this second belief is tied closely to the first, I shall continue with the same example.

## IDEA OF INDISPENSABILITY

Until only two years ago the petroleum industry was pretty much persuaded that there was no competitive substitute for its major product, gasoline—or if there was, that it would continue to be a derivative of crude oil, such as diesel fuel or kerosene jet fuel.

There is a lot of automatic wishful thinking in this assumption. The trouble is that most refining companies own huge amounts of crude-oil reserves. These have value only if there is a market for products into which oil can be converted—hence the tenacious belief in the continuing competitive superiority of automobile fuels made from crude oil.

This idea persisted despite all historic evidence against it. The evidence not only shows that oil has never been a superior product for any purpose for very long but also that the oil industry has never really been a growth industry. It has been a succession of different businesses that have gone through the usual historic cycles of growth, maturity, and decay. Its overall survival is owed to a series of miraculous escapes from total obsolescence, of last-minute and unexpected reprieves from total disaster reminiscent of *The Perils of Pauline*. . . .

## PRODUCTION PRESSURES

Mass-production industries are impelled by a great drive to produce all they can. The prospect of steeply declining unit costs as output rises is more than most companies can usually resist. The profit possibilities look spectacular. All effort focuses on production. The result is that marketing gets neglected.

John Kenneth Galbraith contends that just the opposite occurs.[3] Output is so prodigious that all effort concentrates on trying to get rid of it. He says this accounts for singing commericals, desecration of the countryside with advertising signs, and other wasteful and vulgar practices. Galbraith has a finger on something real, but he misses the strategic point. Mass production does indeed generate great pressure to "move" the product. But what usually gets emphasized is selling, not marketing. Marketing, being a more sophisticated and complex process, gets ignored.

The difference between marketing and selling is more than semantic. Selling focuses on the needs of the seller, marketing on the needs of the buyer. Selling is preoccupied with the seller's need to convert his product into cash; marketing with the idea of satisfying the needs of the customer by means of the product and the whole cluster of things associated with creating, delivering, and finally consuming it.

In some industries the enticements of full mass production have been so powerful that for many years top management in effect has told the sales departments, "You get rid of it; we'll worry about profits." By contrast, a truly marketing-minded firm tries to create value-satisfying goods and services that consumers will want to buy. What it offers for sale includes not only the generic product or service but also how it is made available to the customer, in what form, when, under what conditions, and at what terms of trade. Most important, what it offers for sale is determined not by the seller but by the buyer. The seller takes his cues from the buyer in such a way that the product becomes a consequence of the marketing effort, not vice versa.

## LAG IN DETROIT

The above may sound like an elementary rule of business, but that does not keep it from being violated wholesale. It is certainly more violated than honored. Take the automobile industry, for example.

Here mass production is most famous, most honored, and has the greatest impact on the entire society. The industry has hitched its star to the relentless requirements of the annual model change, a policy that makes customer orientation an especially urgent

[3] John Kenneth Galbraith, *The Affluent Society,* Houghton Mifflin Company, Boston, 1958, pp. 152–160.

necessity. Consequently the auto companies spend millions of dollars a year on consumer research. But the fact that the new compact cars sold so well in the very first year of the "Big Three's" entry into this field indicates that Detroit's vast researches had for a long time failed to reveal what the customer really wanted. Detroit was not persuaded that he wanted anything different from what he had been getting until it lost millions of customers to other small-car manufacturers.

How could this unbelievable lag behind consumer wants have been perpetuated so long? Why did not research uncover consumer preferences before consumers' buying decisions themselves revealed the facts? Is that not what consumer research is for—to find out before the fact what is going to happen? The answer is that Detroit never properly researched the customer's wants. It only investigated his preferences among the kinds of things which it had already decided to offer him. For Detroit was mainly product-oriented, not customer-oriented. To the extent that the customer was recognized as having needs that the manufacturer should try to satisfy, Detroit usually acted as if the job could be done entirely by product changes. Occasionally financing got some attention too, but that was more in order to sell than to enable the customer to buy.

As for taking care of other customer needs, there is not enough being done to write about. The areas of the greatest unsatisfied needs are ignored, or at best get stepchild attention. These areas are at the point of sale and on the matter of automotive repair and maintenance. Detroit considers these problem areas as being of secondary importance. This is underscored by the fact that the retailing and servicing ends of the industry are neither owned and operated nor controlled by the manufacturers. Once the car is produced, things are pretty much in the dealer's inadequate hands. Illustrative of Detroit's arm's-length attitude is the fact that, while servicing holds enormous sales-stimulating, profit-building opportunities, only fifty-seven of Chevrolet's 7,000 dealers provided night maintenance service in 1960.

Motorists repeatedly express their dissatisfaction with servicing and their apprehensions about buying cars under the present selling setup. The anxieties and problems they encounter during the auto-buying and auto-maintenance processes are probably more intense and widespread today than thirty years ago. Yet the automobile companies do not seem to listen to or take their cues from the anguished consumer. If they do listen, it must be through the filter of their own preoccupation with production. The marketing effort is still viewed as a necessary consequence of the product, not vice versa, as it should be. That is the legacy of mass production, with its parochial view that profit resides essentially in low-cost full production.

## WHAT FORD PUT FIRST

The profit lure of mass production obviously has a place in the plans and strategy of business management, but it must always *follow* hard thinking about the customer. This is one of the most important lessons that we can learn from the contradictory behavior of Henry Ford. In a sense Ford was both the most brilliant and the most senseless marketer in American history. He was senseless because he refused to give the customer anything but a black car. He was brilliant because he fashioned a production system designed to fit market needs. We habitually celebrate him for the wrong reason, his production genius. His real genius was marketing. We think he was able to cut his selling price and therefore sell millions of $500 cars because his invention of the assembly line had reduced the costs. Actually he invented the assembly line *because* he had concluded that at $500 he could sell millions of cars. Mass production was the result not the cause of his low prices.

Ford repeatedly emphasized this point, but a nation of production-oriented business managers refuses to hear the great lesson he taught. Here is his operating philosophy as he succinctly expressed it:

> Our policy is to reduce the price, extend the operations, and improve the article. You will notice that the reduction of price comes first. We have never considered any costs as fixed. Therefore we first reduce the price to the point where we believe more sales will result. Then we go ahead and try to make the prices. We do not bother about the costs. The new price forces the costs down. The more usual way is to take the costs and then determine the price, and although that method may be scientific in the narrow sense, it is not scientific in the broad sense, because what earthly use is it to know the cost if it tells you that you cannot manufacture at a price at which the article can be sold? But more to the point is the fact that, although one may calculate what a cost is, and of course all of our costs are carefully calculated, no one knows what a cost ought to be. One of the ways of discovering . . . is to name a price so low as to force everybody in the place to the highest point of efficiency. The low price makes everybody dig for profits. We make more discoveries concerning manufacturing and selling under this forced method than by any method of leisurely investigation.[4]

## PRODUCT PROVINCIALISM

The tantalizing profit possibilities of low unit production costs may create the most seriously self-deceiving attitude that could afflict a company, particularly a "growth" company where an apparently assured expansion of demand already tends to undermine a proper concern for the importance of marketing and the customer.

The usual result of this narrow preoccupation with so-called "concrete matters" is that, instead of growing, the industry declines. It usually means that the product fails to adapt to the constantly changing patterns of consumer needs and tastes, to new and modified marketing institutions and practices, or to product developments in competing or complementary industries. The industry has its eyes so firmly on its own specific product that it does not see how it is being made obsolete.

The classical example of this is the buggy-whip industry. No amount of product improvement could stave off its death sentence. But had the industry defined itself as being in the transportation business rather than in the buggy-whip business, it might have survived. It would have done what survival always entails, that is, change. Even if it had only defined its business as providing a stimulant or catalyst to an energy

[4]Henry Ford, *My Life and Work,* Doubleday & Company, Inc., New York, 1923, pp. 146–147.

source, it might have continued existence by becoming a manufacturer of, say, fan-belts or air cleaners.

What may someday be a still more classical example is, again, the oil industry. Having let others steal marvelous opportunities from it (e.g., natural gas, as already mentioned, missile fuels, and jet engine lubricants), one would expect it to have taken steps to prevent its happening again. But this is not the case. There have been extraordinary new developments in fuel systems specifically designed to power automobiles. Not only are these developments concentrated in firms outside the petroleum industry, but until their delinquency was pointed out to them a few years ago, most petroleum companies almost systematically ignored them, securely content in their wedded bliss to oil. It is the story of the kerosene lamp versus the incandescent lamp all over again. Most big oil companies are still trying to improve hydrocarbon fuels rather than to develop fuels best suited to the needs of their users, whether or not made in different ways and with different raw materials from oil.

Here are some of the things which nonpetroleum companies are working on:

Over a dozen firms now have advanced working models of energy systems which, when perfected, may very well replace the internal-combustion engine and eliminate the demand for gasoline. The superior merit of each of these systems is their elimination of frequent, time-consuming, and irritating refueling stops. Most of these systems are fuel cells designed to create electric energy directly from chemicals without combustion. Most of them use chemicals that are not derived from oil, generally hydrogen and oxygen. The fact that hydrogen-oxygen systems remain crude and now entail serious combustion hazards has tranquilized most oil companies into a comforting reassurance of their own immortality.

Several nonpetroleum companies have advanced models of electric storage batteries designed to power automobiles. One of these firms is an aircraft producer that is working jointly with several electrical utility companies. The latter hope to use off-peak generating capacity to supply overnight plug-in battery regeneration. Another company, also using the battery approach, is a medium-size electronics firm with extensive small-battery experience that it developed in connection with its work on hearing aids. It is collaborating with an automobile manufacturer. Recent improvements arising from the need for high-powered miniature power storage plants in rockets have put us within reach of a relatively small battery capable of withstanding great overloads or surges of power. Germanium diode applications and batteries using sintered-plate and nickel-cadmium techniques promise to make a revolution in our energy sources.

Solar energy conversion systems are also getting increasing attention. One usually cautious Detroit auto executive not long ago ventured that solar-powered cars might be common by 1980.

As for most oil companies, they are more or less "watching developments," as one research director put it to me. Two years ago only a few were doing any research on fuel cells, and that was almost always confined to developing cells powered by hydrocarbon chemicals. None of them was enthusiastically researching fuel cells, batteries, or solar power plants. None of them was spending a fraction as much on research in these profoundly important areas as they are on the usual run-of-the-mill things like reducing combustion-chamber deposit in gasoline engines. One major integrated petroleum company not long ago took a tentative look at the fuel cell and concluded that although "the companies actively working on it indicate a belief in ultimate success . . . the timing and magnitude of its impact are too remote to warrant recognition in our forecasts."

One might, of course, ask: Why should the oil companies do anything different? Would not chemical fuel cells, batteries, or solar energy kill the present product lines? The answer is that they would indeed, and that is precisely the reason for the oil firms having to develop these power units before their competitors, so they will not be companies without an industry.

Management might be more likely to do what is needed for its own preservation if it thought of itself as being in the energy business, as a couple of companies have now announced themselves to be. But even that is not enough if they persist in imprisoning themselves in the narrow grip of their tight product orientation. They have to think of themselves as taking care of customer needs, not finding, refining, or even selling oil. Once they genuinely think of their business as taking care of people's transportation or energy needs, nothing can stop them from creating their own extravagantly profitable growth.

## "CREATIVE DESTRUCTION"

Since words are cheap and deeeds are dear, it may be appropriate to indicate what this kind of thinking involves and leads to. Let us start at the beginning–the customer. It can be shown that motorists strongly dislike the bother, delay, and experience of buying gasoline. People actually do not buy gasoline. They cannot see it, taste it, feel it, appreciate it, or really test it. What they buy is the right to continue driving their cars. The gas station is like a tax collector to whom people are compelled to pay a periodic toll as the price of using their cars. This makes the gas station a basically unpopular institution. It can never be made popular or pleasant, only less unpopular, less unpleasant.

To reduce its unpopularity completely means eliminating it. Nobody likes a tax collector, not even a pleasantly cheerful one. Nobody likes to interrupt a trip to buy a phantom product, not even from a handsome Adonis or a seductive Venus. Hence companies that are working on exotic fuel substitutes which will eliminate the need for frequent refueling are heading directly into the outstretched arms of the irritated motorist. They are riding a wave of inevitability, not because they are creating something which is technologically superior or more sophisticated, but because they are satisfying a powerful customer need.

Once the petroleum companies recognize the customer-satisfying logic of what another power system can do, they will see that they have no more choice about working on an efficient, long-lasting fuel (or some way of delivering present fuels without bothering the motorist) than the big food chains had about going into the supermarket business, or the vacuum-tube companies had about making semiconductors. For their own good the oil firms will have to destroy their own highly profitable assets. No amount of wishful thinking can save them from the necessity of engaging in this form of "creative destruction."

I phrase the need as strongly as this because I think management must make quite an effort to break itself loose from conventional ways. It is all too easy in this day and age for a company or industry to let its sense of purpose become dominated by the economies of full production and to develop a dangerously lopsided product orientation. In short, if management lets itself drift, it invariably drifts in the direction of thinking of itself as producing goods and services, not customer satisfactions. While it probably will not descend to the depths of telling its salesmen, "You get rid of it; we'll worry about profits," it can, without knowing it, be practicing precisely that formula for withering decay. The historic fate of one growth industry after another has been its suicidal product provincialism.

## DANGERS OF R&D

Another big danger to a firm's continued growth arises when top management is wholly transfixed by the profit possibilities of technical research and development. To illustrate I shall turn first to a new industry–electronics–and then return once more to the oil companies. By comparing a fresh example with a familiar one, I hope to emphasize the prevalence and insidiousness of a hazardous way of thinking.

In the case of electronics, the greatest danger which faces the glamorous new companies in this field is not that they do not pay enough attention to research and development but that they pay too much attention to it. And the fact that the fastest-growing electronics firms owe their eminence to their heavy emphasis on technical research is completely beside the point. They have vaulted to affluence on a sudden crest of unusually strong general receptiveness to new technical ideas. Also, their success has been shaped in the virtually guaranteed market of military subsidies and by military orders that in many cases actually preceded the existence of facilities to make the products. Their expansion has, in other words, been almost totally devoid of marketing effort.

Thus they are growing up under conditions that come dangerously close to creating the illusion that a superior product will sell itself. Having created a successful company by making a superior product, it is not surprising that management continues to be oriented toward the product rather than the people who consume it. It develops the philosophy that continued growth is a matter of continued product innovation and improvement.

A number of other factors tend to strengthen and sustain this belief:

1. Because electronic products are highly complex and sophisticated, managements become top-heavy with engineers and scientists. This creates a selective bias in favor of

research and production at the expense of marketing. The organization tends to view itself as making things rather than satisfying customer needs. Marketing gets treated as a residual activity, "something else" that must be done once the vital job of product creation and production is completed.

2. To this bias in favor of product research, development, and production is added the bias in favor of dealing with controllable variables. Engineers and scientists are at home in the world of concrete things like machines, test tubes, production lines, and even balance sheets. The abstractions toward which they feel kindly are those which are testable or manipulatable in the laboratory, or if not testable, then functional, such as Euclid's axioms. In short, the managements of the new glamour-growth companies tend to favor those business activities which lend themselves to careful study, experimentation, and control—the hard, practical realities of the lab, the shop, the books.

What get shortchanged are the realities of the *market.* Consumers are unpredictable, varied, fickle, stupid, shortsighted, stubborn, and generally bothersome. This is not what the engineer-managers say, but deep down in their consciousness it is what they believe. And this accounts for their concentrating on what they know and what they can control, namely, product research, engineering, and production. The emphasis on production becomes particularly attractive when the product can be made at declining unit costs. There is no more inviting way of making money than by running the plant full blast.

Today the top-heavy science-engineering-production orientation of so many electronics companies works reasonably well because they are pushing into new frontiers in which the armed services have pioneered virtually assured markets. The companies are in the felicitous position of having to fill, not find, markets; of not having to discover what the customer needs and wants, but of having the customer voluntarily come forward with specific new-product demands. If a team of consultants had been assigned specifically to design a business situation calculated to prevent the emergence and development of a customer-oriented marketing viewpoint, it could not have produced anything better than the conditions just described.

## STEPCHILD TREATMENT

The oil industry is a stunning example of how science, technology, and mass production can divert an entire group of companies from their main task. To the extent the consumer is studied at all, the focus is forever on getting information which is designed to help the oil companies improve what they are now doing. Most of them generally try to discover more convincing advertising themes, more effective sales promotion drives, what the market shares of the various companies are, what people like or dislike about service-station dealers and oil companies, and so forth. Few companies seem as interested in probing deeply into the basic human needs that the industry might be trying to satisfy as in probing into the basic properties of the raw material that the companies work with in trying to deliver customer satisfactions.

Basic questions about customers and markets seldom get asked. The latter occupy a stepchild status. They are recognized as existing, as having to be taken care of, but not worth very much real thought or dedicated attention. Nobody gets as excited about the customers in his own backyard as about the oil in the Sahara Desert. Nothing illustrates better the neglect of marketing than its treatment in the industry press.

The centennial issue of the *American Petroleum Institute Quarterly,* published in 1959 to celebrate the discovery of oil in Titusville, Pennsylvania, contained twenty-one feature articles proclaiming the industry's greatness. Only one of these talked about its achievements in marketing, and that was only a pictorial record of how service-station architecture has changed. The issue also contained a special section on "New Horizons," which was devoted to showing the magnificent role oil would play in America's future. Every reference was ebulliently optimistic, never once implying that oil might have some hard competition. Even the reference to atomic energy was a cheerful catalogue of how oil would help make atomic energy a success. There was not a single apprehension that the oil industry's affluence might be threatened or a suggestion that one "new horizon" might include new and better ways of serving oil's present customers.

But the most revealing example of the stepchild treatment that marketing gets was still another special series of short articles on "The Revolutionary Potential of Electronics." Under that heading the following article titles appeared in the table of contents: "In the Search for Oil," "In Production Operations," "In Refinery Processes," "In Pipeline Operations."

Significantly, every one of the industry's major functional areas is listed, except marketing. Why? Either it is believed that electronics holds no revolutionary potential for petroleum marketing (which is palpably wrong), or the editors forgot to discuss marketing (which is more likely and illustrates its stepchild status).

The order in which the four functional areas are listed also betrays the past alienation of the oil industry from the consumer. The industry is implicitly defined as beginning with the search for oil and ending with its distribution from the refinery. But the truth is that this industry, as all industries, begins with the needs of the customer for its product. From that primal position its definition moves steadily backstream to areas of progressively lesser importance, until it finally comes to rest at the "search for oil."

## BEGINNING AND END

The view that an industry is a customer-satisfying process, not a goods-producing process, is vital for all businessmen to understand. An industry begins with the customer and his needs, not with a patent, a raw material, or a selling skill. Given the customer's needs, the industry develops backward, first concerning itself with the physical delivery of customer satisfactions. Then it moves back further to creating the things by which these satisfactions are in part achieved. How these materials are created is a matter of indifference to the customer; hence the particular form of manufacturing, processing, or what have you, cannot be considered as a vital aspect of the industry. Finally, the industry moves back still further to finding the raw materials necessary for making its products.

The irony of some industries oriented toward technical research and development is that the scientists who occupy the high executive positions are totally unscientific when it comes to defining their companies' overall needs and purposes. They violate the first two rules of the scientific method—being aware of and defining their companies' problems, and then developing testable hypotheses about solving them. They are scientific only about the convenient things, such as laboratory and product experiments. The reason that the customer (and the satisfaction of his deepest needs) is not considered as being "the problem" is not because there is any certain belief that no such problem exists but because an organizational lifetime has conditioned management to look in the opposite direction. Marketing is a stepchild.

I do not mean that selling is ignored. Far from it. But selling, again, is not marketing. As already pointed out, selling concerns itself with the tricks and techniques of getting people to exchange their cash for your product. It is not concerned with the values that the exchange is all about. And it does not, as marketing invariably does, view the entire business process as consisting of a tightly integrated effort to discover, create, arouse, and satisfy customer needs. The customer is somebody "out there" who, with proper cunning, can be separated from his loose change.

Actually, not even selling gets much attention in some technologically minded firms. Because there is a virtually guaranteed market for the abundant flow of their new products, they do not in truth know what a real market is. It is as if they lived in a planned economy, moving their products routinely from factory to retail outlet. Their successful concentration on products tends to convince them of the soundness of what they have been doing, and they fail to see the gathering clouds over the market. . . .

# 4. THE CONCEPT OF THE MARKETING MIX

*Neil H. Borden*

*Marketing is still an art; and the marketing manager, as head chef, must creatively marshall* all *his marketing activities to advance both the short-term and long-term interests of his firm.*

*This is an overview of the marketing mix.*

I have always found it interesting to observe how an apt or colorful term may catch on, gain wide usage, and help to further understanding of a concept that has already been expressed in less appealing and communicative terms. Such has been true of the phrase "marketing mix," which I began to use in my teaching and writing some fifteen years ago. In a relatively short time it has come to have wide usage. This note tells of the evolution of the marketing mix concept.

The phrase was suggested to me by a paragraph in a research bulletin on the management of marketing costs, written by my associate, Professor James Culliton.[1] In this study of manufacturers' marketing costs he described the business executive as a

> ... "decider," an "artist"–a "mixer of ingredients," who sometimes follows a recipe prepared by others, sometimes prepares his own recipe as he goes along, sometimes adapts a recipe to the ingredients immediately available, and sometimes experiments with or invents ingredients no one else has tried.

[1] James W. Culliton, *The Management of Marketing Costs,* Division of Research, Graduate School of Business Administration, Harvard University, Boston, 1948.

Source: From *Journal of Advertising Research,* vol. 4, June, 1964. pp. 2–7.  Neil H. Borden, Professor Emeritus of Marketing and Advertising, Harvard Graduate School of Business Administration.

I liked his idea of calling a marketing executive a "mixer of ingredients," one who is constantly engaged in fashioning creatively a mix of marketing procedures and policies in his efforts to produce a profitable enterprise.

For many years previous to Culliton's cost study the wide variations in the procedures and policies employed by managements of manufacturing firms in their marketing programs and the correspondingly wide variation in the costs of these marketing functions, which Culliton aptly ascribed to the varied "mixing of ingredients," had become increasingly evident as we had gathered marketing cases at the Harvard Business School. The marked differences in the patterns or formulae of the marketing programs not only were evident through facts disclosed in case histories, but also were reflected clearly in the figures of a cost study of food manufacturers made by the Harvard Bureau of Business Research in 1929. The primary objective of this study was to determine common figures of expenses for various marketing functions among food manufacturing companies, similar to the common cost figures which had been determined in previous years for various kinds of retail and wholesale businesses. In this manufacturer's study we were unable, however, with the data gathered to determine common expense figures that had much significance as standards by which to guide management, such as had been possible in the studies of retail and wholesale trades, where the methods of operation tended toward uniformity. Instead, among food manufacturers the ratios of sales devoted to the various functions of marketing such as advertising, personal selling, packaging, and so on, were found to be widely divergent, no matter how we grouped our respondents. Each respondent gave data that tended to uniqueness.

Culliton's study of marketing costs in 1947–48 was a second effort to find out, among other objectives, whether a bigger sample and a more careful classification of companies would produce evidence of operating uniformities that would give helpful common expense figures. But the result was the same as in our early study: there was wide diversity in cost ratios among any classifications of firms which were set up, and no common figures were found that had much value. This was true whether companies were grouped according to similarity in product lines, amount of sales, territorial extent of operations, or other bases of classification.

Relatively early in my study of advertising, it had become evident that understanding of advertising usage by manufacturers in any case had to come from an analysis of advertising's place as one element in the total marketing program of the firm. I came to realize that it is essential always to ask: what overall marketing strategy has been or might be employed to bring about a profitable operation in light of the circumstances faced by the management? What combination of marketing procedures and policies has been or might be adopted to bring about desired behavior of trade and consumers at costs that will permit a profit? Specifically, how can advertising, personal selling, pricing, packaging, channels, warehousing, and the other elements of a marketing program be manipulated and fitted together in a way that will give a profitable operation? In short, I saw that every advertising management case called for a consideration of strategy to be adopted for the total marketing program, with advertising recognized as only one element whose form and extent depended on its careful adjustment to the other parts of the program.

The soundness of this viewpoint was supported by case histories throughout my volume.[2] In the chapters devoted to the utilization of advertising by business, I had pointed out the innumerable combinations of marketing methods and policies that might be adopted by a manager in arriving at a marketing plan. For instance, in the area of branding, he might elect to adopt an individualized brand or a family brand. Or he might decide to sell his product unbranded or under private label. Any decision in the area of brand policy in turn has immediate implications that bear on his selection of channels of distribution, sales force methods, packaging, promotional procedure, and advertising. Throughout the volume the case materials cited show that the way in which any marketing function is designed and the burden placed upon the function are determined largely by the overall marketing strategy adopted by managements to meet the market conditions under which they operate. The forces met by different firms vary widely. Accordingly, the programs fashioned differ widely.

Regarding advertising, which was the function under focus in the Economic Effects volume, I said at one point:

> In all the above illustrative situations it should be recognized that advertising is not an operating method to be considered as something apart, as something whose profit value is to be judged alone. An able management does not ask, "Shall we use or not use advertising," without consideration of the product and of other management procedures to be employed. Rather the question is always one of finding a management formula giving advertising its due place in the combination of manufacturing methods, product form, pricing, promotion and selling methods, and distribution methods. As previously pointed out different formulae, i.e., different combinations of methods, may be profitably employed by competing manufacturers.

From the above it can be seen why Culliton's description of a marketing manager as a "mixer of ingredients" immediately appealed to me as an apt and easily understandable phrase, far better than my previous references to the marketing man as an empiricist seeking in any situation to devise a profitable "pattern" or "formula" of marketing operations from among the many procedures and policies that were open to him. If he was a "mixer of ingredients," what he designed was a "marketing mix."

It was logical to proceed from a realization of existence of a variety of "marketing mixes" to the development of a concept that would comprehend not only this variety, but also the market forces that cause managements to produce a variety of mixes. It is the problems raised by these forces that lead marketing managers to exercise their wits in devising mixes or programs which they hope will give a profitable business operation.

To portray this broadened concept in a visual presentation requires merely:

1. a list of the important elements or ingredients that make up marketing programs;

[2] Neil H. Borden, *The Economic Effects of Advertising,* Richard D. Irwin, Inc., Homewood, Ill., 1942.

2. a list of the forces that bear on the marketing operation of a firm and to which the marketing manager must adjust in his search for a mix or program that can be successful.

The list of elements of the marketing mix in such a visual presentation can be long or short, depending on how far one wishes to go in his classification and subclassification of the marketing procedures and policies with which marketing managements deal when devising marketing programs. The list of elements which I have employed in my teaching and consulting work covers the principal areas of marketing activities which call for management decisions as revealed by case histories. I realize others might build a different list. Mine is as follows.

## ELEMENTS OF THE MARKETING MIX OF MANUFACTURERS

1. *Product Planning*—policies and procedures relating to:
   a. Product lines to be offered—qualities, design, etc.
   b. Markets to sell: whom, where, when, and in what quantity.
   c. New product policy—research and development program.
2. *Pricing*—policies and procedures relating to:
   a. Price level to adopt.
   b. Specific prices to adopt (odd-even, etc.).
   c. Price policy, e.g., one price or varying price, price maintenance, use of list prices, etc.
   d. Margins to adopt—for company; for the trade.
3. *Branding*—policies and procedures relating to:
   a. Selection of trade marks.
   b. Brand policy—individualized or family brand.
   c. Sale under private label or unbranded.
4. *Channels of Distribution*—policies and procedures relating to:
   a. Channels to use between plant and consumer.
   b. Degree of selectivity among wholesalers and retailers.
   c. Efforts to gain cooperation of the trade.
5. *Personal Selling*—policies and procedures relating to:
   a. Burden to be placed on personal selling and the methods to be employed in:
      (1) Manufacturer's organization.
      (2) Wholesale segment of the trade.
      (3) Retail segment of the trade.
6. *Advertising*—policies and procedures relating to:
   a. Amount to spend—i.e., the burden to be placed on advertising.
   b. Copy platform to adopt:
      (1) Product image desired.
      (2) Corporate image desired.
   c. Mix of advertising: to the trade; through the trade; to consumers.

7. *Promotions*—policies and procedures relating to:
   a. Burden to place on special selling plans or devices directed at or through the trade.
   b. Form of these devices for consumer promotions, for trade promotions.
8. *Packaging*—policies and procedures relating to:
   a. Formulation of package and label.
9. *Display*—policies and procedures relating to:
   a. Burden to be put on display to help effect sale.
   b. Methods to adopt to secure display.
10. *Servicing*—policies and procedures relating to:
    a. Providing service needed.
11. *Physical Handling*—policies and procedures relating to:
    a. Warehousing.
    b. Transportation.
    c. Inventories.
12. *Fact Finding and Analysis*—policies and procedures relating to:
    a. Securing, analysis, and use of facts in marketing operations.

Also if one were to make a list of all the forces which managements weigh at one time or another when formulating their marketing mixes, it w ould be very long indeed, for the behavior of individuals and groups in all spheres of life have a bearing, first, on what goods and services are produced and consumed, and, second, on the procedures that may be employed in bringing about exchange of these goods and services. However, the important forces which bear on marketers, all arising from the behavior of individuals or groups, may readily be listed under four heads, namely the behavior of consumers, the trade, competitors, and government.

The outline below contains these four behavioral forces with notations of some of the important behavioral determinants within each force. These must be studied and understood by the marketer, if his marketing mix is to be successful. The great quest of marketing management is to understand the behavior of humans in response to the stimuli to which they are subjected. The skillful marketer is one who is a perceptive and practical psychologist and sociologist, who has keen insight into individual and group behavior, who can foresee changes in behavior that develop in a dynamic world, who has creative ability for building well-knit programs because he has the capacity to visualize the probable response of consumers, trade, and competitors to his moves. His skill in forecasting response to his marketing moves should well be supplemented by a further skill in devising and using tests and measurements to check consumer or trade response to his program or parts thereof, for no marketer has so much prescience that he can proceed without empirical check.

Below, then, is the suggested outline of forces which govern the mixing of marketing elements. This list and that of the elements taken together provide a visual presentation of the concept of the marketing mix.

## MARKET FORCES BEARING ON THE MARKETING MIX

1. *Consumers' Buying Behavior,* as determined by their:
   a. Motivation in purchasing.
   b. Buying habits.
   c. Living habits.
   d. Environment (present and future, as revealed by trends, for environment influences consumers' attitudes toward products and their use of them).
   e. Buying power.
   f. Number (i.e., how many).
2. *The Trade's Behavior*—wholesalers' and retailers' behavior, as influenced by:
   a. Their motivations.
   b. Their structure, practices, and attitudes.
   c. Trends in structure and procedures that portend change.
3. *Competitors' Position and Behavior,* as influenced by:
   a. Industry structure and the firm's relation thereto.
      (1) Size and strength of competitors.
      (2) Number of competitors and degree of industry concentration.
      (3) Indirect competition—i.e., from other products.
   b. Relation of supply to demand—oversupply or undersupply.
   c. Product choices offered consumers by the industry—i.e., quality, price, service.
   d. Degree to which competitors compete on price vs. nonprice bases.
   e. Competitors' motivations and attitudes—their likely response to the actions of other firms.
   f. Trends technological and social, portending change in supply and demand.
4. *Governmental Behavior—Controls over Marketing:*
   a. Regulations over products.
   b. Regulations over pricing.
   c. Regulations over competitive practices.
   d. Regulations over advertising and promotion.

When building a marketing program to fit the needs of his firm, the marketing manager has to weigh the behavioral forces and then juggle marketing elements in his mix with a keen eye on the resources with which he has to work. His firm is but one small organism in a large universe of complex forces. His firm is only a part of an industry that is competing with many other industries. What does the firm have in terms of money, product line, organization, and reputation with which to work? The manager must devise a mix of procedures that fit these resources. If his firm is small, he must judge the response of consumers, trade, and competition in light of his position and resources and the influence that he can exert in the market. He must look for special opportunities in product or method of operation. The small firm cannot employ the procedures of the big firm. Though he may sell the same kind of product as the big firm, his marketing strategy is likely to be widely different in many respects. Innumerable instances of this fact might be cited. For example, in the industrial goods field, small firms often seek to build sales on a limited and highly specialized line, whereas industry leaders seek patronage for full lines. Small firms often elect to go in for regional sales rather than attempt the national distribution practiced by larger companies. Again, the company of limited resources often elects to limit its production and sales to products whose potential is too small to attract the big fellows. Still again, companies with small resources of the cosmetic field not infrequently have set up introductory marketing programs employing aggressive personal selling and a "push" strategy with distribution limited to leading department stores. Their initially small advertising funds have been directed through these selected retail outlets, with the offering of the products and their story told over the signatures of the stores. The strategy has been to borrow kudos for their products from the leading stores' reputations and to gain a gradual radiation of distribution to smaller stores in all types of channels, such as often comes from the trade's follow-the-leader behavior. Only after resources have grown from mounting sales has a dense retail distribution been aggressively sought and a shift made to place the selling burden more and more on company-signed advertising.

The above strategy was employed for Toni products and Stoppette deodorant in their early marketing stages when the resources of their producers were limited (cf. case of Jules Montenier, Inc.)[3]. In contrast, cosmetic manufacturers with large resources have generally followed a "pull" strategy for the introduction of new products, relying on heavy campaigns of advertising in a rapid succession of area introductions to induce a hoped-for, complete retail coverage from the start (cf. case of Bristol-Myers Company).[4] These introductory campaigns have been undertaken only after careful programs of product development and test marketing have given assurance that product and selling plans had high promise of success.

Many additional instances of the varying strategy employed by small versus large enterprises might be cited. But those given serve to illustrate the point that managements must fashion their mixes to fit their resources. Their objectives must be realistic.

## LONG- vs. SHORT-TERM ASPECTS OF MARKETING MIX

The marketing mix of a firm in large part is the product of the evolution that comes from day-to-day marketing. At any time the mix represents the program that a

[3]Neil H. Borden, and M. V. Marshall, *Advertising Management: Text and Cases,* Richard D. Irwin, Inc., Homewood, Ill., 1959, pp. 498–518.
[4]*Ibid.,* pp. 519–533.

management has evolved to meet the problems with which it is constantly faced in an ever changing, ever challenging market. There are continuous tactical maneuvers: a new product, aggressive promotion, or price change initiated by a competitor must be considered and met; the failure of the trade to provide adequate market coverage or display must be remedied; a faltering sales force must be reorganized and stimulated; a decline in sales share must be diagnosed and remedied; an advertising approach that has lost effectiveness must be replaced; a general business decline must be countered. All such problems call for a management's maintaining effective channels of information relative to its own operations and to the day-to-day behavior of consumers, competitors, and the trade. Thus, we may observe that short-range forces play a large part in the fashioning of the mix to be used at any time and in determining the allocation of expenditures among the various functional accounts of the operating statement.

But the overall strategy employed in a marketing mix is the product of longer range plans and procedures dictated in part by past empiricism and in part, if the management is a good one, by management foresight as to what needs to be done to keep the firm successful in a changing world. As the world has become more and more dynamic, blessed is that corporation which has managers who have foresight, who can study trends of all kinds–natural, economic, social, and technological–and, guided by these, devise long-range plans that give promise of keeping their corporations afloat and successful in the turbulent sea of market change. Accordingly, when we think of the marketing mix, we need to give particular heed today to devising a mix based on long-range planning that promises to fit the world of five or ten or more years hence. Provision for effective long-range planning in corporate organization and procedure has become more and more recognized as the earmark of good management in a world that has become increasingly subject to rapid change.

To cite an instance among American marketing organizations which has shown foresight in adjusting the marketing mix to meet social and economic change, I look upon Sears Roebuck and Company as an outstanding example. After building an unusually successful mail order business to meet the needs of a rural America, Sears management foresaw the need to depart from its marketing pattern as a mail order company catering primarily to farmers. The trend from a rural to an urban United States was going on apace. The automobile and good roads promised to make town and city stores increasingly available to those who continued to be farmers. Relatively early, Sears launched a chain of stores across the land, each easily accessible by highway to both farmer and city resident, and with adequate parking space for customers. In time there followed the remarkable telephone and mail order plan directed at urban residents to make buying easy for Americans when congested city streets and highways made shopping increasingly distasteful. Similarly, in the areas of planning products which would meet the desires of consumers in a fast changing world, of shaping its servicing to meet the needs of a wide variety of mechanical products, of pricing procedures to meet the challenging competition that came with the advent of discount retailers, the Sears organization has shown a foresight, adaptability, and creative ability worthy of emulation. The amazing growth and profitability of the company attest to the foresight and skill of its management. Its history shows the wisdom of careful attention to market forces and their impending change in devising marketing mixes that may assure growth.

## USE OF THE MARKETING MIX CONCEPT

Like many concepts, the marketing mix concept seems relatively simple, once it has been expressed. I know that before they were ever tagged with the nomenclature of "concept," the ideas involved were widely understood among marketers as a result of the growing knowledge about marketing and marketing procedures that came during the preceding half century. But I have found for myself that once the ideas were reduced to a formal statement with an accompanying visual presentation, the concept of the mix has proved a helpful device in teaching, in business problem solving, and, generally, as an aid to thinking about marketing. First of all, it is helpful in giving an answer to the question often raised, "What is marketing?" A chart which shows the elements of the mix and the forces that bear on the mix helps to bring understanding of what marketing is. It helps to explain why in our dynamic world the thinking of management in all its functional areas must be oriented to the market.

In recent years, I have kept an abbreviated chart showing the elements and the forces of the marketing mix, in front of my classes at all times. In case discussion it has proved a handy device by which to raise queries as to whether the student has recognized the implications of any recommendation he might have made in the areas of the several elements of the mix. Or, referring to the forces, we can question whether all the pertinent market forces have been given due consideration. Continual reference to the mix chart leads me to feel that the students' understanding of "what marketing is" is strengthened. The constant presence and use of the chart leaves a deeper understanding that marketing is the devising of programs that successfully meet the forces of the market.

In problem solving the marketing mix chart is a constant reminder of:

1. The fact that a problem seemingly lying in one segment of the mix must be deliberated with constant thought regarding the effect of any change in that sector on the other areas of marketing operations. The necessity of integration in marketing thinking is ever present.
2. The need of careful study of the market forces as they might bear on problems in hand.

In short, the mix chart provides an ever ready checklist as to areas into which to guide thinking when considering marketing questions or dealing with marketing problems.

## MARKETING: SCIENCE OR ART?

The quest for a "science of marketing" is hard upon us. If science is in part a systematic formulation and arrangement of facts in a way to help understanding, then the concept of the marketing mix may possibly be considered a small contribution in the search for a science of marketing. If we think of a marketing science as involving the observation and classification of facts and the establishment of verifiable laws that can be used by the marketer as a guide to action with assurance that predicted results will ensue, then we cannot be said to have gotten far toward establishing a science. The concept of the mix lays out the areas in which facts should be assembled, these to serve as a guide to management judgment in building marketing mixes. In the last few decades American marketers have made substantial progress in adopting the scientific method in assembling facts. They have sharpened the tools of fact finding—both those arising within the business and those external to it. Aided by these facts and by the skills developed through careful observation and experience, marketers are better fitted to practice the art of designing marketing mixes than would be the case had not the techniques of gathering facts been advanced as they have been in recent decades. Moreover, marketers have made progress in the use of the scientific method in designing tests whereby the results from mixes or parts of mixes can be measured. Thereby marketers have been learning how to subject the hypotheses of their mix artists to empirical check.

With continued improvement in the search for and the recording of facts pertinent to marketing, with further application of the controlled experiment, and with an extension and careful recording of case histories, we may hope for a gradual formulation of clearly defined and helpful marketing laws. Until then, and even then, marketing and the building of marketing mixes will largely lie in the realm of art.

# II

# *Organizing the Marketing Function*

*The concept of being marketing-oriented has had a substantial effect on the organizational structure of the firm—from both a formal and an informal point of view.*

*This impact on organization has been duly noted by certain behavioral scientists interested in human organizations such as the business firm. Thus, different philosophies of organization have been brought into clearer perspective as a result of the marketing concept.*

*Organizational changes within the marketing department must occur if the marketing concept is to be implemented. Changes must also occur between the marketing department and other areas within the firm, although they may or may not be reflected in changes in the formal organization of the firm.*

*The impact of marketing generally makes itself felt in attitudinal changes that affect the ways in which individuals cooperate with each other and the points of view taken with respect to problem solving. These attitudinal changes ultimately find their way into new procedures which prescribe relationships between departments. Increasingly it is recognized that the marketing department has a greater role to play in more decision areas than ever before.*

# 5. THE CREATIVE ORGANIZATION

*Gary A. Steiner*

*This material presents an overview of the characteristics of a creative organization and the conditions which foster creativity.*

*Because of the role played by the marketing organization in locating and interpreting demand, it is critical that the firm should function as a creative organization.*

First, a few words about what the key terms in this summary mean: "Creativity" has been defined in a number of ways in the psychological literature, in business discussion, in the arts and sciences generally. Within the transcript of this seminar there appear many explicit, and many more implicit, definitions of varying degrees of generality. We make no attempt to frame a master definition at this point. But for purposes of this overview, it is necessary and hopefully sufficient to make this general distinction: *Creativity* has to do with the development, proposal, and implementation of *new* and *better* solutions; *productivity,* with the efficient application of *current* "solutions."

What "better" means, and who is to say, is one of the sticky methodological issues in the field. What it most often means in these pages is better according to professional colleagues or superiors. The meaning of "solution" obviously varies by field; in the following, solutions range from practical answers to specific problems through new concepts in art, music, or architecture to the most general and abstract conceptualizations that characterize a breakthrough in, say, theoretical physics.

Many of the studies we will cite distinguish "high-creative" from "low-" or "average-creative" groups. It should be clear that "high" and "low" are relative, and not

Source: From *The Creative Organization,* The University of Chicago Press, Chicago, 1965, pp. 4–24, by permission of The University of Chicago Press. Gary A. Steiner: Professor of Psychology, Graduate School of Business, University of Chicago.

absolute, designations. In most of the samples under investigation, both "high" and "low" groups would qualify as highly creative within the population at large and often even within the profession. It would therefore not have been euphemistic—just too clumsy—to use the designations "more highly" and "less highly" creative. Bear in mind, though, that this is what the shorthand distinction between "high" and "low" means.

## I. THE RAW MATERIAL: INDIVIDUAL CREATIVITY

Do individual differences in creativity exist? Does it make sense to speak of more and less creative people in some such way as we speak of more and less intelligent, more or less coordinated, or more or less musical people? Or is personal creativity, like fathering twins, mostly a matter of being in the right place at the right time?

As important as circumstances are in determining who will create what and when, it seems that there are consistent and persistent differences in individual creativity. Holding conditions constant, some people are likely to be more creative than others; and these differences are likely to show up in other situations and at other times. In fact, in most fields, the distribution of creative contributions is something like the distribution of personal income in the United States: a small percentage of people accounts for a large share of the total.

Are these differences in personal creativity specific to particular areas of endeavor, or is there such a thing as general creativity?

That issue involves the distinction between *capacity* and *performance.* Except for a few outstanding historical examples, the most creative people in one field are not likely at the same time to be the most creative in another. But this may be largely a matter of specialization in training and effort. Is an unusually creative architect likely to be highly creative in chemistry also, assuming equal training and opportunity? And are highly creative architects, or chemists, distinguished only by greater creativity in their respective professions, or can they be distinguished from their less creative colleagues in personal capacities and characteristics beyond differential performance on the job?

The results of various testing programs suggest that the qualities and capacities that distinguish more from less creative practitioners of given fields *do* extend beyond the specific area of professional competence. Creative architects, for instance, differ not only in the way they approach architecture but also in the way they approach any number of situations and tasks, some far removed and apparently unrelated to the specific demands of their profession.

What is more, there seem to be at least some differences that hold across diverse fields; for example, some of the same personality characteristics that distinguish between architects of high and average creativity have been observed in studies of creativity not only in industrial research chemists, but even among high school children differing in general creativity.

Granted that people differ in "creativity," are we really talking about anything more than general intelligence?

Yes. General intelligence seems to bear about the same relationship to on-the-job creativity at the professional level as weight does to ability in football. You have to have a lot of it to be in the game at all; but among those on the team–all of whom have a great deal of weight to begin with–differences in performance are only slightly, if at all, related to weight. In short, in the total population, creativity in most fields is associated with high intelligence, probably more so in some (e.g., physics) than in others (art). But within a given group of practitioners, operating at roughly the same professional level, differences in general intelligence provide no significant prediction of differences in creative performance.

What, then, are the characteristics of the creative individual, especially those that might be subject to measurement before the fact so as to make prediction possible?

Although many characteristics of the creative individual, perhaps some of the most important, undoubtedly vary according to the area of creativity, studies of "highs" and "lows" in various fields are beginning to yield some common denominators. The following list concentrates on those differences that are probably more general. In some cases, this assumption of generality stems only from the fact that it seems reasonable on analysis of the characteristics involved *vis-à-vis* the general demands of the creative process. In others, the generality of the finding is actually supported by research from independent studies in diverse areas.

## INTELLECTUAL CHARACTERISTICS

Although measures of general intelligence fail to predict creativity, highs, as a group, typically outscore lows in tests of the following mental abilities:

*Conceptual Fluency.* The ability to generate a large number of ideas rapidly: List tools beginning with the letter *t*; novel uses for a brick; possible consequences of a situation; categories into which the names of a thousand great men can be sorted–to name just a few of the tasks that have actually been used.

*Conceptual Flexibility.* The ability to shift gears, to discard one frame of reference for another; the tendency to change approaches spontaneously.

*Originality.* The ability and/or tendency to give unusual, atypical (therefore more probably new) answers to questions, responses to situations, interpretations of events.

Highs, for instance, are more apt to give rare–as well as more–uses of bricks; they give fewer "popular" interpretations of what an inkblot looks like; in high school, uncommon vs. common career aspirations (e.g., explorer rather than lawyer).

*Preference for Complexity.* Highs often exhibit a preference for the complex, and to them intriguing, as against the simple and easily understood.

When confronted with complex inkblots, for instance, they tend to seek a more difficult "whole" interpretation that takes the entire blot into account, rather than to identify detailed aspects that clearly resemble certain things.

The usual interpretation is that highs take complexity as a challenge; that they enjoy the attempt to integrate and resolve it.

## PERSONALITY

Several closely related personality characteristics distinguish highs and lows in a number of studies:

*Independence of Judgment.* Highs are more apt to stick to their guns when they find themselves in disagreement with others.

In a situation where an artificially induced group consensus contradicts the evidence of their own senses, lows more often yield in their expressed judgment. The same is true when the issue at stake is not a factual one but involves voicing an opinion on an aesthetic, social, or political matter.

*Deviance.* Highs see themselves as more different from their peers and, in fact, they appear to *be* more different in any number of significant as well as trivial characteristics.

At the extreme, highs sometimes feel lonely and apart, with a sense of mission that isolates them, in their own minds, from average men with average concerns.

*Attitudes toward Authority.* A related distinction with far-reaching implications for organizations has to do with the way authority is viewed. The difference between highs and lows is a matter of degree, but to make the point we describe the extremes.

Lows are more apt to view authority as final and absolute; to offer unquestioning obedience, allegiance, or belief (as the case may be), with respect approaching deference; to accept present authority as "given" and more or less permanent. Highs are more likely to think of authority as conventional or arbitrary, contingent on continued and demonstrable superiority; to accept dependence on authority as a matter of expedience rather than personal allegiance or moral obligation, to view present authority as temporary.

Attitudes toward subordinates are related in the appropriate direction; those who pay unquestioned allegiance tend to expect it, and vice versa.

Similarly, and in general, highs are more apt to separate source from content in their evaluation of communications, to judge and reach conclusions on the basis of the information itself. Lows are more prone to accept or reject, believe or disbelieve messages on the basis of their attitudes toward the sender.

*"Impulse Acceptance."* Highs are more willing to entertain and express personal whims and impulses; lows stick closer to "realistic," expected behavior. Highs pay more heed to inner voices, while lows suppress them in favor of external demands.

So, for example, highs may introduce humor into situations where it is not called for and bring a better sense of humor to situations where it is. And, in general, highs exhibit a richer and more diverse "fantasy life" on any number of clinical tests.

Does the more creative man have more inner impulses or fewer inhibitions, or both, and to what degree? The answer is unknown, but there is at least one intriguing finding that suggests a strange combination of two normally opposing traits:

In the genius and near-genius, a widely used personality test shows "schizoid" tendencies (bizarre, unusual, unrealistic thoughts and urges) *coupled* with great "ego strength" (ability to control, channel, and manipulate reality effectively). This line of inquiry begins to speak the cliché that the dividing line between madman and genius is a fine one. According to this finding, the line is fine, but firm.

In sum, highly creative people are more likely than others to view authority as conventional rather than absolute; to make fewer black-and-white distinctions; to have a less dogmatic and more relativistic view of life; to show more independence of judgment and less conventionality and conformity, both intellectual and social; to be more willing to entertain, and sometimes express, their own "irrational" impulses; to place a greater value on humor and in fact to have a better sense of humor; in short to be somewhat freer and less rigidly—but not less effectively—controlled.

## APPROACH TO PROBLEMS

The more detailed aspects of the creative process are taken up in the next section, where we see highs at work. We briefly note three distinctions as personal characteristics of creative problem solvers; all are especially significant in the management of creativity and are elaborated upon later.

*Motivation.* Highs are more perceptive to, and more motivated by, the interest inherent in the problem and its solution. Accordingly, they get more involved in the task, work harder and longer in the absence of external pressures or incentive, and generally place *relatively* greater value on "job interest" versus such extrinsic rewards as salary or status. There is no evidence, however, that the *absolute* importance of external incentives is any less for highs than for lows.

*Orientation.* Along somewhat the same lines.

Lows are more likely to see their future largely within the boundaries of one organization, to be concerned chiefly with its problems and with their own rise within it, and to develop extensive ties and associations within the community; in short, to be "local" in their loyalties and aspirations.

Highs are more apt to think in terms of a larger community, both residential and professional; to view themselves more as members of the profession (whether management, chemistry, or teaching) than as members of Company X; to take their cues from the larger professional community and attempt to rise within it; to be more mobile, hence less "loyal" to any specific organization; in short, to be cosmopolitan in orientation and aspiration.

Hence, the local is more willing to change assignments, even professions (for example, from chemistry or engineering to administration), in the interests of the organization and his own career within it. The cosmopolitan is more likely to change organizations to pursue *his* interests and career within the larger profession. In short highs change jobs to pursue their interests, not their interests to pursue their jobs.

*Pace.* Highs often spend more time in the initial stages of problem formulation, in broad scanning of alternatives. Lows are more apt to "get on with it."

For example, in problems divisible into analytic and synthetic stages, highs spend more time on the former, in absolute as well as relative terms. As a result, they often leave lows behind in the later stages of the solution process, having disposed of more blind alleys and being able to make more comprehensive integrations as a result of more thorough analysis.

One interpretation is that highs have less anxiety to produce, that they are confident enough of their eventual success to be able to step back and take a broad look before making commitments.

Can such differences be measured reliably enough to be of use in selection programs?

Many of these qualities can be measured, at least in part, by simple paper-and-pencil tests or other controlled observations. But the instruments are far from perfect and, perhaps more seriously, the correlation between each of these distinguishing characteristics and on-the-job creativity is limited. The characteristics "distinguish" highs from lows only in the sense that highs, on the average, have more of, or more often exhibit, the particular quality. And that is far from saying that all highs have more of each than all lows.[1]

As a result, as with all actuarial predictions of this sort, the procedure becomes more useful as the number of cases to be predicted increases. If many people are to be selected and it is important that some of them will turn out to be highs, a testing program can improve the odds. This would apply, for instance, in the selection of college or graduate students, Air Force Research and Development Officers, or chemists in a major industrial laboratory.

[1] In general, validity coefficients for specific tests at best attain values around .60, which means that they predict about 36 per cent of the variation in observed creativity.

But if few people are being selected and it is important that almost all of them turn out to be highly creative (the chiefs of staff; the top management team; or the scientists to head a project), it is doubtful that, at present, a testing program will improve the odds beyond those of careful personal appraisal and judgment.

In this connection, there is the interesting suggestion (not documented) that highs may themselves be better judges of creativity in others; that it "takes one to tell one."

As the examples suggest, testing to predict creativity is perhaps least effective where needed most: where the importance of the individual cases is the greatest.

What are the observable characteristics of the creative process; how does it look to an outsider while it is going on?

The appearance of the creative process, especially in its early stages, poses a problem to administrators. Up to a point, it may be hard to distinguish from totally non-productive behavior: undisciplined disorder, aimless rambling, even total inactivity.

*Irregular Progress.* Creativity is rarely a matter of gradual, step-by-step progress; it is more often a pattern of large and largely unpredictable leaps after relatively long periods of no apparent progress.

The extreme example is the sudden insight that occurs after a difficult problem is put aside, and at a time of no conscious concern with the matter. Many anecdotes support the film cliche where the great man cries "Eureka!" in the middle of the night or while shaving—or, as in this famous case, while getting on a bus.

> Just at this time I left Caen, where I was then living, to go on a geological excursion under the auspices of the school of mines. The changes of travel made me forget my mathematical work. Having reached Coutances, we entered an omnibus to some place or other. At the moment when I put my foot on the step the idea came to me, without anything in my former thoughts seeming to have paved the way for it, that the transformations I had used to define the Fuchsian functions were identical with those of non-Euclidean geometry. I did not verify the idea; I should not have had time, as, upon taking my seat in the omnibus, I went on with a conversation already commenced, but I felt a perfect certainty. On my return to Caen, for conscience's sake I verified the result at my leisure.—POINCARÉ

At a level of more immediate concern to most administrators, since few have the problem or the prowess of a Poincaré, the same sort of progress pattern distinguishes creative from merely productive work, and more from less creative activity, in the kind of problem-solving that characterizes the day-to-day activities of the organization.

*Suspended Judgment.* The creative process often requires and exhibits suspended judgment. The dangers of early commitment—sometimes to "incorrigible strategies"—are apparent at various levels. In the perceptual laboratory, for example, people who make an early, incorrect interpretation of a picture in an "ambiguitor" (a device that gradually brings a blurred picture into focus), will tend to retain the wrong perception—actually fail to "see"—even when the picture has been fully and clearly exposed.

Similarly, in the type of small-group problem-solving or decision-making so typical of the modern organization, people will "stick to their guns" to support a position they have taken publicly, beyond its apparent validity and usefulness.

Finally, at the level of the organization itself, financial, technical, or corporate commitments to products, techniques, physical facilities, affiliations, and the like, often stand in the way of change even when it is recognized as necessary and inevitable.

*"Undisciplined" Exploration.* Again, many creators stress the importance of undisciplined thinking, especially in the initial stages, probably because it serves to expand the range of consideration and raw material from which the new solution will emerge.

In this connection, we hear of the use of artificial disorganizers and "boundary expanders," such as alcohol, brain-storming sessions, sometimes even narcotics; and, frequently, the observation that inspiration cannot be willed or worked on, that pressure and preoccupation with the problem are least likely to produce insight–though they may indeed sustain effort in other phases of the process.

The administrative enigma, then, is to distinguish, before the fact, incubation from laziness; suspended judgment from indecision; "boundary expansion" from simple drinking; undisciplined thinking as a deliberate exploratory step from undisciplined thinking as a permanent characteristic; brain-storming from gibberish by committee. In short, how can one tell the temporarily fallow mind–open and receptive, working subconsciously, and just on the threshold of the brilliant flash–from the permanently idle one? There may, of course, not be an answer. In time, outward predictors and distinguishing characteristics (beyond the individual's past history) may emerge. But for the moment, tolerance for high-risk gambles on creativity is probably one of the prerequisites or costs of playing for the higher stakes creativity provides when it does pay off.

What are the characteristics of the psychological state optimal for creative production?

*Motivation.* How much should be at stake; how hard should a man be trying, in order to maximize his chances of being creative? There is an apparent paradox:

First, we often hear that the creative process is characterized by a tremendous sense of commitment, a feeling of urgency, even of mission, that results in enormous preoccupation with the problem and perseverance.

On the other hand, there is evidence that extremely high motivation narrows the focus and produces rigidity, perseveration rather than perseverance, which not only precludes creativity but reduces productivity (freezing up in the clutch). Some go so far as to say that the absence of pressure is a common denominator in situations conducive to creativity.

There are two suggested resolutions: One is that the relationship is curvilinear; that creativity first rises, then falls, with motivation–you need enough to maintain effort at high levels but not so much as to produce panic attempts at immediate solution (jumping out of the window instead of looking for the fire escape). And there is, in fact, good evidence of such a relationship in laboratory studies of human and even animal problem-solving.

The other possible resolution involves a distinction in quality of motivation—between "inner" and "outer," "involvement" and "pressure," "drive" and "stress"—related to the earlier observation that highs are more driven by interest and involvement in the task itself than by external incentives. Perhaps external pressure impedes creativity, while inner drive and task-involvement are prerequisites.

In short, it may very well be that "Genius is 90 per cent hard work" but that inducing hard work is unlikely to produce genius.

The two resolutions are not mutually exclusive. Motivation of both kinds may have a breaking point, a level where they do more harm than good; although it seems reasonable to suppose that higher levels of "intrinsic" than of "extrinsic" motivation are compatible with creativity.

At any rate, other things being equal, interest in and commitment to the problem for its own sake should point to a creative outcome more often than sustained effort purchased by some externally attached reward, simply because the former is more apt to channel energy in the relevant directions.

*Open-Mindedness versus Conviction.* What intellectual attitude toward one's ideas and suggestions is optimal; how much conviction versus continual reappraisal; self-involvement versus objective detachment? Again, both tendencies appear, and in the extreme.

On the one hand, creativity is characterized by a willingness to seek and accept relevant information from any and all sources, to suspend judgment, defer commitment, remain aloof in the face of pressures, to take a stand. On the other hand, creators in the process of creating are often described as having conviction approaching zeal.

There may in fact be a sort of simultaneous "antimony" or interaction between "passion and decorum," "commitment and detachment," domination *by* a problem and yet a view of it as objective and external. The process may involve the continual and conflicting presence of both components. Or it may be a matter of stages. Perhaps the creative process is characterized by open-mindedness in the early, idea-getting phases; then by a bull-headed conviction at the point of dissemination and execution.

There could be at least two reasons. A more open mind, that initially examines more alternatives, is more likely to be convinced of the one it finally selects. An early commitment to a less carefully analyzed approach may be more vulnerable in the face of attack; beliefs developed through more painful and agonizing appraisal are more apt to stand the test of time.

In addition, creators almost always find themselves on the defensive in the period after the idea has been developed but before it has been "sold." There is an inevitable stepping on toes, effrontery to the *status quo* and those responsible for it, that usually leads to some rejection of the maverick, especially if the innovation is not immediately, demonstrably superior. And people on the defensive are apt to overstate their case. In short, open-minded probers may become fervent proselytizers.

As a working summary hypothesis:

In the exploratory, idea-getting stages, there is great interest in the problem; perhaps commitment to its eventual solution but certainly not to any particular approach; an open-minded willingness to pursue leads in any direction; a relaxed and perhaps playful attitude that allows a disorganized, undisciplined approach, to the point of putting the problem aside entirely. But at the point of development and execution, where the selected alternative is pursued, tested, and applied, there is great conviction, dogged perseverance, perhaps strong personal involvement, and dogmatic support of the new way.

## II. THE ORGANIZATION ITSELF

What does all this have to do with organization? What are the characteristics of the creative organization; and what are the implications of individual creativity, if any?

There are various ways to approach this question.

One is to reason, deductively, *from* the characteristics of creators and the creative process *to* the kind of environment that ought to be congenial to them and conducive to creative activity. What does the nature of individual creativity imply about the environmental factors that foster or impede it? For the most part, this is the way we proceed in what follows.

Another approach is to treat the organization, as a whole, as the creative unit. Perhaps some of the characteristics that distinguish "high" and "low" individuals also apply to high and low organization as such.

The characteristics of creative individuals suggest a number of rather direct translations or counterparts at the organizational level; and many of the characteristics independently attributed to creative organizations seem to match items in our description of individual highs.

Here is a brief summary:

| *The Creative Individual* | *The Creative Organization* |
|---|---|
| Conceptual fluency . . . is able to produce a large number of ideas quickly | Has idea men<br>Open channels of communication<br>*Ad hoc* devices:<br>Suggestion systems<br>Brain-storming<br>Idea units absolved of other responsibilities<br>Encourages contact with outside sources |

| | |
|---|---|
| Originality . . . generates unusual ideas | Heterogenous personnel policy<br>Includes marginal, unusual types<br>Assigns non-specialists to problems<br>Allows eccentricity |
| Separates source from content in evaluating information . . . is motivated by interest in problem . . . follows wherever it leads | Has an objective, fact-founded approach<br>Ideas evaluated on their merits, not status of originator<br>*Ad hoc* approaches:<br>Anonymous communications<br>Blind votes<br>Selects and promotes on merit only |
| Suspends judgment . . . avoids early commitment . . . spends more time in analysis, exploration | Lack of financial, material commitment to products, policies<br>Invests in basic research; flexible, long-range planning<br>Experiments with new ideas rather than prejudging on "rational" grounds; everything gets a chance |
| Less authoritarian . . . has relativistic view of life | More decentralized; diversified<br>Administrative slack; time and resources to absorb errors<br>Risk-taking ethos . . . tolerates and expects taking chances |
| Accepts own impulses . . . playful, undisciplined exploration | Not run as "tight ship"<br>Employees have fun<br>Allows freedom to choose and pursue problems<br>Freedom to discuss ideas |
| Independence of judgment, less conformity | Organizationally autonomous |
| Deviant, sees self as different | Original and different objectives, not trying to be another "X" |
| Rich, "bizarre" fantasy life *and* superior reality orientation; controls | Security of routine . . . *allows* innovation . . . , "philistines" provide stable, secure environment that allows "creators" to roam<br>Has separate units or occasions for generating versus evaluating ideas . . . separates creative from productive functions |

This analogizing has serious limitations and it may be misleading. But the table does serve as an organized index to some of the major characteristics attributed to creative organizations, and it is interesting that so many of them sound like the distinguishing characteristics of individual highs.

Finally, there is direct, empirical study of actual creative organizations. This may well turn out to be the most fruitful approach, but it was not the major focus of the seminar. In part, this reflects the state of knowledge; systematic studies of creative organizations, as such, simply do not exist as yet. In part, the composition of the symposium is responsible. A meeting with six psychologists and one psychoanalyst, against three sociologists, inevitably speaks mostly in psychological terms.

At any rate, we make no attempt to represent, let alone do justice to, the sociological investigation and analysis of organizational factors that relate to creativity. In what follows, we reason and abstract mostly from the nature of individual creativity, partly from rather informal observations of actual organizations.

What, specifically, can management do—beyond selecting creative participants—to foster creativity within and on the part of the organization?

*Values and Rewards.* What explicit and implicit goals and values characterize the creative organization? What system of rewards and incentives maximizes creativity?

First the creative organization in fact prizes and rewards creativity. A management philosophy that stresses creativity as an organizational goal, that encourages and expects it at all levels, will increase the chances of its occurrence.

But it is one thing to call for creativity, another to mean it, and still another to reward it adequately and consistently when it occurs. More specifically, creativity as a value should find expression in the following:

*Compensation.* In most areas of day-to-day functioning, productivity rather than creativity is and should be the principal objective; thus, general reward policies tend to measure and stress regular output. But even where creativity is truly desired and encouraged in good faith, activities that are potentially more creative may be subordinated to those more visibly and closely tied to reward policies. (A familiar academic illustration is the "pressure to publish," which may lead to a plethora of relatively insignificant formula-projects that minimize chances of failure—non-publication—but also of creativity.)

In the business enterprise, a similar grievance centers on discrepancies in reward between the sowing and reaping aspects of the operation; with the greater rewards for work that shows immediate, measurable results (e.g., sales) as against that which may pay off in the longer run (such as basic research).

It may be inevitable that work closer to the balance sheet will be more swiftly and fully compensated than efforts that have tenuous, uncertain, and in any case long-range effects on corporate profits. But creativity and guaranteed, immediate results do not go together; not between, nor within, assignments. If creativity is to be fostered, not impeded, by material incentives, they will have to be applied by a different yardstick.

It is probably this simple: Where creativity and not productivity is in fact the goal, then creativity and not productivity should in fact be measured and rewarded. And if creativity is harder to measure and takes longer periods to assess, then this probably requires some speculative investment on the part of the firm that wants to keep and nurture the few men and the few activities that will eventually be worth it.[2]

*Channels for Advancement.* Where concern is with creativity in a professional unit or other specialized function operating within the larger organization, there is this

[2] High potential pay-off and low risk are, unfortunately, incompatible—just as they are in the stock market and at the gambling tables.

related implication: To the extent possible, there should be formal channels for advancement and status within the area of creativity.

Where it is impossible to promote a creative chemist without taking him out of chemistry, he faces a choice between money and position on the one hand, and chemistry on the other. The company is likely to lose his services as chemist in either case: to administration within its own walls or to another organization where a chemist as such can get ahead. (This is one of the chief organizational advantages and attractions of the major university for the research scientist or scholar: parallel channels for advancement, of at least equal status, exist outside of administration.)

To some extent this is a matter of size; it is hard to provide for advancement within a department of one or two persons. But size alone is not enough. The nature and number of status levels established, their labels, and especially their actual value within the firm and the larger community, will determine their worth to individuals who hold them.

*"Freedom."* Within rather broad limits, creativity is increased by giving creators freedom in choice of problem and method of pursuit. In line with the high's greater interest and involvement in his work, greater freedom is necessary, to maximize those satisfactions that are important to him and that channel his efforts into avenues most likely to prove creative. Whether and where there is an upper limit is a point of much contention and no evidence.

But such freedom often puts the appropriate objectives of the organization at odds with the demands of maximum creativity. The symposium itself produced two striking examples.

In one instance, a participant "distracted" himself and the group by working out and presenting an elegant general solution to a mathematical problem that had been mentioned only in passing, as a task assigned to subjects in a creativity experiment. From the point of view of the seminar, he was out of bounds. By following his own interests, he was creative. (Would he have arrived at an equally elegant *psychological* insight had he been constrained to the issue as externally defined?)

More dramatically, after the first few hours of the meeting had been spent in rather academic and abstract discussion, one participant reminded us that the purpose of the meeting was to develop useful and understandable guidelines for management and that we had better get on with it. This precipitated a short but heartfelt donnybrook between the advocates of "No nonsense! Keep your eye on the target," and "Take it easy; it's interesting; let's see where it leads"; between "What good is it if you can't tell us what it means for management?" and "Our job is to create, yours to apply."

Both approaches are valid but as means to different ends. Those responsible for a meeting are rightfully concerned with maximizing its output. By the same token, creative individuals who attend it are not so concerned with the product of the particular conference as with the pursuit of interesting lines of inquiry, whether or not they happen to reach fruition during the session. And curtailing and channeling discussion into areas known to be productive obviously limits the chances of coming up with something outside the range of the ordinary.

This, then, is probably one of the principal costs in the nurture of creativity: Except in the rare and fortunate case where a creative individual's interests exactly match the day-to-day operating objectives of his organization, and continue to do so over time, the organization pays a price, at least in the short run, for giving him his head. What he returns to the organization may or may not compensate it many-fold.

*Communication.* Many observations point to the importance of free and open channels of communication, both vertical and horizontal.

On the one hand, potential creators need and seek relevant information whatever its source, within or without the organization; on the other hand, they are stimulated by diverse and complex input.

Equally important, ideas wither for lack of a grapevine. A possible approach, a feasible but half-baked notion, or even a well worked-out solution must be communicated to those with the power to evaluate, authorize, and implement.

The presence of formal channels is not enough. People must feel free to use them, and channels must not be clogged by routine paperflow that ties up time with "programmed trivia," and creates an air of apathy and neglect toward incoming messages because it is so unlikely that they will contain anything of value.

Since highs tend toward cosmopolitan, professional orientation; the organization must at least provide for and perhaps encourage contact and communication with colleagues and associations on the outside.

As a special case, there is the matter of scientific and professional publication in the appropriate journals, which is often of great personal importance to creators.

There may be problems of security and the natural jealousy of corporate secrets and employee loyalties. But in many cases, these are unrealistic or exaggerated, given the high rate of horizontal mobility, the discretion of the professional, and the fact that most "secrets" are not. At any rate, there may be no reason to think that the balance of payments will be "out"; there should be at least as much information gained as given away in most external contacts. And in many cases, and within broad limits, the net gain in satisfaction, creativity, and perhaps tenure of highs will probably offset the time and trade secrets lost to the outside.

What, specifically, are the costs of creativity? What must an organization be prepared to give up or tolerate if it wants to increase its creativity?

Answers were scattered throughout the preceding, but it may help to pull them together.

First, creativity, by definition, is a high-risk enterprise, not for society or industry, at large, but for any given unit that attempts it. The greater the departure from present practice, the less likelihood that the innovation will work; the greater the potential payoff, the less the odds of its occurring. Conversely, the larger the number of workers or units independently pursuing any problem, the better the chances that one or more of them will succeed.

In the abstract, then, decisions as to whether and where to attempt creativity, and how much to try for, are much like decisions concerning what to insure, and for how much—although the hopes and fears are reversed.

Second, within the unit under consideration, fostering creativity assesses costs in assured productivity. To the extent that energy is consumed in investigation and exploration, it does not go into work known to be productive.

Finally, depending on the personal tastes and preferences of management, there may or may not be costs in "security," "comfort," and "congeniality" of the environment: (*a*) Highs are not as deferent, obedient, flattering, easy to control, flexible to *external* demands and changes, conventional, predictable, and so on, through a long list of desiderata in "good" employees. (*b*) In addition, highs are more mobile, less "loyal"—harder to hold by ordinary extrinsic rewards—but easier to acquire by the offer of interesting opportunities. At any rate, they make for a less stable and secure, more challenging but perhaps more disturbing environment. (*c*) A creative organization itself is more committed to change; operates on a faster track; has a less certain or predictable future than the efficient, me-too operation.

In short, maximizing creativity is not the principal objective of any organization at all times, or even of all organizations at some times. When it is, there are some rough guidelines to how it may be fostered—but not, it is suggested, at no cost.

Consider the organization as a whole, operating within a larger social and economic environment. What type of situation is most likely to produce a creative organization?

The seminar produced little agreement, let alone evidence, on this matter. There was some discussion about the effects of competitive position, size, age, and general success of an organization as they affect its need and chances for creativity. But nothing approaching a conclusion is visible.

One of the more interesting recurrent debates centered on the relative merits of firmly led, "one-man" organizations versus decentralized corporate entities; on charismatic, inspired leadership by a "great man" versus the greater democracy of the professionally managed organization. This debate was not resolved, but it does call attention to some distinctions that may be important.

*Some Final Distinctions.* Last, we take note of some distinctions that may be helpful, suggested simply by the experience of trying to discuss "the creative organization." For instance, the preceding debate may reflect a failure to distinguish between a creative organization and one that produces for a creator.

An organization can be an efficient instrument for the execution of externally created ideas and yet not be in itself creative: for instance, a smooth military unit under a great strategist, a top-notch symphony orchestra, or, in the same terms, a business that hums to the tune of a creative president. These may all implement creativity and yield a product appropriately called creative, but they are not, *ipso facto,* creative organizations. And the characteristics that make for creativity within and on the part of an organization as a whole may in fact be quite different from those that make it the efficient tool of a creative master.

Along the same lines, it may be helpful to distinguish between getting people to be more creative and getting creative people to be more productive. The conditions that induce a Frank Lloyd Wright, an Ogilvy, or a Shockley to turn out more of the same—to repeat or elaborate earlier innovations—may be quite different from those that produce the original and subsequent departures.

In short, organizations, like people, may increase their net yield of creative *products* either by the terms that go into their conception or those that enter into their output. And while the net effects may often be the same, the means are probably not.

For the eventual understanding of "the creative organization," it may be important to learn the difference between creating productivity and producing creativity.

# 6. ORGANIZATION STRUCTURE AND ITS UNDERLYING THEORY OF BUYER BEHAVIOR

*John A. Howard*

*Changing technology—particularly that represented in our knowledge of buyer behavior and the computer—requires that marketing executives look at company organization in new ways.*

*The tremendous amount of marketing information now possible and the availability of formal ways of handling information force him to think in terms of information flows in the company. The marketing executive must be able to use this information, and thus he must be free to specify the information he needs.*

*The information specified by the marketing executives constitutes the company's marketing information system. The system then becomes a part of function of the executives' theory of buyer behavior and the computer's capacity. These developments have a number of implications, both specific and general.*

The writer wishes to discuss a fact long true but only recently recognized. The fact that the executives' theory of buyer behavior influences the nature of the organizational structure of their company. Only with the development of the computer, however, has this fact great significance. To lay a brief background for this discussion it is well to describe a way of looking at company organization.

Source: From John S. Wright and Jac L. Goldstucker (eds.), *New Ideas for Successful Marketing,* American Marketing Association, Chicago, 1966, pp. 87–93. John A. Howard: Professor of Marketing, Graduate School of Business, Columbia University.

## EXECUTIVE THEORY OF BUYER BEHAVIOR

A company's organizational structure can be defined in terms of the flows of information that enable the company to operate. Specifically, these flows can be described by the usual paradigm of communications research: *Who* communicates *what* to *whom* and *when* through which *channel* with what *effect.* The central role of these information flows in a company is not at all obvious, however; and this is one of the reasons why the usual organization chart often hides more than it reveals about the real nature of a company.

Taking this view of company organization as a network of information flows as a background, one must analyze why these flows are what they are, which is another way of saying, "Why the organizational structure is what it is." Any company's organizational structure is the result of many forces, but one of the dominant forces is the way executives think. The way they think, in turn, determines the kinds and amounts of information they want in making their decisions. Normally it has been said that "An executive is a prisoner of his communication network." Now with the new computer technology his information network can be redesigned. Major organizational changes are in the offing.

One of the things that marketing executives obviously think much about is the buyer. The way they think about him determines the information they want about him. In fact, it seems that a greater emphasis upon thinking about buyers is the central characteristic of the marketing concept which has received so much attention.

Not only do executives think about buyers but they think systematically about buyers. Executives soon develop firm views about what causes buyers to behave as they do. These views imply that certain relationships exist. In other words, executives have a theory of buyer behavior. Anyone doing research on the executive decision process quickly finds, however, that executives do not generally articulate these beliefs with ease. The beliefs are implicit. Only upon repeated and insistent interrogation are they usually able to make their beliefs explicit.

Two developments have tended to place the executive in the position of having to articulate his theory of buyer behavior. One of these developments took place some years ago and the other is on the horizon. The first development is market research. It was adopted rapidly by industry after World War II. When they meet to discuss a market research report and they attempt to explain the findings, executives expose their beliefs about the nature of the buyers. The executive seldom has the time to participate in such meetings long enough to fully articulate his beliefs and his theory. By participating more in the original design of the study, however, he would be still more explicit. Unfortunately, one of the greatest weaknesses in rational decision in current marketing is that the executive who uses the report seldom participates in the study design where the decision is made as to what facts to collect.

Only when one looks to the future is it obvious how the executive's theory will shape company organization. Here we find that the second development which is a still more radical innovation than market—computer and its related paraphernalia—is clearly on the near horizon. First, the computer has removed some serious barriers to the use of normative decision models. In using normative decision models, General Electric is finding that automated marketing decisions are far more sensitive to errors in sales estimates than to errors in the other decision inputs such as production cost and the interest rate. Hence, in this way the computer is showing us how essential it is to reduce the error in our estimates of buyer behavior. Second, the computer has made possible the implementation of the concept of a *marketing information system.* What does one mean by a company marketing information system? It has at least two identifying characteristics: it is *centralized* and a *continuous arrangement* for collecting market facts.

By examining these two characteristics of centralization and continuity, it will become more obvious why executives' theories of buyer behavior must now be laid bare. First, in the process of pooling the information collection activities of the marketing operation, each element of the operation such as advertising, distribution, market research, product development, sales and the like is placed in the position of having to defend why it wants some kinds of information and not others. The give and take of the negotiation process of working out this list of information requirements will inevitably give hints as to each executive's theory, and the more articulate executives will describe theirs in some detail. The executive's theory is probably more apparent when he is justifying the facts he wants than in most other circumstances.

Second, the continuity characteristic of a marketing information system requires that fact collection be far better planned than it now tends to be in the typical market research department which is so often deluged by *ad hoc* studies. If the system is to be useful, comparable data must be collected at regular intervals. Hence, a heavy investment is being made. In all areas of decision, the amount of money at stake strongly determines the amount of attention, thought and care given to the decision. Hence, the continuity characteristic will be a force requiring each executive to articulate his theory as best he can.

## THEORY OF BUYERS AND INFORMATION FLOWS

The foregoing comments have implied that an executive's theory of buyers will shape the flows of information which are the structure of the company or organization. Let us now, however, be more explicit about the way in which this is so.

The implementation of a computerized marketing information system requires that all executives in the marketing operation of a company be willing to accept (to internalize psychologically) roughly the same theory of buyer behavior. Contemplating the installation of a marketing information system has a certain diagnostic value. For example, it implies that unless executives do have essentially the same theory the company cannot hope ever to *develop* and *execute* a coherent, unified marketing plan with or without a computer. A strong top executive may force the development of such a plan by sheer leadership; but unless his subordinates believe in it, they will not execute it as effectively. A corollary of this implication is that a company with a coherent, unified marketing plan is evidence that its executives do think alike and do hold to the same theory of buyer behavior.

The following illustrates the point of the consequences of a company's marketing executives holding different theories of buyer behavior. The example concerns the introduction of a new product in the package goods industry, e.g., General Foods, P. & G., or General Mills. Assume that the sales manager holds to the theory that the housewife has a simple information input system. For example, he believes that she is influenced simply in proportion to the brand stimuli that she is exposed to: the more shelf space devoted to a brand, the more likely she is to buy.

The advertising manager, on the other hand, having read some of the perception research, holds to the theory that she has a very complex information input system. He believes that her attitude and values cause her to admit some information and simply not "see" (not perceive) other bits of information though they are directly in front of her on the shelf as she walks down the aisle of the supermarket.

A diagram will show the difference. Figure 1 presents a part of a theory of the process by which buying behavior is affected by marketing.[1] Here is the traditional hierarchy of awareness, knowledge, attitude, intention to purchase and actual purchase. To make it a meaningful and comprehensive analytic framework, motivation, and such inhibitory variables as price, level of availability in the retail store and the like must be added.

More important for the purpose here is the variable, Sensitivity to Information, because it distinguishes the sales manager's theory from the advertising man's theory. The principle underlying this variable is that as a buyer's attitude toward a brand becomes more favorable there is a feedback from his attitude to the buyer's perceptual process. The effect of this feedback is to increase the probability that she will "see" (perceive) anything associated with the brand, such as a verbal statement, an ad, or a box on the shelf. This feedback is shown in Figure 1.

The salesmanager does not believe that this variable exists; the advertising manager believes that it does. As a consequence the salesman will be much less sanguine than the advertising manager about the effects of advertising. Because of his belief in the variable, the advertising manager will argue that advertising has two effects. The first is the traditional effect. It causes the buyer to have a more favorable attitude toward a brand, which will increase the buyer's probability of purchase if she is exposed to the opportunity to buy the brand. The second effect is the more interesting one. The buyer has a greater probability of being exposed to the brand, that is, a greater probability of perceiving the brand when she is confronted with it physically in the supermarket.

[1] For a complete theory of buyer behavior, see a forthcoming book by J. A. Howard and J. N. Sheth, *The Theory of Buyer Behavior.* For a summary of the theory see J. A. Howard, "The Theory of Buyer Behavior." Symposium on Consumer Behavior, University of Texas, April 18 and 19, 1966.

Figure 1. Buyer behavior

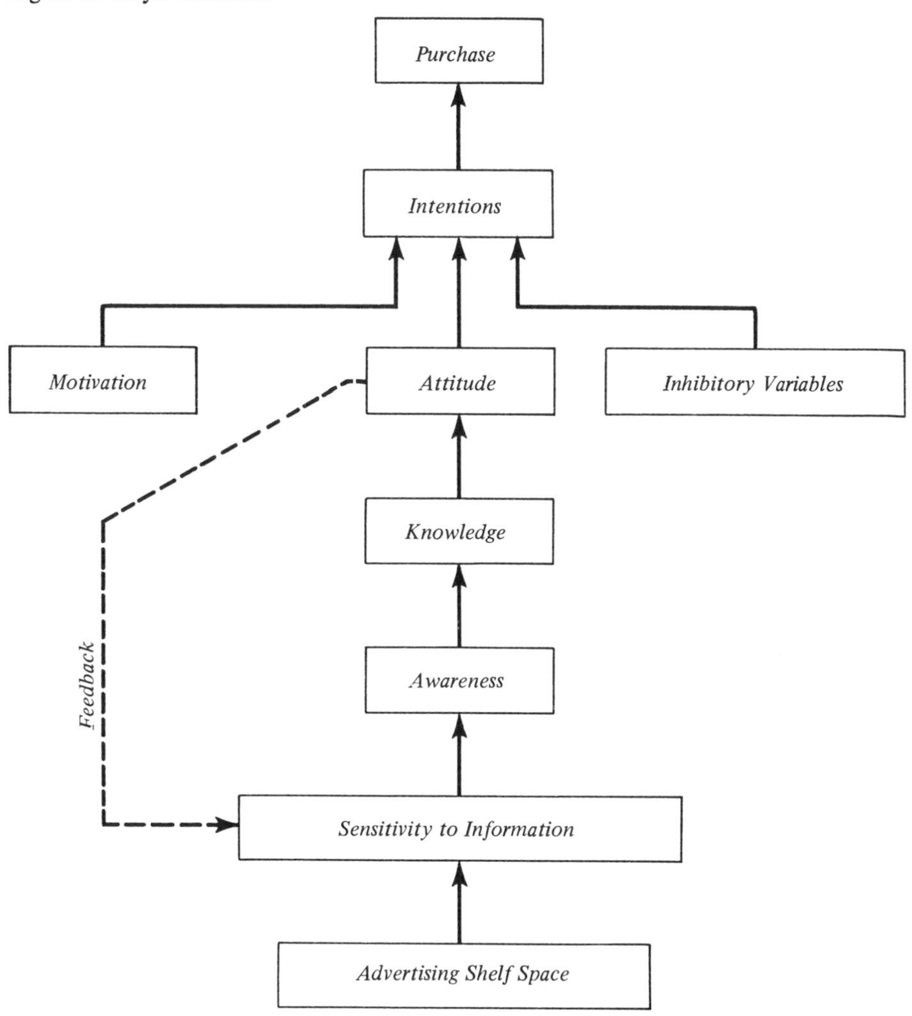


The advertising man as a consequence of his theory will argue in a rational manner that relatively more money should be allocated to advertising and less to getting the product into the supermarket. On the other hand, if both executives hold the same theory, that is, they both believe there is a variable called Sensitivity to Information which operates as described, they are far more likely to agree on a common marketing plan and to execute that plan in good faith rather than with some feeling that they have had something "foisted off" onto them.

A number of implications follow from the analysis here. A company's marketing operation can be organized more simply and its parts can work together far more smoothly if all executives hold the same theory of buyer behavior. Above all, there will be less latent conflict between the executive and his market researcher because the executive will fulfill his true role of being the formulator of the problem and leave the market research department free to collect the data that best measures the variables implied in the executive's formulation and free to develop the more basic theory that should underlie all of the company's market research. The elements of the marketing plan will be coordinated because all executives will be more inclined to think it is the sensible thing to do. There will be greater room for creativity. Finally, this common theory is essential to using the new information collection and processing technology most effectively.

## CONCLUSION

It is well to cite some broader implications. First, the need and urge to have fully articulated and dependable theory of buyer behavior will be very sharp indeed. This need will force a high level of systematic scientific creativity on a broad front, the kind of creative activity which marketing as a field of study has never before experienced. Second, there is the great task of retraining executives to think in these new terms. Third, for the past decade lip service has been given to the marketing concept. Now with a common theory of buyer behavior, the concept can be fully utilized.

A final implication is that we will be relatively ineffective in developing marketing information systems until there is also a far better theory of executive behavior. If there is to be one common model, questions about the intellectual capacities of executives must be answered in order to know the kinds of models that executives can learn to think with. This last broad implication, however, is a topic for another paper.[2]

[2] J. A. Howard and W. M. Moregenroth, "Information Processing Model of Executive Decision" in a forthcoming issue of *Management Science.*

# 7. THE ORGANIZATION OF THE MARKETING DEPARTMENT

*Hector Lazo and Arnold Corbin*

*In their attempts to implement the marketing function, different firms have set up different kinds of marketing department organizations.*

*Several types of organizational structure are explained in the following material.*

Charts showing a variety of techniques of organization are shown in Figures 1 through 7 which follow.

Aside from the over-all organization for customer-oriented marketing, the marketing department itself is organized variously in different companies. Much depends of course upon the level at which marketing is placed in the total organization.

In a typical product division type of organization, if the product division is large enough to warrant its own marketing department, this department is an integral part of the product division. Typical of this type of structure are General Foods (Figure 2) and Sylvania Electric (Figure 6). On the other hand, some product divisions are in reality the combination of various products, none of which is large enough to warrant a complete organization for itself. In such instances, it is not at all unusual to have marketing services organized on a pooled basis, with marketing research, forecasting, sales training, and other staff functions serving all products

Source: From *Management in Marketing: Text and Cases,* McGraw-Hill Book Company, New York, © 1961, pp. 79, 86–89, and 111–120. Used by permission of McGraw-Hill Book Company.
Hector Lazo: Chairman, Marketing Area, and Professor of Marketing, Graduate School of Business Administration, New York University. Arnold Corbin: Professor of Marketing, Graduate School of Business Administration, New York University.

within the division. The organization of the Borden Prescription Products Division (Figure 8) is typical of this arrangement.

There are other types of marketing organization in smaller companies where the marketing concept has been adopted and where the product line is limited. Typically, the marketing director controls and integrates sales, advertising, and other related marketing activities.

Again it should be emphasized that it is not size of company but company philosophy and point of view that is important. How the organization is put together structurally depends upon the individual company's problems, objectives and policies. But regardless of the size and type of organization, certain basic principles are common to all.

**Figure 1. Westinghouse Electric Corporation**

VICE-PRESIDENT – MARKETING

1. Exercises staff supervision over and coordinates all company sales activities with a view to attaining and maintaining competitive leadership.
   - *a.* Pricing
   - *b.* Distribution
   - *c.* Advertising and sales promotion
   - *d.* Market planning
   - *e.* Sales budgets and expenses
   - *f.* Key sales personnel
   - *g.* Sales administration
   - *h.* Field warehousing and inventories
2. Advises the vice-president and general manager on sales matters.
3. Maintains continuous review of organization of company's sales activities.
4. Establishes basic objectives with respect to product lines and assures the development and maintenance of adequate product plans. Studies opportunities for major additions to company's product lines and makes recommendations to top management with respect thereto. Approves elimination of products from the company's line.
5. Makes recommendations to the vice-president and general manager concerning general price policies.
6. Maintains relationships with company's principal customers.
7. Exercises staff supervision over apparatus regional managers on matters pertaining to customers where the interests of more than one product group are involved.

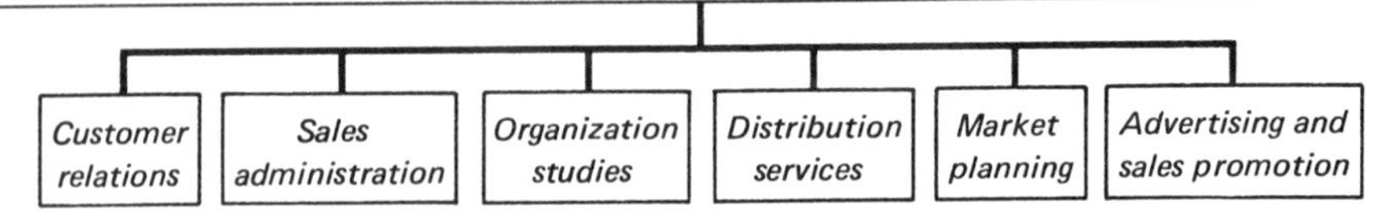


As of May 1, 1957, the office of vice-president–marketing was created; this includes all the above activities and, in addition, a new distribution services department, which is a system of field distribution to handle all company products. *Reproduced by permission.*

**Figure 2. General Foods Jell-O Division: Marketing Department**

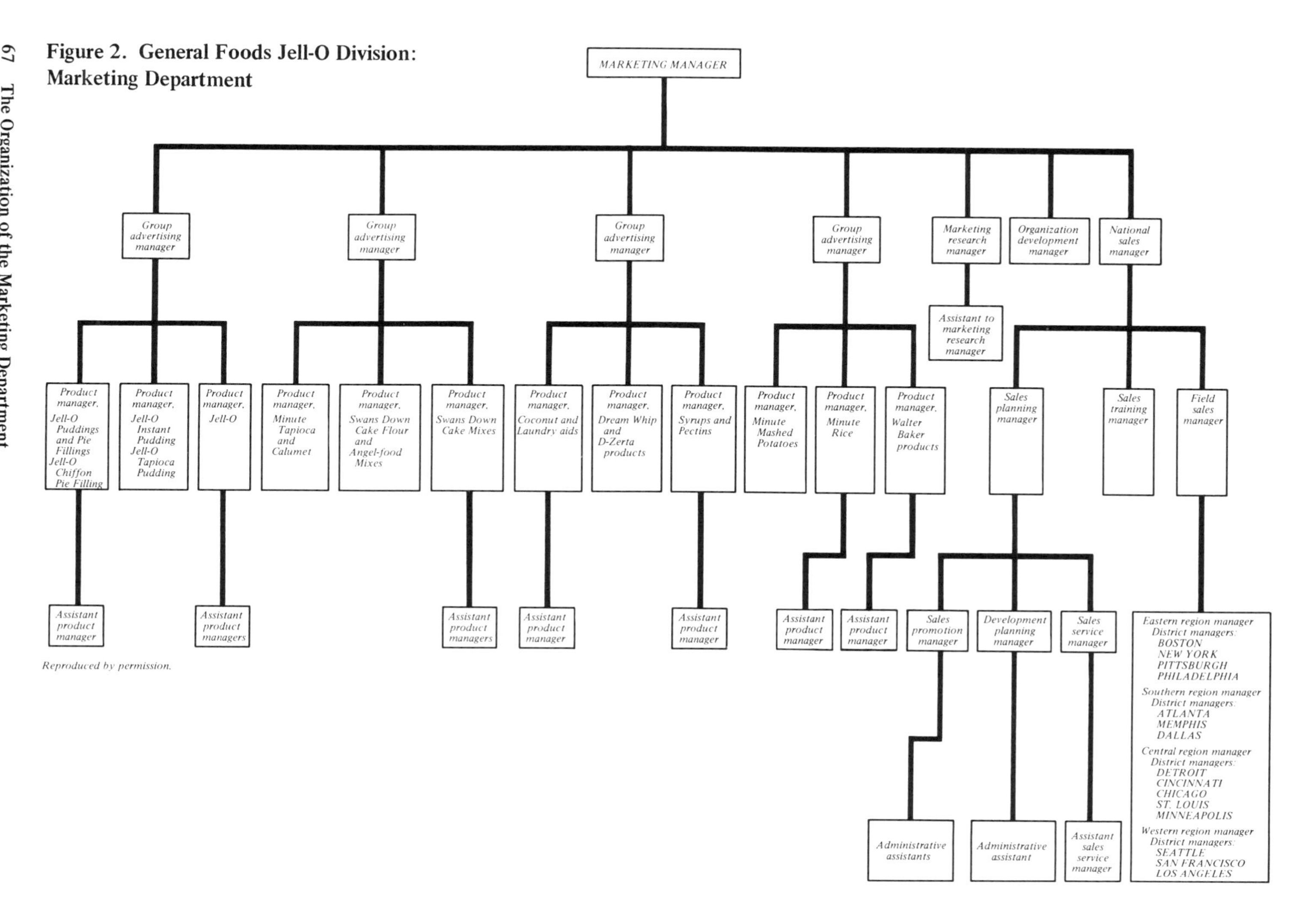


Reproduced by permission.

**Figure 3. Monsanto Chemical Company Organization**

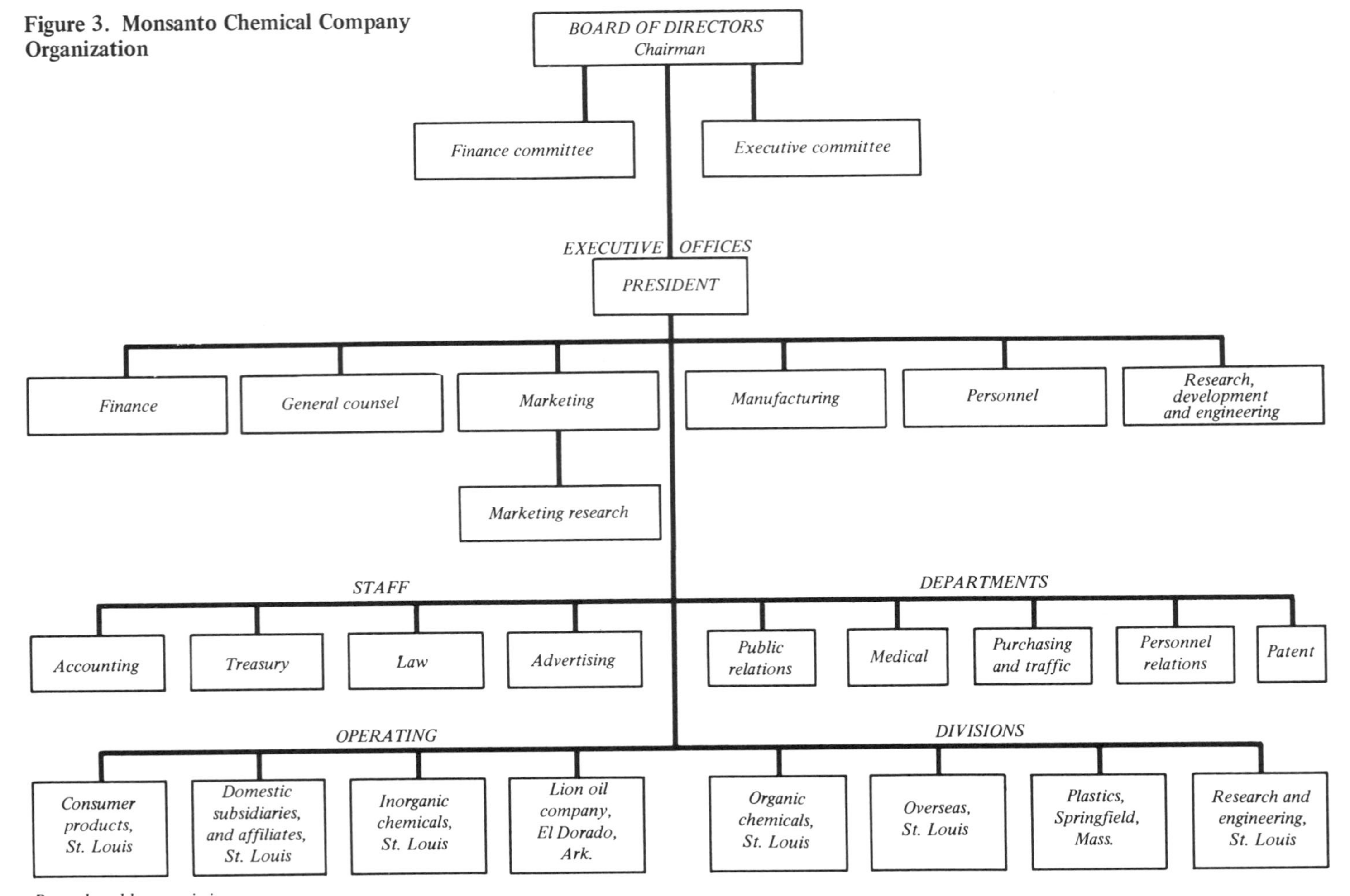


*Reproduced by permission.*

Figure 4. Chrysler Corporation, Dodge Sales Division

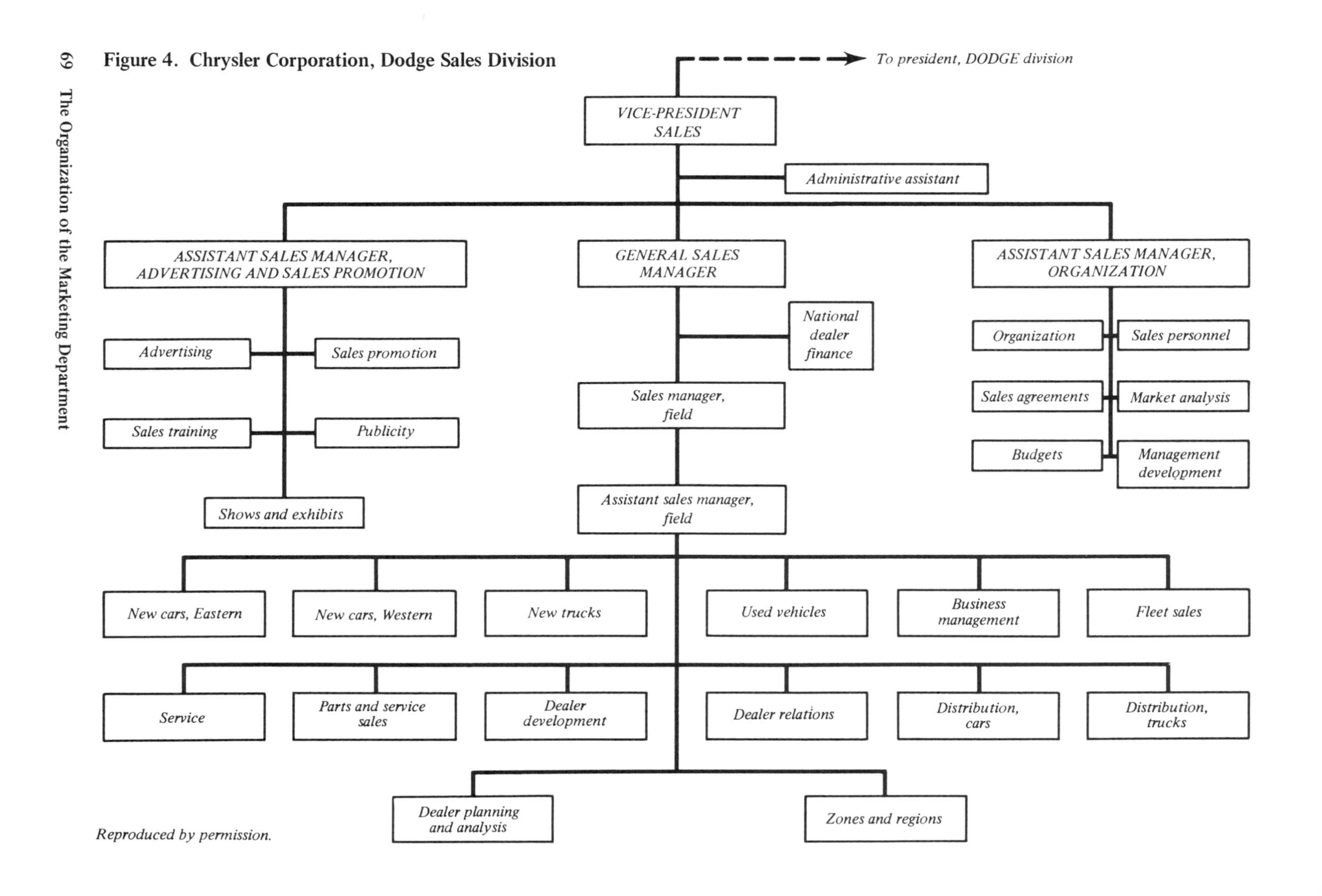


*Reproduced by permission.*

Figure 5. **Falstaff Brewing Corporation**

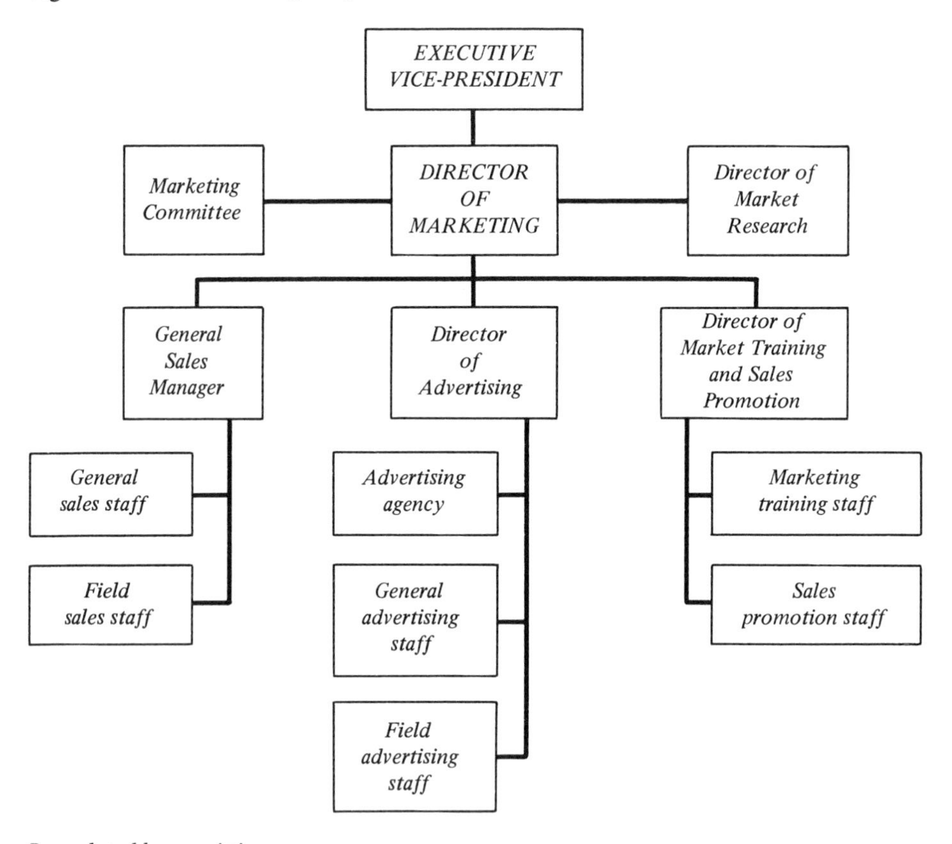


*Reproduced by permission.*

The marketing department must usually provide for three general functions: planning (including controls), sales, and service.

The *planning* function, which naturally should come under the direct supervision of the manager of marketing in a customer-oriented company, includes the development of policies and programs, the establishment of standards for measurement, the coordination and development of the product line, and the integration of marketing plans within the department and in the company as a whole.

The *sales* function includes manpower selection and development, selection and development of trade channels, merchandising policies and methods, and the administration of sales personnel. Responsibility for budgeting and for sales territory determination and organization rests primarily on the sales manager, although usually shared with the marketing manager, since it cuts across the entire operations of the department (and often the company as a whole). Sales is primarily a *line* (operating) function.

**Figure 6. Sylvania Electric Products, Inc.**

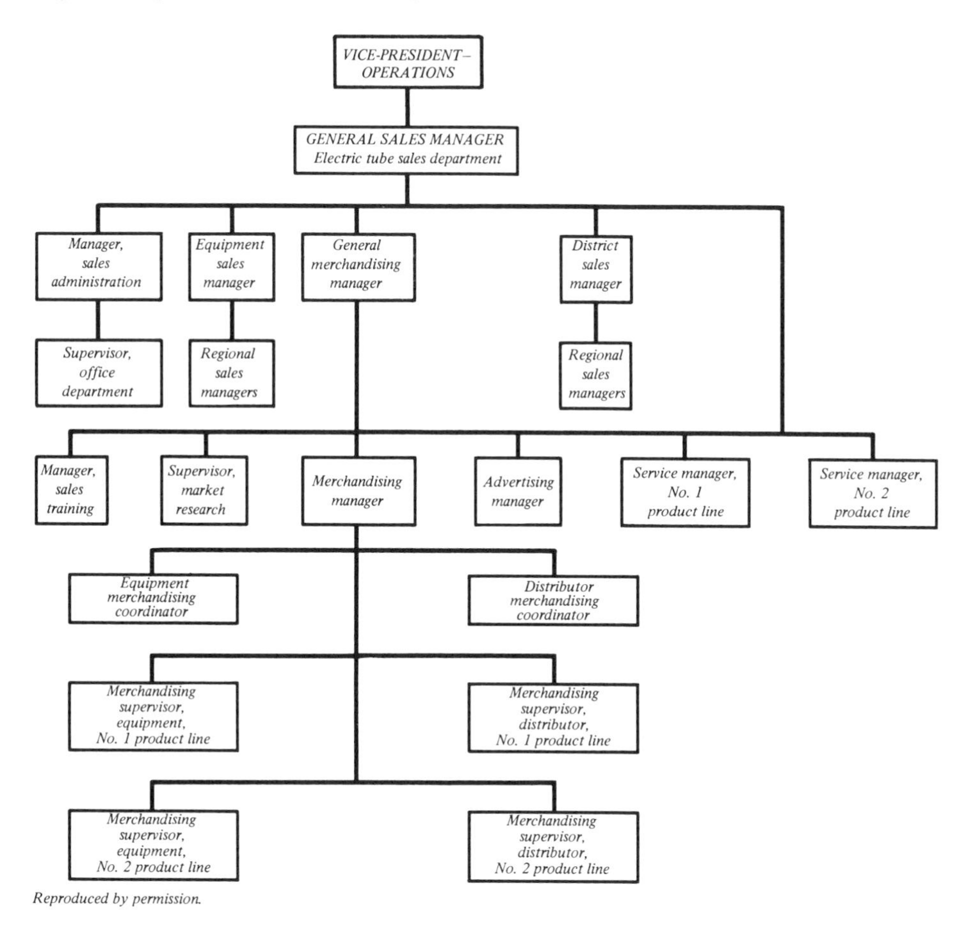


*Reproduced by permission.*

The *services* function includes advertising, sales promotion, public relations, forecasting, and above all, marketing research. In such multidivisional companies as General Electric, marketing services becomes the heart of the marketing division organization; its activities are for the most part staff functions, generally in charge of technical specialists (advertising, research, forecasting, etc.) who serve the various operating departments in an advisory capacity. . . . As a rule, these specialists have little or no line authority. Their work is coordinated at the staff level by an assistant to the general marketing manager, whether such manager carries the title of vice-president–marketing, or vice-president–sales, or any other.

As in all organizational work, the organization of the marketing department calls for a chart, formal or informal, and it calls for people to perform the functions organized. Reconciling and adjusting the people to their functions and to each other is one of the most difficult problems faced in the organization for customer-oriented marketing. In

Figure 7. Philip Morris, Inc., Marketing Division

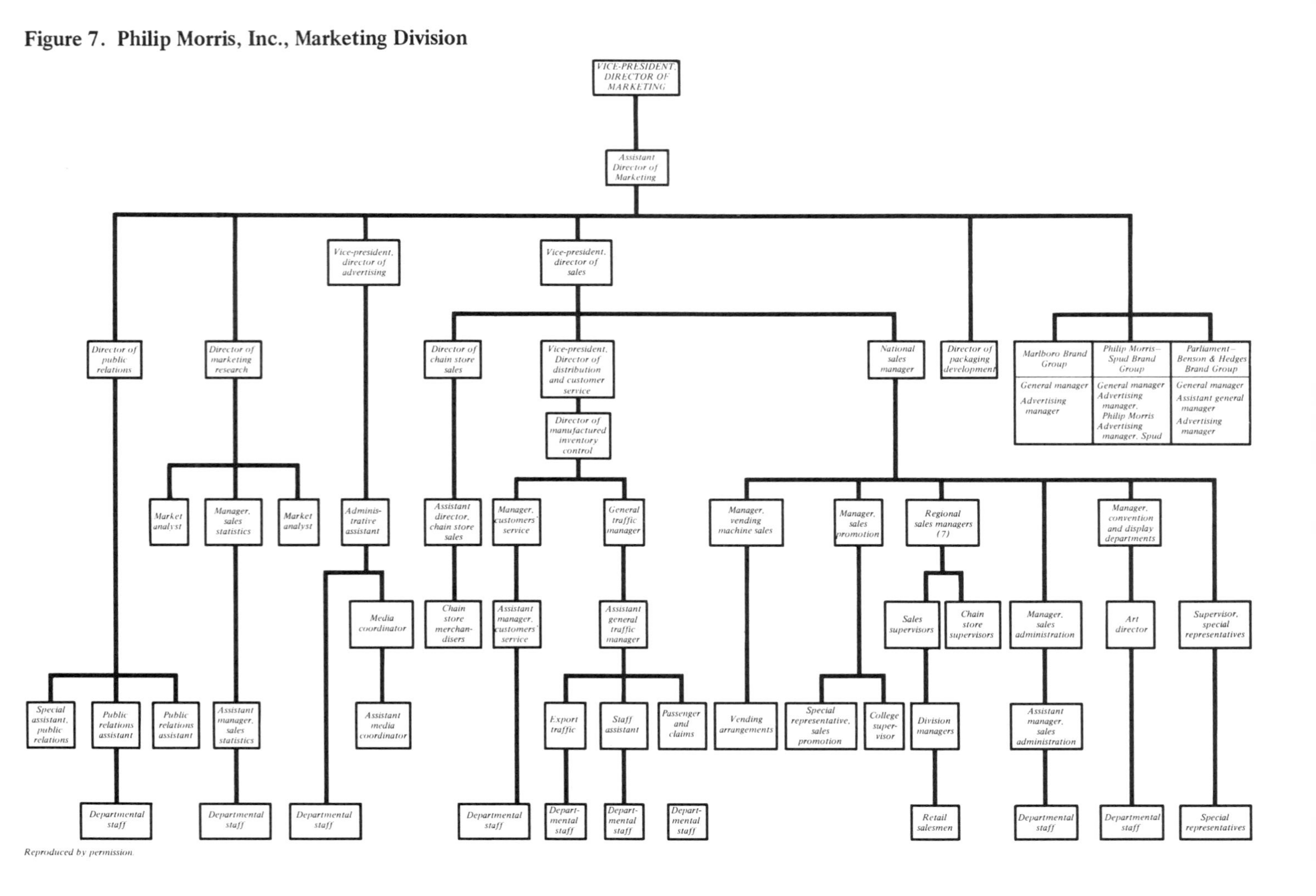


Reproduced by permission.

**Figure 8. The Borden Company, Prescription Products Division**

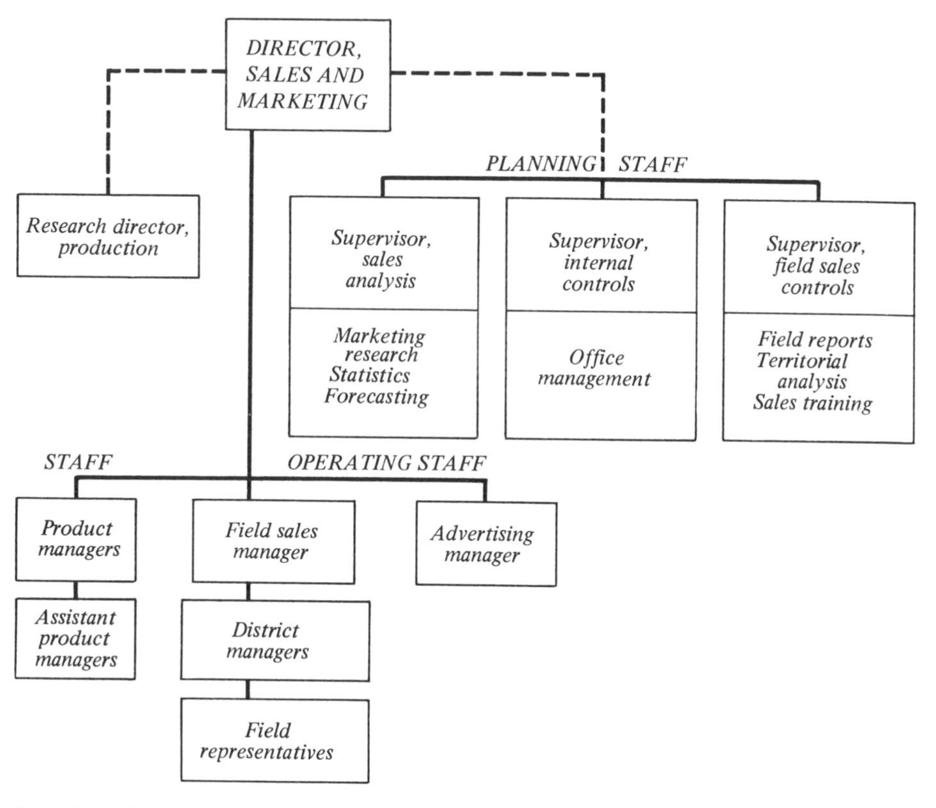


*Reproduced by permission.*

the organization stage, it is particularly important to keep in mind that a good organization is structured around functions and not around *people.* At the same time, every organizer knows that this is easier said than done; for in every organization there exist certain personal and personnel relationships which cannot be overlooked and which often cause major difficulties. Whenever people are being organized together for any purpose whatever, compromises must be made with something less than the "ideal." As a matter of practical common sense, the organization will *start* with an ideal setup but will end with "the best we can get under the circumstances." Judgment, experience, and to a degree, firmness and leadership will play important roles in arriving at this "best-we-can-get" point. . . .

The total marketing department organization, under the marketing concept in its simplest form, would therefore provide three "structural blocks," as shown in Figure 9.

These are the functions that *have* to be provided for; how they are arranged depends upon the needs, objectives, and policies of each individual company. In this basic structured concept, the importance lies in the separation of *services* from *operations* in order

Figure 9. The three structural blocks of marketing department organization

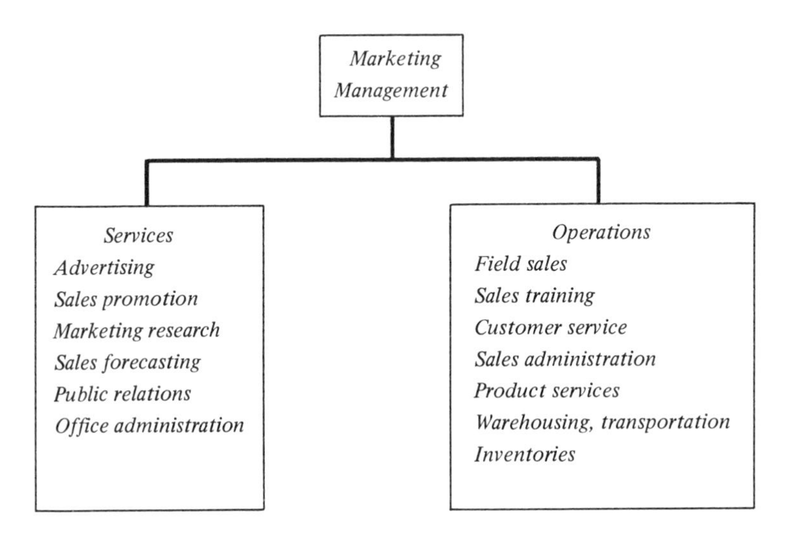


Figure 10. Company organization before marketing reorganization

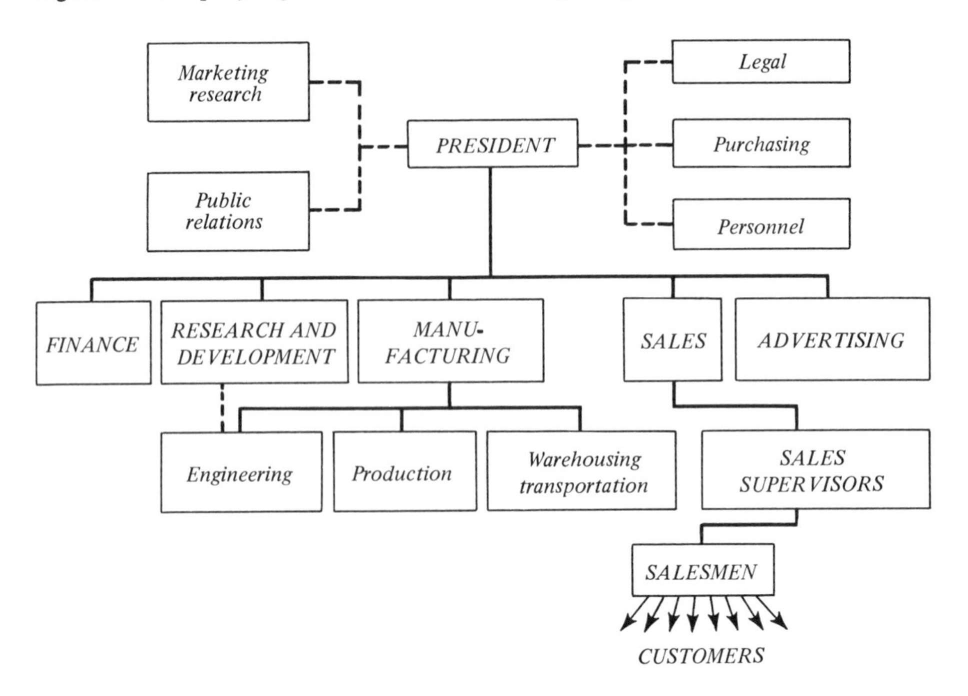

**Figure 11. Company organization after marketing reorganization**

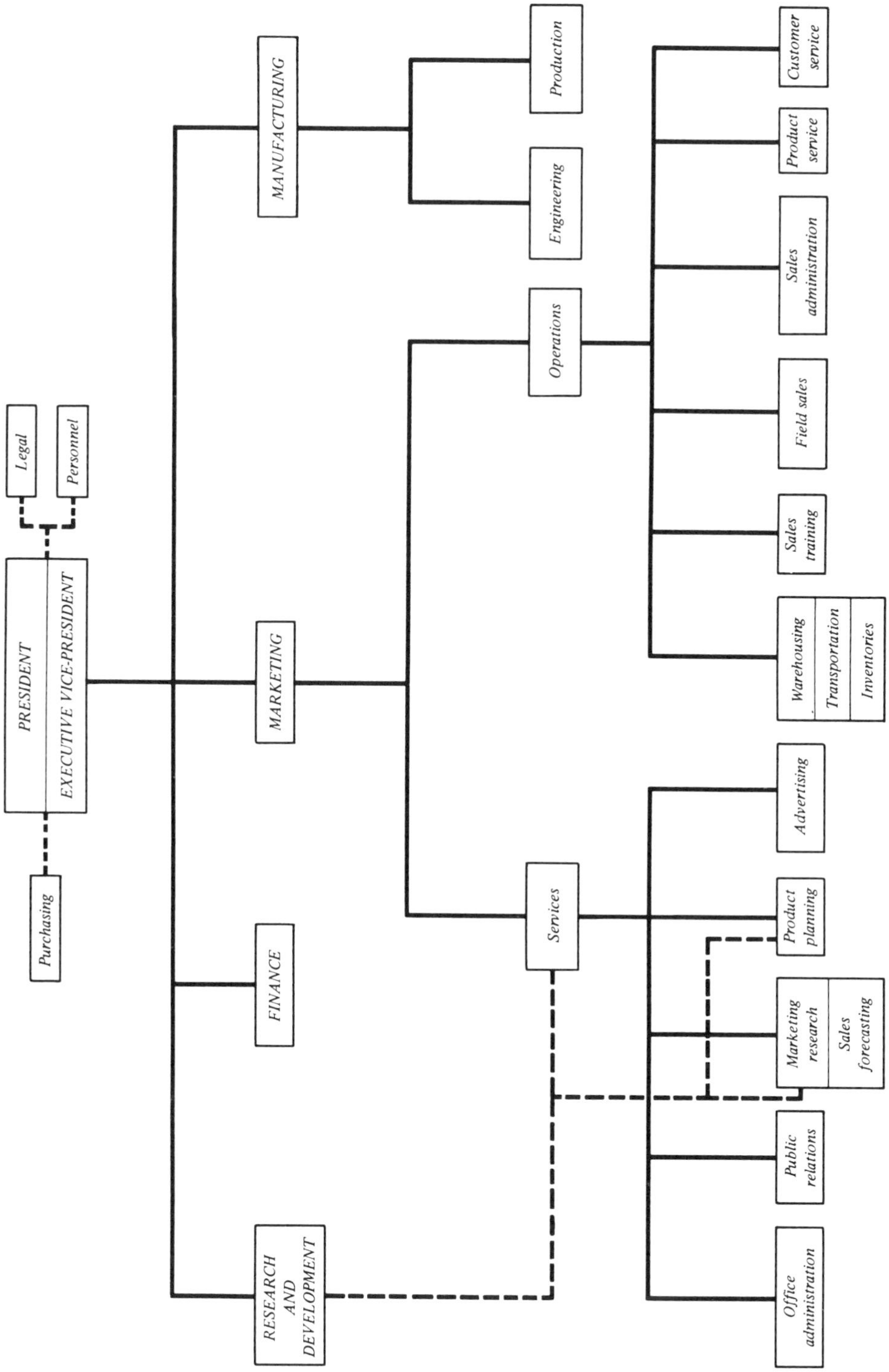

to keep the sales manager's responsibilities directed at selling, the staff or service managers servicing and aiding those sales, and management coordinating both for an integrated total effort. The differences in alignment of functions before and after reorganization to give full effect to integrated marketing are illustrated in Figures 10 and 11.

As brought out before, organization means the logical arrangement of different jobs to be done. The manager delegates as many of the jobs as he can and assigns the jobs to subordinates. Some of these jobs are performed at headquarters; others are carried out in the field. To the extent that decision making is transferred to the field, or at least close to where the action takes place, there is decentralization. It is, clearly, as much a matter of company philosophy as it is of physical setup.

How can a company check on the effectiveness of decentralization in its operations?

To begin with, the administrative unit that covers the total company operations is subdivided into smaller administrative units, sometimes by product division, sometimes geographically. The administrative head is often given complete authority over the line functions of his division, as at General Foods, directs his own staff functions, and is largely autonomous within the corporate structure.

In other cases, a centralized staff of specialists services all the line operations. This staff has the primary responsibility of aiding and advising the chief executive and the line operators; the members of the staff plan, research, compile reports, investigate, make suggestions. Occasionally, the decentralized units have additional staff assistants whose work is then coordinated by the central staff.

The staff activities are headed by specialists in designated fields, and their authority is clearly spelled out. They are carefully trained so that, despite their individual specialties, they reflect the thinking and the philosophy of top management in their relationships with line operators.

Central controls and standards of measurement of performance are established to determine how well the decentralized responsibilities are being discharged and to measure *individual* performance.

At headquarters, busy executives are using an increasing number of capable and trained staff assistants to help them coordinate and integrate the work of specialists as well as line operators. Various types of staff assistants are used: technical specialists, administrative assistants, general assistants. With such staff assistants, the most important consideration is to prevent the chief executive's office from becoming a bottleneck in so far as the particular specialty is concerned. Their most important function is to supply the chief executive with trustworthy information on which major policy and operating decisions of company-wide application can be made. . . .

# 8. THE PRODUCT MANAGER'S JOB

*Gordon H. Evans*

*Product-manager positions are becoming increasingly popular in market-oriented firms. As a vital part of management, the product manager or brand manager guides his product or group of related products through the marketplace, coordinating the total efforts of the firm to do so.*

*However, competition for advertising effort and salesmen's time leads to conflicts among product managers, who must "sell" their product to salesmen and the advertising department.*

*Furthermore, the product managers' problems are complicated by their responsibility for product profit. Yet the many factors contributing to that profit are not within their control.*

*This article is useful as a guide to the duties of a product (or brand) manager.*

A product manager may be a brilliant marketing man, an outstanding salesman, an advertising genius, a peerless planner, an expert in each of the many functions affecting his product; but unless he can coordinate all of these activities, unless the pieces can be fitted together so that they spell "profit," his special skills will have been wasted. More than any other factor, it is his skill in working harmoniously with key people in the various functional disciplines that will heavily influence the success of the product and, of course, his own future with the company.

Source: From *The Product Manager's Job,* American Management Association, Inc., New York; AMA Research Study 69, Copyright © 1964, pp. 49–62. Gordon H. Evans: Survey Associate, American Management Association's Research and Information Service, New York.

## HIS RELATIONSHIP TO SALES

In working to get the sales department to do the best possible job on his products, the product manager can take several different kinds of action. One of his first concerns is likely to be that of securing sufficient actual selling time to be devoted to his goods. In many forward-looking firms this is present by plan, at least in broad terms. Before taking part in planning meetings held for this purpose, the product manager can gather facts which if valid, may win more field selling time than previously allocated to him. Of course, if all product managers are equally diligent, management may be forced to add salesmen in order to tap actual profit potential. One product manager in a large industrial goods firm successfully convinced his superiors that substantial profits were being lost at the field sales level due to inattention to his product; he asked for and got his own small sales force.

Although more and more medium-size and large firms now plan and measure profits at the district sales level, attaining maximum profit in a certain sales district does not automatically lead to maximum total profit for a specific product. The product manager is acutely conscious of product profits, and a number of the product managers interviewed spoke of differences between their viewpoints and those of salesmen. For example, one said:

Sales people are rarely profit-minded. . . . There is a real difference of viewpoints involved. One's attitude changes, coming from sales to product management–you get a broader picture. The sales group has a very serious blind spot in regard to profit. I'm interested in the profit as it appears on this year's income statement. But the sales people have become very lenient with the customer. They may say, "Let's give this man credit," or "Let him return the goods if they're not entirely satisfactory." Either one of these things could ruin today's profits, but they might very well improve future sales. The sales group must live with the customer next year and the year after that. He will remain friendly toward us if we offer him favors. Sales must emphasize customer service and customer accommodation. But too much can ruin the current profit picture, and that's what I'm responsible for. Of course, this difference in our perspectives is not all bad; both have to exist in a company. If you take a narrow profit viewpoint, you are apt to ruin the goodwill on which your success has been based. As a matter of practically managing these matters, I make it a rule that if the sales manager feels very strongly about a problem, much more strongly than I do, I'll go along with him. Unless you're willing to do this, even though you may think it's a downright mistake, you're liable to build up a suspicious and negative attitude in sales. It's very easy to get yourself in such a position.

These sentiments on the importance of the product manager's cooperative coexistence with sales are echoed in the following paragraph taken from a typical product manager's job description:

He [the product manager] must work cooperatively with the sales manager. He must seek the sales manager's counsel and advice, those all-important elements in the product program. Remember, the sales manager and his sales force are those who actually execute the product manager's plans. It thus behooves both the sales manager and the product manager to work in close harmony, and they must do so if maximum results are to be had. However, if opposite points of view are strongly held and a meeting of minds between the two men is impossible, the vice president of marketing will decide between them.

To impress upon the sales department the fact of the product manager's responsibility for profits, many companies make a point of granting the product manager the right to examine sales costs and make suitable recommendations. Indeed, if he is to work effectively, his right to any relevant cost information—or any other information—must be clearly understood by all concerned, and complementing this right is his right to submit suggestions and give advice to both functional personnel and senior management. Product managers stress the crucial importance of both these rights. However, the manner in which the product manager exercises these rights is perhaps an even more critical matter. If he is too demanding, he may defeat his own purpose. He is far more likely to obtain the desired results by persuasion—by making the sales force as profit-conscious as he is. He strives to do this at every possible opportunity, particularly at the district-level meetings where he has a chance to personally hammer this message home.

However, maintaining a cordial working relationship with sales yields its greatest benefits during negotiations for selling time. In a typical multiproduct company which has a shared sales force, the bidding among product managers for selling time is fiercely competitive. Indeed, the product manager's success in selling his product to salesmen and sales management is often a critical factor in his evaluation by higher management. One former product manager remarks: "You must know how to get things done in sales. You may even have to be demanding. If you roll over and play dead, you won't get what you want." Occasionally, the jockeying for selling time goes to extremes. A director of product management comments: "From time to time. things get a little too rough. I have to get everybody together and give them a lecture on good corporate citizenship."

The product manager, lacking any clear-cut authority, must rely heavily on personal tact, diplomacy, and powers of persuasion in selling his product internally. He may frequently find that the dice have been loaded against him; for example, differential commission rates set by higher levels of management may favor other products. In such instances he will have to convince his superiors in the marketing department that *his* product should benefit from such incentives. Here again, his persuasive powers, backed with concrete information and realistic plans for promoting the product, will determine whether he receives this support. Indeed, the sales department looks to the product manager to provide a continuing flow of data about the product, such as periodic bulletins describing price and model changes, special promotions, advertising tie-ins, point-of-purchase displays—anything that will be useful in improving the competitive position of the product. They do not look for this kind of assistance, but they expect it to materialize in the form of useful sales tools such as brochures or flyers depicting new product applications, catalogues, and package-deal promotions rather than gratuitous advice, irksome reminders to watch costs, or unrealistic sales quotas. For this reason, many firms recruit product managers from the field sales force on the assumption that they have a first-hand knowledge of the product, its markets, and customer expectations. These companies feel that the salesman, or sales-manager-turned-product-manager, can acquire the other pertinent skills through practical experience and on-the-job training. At least one major chemical company continues to follow this approach with salutary results. The only difficulty is that a field sales manager is sometimes reluctant to give up his field "command" to become a product manager.

The product manager's face-to-face dealings with field sales people usually occur at planning meetings attended by top-level marketing managers, product managers, field sales managers, and, of course, the salesmen. At these meetings, the group blocks out each salesman's time, and specific product campaigns are scheduled to avoid conflicts. Such meetings provide no guarantee that the following year will be—in the words of Robert Browning—"roses, roses, all the way"; but Lever Brothers, for one, has found that special meetings of this kind have been particularly effective in identifying and resolving difficulties.

One of the most common criticisms of the product manager concept originates with salesmen in the field who feel that the product manager usurps many of their functions—that his "interference" is more of a hindrance than a help. Those in favor of product managers often attempt to minimize such criticism by emphasizing the "value added" potential of the product manager; they point out that he is ideally situated to reinforce their sales efforts by supplying data on special product applications, by expediting special orders, and by making personal sales presentations when necessary. This is especially true of the product manager in an industrial goods company, where his special knowledge of the product's performance characteristics and technological subtleties may provide the clincher in closing an important sale. More often, however, the product manager plays a passive role in relation to field sales. He acts chiefly as an observer. He listens carefully to salesmen, customers, and district office personnel; notes their comments, suggestions, and complaints; and takes these back to the home office for consideration and action. In fact, as a matter of practice some companies go even further to emphasize the nonauthoritarian nature of the product manager's relations with the salesmen. L&F Products Division of Lehn & Fink Products Corporation, for example, states in its comprehensive *Brand Manager's Manual:* "No instructions are to be given to field personnel by brand management personnel unless a specific request to do so is made by the sales manager."

The multiplicity of reports and forms that salesmen must complete is a common source of contention between the product manager and the field. He must constantly evaluate his need for a continual flow of sales data against the reluctance of the salesmen to take time away from their primary function of selling, to fill factual reports and memorandums. If he overpowers them with data-gathering tasks, he may find that the reports are carelessly prepared or even ignored.

## HIS RELATIONSHIP TO ADVERTISING

Although "product manager" and "brand manager" are synonymous terms in many large packaged goods firms, today's product manager is often thought to be a direct descendant of the brand manager; the advertising specialist of the consumer goods company of the late 1920s and early 1930s. While the product manager has acquired considerably broader duties and responsibilities over the years than were held by the original brand managers, he often retains this strong relationship to advertising and exercises a dominant influence in developing and implementing advertising campaigns for his product. He may be authorized to work directly with the advertising agency, plan the overall advertising strategy for his product line, deploy the tactical weapons which implement that strategy, and modify it as the competitive situation dictates or new markets appear. There are exceptions, but in most consumer packaged goods companies the responsibility-without-authority problem does not arise where advertising is concerned. Advertising plans are often approved along conventional reporting lines—that is, by the product manager's own chief.

However, when the organizational setup requires lateral communication, the product manager's goal is to persuade the art, copy, and media experts of the advertising department to create advertising themes and campaigns that will vividly express the consumer's expectations of the product. If the product manager's concept of what the consumer looks for in the product is valid, then half the battle is won. If he miscalculates in choosing the appeals that he wants to build into the product and package design, if the copy does not carry through the basic theme, then no matter what pressure he applies to the sales force and no matter what media he uses to reach his market, his campaign will be seriously compromised and he will spend most of his time attempting to patch up a vessel that was waterlogged before it was launched. However, there are usually others involved in the final decision to proceed with the campaign, and veto power must exist somewhere. Final approval of annual advertising plans may go as high as the president or even the board of directors; but once the budget has been approved, authorization of specific plans often rests with the product group manager or the director of marketing. As regards consumer packaged goods, it is not uncommon for the product manager to be able to say, "no" to ad agency plans.

In contrast, an indication of advertising department power is found in the advertising policy bulletin of a manufacturer of printing equipment, which says, "To insure a consistent external picture, significant changes in advertising styles or approaches are subject to clearance by the General Office Director of Advertising." And the advertising department in one typical pharmaceutical concern is watchdog over ethical standards and may vote down a product manager's proposal for an advertising campaign which it considers marginal.

In many firms, written policies or other guides help to provide common standards for all those responsible for advertising. Salada Foods, Ltd., sets forth some rather firm rules:

- Our advertising must project and reflect quality, and a continuing search for even greater quality, with respect to every product bearing a label of the company.
- No claim should be made in any advertisement which the company would be unwilling to back with an unconditional money-back guarantee. The guarantee itself may or may not be included in any advertisement. Judgment and mechanical requirements will be the deciding factors.

- It must be dynamic in reflecting an active and progressive determination to keep in step with changing consumer habits and tastes.
- It should recognize news, either in the form of new products or new uses of old products, as one of its most vital ingredients.
- It should employ a maximum degree of continuity, recognizing that attitudes are slow to change and that pleasant familiarity with a brand is a powerful selling force.
- In execution, it should build solid confidence through adherence to the following rules:
  *a.* All claims used should be supportable.
  *b.* It must be in good taste by scrupulously avoiding anything that reflects on religious beliefs, or that could offend racial or political minorities. Naturally, also, it should never depend on a suggestive *double entendre* or sexy connotation for attention value or humorous effect.
  *c.* It must not unfairly attack the reputation or product claims of competitors.

The solving of some problems is usually a matter of bargaining and company politics; but in some cases it is reduced to a system. An ingenious system for controlling the allocation of advertising expense has been adopted in a ranking company in the proprietary drug field. The company explains it as follows:

We work on what we call an *advertising-to-sales* ratio. In short, it's called "A to S." Every brand has an A-to-S percentage established for it. This determines what per cent of sales may be spent on advertising. As you see, there is an automatic effect: If sales go down, the budget for that brand automatically goes down. If sales go up, advertising goes up. The thinking is that we should put our money behind our winners, and not behind our losers. The advertising department is constantly reviewing sales and adjusting budgets accordingly. . . . It is their job to drop one budget down and pull another budget up. The result is that the product managers do not have to fight all along the line for their advertising share *most of the time.* This is decided for them. However, there is, of course, always the question of the starting base. The product group may make recommendations for a change in the A-to-S ratio. We may suggest to higher-ups that we spend a higher percentage of money on a given brand.

I don't want to give the impression, however, that we are entirely inflexible. The general thinking is that it is unwise to put money behind a poor seller. Other companies think otherwise. The instinctive reaction of management is to do just the wrong thing in a falling market. However, we are in an industry where sales are very sensitive to advertising. If we get a very hot product (and this may be the result of very good copy or other factors), we are not reluctant to put advertising funds behind it by altering the A-to-S ratio. The percentage is primarily a limit, a protection on the *down side*, but there is no arbitrary ceiling on the *top side.* We're willing to take flyers, and we have taken them. Sometimes, we will spend 50 per cent more than we ordinarily would do on a very high selling brand. But when a brand is declining, and we still have to make a profit on it, profit comes out of advertising savings.

Several degrees of control over the advertising function are possible. The most complete control exists when the company's advertising department, and hence the agencies used by it, report directly to the product manager or to the head of product management. The overriding importance of advertising to consumer goods companies has led some companies to replace competent sales-oriented product managers with executives who have been extremely successful in advertising. In those instances where a manager is particularly adept in one area, he is frequently given a subordinate who is strong in another. In one such case, the product manager was an advertising specialist; he was supported by a field sales contact man whose skills and experience made him a natural complement to the product manager.

A slightly less stringent degree of control is found where the advertising personnel, although they do not report directly to the product manager, still must yield to his judgment on everything substantive about his product and his advertising campaign. Here the product manager can decide the content and wording of the copy, its art, the media in which it will be placed and when it will appear.

Yet, in some companies, the product manager may have even less authority than this. Such instances perhaps are found most often in companies that make technically complex products for industrial customers; here, the product manager may have the right only to reject–veto–advertising copy. He may ask the advertising and sales promotion staff to emphasize certain product advantages in copy and art, may recommend media, and may propose direct mail approaches and lists; but he may not demand that his recommendations be followed. The reason this limited control appears more often in industrial goods firms is that the industrial product manager is rather technically oriented and has been chosen for his background in applications work or engineering rather than for the training and experience in advertising that characterize his counterpart in the consumer goods company. Under the circumstances, the head of marketing may feel that it is better to rely on the skills of an experienced advertising specialist within the company or in an outside agency.

Needless to say, product managers would like as much control as possible over other marketing staffs. More than one product manager mentioned in an interview that it would also be desirable to have market research for his product report to him, or that the market research function report to his director of product management. They feel that only in this way can market research be properly integrated with product management.

Some years ago, when National Biscuit Company first began to use product managers, the rumor spread that the company had a "vice president in charge of Fig Newtons." While this title was invented in jest, it does convey the genuinely high regard that functional chiefs have for product managers. They realize that the product manager bears a considerable portion of the total responsibility for profitable volume for a given product or segment of the line, and they treat him accordingly.

## HIS RELATIONSHIP TO FINANCE

It is common practice for product managers to conduct campaigns to reduce the inequitable allocation of fixed costs to certain items, to study other cost factors, to analyze and evaluate the implications of price changes, and to develop profit plans for a specific product or market. In a conventional marketing organization there may be no one specifically assigned to accomplish these tasks. Consequently a product may be overpriced or underpriced and languish far behind its true market potential, simply because no one has time to explore the revenue and profit possibilities in terms of cost structures and return on investment.

Today's product manager has a working knowledge of financial principles and can discuss them intelligently with cost estimators, accountants, and financial experts in his continuing effort to increase his product's profits, as well as the overall profits of the firm. However, he is not an accountant; even in a small firm, the product manager will have to call on financial specialists to insure a profitable result. And in the large multiproduct, multiplant company, the complexity of product and the frequency of cost, price, or design changes of the product itself will largely determine the number of people assigned to cost analysis and control.

In a conventional functional organization the finance department usually develops the profit plan, if there is to be one. However, many finance men lack the marketing knowledge, experience, and insight of the product manager. The advisability of having a finance man at the product level is, again, a function of profitability. Perhaps the "business teams" of Union Carbide's Chemical Division provide a workable compromise.

In many companies the profit responsibility for a given product rests with the group product manager, or marketing manager, rather than with the product manager himself. However, when profit responsibility is specifically assigned to him, the product manager works closely with accounting or finance people to develop a budget for his product. This budget is essentially a profit plan which will subsequently provide, to a great extent, the basis for evaluating his performance at the end of the year. He plays a major role in developing the estimates that make up the profit plan and, consequently, must bear the responsibility for explaining any undesirable variances that may occur. Over all, the product manager's day-to-day working relationship with finance—either directly or through the group product manager—consists chiefly of arranging for merchandising deals, price changes, premium offers, and occasional unplanned activities arising from changing market conditions or the necessity to counter a competitor's tactical moves.

## HIS RELATIONSHIP TO MANUFACTURING

The extent to which the product manager becomes involved in manufacturing depends mainly on the nature of the product. If the product is relatively easy to make and represents a minimal capital investment, his dealings with manufacturing will be occasional and informal. If, however, the product requires a sizable investment in raw stock, expensive machinery, and technical manpower, then the product manager will devote a significant portion of his time to the analysis of costs, schedules, productive capacities (including make-or-buy decisions), and quality control.

Few product managers qualify as experts in developing shop costs, but those fortunate enough to have had some experience in production can at least recognize when manufacturing costs seem out of line. In one chemical manufacturing company, for example, a product manager objected to the manufacturing expenses charged to his product. He made a detailed analysis of these costs and was able to prove that the costs were overstated. Thus, because he knew something of the manufacturing process, the materials involved, and the man-machine requirements, he was able to control an important component of his total cost picture and improve his profit potential accordingly. Such knowledge not only minimizes the possibility of manufacturing overcharges but can be instrumental in developing competitive price structures.

There are difficulties in estimating shop costs, of course. It is not simply a question of applying historical data and the cost of current facilities. A competitor may enter the field with new and more efficient equipment that will permit him to lower his costs and selling price—and perhaps run away with the market. One method of preventing just such occurrences is through the development of "design-cost systems." This approach provides estimates based on the use of the best possible equipment and facilities, rather than the existing plant capabilities. As one executive commented:

> By using "design costs" we can arrive at a hypothetical price based on the use of the most advanced and efficient processes, materials, handling techniques, and the like. This is the lowest cost at which our product could be made.

By constantly referring to the difference between the ideal design cost and the actual shop costs, the product manager is in a position to exert pressure for low-cost production. He has a reliable yardstick for measuring cost improvements. Furthermore, he is able to anticipate the effect of competitive activities if it becomes apparent that the competition is installing the same type of machines upon which the ideal design costs were based.

The problems of scheduling, inventory control, and production lot sizes are second in importance; only manufacturing costs deserve more attention. Again, these problems will be of more or less interest to the product manager, depending on the nature of his product. They are virtually nonexistent in some companies. A producer of proprietary drugs comments:

> Our product is physically very small and chemically very simple. We can keep a year's inventory in a medium-size room. Our manufacturing process is almost primitive and capital equipment is inexpensive. I have little to worry about in my relations with manufacturing.

When the product is bulky and costly to produce and distribute, however, the product manager may find it advisable to become more deeply involved in production problems. If the product requires long production runs and extensive warehousing facilities or has a markedly seasonal sales pattern, then the product manager probably should investigate the pros and cons of economic lot quantity planning (ELQ), which attempts to balance output costs against warehouse costs and deterioration losses. He might find that costs could be reduced significantly by the use of ELQ planning.

In many companies, the product manager is responsible for telling manufacturing how much of a given item will be needed per year, quarter, or month; in such a situation, his statement is often binding on manufacturing. The manufacturing manager may ask the product manager: "How much of product X will you need during the next year, and how much should I make?" "Will you verify that our inventory level is such and such?" The product manager often must answer these questions. From manufacturing's viewpoint, this is all to the good. As one executive puts it: "Manufacturing now has someone to put its finger on, someone who will give a hard, quantitative answer." It is not surprising that in many companies manufacturing is not at all unfriendly toward the product manager in this connection.

Another area of consideration for some product managers arises when they become involved in the formulation of plant expansion or contraction decisions. Since the product plan must include forecasts[1] of future demand, the question of capacity must arise. Often it is part of the product manager's job to act as a liaison with manufacturing on this question. Manufacturing is of course most interested in the product manager's predictions of future sales levels. He is the specialist on the market; and if his judgment is trusted, manufacturing will listen keenly to his views on how much more or less capacity will be needed next year, or five years from now. This is especially true with the introduction of new products. Production routine has not yet been set, and manufacturing must rely heavily on the product manager's ideas of sales level and production timing. Conversely, the product manager must be careful to see that he does not stimulate a premature demand which manufacturing is incapable of meeting. As one company puts it in its product manager job description: "Specific planning must be done on end product requirements. They must be announced early enough for production to have merchandise ready in kind and quantity."

Make-or-buy decisions constitute potentially one of the most difficult problems facing the product manager in his dealings with manufacturing. As guardian of a product's profitability, he may discover that it is easier and cheaper to buy his supply outside the company rather than to manufacture it in-house. At this point, a conflict with manufacturing is almost sure to arise. Alfred N. Watson, professor of business at the Graduate School of Business Administration of Columbia University and a former vice president–marketing of U.S. Rubber, says:

> This problem arises because in some industries, as, say, the chemical industry, productive capacity is growing faster than consumption. Certain companies will have difficulty even keeping plants open and reaching their break-even points. Beyond this, they [the products] can sell at lower *incremental costs.* The product manager of a potential buyer will realize that his plant's production will be charged to him at *average* cost. If he buys astutely–and certainly this is one of the qualifications of a product manager–he will see chances to buy cheaper outside. The manufacturing function will, of course, fear being put out of business. So it must be equally astute in meeting competitive production prices.

The coordination of the interest of marketing and production with the overall interests of the company is often a major problem of senior management. An executive may wonder, for example, if he should place the company at the mercy of a competitor-supplier, even if a great temporary advantage might be secured by purchasing products from it.

[1]For an example of the form the product manager's forecast may take, see "The Product Manager: A Forecast of Bookings and Required Shipments," *Successful Production Planning and Control,* AMA Special Report No. 5, 1955, pp. 142–145.

Finally, the product manager must keep in touch with product quality. In many lines, quality is a significant factor in product sales. Traditionally, quality control has been the responsibility of manufacturing, and in most companies this is still the rule.

But the product manager must be concerned with the costomers' reaction to the overall quality level. He has a valid interest in complaints, especially where the alleged defect may be serious or frequent enough to undermine the product's reputation. He is often charged with making sure an investigation is made and corrective action is taken.

## HIS RELATIONSHIP TO RESEARCH AND DEVELOPMENT

As with manufacturing, the product manager's relationship to research and development will depend to a great extent on his product. If the product is subject to innovation, or requires frequent customer service of a highly technical nature, the product manager will work closely with the R&D people; if not, he will seldom have occasion to see them. In most organizations, the research and development group is a separate entity and has few day-to-day dealings with marketing and the product manager. Celanese Fibers Company, a division of Celanese Corporation of America, is an exception to this rule. Dr. Robert D. Williams, who has charge of both product management and the division's research and development activities, cites some of the advantages of his dual responsibility:

> The advantage of having R&D in the same house with product management is that we have available a large number of competent people who are able to think analytically. They are able to act as a kind of auxiliary marketing staff. This definitely improves the working relationship. Otherwise, our access to our R&D people would be slower and less close. In the same house we have a tremendous benefit in terms of quick responses to new product developments. All the complaints one hears about the marketing department being unable to get service from R&D may be true enough, but not in this division.

Perhaps it is in the area of new product development that the product manager finds his closest working relationship with research and development. His knowledge of customer expectations and market requirements is of particular significance in this phase of the product's life. If he can persuade the research and development scientists and engineers to build these expectations and requirements into the design and packaging components of the product, then he will have served his company well.

### *THE PRODUCT MANAGER'S AUTHORITY*

Typically, the product manager has the authority to make a wide range of analyses and marketing plans for the product line assigned to him, subject of course to budget and policy limits. He may have authority over promotional aids or advertising copy. Occasionally he has authority to set prices in his line. He has almost unlimited authority to communicate with persons in other departments which design, sell, schedule, make, inspect, or bill for his product line. But, as a rule, he may only request, or persuade, these people to act in the ways he believes will advance the sales and net income from the product line.

## RESPONSIBILITY FOR PROFITS

Marketing executives consulted in the preparation of this AMA Study repeatedly spoke of the product manager as "the watchdog for profits." In what sense is this true? And to what extent is he accountable for the components of profits–sales and costs? The profit of the product line for which he is responsible is a very real concern of the product manager, and is constantly in his mind. Yet, paradoxically, there is a very real question of how much direct authority he has over the conditions which create or destroy profit. J. M. Juran has sketched the situation in this way:

> This man is a planner and coordinator for a particular product or market. He has the main voice as to some matters–the content of the product line, through what channels it should be sold, how it should be promoted and priced. He is decisive [as] to the sales forecast and the profit budget. He has the right and duty to sound the alarm when an impasse looms ahead. However, he does not command the technical departments, the manufacturing departments, or the field sales forces. When we tell this man, "You are responsible for profit," we are more wrong than right. He *is* responsible for the profit planning, for some of the ingredients of profit performance, for coordinating, and for needling. Whether a profit results from all this depends on many things beyond him–so many, in fact, that to hold him "responsible" is usually unrealistic and sometimes ludicrous. Paying him based on this profit is another matter. Even if he is not "responsible," it may be a good thing to make his bonus (and, for that matter, the bonus of the others) depend on the profit.[2]

A senior marketing executive interviewed for this study puts it this way:

> You cannot really be responsible for anything unless you have it under your direct control. The product manager can't be responsible for manufacturing costs, because he doesn't run the factory. He can't be directly responsible for sales, because he doesn't have working control of the salesmen. You simply can't eliminate either, or both, of these aspects of profit and say that the product manager is responsible for the end result. I suppose in some companies you could make a case that since he is part of marketing, his influence with the sales people is greater. Perhaps in some places he is the dominant factor in field sales, or at least his superior is. But in very few companies is this true with manufacturing. If either one of the manufacturing or sales elements is taken away from a fellow, you can't say that he is running the whole product–he is only having something to do with running it.

The general manager of a product division has authority over more of the factors that govern profit. Thus he may reasonably be charged with a greater degree of profit responsibility than can be attached to the product manager. To quote J. M. Juran:

> This man is put in charge of a profit center or division of the company. He has broad responsibility over design, manufacture, and marketing of the product, including command of the respective departments. He also commands some but not all of the supporting services. He does not have the full latitude that is enjoyed by the head of an independent company, but he has a lot to say. When we tell the general manager, "You are responsible for profit," we are more right than wrong. When we go a step further and tell him, "We will make your bonus depend on this profit," we are on sound ground.[3]

[2] J. M. Juran, *Managerial Breakthrough,* McGraw-Hill Book Company, New York, 1964, pp. 190–91.
[3] *Ibid.,* p. 190.

This element of authority is a key distinction between the product manager arrangement and the general manager arrangement. The typical product manager cannot be held fully accountable for profit in the same sense that the general manager can. Yet the product manager has a very real *influence* over profit and may be the key factor in making a profit exist for a specific product. His special knowledge, plans, stimulus, and persuasion can clearly give the needed competitive edge to his product.

## CAN HIS AUTHORITY BE INCREASED?

Basically, marketing executives point out that a good product manager has the possibility of spurring sales and profits in his field, yet can be blocked in his efforts by one or two intransigent executives in other functions–particularly sales, advertising, or production. In this respect he is in a position which is similar to that of the personnel manager or the director of industrial engineering. If the full potential of any of these positions is to be realized, the executive in charge must be able to communicate and persuade. It is impractical to give him formal authority to command everyone his job touches, so he must earn much of his authority with the quality of his ideas.

The product manager often wishes he had command authority over each of the various groups which play important parts in marketing or producing the products he is concerned with. There are only two ways this could be done. One is to give any such group as many bosses as there are product managers. The image of confusion, missed schedules, uncontrolled costs, and frustrated group supervisors brought to mind by this idea normally causes it to be dismissed without further thought.

The second possibility is to subgroup the people engaged in a particular function according to product specialization and place the subgroup under the direction of the product manager responsible for the same product. This has been found to be somewhat more practicable. When carried to its extreme in most of the major functions, this arrangement becomes a general manager system as defined in this report.

However, many in-between applications of this concept also are found in practice; in a number of companies the product manager has direct authority over one or two functions vital to his success. The limiting factors are duplication of jobs and facilities and difficulties in coordinating the subgroups, training them, and balancing their workloads. Where these factors are paramount–as in production–the product manager is rarely given line authority. Where they are less serious as liabilities, the product manager is sometimes given authority. Advertising is perhaps the best example. Some companies (for example, Vick Chemical Division of Richardson-Merrell) assign an advertising man to the product manager. Others (Colgate-Palmolive and Mennen, to name only two) have organized to give the product manager direct access to an advertising agency; in effect, he serves as advertising manager for his line of products. In such arrangements the product manager gains in control over results but in exchange for some disadvantage in other sectors. Obvious among these is greater difficulty in coordinating advertising programs on a companywide basis, since the authority gained by the product manager has been lost by the manager who had companywide authority over advertising. Now *his* mission must be carried out largely through persuasion.

In most of the major company functions, the problems that would be generated by giving the product manager direct authority seem too great to be tolerated. So, as noted earlier, he must generally keep work moving by explaining and persuading. This is not to say that the product manager's superiors cannot help to make his responsibility for product success tenable. Where it is impractical to give him formal authority, they can help the product manager to break down roadblocks by giving their support and by setting up procedural guidelines.

## RESOLVING THE PROBLEM OF LIMITED AUTHORITY

In any organizational arrangement, a man consults his chief if he finds his work seriously or consistently hampered by someone whose cooperation he needs to reach his goal. The superior then negotiates for a better solution at a higher level. If he fails to get one, he can take the issue to a still higher level. The outcome of a number of such debates over a period of months or years does much to establish the informal authority—or lack of authority—of the product manager. A kind of case law develops. If a product manager differs with an advertising man on specifics of copy a number of times, for example, and the judgment of the superiors goes generally with the product manager, then usually the advertising man finds it prudent to allow fewer copy matters to reach the appeal stage. In this case the product manager gains informal authority. If, on the other hand, the advertising man's ideas are more often supported, then the product manager loses informal authority in this area. The aggregate of such decisions in many fields does much to establish the image of importance or unimportance of the job of product manager in the company as a whole, and so to influence the willingness of others to honor his requests.

In this and other ways the attitude of top management is revealed and comes to be reflected by people of the various departments who work with the product manager. The respect higher managers show for the job—in deeds even more than in words—is a vital factor. The caliber of person they choose for the post of product manager is one such signal to the organization. In one company he may be paid $24,000 a year; in another, $10,000.[4] If the salary is low, it may be necessary to accept a candidate of limited qualifications. Because of his inexperience this man may make quite a few decisions which do not work out well; or he may make recommendations which are not accepted by the departments to which they are directed and, on appeal, the recommendations are found inadequate. The result is low informal authority. Where the top marketing executive wants to strengthen the hand of the product manager he must be prepared not only to act in a supportive way but also to select product managers of knowledge and experience so their day-to-day actions will be supportable.

## MINIMIZING FRICTION

To sum up: Prudent management will go a long way to prevent problems in the relationships between product managers and functional units, through careful selection of

[4] Detailed information on the compensation of product managers is available, from surveys of AMA's Executive Compensation Service, on a subscription basis.

people. But even in the best-managed firms there will be unavoidable friction, misunderstanding, and disagreement. The means used to minimize the frequency of unpleasant incidents include:

- Periodic planning meetings to allocate time and spell out special responsibilities for specific products.
- "As needed" meetings between product management and functional units to discuss unforeseen problems.
- Written procedures to clarify, where necessary, relationships between product managers and functional specialists. These descriptions also may spell out limits of activity with respect to advertising and other outside agencies.
- Appointment of counterparts to each product manager, in manufacturing, finance, and other functions, to complement his efforts and thus speed action on specific product needs.
- Coordination of product managers' recommendations to functional groups, to minimize any tendency to favor one man's products at the expense of those of others.

A number of executives have pointed out the importance of establishing a favorable climate when the position of product manager is first set up. When the job is first created and the product manager (or his immediate superior, the group product manager) is made responsible for a profit center, these executives feel it is vital to communicate his role in creating revenue and profit to the managers of the departments he will be dealing with. Some suggest that it is valuable, especially in early stages, for higher-level marketing, production, and other managers to aid in establishing direct lines of communication between the product manager and those at the same managerial level in sales, advertising, production control, quality control, accounting, and other functional areas.

It is common for a higher-level marketing executive to arrange periodic meetings between product managers and the sales manager, the advertising manager, and other functional managers concerned to allocate time and efforts. Since the several product managers are usually competing with each other for time of the same group of salesmen, for example, it is necessary to take some such approach to reconciling their pressures by agreeing on priorities or time allocations. There is apt to be a similar need to work out priorities for work in the factory, particularly where the products are made on a job-order basis.

Because the work of the product managers interacts with that of so many people in the company, managerial-level procedures may be written to facilitate crossing organizational lines where promotional arrangements, packaging modifications, price changes, complaint handling, and other important actions are involved. Such memos or manuals clarify the part that is to be played by each department, the clearances that have to be secured on various kinds of proposals or plans, the lead time that is normally to be allowed, and like matters.

Finally, of course, special conferences may be called, as needed, to smooth the way for specific programs or resolve conflicts between the product manager and representatives of other departments.

# Establishing the Marketing Objectives

*The heart of the marketing concept is that the wants and needs of the consumer form the basis for all activities of the business firm. The satisfaction of these wants and needs provides the rationale for the firm's existence, and the degree to which they are satisfied provides information as to the efficiency of the way in which the firm is managed.*

*Today, as never before, the tempo of technological change has forced obsolescence to become a fact of life. Thus, management must constantly seek out better ways of satisfying consumer wants and needs and* not *concentrate only on products which may be displaced by other products more satisfactory to the consumer. If the management of a company persists in being product-oriented rather than consumer-oriented, that business ultimately will fail.*

*The customer-use concept is especially important in the life of a firm which produces industrial goods, because the market may be several-fold removed from the firm's immediate customers. Any changes in the wants of the ultimate customers will often have dramatic effects on the success or failure of the firm. This means that marketing management must be knowledgeable about the wants and needs of the ultimate consumers and must strive to create goods and services which in turn will help others to do a better job of satisfying these wants and needs.*

*The firm's objectives lie in the marketplace; but these objectives will change over a period of time, since customer wants are anything but static. But a firm must not attempt to be all things to all customers; and most firms must confine their basic objectives to certain parts or segments of the market.*

# 9. MARKET KNOWLEDGE–SOURCE OF OBJECTIVES

*William Travers Jerome III*

*Any statement regarding the objectives of a business must be rooted in the market. Knowledge of both a qualitative and a quantitative nature is essential if management is to plan ahead and develop performance measurements.*

*The following article contrasts marketing with selling and industrial with consumer markets–especially as to knowledge and information available.*

For the purpose of our analysis, the meaning of markets is quite simple. First, markets exist only when there are either goods or services that can be bought and sold. Second, markets presuppose a number of willing buyers and sellers.

Top management's great interest in *product* research (as judged by the billions spent) stands in striking contrast to its far lesser interest in *market* research. The disparity in these two types of research leads to an interesting conclusion: people prefer to spend money on something tangible like a new product. It takes considerably more courage to invest in intangibles–even though these ultimately may lead to greater sales and profits. Notwithstanding, progress has been made toward achieving increased understanding of consumer motivation. More refined techniques are also being developed to measure market potential, as well as the success a company is having in capitalizing upon that potential. These are important areas holding extreme significance for any system of executive control, especially since the marketplace is the ultimate arbiter of management's success.

Source: From *Executive Control–The Catalyst,* John Wiley & Sons, Inc., New York, 1961, pp. 77–89.
William Travers Jerome III: Dean of College of Business Administration and Professor of Business Administration, Syracuse University.

The key role of market knowledge in any system of executive control can be expressed in yet another way. All planning, programming, and budgeting reflect the firm's best appraisal of the public's expected demand for the product or service being offered. Near-term expenditures are based on estimated demand for goods and services now in existence, whereas long-term capital expenditures are made in anticipation of changes now taking place in both research laboratories and consumers' tastes.

Similarly, in the area of organization, many changes in recent years have been dictated largely by market needs. Carrier Corporation, for example, completely revamped its organization around three basic product lines. General Electric has pushed its policy of decentralization down to product groupings.

The importance of market knowledge is likewise evident in the area of information. Thus, most of the vital statistics collected have to do with the life cycle of particular products or services. Key questions are inevitably concerned with price–volume relationships, with how much is being produced and sold, and with costs and prices.

A further purpose of this chapter is to indicate the changes that are taking place in the marketing or sales function of many successful companies. Such changes are significant both in terms of the internal organization of a firm and in terms of relationship of the marketing function to a firm's other activities. These changes are not always obvious, nor are the implications necessarily clear, to those who live in the midst of them. Yet, these changes have defininte bearing upon this subject of executive control. Thus the product (or service) and the market, if properly defined and identified, become a primary goal for all corporate effort. The product and the market are a way of pulling together all the other activities of the business. Indeed the product and the market serve as the justification for the existence of the various activities performed by the organization. It becomes possible to think of production, distribution, and various aspects of the financial–accounting operations as attributes of a continuous flow of services to the consumer.

For that matter, the product is often the basis of the individual's pride in company, in job, and in self. If properly understood and symbolized, the product or service can be used by management as a substantial motivating factor. The desire to perform services under the most trying of circumstances has become a tradition of the American Telephone Company because its management long ago recognized the importance of this. Few are the jobs that cannot be similarly glamorized in the sort of advanced technological society in which we live. Even more significantly, few are the people who can do a job well without some such glamorization. Most of us need to believe that our contribution to society, no matter how small, is nonetheless significant.

The following facts should serve to show the importance of market knowledge to a system of executive control. Moreover they provide evidence that market knowledge is not something passive or abstract.

1. Eight out of ten new products are failures, according to Department of Commerce estimates. This is a high mortality rate, particularly when new products are the stuff from which considerable business success has come since World War II.

2. Over 50 per cent of the sales of some of the country's largest companies are of products developed and marketed since World War II. The per cent of sales volume resulting from products introduced in the past five years is suggested by the following sample of industrial companies. Thus in the electronics industry, 45 per cent of sales volume is of products introduced in the past five years; in the chemical, pharmaceutical, and petroleum industries–26 per cent; in business equipment–26 per cent; in industrial products–19 per cent; and in the basic materials industry (steel, copper, glass, paper, and rubber)–12 per cent.[1] This outpouring of new products is the result of the intensive research being done by many of these companies.
3. Approximately six times as much money has been spent on *product* development as on *market* development. This may be one reason why the mortality of new products is so high in so many companies.

## KNOWLEDGE OF MARKET–SOURCE OF ORGANIZATIONAL OBJECTIVES

The importance of setting objectives (i.e., desired results) in order to guide and to evaluate performance is emphasized in other chapters. We must make clear now the overriding influence of the market on the fashioning of these objectives.

This need for understanding the importance of the market on company objectives is especially urgent for older, well-established companies. Thus, in a period of three decades these firms have seen the economy move from semistagnation, through two wars, to a burgeoning era of new products and growing markets. Consequently, so great are the present opportunities for any well-organized and imaginative business that the temptation is almost irresistible to dabble in many products and in many markets. Under these circumstances, management's job is the difficult one of attempting to determine what its firm can do best in order to concentrate always limited resources on this activity.

A case in point is the Minneapolis-Honeywell Company, originally founded to produce and to market a thermostatic heat regulator. After rescuing the company from the edge of bankruptcy in the 1880s, the father of the present Chairman of the Board declared that the objective of the business was to make thermostats and, as a matter of policy, it should never compete with its customers by trying to make furnaces. After World War II, Minneapolis-Honeywell was tempted to enter into what looked like the profitable manufacture of air conditioners. Instead of succumbing to this temptation, however, the company resolved to adhere to its basic objective, namely, the making of automatic controls. As it developed, the market for air-conditioning controls which Minneapolis-Honeywell made was very profitable, whereas the manufacture of air conditioners became highly competitive.

Another temptation, after the war, was for Minneapolis-Honeywell to enter television, especially as the postwar demand for this and similar household appliances appeared

[1] "What Does a New Product Mean to Your Company?" a report on the answers of ninety-one industrial companies, in *Sales Management,* November 20, 1959.

insatiable. Instead, the company again decided to stick to its basic objective and to concentrate on producing the sort of precision instruments and controls that management recognized were being made increasingly necessary by air power. Thus, the company stepped up its aviation research at a time when most companies were deserting military for civilian products. When the company ranged the field to buy up new businesses, it was always with one objective in mind—the new acquisitions had to be in, or related to, the business of making control instruments.

Adherence to the original goal or objective of concentrating company efforts on the production of control equipment reinforced still another fundamental objective: the desire to be the only company in the control industry capable of supplying a complete line of industrial controls. This meant expanding into such areas as controls for servomechanisms and for guided missiles.

The foregoing illustrates one very significant point: the process of determining the kind of company that managers think they are running depends on a proper identification of the sort of market they wish to serve. For Minneapolis-Honeywell the market was specifically defined to include automatic controls only. Manufacture of finished products like television or air conditioners, which used the company's control components, was left to others. A decision to produce television sets or air conditioners in all probability would have materially changed the character of the company's market and added a host of new problems.[2]

The Monsanto Chemical Company, for example, ran into difficulties when it departed from its traditional industrial market to vend to consumers a promising detergent developed in its laboratories. The venture was unsuccessful because Monsanto was not organized to handle profitably the required promotional and distributive job. A soap company to which the detergent was later sold found this product an immediate success. Presumably the soap company's established manufacturing and distributive facilities permitted the low costs and high volume required if profits were to be earned in the highly competitive soap markets.

Such illustrations have a common deficiency—they talk about products and markets as though they were solely physical things. Actually both products and markets take on different shapes and sizes as the *ideas* of the buyers are themselves transformed. These ideas may concern characteristics attributed to the products themselves, such as service, reliability, styling, and economy. Or these ideas may reflect external changes over which a single firm has little direct influence, such as changes in taste, national income, or defense spending.

The important point is that the objectives of a firm should not be regarded solely as the response to an existent market already being served. These objectives also need to be an affirmation of faith in the kind of market that management believes either can or will be created for its product or services. The problem here lies in first seeing the general outline and characteristics of the market and in then identifying the corresponding resources available to a firm to cultivate this market.

[2] This illustration is drawn largely from material found in "The Restless House of Honeywell," *Forbes*, December 15, 1956, pp. 15–18.

Objectives are thus the ultimate results desired from performing the particular tasks required to develop the market. The tasks themselves spring from management's knowledge of the market, and so do the objectives. These objectives are only another way of answering the question, "What kind of company are we?" They answer it by saying in effect, "Here are the markets that we seek to serve and these are the results that we want to achieve."

Furthermore, objectives born of the market place are a necessary first step in any system of management control in at least two respects: they provide relatively clear-cut targets for planning the work; and they also provide some useful norms against which to compare actual performance. Knowledge of a firm's present market, therefore, is simply one step in making necessary plans to create the firm's future market.

## MARKETING VERSUS SELLING

The importance of knowledge of product and market to the development of an effective system of executive control can be studied in still another way, namely, through an examination of the marketing function itself. Not so long ago selling and marketing were substantially synonymous, but this is no longer true. The marketing function calls for a broader, more systematic, approach both to the other functions of the business and to the market itself than was true of the sales approach. This difference between marketing and selling is well expressed by Dr. Henry Bund, Vice President and Director of the Research Institute of America:

> Right or wrong, marketing has come to mean a great deal more than just selling. Selling, traditionally—and in many companies to this day—means getting the order, then dealing with the customer.
>
> Marketing is a responsibility that extends beyond sales. It entails cooperation and coordination with other parts of the organization, specifically production and finance. It means taking their viewpoint into consideration so as to produce the kind of sales volume and dynamics that will give the company the greatest net profit as well as the greatest potential growth.[3]

This point of view makes possible an approach to executive control that can be understood first in terms of the relationship of the marketing function to the other activities of a company, and second, in terms of marketing's own internal organization. Thus, this change in selling approach is apparent in the way that some companies use the marketing function to pull together all the other activities of a business. Historically, for example, goods were manufactured and then given to the salesmen to sell. Subsequently, the power of advertising and sales promotion was exploited in order to develop demand for the goods manufactured. In even more recent years, sales have been stimulated through the use of credit or installment terms in order to exploit and to broaden the market. The challenge today is to discern the motivation of buyers and to tailor products appealing to this market. This is especially necessary for those companies selling in a highly competitive market.

[3] "Marketing: New Harness for Management," a round-table discussion in *Printer's Ink,* November 23, 1956, p. 21.

The change in emphasis from one of manufacturing goods and then selling them to one of identifying the market and then producing for known consumer preferences requires a great deal of cooperation and coordination from all executives in a firm. After the sales estimates are made, it is necessary to agree on inventory levels, to work out production schedules, to determine plant and equipment requirements, and to relate all these to the availability of capital and to the generation of satisfactory profits. It does not suffice, for example, to develop the sales estimates and to let it go at that. Further meetings with the production people, and those in finance, will usually be necessary. Thus, the original estimates may indicate that the volume anticipated is too low if costs are to be kept down to a profitable level. Or, it may be that plant and equipment, or skilled labor, cannot be provided in time to meet the particular sales estimates.

In the sense just mentioned marketing tends to pull together to some agreed-on goal all the various activities of the company. It is in this sense, too, that a knowledge of market and product helps to lay the basis for effective executive control.

The second significant aspect of this change in selling approach concerns the internal operation of the marketing function. There is a need to combine and to coordinate such activities as advertising, promotion, personal selling, and research and analysis. To the degree that there is absence of coordination, the marketing function loses direction and vitality. To that degree, too, it may be difficult to instill throughout the company the knowledge of product and market so necessary to good executive control.

At the risk of oversimplification, the significance of the marketing as contrasted with the sales approach might be highlighted as follows:

The marketing manager starts off with the customers' viewpoint and stresses their needs. The sales manager, on the other hand, starts from the narrower, company viewpoint, with emphasis on the need to sell the products of that company. The marketing manager is trained and disciplined to plan and coordinate his activities, ranging from design of product and its packaging, to setting quotas and to concentrating on areas of greatest sales and profit potentials. The sales manager, on the other hand, is typically the actor or doer, anxious to use the art of persuasion and showmanship, if necessary, to make the sale. Finally, the marketing manager is very profit conscious and recognizes the effect of his actions on other company activities. The sales manager, on the other hand, tends to be sales or volume conscious, often anxious to carry complete lines or to perform any number of services, unmindful that their cumulative effects may be detrimental to company profits.

The contrast suggested above and its significance is well described by Charles W. Smith, former President of the American Marketing Association:

> The difference in concept between the sales manager and the marketing manager is that the marketing manager has to develop a proposition that is going to be sold. In order to do that he has to think a lot deeper and a lot broader. He has to get things into much better focus than the average sales manager.

If the vice-president in charge of sales has been doing that, then you have no problem. But if he hasn't, then that is the gap companies are trying to fill.

Top management simply can't afford to stumble any more in the area of long-range planning. Operations are getting so complex and so big that to make a mistake in planning may ruin the profit structure of the company, maybe for a year, maybe for a long time.[4]

## INDUSTRIAL VERSUS CONSUMER MARKETS

The foregoing discussion draws no distinction between industrial and consumer markets. The question must now be raised whether knowledge of product and market is also important for firms selling to other manufacturers. The difference in the two markets seems to be largely a matter of degree. The sort of knowledge required for executive control is necessary whether a company is producing for the industrial or consumer market.

In fact, because industrial producers have tended to underplay the marketing function, it could be argued that the previous discussion is more relevant to the producer of industrial as contrasted with consumer goods. Thus, industrial producers seem to regard marketing costs as a necessary evil, rarely as an investment contributing to future earnings. In other words, marketing expenditures appear to be viewed as something to be reduced wherever possible rather than to be increased. Similarly, advertising, which averages 3 per cent of the sales of consumer goods producers, constitutes less than 1 per cent of sales for industrial producers. To be sure, the appeal is to buyers with somewhat different motivations. On the other hand, advertising and promotional work are no longer solely for pushing sales. Promotional programs seem to have significant influence on the attitudes of the workers in a given company as well as on the community in which that corporation is domiciled.

Recruiters, for example, are finding that their company's institutional advertising has often paid dividends because of the prestige value associated with the company's name. Industrial advertising, by periodically stressing certain product or service characteristics, also provides a method for supplementing the presentation of company salesmen as well as for "educating" them as to the most telling points to drive home. In other words, getting a company's story across to potential *buyers* is only one part of the marketing problem. Every company has an equally important, if somewhat different, story about itself to market right in its own backyard.

The importance of the knowledge of product and market to industrial producers can also be seen in the widespread attempt to achieve diversification through mergers. Underlying many of these attempts have been product and market considerations. From the standpoint of management control, the problems raised by these mergers concern a whole host of matters that directly relate to the market place. Objectives need to be restated, plans and programs must be reworked, and usually financial and budgetary controls need to be restudied.

[4] *Ibid.*, p. 22.

In yet other ways the influence of the market is inescapable for industrial producers. Thus, the effect of research upon product lines has just as far-reaching repercussions for industrial producers as for consumer producers. In a similar way the success of any value analysis type program depends considerably on knowledge of market and product. By value analysis I have reference to the practice of an increasing number of companies to examine the cost effects of their product design or material specifications or procurement sources. Whenever goods are mass-produced, a modest change in design specifications can frequently reduce cost without detracting from product performance in any way. A slight change in machining, for example, or the use of coldforms rather than of heat-treated parts, can represent savings amounting to thousands of dollars.

The importance of marketing (and therefore to a degree of executive control) to companies producing for the industrial market has perhaps been minimized for an interesting reason. Industrial producers generally have been much closer to the buyer or user of their product than the typical consumer goods producer. Because of this close relationship between user and manufacturer, industrial producers have always had an integrated marketing concept, although one far more limited in scope than the one we have been discussing.

In commenting on industrial marketing, Professor Neil H. Borden, of the Harvard Business School, put it this way:

> Lots of industrial manufacturers still are (as contrasted with consumer-goods operations) relatively smaller organizations in the number of people that may be involved in the marketing side of the business. At least in these small organizations we haven't had the question of the span of control coming in as it does in some of these other larger businesses, so the coordinating job is thrown back to the president.
>
> The big question then becomes: "Do we have a man at the top who has a good concept of what should be done in marketing?" It isn't a question of whether there should be an extra man in the organization, because it probably doesn't need another man.[5]

The very fact that industrial goods manufacturers in the past have succeeded with a simple, down-to-earth marketing arrangement may spell trouble for the future. With more money than ever before being poured into research and development, the need for quick and thorough market coverage is most important. Du Pont, for example, has learned that it must often help its customers both find and develop new uses (e.g., markets) even though the benefit to Du Pont is somewhat indirect.

As industrial companies grow larger, and as those executives with technical training rise within the management ranks, there may also be an even greater tendency to take the marketing function for granted. The reason for this is that engineers usually are disposed to think in terms of things rather than in terms of people and their motivations. Some companies have learned to their sorrow that it is not enough to build a better mousetrap. It is still necessary to entice the world to beat a path to the door. Equally as important, too, is the necessity to instill an organization with pride and

[5] *Ibid.*, p. 72.

satisfaction in the work of the corporation, since such pride helps to cut costs and to maintain quality leadership. The marketing job also involves creating a corporate reputation for respectability in the minds of the public at large.

## ORGANIZATIONS WITHOUT PRODUCTS TO "SELL"

It is now necessary to digress long enough to consider the effects on systems of executive control arising from the differences between markets in the private sector of the economy and those in the public sector. Knowledge of the market, I have asserted, is one of four key elements in any system of executive control. Since the market served by government is quite different from that served by private business, it is necessary to show how organizations in the public sector either can or cannot operate under a system of control similar to profit-making organizations.

The Department of Defense, for example, is making intensive efforts to institute an integrated financial plan. To encourage better management, certain self-contained units like an arsenal or a depot are supposed to charge all users (i.e., "customers") for services rendered. In this way, users are obliged to consider the cost of these services both in developing their own programs and budgets and later in living within the funds allotted to them. The arsenals and depots, for their part, have to live within the "income" that they earn from the "sale" of their services.

Something resembling a "market" economy, in other words, is being created in the armed services, not unlike the interdivisional "sales" of private corporations. Despite the apparent similarity between some of these newer practices in government and practices that have proved successful in business, the question still remains whether the creation of this pseudo market economy will enable government to pattern its system of management control after successful business prototypes.

In his book, *The Practice of Management,* Peter Drucker takes the position that "any organization in which marketing is either absent or incidental is not a business and should never be run as if it were one."[6] Unfortunately, Drucker does not develop the reasoning leading to this brusque conclusion–brusque in the sense that he seems to have serious doubt about the wisdom of postwar efforts to incorporate so-called business principles into government operations.

Drucker's belief, however, appears to be based on a line of reasoning similar to that pursued in this chapter. Thus, he seems to regard the market as both the starting point for management control as well as the key determinant of a business' objectives. "There is only one valid definition of business purpose: *to create a customer. . . .* Marketing is the distinguishing, the unique function of the business. A business is set apart from all other human organizations by the fact that it markets a product or a service."[7] From this sort of reasoning, he apparently drew his conclusion that an organization without a product or service to sell is not a business and should never be run as though it were one.

[6]Peter F. Drucker, *The Practice of Management,* Harper & Brothers, New York, 1958, p. 38.

[7]*Ibid.,* p. 37.

Governmental or other nonprofit organizations unquestionably are subject to different forces than those characterizing the markets in the private sector of the economy. In this sense, Drucker's comments are valid. Nonetheless, governmental organizations still must derive their ultimate justification (i.e., their objectives) from the needs of society. To be sure, the mechanism for expressing these needs may be the ballot box or the politician's smoke-filled room rather than the market place. But certainly the necessity for establishing objectives, as the first step in any system of management control, cannot in good conscience be escaped. It also seems incontrovertible that these objectives should be spun by following the same approach as that used by private business, namely, through developing answers to such questions as: "What is this organization's basic purpose?" and "How may this purpose best be accomplished?" Although government has been as superficial as business in stating objectives and in measuring performance, objectives still must be shaped from the needs of those served.

Governmental organizations can get the country into trouble, however, if in developing their objectives they adopt too uncritically practices of the marketplace better left to profit-making firms. A well-managed business, we have seen, is always on the move to create new demands and new markets in order to optimize profits and to achieve self-perpetuation, but similar behavior on the part of government is a certain way of leading to an even larger bureaucracy. It also leads to self-duplication and waste as in the guided missile rivalry among the three military services.

The absence of profits is yet another characteristic of markets in the public sector. This lack is most detrimental to the effective operation of systems of management control in the public sector, not because of the absence of the profit incentive, as is so often believed, but because no impartial mechanism exists for putting a price on the services offered. Absence of a price mechanism makes it extremely difficult to *measure* either the value of the services provided in the government sector or the effectiveness with which they are performed.

The merit of a market economy, assuming the existence of several buyers and sellers, lies in the opportunity to judge the value which the public affixes to a firm's goods and services. If these goods and services are well received and properly priced, the profits earned confirm the wisdom (or unwisdom) of management's decisions. Furthermore, profits aid planning by providing some objective criteria for deciding the merits of either increasing expenditures or of budget cutting. In government, where managers lack any very objective measures of accomplishment, most financial control is "expense control," exercised through across-the-board cuts. Under these circumstances where generally accepted objectives or criteria of performance are lacking, it is difficult for a system of executive control to function with maximum effectiveness. Absence of the profit test is by no means fatal. It simply means that certain aspects of the job of managing in government are rendered more complex.

Interestingly enough, the creation of a pseudo market economy in the public sector does nothing to temper the tenor of the preceding remarks. Funding arsenals and depots, for example, and requiring each organizational unit to "buy" its needs will do little to make for better management. Thus, these individualized segments are still "government" and government is the sole buyer and, in most instances, the sole seller—which is the antithesis of a market economy. Furthermore, the effectiveness of this whole intricate operation still depends on the amount and timeliness of the monies appropriated each year by Congress. Even the management of an arsenal with its own funds is subject to the whims of Congress, since its "sales" are dependent on the monies made available to customers. Thus, without long-range planning, programming, and budgeting, plus the determination to make these work, many of the "modern" practices being introduced into the government are all but worthless.

# 10. WHAT KIND OF CORPORATE OBJECTIVES?

*Harper W. Boyd, Jr., and Sidney J. Levy*

*What are the most effective ways of devising overall corporate objectives?*

*Here are analyses of six different categories of marketing objectives, especially useful to top management.*

An overriding objective is critical to the successful functioning of a business enterprise.

Lack of specificity in objectives often causes management to fall back on vague, overgeneralized statements. When this happens, the decisions relating to such major strategies as product and product line, pricing, personal selling, advertising, channels, R & D, and plant location are poorly coordinated. Too often the decisions are made by merely following industry practice ("all companies have their own sales force"); by historical precedent ("we have always had exclusive dealers"); and by tradition, uncertainty, and imitation, as well as by sound precedent and experienced insight.

As corporations have grown in size, executive problems have increased in complexity. Consider the desires of certain departments with respect to length of product line. The marketing group wants a long product line because it means a better position in the marketplace. But the production people want long production runs in order to minimize manufacturing costs. And the financial executives want to minimize capital investments in inventory and the extra production equipment needed to produce the longer line.

Source: From *Journal of Marketing,* vol. 30, October, 1966, pp. 53–58. Harper W. Boyd, Jr.: Professor of Marketing, Graduate School of Business, Stanford University. Sidney J. Levy: Professor of Marketing, Graduate School of Business, Northwestern University.

Reference to the firm's *overall objectives* is the only effective way of resolving such differences.[1]

Operations researchers long have been interested in the setting of objectives, both from the point of view of individual executives and the organization as a whole. Some have documented both the need and the difficulty of specifying objectives, and conclude that most organizations are unable to describe their specific goals satisfactorily.[2]

Multiple objectives can be stated in terms of departmental objectives or area responsibilities, such as those suggested by Peter F. Drucker—market standing, innovation, productivity, physical and financial resources, profitability, manager performance and development, worker performance and attitudes, and public responsibility.[3]

Such objectives, often conflicting, raise the question of *suboptimization*. A "best" solution to such a problem requires the assigning of relative weights to the objectives involved, and determining their substitutability.[4] Clearly the presence of a *governing objective* would increase greatly the efficiency of solutions to the problems of suboptimization. Thus, despite the conclusions drawn by some operation researchers, continuation of the search for some way to set forth an overriding objective is needed.

There have been a number of attempts to get at this problem. Typically the "procedures" center around the kind of businesses in which the firm should be engaged, what market niche the company should attempt to occupy, what product or products the company should produce, and where the company wants to be in the next five to ten years. All have one thing in common: lack of the precision necessary *if* the firm is to have a true rationale for existence.

## CATEGORIES OF OBJECTIVES

Our purpose here is to discuss only the overriding or "broader" corporate objective, in contrast with the sub-objectives which would be used to accomplish the large objective.[5]

Although there is no simple solution and no easy formula available by which to accomplish our task, it should be helpful to discuss those aims an enterprise might have—growing out of what it has to sell, the utilization of its products or services, and its relationships to its customers.

[1] C. West Churchman, Russell L. Ackoff, and E. Leonard Arnoff, *Introduction to Operations Research,* John Wiley & Sons, Inc., New York, 1957, p. 5.

[2] David M. Miller and Martin K. Starr, *Executive Decisions and Operations Research,* Prentice-Hall, Inc., Englewood Cliffs, N. J., 1960, p. 44.

[3] Peter F. Drucker, *The Practice of Management,* Harper & Brothers, New York, 1965, p. 63; also Miller and Starr, *op. cit.*, pp. 44–45.

[4] Russell L. Ackoff, *The Design of Social Research,* The University of Chicago Press, Chicago, 1953, pp. 375–376.

[5] See Charles H. Granger, "The Hierarchy of Objectives," *Harvard Business Review,* vol. 42, May–June, 1964, pp. 63–74.

Study of more than 200 statements received from a research inquiry which pertained to corporate objectives, many discussions with corporate executives, and results from numerous research projects suggest different sources of objectives which have the potential of generating goals from which relatively specific plans can be developed. Here are six for consideration:

1. Focus on material resources,
2. Concern with fabricated objects,
3. Major interest in events and activities, requiring certain products or services,
4. Emphasis on kind of person whose needs are to be met,
5. Catering to specific physical parts of a person,
6. Examination of wants and needs, and seeking to adapt to them.

These categories are *not* mutually exclusive and do *not* include such nondifferentiating objectives as the making of profits, the generating of increased sales, the desire to perpetuate the firm, and other such management-centered aims.

Also, the discussion of the six categories centers largely around firms producing consumer goods, although the principles apply for the most part to industrial-goods firms.

### 1. Focus on Material Resources

Many modern companies owe their origin and continued existence to having owned or been granted rights to drill, mine, and hew. Still others were founded to process certain natural resources, including those derived from agriculture, for example, grain crops, meats, and milk. Earlier, the main problems were to get the raw materials and to overcome the transportation difficulties in bringing them to an expanding market.

The companies that were founded to process agricultural products were the first to change, or else die. The very efficiency of the American farmer "choked" many to death. The growth of standardized processing methods, the development of substitute products via the laboratory, and the difficulty and cost of marketing also took their toll.

The milling and dairy industries are but two examples of the evolution that took place in the growth of large diversified companies. In natural fibers, the growth of the man-made synthetics altered substantially the viewpoints of those in the carpeting and clothing industries.

The metal, oil, and gas industries have not escaped the technological revolution. The competition among metals and between metals and plastics has been intense, with important effects on the management philosophies of the firms involved. The attention paid to the market and its needs by basic-plastics producers and by the aluminum companies has forced some of the old-line companies to accelerate their R & D efforts and do a better job of satisfying customer needs as an example, through the development of certain metal alloys.

The plastic companies rely on chemical research and recognize the inevitability of a product life cycle, with the superseding of one plastic by another. In order to capitalize on innovations they engage heavily in market-development programs. Thus, to promote its polystyrene, the Dow Chemical Company established a product-evaluation program designed to evaluate end-products on the following basis:

1. General plastics application–should *any* plastic material be used?
2. Specific material application–should Dow styron be used, and if so, what formulation?
3. Product design.
4. Workmanship.

In recent years many producers of raw materials have devoted considerable effort to increasing demand by finding new and attractive uses for their products. Thus, the producers of raw asbestos fibers have expanded their market by producing asbestos woven sheets which will withstand extremely high temperatures and which can be used by a variety of industries. Such producers have been led from merely supplying industry to thinking about ultimate consumption. They often start with the need to sell byproducts of raw materials and as they think about how to foster consumption of their products, they may start to use and sell other products in conjunction with their own.

The fact that the oil companies typically sell certain chemical products as well as tires, batteries, accessories, mechanical repairs, soft drinks, travel items, and food, is a case in point.

Although raw-material oriented companies have come to be highly concerned about their markets, many tend to remain heavily preoccupied with the discovery of new supplies, new techniques for shipping, automated processing, negotiations with governments, geo-political problems of extracting minerals, large-scale effects of laws, fiscal policies, and economic patterns.

Thus, the attempt to be market-oriented centers mainly on helping the customer to sell, and the customer's customer to sell. Personal selling and the heavy use of consumer advertising are the means used. But while these activities may have a beneficial effect on market share, they rarely solve the long-range problems of finding new and better ways to satisfy the needs and wants of the ultimate consumer.

Individuals who manage "raw-materials" companies probably are more "tough-minded," more dedicated to a single-minded purpose, and more centered on inner-oriented activities of the company than those managers who, at the other extreme, are concerned with examining human wants and needs and seeking to adapt to them. The latter survive not by battling nature but by ingratiation and catering to whims. Compare, if you will, the food company to an oil company.

The danger of being materials-oriented in objectives is obvious. Given the fast pace of technological change, a company that concentrates narrowly on its materials power can easily be rendered obsolete. The management of such a company would find it difficult to change successfully the company's mission. The very attributes which make for a successful manager of a raw-materials company would serve as liabilities, given a set of objectives that are market-oriented.

## 2. Concern with Fabricated Objects

A significant center of energy and attention is the manufactured object. It has been and remains a major source of interest and dedication to many company executives.

The main objective of many companies is the production of a "thing" (or "things"). Attention focuses on what it is, what its characteristics are, how it gets made, its contents and specifications, and how it works. Questions dealing with who uses it, what is done with it, and why people might or might not want it may be left unanswered.

Clearly, product-orientation and concern with production problems are uppermost in the minds of such managements. This preoccupation with production restricts the horizons of company thinking. This means that the urge to perfect the product may be greater than the willingness to change it radically, or to make variations that might lead to a product line, or to develop alternatives to replace it.

As an example, the president of a large and well-known quality producer of men's suits reacted to synthetic fibers by indicating that they did not fit into his way of doing business. He said that his buyers were wool buyers, not synthetic buyers.

It is also likely that a company's interest in just *selling more* of a product can become the main goal of management, since the channeling of energy into production makes increased productivity the only apparent avenue to profits. Given a stable history and growing demand for the product, such a production-orientation is likely to build a strong feeling of security and confidence.

On the other hand, when market changes occur that affect the demand for the product, such managements are vulnerable. The area where they exert the greatest control—within the plant—is least helpful in modifying their relationship to the external environment. Many traditionally-minded small businessmen often find themselves in such difficult situations.

The focus on material resources and the concern with fabricated objects are basically oriented *away* from the consumer, or at least are not specifically aimed at him. He is largely taken for granted. The sources of objectives which follow tend to develop an awareness of the consumer; there is some more or less direct concern with meeting his needs and wants, and gratifying him or stimulating him.

### 3. Major Interest in Events and Activities

If the major interest of the management of a company is to sell products or services which fit into a consumer's life in a special way, then this will serve as a useful source of company vitality.

If a management perceives its objective as that solely of producing a golf ball, then it is likely to be less flexible and responsive to change than a management which thinks of itself as making products which are to be used in golfing, or in sports activities, or in recreation. This larger definition which deals with what people are doing in the sporting world, or in the changing world of recreation, enlarges the scope of management's thinking about what the company should be trying to accomplish. Management will be more likely to search out new lines, and to anticipate or foster new trends.

Events and activities can be a useful way of segmenting the market. Emery Air Freight developed a unique service "to handle emergencies" through the use of a complex network of air carriers and delivery trucks. Emery even took into account the psychological aspects of an emergency by offering, at extra cost, a time of delivery service which informed the buyer exactly where his shipment was and when it would be delivered.

Events and activities which tie to style considerations tend to generate flexibility and sensitivity to change in the management of those companies which cater to such objectives, for example, clothing for holidays or vacations. When the consumer's goals transcend the significance of the product itself and management recognizes this fact, then the firm is also likely to be more sensitive to the external environment and the opportunities inherent in the process of change.

In recent years the American public has taken up in increasing numbers "new" sporting activities–including skiing, surfing, and skin-diving. Golf is more popular than ever. These changes in our avocations have provided many manufacturers with new and lucrative markets.

Another illustration has to do with high-school graduation. This used to be an occasion celebrated with the gift of a watch. But today fewer watches are given if only because the new graduate is likely already to possess one.

### 4. Emphasis on Kind of Person

Through various historical circumstances, the managements of some companies have come to think of themselves as serving the needs and wants of a particular kind of person. They are focused on a certain market segment, rather than on supplying a product line to different kinds of people.

This makes a great difference in what policies are pursued. Gerber advertises "Babies Are Our Business–Our Only Business." If Gerber were to extend this policy (and it has done so to some extent) it might end up with a diversified line of clothing, furniture, and other articles–all designed solely for babies.

This "targeting" on a certain kind of person, depending on how the "kind" is defined, can make a great deal of sense. Many small specialized retailers or service establishments build business around such an objective–for instance, a quality haberdasher. But if the objective centers on a disappearing "kind" of person, then the firm will experience trouble. A publisher who caters to the education and amusement of the wives of blue-collar workers might, over the next decade or two, experience a substantial reduction in his potential market.

The ability to be successful in serving people, as contrasted with producing things for people, has merit, of course, since the executives of a firm must understand what is different about "their kind of people" as compared with other kinds. And a preoccupation with a type of person may induce great sensitivity to any changes in such individuals, as retailers who have catered successfully to college students over the past decade can testify.

The behavioral sciences have provided some insightful information about certain groups of individuals. For example, knowledge of how social classes differ with respect to their life style and buying behavior is helpful in the establishment of market segments.[6]

## 5. Catering to Specific Physical Parts of a Person

Consider the concern of companies as to eyes (Maybelline), teeth (Dr. West), feet (Florsheim), skin (Noxema), hair (Alberto Culver), beard (Gillette), and legs (Hanes).

However, the physical part of a person for which concern is expressed is merely part of a person's total *gestalt*. The use of lip rouge and hair dye and the colors involved are affected by cultural norms as well as by the life style to which a woman aspires.

Still, the "parts" objective has considerable appeal. By focusing on a relatively small and specialized part of a person, a firm can build a relatively secure market. But it may be difficult to build up sufficient sales to compete against a larger and more diversified seller.

A related problem has been experienced in the channels of distribution. Companies producing products having to do with the feet and legs, that is, shoes and stockings, have had difficulty in obtaining specialty-type selling without setting up their own outlets or leased departments. Only the larger firms have been able to afford such expenditures.

[6]Pierre Martineau, "Social Classes and Spending Behavior," *Journal of Marketing,* vol. 23, October, 1958, pp. 121–130. For an example of another classification system, see Janet Fisher, "Family Life Cycle, Analysis in Research on Consumer Behavior," from Lincoln H. Clark, Ed., *Consumer Behavior: The Life Cycle and Consumer Behavior,* vol. 2, New York University Press, New York, 1955, pp. 28–35.

## 6. Examination of Wants and Needs

To have real meaning, an objective must be specific—as to what wants and needs of what parts of the market are to be satisfied.

This objective can be accomplished with some probability of success if the management of a firm considers (1) what generic use is to be satisfied, and (2) what consumption systems are operating to satisfy these generic uses.

*Generic Use.* Too broad an affirmation of corporate intentions provides little guidance to planning. It makes considerable difference whether a company defines its goals as being primarily financial, and sets about acquiring divisions chosen for their tax advantages rather than for their product fit; whether it aims to cater to, say, the textbook market and develop academic contacts to attract authors; or whether it wants to provide a congenial environment for bright and inventive engineers.

One important aspect of defining need objectives has to do with a product's *generic use.* Companies not only sell their products, but the functions which these products can serve in satisfying customers' wants.

In this sense, companies sell transportation, nutrition, energy, comfort, self-expression, escape, intellectual development, and conformity—rather than cars, bread, gasoline, pillows, pens, novels, textbooks, and uniforms. Transportation can be served by objects other than cars, and bread serves other functions than nutrition, and so on.

This means that objectives can be phrased and interpreted in different ways by companies in the very same industry. A company that centers its objectives on helping people to express their individual styles of communication might do better with the market by creating a new, more malleable pen, rather than by devising a cigarette lighter just because it happens to have the equipment to turn out small gadgets.

A logical starting point in the setting of need objectives would be to state the end-uses to which the product applies, and the basic needs that the end-use is attempting to satisfy. For example, a manufacturer of wristwatches might state that the basic need for the product is to measure time. The human outlook here rests in compulsive attention to precision and accuracy. Less literally, there is the definition of the wearer as mature enough to control the organization of his timed activities, and to relate to other people in a "socially synchronized" way.

If precision and accuracy are to be the main factors, then the necessity for fineness and quality of workmanship follows. If control of timed activities is given precedence, the company may begin to develop activating mechanisms and miscellaneous automatic timing devices. If social relationships and synchronization are emphasized, the company may turn toward making watches for children, for cocktail wear, and for jewelry adornment.

The petroleum industry will take quite different courses—depending on whether company managers see themselves as providing power, automotive service, transportation, or as being a conveniently located channel of distribution for a variety of products.

*Generic use* refers to the satisfaction of fairly general consumer needs and wants. But how they are gratified can vary and change through time.

People need food, shelter, and sex if they and their kind are to survive; but overweight people, "high-rise" dwellers, and contraceptive-users have made some significant modifications in their diet, environmental control, and sensual gratifications. It is necessary to keep abreast of changing social, cultural, and psychological situations and what they imply for product variation and innovation.

*Consumption Systems.* It is useful to think of the consumer as a decision-maker who individually or in conjunction with others control the operation of a system comprised of products, effort (labor), and machines.[7]

Every product is, therefore, by definition a part of some consumption system. The totality of the system exists to satisfy some basic need or want—that is, to solve a problem.

This "solving a problem"—or goal-directedness—is critical. A failure to understand the nature of the goals and the standards set by the consumer will inevitably result in difficulties. Typically, there are a "constellation" of goals; for example, the housewife cleans a floor to remove dirt, to show that she is a competent housewife, to demonstrate to her family that she loves them, and so on. The housewife uses many systems as she goes about her household tasks. Cleaning house, preparing food, washing clothes, caring for the baby, and getting ready to go out provide examples of consumption systems in operation.

Here the consumer is like an economic entity—engaged in buying, transporting, changing raw materials into finished products in a sequence of events that is more or less efficient, and more or less satisfying to the participants. A manufacturer wishing her business has to produce and sell a product that will "fit." He has to understand what she is doing behavioristically (her actions), as well as teleologically (her goals).

Knowledge of the consumption system, more fully and carefully dissected, can alert the manufacturer to the fact that the housewife is acting in an orderly or purposeful way, according to her likes and dislikes; that there is a series of interrelated steps which require decision-making based on knowledge, expectations, standards (as well as ignorance, surprise, and uncertainty), and that the product is used with other products with which it must be compatible.

When the manufacturer knows these systems in detail and keeps his knowledge current, then he is in a position to assess opportunities (perhaps he can meet the standards of a housewife better with a new or modified product) as well as threats (for example, the development of a new washing machine which cleans by vibration).

We can also assume that a knowledge of the more important systems will help him to innovate, or at least provide him with a better understanding of the opportunities to do

[7] See, for example, Churchman, Ackoff, and Arnoff, *op. cit.,* pp. 8–9, 20–56, and 107–114.

so. Certainly he has a point of reference, since time as well as the actions of competitors no doubt will change the system, thereby providing him with new opportunities.

A seller of industrial equipment or supplies should easily be able to perceive the usefulness of the systems approach to objectives. Manufacturing systems are more precise and logical in their operation than are consumer systems. They center around a "flow," so that a manufacturer can predict with a fair degree of accuracy what he must do to "plug into" a given system at a specific point.

# 11. ON KNOWING THE CONSUMER–AN OVERVIEW

*Joseph W. Newman*

*This selection represents an excellent summary of what is known, or probably known, about the behavior of consumers in the marketplace.*

*The author is summarizing some of the principal points of a special symposium "on knowing the consumer"; and he presents an effective integration of several different research approaches.*

In this chapter, I have attempted to summarize the product of the Symposium in the form of answers to the major questions considered. Its preparation entailed reviewing the transcript of the proceedings, to formulate answers to such questions where answers seemed to be present. Of primary interest were conclusions or ideas supported by research findings. The distinction between opinions and supportable conclusions, however, often was a difficult one to make. Knowing is a matter of degree, and the participants in the give and take of their discussions did not always make clear the extent to which they felt their statements rested on empirical evidence.

In any case, no one pretended to have a great amount of "solid knowledge." The experience of other fields shows that it is well to regard "knowledge" as tentative, existing only until rendered obsolete by new findings that lead to new insights. The participants appeared to be very much aware of the limitations of knowledge in as young a field of study as consumer behavior. Inasmuch as relatively little is known, theories, concepts, and opinions, as well as research findings, which suggest promising avenues of inquiry, are of more than usual interest.

Source: From Joseph W. Newman (ed.), *On Knowing the Consumer,* John Wiley & Sons, Inc., New York, 1966, pp. 3–20. From a chapter "On Knowing the Consumer–an Overview," by Joseph W. Newman. Joseph W. Newman: Professor of Business Administration, Graduate School of Business Administration, The University of Michigan.

For the most part, the integration of ideas that follows represents answers only as they were suggested in the Symposium. Many represent a consensus or, at least, main points made which encountered little opposition. An attempt was made to reflect important differences of opinion when they appeared. A good many of the answers are based directly on what was said, but others involve interpretations for which I assume responsibility.

The summary follows:

## TRENDS IN THE AMERICAN MARKET

*What important changes have taken place in the American market in the last 15 years?*

Information supplied largely by studies of the Survey Research Center at The University of Michigan showed the following:

1. One household in every six is headed by a retired person or a person over 65 years of age. Relatively little is known about the distinctive market behavior of this group.
2. A marked rise has taken place in the educational level. There is evidence that it has been accompanied by an increase in deliberate decision-making and greater interest in product information.
3. A dramatic increase has taken place in discretionary purchasing power. Implications have not been fully explored, but a larger part of total purchasing power now is devoted to non-necessities. There is evidence of a proliferation of wants and increased latitude in the timing of purchases. It is not known how increasing affluence affects price consciousness or the care with which buying decisions are made.
4. The proportion of suburban residents has increased. The trend implies a continuing preference for an informal life style and outdoor activities.
5. The proportion of households with working wives has increased to 37 per cent. Many implications of this change remain to be studied, but indications are that working wives place greater than average emphasis on convenience and timesaving.

## BUYING DECISIONS

*Who makes the household buying decisions?*

Information on this point is surprisingly scarce and sometimes contradictory. A distinction has been made among the purchaser, the user, and the authority. The influence of each varies by product category. Family members exert considerable influence on the housewife's buying decisions. Children not only are big buyers of some products (gum, toys, soft drinks), but they are very influential on their parents' purchasing. Brand choice in some product categories is determined by the process of "passive dictation"; i.e., trying a number of brands and continuing to buy the one the child (or the dog) will eat. The housewife is most aware of her family's preferences for products on which the brand name is clearly visible in use. Whether she takes the preferences into account depends on the product concerned, on whether she thinks her family can distinguish among brands, and on the ease of accommodating individual preferences.

*How deliberate are consumer buying decisions?*

Neither the stereotyped economist's image of the "rational" consumer nor the opposite image of the casual or impulsive buyer easily swayed by emotional appeals is the true one. The amount of deliberation varies among people and by circumstance. Deliberation can be directed at allocating income by types of expenditures, or making specific purchases within those allocations, or both. Unsuccessful attempts to talk to people about their budgeting procedures have led to the tentative conclusion that determination is a more effective control device than a plan developed on paper. It appears that people resort to formal budgets because their self-control has not proved sufficient.

Much of what has been referred to as "impulse buying" actually is deferred purchasing. The consumer has a background of product experience, and when he sees what he wants under the correct circumstances, he buys. The planning matrix is in the mind, rather than in the form of a written shopping list. Shoppers know from experience that they can not come back later and expect to find the same item available, especially in certain product categories.

Consumer planning periods typically are short and people readily change their minds. One-half of the purchases of durable household goods appear to be planned no more than two months in advance; the planning period for smaller purchases is shorter still. The proportion of unplanned purchases tends to be higher in years of particularly active demand. Given latitude in timing of major purchases, large masses of people at certain periods often all decide at the same time either to accelerate or to postpone discretionary outlays, the timing being influenced by financial and attitudinal factors.

Consumers appear to be more aware of the costs of search and decision than do some of the critics of their buying behavior. Consumers recognize that obtaining personally useful information can be time-consuming and difficult. Getting help from friends, for example, may be a complex process of searching out people whose values and information the prospective purchaser feels will be meaningful to him and interpreting what is said.

Consumers seek buying information by talking to friends, having family discussions, visiting more than one store, and comparing goods on price and easily understandable properties of the merchandise. But they seldom do all of these things. Because of the desire to economize in the decision-making process, the degree of deliberation varies with the amount of money involved in the purchase, its meaning and importance to the buyer, his previous satisfaction or dissatisfaction with similar products, the urgency of his wants, the presence of strong stimuli, and his education.

Although people are gaining increasing latitude in the use of their funds, they do not appear to be willing to devote increasing amounts of time and interest to their economic decisions. Instead, they prefer to enter into a number of contractual savings schemes and buy on the installment plan, as means of regularizing their payments and simplifying the systematic handling of family finances.

*How do people acquire market information and make buying decisions which involve considerable risk?*

Little specific information exists on the processes involved. Recognizing the void, the Marketing Science Institute has launched a study of how new resident households in a community accumulate information on their new social and economic environment. The project seeks to explain both the process and the quantity of search activity in terms of socioeconomic and psychological variables. It focuses on the dynamics of the decision processes in the choices of a bank, an automobile dealer, furniture dealer, major appliance dealer, automobile repairman, television or appliance repairman, plumber or carpenter, hairdresser, doctor (general practitioner), doctor (pediatrician), dentist, and babysitter.

*How do people make decisions with regard to the acquisition and use of information that reduces uncertainty?*

At present, little is known. A project is now under way at the Management Science Center at the University of Pennsylvania, which seeks to determine whether people react to uncertainty as the Bayesian decision model says they should. Experiments conducted so far showed that they do not conform closely to the model. They typically did not use all of the information available to them and overbought information in cases where their prior uncertainty about the outcome should have been low. In a sequential sampling game, they almost invariably purchased too little information. Large differences were noted among people. Those sensitive to information were found by tests to be open-minded and confident in regard to their control over their environment. People not sensitive to information tended to have closed minds and a fatalistic attitude about the future.

## INFLUENCE AND CONSUMER CHOICE

*What is involved in getting a person to value a product favorably?*

Influencing is not simply a matter of informing people about values innate to products. Contrary to past notions, people are not passive recipients of messages. Both the communicator and the audience are out after something. Value is derived from three interrelated spheres of consumer experience: the cultural definition of the generic product category; the image of the brand; and the physical-sensory product itself. Coming from their own worlds of experience with their own identities, consumers bring more values to products and advertisements than they take from them. The experience of value is more than an economic decision based on the traditional quality-price ratio. It depends upon the extent to which a product fits appropriately into the total life style of the consumer. Advertising alone cannot modify cultural values and consumer product definitions.

*Are some people more susceptible to persuasion than others?*

Yes. Results of recent research, however, varied somewhat from the traditional beliefs that persuasibility tends to be greatest for persons low in self-esteem and persons facing difficult decisions. While persuasibility appears to be inversely related to self-confidence with men, it has been found to be greater for women of medium self-confidence. A possible explanation is that women low in self-confidence resisted persuasion in ego defense and those high on the scale felt no need for outside help. In one experiment, the difficulty of assigned tasks was varied. Women's reactions to persuasion remained the same, however, because they shifted their strategies when they faced the more complex assignment.

*Does advertising have to be believed to be influential?*

No, at least not at first. A consumer will believe an ad which reminds him of what he already knows, but he will rarely change his attitude completely as a result of exposure to a single advertisement. Attitude change involves moving through a stage of non-belief, during which the person will try to resolve the conflict between his past beliefs and the new information. It is more important, therefore, that individual messages contribute to a flow of communication which, *in toto*, is designed to change attitudes than it is that a single message be believed.

*How does the reputation of the source affect a message's influence?*

Messages from sources regarded as high on competence and trustworthiness produce the greatest change in attitudes and the strongest defense against exposure to counter-propaganda taking place almost immediately afterwards. A recent experiment, however, found that messages from such sources also left people vulnerable to counter-attack later. Messages from sources seen as high in competence and low in trust resulted in the best defense to counterpropaganda. A possible but undocumented explanation is that in the latter case, people had thought the matter through more carefully, and the process served to inoculate them against attempts to change their minds.

*How important is recency of advertising exposure?*

In an experiment that simulated a jury trial, it was found that the argument last heard overwhelmingly was the one that persuaded people to vote one way or the other regardless of their previous exposure to arguments. Little is known about whether this holds true for advertising. The importance of recency of exposure was supported, however, in an experiment that measured the sales effectiveness of a new advertising medium consisting of 36-inch, three-dimensional displays in supermarkets. The results showed striking sales effectiveness for the in-store displays.

*Is an advertisement more likely to be seen by a person after he has tried the advertised product?*

Yes. Experimental findings support the idea that people read advertisements to resolve dissonance left in the wake of the purchase.

*Can advertising and promotional deals adversely affect product sales?*

Yes. Experiments have produced evidence that advertising can have a negative effect if the message is inconsistent with attributes of the brand that can be evaluated by the consumer. One study found that market share for one brand decreased as the amount of advertising increased. Some promotional deals appear to have left consumers less likely to buy a brand after the deal was removed than they would have been had no deal been offered.

*Is there a direct relationship between a product's share of advertising and share of sales?*

This question provoked extensive discussion and some disagreement. Exceptions to the direct relationship were cited. There was substantial agreement that share of advertising was a relevant consideration in setting the advertising budget, but that the problem is current inability to tell advertisers how they should take competitors' advertising expenditures into account. One case of success was reported in arriving at an optimum advertising investment by experimentation, but studies in which expenditures have been varied generally have not been very successful because of lack of adequate control and measurement of other variables affecting sales. Advertising budgeting has been the subject of much study which has made use of mathematical models and experimentation. So far, however, knowledge of how to allocate funds to regions or products with varying sales trends has not progressed much beyond the rules of thumb and hunches that long have been used by operating management.

## MARKET SEGMENTATION

*How can people be categorized meaningfully for marketing considerations other than by the usual demographic factors?*

Of the many possible ways of grouping consumers, the following received special attention:

*Social Class.* The existence of social classes reflects the fact that groups in our society do different kinds of work, get different types and amounts of financial reward, and are evaluated differently along various dimensions of social esteem and importance to the community. As a consequence, they think of themselves differently, want differently, and behave differently. The social classes differ in respect to their values, the character of their interpersonal relations, their self-perceptions, and how they live their daily lives. Social status affects how people feel about where they should shop, and how they go about their shopping; their use of different advertising media; their reactions to kinds of advertising appeals; the products they want to consume, and the reasons for consumption; how they regard and use food; their tastes in furniture, housing, clothing, etc.; and brand selections. Social class variations in life style are often subtle and are more important to the marketing of some products than others.

*Race.* Racial and ethnic groups may differ substantially from the population at large in their purchasing and consumption. Evidence was presented that the Negro market is self-segmenting on the basis of whether the individual is striving for the white race standard in material goods or has abandoned the attempt. In general, Negroes tend to take whites as their reference group, and they concentrate seriously on products as elements for attaining the status they want in society. Negro consumers show much anxiety about products and shopping decisions. They are very brand conscious, apparently relying on brands as insurance against making mistakes, but they tend to be ready to shift brands.

*Stage in Career as a Consumer.* Certain purchases occur at very different points in a person's career as a consumer, and there are times in a person's life when he is more apt to change products and brands than at other times. Some consumer research has made the career rather than the purchase the unit of study. One aspect is that some people are experienced buyers while others are still learning. Great differences have been found between people who acquire an appliance for the first time and those making a replacement purchase. The buying behavior of people making original acquisitions tends to be similar for all major appliances.

*Children.* Marketers may be interested in special studies of children as consumers because there are many children, they are influential, and they differ from adults. Certain types of motivating scenes in television commercials have been found to make a lasting impression on children. Their reactions to commericals cannot be reliably predicted from their reactions to programs. Some advertisers have been more successful than others in distinguishing their brands from the product type. Although television is a favorite of children, outdoor play is an important competitor which affects the hours of viewing. Interviewing of children entails problems that require special skills.

*Consumer Requirements of Products.* An approach was presented which involved grouping people by measures of various requirements of food within these classifications: nutritive-health; sensory; convenience; social-psychological; and economic value.

*People Who Move.* Available information suggests that about 5 per cent of the population moves across county lines in a year. They typically are professional people who are well-educated, do not get into financial troubles, and associate moving with advances in status and consumption levels. A study being conducted by the Marketing Science Institute is directed at learning more about the characteristics and problems of new resident households, the roles played by marketing institutions in their adjustment to the new towns, and the feasibility and value of measuring mobility and adjustment.

*Personality.* The influence of personality on consumer choice was the subject of much discussion and limited but conflicting evidence as to its importance was presented.

Several attempts to relate personality to brand loyalty and the amount of consumption have failed to produce anything of importance. Opinions were expressed that these failures occurred because environmental factors often are much more important than personality; personality characteristics tend to be stable as contrasted with attitudinal variables, which change more readily; it is difficult to measure personality; the consumer purchase data used in the studies may be unreliable; and general personality inventories which were not prepared in accordance with criteria relevant to product or brand choice are used.

Success was reported in the use of tailor-made scales to differentiate among buyers of food on the basis of such factors as nutrition anxiety. Mention was made of data showing that people who place a high value on durability tend to buy brands of appliances regarded as representing durability. Success in predicting brand-loyal and brand-switching tendencies from scores on personality tests and people's behavior in experimental games was reported from one study. Systematic differences have been found in personality among the social classes. All in all, however, relatively little progress appears to have been made in relating consumer behavior to personality.

*Heavy versus Nonheavy Buyers.* Heavy buyers are very important. The top 20 per cent account for more than half of the total volume of many frequently purchased products. Significant demographic differences exist among heavy, medium, and light users of several classes of food products, and the differences tend to be stable over time. Within demographic groupings, heavy and light users have been found to differ sharply in attitudinal dimensions, but not in personality characteristics as measured by two standard tests. Data from studies of three products in three stages of their life cycles suggest that for mature products, the basic pattern of attitudes separating heavy from light buyers remains stable over time. For growth products, however, increases in the number of heavy users may be a function of evolving new sets of attitudes that lead to heavy usage. Although marketing activities directed at populations from which heavy buyers are drawn may be sound, the practice of following a marketing strategy directed at identifying heavy users of competitive brands and converting them to one's own brand might be very expensive, because people move in and out of the heavy buyer classification in some product categories in short periods of time.

## CONSUMER-BRAND RELATIONSHIPS

*Are people loyal to brands?*

They do not purchase brands in a purely random fashion, but it is not clear on the basis of empirical data whether this is due to a feeling of loyalty, inertia, or something else. The reason is that the definition of loyalty, which typically has been used, specifies only that a certain percentage of a household's purchases go to one brand within a given time period. It says nothing about whether the purchaser feels an attachment to the brand and, if so, how strong the feeling is.

Using the standard definition, we find that the amount of brand loyalty varies by product category. Within certain food products, loyal buyers (giving 50 per cent or more of their purchases to one brand) contribute 60 per cent to 85 per cent of a brand's total volume, and 35 per cent to 60 per cent of the buyers of brands would be classified as loyal. Little exists by way of explanation for loyalty that can be supported by empirical data, and failure was reported from attempts to predict which families will become loyal to a new brand. Statistically significant demographic differences have been found among loyal buyers of some leading nationally advertised brands. While some believe these differences have resulted from the marketing strategies and media patterns used by the brands, this conclusion is difficult to document. Families loyal to a given brand tend to respond to changes in price and promotion in the same way and to about the same extent as do families not loyal to the brand.

Most families purchase a relatively stable mix of brands within a product category (apart from the influence of deals), whether for variety, regular use of different brands by individual family members, use of different brands for different applications, or because of shopping in a mix of stores. Patterns of high switching among brands from purchase to purchase may indicate that the brands are regarded as close substitutes for one another, but empirical evidence was notable by its absence. One reason for the absence is that interpretation of brand interaction depends on data beyond that usually available from consumer panel purchase records. Brand loyalty studies typically have consisted of applications of quantitative techniques to existing purchase data, and have not included the gathering of new data. Considerable research using mathematical models has been done on brand switching, but little agreement exists as to what has been learned aside from additional insight into the nature of the problem of study.

In one major product class, long-term buyer flow studies showed that change in share and volume were at least as much related to movement of loyal buyers in and out of the market or changes in purchase rates among loyal buyers as they were to shifts in loyalty from one brand to another. Fifty per cent of the families who were in the market one quarter, for example, dropped out the second quarter, being replaced by a comparable number of new families who had not been in the market the preceding quarter. Such observations, coupled with the limitations of the typical definition of loyalty, have prompted questioning of the value of brand loyalty as an operational concept.

The above comments are based, to a large extent, on studies of grocery buying, which has received much of the attention because of the high frequency of purchase and the availability of consumer panel data.

In hard goods, studies have shown little loyalty to brands, though brand share trends have proved to be strong nevertheless.

*Are consumers loyal to families of brands?*

The answer appears to be "Yes" for food products. One study found that people who purchase a particular brand in one food product class are likely to purchase it in another. The tendency, however, is much greater when items are grouped by brand rather than by product type in the retail store. In another study, greater joint loyalty and greater joint purchase of products bearing the same brand were observed than would be expected on the basis of chance alone. Little loyalty has been reported to brand lines of hard goods.

*Who is most likely to adopt a new product or a new brand?*

Relatively little is known, although the question has been the subject of some interesting work. One means of predicting mass marketability of new products was described, which involved categorizing people on the basis of how satisfied they were with their self-images. Some empirical data were presented in support of the proposition that the buying behavior of those who were somewhat dissatisfied with their current self-images and wanted to upgrade their life styles in realistic ways was predictive of the future acceptance of new products by the mass market. People who were satisfied with their current self-images, or who were so dissatisfied that they wanted change they could not expect to achieve, tended to be followers rather than leaders in adopting new products and activities.

## RESEARCH APPROACHES

*What trends are evident in research approaches to consumer behavior?*

A continuing growth is apparent in the amount and quality of research being done in both business and universities. A greater portion of the work is of a more fundamental character than has been typical of past years. The research increasingly is being directed by professional people who have formal graduate training in one of the social sciences, mathematics, or statistics. Greater use is being made of all of the main methods of gathering data, particularly experimentation. The development that has captured more attention than any other in recent years, however, probably is the application of various quantitative techniques of analysis, usually to data that already were in existence.

*What has been the product of research based on mathematical models of consumer behavior?*

The picture is mixed. The contribution to knowledge has not been large so far because of limitations of basic inputs and assumptions underlying the models. Researchers have yielded to the temptation of trying to fit problems to readily available analytical techniques such as regression analysis and linear programming, rather than concentrating on developing adequate statements (models) of the marketing processes to be studied before choosing or developing appropriate tools. Mathematical models, however, have served the valuable function of imposing needed discipline on thinking. They offer the advantages of precision of expression, the power of mathematics in deriving logical implications of such expressions, and a base for extension of research effort. Approached in the context of a systematic long-term research program, models would appear to have much to offer.

*Is an interdisciplinary approach needed for substantial future progress in knowledge of consumer behavior?*

Yes. Research must draw upon the social sciences because understanding specific aspects of consumer behavior depends upon understanding the human beings who are the consumers. (Although most of the participants appeared to hold this view, there were differences of opinion as to the desirable extent and form of interdisciplinary efforts.) Economic, psychological, cultural, sociological, physical, and marketing variables all are important in the total realm of consumer behavior. It does not follow, however, that the outside disciplines can be of help on all marketing problems. There is a need to further specify what the people in the various disciplines can and cannot do, and establish guidelines as to when they should be consulted. Special problems are encountered in attempts to borrow concepts and methods from other fields. Considerable revamping is often necessary.

*What is the function of theory in regard to consumer behavior?*

Theory cannot tell you what marketing action to take in a given situation or how many people will buy a given product brand under certain conditions. The function of theory is to guide thinking about the nature of problems, suggest promising inquiries, and aid in the interpretation of data in the search for answers that are operationally meaningful.

*How can the benefits of other disciplines best be realized?*

There is no one answer because problems vary in their requirements, and opinions differ as to what working arrangements can produce best results. There is substantial agreement, however, on the need for greater tolerance of diverse approaches and for removal of barriers that long have separated different disciplines. One approach to making use of the resources of several fields is that of composing interdisciplinary teams of people with relevant backgrounds. Successful performance is more likely if the team members (1) are especially good in their own specialities; (2) have a mutual respect for one another and a desire to work together; (3) have learned how to complement one another; (4) have a mutual understanding of the nature of the problem and a real interest in working on it. People who are strongly devoted to their own disciplines tend to find it difficult to entertain ideas of others. A problem orientation rather than a disciplinary or technique orientation is important. It may be well to have marketing management represented on the team for this reason as well as for the value of practical experience. Temporary interdisciplinary groups frequently never become well functioning teams. Long range interdisciplinary efforts, however, can be very productive. Some specialists will not join interdisciplinary groups but can nevertheless make a contribution to the work if they are approached on specific aspects of the problem in the right way.

## CONCLUSION

The term "consumer behavior" generally is used to refer to both buying and consuming. The Symposium discussions, however, were largely concerned with aspects of purchasing as is most of the literature in the field. Actually, very little is known about the meaning of consumption in specific situations in any product category.

The discussions served to point up a number of problems which demand future attention, as has been indicated in the preceding paragraphs. Relatively little is known, for example, about the processes of making different buying decisions, and the character and meaning of shopping activity. The operational value of the concept of brand loyalty was challenged as was the wisdom of marketing strategy designed to switch heavy users from one brand to another. The question of what advertising a marketer should do in a given situation still awaits a specific answer. When disagreement appeared in the discussions, it frequently concerned the shape of curves for describing relationships. This served as a striking reminder that it is not enough to indicate the direction of a relationship; something more specific is needed to aid management decision-making.

Everyone would agree that knowledge of consumer behavior is still very limited. A tremendous amount of work needs to be done to identify relevant variables, and to establish relationships between controllable stimuli and responses to them before marketing laws can emerge, which might be integrated by theory. While the frontier is large, it clearly is being subjected to explorations of both number and kind which marketing has not known in the past. This is highly important because an understanding of people's needs and the fulfillment of those needs which can be met by goods and services is basic to the existence as well as the performance of marketing.

# 12. WHAT ABOUT CONSUMER BEHAVIOR AND THE BEHAVIORAL SCIENCES?

*Steuart Henderson Britt*

*The author of the following selection indicates how various behavioral-science materials can result in useful insights into certain aspects of consumer motivation and behavior.*

*After a brief philosophical background, he discusses what is meant by the phrase "the behavioral sciences," and he contrasts some misconceptions about consumer motivation with the findings of behavioral scientists.*

One might say that reading
Is not to make anything of anyone
But simply to open the mind of everyone
To go from *cocksure ignorance*
To *thoughtful uncertainty!*

In a sense, the statement above is the theme of this brief discussion regarding the influence of the materials from the behavioral sciences on consumer behavior. There is an enormous literature, both in the field of the behavioral sciences and in the field of marketing; and the more that one reads, the more he moves from "cocksure ignorance" to "thoughtful uncertainty."

For a marketing practitioner or marketing teacher to make use of materials from the behavioral sciences requires an overwhelming amount of "digging," reading, and

Source: From Steuart Henderson Britt (ed.), *Consumer Behavior and the Behavioral Sciences: Theories and Applications,* John Wiley & Sons, Inc., New York, 1966, pp. 16–21. From a chapter "What About Consumer Behavior and the Behavioral Sciences?" by Steuart Henderson Britt. Steuart Henderson Britt: Professor of Marketing and Advertising, Northwestern University; Editor, *Journal of Marketing.*

studying. The marketing man has to become an interdisciplinarian. That is, he must introduce into the discipline known as marketing those theoretical considerations, experimental techniques, and empirical results from the disciplines of anthropology, sociology, and psychology that help to provide increased understanding of consumer behavior.

## BACKGROUND IN PHILOSOPHY

But before attempting to deal with recent literature in these fields of thought, the true marketing scholar should be well read in certain European literature in philosophy, psychology, and sociology—especially that of the last half of the 17th century and of the 18th and 19th centuries.

This takes us all the way from Descartes to Wundt. Consider such works, for example, as the following:

| | |
|---|---|
| Descartes | *Passions de L'Ame* (1649) |
| Hobbes | *Human Nature* (1650) |
| Locke | *An Essay Concerning Human Understanding* (1690) |
| Berkeley | *Principles of Human Knowledge* (1710) |
| Hume | *Treaty on Human Nature* (1739) |
| Lamettrie | *L'Homme Machine* (1748) |
| Hartley | *Observations on Man, His Frame, His Duty, and His Expectations* (1749) |
| Herbart | *Lehrbuck zür Psychologie* (1816) |
| James Mill | *Analysis of the Phenomena of the Human Mind* (1829) |
| Spencer | *The Principles of Psychology* (1855) |
| Fechner | *Elemente der Psychophysik* (1860) |
| Darwin | *The Expression of the Emotions in Man and Animals* (1872) |
| Brentano | *Psychologie vom Empirischen Standpunkte* (1874) |
| Müller | *Zür Grundlegung der Psychophysik* (1878) |
| Sully | *Outlines of Psychology* (1884) |
| Galton | *Inquiries into Human Faculty and Its Development* (1883) |
| Binet | *La Psychologie du Raisonnement* (1886) |
| LeBon | *Les Lois Psychologiques de L'Évolution des Peuples* (1894) |
| Durkheim | *Les Règles de la Méthode Sociologique* (1895) |
| Wundt | *Grundriss der Psychologie* (1896) |

These examples of philosophical thought are mentioned for three reasons.[1]

[1] For further examples, see Steuart Henderson Britt, "European Background (1600-1900) for American Psychology," *The Journal of General Psychology*, vol. 27, October, 1942, pp. 311-329; also, such works as Edwin G. Boring, *A History of Experimental Psychology*, Century Company, New York, 1929; Fay Berger Karpf, *American Social Psychology: Its Origins, Developments, and European Background,* McGraw-Hill Book Company, 1932; and Robert I. Watson, *The Great Psychologists: Aristotle to Freud,* Philadelphia, J. B. Lippincott Company, 1963.

First, some of these works are even more significant to the development of psychological and sociological thinking than the classical writings of Plato and Aristotle, the sixth-century writings of St. Augustine, or the thirteenth-century works of Albertus Magnus and Thomas Aquinas.

Second, the period from Descartes and Hobbes to that of Durkheim and Wundt may be said to represent roughly the beginnings of the modern experimental method.

Third, and perhaps most important, all of these works, plus many others by the same authors and by other philosophers, psychologists, and sociologists—such as Spinoza, Leibniz, Kant, Bentham, Comte, John Stuart Mill, Helmholz, Bagehot, Tarde, and Ward—are an important background for an appreciation of the publications in the behavioral sciences during the past decade or so.

## THE BEHAVIORAL SCIENCES

What is really meant by the behavioral sciences? Curiously enough, there is no general agreement among scholars. But it is agreed that the phrase "behavioral sciences" is not synonymous with "social sciences"; the latter phrase includes the former.

The social sciences include:

*Anthropology* (*Behavioral* science, especially *cultural anthropology*)

Economics
Education
History
Jurisprudence (law)
Political science

*Psychology* (*Behavioral science*, especially *social psychology*)

*Sociology* (*Behavioral science*, especially *psychological sociology*)

Note that economics, education, history, jurisprudence, and political science are listed among the social sciences. However, as indicated above, there are three fields of knowledge that help to provide the greatest understanding of consumer motivation and behavior: anthropology, psychology, and sociology. For our purposes these may truly be called *behavioral sciences.*

And the very basis of these behavioral sciences is much the same as for the physical sciences, that is, the use of empirical methods: *experimentation, observation,* and *quantification.*

Within the disciplines of anthropology, psychology, and sociology the special fields of *cultural anthropology, social psychology,* and *psychological sociology* provide the greatest insights into consumer behavior.

Thus, the field of *anthropology* can be divided into archaeology, physical anthropology, and cultural anthropology. The first two areas do not provide much "grist for the mill" for those of us trying to fathom modern *consumer behavior.*

On the other hand, in the field of *cultural anthropology* we have many investigations of primitive peoples—everything from studies of the Trobriand Islanders to the Dobuans, Zuñi, and Kwakiutl, for example, to the Samoans—that reveal special nuances of human nature. And there are the studies of present-day communities and groups, as exemplified in the writings of such behavioral scientists (not necessarily anthropologists) as Lloyd Warner, John Dollard, Gunnar Myrdal, and Alfred Kinsey, that stimulate us to think about consumer behavior in new ways.

Likewise, not all the materials of *psychology* are by any means useful in understanding *consumer behavior.* After all, the great majority of psychological literature deals with such areas as physiological psychology, animal psychology, therapy and guidance, abnormal psychology, and educational psychology—rarely of value to the marketing practitioner studying consumer behavior.

On the other hand, there is a vast literature on subjects such as learning and remembering, perception, thinking, language, attitudes and opinions, personality, motivation, and emotions, within which can be found real "nuggets of wisdom" for the marketing man. Instead of all phases of psychology being useful for our purpose, the materials that are of special interest to marketers are those from *social psychology.*

And by no means is the great majority of literature in *sociology* significant in gaining a more complete understanding of *consumer behavior.* Important though such investigations and their results are, what can we possibly learn about consumer behavior from the literature on crime, delinquency, prejudice, and race differences?

On the other hand, studies of social-class structure, social mobility, leadership, and group interactions, plus techniques such as scaling devices and measurement of social norms are very significant for our purposes. This is the area of what might be called *psychological sociology.*[2]

However, even in the anthropological literature on cultural antecedents of behavior, for example, or in the psychological literature on learning, as another example, or in the sociological literature on social-class structure, as another example, there is a paucity of literature actually dealing with *consumer behavior.*

In fact, only a rare behavioral scientist has the slightest interest in the field of marketing, and particularly in the psychology of consumer motivation and behavior. During 1963–1964, when I served as President of the Division of Consumer Psychology of the American Psychological Association, only 242 (1 per cent) of the 22,119 Members and Fellows of the American Psychological Association were Members or Fellows of the Division of Consumer Psychology.

The applications of both theoretical and empirical studies in cultural anthropology, social psychology, and psychological sociology must be developed by those marketing scholars who truly are interdisciplinarians. The task is to discover those kinds of

[2]See Steuart Henderson Britt, "Social Psychologists or Psychological Sociologists—Which?" *The Journal of Abnormal and Social Psychology,* vol. 32, October–December, 1937, pp. 314–318.

information in the behavioral sciences in which effective techniques have been used, and then to try to interpret consumer behavior in terms of the results obtained by use of these techniques.

This is where the *newer* techniques of the behavioral sciences enter in, such as:

Cybernetics
Decision-making theory
Game theory
Information theory
Linguistics

After all, the consumer is not some rarefied kind of a "purchasing unit" whose motives can be pried into, and whose purchasing behavior, therefore, can be predicted precisely.

In this connection, although economics and especially economic theory is important as a background for certain aspects of marketing, it is truly astonishing how little of the materials from economists really are of any use at all in getting new insights into consumer behavior.

Careful and thorough study of the principal works of both tranditional and modern-day economists reveals that economists almost never observe consumer behavior at all. They just theorize about it.

Classical economic theory implies that consumer choices are completely rational . . . that the consumer is completely informed at all times . . . that his preference patterns are constant . . . that he knows all the products from which he can choose . . . and that he can intelligently and logically make choices that provide maximum utility. And the consumer is pictured by many economists as allocating his theoretical, disposable income to buy theoretical units based on theoretical prices.

In contrast, cultural anthropologists, social psychologists, and psychological sociologists are concerned with the real world of human beings: their cultural milieu, their socialization and personality development, their wants and aspirations, and their role expectations, for instance. From scholars in these fields we can learn about some of the nonrational aspects of human behavior, the emotional factors involved, the conflicts of decision, the personality problems, the symbolic influences on human behavior and so on.

*Misconceptions About Consumer Motivation.* Far too many practitioners of marketing and teachers of marketing are handicapped by "cocksure ignorance" about consumer motivation, instead of having "thoughtful uncertainty" about consumers. As examples of some misconceptions about consumer motivation, consider the beliefs that:

1. Motivation can be divided neatly into rational and emotional categories.
2. Consumer motivation tends to be on one level only.

3. Consumer motivation is relatively static.

4. Most motivation is based on conscious decisions.

5. By just asking questions and getting answers, adequate information can be obtained from consumers.

Contrary to these beliefs, studies by behavioral scientists demonstrate that:

1. There is no such thing as a universal set of explanatory motives.
2. There are many different levels of motivation.
3. Consumer decisions are relatively changeable.
4. Consumer decisions are based on both unconscious as well as conscious factors.
5. Useful information from consumers needs to go far beyond mere question-and-answer procedures.

Certain behavioral scientists increasingly are providing factual information as well as theory about actual behavior in this real world. Some of their empirical investigations are giving us greater knowledge than ever in the past about consumer behavior.

Thus, in recent years we have greater insights than ever before into:

1. *The behavior of the business firm with relation to the consumer,* including psychological segmentation of the market and also psychological interactions in the marketplace,
2. *Product attributes as they affect the consumer,* including the brand, the package, the price, and the buying environment,
3. *Promotion activities as they influence the consumer,* that is, various types of communication and persuasion, including advertising, selling, and sales promotion,
4. *Decision-making by consumers,* including both predictions and evaluations of consumer behavior.

## SOME PROBLEMS

The degree of overlapping between information in the behavioral sciences and information about the consumer should not be exaggerated, of course. Unfortunately, too many marketing practitioners and marketing teachers seem to think that there is some body of knowledge in the behavioral sciences that somehow can be "lifted out" and applied to marketing problems, especially those involving the consumer.

In actuality, specific materials applicable to a better understanding of consumer behavior must be searched for and searched for—almost like looking for the proverbial needle in the haystack. Even though so little relatively can be found that really "bridges the gap" between the behavioral sciences and the field of consumer psychology, there are some significant behavioral-science studies that can be utilized by the interdisciplinarian interested in consumer behavior.

But there is the problem, by no means an easy one, of trying to *apply* the findings of the behavioral scientists to specific marketing problems. The answer is that when materials are found in the literature of the behavioral sciences that seem useful, they may be utilized in two ways. Both involve what psychologists call "transfer of training."

The materials may be applied in helping to solve a specific problem of consumer behavior; that is, the facts are "transferred." Or much more likely, the materials may be digested in the sense that they affect the attitudes of marketing men as they study consumers; that is, the ideas are "transferred" attitudinally.

*Behavioral Science and Marketing.* In any case, though, there are a great many differences in the backgrounds, attitudes, and methods of behavioral scientists as compared with marketing practitioners and marketing teachers:

1. *History.* The literature of the behavioral sciences extends back in history at least a few hundred years, perhaps a few thousand. In contrast, the history of marketing literature is measured in decades only.

2. *Scope of literature.* The number of professional periodicals in the behavioral sciences in English alone is at least 75; and the total number of books, monographs, and articles in the behavioral sciences in all languages is some 12,000 to 15,000 a year. In contrast, the professional periodicals in marketing in English alone can be counted on the fingers of one hand; and the total number of books, monographs, and articles on marketing in all languages is a few hundred a year at most.

3. *Theory.* The theoretical literature in the behavioral sciences is simply enormous–a plethora of materials. In contrast, the theoretical literature in marketing is sparse–perhaps a few hundred thousand words at most.

4. *Schools of thought.* The literature of the behavioral sciences is replete with differences in interpretations of behavior, depending upon the "school of thought," such as functionalism, purposivism, behaviorism, and so on. In contrast–aside from some discussions of a functional, institutional, or commodity approach to the study of marketing–the literature of marketing contains almost no diverse theories or "schools of thought."

5. *Science and art.* Most behavioral scientists have stressed the science of behavior and its scientific methodologies. In contrast, most marketing men have stressed the art of marketing and its practical uses.

6. *Objectives.* Most behavioral scientists are concerned with a scientific understanding of behavior, and not necessarily with applying this information. In contrast, most marketing men are concerned with the prediction and control of behavior in the most practical terms possible.

7. *Attitudes.* Behavioral scientists traditionally have been concerned with data that represent pure scientific findings. In contrast, marketing men traditionally have been interested in information that can be applied.

8. *Motivation.* Most behavioral scientists are motivated to explain behavior, and are not content with description only. In contrast, most marketing men usually are content with describing behavior, and not overly concerned with explaining behavior.

9. *Methods.* For a great many years experimentation, observation, and quantification have been the hallmarks of behavioral scientists. In contrast, only within the most recent years have a tiny fraction of marketing men carried out significant experimental, observational, and quantitative studies.

10. *Reading habits.* Most anthropologists, psychologists, and sociologists follow literature in their own fields of specialization, but rarely in marketing. In contrast, most marketing men read marketing literature, but rarely read in the fields of the behavioral sciences.

11. *Meetings.* Most anthropologists, psychologists, and sociologists attend their own congresses and conventions, and only rarely those in the field of marketing. Likewise, most marketing people attend their own congresses and conventions, and only rarely those in any of the behavioral sciences.

## SOME ANSWERS

In spite of these many problems, there are some answers.

It is true that almost no significant materials in the behavioral sciences really are applicable to *certain* aspects of consumer behavior—such as channels of distribution, for example, or pricing, as another example. On the other hand, marketing men can learn from cultural anthropology the extent to which certain antecedents of behavior can affect the consumer's perception of packages; from social psychology how the order in which promotional points are made can influence the consumer's attitudes about various products; and from psychological sociology the influences of innovators and opinion leaders on consumer purchases.

From the behavioral sciences we can gain useful insights into many other aspects of consumer motivation and consumer behavior in the marketplace—especially of the business firm with relation to the consumer; of product attributes as they affect the consumer; of promotional activities as they influence the consumer; and of decision-making by consumers.

The implications are clear. Those engaged in the development of the scientific aspects of marketing really should be called "marketologists."[3] And if marketologists are to move from cocksure ignorance to thoughtful uncertainty about consumer motivation and behavior, they have no choice but to use experimental, observational, and statistical methods to a greater extent than ever before, especially some of the newer techniques.

[3] "Sociologists and Marketologists," *Journal of Marketing,* vol. 24 (October, 1959), pp. 37–44.

# 13. CONSPICUOUS CONSUMPTION

*Thorstein Veblen*

*The thesis of the classic book* The Theory of the Leisure Class *is that, in general, people tend to use their financial surplus so as to impress other people with the fact that they have a surplus.*

*The ways and means for creating that impression are called "conspicuous consumption."*

Conspicuous consumption of valuable goods is a means of reputability of the gentleman of leisure. As wealth accumulates on his hands, his own unaided effort will not avail to sufficiently put his opulence in evidence by this method. The aid of friends and competitors is therefore brought in by resorting to the giving of valuable presents and expensive feasts and entertainments. Presents and feasts had probably another origin than that of naïve ostentation, but they acquired their utility for this purpose very early, and they have retained that character to the present; so that their utility in this respect has now long been the substantial ground on which these usages rest. Costly entertainments, such as the potlatch or the ball, are peculiarly adapted to serve this end. The competitor with whom the entertainer wishes to institute a comparison is, by this method, made to serve as a means to the end. He consumes vicariously for his host at the same time that he is a witness to the consumption of that excess of good things which his host is unable to dispose of single-handed, and he is also made to witness his host's facility in etiquette.

In the giving of costly entertainments other motives, of a more genial kind, are of course also present. The custom of festive gatherings probably originated in motives

Source: From *The Theory of the Leisure Class: An Economic Study of Institutions* [1899], Modern Library, Inc., New York, 1934, pp. 75–76, 83–84, and 97–98. Present owner of publication rights, The Viking Press, Inc. Thorstein Veblen: Economist and Managing Editor, *Journal of Political Economy.*

of conviviality and religion; these motives are also present in the later development, but they do not continue to be the sole motives. The latter-day leisure-class festivities and entertainments may continue in some slight degree to serve the religious need and in a higher degree the needs of recreation and conviviality, but they also serve an invidious purpose; and they serve it none the less effectually for having a colourable non-invidious ground in these more avowable motives. But the economic effect of these social amenities is not therefore lessened, either in the vicarious consumption of goods or in the exhibition of difficult and costly achievements in etiquette. . . .

The requirement of vicarious consumption at the hands of the wife continues in force even at a lower point in the pecuniary scale than the requirement of vicarious leisure. At a point below which little if any pretence of wasted effort, in ceremonial cleanness and the like, is observable, and where there is assuredly no conscious attempt at ostensible leisure, decency still requires the wife to consume some goods conspicuously for the reputability of the household and its head. So that, as the latter-day outcome of this evolution of an archaic institution, the wife, who was at the outset the drudge and chattel of the man, both in fact and in theory—the producer of goods for him to consume—has become the ceremonial consumer of goods which he produces. But she still quite unmistakably remains his chattel in theory; for the habitual rendering of vicarious leisure and consumption is the abiding mark of the unfree servant.

This vicarious consumption practised by the household of the middle and lower classes can not be counted as a direct expression of the leisure-class scheme of life, since the household of this pecuniary grade does not belong within the leisure class. It is rather that the leisure-class scheme of life here comes to an expression at the second remove. The leisure class stands at the head of the social structure in point of reputability; and its manner of life and its standards of worth therefore afford the norm of reputability for the community. The observance of these standards, in some degree of approximation, becomes incumbent upon all classes lower in the scale. In modern civilized communities the lines of demarcation between social classes have grown vague and transient, and wherever this happens the norm of reputability imposed by the upper class extends its coercive influence with but slight hindrance down through the social structure to the lowest strata. The result is that the members of each stratum accept as their ideal of decency the scheme of life in vogue in the next higher stratum, and bend their energies to live up to that ideal. On pain of forfeiting their good name and their self-respect in case of failure, they must conform to the accepted code, at least in appearance. . . .

The use of the term "waste" is in one respect an unfortunate one. As used in the speech of everyday life the word carries an undertone of deprecation. It is here used for want of a better term that will adequately describe the same range of motives and of phenomena, and it is not to be taken in an odious sense, as implying an illegitimate expenditure of human products or of human life. In the view of economic theory the expenditure in question is no more and no less legitimate than any other expenditure. It is here called "waste" because this expenditure does not serve human life or human well-being on the whole, not because it is waste or misdirection of effort or expenditure as viewed from the standpoint of the individual consumer who chooses it. If he chooses it, that disposes of the question of its relative utility to him, as compared with other forms of consumption that would not be deprecated on account of their wastefulness. Whatever form of expenditure the consumer chooses, or whatever end he seeks in making his choice, has utility to him by virtue of his preference. As seen from the point of view of the individual consumer, the question of wastefulness does not arise within the scope of economic theory proper. The use of the word "waste" as a technical term, therefore, implies no deprecation of the motives or of the ends sought by the consumer under this canon of conspicuous waste.

# 14. FOOD AND SEX AS SYMBOLS

*David Riesman*

*The sociologists who wrote the following material have developed an interesting theory about being "inner-directed" or "other-directed."*

*Here they discuss the symbolic meanings of food and sex. These are, of course, important considerations with respect to many products.*

*But it must not be supposed that in the midst of all their toils the people who live in democracies think themselves to be pitied; the contrary is noticed to be the case. No men are fonder of their own condition. Life would have no relish for them if they were delivered from the anxieties which harass them, and they show more attachment to their cares than aristocratic nations to their pleasures.*

*Tocqueville,* Democracy in America

The only thing that has changed since Tocqueville wrote (no small change, it is true) is that the sphere of pleasures has itself become a sphere of cares. Many of the physical hardships of the older frontiers of production and land use have survived in altered, psychological form on the newer one of consumption. Just as . . . the day shift of work-mindedness is invaded by glad-hand attitudes and values that stem in part from the sphere of leisure, so the night shift of leisure-mindedness is haunted by the others with whom one works at having a good time.

First of all, however, with the rise of other-direction, we see the passing both of the acquisitive consumers and of the escapists of the earlier era. The passion for acquisition diminishes when property no longer has its old stability and objective validity; escape

Source: From David Riesman, in collaboration with Reuel Denney and Nathan Glazer, *The Lonely Crowd: A Study of the Changing American Character,* Yale University Press, New Haven, 1961, pp. 141–148.
David Riesman: Professor of Social Sciences, University of Chicago.

diminishes by the very fact that work and pleasure are interlaced. We can see these new tendencies, in what is perhaps their most extreme form, the attitudes toward food and sexual experience prevailing among some upper middle-class groups.

## I. CHANGES IN THE SYMBOLIC MEANING OF FOOD AND SEX

*From the Wheat Bowl to the Salad Bowl.* Among inner-directed types there is of course great variation as to interest in food. In America—the story is different among the food-loving peoples of the rest of the world—puritans and nonpuritans of the recent past might use food for display, with relatively standardized menus for company and dining out; what was put on display was a choice cut of meat, an elegant table, and good solid cooking. All this was an affair largely of the women, and in many circles food was not a proper topic for dinner conversation. Having the proper food was something one owed to one's status, one's claim to respectability, and more recently to one's knowledge of hygiene with its calories and vitamins. (This last pattern did not spread to the South, where an older, more gastronomically rugged tradition of ceremonial fondness for food prevailed.) The earlier editions of the *Boston Cooking School Cookbook* breathe this air of solidity, conservatism, and nutrition-mindedness.

The other-directed person of the midtwentieth century in America, on the contrary, puts on display his taste and not directly his wealth, respectability, cubic capacity, or caloric soundness. Indeed . . . the radio begins the other-directed person's training in food taste even before the child goes to school and he takes his lessons seriously. While well-educated upper middle-class parents are becoming hesitant to tell children to eat someting because it is good for them—lest they create oral complexes—they join the radio in discussion of what is "good" as a matter of taste. Often, in fact, this merely disguises the emotion focused on the child's eating habits, almost as much emotion as their parents concentrated on the regimen of no-nonsense plate cleaning. The other-directed person is thus prepared for the search for marginal differentiation not only in what he sets before his guests but in how it is talked about with them.

Earlier there existed a small coterie of gourmets; fastidious enjoyment of food was one hobby, among others, that inner-directed people might choose. Today, in wide circles, many people are and many more feel that they must be gourmets. The abundance of America in the phase of incipient population decline is perhaps the most important factor in this development; it has made the good foods available to nearly everybody. The seasonal and geographic limitations that in the earlier period narrowed food variations for all but the very rich have now been largely done away with by the network of distribution and the techniques of preserving food—both being legacies from the phase of transitional population growth. The consumer's choice among foods need therefore no longer be made on the basis either of tradition or of Malthusian limits.

As a result, both the setting of the meal and its content are affected. Informality breaks down the puritan inhibition against talking about food and drink, just as Mexican casseroles and copper kettles replace the white napery and classic decor of the nineteenth-century middle-class table. More important still, the housewife can no longer blame the preferential and limited cuisine offered by a kitchen servant for her failure to personalize her own tastes in food. In the period of incipient population decline servants disappear from the middle-class home, and where they do not, they lack any traditional pattern of prerogatives that allows them, rather than the host and hostess, to control the menu and its stylized serving. No walls of privacy, status, or asceticism remain to protect or prevent one from displaying personalized taste in food and decor as an element in one's competition with others. The diner has the power, unlike Jiggs, to decide that corned beef and cabbage is an amusing dish; he can ransack immigrant cookeries or follow the lead of food columnist Clementine Paddleford toward exoticism. Only at the conventional conventions can one still find the uniform menu of steak or chicken, potatoes, and marbled peas. And at home, in place of the staple menu, the hostess today is encouraged to substitute her own specialty, such as lasagna or rüstoffel. Men are involved almost as much as women, and in the kitchen as well as at the back-yard grill.

The most popular cookbook today is said to be *The Joy of Cooking,* and the number of specialized cookbooks–ethnic, chatty, and atmospheric–constantly increases to meet the demand for marginal differentiation. The very change in titles–from the *Boston Cooking School Cookbook* to *How to Cook a Wolf* or *Food Is a Four Letter Word*–reveals the changing attitude. For the other-directed person cannot lean on such objective standards of success as those which guided the inner-directed person: he may be haunted by a feeling that he misses the joy in food or drink which he is supposed to feel. Mealtime must now be "pleasurable"; the new *Fireside Cookbook* is offered to "people who are not content to regard food just as something one transfers periodically from plate to mouth." And if one still fails to get much joy out of the recipes given there, he may search in books like *Spécialité de la Maison* to see what "others" are eating–to get the "favorite recipes" of such people as Noel Coward and Lucius Beebe. Fred MacMurray and Claudette Colbert testify to the delights of new concoctions such as "The Egg and I Julep"; and "There is nothing," writes MacMurray in a little collection of his favorite egg recipes, "so appealing as a pair of fried eggs with their limpid golden eyes gazing fondly at you from the center of a breakfast plate, festooned with strips of crisp bacon or little-pig sausage. Or poached, gaily riding a raft of toast." The most popular translation of an old French cookbook, *Tante Marie,* is also extremely chatty, and *The Joy of Cooking* explains its chattiness by saying that originally the recipes were collected and written down for the author's daughter, who in turn thought "other daughters" might like them. (As there is today less teaching of daughters by mothers, the daughter must rely on the instruction of an outsider, if she is to cook at all.) In short, the other-directed person in his approach to food, as in his sexual encounters, is constantly looking for a qualitative element that may elude him. He suffers from what Martha Wolfenstein and Nathan Leites call "fun-morality."[1]

Of course, putting matters this way exaggerates the disadvantages of the shift: undeniably, many more people today really enjoy food and enjoy talk about food than they did when the monotony of the American diet was notorious.

[1] In *Movies,* Free Press, Glencoe, Ill., 1950.

Many people, to be sure, follow the new fashions in food without being other-directed in character, just as many personnel directors in industry are zealous inner-directed believers in the glad hand. Even so, if we wanted to demarcate the boundaries of other-direction in America, we might find in the analysis of menus a not too inaccurate index. As tossed salads and garlic, elaborate sauces, dishes *en casserole, Gourmet* magazine, wine and liqueurs, spread west from New York and east from San Francisco, as men take two-hour lunch periods and exhibit their taste in food and wine, as the personalized cookbook tends to replace the Boston Cooking School type–in all these signs of the times we see indications of the new type of character. Recently, Russell Lynes, in his article, "Highbrow, Lowbrow, Middlebrow,"[2] sought to delineate the contemporary urban American social system in terms of similar consumption indexes. Thus, the tossed salad is the sign of the high-brow, who may also be tagged by his taste in cars, clothes, and posture. What we really see emerging is an embryonic social system whose criteria of status are inconsistent with the criteria of the more traditional class system. This has been seen by Lloyd Warner, who actually defines class less in terms of wealth or power and more in terms of who is sociable with whom, and of styles of consumer behavior. These observers, however, are exceptional; . . . most Americans continue to see their social structure in terms of an older one based on wealth, occupation, and position in the society-page sense. But beneath these older rubrics, I believe that a much more amorphous structure is emerging in which opinion leadership is increasingly important, and in which the "brow" hierarchy competes for recognition with the traditional hierarchies based on wealth and occupational position.

*Sex: the Last Frontier.* In the era depending on inner-direction sex might be inhibited, as in classes and areas affected strongly by the Reformation and Counter Reformation. Or its gratification might be taken for granted among men and within given limits, as in Italy, Spain, and the non-respectable elements, such as the "riverbottom people," in every population. In both cases there was a certain simplification of sex, in the one instance by taboos, in the other by tradition. The related problems of livelihood and of power, problems of mere existence or of "amounting to something," were uppermost; and sex was relegated to its "proper" time and place: night, the wife or whore, occasional rough speech, and daydreams. Only in the upper classes, precursors of modern other-directed types, did the making of love take precedence over the making of goods (as alleged in France) and reach the status of a daytime agenda. In these circles sex was almost totally separated from production and reproduction.

This separation, when it goes beyond the upper class and spreads over almost the whole society, is a sign that a society, through birth control and all that it implies, has entered the population phase of incipient decline by the route of industrialization. In this phase there is not only a growth of leisure, but work itself becomes both less interesting and less demanding for many; increased supervision and subdivision of tasks routinize the industrial process even beyond what was accomplished in the phase of transitional growth of population. More than before, as job-mindedness declines, sex

[2] *Harper's,* 198 (1949), 19.

permeates the daytime as well as the play-time consciousness. It is viewed as a consumption good not only by the old leisure classes but by the modern leisure masses.

The other-directed person, who often suffers from low responsiveness, may pursue what looks like a "cult of effortlessness" in many spheres of life. He may welcome the routinization of his economic role and of his domestic life; the auto companies may tempt him by self-opening windows and self-shifting gears; he may withdraw all emotion from politics. Yet he cannot handle his sex life in this way. Though there is tremendous insecurity about *how* the game of sex should be played, there is little doubt as to *whether* it should be played or not. Even when we are consciously bored with sex, we must still obey its drive. Sex, therefore, provides a kind of defense against the threat of total apathy. This is one of the reasons why so much excitement is channeled into sex by the other-directed person. He looks to it for reassurance that he is alive. The inner-directed person, driven by his internal gyroscope and oriented toward the more external problems of production, did not need this evidence.

While the inner-directed acquisitive consumer could pursue the ever-receding frontiers of material acquisition, these frontiers have lost much of their lure for the other-directed person. . . . The latter begins as a very young child to know his way around among available consumer goods. He travels widely, to camp or with his family. He knows that the rich man's car is only marginally, if at all, different from his own—a matter at best of a few additional horsepower. He knows anyway that next year's model will be better than this year's. Even if he has not been there, he knows what the night clubs are like; and he has seen television. Whereas the deprived inner-directed person often lusted for possessions as a goal whose glamour a wealthy adulthood could not dim, the other-directed person can scarcely conceive of a consumer good that can maintain for any length of time undisputed dominance over his imagination. Except perhaps sex.

For the consumption of love, despite all the efforts of the mass media, does remain hidden from public view. If someone else has a new Cadillac, the other-directed person knows what that is, and that he can duplicate the experience, more or less. But if someone else has a new lover, he cannot know what that means. Cadillacs have been democratized. So has sexual glamour, to a degree: without the mass production of good-looking, well-groomed youth, the American pattern of sexual competition could not exist. But there is a difference between Cadillacs and sexual partners in the degree of mystery. And with the loss of submergence of moral shame and inhibitions, but not completely of a certain unconscious innocence, the other-directed person has no defenses against his own envy. He is not ambitious to break the quantitative records of the acquisitive consumers of sex like Don Juan, but he does not want to miss, day in and day out, the qualities of experience he tells himself the others are having.

In a way this development is paradoxical. For while cookbooks have become more glamorous with the era of other-direction, sex books have become less so. The older marriage manuals, such as that of Van der Velde (still popular, however), breathe an ecstatic tone; they are travelogues of the joy of love. The newer ones, including some high school sex manuals, are matter of fact, toneless, and hygienic—Boston Cooking

School style. Nevertheless, much as young people may appear to take sex in stride along with their vitamins, it remains an era of competition and a locus of the search, never completely suppressed, for meaning and emotional response in life. The other-directed person looks to sex not for display but for a test of his or her ability to attract, his or her place in the "rating-dating" scale—and beyond that, in order to experience life and love.

One reason for the change is that women are no longer objects for the acquisitive consumer but are peer-groupers themselves. The relatively unemancipated wife and socially inferior mistresses of the inner-directed man could not seriously challenge the quality of his sexual performance. Today, millions of women, freed by technology from many household tasks, given by technology many "aids to romance," have become pioneers, with men, on the frontier of sex. As they become knowing consumers, the anxiety of men lest they fail to satisfy the women also grows—but at the same time this is another test that attracts men who, in their character, want to be judged by others. The very ability of women to respond in a way that only courtesans were supposed to in an earlier age means, moreover, that qualitative differences of sex experience—the impenetrable mystery—can be sought for night after night, and not only in periodic visits to a mistress or brothel. Whereas the pattern of an earlier era was often to make fun of sex, whether on the level of the music hall or of Balzac's *Droll Stories,* sex today carries too much psychic freight to be really funny for the other-directed person. By a disguised asceticism it becomes at the same time too anxious a business and too sacred an illusion.

This anxious competitiveness in the realm of sex has very little in common with older patterns of social climbing. To be sure, women still use sex as a means to status in spheres controlled by men. But they can do this chiefly in industries that are still competitive in the pre-monopolistic patterns. Thus until recently the theater and the movies were controlled by *novi homines* who remind us of those early nineteenth century British mill owners who, before the Factory Acts, relied on their mills as a harem.[3] And Warner, Havighurst, and Loeb in *Who Shall Be Educated?*[4] describe how women schoolteachers may still cabin-date their way up the relatively unbureaucratized hierarchies of local school systems. These, however, are exceptional cases; the search for experience on the frontier of sex is, in the other-directed era, generally without ulterior motives.

[3]See G. M. Young, *Portrait of an Age,* Oxford University Press, London, 1936, p. 16, n. 1.

[4]W. Lloyd Warner, Robert J. Havighurst, and Martin Loeb, *Who Shall Be Educated?,* Harper & Brothers, New York, 1944, p. 103.

# 15. BEHAVIORAL MODELS FOR ANALYZING BUYERS

*Philip Kotler*

*What happens in the buyer's mind between the acts of receiving impressions about products and making his purchasing decisions? Several theories exist, but there is no generally accepted comprehensive theory.*

*Here the author contrasts buyer behavioral models based on five major theories, and shows how each has unique marketing applications.*

In times past, management could arrive at a fair understanding of its buyers through the daily experience of selling to them. But the growth in the size of firms and markets has removed many decision-makers from direct contact with buyers. Increasingly, decision-makers have had to turn to summary statistics and to behavioral theory, and are spending more money today than ever before to try to understand their buyers.

Who buys? How do they buy? And why? The first two questions relate to relatively overt aspects of buyer behavior, and can be learned about through direct observation and interviewing.

But uncovering *why* people buy is an extremely difficult task. The answer will tend to vary with the investigator's behavioral frame of reference.

The buyer is subject to many influences which trace a complex course through his psyche and lead eventually to overt purchasing responses. This conception of the

Source: From *Journal of Marketing,* vol. 29, October, 1965, pp. 37–45. Philip Kotler: Associate Professor of Marketing, School of Business, Northwestern University.

Figure 1. The buying process conceived as a system of inputs and outputs

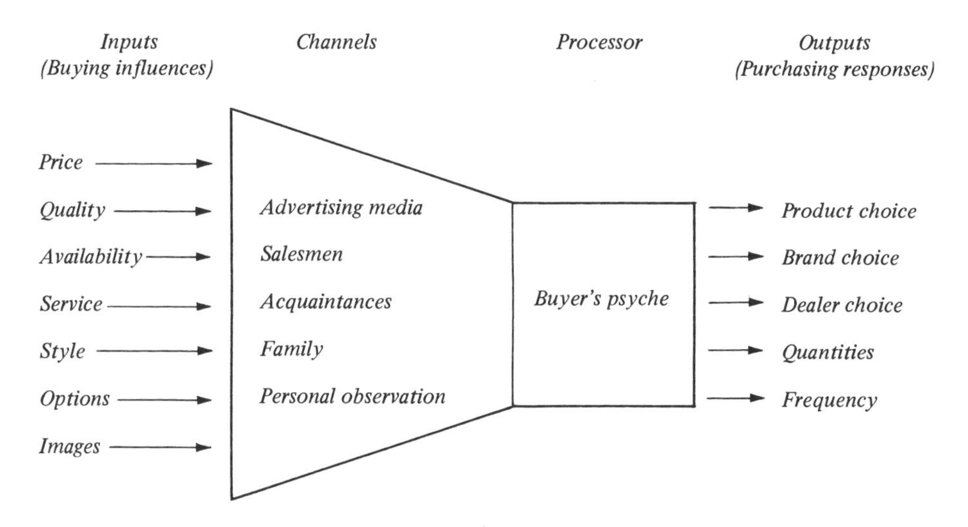


buying process is illustrated in Figure 1. Various influences and their modes of transmission are shown at the left. At the right are the buyer's responses in choice of product, brand, dealer, quantities, and frequency. In the center stands the buyer and his mysterious psychological processes. The buyer's psyche is a "black box" whose workings can be only partially deduced. The marketing strategist's challenge to the behavioral scientist is to construct a more specific model of the mechanism in the black box.

Unfortunately no generally accepted model of the mechanism exists. The human mind, the only entity in nature with deep powers of understanding, still remains the least understood. Scientists can explain planetary motion, genetic determination, and molecular behavior. Yet they have only partial, and often partisan, models of *human* behavior.

Nevertheless, the marketing strategist should recognize the potential interpretative contributions of different partial models for explaining buyer behavior. Depending upon the product, different variables and behavioral mechanisms may assume particular importance. A psychoanalytic behavioral model might throw much light on the factors operating in cigarette demand, while an economic behavioral model might be useful in explaining machine-tool purchasing. Sometimes alternative models may shed light on different demand aspects of the same product.

What are the most useful behavioral models for interpreting the transformation of buying influences into purchasing responses? Five different models of the buyer's black box are presented in the present article, along with their respective marketing applications:

1. the Marshallian model, stressing economic motivations;

2. the Pavlovian model, learning;
3. the Freudian model, psychoanalytic motivations;
4. the Veblenian model, social-psychological factors; and
5. the Hobbesian model, organizational factors. These models represent radically different conceptions of the mainsprings of human behavior.

## THE MARSHALLIAN ECONOMIC MODEL

Economists were the first professional group to construct a specific theory of buyer behavior. The theory holds that purchasing decisions are the result of largely "rational" and conscious economic calculations. The individual buyer seeks to spend his income on those goods that will deliver the most utility (satisfaction) according to his tastes and relative prices.

The antecedents for this view trace back to the writings of Adam Smith and Jeremy Bentham. Smith set the tone by developing a doctrine of economic growth based on the principle that man is motivated by self-interest in all his actions.[1] Bentham refined this view and saw man as finely calculating and weighing the expected pleasures and pains of every contemplated action.[2]

Bentham's "felicific calculus" was not applied to consumer behavior (as opposed to entrepreneurial behavior) until the late nineteenth century. Then, the "marginal-utility" theory of value was formulated independently and almost simultaneously by Jevons[3] and Marshall [4] in England, Menger[5] in Austria, and Walras[6] in Switzerland.

Alfred Marshall was the great consolidator of the classical and neoclassical tradition in economics; and his synthesis in the form of demand-supply analysis constitutes the main source of modern micro-economic thought in the English-speaking world. His theoretical work aimed at realism, but his method was to start with simplifying assumptions and to examine the effect of a change in a single variable (say, price) when all other variables were held constant.

He would "reason out" the consequences of the provisional assumptions and in subsequent steps modify his assumptions in the direction of more realism. He employed the "measuring rod of money" as an indicator of the intensity of human psychological desires. Over the years his methods and assumptions have been refined into what is now

[1] Adam Smith, *An Inquiry into the Nature and Causes of the Wealth of Nations* [1776], The Modern Library, New York, 1937.

[2] Jeremy Bentham, *An Introduction to the Principles of Morals and Legislation* [1780], Clarendon Press, Oxford, England, 1907.

[3] William S. Jevons, *The Theory of Political Economy,* The Macmillan Company, New York, 1871.

[4] Alfred Marshall, *Principles of Economics* [1890], The Macmillan Company, London, 1927.

[5] Karl Menger, *Principles of Economics* [1871], Free Press, Glencoe, Ill., 1950.

[6] Leon Walras, *Elements of Pure Economics* [1874], Richard D. Irwin, Inc., Homewood, Ill., 1954.

known as *modern utility theory*: economic man is bent on maximizing his utility, and does this by carefully calculating the "felicific" consequences of any purchase.

As an example, suppose on a particular evening that John is considering whether to prepare his own dinner or dine out. He estimates that a restaurant meal would cost $2.00 and a home-cooked meal 50 cents. According to the Marshallian model, if John expects less than four times as much satisfaction from the restaurant meal as the home-cooked meal, he will eat at home. The economist typically is not concerned with how these relative preferences are formed by John, or how they may be psychologically modified by new stimuli.

Yet John will not always cook at home. The principle of diminishing marginal utility operates. Within a given time interval–say, a week–the utility of each additional home-cooked meal diminishes. John gets tired of home meals and other products become relatively more attractive.

John's *efficiency* in maximizing his utility depends on the adequacy of his information and his freedom of choice. If he is not perfectly aware of costs, if he misestimates the relative delectability of the two meals, or if he is barred from entering the restaurant, he will not maximize his potential utility. His choice processes are rational, but the results are inefficient.

*Marketing Applications of Marshallian Model.* Marketers usually have dismissed the Marshallian model as an absurd figment of ivory-tower imagination. Certainly the behavioral essence of the situation is omitted, in viewing man as calculating the marginal utility of a restaurant meal over a home-cooked meal.

Eva Mueller has reported a study where only one-fourth of the consumers in her sample bought with any substantial degree of deliberation.[7] Yet there are a number of ways to view the model.

From one point of view the Marshallian model is tautological and therefore neither true nor false. The model holds that the buyer acts in the light of his best "interest." But this is not very informative.

A second view is that this is a *normative* rather than a *descriptive* model of behavior. The model provides logical norms for buyers who want to be "rational." Although the consumer is not likely to employ economic analysis to decide between a box of Kleenex and Scotties, he may apply economic analysis in deciding whether to buy a new car. Industrial buyers even more clearly would want an economic calculus for making good decisions.

A third view is that economic factors operate to a greater or lesser extent in all markets, and, therefore, must be included in any comprehensive description of buyer behavior.

Furthermore, the model suggests useful behavioral hypotheses such as: (a) The lower the price of the product, the higher the sales. (b) The lower the price of substitute products, the lower the sales of this product; and the lower the price of complementary products, the higher the sales of this product. (c) The higher the real income, the higher the sales of this product, provided that it is not an "inferior" good. (d) The higher the promotional expenditures, the higher the sales.

[7] Eva Mueller, "A Study of Purchase Decisions," part 2, in Lincoln H. Clark (ed.), *Consumer Behavior, The Dynamics of Consumer Reaction,* New York University Press, New York, 1954, pp. 36–87.

The validity of these hypotheses does not rest on whether *all* individuals act as economic calculating machines in making their purchasing decisions. For example, some individuals may buy *less* of a product when its price is reduced. They may think that the quality has gone down, or that ownership has less status value. If a majority of buyers view price reductions negatively, then sales may fall, contrary to the first hypothesis.

But for most goods a price reduction increases the relative value of the goods in many buyers' minds and leads to increased sales. This and the other hypotheses are intended to describe average effects.

The impact of economic factors in actual buying situations is studied through experimental design or statistical analyses of past data. Demand equations have been fitted to a wide variety of products–including beer, refrigerators, and chemical fertilizers.[8] More recently, the impact of economic variables on the fortunes of different brands has been pursued with significant results, particularly in the case of coffee, frozen orange juice, and margarine.[9]

But economic factors alone cannot explain all the variations in sales. The Marshallian model ignores the fundamental question of how product and brand preferences are formed. It represents a useful frame of reference for analyzing only one small corner of the black box.

## THE PAVLOVIAN LEARNING MODEL

The designation of a Pavlovian learning model has its origin in the experiments of the Russian psychologist Pavlov, who rang a bell each time before feeding a dog. Soon he was able to induce the dog to salivate by ringing the bell whether or not food was supplied. Pavlov concluded that learning was largely an associative process and that a large component of behavior was conditioned in this way.

Experimental psychologists have continued this mode of research with rats and other animals, including people. Laboratory experiments have been designed to explore such phenomena as learning, forgetting, and the ability to discriminate. The results have been integrated into a stimulus-response model of human behavior, or as someone has "wisecracked," the substitution of a rat psychology for a rational psychology.

The model has been refined over the years, and today is based on four central concepts–those of *drive, cue, response,* and *reinforcement.*[10]

[8] See Erwin E. Nemmers, *Managerial Economics,* John Wiley & Sons, Inc., New York, 1962, Part II.

[9] See Lester G. Telser, "The Demand for Branded Goods as Estimated from Consumer Panel Data," *Review of Economics and Statistics,* vol. 44, August, 1962, pp. 300–324; and William F. Massy and Ronald E. Frank, "Short Term Price and Dealing Effects in Selected Market Segments," *Journal of Marketing Research,* vol. 2, May, 1965, pp. 171–185.

[10] See John Dollard and Neal E. Miller, *Personality and Psychotherapy,* McGraw-Hill Book Company, New York, 1950, chap. III.

*Drive.* Also called needs or motives, drive refers to strong stimuli internal to the individual which impels action. Psychologists draw a distinction between primary physiological drives—such as hunger, thirst, cold, pain, and sex—and learned drives which are derived socially—such as cooperation, fear, and acquisitiveness.

*Cue.* A drive is very general and impels a particular response only in relation to a particular configuration of cues. Cues are weaker stimuli in the environment and/or in the individual which determine when, where, and how the subject responds. Thus, a coffee advertisement can serve as a cue which stimulates the thirst drive in a housewife. Her response will depend upon this cue and other cues, such as the time of day, the availability of other thirst-quenchers, and the cue's intensity. Often a relative change in a cue's intensity can be more impelling than its absolute level. The housewife may be more motivated by a 2-cents-off sale on a brand of coffee than the fact that this brand's price was low in the first place.

*Response.* The response is the organism's reaction to the configuration of cues. Yet the same configuration of cues will not necessarily produce the same response in the individual. This depends on the degree to which the experience was rewarding, that is, drive-reducing.

*Reinforcement.* If the experience is rewarding, a particular response is reinforced; that is, it is strengthened and there is a tendency for it to be repeated when the same configuration of cues appears again. The housewife, for example, will tend to purchase the same brand of coffee each time she goes to her supermarket so long as it is rewarding and the cue configuration does not change. But if a learned response or habit is not reinforced, the strength of the habit diminishes and may be extinguished eventually. Thus, a housewife's preference for a certain coffee may become extinct if she finds the brand out of stock for a number of weeks.

Forgetting, in contrast to extinction, is the tendency for learned associations to weaken, not because of the lack of reinforcement but because of nonuse.

Cue configurations are constantly changing. The housewife sees a new brand of coffee next to her habitual brand, or notes a special price deal on a rival brand. Experimental psychologists have found that the same learned response will be elicited by similar patterns of cues; that is, learned responses are *generalized.* The housewife shifts to a similar brand when her favorite brand is out of stock. This tendency toward generalization over less similar cue configurations is increased in proportion to the strength of the drive. A housewife may buy an inferior coffee if it is the only brand left and if her drive is sufficiently strong.

A counter-tendency to generalization is *discrimination.* When a housewife tries two similar brands and finds one more rewarding, her ability to discriminate between similar cue configurations improves. Discrimination increases the specificity of the cue-response connection, while generalization decreases the specificity.

*Marketing Applications of Pavlovian Model.* The modern version of the Pavlovian model makes no claim to provide a complete theory of behavior–indeed, such important phenomena as perception, the subconscious, and interpersonal influence are inadequately treated. Yet the model does offer a substantial number of insights about some aspects of behavior of considerable interest to marketers.[11]

An example would be in the problem of introducing a new brand into a highly competitive market. The company's goal is to extinguish existing brand habits and form new habits among consumers for its brand. But the company must first get customers to try its brand; and it has to decide between using weak and strong cues.

Light introductory advertising is a weak cue compared with distributing free samples. Strong cues, although costing more, may be necessary in markets characterized by strong brand loyalties. For example, Folger went into the coffee market by distributing over a million pounds of free coffee.

To build a brand habit, it helps to provide for an extended period of introductory dealing. Furthermore, sufficient quality must be built into the brand so that the experience is reinforcing. Since buyers are more likely to transfer allegiance to similar brands than dissimilar brands (generalization), the company should also investigate what cues in the leading brands have been most effective. Although outright imitation would not necessarily effect the most transference, the question of providing enough similarity should be considered.

The Pavlovian model also provides guide lines in the area of advertising strategy. The American behaviorist, John B. Watson, was a great exponent of repetitive stimuli; in his writings man is viewed as a creature who can be conditioned through repetition and reinforcement to respond in particular ways.[12] The Pavlovian model emphasizes the desirability of repetition in advertising. A single exposure is likely to be a very weak cue, hardly able to penetrate the individual's consciousness sufficiently to excite his drives above the threshold level.

Repetition in advertising has two desirable effects. It "fights" forgetting, the tendency for learned responses to weaken in the absence of practice. It provides reinforcement, because after the purchase the consumer becomes selectively exposed to advertisements of the product.

The model also provides guidelines for copy strategy. To be effective as a cue, an advertisement must arouse strong drives in the person. The strongest product-related drives must be identified. For candy bars, it may be hunger; for safety belts, fear; for hair tonics, sex; for automobiles, status. The advertising practitioner must dip into his cue box–words, colors, pictures–and select that configuration of cues that provides the strongest stimulus to these drives.

[11] The most consistent application of learning-theory concepts to marketing situations is found in John A. Howard, *Marketing Management: Analysis and Planning*, Richard D. Irwin, Inc., rev. ed., 1963.

[12] John B. Watson, *Behaviorism,* The People's Institute Publishing Company, New York, 1925.

## THE FREUDIAN PSYCHOANALYTIC MODEL

The Freudian model of man is well known, so profound has been its impact on twentieth-century thought. It is the latest of a series of philosphical "blows" to which man has been exposed in the last 500 years. Copernicus destroyed the idea that man stood at the center of the universe; Darwin tried to refute the idea that man was a special creation; and Freud attacked the idea that man even reigned over his own psyche.

According to Freud, the child enters the world driven by instinctual needs which he cannot gratify by himself. Very quickly and painfully he realizes his separateness from the rest of the world and yet his dependence on it.

He tries to get others to gratify his needs through a variety of blatant means, including intimidation and supplication. Continual frustration leads him to perfect more subtle mechanisms for gratifying his instincts.

As he grows, his psyche becomes increasingly complex. A part of his psyche–the id–remains the reservoir of his strong drives and urges. Another part–the ego–becomes his conscious planning center for finding outlets for his drives. And a third part–his super-ego–channels his instinctive drives into socially approved outlets to avoid the pain of guilt or shame.

The guilt or shame which man feels toward some of his urges–especially his sexual urges–causes him to repress them from his consciousness. Through such defense mechanisms as rationalization and sublimation, these urges are denied or become transmuted into socially approved expressions. Yet these urges are never eliminated or under perfect control; and they emerge, sometimes with a vengeance, in dreams, in slips-of-the-tongue, in neurotic and obsessional behavior, or ultimately in mental breakdown where the ego can no longer maintain the delicate balance between the impulsive power of the id and the oppressive power of the super-ego.

The individual's behavior, therefore, is never simple. His motivational wellsprings are not obvious to a casual observer nor deeply understood by the individual himself. If he is asked why he purchased an expensive foreign sports-car, he may reply that he likes its maneuverability and its looks. At a deeper level he may have purchased the car to impress others, or to feel young again. At a still deeper level, he may be purchasing the sports-car to achieve substitute gratification for unsatisfied sexual strivings.

Many refinements and changes in emphasis have occurred in this model since the time of Freud. The instinct concept has been replaced by a more careful delineation of basic drives; the three parts of the psyche are regarded now as theoretical concepts rather than actual entities; and the behavioral perspective has been extended to include cultural as well as biological mechanisms.

Instead of the role of the sexual urge in psychic development–Freud's discussion of oral, anal, and genital stages and possible fixations and traumas–Adler[13] emphasized

[13] Alfred Adler, *The Science of Living*, Greenberg Publisher, Inc., New York, 1929.

the urge for power and how its thwarting manifests itself in superiority and inferiority complexes; Horney[14] emphasized cultural mechanisms; and Fromm[15] and Erickson[16] emphasized the role of existential crises in personality development. These philosophical divergencies, rather than debilitating the model, have enriched and extended its interpretative value to a wider range of behavioral phenomena.

*Marketing Applications of Freudian Model.* Perhaps the most important marketing implication of this model is that buyers are motivated by *symbolic* as well as *economic-functional* product concerns. The change of a bar of soap from a square to a round shape may be more important in its sexual than its functional connotations. A cake mix that is advertised as involving practically no labor may alienate housewives because the easy life may evoke a sense of guilt.

Motivational research has produced some interesting and occasionally some bizarre hypotheses about what may be in the buyer's mind regarding certain purchases. Thus, it has been suggested at one time or another that

- Many a businessman doesn't fly because of a fear of posthumous guilt–if he crashed, his wife would think of him as stupid for not taking a train.
- Men want their cigars to be odoriferous, in order to prove that they (the men) are masculine.
- A woman is very serious when she bakes a cake because unconsciously she is going through the symbolic act of giving birth.
- A man buys a convertible as a substitute "mistress."
- Consumers prefer vegetable shortening because animal fats stimulate a sense of sin.
- Men who wear suspenders are reacting to an unresolved castration complex.

There are admitted difficulties of proving these assertions. Two prominent motivational researchers, Ernest Dichter and James Vicary, were employed independently by two separate groups in the prune industry to determine why so many people dislike prunes. Dichter found, among other things, that the prune aroused feelings of old age and insecurity in people, whereas Vicary's main finding was that Americans had an emotional block about prunes' laxative qualities.[17] Which is the more valid interpretation? Or if they are both operative, which motive is found with greater statistical frequency in the population?

Unfortunately the usual survey techniques–direct observation and interviewing–can be used to establish the representativeness of more superficial characteristics–age and family size, for example–but are not feasible for establishing the frequency of mental states which are presumed to be deeply "buried" within each individual.

[14] Karen Horney, *The Neurotic Personality of Our Time,* W. W. Norton & Company, Inc., New York, 1937.

[15] Erich Fromm, *Man For Himself,* Holt Rinehart & Winston, Inc., New York, 1947.

[16] Erik Erikson, *Childhood and Society,* W. W. Norton & Company, Inc., New York, 1949.

[17] L. Edward Scriven, "Rationality and Irrationality in Motivation Research," in Robert Ferber and Hugh G. Wales (eds.), *Motivation and Marketing Behavior,* Richard D. Irwin, Inc., 1958, pp. 69–70.

Motivational researchers have to employ time-consuming projective techniques in the hope of throwing individual "egos" off guard. When carefully administered and interpreted, techniques such as word association, sentence completion, picture interpretation, and role-playing can provide some insights into the minds of the small group of examined individuals; but a "leap of faith" is sometimes necessary to generalize these findings to the population.

Nevertheless, motivation research can lead to useful insights and provide inspiration to creative men in the advertising and packaging world. Appeals aimed at the buyer's private world of hopes, dreams, and fears can often be as effective in stimulating purchase as more rationally-directed appeals.

## THE VEBLENIAN SOCIAL-PSYCHOLOGICAL MODEL

While most economists have been content to interpret buyer behavior in Marshallian terms, Thorstein Veblen struck out in different directions.

Veblen was trained as an orthodox economist, but evolved into a social thinker greatly influenced by the new science of social anthropology. He saw man as primarily a *social animal*–conforming to the general forms and norms of his larger culture and to the more specific standards of the subcultures and face-to-face groupings to which his life is bound. His wants and behavior are largely molded by his present group-memberships and his aspired group-memberships.

Veblen's best-known example of this is in his description of the leisure class.[18] His hypothesis is that much of economic consumption is motivated not by intrinsic needs or satisfaction so much as by prestige-seeking. He emphasized the strong emulative factors operating in the choice of conspicuous goods like clothes, cars, and houses.

Some of his points, however, seem overstated by today's perspective. The leisure class does not serve as everyone's reference group; many persons aspire to the social patterns of the class immediately above it. And important segments of the affluent class practice conspicuous underconsumption rather than overconsumption. There are many people in all classes who are more anxious to "fit in" than to "stand out." As an example, William H. Whyte found that many families avoided buying air conditioners and other appliances before their neighbors did.[19]

Veblen was not the first nor the only investigator to comment on social influences in behavior; but the incisive quality of his observations did much to stimulate further investigations. Another stimulus came from Karl Marx, who held that each man's world-view was determined largely by his relationship to the "means of production."[20]

[18] Thorstein Veblen, *The Theory of the Leisure Class,* The Macmillan Company, New York, 1899.

[19] William H. Whyte, Jr., "The Web of Word of Mouth," *Fortune,* vol. 50, November, 1954, pp. 140 ff.

[20] Karl Marx, *The Communist Manifesto* [1848], Martin Lawrence, Ltd., London, 1934.

The early field work in primitive societies by social anthropologists like Boas[21] and Malinowski[22] and the later field work in urban societies by men like Park[23] and Thomas[24] contributed much to understanding the influence of society and culture. The research of early Gestalt psychologists—men like Wertheimer,[25] Köhler,[26] and Koffka[27]—into the mechanisms of perception led eventually to investigation of small-group influence on perception.

*Marketing Applications of Veblenian Model.* The various streams of thought crystallized into the modern social sciences of sociology, cultural anthropology, and social psychology. Basic to them is the view that man's attitudes and behavior are influenced by several levels of society—culture, subcultures, social classes, reference groups, and face-to-face groups. The challenge to the marketer is to determine which of these social levels is the most important in influencing the demand for his product.

*Culture.* The most enduring influences are from culture. Man tends to assimilate his culture's mores and folkways, and to believe in their absolute rightness until deviants appear within his culture or until he confronts members of another culture.

*Subcultures.* A culture tends to lose its homogeneity as its population increases. When people no longer are able to maintain face-to-face relationships with more than a small proportion of other members of a culture, smaller units or subcultures develop, which help to satisfy the individual's needs for more specific identity.

The subcultures are often regional entities, because the people of a region, as a result of more frequent interactions, tend to think and act alike. But subcultures also take the form of religions, nationalities, fraternal orders, and other institutional complexes which provide a broad identification for people who may otherwise be strangers. The subcultures of a person play a large role in his attitude formation and become another important predictor of certain values he is likely to hold.

*Social Class.* People become differentiated not only horizontally but also vertically through a division of labor. The society becomes stratified socially on the basis of wealth, skill, and power. Sometimes castes develop in which the members are reared for certain roles, or social classes develop in which the members feel empathy with others sharing similar values and economic circumstances.

Because social class involves different attitudinal configurations, it becomes a useful independent variable for segmenting markets and predicting reactions. Significant differences have been found among different social classes with respect to magazine

[21] Franz Boas, *The Mind of Primitive Man*, The Macmillan Company, New York, 1922.

[22] Bronislaw Malinowski, *Sex and Repression in Savage Society*, Meridian Books, Inc., New York, 1955.

[23] Robert E. Park, *Human Communities*, Free Press, Glencoe, Ill., 1952.

[24] William I. Thomas, *The Unadjusted Girl*, Little, Brown and Company, Boston, 1928.

[25] Max Wertheimer, *Productive Thinking*, Harper & Brothers, New York, 1945.

[26] Wolfgang Kohler, *Gestalt Psychology*, Liveright Publishing Company, New York, 1947.

[27] Kurt Koffka, *Principles of Gestalt Psychology*, Harcourt, Brace and Company, Inc., New York, 1935.

readership, leisure activities, food imagery, fashion interests, and acceptance of innovations. A sampling of attitudinal differences in class is the following:

> Members of the *upper-middle* class place an emphasis on professional competence; indulge in expensive status symbols; and more often than not show a taste, real or otherwise, for theater and the arts. They want their children to show high achievement and precocity and develop into physicists, vice-presidents, and judges. This class likes to deal in ideas and symbols.
>
> Members of the *lower-middle* class cherish respectability, savings, a college education, and good housekeeping. They want their children to show self-control and prepare for careers as accountants, lawyers, and engineers.
>
> Members of the *upper-lower* class try to keep up with the times, if not with the Joneses. They stay in older neighborhoods but buy new kitchen appliances. They spend proportionately less than the middle class on major clothing articles, buying a new suit mainly for an important ceremonial occasion. They also spend proportionately less on services, preferring to do their own plumbing and other work around the house. They tend to raise large families and their children generally enter manual occupations. This class also supplies many local businessmen, politicians, sports stars, and labor-union leaders.

*Reference Groups.* There are groups in which the individual has no membership but with which he identifies and may aspire to—reference groups. Many young boys identify with big-league baseball players or astronauts, and many young girls identify with Hollywood stars. The activities of these popular heroes are carefully watched and frequently imitated. These reference figures become important transmitters of influence, although more along lines of taste and hobby than basic attitudes.

*Face-to-face Groups.* Groups that have the most immediate influence on a person's tastes and opinions are face-to-face groups. This includes all the small "societies" with which he comes into frequent contact: his family, close friends, neighbors, fellow workers, fraternal associates, and so forth. His informal group memberships are influenced largely by his occupation, residence, and stage in the life cycle.

The powerful influence of small groups on individual attitudes has been demonstrated in a number of social psychological experiments.[28] There is also evidence that this influence may be growing. David Riesman and his coauthors have pointed to signs which indicate a growing amount of *other-direction*, that is, a tendency for individuals to be increasingly influenced by their peers in the definition of their values rather than by their parents and elders.[29]

For the marketer, this means that brand choice may increasingly be influenced by one's peers. For such products as cigarettes and automobiles, the influence of peers is unmistakable.

[28] See, for example, Solomon E. Asch, "Effects of Group Pressure Upon the Modification & Distortion of Judgments," in Dorwin Cartwright and Alvin Zander, *Group Dynamics,* Row, Peterson & Company, Evanston, Ill., 1953, pp. 151–162; and Kurt Lewin, "Group Decision and Social Change," in Theodore M. Newcomb and Eugene L. Hartley (eds.), *Readings in Social Psychology,* Henry Holt and Comapny, New York, 1952.

[29] David Riesman, Reuel Denney, and Nathan Glazer, *The Lonely Crowd,* Yale University Press, New Haven, Conn., 1950.

The role of face-to-face groups has been recognized in recent industry campaigns attempting to change basic product attitudes. For years the milk industry has been trying to overcome the image of milk as a "sissified" drink by portraying its use in social and active situations. The men's-wear industry is trying to increase male interest in clothes by advertisements indicating that business associates judge a man by how well he dresses.

Of all face-to-face groups, the person's family undoubtedly plays the largest and most enduring role in basic attitude formation. From them he acquires a mental set not only toward religion and politics, but also toward thrift, chastity, food, human relations, and so forth. Although he often rebels against parental values in his teens, he often accepts these values eventually. Their formative influence on his eventual attitudes is undeniably great.

Family members differ in the types of product messages they carry to other family members. Most of what parents know about cereals, candy, and toys comes from their children. The wife stimulates family consideration of household appliances, furniture, and vacations. The husband tends to stimulate the fewest purchase ideas, with the exception of the automobile and perhaps the home.

The marketer must be alert to what attitudinal configurations dominate in different types of families, and also to how these change over time. For example, the parent's conception of the child's rights and privileges has undergone a radical shift in the last thirty years. The child has become the center of attention and orientation in a great number of households, leading some writers to label the modern family a "filiarchy." This has important implications not only for how to market to today's family, but also on how to market to tomorrow's family when the indulged child of today becomes the parent.

*The Person.* Social influences determine much but not all of the behavioral variations in people. Two individuals subject to the same influences are not likely to have identical attitudes, although these attitudes will probably converge at more points than those of two strangers selected at random. Attitudes are really the product of social forces interacting with the individual's unique temperament and abilities.

Furthermore, attitudes do not automatically guarantee certain types of behavior. Attitudes are predispositions felt by buyers before they enter the buying process. The buying process itself is in learning experience and can lead to a change in attitudes.

Alfred Politz noted at one time that women stated a clear preference for G.E. refrigerators over Frigidaire, but that Frigidaire continued to outsell G.E.[30] The answer to this paradox was that preference was only one factor entering into behavior. When the consumer preferring G.E. actually undertook to purchase a new refrigerator, her curiosity led her to examine the other brands. Her perception was sensitized to

[30]Alfred Politz, "Motivation Research–Opportunity or Dilemma?", in Ferber and Wales, *op. cit.*, pp. 57–58.

refrigerator advertisements, sales arguments, and different product features. This led to learning and a change in attitudes.

## THE HOBBESIAN ORGANIZATIONAL-FACTORS MODEL

The foregoing models throw light mainly on the bheavior of family buyers.

But what of the large number of people who are organizational buyers? They are engaged in the purchase of goods not for the sake of consumption, but for further production or distribution. Their common denominator is the fact that they

1. are paid to make purchases for others and
2. operate within an organizational environment.

How do organizational buyers make their decisions? There seem to be two competing views. Many marketing writers have emphasized the predominance of rational motives in organizational buying.[31] Organizational buyers are represented as being most impressed by cost, quality, dependability, and service factors. They are portrayed as dedicated servants of the organization, seeking to secure the best terms. This view has led to an emphasis on performance and use characteristics in much industrial advertising.

Other writers have emphasized personal motives in organizational buyer behavior. The purchasing agent's interest to do the best for his company is tempered by his interest to do the best for himself. He may be tempted to choose among salesmen according to the extent they entertain or offer gifts. He may choose a particular vendor because this will ingratiate him with certain company officers. He may shortcut his study of alternative suppliers to make his work day easier.

In truth, the buyer is guided by both personal and group goals; and this is the essential point. The political model of Thomas Hobbes comes closest of any model to suggesting the relationship between the two goals.[32] Hobbes held that man is "instinctively" oriented toward preserving and enhancing his own well-being. But this would produce a "war of every man against every man." This fear leads men to unite with others in a corporate body. The corporate man tries to steer a careful course between satisfying his own needs and those of the organization.

*Marketing Applications of Hobbesian Model.* The import of the Hobbesian model is that organizational buyers can be appealed to on both personal and organizational grounds. The buyer has his private aims, and yet he tries to do a satisfactory job for his corporation. He will respond to persuasive salesmen and he will respond to rational product arguments. However, the best "mix" of the two is not a fixed quantity; it

[31] See Melvin T. Copeland, *Principles of Merchandising*, McGraw-Hill Book Company, New York, 1924.

[32] Thomas Hobbes, *Leviathan* [1651], G. Routledge and Sons, London, 1887.

varies with the nature of the product, the type of organization, and the relative strength of the two drives in the particular buyer.

Where there is substantial similarity in what suppliers offer in the way of products, price, and service, the purchasing agent has less basis for rational choice. Since he can satisfy his organizational obligations with any one of a number of suppliers, he can be swayed by personal motives. On the other hand, where there are pronounced differences among the competing vendors' products, the purchasing agent is held more accountable for his choice and probably pays more attention to rational factors. Short-run personal gain becomes less motivating than the long-run gain which comes from serving the organization with distinction.

The marketing strategist must appreciate these goal conflicts of the organizational buyer. Behind all the ferment of purchasing agents to develop standards and employ value analysis lies their desire to avoid being thought of as order-clerks, and to develop better skills in reconciling personal and organizational objectives.[33]

## SUMMARY

Think back over the five different behavioral models of how the buyer translates buying influences into purchasing responses.

Marshallian man is concerned chiefly with economic cues—prices and income—and makes a fresh utility calculation before each purchase.

Pavlovian man behaves in a largely habitual rather than thoughtful way; certain configurations of cues will set off the same behavior because of rewarded learning in the past.

Freudian man's choices are influenced strongly by motives and fantasies which take place deep within his private world.

Veblenian man acts in a way which is shaped largely by past and present social groups.

And finally, Hobbesian man seeks to reconcile individual gain with organizational gain.

Thus, it turns out that the black box of the buyer is not so black after all. Light is thrown in various corners by these models. Yet no one has succeeded in putting all these pieces of truth together into one coherent instrument for behavioral analysis. This, of course, is the goal of behavioral science.

[33] For an insightful account, see George Strauss, "Tactics of Lateral Relationship: The Purchasing Agent," *Administrative Science Quarterly,* vol. 7, September, 1962, pp. 161–186.

# 16. NEW DIMENSION IN CONSUMER ANALYSIS

*Harper W. Boyd, Jr., and Sidney J. Levy*

*Marketing managers tend to plan and act in terms of their own understanding of consumer needs and behavior patterns. However, the authors of this article explain how these managers can gain greater marketing effectiveness if they study and analyze the total consumption system in which their products and services play a part.*

In recent years there has been an outpouring of management literature dealing with a subject which has become known as "the marketing concept."[1] This line of thinking has been well summarized by Peter F. Drucker:

> "If we want to know what a business is we have to start with its purpose. And its purpose must lie outside of the business itself. In fact, it must lie in society, since a business enterprise is an organ of society. There is only one valid definition of business purpose: to create a customer."[2]

A logical starting point, under this approach, is to concentrate on the *functions* that the product serves in satisfying a customer's needs instead of becoming preoccupied

AUTHORS' NOTE: We wish to acknowledge the helpful insights contributed by Professor Edward C. Bursk.

[1] See, for example, Theodore Levitt, "Marketing Myopia," *Harvard Business Review*, July–August, 1960, p. 56; Fred J. Borch, "The Marketing Philosophy as a Way of Business Life," American Management Association, Inc., Marketing Series No. 99, 1957; and J. B. McKitterick, "What Is the Marketing Management Concept?" *The Frontiers of Marketing Thought and Science,* The American Marketing Association, Chicago, 1957, pp. 71–82.

[2] *The Practice of Management,* Harper & Brothers, New York, 1954, p. 37.

Source: From *Harvard Business Review,* vol. 41, November–December, 1963, pp. 129–140. Harper W. Boyd, Jr.: Professor of Marketing, Northwestern University, and Visiting Professor of Marketing in International Business, Stanford University. Sidney J. Levy: Professor of Marketing, Northwestern University.

with the physical aspects of the product itself. Phrased in terms of functions, companies sell such things as transportation, nutrition, energy, comfort, self-expression, escape, intellectual development, and conformity; rather than cars, bread, oil, pillows, pens, novels, textbooks, and uniforms.

Certainly, this is a good start. By taking such a conceptual approach, many companies have sharpened their marketing effort by

1. researching and analyzing why customers (or potential customers) buy (or don't buy) particular kinds of products or services, and

2. surveying and identifying particular groups of customers (or potential customers) who differ from one another in why they buy (or don't buy) the products or services in question.

Many of the same companies have also used the marketing concept to instill more sense of direction in the nonmarketing functions of the business and to unify their over-all organizational effort.

## FOR FULL EFFECTIVENESS

But general adoption of a customer orientation is not enough. Such an approach can still fall short of full effectiveness. The trouble is that it does not *ensure* that customers' needs and wants will be understood and spelled out in the comprehensive, meaningful detail that they could and should be.

It is the purpose of this article to point out the value of thinking and making decisions in terms of *consumption systems.* This, we will show, is an effective way to avoid use of generalizations or unrelated specifics, and of achieving more innovation, greater market penetration, and more coordinated planning of the total marketing (and corporate) effort.

By the term *consumption system* we mean the way a purchaser of a product performs the total task of whatever it is that he or she is trying to accomplish when using the product—not baking a cake, but preparing a meal; not installing a transmission, but building an automobile.

There are at least three layers of increasingly greater depth in the analysis of customers for full marketing effectiveness:

1. *Looking beyond purchase behavior to use behavior.* Whatever reasons people have for buying (or not buying) a *particular* product are clearly rooted in how they use that product; and how well it serves the use to which they put it becomes particularly important at times of repurchase. Here focusing on the consumption system, though this is broader than the use of the particular product, does ensure that the use behavior of the consumer will not be overlooked since it has to be included as part of the consumption system.

2. *Deliberately studying the total consumption system for the sake of additional insights.* The use behavior for a particular product is bound to be affected not only by the problem to be solved or the task to be performed by the use of that product but also by the related products and related use behaviors that make up the *total* consumption system in which it plays a part; and these effects are subject to marketing applications.

3. *Analyzing the consumption system in the further detail of the many interrelated subsystems resulting from different kinds of people making different use of the same product or the same use of different products.* Here we can combine market segmentation with consumer motivation for maximum effectiveness. Because these different subsystems reflect the different goals that people have in using products to solve their problems or perform their tasks, it is possible to pinpoint marketing action to each individual subsystem and/or to reassemble such individual marketing actions into a coordinated master strategy.

Let us now look at these three layers of successively greater depth in more detail. As we shall see, many marketers already look at use behavior, and a number study the consumption system (sometimes without labeling it as such, sometimes in the narrower version of "behavior patterns"); but there are very few, if any, who carry their analysis to the ultimate step of interrelated subsystems.

*Use Behavior.* Many companies are sophisticated enough to realize that purchases are made not for the sake of the product but of the product's functions–that is, what the product will do in satisfying needs and wants. But unless they actually think in terms of *how* the consumer is using the product, they may slip into the error of taking product-oriented action. And one way of making use orientation inescapable is to think in terms of the consumption system in which the product plays a part. Thus:

A manufacturer of wristwatches will recognize that he is serving people's needs to know what time it is. Yet he might still concentrate on making his watch simply a better timekeeper for the money, and pay major attention to the accuracy and dependability that lead people to buy or not buy his particular brand or model.

But the customers' need for such features depends, in turn, on the use to which they put watches in actual practice. First of all, what is the problem to be solved or the task to be performed: the scheduling of events, the organization of individual effort, the synchronization of related activities, the meeting of social obligations, or what? Secondly, what other products or services do people use to solve their time problem (e.g., clocks, bells, telephones, other people's actions or statements); and what are the circumstances (light, physical position, degree of hurry, presence of others, nearness of clocks, and so on)? It could turn out, for example, that for most people it is *more* important to be able to read the time quickly and clearly than to have it actually measured to the precise second. In any event, understanding the use behaviors of watch wearers *forces* attention on the product features and selling appeals that will lead to more effective marketing.

*Total System.* However, if marketers only look at the use behavior for their particular product or service, and do not go on to wring the full meaning out of the way that product fits into the total consumption system representing the wider problem or task which it is being used to solve or perform, they still may miss valuable leads to marketing action.

Consider the housewife. She uses many different systems as she goes about her household tasks—cleaning house, preparing food, laundering clothes, caring for the baby, getting ready to go out, and the like. Here the housewife, like other consumers, functions much as do other economic entities. She buys, transports, and changes raw materials into finished products in a sequence of events that is more or less efficient, more or less satisfying. Thus, a manufacturer who wants the housewife's "business" has to produce and sell a product which will, in meaningful ways, "plug into" the systems relevant to her. He has to have a practical understanding of what she is doing—the various products she uses, the different actions she takes—the total system in question.

EXAMPLE. Here is a general description of the steps involved in laundering clothes. In studying this system, the reader should keep in mind that only a bare skeleton is being presented; for the system to be truly meaningful much more would have to be known about housewives' feelings, thoughts, and attitudes about what they are doing. (Some speculative marketing implications are added in parentheses simply to illustrate the kinds of possibilities.)

The week's accumulation of laundry is sorted into piles. The housewife classifies the clothes to be processed, either by observation or by some predetermined set of "rules." Thus:

- Men's white shirts may be handled routinely, but an unusually soiled pair of trousers may require a decision to be made. The housewife may use such standards as appearance, soiling, wrinkling, odor, length of wearing, and type of cloth as bases for her decisions.
- Perhaps the men's shirts will be delivered to a Chinese laundry some distance away. (Here a special service is being used. Why is this service so unique? On the other hand, how much of a nuisance is it? Might the Chinese laundry begin pickup and delivery? Couldn't the large commercial laundries duplicate this type of laundering?)
- The sorting continues. (How distateful is sorting to the housewife? Perhaps a powder to reduce odor and mildew in the laundry hamper would be useful. Or perhaps a method of precleaning clothes so that soaking is eliminated would be welcome. Could some kind of sorting rack attachment to an appliance facilitate the process?)
- White goods form one pile—sheets, pillowcases, towels, underwear, and so on. This requires hot water and bleach. Especially dirty spots may need individual attention with a brush. (Perhaps a tube of aerosol spray of a special cleaning substance could take care of these.)
- Another pile includes the colorful items—blouses, linen napkins, girls' frocks. These may or may not need hot water. They may possibly need a bit of mending. (Maybe a little laundry sewing kit would be handy for this.)
- Still another pile needs very special handling. Perhaps it includes socks, delicate undergarments, synthetics, woolens, to be subdivided into those needing cold water, warm water, hand washing, and so on. (Possibly the sink that has been designed out of laundry rooms still has its place after all.)
- Some things are to be dry cleaned—sent out or taken to a coin-operated machine. (When will home dry cleaning machines be available? And will there be a market for them?)

In doing the laundry the products that will be used must be at hand—often a messy array of boxes, bottles (glass and plastic), spray cans, and jars. Like an alchemist the woman will juggle an assortment that may include more than one brand of detergent, bluing, starch, bleach, water softener, fabric softener, spot remover, soap, and hand lotion! (Conceivably, there is room for an integrated line of laundry products with compatible ingredients and matched containers to help organize the array of cleaning staples.) Let's see how the system continues and note what other questions arise:

- Piles of clothes are put into the washing machine. Since the piles are of different volume and weight, there are problems in loading. Overloading is not uncommon; underloading is a wasteful irritation. (This problem has been solved by new models that adapt to smaller loads, but are there other refinements still possible?)
- There are different kinds of washing machines. The consumer has to judge which is best for her and then live with it. "I'd like one that does everything automatic, but my service man says those give more trouble, and that I'm better off with my simpler machine," is a statement commonly heard among housewives. (Clearly, reliability is still an area with marketing potential.)
- Nearby is the box of detergent. The giant box is a real chore to handle and to lug from the supermarket. (Volume delivery would seem a good solution; and perhaps home delivery of barrel-size containers would offer possibilities. Also, since laundries are such wet places, why don't they do something about the boxes that collapse? Plastic containers or plastic-bottom boxes would alleviate this problem.)
- Frequently the detergent is added to the wash by pouring from the box "about one cup." There is a general problem of imprecision; women are likely to overdo. (Perhaps the directions should be more explicit, or there should be warning lights or bells; and perhaps the detergent manufacturer could include measuring cups or one-cup automatic dispenser chutes.)
- What to do about bleach is a question that needs to be resolved. It is strong and threatening, but routinely useful; powder is safer, but possibly less effective. Bleach may be hard on clothes. It is disheartening to have clothes get frayed and threadbare. On the other hand, they *will* wear out and it is exciting to contemplate the possibility of a new garment. (The rapidity with which new types of bleaches enter the market indicates that there remains an unsatisfied need here.)
- Washing chores vary with the kind of machines women have—whether a washer-dryer, or separate appliances. As the process goes on, the clothes are spread around in different states of handling—dirty, wet, dry, ironed, waiting ironing, from last time, poorly done pieces that need re-doing, things that need touching up. (Laundries and utility rooms are not always well planned, even in new homes. There is still a market for intelligent architectural attention to working space and its organization. On the other hand, may there not also be a certain amount of pleasure in being ankle deep in clothes that are gradually working their way to cleanliness?)
- Dealing with lint is a problem. Lint removers (Scotch tape, sticky drums, and the like) for dry clothes, and lint removers in appliances are helpful, but still a bother. Washer and dryer lint traps are commonly neglected and may lead to mechanical problems. Many housewives end up washing dark things by hand to avoid lint. (Surely improvements are possible here.)

The housewife continues with the laundry task, perhaps also attending to children, preparation of meals, alert to clicks, buzzers, bells, agitator rhythm, and so on. Strangely enough, doing the home laundry is more complicated and more time consuming than it used to be, owing to the proliferation of fabrics, machines, and washing ingredients. All the way through the system, many products are being used—softened water, implements, appliances, cleansers, aids—some casually, some with irritation, some with pleasure. Too much detergent may produce too many suds; too much softener makes the clothes feel too smooth (even "slimy"); too much bleach is a hazard; the iron may scorch; a pipe leaks; buttons pop off; the dryer burns too hot—but the result may be, to the housewife, a fragrant, warm, fluffy pile of gratified accomplishment.

This analysis of the home laundry system is meant only to be suggestive; a properly done, more intensive, detailed analysis would be voluminous. But, hopefully, even this overly general analysis does indicate how knowledge of the total system, more fully and carefully dissected, can alert the manufacturer to certain facts:

- The housewife is acting in an orderly or purposeful way, in the terms in which she defines her problems and tasks.
- There are a series of interrelated steps which require consumer decision making based on knowledge, expectations, and standards (as well as on ignorance, surprise, and uncertainty).
- Any laundry product is used with other products with which it must be compatible.
- Questions arise from this type of analysis that point the way to new products or to a clearer understanding of consumer motivations by which old products can be marketed more effectively.

Figure 1 illustrates this total home laundering system. The various circles also indicate how it is made up of several (to some extent overlapping) subsystems.

*Interrelated Subsystems.* Many companies have gone quite far in another direction: identifying consumer groups, usually called market segments, that have different characteristics which (a) make them particularly good prospects for different varieties of product or service, and (b) make special product designs or marketing efforts directed at them enough more effective to more than repay the added cost of the specialization. But note how much more effective such segmentation can be if, again, it is tied not only into consumer characteristics (like income, geographic location, or education) but also into the different consumer goals that distinguish various consumption systems *and subsystems.*

Not only is every product (or service) part of some total consumption system, but also there are usually several distinct and definable subsystems in operation, because:

1. Most problems can be solved with several different products, and most tasks can be performed in several different ways. Think of the various activity patterns which are in operation merely in the process of washing men's shirts—by hand or machine at home, commercial laundry, the laundromat, Chinese laundry, bachelor service, and so on.
2. Different people have different goals in solving a problem or performing a task. Thus:

- Our wristwatch manufacturer can focus on occupational use—railroad engineers, executives, secretaries, night watchmen, and so on (with a different subsystem for each, if he finds it worthwhile to go that far). Or he can focus on social use, in which case he may find problems and opportunities among people who are obsessive about being on time (which suggests automatic timing devices) versus people who use time maturely as a way of relating to other people in a socially synchronized way (and just how they do it may give him clues to watches for children, cocktail wear, and jewelry adornment).
- Similarly, a manufacturer of a fabric softener will develop one kind of orientation if his interest is in consumption systems which relate to fabric protection. Longevity, resistance to weather and insects, odor, and hygiene—these will be the basic functions he will focus on. But if his interest

Figure 1. Picture of a home laundry system

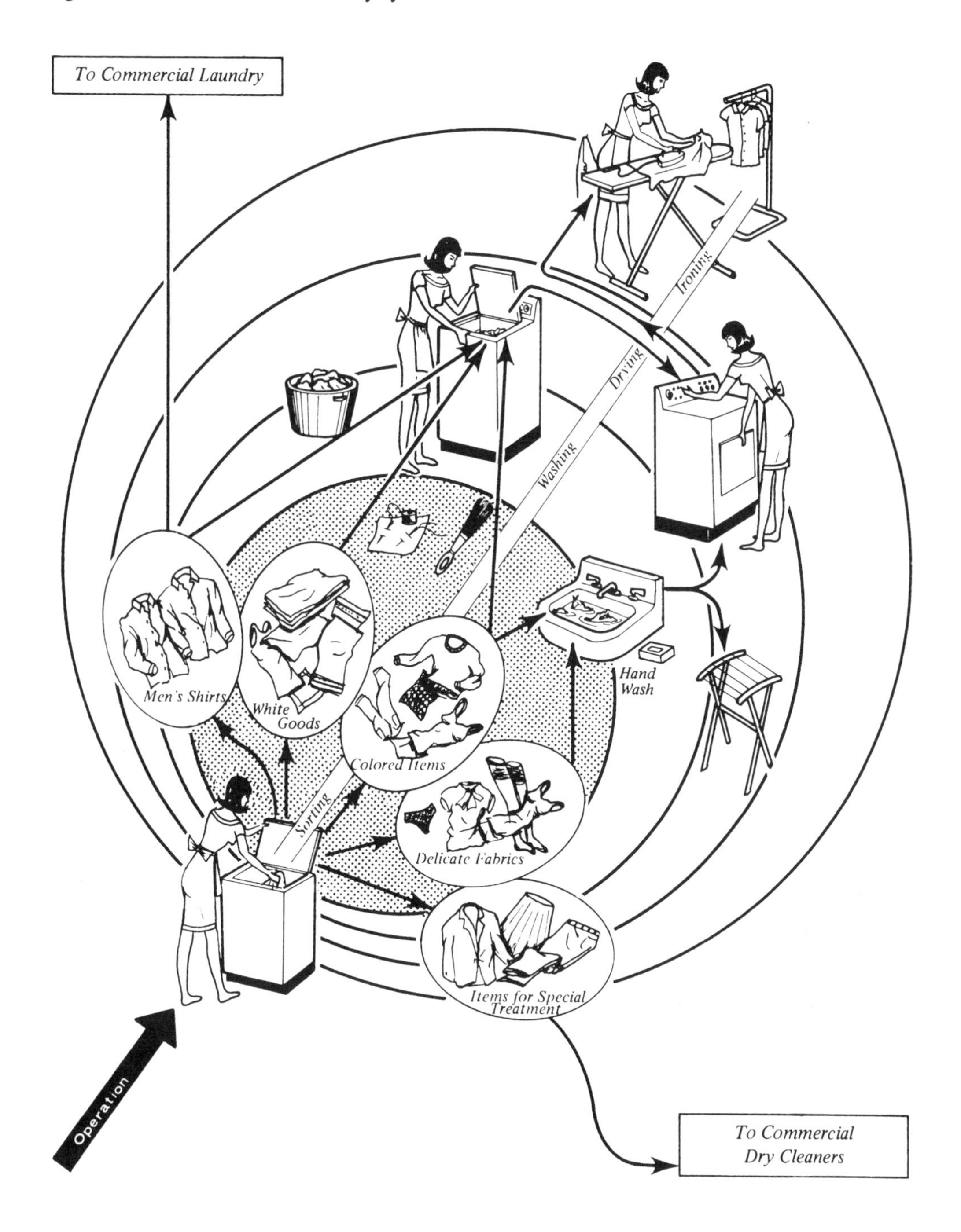

primarily relates to fabric beautification, then softness, wrinkle-resistance, color enhancement, and so on will be the functions of interest to him.

- A company in the petroleum industry will follow quite different courses, depending on whether it sees itself as fitting into a system which provides power, automotive service, transportation facilitation, or, as some companies are tending, as part of a system involving a conveniently located channel of distribution for a variety of products.

3. People have different goals for different parts of a total consumption system. For example, a home gardener may want to cut his grass as painlessly and quickly as possible, but he may enjoy lavishing great care on his rose bushes.

   EXAMPLE. Now, see what happens when we combine all of these differences–people, products, and goals–into a network of subsystems. For this purpose let us develop our gardening example in detail.

   Suppose there are three major types of gardeners: (a) owners of small properties, casual about gardening; (b) owners of small properties, careful about gardening; and (c) owners of large properties, casual about gardening. In real life, the lines would not be drawn so sharply, there would be much overlap, and there would be other types of gardeners; but let us assume that for practical purposes they comprise most of the market.

   Further, let us take three kinds of gardening products–lawn mowers, sprinklers, and chemical sprays–and see how they fit into the three separate systems of the three major types of gardeners. Actually, the three consumer groups differ among themselves in the goals that they have for each of the products. Even more significantly, within each consumer group the gardeners have different goals for the three different products, springing from the different ways they use the products in their total gardening consumption systems. Thus, there is a constellation of goals in each case (in real life there would of course be as many more sets of goals as there would be different products or different uses involved).

   Consider, first, the three different gardening systems for the three different types of gardeners (identified by the relative size of their property and their general attitude) as far as their lawns and roses are concerned:

- The small, casual gardener drags out the lawn mower when the grass begins to look untidy (to his wife, most likely), gets the job over with as quickly and easily as he can. But he loves and enjoys his roses, in part because they do not seem to call for the same effort, in part because they are more rewarding. So on other, more numerous occasions, he tends his roses, pruning them a little, raking around them a little; and if the bugs are eating the leaves, he will eagerly buy some chemical preparation and spray them, with much concern that he has the right brand. On still other occasions, when the grass looks dry (to his wife) or the roses look thirsty (to him), he'll do some watering, letting the spray cover grass and bushes alike.
- The small, careful gardener, however, will treat both his lawn and his roses with great care, on a planned schedule, with different amounts of care and different kinds of treatment for each. He is particular about having his grass just the right height–not letting it get so high it looks shaggy or cutting it so low it burns–but also varying it according to the season and weather. He applies his insecticide and does his watering *before* it is needed, being sure the spray doesn't wash the chemical

off the roses, never watering the lawn in the heat of the sun, and doing a lot of deep soaking around the roots of the rose bushes. Note that he needs a watering device which will not just take care of the lawn but will be right, in a quite different application, also for the roses; that he will buy different kinds of chemicals, whose properties he knows from reading a horticultural magazine; and that it is more important for his lawn mower to have adjustable blades than to be easy and simple to use.

- As for the large, casual gardener, every Saturday morning (if he plays golf in the afternoon, or every Saturday afternoon (if he plays golf in the morning), he gets out his power mower and begins to enjoy the spectacle of himself riding up and down on his flashy steed. From time to time he dismounts, for a quick drink or to get the watering started where he has just mowed, or both. Finally, he gives the roses a quick going over, not noticing the destructive work of the bugs unless it gets so bad that it mars the appearance of the total landscape—and then, if it does, he sends out impatiently, and with some annoyance, for something—anything—with which to spray them. He really enjoys the mowing, because it shows him off, but the roses are only a necessary background, and the watering is a nuisance.

Next, note that each of the *three* gardener types has a different set of goals for each of the *three* different products, depending on how he uses them; and even though all are gardeners, interested in lawns and roses, their use behaviors for just this much of their total gardening add up to three times three, or *nine*, subsystems (see Table 1).

Now consider, more fully, some of the marketing implications of looking at gardening as a consumption system made up of consumption subsystems:

1. Mention has already been made of the implications for product design in the case of one product—lawn sprinklers. In the same way—but with different results, because the subsystems of consumption are different for the other two products—the insecticide manufacturer and the lawn-mower manufacturer can design their products to fit the needs of the three major types of gardeners. There are also implications if any one of these manufacturers is thinking of diversifying into other products. If an insecticide manufacturer with a strong following in the small, casual group wants to capitalize on this fact in the mower market, then he must have an economy-model mower to go with his high-quality spray.

2. In the matter of distribution channels, the same insecticide manufacturer faces a dilemma. His lawn mowers may sell through hardware stores and discount houses, but the same people who buy mowers there will go to a garden center for their rose bush sprays (for the sake of professional advice). His alternative, then, might be to expand his line of sprays and attract the small, careful group B, thus capitalizing on his position in that type of outlet. On the other hand, the manufacturer of lawn mowers bought principally by the small, casual group could easily diversify into sprinklers, since they would be bought by the same people at the same kind of outlet.

3. As for advertising, there would be the same crisscross (in some cases, re-enforcing; in other cases, conflicting) of quality and complexity versus economy and convenience. Involved would be not only the kinds of appeals to be used, but also the media to convey them, the amount of money to be spent, and even the timing. Manufacturers of lawn mowers and sprinklers for groups A and C would spend less on national

**Table 1. Analysis of three different products in context of total gardening consumption system (much abbreviated) with nine subsystems (three different types of gardeners, or market segments, with three subsystems each)**

| *Three major types of gardeners* | *Lawn mowers (for grass)* | *Watering devices (for grass and rose bushes)* | *Insecticides (for rose bushes)* | *Marketing application* |
|---|---|---|---|---|
| A<br>"SMALL, CASUAL"<br>Owner of small property<br>Attitude toward gardening: casual, pleasurable<br>Gardening work habits: little-by-little, intermittently<br>Schedule: random, impulsive<br>Interests: grass for cover and durability, roses for fun | Wants a product that is simple, rugged, easy to use | Wants anything that promises coverage of lawn | Wants one good formulation, easy to apply | Product design |
| | Will buy anywhere he can inspect it and buy it cheaply | Will buy anywhere it can be sold cheaply and inspected | Will buy where he can get advice | Channel of distribution |
| | Goal: to get the job done quickly and conveniently | Goal: to cover the lawn with minimum of moving (no special thought about roses) | Goal: to rescue attacked plants and bring them back to health | Advertising |
| | Wants a bargain | Wants a bargain | Will pay a high price, if product promises to be successful | Pricing |
| B<br>"SMALL, CAREFUL"<br>Owner of small property<br>Attitude toward gardening: careful, precise<br>Gardening work habits: constantly, all leisure time<br>Schedule: planned timing for lawn and roses with proper proportions of care for each<br>Interests: obsessive desire for perfection of both lawn and roses | Wants adjustable blades, special attachments | Wants a small device, with fine, slow, manipulatable spray, and special attachment for soaking | Wants a complex formulation several varieties, which can be applied precisely | Product design |
| | Will buy where quality is assured | Will buy where quality is assured | Will buy where quality is assured | Channel of distribution |
| | Goal: to secure precise, tailored lawn | Goal: to give different objects the kind of watering they individually require | Goal: to protect plants so they will never be attacked by disease | Advertising |
| | Will pay a high price if product has proper features | Will pay a high price if product has proper features | Will pay a high price, but it must promise economy for effect secured | Pricing |
| C<br>"LARGE, CASUAL"<br>Owner of medium-size to large property<br>Attitude toward gardening: casual, expansive, and sporty<br>Gardening work habits: makes a big production of everything<br>Schedule: does chores in regular sequence<br>Interests: great sweeps of lawn, great clumps of roses | Wants something big and pretentious (with fancy gadgets) | Wants anything that promises wide coverage of lawn | Wants any formulation, easy to apply | Product design |
| | Will buy where appropriate for "estate" owners to go | Will buy anywhere convenient | Will buy anywhere convenient | Channel of distribution |
| | Goal: to cover a lot of lawn quickly and show off while doing it | Goal: to cover the maximum amount of lawn with a lot of water (no special thought about roses) | Goal: to restore attacked plants to decent appearance | Advertising |
| | Will pay a high price if product has proper features | Will pay a high initial price, but the product must be economical when expanded into a system | Wants a bargain | Pricing |

advertising, more on cooperative advertising (with dealers) or promotion of sales in local newspapers. Manufacturers of insecticides would stress chemical quality, early in or ahead of the season, in horticultural journals, in order to reach group B; and do dealer promotion with garden centers during the season, for group A. And so on.

4. In pricing, too, the problems and opportunities for the nine subsystems shown in Table 1 would differ because of the different uses (and attendant goals) of the three market segments for the three products. The insecticide manufacturer can charge a high price for his product sold through garden centers to groups A and B, but he had better have a cheap product (under another brand name, perhaps) for sale through hardware stores to group C. And the lawn-mower manufacturer who observes many group A gardeners paying a high price for insecticides dares not conclude that these same gardeners will also pay a high price for his mowers.

The important point is that many of these insights would not result from generalizations either about market segments or product use, generalizations which would hide the sharp differences that become apparent from looking at the total consumption system and the nine subsystems corresponding to the three different products and the three different types of gardeners.

If one thinks of the consumer as operating a manufacturing process by which some end product emerges, it is easy to see that a variety of systems and subsystems would be in operation at any one time and that they would have some degree of relationship. While we have no desire to complicate the system concept further by introducing the notion of still wider systems, it is important for any seller to go far enough in his thinking to relate one consumption system to any wider systems which exist and which have an important effect on the operation of the system in which he has an immediate interest. For example, a marketer would be ill-advised to define a consumption system for a gardening product without recognizing that this system is related to and dependent on a wider system of acts and ideas pertaining to the whole changing pattern of leisure time in this country.

## INDUSTRIAL PRODUCTS

Systems for industrial products are in some ways easier to specify if only because they are more precise and logical in their operation. It can be well argued that anyone producing an industrial good should develop a system which starts with the consumer and moves all the way back to the production of the goods that, in turn, produce the goods (and so on) which are consumed by the consumer. The producer of industrial goods or supplies can typically be more successful if he helps his potential customers "create a customer." To do this requires that he understand the (relative) totality of the system even if, at best, he learns this primarily from research done by customers.

At the very minimum, a seller of an industrial product should concern himself with "where" his product fits into the manufacturing process of his potential customers. It must be compatible with prior parts of the process as well as with subsequent steps.

Any change in any part of the process is likely to have an effect on all other parts—a fact that the manufacturer selling into the system must keep in mind. He can better protect against obsolescence, as well as do a better job of selling, if he knows his constraints; that is, if he understands the needs of the system.

Take, for example, the manufacturer of plastic materials designed to be used in the packaging of food:

This manufacturer would—or should—be concerned with a protection system which would solve such problems as spoilage, prevention of color fading, shrinkage, product visibility, and ease of storage and shipment. To market his product effectively, he would have to know and understand the various production systems currently in use by manufacturers of different food products: for example, fresh fruits and vegetables, smoked meats, poultry, fish and seafoods, and cheese. In addition, he would have to know the distribution systems in use, including physical handling, shipment, storage, shelf life, exposure to store traffic, markups, and amount of handling. Further, he would be interested in the consumer system that the product is a part of, including place of storage, product life span in terms of replacement rate, and need for resealing.

As an actual case in point, the Cryovac Division of W. R. Grace & Company developed a vacuum-sealing process which in actuality was a major component of the total production, distribution, and consumer systems for meat, poultry, cheese, and fish. Since the Cryovac process necessitated the use of manual or automatic machines, company salesmen had to perform such activities as helping train labor, helping in the promotion of Cryovac-wrapped products to the trade, and helping to show how to install a product line using the Cryovac process.

Agricultural machinery also illustrates the value of the system concept, although there is little to suggest that most such manufacturers have applied themselves diligently to learning about the various farm systems in effect. With the growth in the number of large farms, we find many analogies between farming and manufacturing. More and more machinery is being required to displace high-cost labor. Yet it is doubtful if many manufacturers consider the farm as a systematic production unit, and have studied the nature of the job to be done (for instance, on a time and motion basis) to determine the most efficient "factory layout" and machinery required.

On the other hand, farm machines have been developed which represent integral systems unto themselves. Some of these machines might have been developed earlier if manufacturers had analyzed the total process. Take, for example, the harvesting of corn:

Until recently the corn combine piece of machinery was limited to harvesting shelled corn in either a moist or dry state. Corn cobs were left in the field. Such a machine, of course, represented a radical improvement over earlier machines, since it picked and shelled, whereas previously, different machines were required. Now corn can be picked, shelled, and mixed or combined in the form of whole shelled corn with broken cobs by a single machine. In fact, some machinery manufacturers sell in terms of "systems" which require the use of two or more pieces of machinery to do a total job. Thus, in corn harvesting, one can by the addition of a dryer, a wagon dump, a chuck (storage) wagon, and escalators (for moving corn into the bins) complete the entire process with one basic machine.

In the past few years, the agricultural industry has experienced substantial unrest caused by the innovative tactics of smaller firms versus the giants who have continued largely to sell machinery on a dollar-per-pound-of-iron basis. Much of this new machinery gives evidence that the inventors understand, at least pragmatically, the nature and functioning of the system approach. Thus, for example, a new ingenious mechanized potato harvester has been developed that permits a crew of eight to do the work of thirty diggers.

## MARKETING DECISIONS

The analysis of consumption systems should be helpful to the management of a firm in many ways. It can serve to identify more precisely the company's corporate objectives, construct a plan of action, organize to carry out the plan (including finance, R & D, and production as well as marketing), and set up a control-reappraisal system. Here, however, we will discuss the relation of consumption systems to marketing strategy and gather together a few of the more important implications to show how this focus on consumption systems helps to enrich and coordinate various planning and decision-making areas in marketing.

*Product & Product Line.* When the manufacturer knows and keeps current the details of the consumption systems pertinent to his products, then he is in a better position to assess opportunities (perhaps he can meet housewife standards with a new or modified product) as well as threats (for example, the development of new washing machines which clean by vibration). We can also assume that a knowledge of the more important systems will help him to innovate, or at least provide him with a better understanding of the chances to innovate. The part his product plays in the total system, when made reasonably explicit, should enable him to gain a better understanding of his role in the consumer's life. Further, he has a point of reference from which to judge how the passage of time and the actions of his competitors may be changing the system. Consequently, he will be better able to spot new opportunities as they arise.

More often than not, innovations are actually little more than a rearrangement or collapsing of the parts of a given system. This rearrangement usually represents an easier, or less costly, or more attractive, or more efficient way of solving the basic need.[3] In most cases, the rearrangement of steps involves combining and shortening. Most consumer goods innovations have, in recent years, been of this type. Many new products have been created when several "specialized" products have been combined into one. Thus:

- A classic example is in the home laundry field where detergents, bluing, and softeners have been combined.

[3]See Elting E. Morison, "A Case Study of Innovation," *Engineering and Science Monthly,* April 1950.

- Combination has been accomplished with a number of food products such as ready-to-eat cereals with sugar added, lemon-flavored sugar lumps for tea, frozen vegetables with butter sauce, cake mixes which include eggs, and, of course, precooked meals.
- In the world of machines for use in the home, the electric refrigerator with automatic defrosting, the gas or electric stove with its automatic timer, the radios and hi-fi sets which turn themselves off, the TV sets with their armchair controls, and the garage doors that open on signal, all are examples of admirable ingenuity that did not require tapping novel scientific principles.
- The car has been the locale of many innovations, all involving a shortening of steps—automatic transmissions, longer greasing intervals, more miles to an oil change, push-button window washers, to note a few.
- The innovations in cameras have centered recently around doing away with the light meter, the range finder, and even the developer as separate parts of the system.

If a manufacturer knows where his product fits into the steps in a system, he can better estimate the possibility of effecting innovation. This is accomplished by an examination of the steps prior to and subsequent to the point at which the product in question enters the system. He can frequently estimate the vulnerability of his current product by evaluating the other products which enter the system before and after his own product or are used in direct conjunction with it. Innovation by reaching back or by reaching forward in the system is, as has been stressed earlier, a common fact of life.

Research and development personnel need such a precise frame of reference within which to work. Knowledge of the steps in the individual consumption systems as well as the variety of alternative systems employed should provide them with the challenge, as well as the operational objectives, they so badly need. Assessing what they can do, both with current technology and with probable future technological changes, can help them provide the company with a higher return on R & D investments.

It is important, also, not to let one's thinking become too behavioristic. Just analyzing the mechanical steps in a system may not in itself generate useful ideas. In analyzing any consumption system, the engineer should think about the "problem" that users may feel at any given point. People are not always looking for efficiency, economy, and the like, as most impersonal analyses tend to assume. They may want distraction, aesthetics, individual expressiveness, pretentiousness, speed, and quiet.

*Advertising Strategy.* Advertising effectiveness obviously depends on the availability of a considerable amount of detailed information which will permit the determination of the role to be played by advertising, the advertising objectives, the proper choice of advertising copy, the coordination of advertising with other sales promotion activities, and the preparation of the advertising budget. Since consumers typically think in terms of product functions subjectively, and concern themselves with the ways in which products fit into their activities, it would seem that the systems approach would prove extremely helpful in advertising—if only because it presents a unified picture of the process by which a given task is accomplished, *including* the rationale, standards, and emotions involved. At the least, such a wholeness would help the advertiser see his product in relation to the total operation, to see its relative importance to other products used in the system, to understand more fully what its real contribution is to the user, and to learn more about *why* it is used.

Knowing the point of entry of the product into the consumption pattern makes the appropriate appeals more apparent. It poses this question: What is the unique role the product plays in bridging the gap between prior and subsequent steps? Sometimes after analysis of the *true* action system, rather than the presumed, an advertiser may call for changes in his appeals that go counter to the overly generalized beliefs about consumer behavior that are accepted in his industry. Here are two examples:

1. The decision to sell fresh chilled orange juice as a "refreshing drink always available from your refrigerator" is a case in point. But an analysis of the consumption system for fresh squeezed juice shows obstacles to this idea. Housewives typically serve juice in small glasses and have not prepared it in quantities to be stored. They regard it as precious. Also it is acid in content, they believe; too much is not healthy. And if it stands, its value declines. In the light of this analysis, what should the advertiser do to modify the situation?

2. Aiming Gleem toothpaste at "people who can't brush after every meal" represents an interesting recognition and exploration of an actual system with which many people feel uncomfortable because it is not the sanctioned system. The TV situations showing why a busy life precludes brushing after every meal are ones with which the housewife can readily identify. Here the advertiser is adapting to reality.

*Pricing Policy.* As part of solving his price problems, the manufacturer explores the preferences and educability of his consumers. An analysis of the consumer systems employing his products will be extremely helpful. If, for example, a "new" product has little effect on the totality of the way consumption is currently organized in terms of time, general cost, and final satisfaction in the goal, there is little reason to believe that it will command a premium price. All too often the manufacturer exaggerates the importance of his new item, failing to realize that it is but a very small part of a ramified pattern.

Conversely, he may underestimate the importance of a small item which actually may have much to offer in a lengthy or relatively unpleasant system. Here is an interesting illustration:

A manufacturer of point-of-sale displays used at trade shows and conventions designed a prefabricated unit consisting of a number of panels that could be locked together with fiber plugs. The appearance of this prefab unit was equal to that of the highest priced wooden displays and could be set up by two men in less than one hour.

Rather than take essentially a cost approach to the problem of what initial price to charge for such a new unit, this manufacturer would have been well advised to study the consumption system for all such units and determine what effect the prefab unit would have on the total system. The costs and time involved in the selling process, the shipping costs (from one show to another), the deterioration owing to improper handling during shipment, the assembly time at the convention site, the dismantling time, the frequency and extent of refurbishing–all these and other components of the use system involved (attitudes and feelings of workers at these various steps) should have been analyzed before an attempt was made to arrive at a "best" market price.

Pricing may also be related to the expected life span of a product. Instead of waiting to see how long an object lasts in wear, manufacturers should maintain an up-to-date, ongoing knowledge of how well and how long the product keeps functioning in the system. A far more realistic pricing strategy will be the result.

*Personal Selling.* The salesman's role or mission is changing in many firms—especially those selling technical products to industry. More and more, he is looked upon as a communication link between the seller and the marketplace. Increasingly, he is the "feedback" agent as to what the market wants and needs, as well as being the vertical thrust agent who sells the product. It is obvious that to execute these roles with efficiency requires an understanding on his part of the systematic process facilitated by his product. For example:

A salesman selling building materials must be able to demonstrate to architects, contractors, and engineers that his product is not only compatible with other products in the system, but that it is not at odds with the human factors which may be involved, for instance, existing skills of labor.

House-to-house and route salesmen should be aware of the characteristic ongoing patterns of living they are attempting to break into. A route man is asking an established system to alter and make a position for him in the stream of events. Thus:

A study for the Jewel Tea Company by Social Research, Inc. found that a large number of "customers wanted a route man who was friendly, congenial but 'not too nice,' submissive, and conforming to requests and routines. He should be sensitive to the amount of socializing desired by the customer, allow her to set the pace, and then follow it quickly and willingly. He should follow a regular schedule of visits."[4]

## CONCLUSION

An analysis of consumption systems should provide manufacturers with data which are useful in many marketing decision areas. Such analyses give a perspective of the process by which consumers satisfy their basic wants and needs, they make available a framework within which the company can exercise its imagination in product innovation, in advertising strategy development, in pricing policy, and in sales activities.

But systems can only be understood if they are seen as a series of interlocking steps. This coherent, connected view avoids the distortion resulting from studying bits and pieces of market information which are the usual fare of the marketer. In particular, the systems approach should facilitate innovations, since most "new" products are new only in the sense that they are a combination of products used in two or more steps in a system.

[4]See Joseph W. Newman, *Motivation Research and Marketing Management,* Division of Research, Harvard Business School, Boston, 1957, p. 355.

Today's rapidly increasing expenditures for R & D require that the efforts of creative personnel be directed toward obtainable and meaningful innovations. These can best be achieved through an understanding of consumer systems relevant to their companies' products. Such an approach should be welcomed by technical personnel once they are trained to think along such lines.

# 17. APPLYING THE STRATEGY OF MARKET SEGMENTATION

*Alan A. Roberts*

*Market segmentation is of vital importance to most sellers, for only rarely can a product and a service be all things to all people. Market segmentation is based on the generally true concept that the market for a product is not homogeneous as to its needs and wants. By implication this concept means that one part of the market is worth more than another. It also implies that different marketing strategies will be employed in selling to the various parts.*

*This article is a case study in which the author discusses the opportunities inherent in market segmentation.*

Market segmentaton is the strategy of dividing markets in order to conquer them. Its philosophy is "something for everybody," within practicable limits. As a definition, this is less formal but more useful than those found in marketing textbooks.

Textbooks define a market segment as any subsection of a total market that is worth cultivating. They add that in order to implement a strategy of segmentation a firm must first identify the segment and then take marketing action based upon that identification. Unfortunately, bookish definitions like these do not cast much light upon the process whereby businessmen decide whether a segment worth cultivating truly exists. Moreover, they seldom give a basis for relating the single decision of whether or not to segment a market to any dynamic, over-all corporate strategy that implies continuity in this decision-making process.

Source: From *Business Horizons,* vol. 4, Fall, 1961, pp. 65–72. Alan A. Roberts: Vice-president–Research of the Western Division of Geyer, Morey, Madden & Ballard, Inc., Chicago.

It is well known that all companies more or less segment their markets. What we are interested in is this: Are the company's criteria for deciding whether a submarket is worth cultivating so general that the decision to segment is frequently made, or are they so specific that the company seldom moves in this direction? Looking at the same set of objective marketing facts, one firm may decide to segment progressively, while another firm may decide not to segment at all, depending on their relative enthusiasm for segmentation as general strategy behind their marketing approach. Moreover, marketing action, following the decision to segment, may take different forms.

## AGGREGATION VERSUS SEGMENTATION

Perhaps the best way to understand this concept and its implications is to consider simultaneously the approach and the rationale of each of these opposite strategies. The opposite of market segmentation could be called market aggregation, suggesting the policy of lumping together into one mass market many groups of buyers who might otherwise be marginally differentiated one from another into smaller submarkets.

The strategy of market aggregation is sometimes related to such considerations as cost of production, warehousing, and transporting. The idea here is that long production runs are more economical than short runs, that inventory costs may be minimized if fewer lines are offered, and so forth. Another set of reasons supporting market aggregation focuses upon measurements of the buying efficiency of promotional funds. Within certain dollar ranges, at least, the efficiency of promotional budgets may respond elastically to changes in size. That is, each dollar added to the promotional investment in a single product may result in a proportionately larger increase in promotional efficiency. The explanation of this lies in the basic per-thousand costs of advertising media. Media costs tend to follow this law: The larger and more general the medium, the smaller the cost per thousand; the more limited or specialized the medium, either geographically or by editorial or audience appeal, the greater the cost per thousand. The more that markets may be aggregated, the lower the cost per thousand in buying advertising to reach that mass market, at least within the range of certain promotional budgets.

For the major consumer advertisers, however, promotional budgets frequently pass the range of efficiency discussed above. The size and diversity of the mass-consumer markets require supplemental advertising investment in local and/or specialized audience media. The latter then become an important part of the company's total national advertising program. At this point, one rationale for the strategy of aggregation tends to disappear; indeed, national advertisers move toward segmentation strategy in proportion to their trageting of selective local and/or specialized markets.

The strategy of market segmentation suggests a continuous policy of looking for differences, geographical or otherwise, in the total market and the continuous exploitation of these differences. Often they are quite marginal, and their exploitation may require imaginative thinking on merchandising and promotion. Thus, some of the finest examples of market segmentation entail really creative actions. These may be the creation of new buyer needs, or at least the crystallization of needs previously felt only vaguely or to a slight degree. The effective crystallization of such needs in the minds of some consumers invokes demand for a new specialized product where previously there was reasonable satisfaction with a more generalized product.

Segmentation may also be practiced in many facets of marketing other than the product mix—for example, the penetration of new markets for existing products through sales force specialization, or the greater diversification of distribution channels.

As a consistently practiced strategy, segmentation seems to be oriented toward high sales volume, more so than the opposite policy of aggregation. It is ordinarily demonstrable that total sales may be increased with a more diversified product line sold through more diversified channels. The operative consideration is, traditionally, whether the line can thus be expanded profitably. This in turn may lead to the weighing of average unit profits versus marginal unit profits. These are always changing relationships, but important secular trends seem to be altering the equation in favor of market segmentation as more generally advantageous strategy.

Some of these trends relate to simple demographic factors, which tend to make markets larger and more segmentable. Such factors include increased population, income, leisure time, home ownership, educational level, and so forth. A perhaps less obvious factor in increasing the acceptance of market segmentation as a corporate strategy has been the advance of technique in market research, which always seems to be finding better ways to identify consumers and their buying motivations.

*Common Examples.* All around us we can see the fruits of market segmentation as practiced by major national manufacturers of consumer goods. Taking the period just before World War II as our reference point, we find everywhere examples of companies that have followed a pattern of progressive segmentation of their markets. Remember when most cigarette smokers were users of only four brands, all standard size, soft-packaged, nonfilter, nonmentholated? Cigarettes are perhaps a noteworthy example, but they are surely not unique. Package foods, cosmetics, soaps, liquor, and automobiles are other obvious examples.

Some consumer product-line manufacturers have practiced segmentation so assiduously over so many years that they are now in danger of losing their corporate identity in the minds of consumers. Even the most confirmed segmenters acknowledge that the "family of products" effect can be beneficial. It is then that they turn to umbrella devices, like the Betty Crocker name and the spoon on the General Mills packages.

Few companies that have chosen the strategy of market segmentation, however, have reached such a point. For most would-be segmenters the immediate problem is how to diversify rather than unify their offerings. They tend to use corporate emphasis only for special purposes—on a temporary basis when introducing a product or at trade rather than at consumer promotional levels.

Management's widespread adoption of segmentation—made obvious by the postwar boom of new brands and sales outlets—must be recognized as a marketing strategy that takes account of more than just simple economic or demographic changes in American life. For example, as consumers and as businessmen, we are subject to a constantly increasing volume of advertising messages. So great is the total number of advertising messages with which we are daily bombarded that this fact alone tends to outmode one implication in the strategy of market aggregation. The marketer who formerly preferred to concentrate his promotion on a tightly limited product line had in the back of his mind that he could, perhaps, overwhelm his buying public with the sheer volume of his repeated advertising messages. This has become an impossibility in recent years.

More and more the successful advertiser has to depend on the uniqueness of his selling message in order to win consumer interest. And product differentiation, however marginal, is one of the more obvious ways of finding a unique selling message. Even the Coca-Cola Company, that steadfast proponent of market aggregation that has been in the mind of man and boy one brand, one product, and one bottle, has in recent years edged slightly toward segmentation with its multisized bottles, and thus has found new selling appeals.

Sociologists and others have commented on the increasing sameness in many aspects of American life. The other side of this coin of sameness is that it forces us as consumers to distinguish ourselves from our development-housing neighbors, increasing our demand for at least minor distinctions in the products that we consume. This, of course, plays right into the hands of the market segmenters.

The postwar onset of television has furnished a most convenient springboard for market segmentation as a strategy to be more widely and systematically applied. In the introduction of new products, a regular condition of life for thoroughgoing market segmenters, a common approach is market-by-market. Spot TV is a powerful, well-adapted medium for promoting new products in selective markets. Another recent development in advertising—the multiplication of state and regional editions of magazines formerly available only as single national buys—may be understood both as an applied form of market segmentation by the magazines and a stimulus toward the strategy of market segmentation on the part of advertisers.

## BUSINESS AND AGRIBUSINESS

Leaving the more familiar realm of consumer goods, we encounter dramatic insights into segmentation strategy everywhere in industrial marketing. Recently, a manufacturer of industrial metal buildings, aiming to sell store buildings to large retail chain organizations, shifted its tactics to allow its dealer organization to carry the ball in promoting such national construction contracts. Previously, this manufacturer had tried, not too successfully, to handle these retail chains as house accounts, and to offer them a standardized, prototype building. The dealer organization was finally recognized as the key to unlocking this market, because dealers are better able to tailor their product offering to the buyers' local needs, even when the buyer is a large national chain. In other words, what had been considered as a single aggregated market proved through hard experience to be more correctly defined as a segmentable market.

Another broadly segmentable market is represented by American agribusiness in its role as purchaser of numerous production inputs. Despite some widespread stereotypes about agriculture—as in the expression "the farm problem," which implies that agriculture could be considered as a unit—today's agricultural organization is rich in variations. It actually makes segmentation strategy mandatory for suppliers who would penetrate agricultural markets in any depth. In agriculture, the problem for marketers is not whether to segment this vast buying potential, but how and to what degree. In the last analysis, no two farms are precisely the same in their significant demand characteristics, nor do they have precisely the same enterprises. As in consumer marketing, the firm selling in agricultural markets must aggregate its final customers at least to the extent of dealing with groups rather than individuals. There is no point in analytically subdividing agriculture into purposeless fragments, or even going beyond some of the broader, more obvious subdivisions.

Since the tree of agriculture has too much foliage for us to examine every leaf, we propose to strip back the bark from just one branch, and see how the sap runs.

The two most basic branches in agribusiness are crop production and livestock-poultry production, although the interrelations and overlappings between the two are so complex that their presentation as a dichotomy could mislead. Of these two, the livestock-poultry sector is the more important in terms of total income to farmers. Moreover, secular trends in American consumption patterns toward higher protein diets indicate even greater future importance for this sector. In general, livestock-poultry is a more dynamic and challenging example for the purposes of this article.

## LIVESTOCK CHEMICALS

Among the most important of the industrially purchased inputs used for livestock-poultry production are fine chemicals and drugs. Indeed, the annual expenditure of $250 million for these represents about 1 per cent of all farmers' total reinvestment in productive goods and services. A shortened term for this particular reinvestment volume is the market for livestock chemicals.

The balance of this article will focus on experience gained by companies that are trying, in various ways, to segment the market for livestock chemicals, and generalized conclusions will be developed from their experiences.

### The Structure: Submarkets

One consideration in focusing upon the marketing of livestock chemicals is that it involves definite submarkets that are representative of (1) quasi-professional or ethical product marketing; (2) industrial bulk product marketing; and (3) quasi-consumer packaged product marketing. These natural submarkets are briefly explained below.

*The Licensed Veterinarian.* When compared with the professional marketing of drugs for humans, the marketing of livestock drugs through professional veterinarians offers points of both similarity and dissimilarity. The essential difference, of course, is that the veterinarian operates on an economic rather than a humanitarian rationale. Nevertheless, veterinarians are motivated to some extent at least by a service concept, and they tend to be quite "touchy" about their professional status. In short, veterinarians think of themselves, and foster an image of themselves, in ways to set them apart as a distinct submarket and an obvious target for segmenting strategy by chemical and drug manufacturers.

*The Feed Industry.* In selling to major feed manufacturers, the appropriate marketing mix is that required in many industrial marketing situations, such as the selling of bulk chemical intermediates. It happens, however, that concentration in the feed industry is very low, compared with other basic manufacturing industries. More than 50 per cent of total manufactured feed volume is accounted for by some 5,000 small operators. At the lower end of the feed-tonnage spectrum, these 5,000 merge into the manufacturing retailers, who sell over the counter in package form many of the same drugs that they buy in bulk for mixing in their registered and/or custom feeds.

*Over-the-Counter Packaged Products.* Some 25,000 assorted drugstores, feedstores and mills, country elevators, hatcheries, cooperatives, farm-to-farm salesmen, and other retailers sell livestock chemicals over the counter in both feed and nonfeed forms. Drug promotion to farmers through these unrestricted channels stimulates consumer goods marketing, with manufacturers using all the techniques of mass promotion and advertising. This occurs despite the fact that the products involved are production inputs and should (theoretically) be bought by the farmer not in his capacity as consumer but as purchasing agent for his livestock enterprise.

Before analyzing how manufacturers have implemented their identification of these three segments of the livestock-chemical market, we should understand that many firms limit themselves agriculturally to a cream-skimming operation, confined to a single submarket. For example, a large variety of firms—some not essentially chemical or drug companies such as distillers, brewers, Eastman Kodak, Borden's, and others—simply sell bulk vitamins or antibiotics to the commercial feed industry. For them, as well as for other firms that confine their involvement to the veterinarian submarket (as do some ethical drug manufacturers) or to the over-the-counter package goods submarket, the opportunities to practice market segmentation are much fewer. Our main interest here is in approaches employed by those firms that aim for substantial operations in all three of the major submarkets of the livestock-chemical industry.

## Implementation

Marketing management's problems begin, not end, with the identification of the above three submarkets. Complicatons arise from the fact that they overlap.

Broadly speaking, drug and chemical manufacturers have sought to segment these submarkets through two approaches:

1. Sales force separation, which, carried to its logical conclusion, entails operating in each submarket through quasi-independent, differently named corporate subsidiaries.
2. A less formalized approach, with somewhat lower-key emphasis on product-line multiplication under one label and one management.

Firms that have sought to keep their marketing efforts in each of the three submarkets completely separate have commonly used the cover device of different corporate names. Partly, they aim for greater sales and deeper penetration by fostering specialization; the marketing effort of each subsidiary is tightly compartmentalized to one or, at the most, two of the major submarkets. Their aim is also to prevent one submarket–especially the veterinarian segment–from knowing what happens in another. For example, Vick splinters off the veterinarian submarket for development by its Jensen-Salsbery subsidiary, while its Hess & Clark subsidiary operates over the counter; American Home Products markets ethically as Fort Dodge Laboratories, and over the counter as Wyeth; Lilly appears as Corn States to veterinarians, but sells to the feed industry under the Lilly name, Elanco division. There are numerous other examples.

A special consideration for some human drug companies, which are greatly concerned with maintaining a 100 per cent ethical image in the eyes of druggists, is that they wish to sell farmers packaged animal-health products while avoiding the hurly-burly of shelf competition within the drugstore itself. With retail druggists controlling about 25 per cent of the packaged animal-health business, this image is hard to maintain without benefit of a cover organization. Schering handles this by selling its own labelled animal-health products through licensed veterinarians, while its American Scientific subsidiary sells through unrestricted channels, including drug outlets.

The other general approach to market segmentation–emphasis on product-line diversification under one label–is the favorite of the large companies that have entered agriculture from fine chemicals. The idea here is to offer the same basic product in a wide array of forms, package sizes, "formulas," and convenient combinations. The objective is to cover by product: all species of livestock and poultry; all routes of entry into the animal; types that typically move over the counter (such as growth stimulants); and types that are usually distributed to veterinarians (such as certain biologicals). All are under one corporate name and/or umbrella-brand label. Because the three submarkets tend to blend together in certain areas, this approach permits the same salesman to "sell everybody in town," while the advertising "gets more mileage." Heavy consumer and trade promotion is a concomitant of this species of market segmentation, which relies on the pulling power of advertising to compensate, in some instances, for loss of veterinarian and/or dealer incentive to push merchandise.

In other words, the product-line diversification approach can be developed to modify or even overcome the traditional attitudes held by some veterinarians, druggists, and other retailers who might expect local "exclusives" in animal-health products. Merck,

American Cyanamid, and Pfizer have all been notably successful in operating on this basis. Pfizer, for instance, has been most ingenious in multiplying its brand of oxy-tetracycline into a profusion of forms, package sizes, combinations, and special formulas, some rather marginally differentiated one from another, and then backing all this up with a saturation distribution and promotion program to farmers and to all three of the submarkets.

## Evaluation of Techniques

The separate sales force approach, institutionalized into operation through differently named corporated subsidiaries, is firmly rooted in the traditions and predilections of veterinarians and, to a lesser extent, of druggists and feed manufacturers.

For the many manufacturers that so far have made only a token entry into livestock chemicals, this particular segmentation route undoubtedly offers interesting possibilities for achieving wider and deeper market penetration. It does suffer, however, from the ultimate limitation of being oriented toward the *status quo* of the agribusiness. With the organization of American livestock and poultry production rapidly moving toward thoroughgoing specialization, larger unit size, and more integration—both horizontal and vertical—these changes are being reflected in the relative importance of various channels in distribution of livestock chemicals.

In Western commercial cattle feedlots, for instance, veterinarians are tending toward more specialized diagnostic-advisory functions with less dispensing, and with control (particularly application) of health products passing heavily into the hands of laymen. Even in the Midwest, hypodermic syringes, ownership of which was once the hallmark of the professional veterinarian, are now in the hands of one-third of all livestock farmers. More than 50 per cent of all large animal injectable products are estimated now to be applied by farmers themselves.

Developments such as these, plus the already mentioned dispersal of the feed industry, create difficulties for the segmentation approach based on separate subsidiaries operating in rigidly defined submarkets. Within the parent corporation, need may frequently arise to arbitrate jurisdictional problems caused by these shifting areas between submarkets.

In contrast, the segmentation approach, which is based mostly on product diversification, allows more flexibility in the matching of products to channels. The trade classifies itself, so to speak, with minimum intraorganization friction and with no bases left untouched. It is easy, then, to handle the many overlapping trade classifications, such as the integrated broiler organization, or the veterinarian in the wholesale feed supply business. No matter what buyer wants a particular drug in whatever form, quantity, or package size, any of the manufacturer's territorial salesmen can service the account. The extreme diversity of production patterns in different species of livestock and poultry, and in the various regions, is reflected by how producers buy livestock chemicals. It puts a premium on flexibility of the marketing organization in firms that would sell livestock chemicals in great volume.

Thus, the most generally successful approach to segmenting the market for livestock chemicals appears to involve:

1. a single marketing management;
2. multiplication of product offering to suit the needs of every major type and size of buyer; and
3. full-line offering in the field.

This is recognized as a somewhat less aggressive response to the segmentation possibilities inherent in the three major submarkets than its alternative—split operations through quasi-independent corporate subsidiaries.

The latter approach seems, eventually, to become a type of overresponse to the inherent segmenting possibilities. This conclusion suggests that there is an implied time dimension in identification of market segments. In the short run, before deep market penetration can be programmed, market segments can be identified by their close correspondence to prototype. In the long run, after enough time has elapsed to sell a market segment in real depth, this deeper penetration takes the marketer past the clear-cut, close-to-prototype customers, and into the areas populated by cross-over customers who are only partly in that segment. It is not a matter of the market segment becoming illusory; these are real concepts. Rather, it is a case where the validity limits of the segment identification have been finally reached.

In contrast, the more flexible approach toward segmenting the livestock chemical submarkets—exemplified by Cyanamid, Merck, and Pfizer—represents a more mature form of segmentation strategy, in this industry at least. A view of the organizational history of these firms tends to verify this thesis. At one point or another in the past, all three of these firms have had marketing organizations that incorporated some of the philosophy of the completely separate-sales-force-*cum*-different-label approach. For example, the licensed veterinarian submarket was, in the past, singled out by Cyanamid to sell under the Lederle label, by Merck under the Merck, Sharp & Dohme label, and by Pfizer under a special brown label. In time, however, with deeper market penetration accompanied by a stream of new products, these special submarket labels were sloughed off as the present segmentation strategy crystallized and emphasis shifted to offering many products tailored to submarkets under one corporate label and one marketing management.

Market segmentation is the strategy of divide-and-conquer, and its implementation takes many forms. Like Molière's character who had been speaking prose all his life without realizing it, all firms practice market segmentation to some degree, mostly without conscious formalization of it as corporate strategy. In order that market segmenting action by any firm qualify as part of a general strategy, there should be a background of a more or less *continuous* search for identifiable submarkets plus *continuous* exploitation of them.

In their purest form, segmentation actions require imagination and creativity but are compensated for by higher sales volume. The operative criterion, however, in weighing such segmenting action as product-line diversification has traditionally been profitability.

Numerous examples from everyday life suggest that secular trends are altering certain equations in favor of more extensive segmentation as the profit-maximizing strategy for more and more firms. A few of the postwar demographic, sociological, and business factors contributing to this development were mentioned.

The livestock-chemical industry was analyzed for applications of segmentation strategy. Three major submarkets were described. Companies broadly involved in livestock chemicals were found to practice two kinds of market segmentation: one based on sales force diversification, which in its purest form is operation under differently named quasi-independent subsidiaries in each submarket; the other emphasizing product-line diversification under one label and one marketing management. While the first approach is widely used, and undoubtedly is a promising avenue of expansion for firms now only modestly involved in livestock chemicals, it was concluded that long-run sales maximization in the interrelated and shifting livestock-chemical markets requires the greater flexibility of the second approach. The areas of cross-over products and mixed channels of distribution emphasize the need for flexibility, in order to be sure that all bases are covered—by product as well as by field sales effort.

It was concluded that the other market segmentation approach in livestock chemicals, based on split operations through separate corporate subsidiaries, becomes in the long run a form of overresponse to the segmenting possibilities inherent in identification of the three submarkets. This conclusion led to the suggestion that there may be a time dimension implied in the identification of any market segment. In the short run, a firm can identify a market segment by the close correspondence of customers to a prototype. In the long run, after that market segment has been sold in depth, the marketer works himself into areas populated by cross-over customers who are only partly true to prototype. Thus, the validity limits of the segment are finally reached. And it is at that point that a too rigid marketing organization, one that attempts to institutionalize segmental distinctions, becomes an instrument of less than optimum efficiency.

# 18. NEW CRITERIA FOR MARKET SEGMENTATION

*Daniel Yankelovich*

*Demography is not the only or the best way to segment markets.*

*Even more crucial to marketing objectives are differences in buyer attitudes, motivations, values, patterns of usage, aesthetic preferences, and degree of susceptibility.*

*Through a number of examples the author points out how criteria other than demographic ones have led to a creative form of segmentation, which in turn have provided new marketing opportunities for a firm.*

The director of marketing in a large company is confronted by some of the most difficult problems in the history of U.S. industry. To assist him, the information revolution of the past decade puts at his disposal a vast array of techniques, facts, and figures. But without a way to master this information, he can easily be overwhelmed by the reports that flow in to him incessantly from marketing research, economic forecasts, cost analyses, and sales breakdowns. He must have more than mere access to mountains of data. He must himself bring to bear a method of analysis that cuts through the detail to focus sharply on new opportunities.

In this article, I shall propose such a method. It is called *segmentation analysis.* It is based on the proposition that once you discover the most useful ways of segmenting a market, you have produced the beginnings of a sound marketing strategy.

Source: From *Harvard Business Review*, vol. 42, March–April, 1964, pp. 83–90. Daniel Yankelovich: President of Daniel Yankelovich, Inc., marketing consultants.

## UNIQUE ADVANTAGES

Segmentation analysis has developed out of several key premises:

- In today's economy, each brand appears to sell effectively to only certain segments of any market and not to the whole market.
- Sound marketing objectives depend on knowledge of how segments which produce the most customers for a company's brands differ in requirements and susceptibilities from the segments which produce the largest number of customers for competitive brands.
- Traditional demographic methods of market segmentation do not usually provide this knowledge. Analyses of market segments by age, sex, geography, and income level are not likely to provide as much direction for marketing strategy as management requires.

Once the marketing director does discover the most pragmatically useful way of segmenting his market, it becomes a new standard for almost all his evaluations. He will use it to appraise competitive strengths and vulnerabilities, to plan his product line, to determine his advertising and selling strategy, and to set precise marketing objectives against which performance can later be measured. Specifically, segmentation analysis helps him to:

- direct the appropriate amounts of promotional attention and money to the most potentially profitable segments of his market;
- design a product line that truly parallels the demands of the market instead of one that bulks in some areas and ignores or scants other potentially quite profitable segments;
- catch the first sign of a major trend in a swiftly changing market and thus give him time to prepare to take advantage of it;
- determine the appeals that will be most effective in his company's advertising; and, where several different appeals are significantly effective, quantify the segments of the market responsive to each;
- choose advertising media more wisely and determine the proportion of budget that should be allocated to each medium in the light of anticipated impact;
- correct the timing of advertising and promotional efforts so that they are massed in the weeks, months, and seasons when selling resitance is least and responsiveness is likely to be at its maximum;
- understand otherwise seemingly meaningless demographic market information and apply it in scores of new and effective ways.

These advantages hold in the case of both packaged goods and hard goods, and for commercial and industrial products as well as consumer products.

*Guides to Strategy.* Segmentation analysis cuts through the data facing a marketing director when he tries to set targets based on markets as a whole, or when he relies primarily on demographic breakdowns. It is a systematic approach that permits the marketing planner to pick the strategically most important segmentations and then to design brands, products, packages, communications, and marketing strategies around them. It infinitely simplifies the setting of objectives.

In the following sections we shall consider nondemographic ways of segmenting markets. These ways dramatize the point that finding marketing opportunities by depending solely on demographic breakdowns is like trying to win a national election by relying only on the information in a census. A modern census contains useful data, but it identifies neither the crucial issues of an election, nor those groups whose voting habits are still fluid, nor the needs, values, and attitudes that influence how those groups will vote. This kind of information, rather than census-type data, is the kind that wins elections—and markets.

Consider, for example, companies like Procter & Gamble, General Motors, or American Tobacco, whose multiple brands sell against one another and must, every day, win new elections in the marketplace:

> These companies sell to the whole market, not by offering one brand that appeals to all people, but by covering the different segments with multiple brands. How can they prevent these brands from cannibalizing each other? How can they avoid surrendering opportunities to competitors by failing to provide brands that appeal to all important segments? In neither automobiles, soaps, nor cigarettes do demographic analyses reveal to the manufacturer what products to make or what products to sell to what segments of the market. Obviously, some modes of segmentation other than demographic are needed to explain why brands which differ so little nevertheless find their own niches in the market, each one appealing to a different segment.

The point at issue is not that demographic segmentation should be disregarded, but rather that it should be regarded as only one among many possible ways of analyzing markets. In fact, the key requirement of segmentation analysis is that the marketing director should never assume in advance that any one method of segmentation is the best. His first job should be to muster all probable segmentation and *then* choose the most meaningful ones to work with. This approach is analogous to that used in research in the physical sciences, where the hypothesis that best seems to explain the phenomena under investigation is the one chosen for working purposes.

## TEN MARKETS

In the following discussion we shall take ten markets for consumer and industrial products and see how they are affected by seven different modes of nondemographic segmentation. The products and modes are shown schematically in Figure 1. Of course, these segments are not the only ones important in business. The seven I have picked are only *examples* of how segmentation analysis can enlarge the scope and depth of a marketer's thinking.

### I. Watches

In this first case we deal with a relatively simple mode of segmentation analysis. The most productive way of analyzing the market for watches turns out to be segmentation by *value*. This approach discloses three distinct segments, each representing a different value attributed to watches by each of three different groups of consumers:

Figure 1. Example of segmentation in different industries

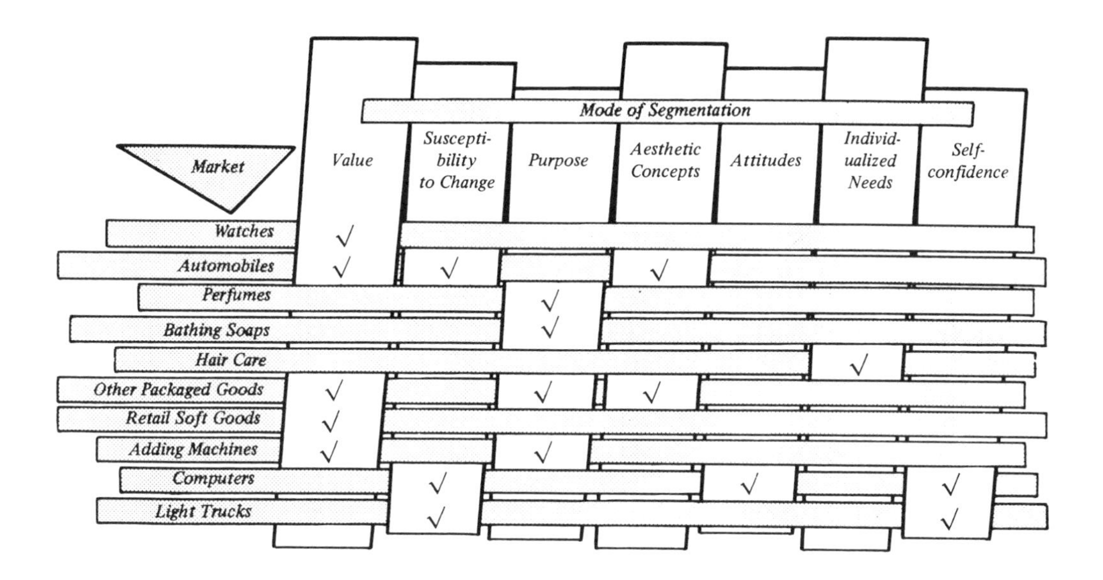


1. People who want to pay the lowest possible price for any watch that works reasonably well. If the watch fails after six months or a year, they will throw it out and replace it.
2. People who value watches for their long life, good workmanship, good material, and good styling. They are willing to pay for these product qualities.
3. People who look not only for useful product features but also for meaningful emotional qualities. The most important consideration in this segment is that the watch should suitably symbolize an important occasion. Consequently, fine styling, a well-known brand name, the recommendation of the jeweler, and a gold or diamond case are highly valued.

In 1962, my research shows, the watch market divided quantitatively as follows:

- Approximately 23 per cent of the buyers bought for lowest price (value segment #1).
- Another 46 per cent bought for durability and general product quality (value segment #2).
- And 31 per cent bought watches as symbols of some important occasion (value segment #3).

Defining and quantifying such segments is helpful in marketing planning—especially if a watch company's product happens to appeal mostly to one segment or if the line straddles the three segments, failing to appeal effectively to any. Without such an understanding, the demographic characteristics of the market are most confusing. It turns out, for example, that the most expensive watches are being bought by people with both the highest and the lowest incomes. On the other hand, some upper income consumers are no longer buying costly watches, but are buying cheap, well-styled watches to throw away when they require servicing. Other upper income consumers, however, continue to buy fine, expensive watches for suitable occasions.

*Timex's Timely Tactics.* The planning implications in value segmentation are very broad for the industry. For one thing, many of the better watch companies in the years between 1957 and 1962 were inadvertently focusing exclusively on the third segment described—the 31 per cent of the market that bought a watch only as a gift on important occasions—thus leaving the bulk of the market open to attack and exploitation.

The U.S. Time Company took advantage of this opening and established a very strong position among the more than two-thirds of America's watch buyers in the first two segments. Its new low-price watch, the Timex, had obvious appeal for the first segment, and it catered to the second segment as well. At that time, higher-priced watches were making the disastrous mistake in their advertising of equating product quality with waterproof and shock-resistant features. The Timex also offered these low-cost features, at lower prices, thus striking at a vulnerable area which the competition itself created. When Timex pressed its attack, it was able within a few years to claim that "Timex sells more watches than any other watch company in the world."

Even the *timing* of Timex's watch advertising was involved. Much of the third segment was buying watches only during the Christmas season, and so most of Timex's competitors concentrated their advertising in November and December. But since buying by the other two segments went on all the time, Timex advertised all year-around, getting exclusive attention ten months of the year.

Thus, nondemographic segmentation in the watch industry has directly affected almost every phase of marketing, including the composition of the product line. Major watch companies know that they must plan product line, pricing, advertising, and distribution within the framework of the three basic value segments of this market.

## II. Automobiles

The nondemographic segmentation of the automobile market is more complex than that of the watch market. The segments crisscross, forming intricate patterns. Their dynamics must be seen clearly before automobile sales can be understood.

Segmentation analysis leads to at least three different ways of classifying the automobile market along nondemographic lines, all of which are important to marketing planning.

*Value Segmentation.* The first mode of segmentation can be compared to that in the watch market—a threefold division along lines which represent how different people look at the meaning of *value* in an automobile:

1. People who buy cars primarily for economy. Many of these become owners of the Falcon, Ford, Rambler American, and Chevrolet. They are less loyal to any make than the other segments, but go where the biggest savings are to be found.
2. People who want to buy the best product they can find for their money. These prospects emphasize values such as body quality, reliability, durability, economy of operation, and ease of upkeep. Rambler and Volkswagen have been successful because so many people in this segment were dissatisfied.
3. People interested in "personal enhancement" (a more accurate description than "prestige"). A handsomely styled Pontiac or Thunderbird does a great deal for the owner's ego, even though the car may not serve as a status symbol. Although the value of an automobile as a status symbol has declined, the personal satisfaction in owning a fine car has not lessened for this segment of the market. It is interesting that while both watches and cars have declined in status value, they have retained *self-enhancement* value for large portions of the market.

Markets can change so swiftly, and the size of key segments can shift so rapidly, that great sensitivity is required to catch a trend in time to capitalize on it. In the automobile market, the biggest change in recent years has been the growth in segment two—the number of people oriented to strict product value. Only a few years ago, the bulk of the market was made up of the other segments, but now the product-value segment is probably the largest. Some automobile companies did not respond to this shift in the size of these market segments in time to maintain their share of the market.

*Aesthetic Concepts.* A second way of segmenting the automobile market is by differences in *style* preferences. For example, most automobile buyers tell you that they like "expensive looking" cars. To some people, however, "expensive looking" means a great deal of chrome and ornamentation, while to others it means the very opposite—clean, conservative lines, lacking much chrome or ornamentation.

Unfortunately, the same *words* are used by consumers to describe diametrically opposed style concepts. Data that quantify buyers according to their aesthetic *responses*—their differing conceptions of what constitutes a good looking car—are among the most useful an automobile company can possess.

The importance of aesthetic segmentation can be pointed up by this example:

> When Ford changed from its 1959 styling to its 1960 styling, the change did not seem to be a radical one from the viewpoint of formal design. But, because it ran contrary to the special style expectations of a large group of loyal Ford buyers, it constituted a dramatic and unwelcome change to them. This essential segment was not prepared for the change, and the results were apparent in sales.

*Susceptibility to Change.* A third and indispensable method of segmenting the automobile market cuts across the lines drawn by the other two modes of segmentation analysis. This involves measuring the relative susceptibility of potential car buyers to changing their choice of make. Consider the buyers of Chevrolet during any one year from the point of view of a competitor:

- At one extreme are people whose brand loyalty is so solidly entrenched that no competitor can get home to them. They always buy Chevrolets. They are closed off to change.
- At the other extreme are the open-minded and the unprejudiced buyers. They happened to buy a Chevrolet because they preferred its styling that year, or because they got a good buy, or because someone talked up the Fisher body to them. They could just as easily have purchased another make.
- In the middle of this susceptibility continuum are people who are predisposed to Chevrolet to a greater or lesser degree. They can be persuaded to buy another make, but the persuasion has to be strong enough to break through the Chevrolet predisposition.

The implications of this kind of a susceptibility segmentation are far-reaching. Advertising effectiveness, for example, must be measured against each susceptibility segment, not against the market as a whole. Competitors' advertising should appear in media most likely to break through the Chevrolet predisposition of the middle group. In addition, the wants of those who are not susceptible must be factored out, or they will muddy the picture. Marketing programs persuasive enough to influence the uncommitted may make no difference at all to the single largest group—those who are predisposed to Chevrolet but still open enough to respond to the right stimulus.

If the marketing director of an automobile company does not break down his potential market into segments representing key differences in susceptibility, or does not clearly understand the requirements of each key segment, his company can persevere for years with little or no results because its promotion programs are inadvertently being aimed at the wrong people.

### III. Perfume

A segmentation analysis of the perfume market shows that a useful way to analyze it is by the different *purposes* women have in mind when they buy perfume.

One segment of the market thinks of a perfume as something to be added to what nature has supplied. Another segment believes that the purpose of fragrance products is to help a woman feel cleaner, fresher, and better groomed—to correct or negate what nature has supplied. In the latter instance, the fragrance product is used to *cancel out* natural body odors; in the former, to *add* a new scent. To illustrate this difference in point of view:

- One woman told an interviewer, "I like a woodsy scent like Fabergé. It seems more intense and lingers longer, and doesn't fade away like the sweeter scents."
- But another woman said, "I literally loathe Fabergé. It makes me think of a streetcar full of women coming home from work who haven't bathed."

These differences in reaction do not indicate objective differences in the scent of Fabergé. They are subjective differences in women's attitudes; they grow out of each woman's purpose in using a perfume.

Purposive segmentation, as this third mode of analysis might be called, has been of great value to alert marketers. For instance:

A company making a famous line of fragrance products realized that it was selling almost exclusively to a single segment, although it had believed it was competing in the whole market. Management had been misled by its marketing research, which had consistently shown no differences in the demographic characteristics of women buying the company's products and women buying competitors' products.

In the light of this insight, the company decided to allocate certain lines to the underdeveloped segments of the market. This required appropriate changes in the scent of the product and in its package design. A special advertising strategy was also developed, involving a different copy approach for each product line aimed at each segment.

In addition, it was learned that visualizations of the product in use helped to create viewer identification in the segment that used perfume for adding to nature's handiwork, but that more subtle methods of communication produced better results among the more reserved, more modest women in the second segment who want the "canceling out" benefits of perfume. The media susceptibilities of women in the two segments were also found to be different.

Thus, from a single act of resegmentation, the advertising department extrated data critical to its copy platform, communication strategy, and media decisions.

## IV. Bathing Soap

A comparable purposive segmentation was found in the closely related bathing soap field. The key split was between women whose chief requirement of soap was that it should clean them adequately and those for whom bathing was a sensuous and enjoyable experience. The company (a new contender in this highly competitive field) focused its sights on the first segment, which had been much neglected in recent years. A new soap was shaped, designed, and packaged to appeal to this segment, a new advertising approach was evolved, and results were very successful.

## V. Hair-Care Market

The Breck-Halo competition in the shampoo market affords an excellent example of another kind of segmentation. For many years, Breck's recognition of the market's individualized segmentation gave the company a very strong position. Its line of individualized shampoos included one for dry hair, another for oily hair, and one for normal hair. This line accurately paralleled the marketing reality that women think of their hair as being dry, oily, or normal, and they do not believe that any one shampoo (such as an all-purpose Halo) can meet their individual requirements. Colgate has finally been obliged, in the past several years, to revise its long-held marketing approach to Halo, and to come out with products for dry hair and for oily hair, as well as for normal hair.

Other companies in the hair-care industry are beginning to recognize other segmentations in this field. For example, some women think of their hair as fine, others as coarse. Each newly discovered key segmentation contains the seeds of a new product, a new marketing approach, and a new opportunity.

## VI. Other Packaged Goods

Examples of segmentation analysis in other packaged goods can be selected almost at random. Let us mention a few briefly, to show the breadth of applicability of this method of marketing analysis:

- In *convenience foods,* for example, we find that the most pragmatic classification is, once again, purposive segmentation. Analysis indicates that "convenience" in foods has many different meanings for women, supporting several different market segments. Women for whom convenience means "easy to use" are reached by products and appeals different from those used to reach women for whom convenience means shortcuts to creativity in cooking.
- In the market for *cleaning agents,* some women clean preventively, while others clean therapeutically, i.e., only after a mess has been made. The appeals, the product characteristics, and the marketing approach must take into account these different reasons for buying—another example of purposive segmentation.
- In still another market, some people use *air fresheners* to remove disagreeable odors and others to add an odor. A product like Glade, which is keyed to the second segment, differs from one like Airwick in product concept, packaging, and type of scent.
- The *beer market* requires segmentation along at least four different axes—reasons for drinking beer (purposive); taste preferences (aesthetic); price/quality (value); and consumption level.

## VII. Retail Soft Goods

Although soft-goods manufacturers and retailers are aware that their customers are value conscious, not all of them realize that their markets break down into at least four different segments corresponding to four different conceptions of value held by women.

For some women value means a willingness to pay a little more for quality. For others, value means merchandise on sale. Still other women look for value in terms of the lowest possible price, while others buy seconds or discounted merchandise as representing the best value.

Retailing operations like Sears, Roebuck are highly successful because they project *all* these value concepts, and do so in proportions which closely parallel their distribution in the total population.

## VIII. Adding Machines

In marketing planning for a major adding machine manufacturer, analysis showed that his product line had little relationship to the segmented needs of the market. Like most manufacturers of this kind of product, he had designed his line by adding features to one or several stripped-down basic models—each addition raising the model price. The lowest priced model could only add; it could not subtract, multiply, divide, or print, and it was operated by hand.

Since there are a great many features in adding machines, the manufacturer had an extremely long product line. When the needs of the market were analyzed, however, it became clear that, despite its length, the line barely met the needs of two out of the three major segments of the market. It had been conceived and planned from a logical point of view rather than from a market-need point of view.

The adding machine market is segmented along lines reflecting sharp differences in value and purpose:

- One buyer group values accuracy, reliability, and long life above all else. It tends to buy medium-price, full-keyboard, electric machines. There are many banks and other institutions in this group where full-keyboard operations are believed to ensure accuracy.
- Manufacturing establishments, on the other hand, prefer the ten-key machine. Value, to these people, means the maximum number of laborsaving and timesaving features. They are willing to pay the highest prices for such models.
- Both these segments contrast sharply with the third group, the small retailer whose major purpose is to find a model at a low purchase price. The small retailer does not think in terms of amortizing his investment over a period of years, and neither laborsaving features nor full-keyboard reliability count for as much as an immediate savings in dollars.

Despite the many models in the company's line, it lacked those demanded by both the manufacturer and small retailer segments of the market. But, because it had always been most sensitive to the needs of financial institutions, it had developed more models for this segment than happened to be needed. Product, sales, and distribution changes were required to enable the company to compete in the whole market.

## IX. Computers

One pragmatic way of segmenting the computer market is to divide potential customers between those who believe they know how to evaluate a computer and those who believe they do not. A few years ago only about 20 per cent of the market was really open to IBM's competitors—the 20 per cent who believed it knew how to evaluate a computer. By default, this left 80 per cent of the market a virtual captive of IBM—the majority who did not have confidence in its own ability to evaluate computers and who leaned on IBM's reputation as a substitute for personal appraisal.

Another segmentation in this market involves differences in prospects' attitudes toward the inevitability of progress. Although this factor has been widely ignored, it is a significant method for qualifying prospects. People who believe that progress is inevitable (i.e., that change is good and that new business methods are constantly evolving) make far better prospects for computers than those who have a less optimistic attitude toward progress in the world of business.

## X. Light Trucks

The market for light trucks affords us another example of segmentation in products bought by industry. As in the computer example, there are both buyers who lack confidence in their ability to choose among competing makes and purchasers who feel they are sophisticated about trucks and can choose knowledgeably. This mode of segmentation unexpectedly turns out to be a key to explaining some important dynamics of the light truck market:

> Those who do not trust their own judgment in trucks tend to rely very heavily on both the dealer's and the manufacturer's reputations. Once they find a make that gives them reliability and trouble-free operation, they cease to shop other makes and are no longer susceptible to competitive promotion. Nor are they as price-sensitive as the buyer who thinks he is sophisticated about trucks. This buyer tends to look for the best price, to shop extensively, and to be susceptible to the right kind of competitive appeals, because he puts performance before reputation.

These ways of looking at the truck market have far-reaching implications for pricing policy, for product features, and for dealers' sales efforts.

## CONCLUSION

To sum up the implications of the preceding analysis, let me stress three points:

1. We should discard the old, unquestioned assumption that demography is always the best way of looking at markets.

   The demographic premise implies that differences in reasons for buying, in brand choice influences, in frequency of use, or in susceptibility will be reflected in differences in age, sex, income, and geographical location. But this is usually not true. Markets should be scrutinized for important differences in buyer attitudes, motivations, values, usage patterns, aesthetic preferences, or degree of susceptibility. These may have no demographic correlatives. Above all, we must never assume in advance that we know the best way of looking at a market. This is the cardinal rule of segmentation analysis. All ways of segmenting markets might be considered, and *then* we must select out of the various methods available the ones that have the most important implications for action. This process of choosing the strategically most useful mode of segmentation is the essence of the marketing approach espoused in this article.

   In considering cases like those described, we must understand that we are not dealing with different types of people, but with differences in peoples' *values.* A woman who buys a refrigerator because it is the cheapest available may want to buy the most expensive towels. A man who pays extra for his beer may own a cheap watch. A Ford-owning Kellogg's Corn Flakes-eater may be closed off to Chevrolet but susceptible to Post Toasties; he is the same man, but he has had different experiences and holds different values toward each product he purchases. By segmenting markets on the basis of the values, purposes, needs, and attitudes relevant to the product being studied, as in Figure 1, we avoid misleading information derived from attempts to divide people into types.

2. The strategic-choice concept of segmentation broadens the scope of marketing planning to include the positioning of new products as well as of established products.

It also has implications for brand planning, not just for individual products but for the composition of a line of competing brands where any meaningful segment in the market can possibly support a brand. One explanation of the successful competing brand strategy of companies like Procter & Gamble is that they are based on sensitivity to the many different modes of market segmentation. The brands offered by P & G often appear very similar to the outsider, but small, marginal differences between them appeal to different market segments. It is this rather than intramural competition that supports P & G successes.

3. Marketing must develop its own interpretive theory, and not borrow a ready-made one from the social sciences.

Marketing research, as an applied science, is tempted to borrow its theoretical structures from the disciplines from which it derives. The social sciences offer an abundance of such structures, but they are not applicable to marketing in their pure academic form. While the temptation to apply them in that form is great, it should be resisted. From sociology, for example, marketing has frequently borrowed the concept of status. This is a far-reaching concept, but it is not necessarily the most important one in a marketing problem, nor even one of the important ones. Again, early psychoanalytic theory has contributed an understanding of the sexual factor. While this can sometimes be helpful in an analysis of buying behavior in a given situation, some motivation researchers have become oversensitive to the role of sex and, as a result, have made many mistakes. Much the same might be said of the concept of social character, that is, seeing the world as being "inner-directed," "other-directed," "tradition-directed," "autonomous," and so forth.

One of the values of segmentation analysis is that, while it has drawn on the insights of social scientists, it has developed an interpretive theory *within* marketing. It has been homegrown in business. This may explain its ability to impose patterns of meaning on the immense diversity of the market, and to provide the modern marketing director with a systematic method for evolving true marketing objectives.

# 19. SEGMENTATION BY PERSONALITY TYPES

*Morris J. Gottlieb*

*Since there are so many different ways in which a market can be segmented, it is important to consider various methods.*

*The following selection is an interesting example of segmentation by personality types.*

Every practitioner of marketing research has at one time or another been approached by a sales or advertising executive with a problem stated in terms such as these– "Look," the executive will say, "it's really quite simple. All I want to do is to talk to the people who are buying my product and ask them why they buy it. Then, I want to get the people who are not buying it and ask them why they're *not* buying it."

Really, this is a very reasonable request. It has only three false premises:

1. That it's really quite simple. It practically never is.
2. That you can find out why by asking.
3. That it would necessarily be helpful to know why.

Nevertheless, the request generally stems from a genuine need to know and it is the market researcher's job to find out enough of why people do or do not buy one product rather than another or one brand rather than another to help management do a better marketing job.

Source: From Lynn H. Stockman (ed.), *Advancing Marketing Efficiency,* American Marketing Association, Chicago, 1958, pp. 148–158. Morris J. Gottlieb: Vice-president, Market Facts, Inc., Chicago.

One of the modest but important trends in modern marketing research has been to transform these "why" questions into "who" questions. The general idea is that if you know in sufficiently meaningful terms *who* is and *who* is not buying the product or who is and who is not a *potential* customer you really know *why* as well.

I'd really like to be able to say that I am going to expound the strategy of market segmentation by personality types, but it will be helpful to think of this segmentation as a research strategy rather than a marketing strategy. Hopefully, it will yield results which would suggest market segmentation strategies.

Rather than attempting to outline a general technique, I shall restrict myself to illustrating some cases where this concept seemed to be useful and discuss some of the limitations as well as the possibilities of this approach.

The first product is a proprietary medicine. It is an antacid and analgesic or pain killer which is sold mainly through drug stores and does not require a prescription. Let's call it Brominex. There are many directly competitive products in the proprietary field. However, the product class boundaries tend to become rather vague—extending from home remedies such as bicarbonate of soda or even water or orange juice on the one hand to analgesics such as aspirin on the other. In addition, many products in this category are prescribed by doctors.

For the purposes of this discussion, the product class was defined as proprietary products which are primarily combinations of antacids and analgesics. The bulk of this market is divided among seven or eight well-known products.

Our hope is that if we can find out how users of antacid-analgesics differ from non-users or how frequent users differ from infrequent users we can learn enough to help us locate the potential Brominex user and to reach him successfully.

At first thought it might seem a very simple matter to define the market for this type of product as simply the people who have upset stomachs and headaches. But it might be of use to know whether any particular type of person tends to have these symptoms. A little introspection will probably convince you of the difficulty of trying to pin down these symptoms. There is actually a considerable element of discretion in judging at what point you have an upset stomach or a headache bad enough to make you use an analgesic.

One person will choose to put up with any amount of pain or discomfort rather than take anything. Another will take something at the slightest suggestion of anything wrong, or as a preventive measure. Another will choose to see a doctor who may prescribe something else.

It is precisely in this kind of a situation that the "who" question is interesting. By understanding the differences between users and non-users—or between frequent and infrequent users of a completely discretionary product we can understand more precisely what needs the product class is satisfying and hopefully how the marketing of our product can be effectively geared to this need.

Now, most of the trick in getting useful answers to the "who" question is to ask it the right way. The more thought given to outlining the various dimensions along which to compare users and non-users the more useful the answers will be.

It is generally stated that at this stage of an investigation depth interviewing is of the most use. However, the older I get, the more it is brought home to me that depth interviewing is at best a supplement to and not a substitute for deep thinking.

The only method is to learn the subject thoroughly, to observe carefully with an open mind, to listen to the experts in the field—whether there are any real experts or not. Past experience will suggest many possibilities. Finally, it helps to be insightful, incisive, and wise.

In the Brominex problem, we started by getting some medical counsel. Doctors told us that middle-aged men are the most frequent sufferers from this kind of condition.

One could further anticipate that frequent users of such products would be common among the lower income groups and groups with a lower educational level because of cultural and economic factors. In any event, one always tries segmenting the market by age, sex, and income whenever there is an adequate sample and in this case there was one.

This analysis showed that age and sex were dominant factors in use, and that use tends to be greater at the lower educational levels in each of the age and sex groups. However, since use is not *completely* universal in the higher usage groups nor completely absent in the lower usage groups, one feels that *other* factors must be operating as well.

It seems a fairly sound principle to examine any factors which reflect group or other cultural influences before turning to an examination of individual characteristics distinguishing users and non-users.

One might suspect that geographic factors would influence usage. However, while usage *is* higher in the South—among white as well as non-white—it turns out upon analysis that this is almost entirely a reflection of income and education. Similarly, a greater usage among non-white in the North also reflects income and educational factors. In fact, since education is an important factor in use, one would expect any cultural factors—such as differing ethnic origin—to be cancelled out by education, and in fact this seems to be the case.

Now, one form of education that bears directly on use of this kind of product is based on contact with doctors. One would suspect that people who have more contact with doctors tend to use these products less, since doctors tend to focus on the cause of these symptoms and would be inclined to counsel changes in diet or some form of medical treatment, rather than on the use of proprietary products. However, this study showed that exposure to doctors had no effect on usage for two different reasons:

1. Since there was no accurate way of determining who had the symptoms more frequently, the two factors—existence of symptoms leading to increased usage, and

exposure to doctors presumably leading to decreased usage—tended to be confounded and to cancel each other out.

2. Examination of some medical histories showed that doctors rarely discussed the use of this type of product with their patients, so that it would be quite possible that while the doctors might have counseled the patient against the use of such products had the subject come up, the subject rarely came up.

At this point it would seem natural to consider some of the social pressures that might be operating to influence usage of this type of product. However, the social class position information was found to add relatively little to education data.

Now, the use of this type of product is generally a pretty personal affair, so that one suspects that there is a great deal of room for individual personality variables to affect the use of antacid-analgesics.

Given one's cultural background and susceptibility to the relevant symptoms, one suspects that attitudes towards one's own health would affect the decision to use a proprietary medicine. It is significant that use tends to be higher among hypochondriacs—or at least among people who show a greater than average concern with their health. Thus, in the accompanying chart, people who expect a great deal of illness tend to use antacid-analgesics more frequently.

This chart is about men. Note that for every age group and for each educational level, usage is greater among people with a *poor* opinion of their health than among those with a good opinion of their health—with only one exception.

*Usage Related to Health Attitudes*

| | *Average annual dosage* | | | | | |
|---|---|---|---|---|---|---|
| *Age* | *35 or under* | | *36–50* | | *Over 50* | |
| *Health attitude* | *Poor* | *Good* | *Poor* | *Good* | *Poor* | *Good* |
| Low educational level | 4.1 | 3.9 | 14.2 | 12.2 | 13.5 | 5.8 |
| High educational level | 3.2 | 3.4 | 15.7 | 10.8 | 11.5 | 4.9 |

The questions I'd like to answer here are:

1. How do you decide which attitude or temperament variables to examine?
2. Of what earthly use is the information?

Answer the first question by saying—deep thinking. But the fact is that while this finding of the relation between hypochondria and antacid-analgesic usage seems just what you'd expect after you see it, it was called to our attention rather dramatically by some depth interviews which were really intensive case histories. In some twenty case histories it was obvious that the more frequent users were all marked hypochondriacs and the non-users were people who were aggressive in their assertions that they enjoyed perfect health.

Back in the early days of marketing research—three or four years ago—there would have been many people in the marketing research business who would have been content to take the results of these twenty interviews and form conclusions. But enough of us feel the need for a sample large enough to permit an analysis of the relation between different factors.

The answer to the second question is that to be effective, the advertising message must take into account the health attitudes of the potential user. One would expect to communicate one way with a person who hated to admit that he was ill and was only seeking relief for a well-localized symptom, and another way with a person who complained about various vague aches and pains and was possibly seeking to allay non-specific anxieties.

Another personality variable which appears to differentiate users of this product class is what one might call "compulsiveness." This is measured by the extent of agreement or disagreement with such statements as:

- I like to set up a schedule for my activities and then stick to it.
- I never seem to be able to throw things away.
- Most people don't keep themselves as clean as they should.
- I make decisions only after a great deal of thought.

The following chart shows the effect of compulsiveness—as measured by agreement with the first of these statements on antacid-analgesic usage.

*Usage Related to Compulsiveness*

| | *Average annual dosage* | | | | | |
|---|---|---|---|---|---|---|
| *Age* | *35 or under* | | *36–50* | | *Over 50* | |
| | *Compulsive* | *Non compulsive* | *Compulsive* | *Non compulsive* | *Compulsive* | *Non compulsive* |
| Low education | 6.5 | 4.2 | 14.5 | 9.9 | 9.2 | 10.0 |
| High education | 3.5 | 2.8 | 13.9 | 12.9 | 8.2 | 4.5 |

The significance of this factor is illustrated by the fact that our client had been having considerable success with an advertising campaign based on a principal theme which was in itself ineffective. However, the advertising presented Brominex in the context of a routine or schedule or regimen. It seemed to be this element of imposed orderly routine which was appealing to the compulsive tendencies of the users of this product class. Incidentally, establishing this conjecture required a secondary analysis to show that compulsives were more attracted by the advertisement in question than non-compulsives.

Still another area which was relevant in the examination of this product class was the attitude toward discipline and punishment. Some people tend to be punitive or puritanical, others permissive. People who tend to be more self-punitive rather than hedonistic in their outlook might want a medicine that gives relief to taste bad in order to do them good. The analysis of this factor is interesting because it illustrates an ever-present pitfall in considerations of this sort. Our first conclusion was that *punitiveness* is positively associated with usage. Here, punitiveness is measured by agreement with such statements as:

- People learn a great deal from suffering.
- Discipline is the single most important factor in building children's character.

However, it can be seen from the following chart that if one shows the appropriate regard for the basic variables of age and education, the opposite is the case. Within any age-education cell, punitive people use less than non-punitive ones. What misled us at the outset was the compound effect that:

1. Lower education groups tend to have more punitive attitudes, and
2. Lower education groups tend to use more antacid-analgesics.

The fallacious conclusion that antacid-analgesic users tend to have more punitive attitudes was avoided by observing that *within* a given age-education stratum, usage is *negatively* rather than positively associated with punitiveness. In other words, it is *not* necessary or desirable that the product should taste bad.

*Usage Related to Punitiveness*

| | *Average annual dosage* | | | | | |
|---|---|---|---|---|---|---|
| *Age* | *35 or under* | | *36–50* | | *Over 50* | |
| | *Punitive* | *Non-punitive* | *Punitive* | *Non-punitive* | *Punitive* | *Non-punitive* |
| Low education | 6.4 | 4.5 | 12.7 | 17.7 | 7.4 | 9.1 |
| High education | 3.1 | 3.9 | 13.6 | 15.5 | 4.7 | 5.1 |

Now let's try to make the transition from research strategy to marketing strategy. On the basis of these findings one would expect the most successful product in this class to be a lower class product which made extensive claims,[1] advertised regular use, and tasted good. Actually the *single* dominant product in the field was one used widely by the higher status groups, which advertised very specific use and made fewer broad claims than other products. It was a product which had higher approval by doctors and hospitals than most others. It didn't taste particularly good but was in the process of correcting this defect; it was not our client's product.

The reason for the unexpected success of this leading product was simple. Instead of competing with other products for the most profitable segments of the antacid-analgesic market, that contrary product had captured the less prominent—but still highly significant minority segments—where it had no competitor.

Incidentally, this was a pleasant by-product of the study. Our client had been developing a different type of analgesic beamed toward this segment. The study confirmed his hunch that there was room for a competitive product here.

So, answering the *why* question with a *who* question had these positive results:

1. It pointed to an important segment which offered potential for a new product which our client was developing to supplement his present major product.
2. It enabled him to direct the advertising for his present major product more effectively since he knew whom he was speaking to.

Now let's examine some of the limitations and difficulties of this approach of segmentation by personality types.

It is interesting that the difference in usage between the various personality groups is not very large. Thus, it is not as large as the difference between age or sex groups or between social class groups.

This phenomenon occurs rather frequently. One might think that it was a function of scales or tests to characterize these groups. It is true that where one is dealing with a scalable characteristic and where it is possible to pick out the extremes, the differences between these extremes are a little larger, but even then the differences are often small.

It is probably not possible to address oneself to a clearly delineated compulsive group. *What one should do is to address himself to the compulsive in all of us.*

Social and personality variables operate in a kind of residual area left by the product considerations. The residual nature of these variables becomes even more pronounced for large ticket items where product or price considerations are more important.

For conspicuous consumption items, social class considerations are likely to outweigh personality factors. To illustrate this, another product generally consumed in public has implications of social status. This is a liquor product somewhat like a liqueur or cordial but used more widely than products of that type are generally. Let's call it *Bayou Rum.*

[1] It would have to cure many things to satisfy the hypochondriac.

Since this is a drink that would often be served in company, it is not surprising that it has a very definite social position. A broad cut at the subject by such variables as income and education shows that usage is greater *towards* but not *at* the upper end of the scale. (See Figure 1.)

This impression is reinforced by our looking at the relation between objective social class as measured by occupation and status orientation as measured by the person's assignment of himself to a social class. (See Figure 2.)

Here it is clear that our product is really a middle class drink.

The social position is spelled out even more clearly by relating usage to social mobility. Its use is by far the greatest among stable members of the middle class. (See Figure 3.)

How does one know whether he should be looking at social characteristics, at personality or temperament traits? Which traits are likely to be important? How deep should one go into motivations?

A passage from a recent book on Motivational Research by Harry Henry puts the matter interestingly. It says:

> This sort of case-history makes fascinating reading, for a time. But sooner or later the profit-conscious business-man is bound to ask himself what guidance this gives him for the formulation of manufacturing, marketing, or advertising policies. And it is for this reason that, . . . constructive and useful Motivation Research is concerned only with getting *sufficiently* below the surface to do the necessary job.

I don't think that anyone can disagree with this statement any more than anyone can use it for practical guidance. It is patently uneconomical to get more information or more depth than one needs. But I don't know of anyone who can be certain that he

**Figure 1. Bayou rum usage by education**

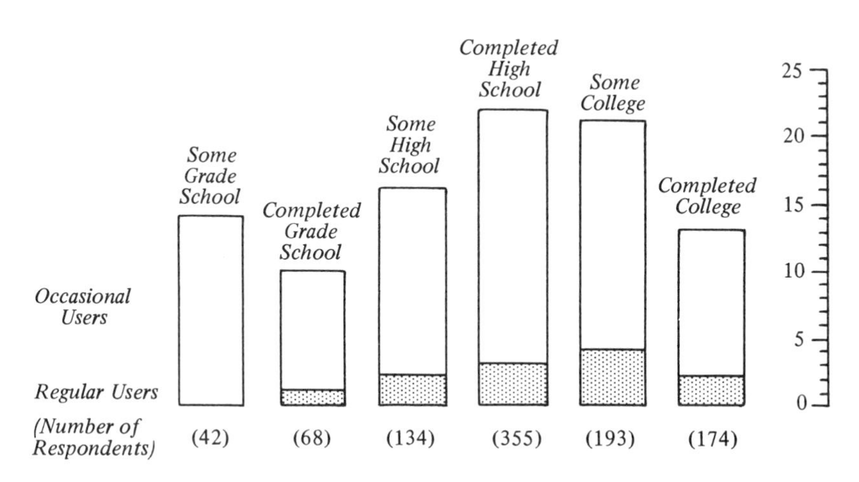

Figure 2. Bayou rum usage by social class

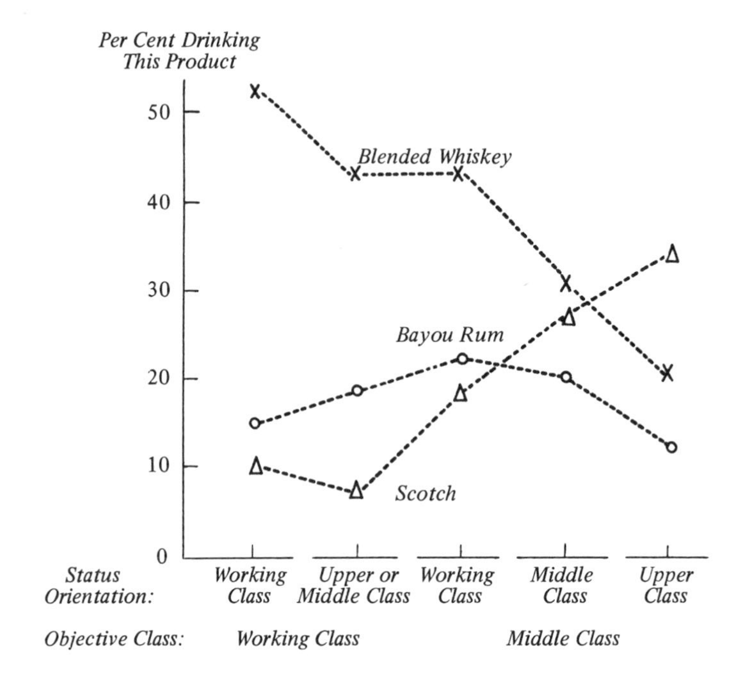


Figure 3. Bayou rum usage by social mobility

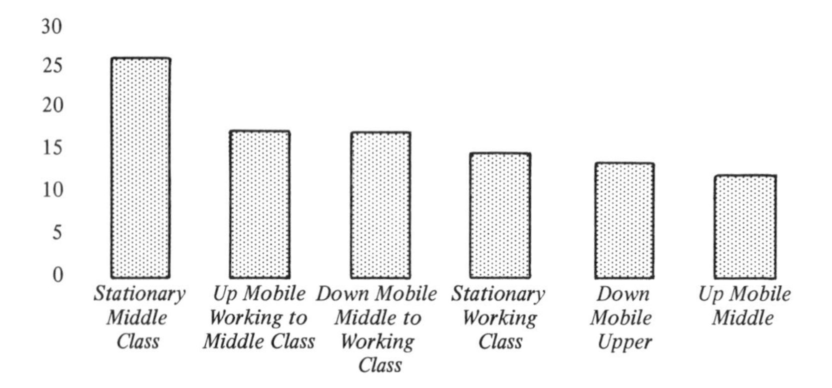

has enough information unless he has too much—at least in the sense of being able to select and reject, or who can be sure he's thought enough about something until he's thought too much.

Many of us in the marketing research profession pride ourselves on the desire to focus research on a specific marketing decision. True, this makes for efficient research. But I wonder if there isn't failure to understand all aspects of a problem. In fact, it is only when the researcher knows much more about a situation that he can profitably communicate an airtight case to management.

Finally, no matter how skillfully such an analysis has been conducted, the road to a marketing strategy is still tortuous. What starts out as a good idea based on sound research may lead to a poor strategy.

As we get more sophisticated in developing research which produces ideas leading to marketing strategies, we will have to start tackling seriously the tremendously difficult problem of testing these strategies—of measuirng advertising and marketing success and relating it to the specific components of the strategies developed.

# 20. FAMILY LIFE CYCLE AS AN INDEPENDENT VARIABLE[1]

*John B. Lansing and Leslie Kish*

*Family life cycle is a more accurate predictor of spending-unit consumption behavior than is age, according to sociologists Lansing and Kish.*

*Statistical data presented here imply that life-cycle status correlates with spending patterns better than do age groupings. It seems that life-cycle stages are in themselves partial causes of spending behavior and are more important causatives than ages of household heads or of housewives.*

Demographic variables, all too frequently, are used as independent variables in a mechanical way, without theory to guide in the selection of the variables appropriate to the study of the dependent variable under consideration, and without theory to guide the definitions of the variables themselves.[2] Sometimes this is due to the fact that data used in demographic research were collected primarily for other purposes. It is

[1] Expanded version of a paper presented at the 1956 meeting of the Population Association of America.

[2] The terms "independent variable" and "dependent variable" are in common use in regression analysis. This is unfortunate because of the possible confusion with "independent" as used in probability and statistics. Kendall suggests the use of two other terms, perhaps "predicated variate" and "predictand." See Maurice G. Kendall and William R. Buckland, *A Dictionary of Statistical Terms,* Oliver and Boyd for the International Statistical Institute, London, 1957, pp. 136, 225, 244–245.

Source: From *American Sociological Review,* vol. 22, October, 1957, pp. 512–518. John B. Lansing: Associate Professor of Economics, and Program Director in Survey Research Center of Institute for Social Research, University of Michigan. Leslie Kish: Associate Professor of Sociology, and Head of Sampling Section in Survey Research Center of Institute for Social Research, University of Michigan.

important in using demographic variables as predictors of behavior to pay close attention to the meaning of the variables. This paper reports the results of an attempt to increase the usefulness of one variable.

Age of person or of the head of a famliy is a traditional variable. It has several advantages such as uniformity of measurement, relatively easy and uniform acceptance, and the fact that it is a continuous metric scale. The advantage of age as a metric scale may be considerable when one works out formal correlations. But this advantage of age is not obtained when the results are analyzed and presented only in tables showing age in class intervals. In this paper we propose the "family life cycle" (FLC) as an alternative variable and will show some of its advantages, particularly in its greater "explanatory" power illustrated with several dependent variables. It is well known that changes occur in people's attitudes and behavior as they grow older, but many of these changes may be associated less with the biological process of aging than with the influence of age upon the individual's family memberships. Thus, the critical dates in the life of an individual may not be his birthdays so much as the days when a change occurs in his family status, for example, when he marries, or when his first child is born. (In this respect there is realism in the attitude of some primitive societies whose members are cognizant of their FLC status, but not of their birthdays.) To understand an individual's social behavior it may be more relevant to consider which stage in the life cycle he has reached than how old he is.

Much work on the life cycle has centered on the demographic problems of ascertaining the proportions of different life cycle classes in the population and of finding the ages at which people move from one stage to another. Some interesting time trends and urban-rural differences have been found.[3] We have discovered but few instances of quantitative results in which the life cycle was used as the independent variable, i.e., as a tool to "explain" variations in other social and economic variables.[4] It has been proposed that some mental disorders of old age may be "caused" more by life cycle roles within our social system than by age-determined biological deterioration.[5]

In the course of this research some theory of the life cycle has been built up, including some cross-cultural comparisons.[6] This theory is necessary to fit our empirical results into the web of broad social theory. Life cycle analysis depends on the existence of the conjugal family. An isolated conjugal family is needed to permit assignment

[3]Paul C. Glick, *American Families,* John Wiley & Sons, Inc., New York, 1957, especially pp. 53–70; Charles P. Loomis and J. Allan Beegle, *Rural Sociology,* Prentice-Hall, Inc., Englewood Cliffs, N.J., 1957, pp. 79–81; Charles P. Loomis and J. Allan Beegle, *Rural Social Systems,* Prentice-Hall, Inc., New York, 1950, pp. 77–87.

[4]John B. Lansing and James N. Morgan, "Consumer Finances Over the Life Cycle," in *The Life Cycle and Consumer Behavior,* edited by Lincoln Clark, New York University Press, New York, 1955; Gordon W. Blackwell, "Correlates of Stage of Family Development Among Farm Families on Relief," *Rural Sociology,* no. 7, June, 1942, pp. 161–174.

[5]Ivan Belknap and Hiram J. Friedsam, "Age and Sex Categories as Sociological Variables in the Mental Disorders of Later Maturity," *American Sociological Review,* no. 14, June, 1949, pp. 367–376.

[6]Charles P. Loomis, "Study of the Life Cycle of Families," *Rural Sociology*, no. 1, June, 1936, pp. 180–199.

of definite life spans and categories to each family; life cycle classification would be difficult in societies with consanguine families. Finally, the ordering of the FLC classes presupposes that most families make an orderly progression through a few life cycle classes. Actually, 3.8 per cent of our spending units are of unusual types so that we could not fit them into one of our seven categories at the time of interview.

We do not mean to insist on the particular classification of stages in the life cycle presented here. Other classifications have been suggested and used. To choose between two proposed classifications, we suggest the use of the measures employed here in comparing age with stage in the life cycle.

The dependent variables in this study are the income and spending of consumers as measured in a nationwide survey.[7] Table 1 presents the data on which the analysis is based. The two right hand columns show the distribution of the independent variables, and the remaining columns show the proportion of those of each age or in each stage with specified characteristics. We believe, however, that the essential features of these data can be best seen by looking at Figures 1–6.

**Figure 1. Per cent of spending units who own their own homes**

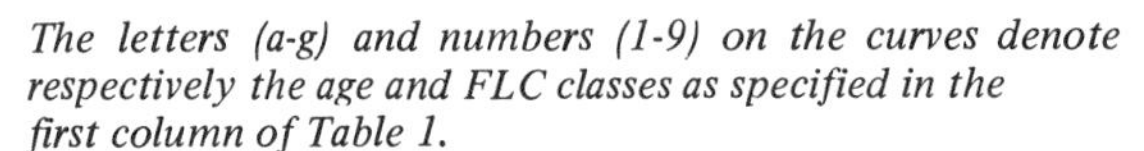


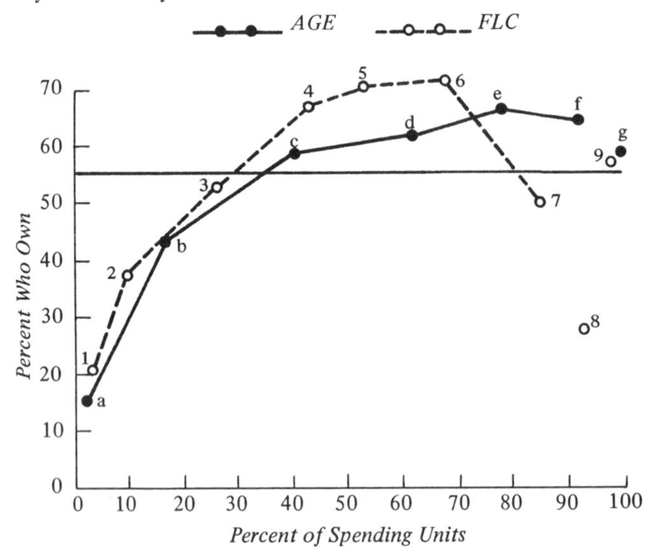


[7]The data reported are taken from the 1955 Survey of Consumer Finances conducted by the Survey Research Center in cooperation with the Federal Reserve Board.

Each figure shows the proportion of those in different classes who did something or have a certain characteristic. One problem that faced us was where to place the abscissa

**Table 1. Six economic characteristics for age classes and for stages in the family life cycle**

| | | *Proportions of spending units with each characteristic* | | | | | | *Proportions of independent variable* | |
|---|---|---|---|---|---|---|---|---|---|
| *Independent variable* | | *Own home* | *Have debts* | *Wife working* | *Income over $4000* | *Bought new car* | *Bought TV* | *Weight of class*†* *(a)* | *Midpoint of weight class†* *(b)* |
| *Age of head of spending unit* | | | | | | | | | |
| (a) | 18-24 | 15.4 | 58.7 | 14.2 | 15.5 | 6.0 | 10.7 | 8.0 | 4.0 |
| (b) | 25-34 | 43.0 | 76.3 | 24.8 | 55.0 | 9.5 | 18.2 | 23.0 | 19.5 |
| (c) | 35-44 | 58.7 | 76.1 | 25.9 | 61.2 | 10.8 | 16.8 | 22.6 | 42.3 |
| (d) | 45-54 | 61.4 | 65.2 | 23.6 | 56.2 | 8.1 | 14.1 | 17.3 | 62.2 |
| (e) | 55-64 | 65.9 | 48.2 | 14.5 | 40.6 | 7.0 | 12.7 | 14.0 | 77.9 |
| (f) | 65 and over | 63.4 | 31.2 | 5.5 | 12.7 | 2.2 | 5.8 | 12.9 | 91.3 |
| (g) | Not ascertained | 57.5 | 77.5 | 22.5 | 57.1 | 7.7 | 20.9 | 2.2 | 98.9 |
| | *All ages* | 55.2 | 63.2 | 20.0 | 46.0 | 7.9 | 14.0 | 100.0 | |
| *Stage in the life cycle of the family* | | | | | | | | | |
| (1) | Young single | 20.2 | 43.7 | 0.6 | 19.0 | 6.0 | 5.0 | 10.4 | 5.2 |
| (2) | Young married, no children | 37.3 | 72.2 | 57.2 | 66.4 | 14.3 | 12.9 | 7.1 | 14.0 |
| (3) | Young married, youngest child under six | 52.5 | 84.8 | 21.0 | 60.1 | 9.6 | 21.6 | 22.9 | 28.9 |
| (4) | Young married, youngest child six or older | 66.7 | 83.6 | 39.6 | 71.8 | 12.8 | 19.4 | 8.5 | 44.8 |
| (5) | Older married, children | 69.9 | 75.3 | 27.1 | 58.2 | 8.2 | 16.5 | 10.2 | 54.0 |
| (6) | Older married, no children | 71.4 | 48.5 | 21.8 | 47.9 | 7.7 | 12.2 | 18.2 | 68.2 |
| (7) | Older single | 49.2 | 32.6 | 0.3 | 15.6 | 1.9 | 6.7 | 13.2 | 83.9 |
| (8) | Others | 27.1 | 63.4 | 3.8 | 15.9 | 1.9 | 13.5 | 3.8 | 92.4 |
| (9) | Not ascertained | 56.3 | 65.4 | 14.2 | 37.7 | 7.8 | 15.9 | 5.7 | 97.1 |
| | *All stages* | 55.2 | 63.2 | 20.0 | 46.0 | 7.9 | 14.3 | 100.0 | |

*For home ownership the weights were slightly different because they were based on nonfarm families: for age they were 4.4, 23.8, 23.5, 18.3, 13.9, 13.7 and 2.4; for FLC they were 5.4, 7.6, 24.9, 9.2, 10.4, 19.2, 13.7, 3.7 and 5.9

†In column (a) are given the $w_1$, the proportion of the sample contained in the $i^{th}$ class. In column (b) are given the midpoints $\overset{a-1}{\Sigma} w_1 + \frac{w_1}{2}$ of the $a^{th}$ class interval.

**Figure 2. Per cent of spending units who owe any debts**

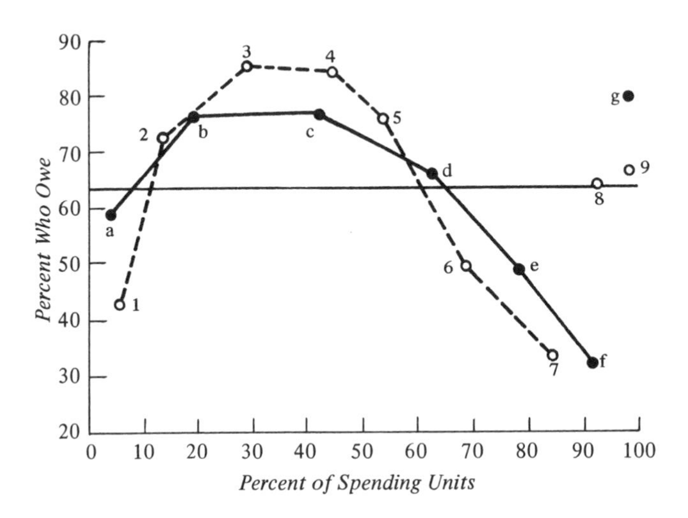


for each class so that the two curves could be plotted on the same figure. The classes of both independent variables could be ordered, except for the category "others" in FLC and the class "not ascertained," which were placed at the ends of the curves. We transformed the classes of each variable to a scale in terms of the proportion of the

**Figure 3. Per cent of spending units including a working wife**

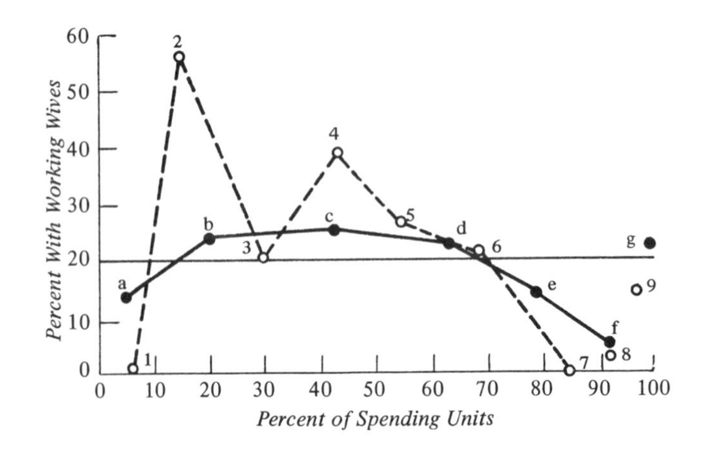

**Figure 4. Per cent of spending units with income over $4,000**

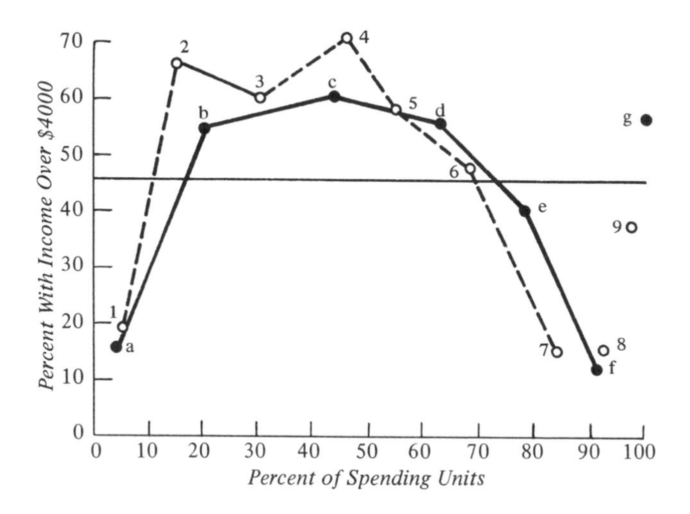


entire sample (hence approximately of the population) contained in each class of the independent variables. Then, at the midpoint of the class, the height of the dependent variable was plotted. These heights are given respectively in the six columns of the six independent variables; the midpoints of the age and FLC classes are given in the last column of Table 1.

**Figure 5. Per cent of spending units who bought a new car in one year**

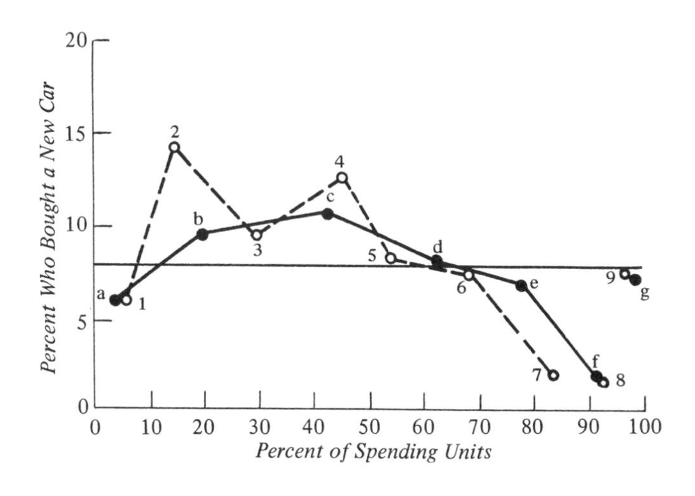

**Figure 6. Per cent of spending units who bought a television set in one year**

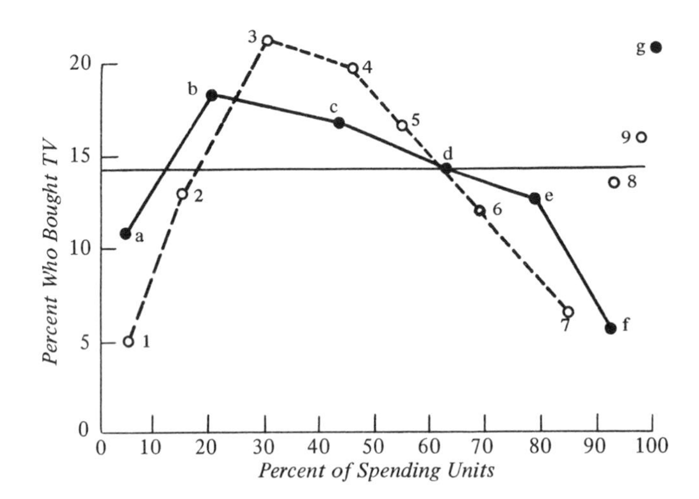


This method of plotting has some advantages. An entire column with unit base represents the same proportion of the total sample for one variable as for the other. The areas under the curves represent the total number of people who possess a certain characteristic. The areas of deviation from the height of the mean of the dependent variable represent the amount of "deviant" behavior "explained" by the corresponding portions of the independent variable scale.

The curves for home ownership (Figure 1) are both rather smooth but not entirely similar. There is an increase in the proportion of units owning their homes with the passage of time whether the time is measured in years or in stages. The life cycle approach, however, shows a sharp drop in the proportion of home owners among older, single people as compared to older units where both husband and wife are still present. This decline barely appears from age 55–64 to age 65 or over. The presence of older, single people under age 65 and of older married couples over 65 obscures the underlying fact that widows and widowers do tend to give up their houses. The relevant fact is widowhood rather than age.

Figure 2 plots consumers' indebtedness. A spending unit is classified as indebted if it owes money on a mortgage, installment debt, or other personal debt. The proportion who owe money is rather low in the early stages of the life cycle and in the younger age groups. For both curves there is an increase followed by a steady but important falling off to the end of the cycle, but the FLC curve shows greater variation than the age curve.

The advantages of the FLC curve over the age curve are perhaps best shown in Figure 3: the proportion of spending units with a working (income earning) wife. The smooth age curve hides what appears as distinctly bimodal behavior on the FLC scale. To look at the age curve one would think that young women tend to work indefinitely without interruption. The FLC curve shows that young wives with no children are much more likely to work than those who have young children.

The proportion of spending units with income over $4,000 (Figure 4) on the FLC curve shows a bimodality which is related to that on the previous curve. Again, this relationship is hidden on the unimodal age curve.

Bimodality shows up also in the FLC curve for buyers of new cars (Figure 5). Again there is a smooth and unimodal curve for the age variable. Both curves rise to maximum within the first half of the life cycle (or the first half of the age groups) with a slow decline to the end of the figure.

Similar declines from a maximum in the first half toward the end of the FLC are shown on both curves of buyers of TV sets (Figure 6). Here both curves are unimodal, but again the FLC curve shows the greater variation. The maximum is for parents with young children. Note that proportionately *fewer* parents with young children bought new cars or had incomes over $4,000 than those in the stages preceding the following, but *more* bought TV.

The category of "not ascertained" (denoted by g and 9 on the figures) is generally near the average, mostly between the mean and the modal classes. While this may not be surprising, it is reassuring to survey researchers. It would seem that this source of non-response does not contribute greatly to the biases of surveys.

The category of "others" in the FLC classification (denoted by 8 on the figures) is a class with a distinct and deviant behavior. It includes spending units who did not fit into our ordered seven categories of a "normal" family life; for example, units which contain only one adult and also children under 18. On four of the curves it shows a lower economic activity. For the amount of debt and for TV buying it is close to the average of the entire sample.

The data in Table 1 and Figures 1–6 show that the FLC variable brings out more of the variation in each of the six dependent variables than age does. Further, in each case an argument can be made that the influences of age are effected in large part through changes in the life cycle. Since age is not the only factor determining stage in the life cycle, stage in the life cycle is the more powerful independent variable. To test this reasoning it is desirable to obtain an objective measure of how well the two independent variables account for the variation in the dependent variables. Such a measure will permit the comparison of the relative effectiveness of the two independent variables for any dependent variable. It will also permit comparisons among the dependent variables as to the amount of variation explained by the independent variables.

The sorting by an independent variable would be complete if all individuals in each class were exactly alike with respect to the dependent variable. For a binomial dependent variable this would mean percentages of either 0 or 100 for each class. While complete sorting is impossible, we aim at maximizing the homogeneity of the dependent variable within classes. For a given total variation, this amounts to maximizing the differences between classes.

Variation is most generally measured in terms of the variance. The total variance may be broken into two components, the variance "between" classes and the variance "within" classes. The coefficient of intraclass correlation (*rho*) measures the proportion of the variance among the class means as a proportion of the total variance among the individuals comprising the population.

In the first two rows of Table 2 are the rhos for the age and for the FLC variable respectively. The latter seem to be higher on each of the six comparisons. The third row shows the ratio of the rho's. Advantage in explanatory power is largest–fivefold–for the "wife working" characteristic, as expected. For the other characteristics ratios of 1.23 to 2.06 are found, indicating gains in explanatory power of roughly 25 to 100 per cent. The order of the remaining variables is as follows: bought TV, bought new car, home ownership, owe money, and income over $4,000.

One may wonder to what extent the advantage of the FLC variable over the age variable should be attributed to the use of nine classes for the former to seven for the latter. Although this difference works in the direction of putting the FLC variable in a more favorable light, the effect is not great. We recomputed the rho for home ownership using twelve age classes and found a rho of .0618 as against .0547 using seven age classes. This still leaves a ratio of .0829/.0618 = 1.34 in favor of the FLC variable with nine classes. A similar check on TV ownership yielded the same rho when eleven age classes were used as compared with seven age classes.

We feel that rho is the most relevant measure of the "explanatory" value of the independent variables. However, we present two other measures as well, and on both of these tests the FLC performs better than age. A measure was computed in terms of the sum of the weighted absolute deviations from the overall means:

Sum of deviations = $\sum^{M} |w_1 (p_1 - p)|$. The sums of deviations are shown in Part II of Table 2. (Incidentally they are equal to the areas between the horizontal line representing the mean and the respective curves.) These are reduced to "relative deviations" (also shown in the table) by dividing each value by p. The ratios of these relative deviations show the FLC variable with greater relative deviations for each of the six characteristics.

Finally we sorted the age classes into "high" and "low" groups, according to whether the mean of the characteristic was higher or lower than the overall mean. Then we computed the means for the "highs" and "lows" to make a simple contrast; the FLC classes were sorted similarly into highs versus lows (Part III, Table 2). For each of the variables rather large differences between "high" and "low" groups are obtained showing that the independent variables are important "explanatory" variables for each of

Table 2. **Three methods for measuring and comparing the "explanatory" powers of age and of the family life cycle (FLC)**

| | | Own Home | Have Debts | Wife Working | Income Over $4000 | Bought New Car | Bought TV |
|---|---|---|---|---|---|---|---|
| I. | Age: Rho | .0547 | .1045 | .0288 | .1239 | .0078 | .0117 |
| | FLC: Rho | .0829 | .1542 | .1471 | .1522 | .0135 | .0240 |
| | Ratio of Rhos | 1.52 | 1.48 | 5.11 | 1.23 | 1.79 | 2.06 |
| II. | Age: Sum of deviations | .0931 | .1318 | .0621 | .1498 | .0212 | .0329 |
| | Relative deviations | .1686 | .2085 | .3105 | .3257 | .2678 | .2298 |
| | FLC: Sum of deviations | .1157 | .1749 | .1118 | .1692 | .0258 | .0496 |
| | Relative deviations | .2096 | .2767 | .5588 | .3678 | .3268 | .3472 |
| | Ratio of deviations | 1.24 | 1.33 | 1.80 | 1.13 | 1.22 | 1.51 |
| III. | Age: High classes | 61.7 | 73.3 | 24.8 | 57.5 | 9.6 | 17.7 |
| | Low classes | 38.7 | 43.3 | 11.1 | 24.5 | 5.1 | 11.1 |
| | Difference | 23.0 | 29.0 | 13.7 | 33.0 | 4.5 | 6.6 |
| | FLC: High classes | 68.1 | 78.2 | 28.4 | 58.3 | 10.6 | 19.6 |
| | Low classes | 44.7 | 42.3 | 3.1 | 20.4 | 5.4 | 9.6 |
| | Difference | 23.4 | 35.9 | 25.3 | 38.3 | 5.2 | 10.0 |

these characteristics. The FLC variable produces larger differences than the age variable for all six dependent variables.

We cannot now make proper tests of the null hypothesis that the two rhos for any characteristic came from the same population. One difficulty is that the data came from a complex sample design.[8] Any test is further complicated by the fact that the two rhos are based on the same set of data, and are highly (and positively) correlated. We hope to be able to work out satisfactory tests.

## SUMMARY

Stages of the family life cycle (FLC) were used as an independent variable for investigating variations in six economic characteristics. For each of these characteristics it proved itself superior in "explanatory" power to age classes. This result is consistent with social theory since the FLC should be a better reflection than age of the individual's social role.

Advantages of the family life cycle over age probably can be shown for many economic, social, political, and psychological variables as well as for the few shown here. Of course, contrariwise, there are characteristics for which age is a better explanatory variable; mortality and morbidity come to mind immediately. Laws and contracts are often written in terms of age. But we believe that the life cycle should be adopted more widely as an independent variable to be used in place of or parallel to age.

[8]See Leslie Kish, "Confidence Intervals for Clustered Samples," *American Sociological Review,* no. 22, April, 1957, pp. 154–165.

# 21. REVIEW AND SUMMARY OF "WORKINGMAN'S WIFE"

*Seymour Banks*

*The blue-collar worker represents a very important segment of the market for most goods. This review and summary of the book* Workingman's Wife *describes the day-in, day-out life of a working class woman, with emphasis on her goals, her attitudes toward her daily tasks, and her feelings about various people in her life.*

*This material is then, in reality, a detailed view of the distaff component of a large social class.*

This is a study of the social and psychological values of the wife of the blue-collar worker; the work is concerned with her personality, world and life-style. However, before discussing this book, I want to say something about a fundamental concept that pervades it–social class. The concept of social class in America has been most thoroughly developed and promoted by W. Lloyd Warner, originally an anthropologist, who has studied American communities with the techniques that he had used in the investigation of the social life of Australian tribes.

Social class refers to groupings which are recognizable by the general behavior and social attitudes of the people of the community where these groupings exist. Social class in America is not the same as economic class. Although economic factors are of prime importance and are some of the principal determinants of social class, they are insufficient to account for all the social class behavior which people have become aware of, or for its presence in American life.

Source: This review of Lee Rainwater, Richard P. Coleman, and Gerald Handel, *Workingman's Wife: Her Personality, World, and Life Style,* Oceana Publications, Inc., New York, 1959, has not previously been published. Seymour Banks: Vice-president, Leo Burnett Company, Inc., Chicago.

Basically, the class systems of different communities in the several regions of the United States are similar. However, variations do exist in the number of class levels, and the proportion of the population in each level from region to region and from city to city. Typically, the East and South have more highly-organized class systems than the West. Overall, one might say that somewhere around 60 to 70 per cent of the nonfarm population falls into what is called the common man level, or the "middle majority." This group is made up of two categories: the lower middle class and the working class. These two categories shade into one another. However, there are some differences between them. The lower middle class represents white collar workers in government and business, small businessmen and some professionals. Very often, they are high school graduates. These are the model for the perhaps popular stereotype of America's average man. The other group within this middle majority represents the factory employees and similar semi-skilled workers. These are the blue-collar workers whose wives will be discussed in the book review which follows. The husbands in this class work from day to day; they live adequately but on a small margin; they have little hope of rising and aim at getting by.

Undoubtedly, there is considerable variation of personality and attitude structure, mode of life and patterns of response among the members of any social class. The descriptions which follow should be considered as expressing general tendencies, not as individual analyses.

These women make up a large proportion of the population with a significant share of American purchasing power. They represent a very high proportion of the audiences to radio and TV daytime serials and their print equivalent—the "true story" magazines. In addition, they probably are in the audiences, to a considerable extent, of newspaper supplements and of the following types of evening TV programs: adventure, quiz, and audience participation.

For those who would like to read further about social classes in America, how the concepts were developed and the ramifications of this method of studying American life, I refer you to the following two books: Joseph A. Kahl, *The American Class Structure* and W. Lloyd Warner, *American Life, Dream and Reality.*

## THE REVIEW ITSELF

*Day-in, Day-out.* This section has to do with a description of the day-to-day activities of working class women, principally those with young children. The working class wife's daily life is centered on the tasks of homemaking, child-rearing and caring for her husband. These domestic demands may be exactly the same as those of middle class women but the working class wife has a different set of attitudes toward them.

The working class woman feels that she is extremely busy with her housework. She fixes breakfast, washes clothes, dresses children, cleans the house, does the dishes, makes lunch, irons the clothes, makes supper, makes light snacks, makes beds, dusts, mops, sweeps, mends old clothes, washes windows, scrubs the kitchen, works out in the yard, shops for groceries, and sews on new clothes or curtains; and does this every day. She also views her children as a source of considerable concern in her daily life. She must feed them, clothe them, bathe them and put them to bed, and also keep a continual weather-eye out for them even when she is not actually taking care of them.

In the description of daily routines, husbands seem to come in a poor third in the attention they get.

The working class wife classified her daily routine as busy, crowded, a mess, humdrum or just dull. Although she feels her own life is one of monotony, she is consoled by her belief that this does not make her different from most of the other women she knows.

Weekends aren't really too much different from the rest of the week for working class wives. Working class women often do not actually experience a weekend as it is known by most white collar Americans. Many of the husbands have extra jobs on Saturday or Sunday; another large portion of the husbands are required by the nature of their jobs to work during the weekend, taking their days off in the middle of the week.

Just as there is little or no difference between the weekday and the weekend for the working class wife, so there is little difference in her life from season to season; summer is dull and normal just like winter. The only difference she sees is a chance to stay outside in her yard more often during the summer. Working class wives do not usually have vacations which they can devote to travel. What they do with their vacation time is very much influenced by the wife's age or child-rearing status. The mothers of older children do take trips now and then, even if the only purpose is to visit a relative in a near-by city. For many working class women, the celebration of one of the big holidays–Christmas, Easter or Thanksgiving–is the nearest thing to a vacation. These holidays are usually celebrated in family-clan fashion at the grandparents' home. This is in contrast to the middle class pattern of spending such holidays with only the immediate family or with friends.

*Inner Life and the Outer World.* The authors point out that statements describing the personality of the working class woman should be regarded merely as broad generalizations. No individual would match perfectly with the various characteristics of personality that they describe. However, they believe the picture represents this group as a whole.

The central characteristic of the personality of the working class wife is her underlying conviction that most significant things originate from the world outside of herself, rather than from within herself. For her, the world is a kind of massive, immovable apparatus to which she responds. She regards herself as a "little" person. These women rely upon having the outer world appear to them, or presented to them, in terms that are specific, clearly defined and readily understood. Lacking such specific stimulation, they do not know how to go about taking suitable action in unfamiliar areas. In fact, they do not know even how to begin. They require, indeed crave, explicit guidance: they feel grateful when it is presented in a form they can use. Without it, they feel self-conscious, painfully conspicuous and quite uncertain.

This feeling of smallness before the world is not restricted to a specific context but runs through their entire outlook. The working class woman's education and upbringing have acquainted her with a relatively small segment of the world. She knows only that which is close to home. She tends to see the world beyond her doorstep and immediate neighborhood as chaotic and potentially catastrophic. The working class wife's outlook is shaded by a fairly widespread anxiety over possible losses or deprivations—she is anxious about her physical safety, stability of affection from her husband and children and, of course, the loss of income from layoffs, strikes, reductions in hours of work.

The most important elements in the working class wife's world are the people in her family. This is, of course, largely true for other women, but the working class wife is so overwhelmingly bound up with her family and has so few significant connections to anything beyond, that she is very much concerned with the problem of what her life would be like if anything happened to that family. Among the working class wives, loneliness is widely feared. Though it is not necessarily in the forefront of their minds, it looms as a disquieting possibility.

To the working class woman, life is often a somewhat chancy affair. She is basically a person who waits for what life might bring to her door, and she is never quite sure of what will happen. Two major aims are evident in an analysis of the working class wives' characters: One central motive is the search for a stable world. This comes about because of their deep conviction that, with good fortune, one can be saved from or spared unpleasantness, but one cannot be personally successful against it. Wishfulness is her most easily summoned resource. However, the content of her wishes are usually relatively modest and not extravagant. In addition to simple wishing, many of these women also put faith in prayer as a way to see them through difficulties or to drive away the source of the difficulties.

The second major aim of the working class wife is to add some brightness to life. One very important way she can do this is to make herself and her surroundings as attractive as she can. These women often tend to be highly self-conscious; prettying up themselves and their surroundings reassures them life is not so bad after all. She tries to enhance her attractiveness in her own eyes, in hopes that others, particularly her husband, will be able to see her as she wants to see herself.

In comparison with the middle class woman, the working class woman's emotional structure is not well organized nor are her emotions easily controlled. The working class woman's tendency to a somewhat volatile set of emotions is one of the factors that contributes to her moral concern. She wants to be a good person and do the right thing, but is often dismayed by some of the feelings that she finds in herself from time to time. Like most people, she wants to be a decent person, respectable and unashamed; she differs from the middle class woman in the ways she maintains her sense of moral goodness—the working class wife is governed more immediately by what others think of her than by her own conscience. Incidentally, the working class wife is much more ready than is a middle class woman to believe that a person is entitled to make a mistake or two. This belief adds a dimension of complexity to her moral outlook, but perhaps it can be understood in terms of her feeling that life is hard enough and what one needs is less trouble rather than more.

*The Man in Her Life.* The previous discussion of the personality of working class wives points out that their view of the world is essentially a personal one; thus they perceive the people in that world much more clearly and find them much more meaningful than the impersonal forces of social institutions. For the working class housewife, marriage, being a wife and having a husband, is very important. These women have always known that their reason for existence is to be wives and mothers, and much went into thinking about that day when they would become married. They tend to marry at a substantially younger age than do middle class women. The working class woman does not seem to feel comfortable without a clear-cut role in a family; when she outgrows the daughter role, she appears to move as quickly as possible to the wife-mother role.

Thus, the husband is the central person in the lives of these working class women. This relationship is of crucial emotional and realistic significance to them. Because these women feel as unsure as they do about themselves and about how acceptable they are to the world around them, they are heavily dependent on having a husband as a sign that they are full members in the society of mature women. Yet these women frequently feel isolated from their husbands in many ways and retain lingering doubts as to their hold on their affections.

Before discussing how the working class wife deals with her husband, let us point out that her feelings toward him are an integral part of her total personality structure. The working class woman sees men as dominant and controlling. Men, including her husband, are in a sense representatives of the external world and she feels that she has no more effective power with men than she has with any other force or power in the world.

Tenderness, care, affection seem to be exceptions in relations with men; and, in the eyes of working class women, the woman who is sure of receiving these from a man is fortunate. Often, this kind of woman considers herself lucky to be able to settle for permanence in a relationship, whether or not it also has the elements of closeness and tenderness she longs for in fantasy. These women feel that it is hard to get a husband to do what they want or to change his ways. Men go their own ways and often, as not, the working class wife feels that she has little influence. She believes that men are quite independent and can easily leave. This is frustrating. It seems to be accepted with resignation, rather than a sense of defeat.

The middle class woman typically has an entirely different set of attitudes toward her husband. She seeks to direct and control his behavior and feels reasonably confident, in fact, that she can do so.

When one turns from a consideration of the subjective aspects of a woman's relationship to her husband and her family activities, a pattern of roles is found to be rather sharply separated; in a variety of areas, the husband and wife go separate ways. The couple's day seems to be spent in isolated activity with the minimum amount of time spent around shared interest. There seems to be a greater division of labor and interest between husband and wife in the working class than in the middle class. Often it becomes apparent that the working class wife must stay at home while her husband has fun. The wife and mother tends to be almost totally absorbed in her homemaking chores and interests; her husband has outside recreatoinal interests and, often, does not want her to share them.

One of the areas of greatest interest to advertisers, arising from the division of labor within a working class household, has to do with the family financial management. In general, the working class wife is dominant in family financial matters. The prevailing notion is that earning the money is a man's responsibility; spending it wisely is the wife's duty.

*Nature's Law: Motherhood.* The attitudes of working class wives toward their children are fundamental in her entire pattern of behavior. They are exaggeratedly concerned over their children's well-being and happiness, calling them "the most prized possession in our house." At the same time, they feel tied down by their children, considering them a terrific nuisance and bother. It is precisely because they are so involved in their children that they are so heavily caught up in child-caring chores.

Just as marrying signifies to her that she is truly grown up and a socially acceptable person, having children establishes her in her own eyes, and she hopes in others', as a normal, respectable woman. Pregnancy and childbirth have a strong fascination for the working men's wives and they are perhaps more deeply involved emotionally in these physical experiences than are middle class women.

The working class woman looks for gratification from her children in the present rather than in the future. She has some tendency to regard children as though they were a combination of animated toy, stuffed animal and sparkling bauble. A child is for her, very often, a passive object to be hugged close or to be decked out in appealing clothes, or to be enjoyed for its antics. These women tend not to see their children as persons; they are not greatly interested in the child's individuality, except perhaps for his entertainment value. Thus, they are not easily able to see a child as being an individual with an integrity of his own and one which is worthy of respect.

The working class mother feels it is difficult to influence the behavior of her children. The mother is often uncertain in disciplining her children, since she is likely to see her child's behavior as being mysterious and beyond understanding. She consequently looks for rules or authoritative guidance which she hopes will work and take hold on the child.

Middle class and working class mothers have a different set of desires for their children.

The working class mother is interested in activities only if her children recognize them and reward her with affection. Middle class mothers, on the other hand, are willing to aid their children to achieve goals which they themselves never achieved; success of their children, by itself, is sufficient reward for the middle class mother. She does not seem to care too deeply if the children do not reciprocate with undying love. To say this in another way, middle class mothers invest in their children; the working class mothers indulge them.

This set of differences between immediate and long-range orientation between working and middle class mothers appears in their attitudes toward school and education. In general, the working class mother thinks of schools as a somewhat necessary evil, providing knowledge and social approval; however, school is generally an institution which they do not look upon with confidence but rather with a kind of wary hopefulness. Rather few working class mothers belong to PTA's; if they do, it's to look after their own children's interest.

*Friendly Relations.* Working class wives are family-type people, and relatives are the people they like best. Whenever working class women mention doing anything with other people—going to a picnic, shopping, getting together for dinner, etc.—the other people are relatives more frequently than not. This is in considerable contrast to the middle class women's habits of dealing with people outside their own family, often in preference to relatives.

One source of concern of the working class wife regarding her close ties of affection with her relatives seems to be that, outside of this family circle, she is friendless and lonely; thus, quite a few working class women are family-type people through default. Within the circle of the extended family, they find the security, affection and acceptance which they feel is so much more difficult to obtain from the wider world of "unknown" other people. They fear that they lack the personal skills for making friends easily.

Working class women very much want to "do unto others as you would have them do unto you." In their search for friends, they recognize the values of doing for others because they want the reciprocal act. They are fond of bestowing physical tokens of their esteem upon other people; many find their greatest pleasure in buying gifts. They do not draw a boundary line on their gift-giving; they enjoy gift-giving on any and all possible occasions and sometimes say that the money that they have spent most pleasurably was "whenever I've given people a gift and made them happy."

*Not All Americans Are Joiners.* If we look at the working class wife in relationship to the environment outside her own immediate family and relatives, we find that the working class woman is not a joiner. She is not a club woman. If she joins a club, it is very often an occupational auxiliary or a woman's auxiliary of a man's organization. The working class women who are actively engaged in club enterprises often justify it by saying this activity represents an expression of their great concern for their families and children.

This non-groupiness is an area of considerable contrast with middle class women.

*Working Class Women Are Deeply Religious.* Religion means many things to them; but one of the greatest benefits is peace of mind and help in time of trouble.

Religion not only helps in time of trouble, it also helps the working class wife stay out of trouble.

Despite the strong feelings toward religion, working class women are not church-goers, typically going to church occasionally, maybe once a month or just for the big holidays like Easter and Christmas. It is believed that the working class woman is not a church-goer for approximately the same reason that she is not a club member. She is afraid that she might feel out of place somehow in a church. And, furthermore, she is too tied down with young children and other responsibilities at home to take the time or make the effort to go to church.

*Dollar Decisions.* Most working class women realistically assess the family's income as average or a little bit below. They tend to think of themselves as people for whom ends meet, but not as comfortably as they should, and sometimes only by a sacrifice in the mid-section. As a group, they are not confident that their economic futures hold promise of improvement. In many ways, for working class women, expenses for housing (and neighborhood) form the basic skeleton of their spending pattern, the flesh of the good life is added by appliances, food and furnishings. For middle class women, on the other hand, the housing and neighborhood are of greater interest.

Working class families, by and large, have modest desires for housing: they want an adequate house in terms of room for the family, they want something in reasonably good condition, and preferably the house should look nice also. The majority of them own their own homes and many more aspire to. However, they are not willing to sacrifice the contents of a house for its external appearance, or for a better neighborhood, once a minimum standard of decency is achieved. Once a house is purchased, it is stocked with appliances. In many ways, the working class housewife expects to put much the same appliances in her home that the middle class woman does, and she is willing to sacrifice a more expensive house if she can appliance it as she wishes.

Typically, working class housewives practice a "tin can" or "envelope" budgeting system. What she does is to set up a series of tin cans or envelopes in which she places money from her husband's paycheck to cover expected expenses of various kinds until the next paycheck comes in. She finds it difficult to do abstract thinking on budgeting and finds paper budgets more confusing than helpful. Her attitudes are strongly against installment plans, preferring to make payments with cash; however, behavior is quite the reverse. Two-thirds of the working class respondents studied by the authors were carrying some kind of installment debt other than their house mortgage. The desire to pay cash had fallen victim to the more urgent desire for the benefit of an appliance or other items.

Generally speaking, these women have a pessimistic attitude toward goods in the market place, partly because they fear their own proclivity for buying incidentals or knickknacks for the children. They lack confidence in their own buying skills and exhibit a distrust of the business community. Many working class women exhibit extremely narrow horizons in their choice of shopping places. In comparison with middle class women, they are very provincial shoppers, confining most of their shopping expeditions to neighborhood stores. They prefer to make their big ticket purchases through connections such as relatives or friends who run businesses themselves or who have connections with people who do. Sometimes this reliance upon relatives or friends has a real bargain or discount as its objective; equally frequently, however, such reliance is a means of avoiding the unknown in stores or salespeople where the outcome of the purchasing venture is more threatening.

The working class housewife likes to buy nationally advertised brands. In name-brand purchases, she feels the security of doing what millions of others are doing. She feels that name brands are good brands, or else the brand could not have stayed in business so long or have been advertised so widely, and she finds in name-brand purchases the greatest degree of certainty that she will not get gypped. Working class women rely upon advertisements and pictures in the mass media to educate them about the latest ideas in home decoration and appliances, as well as to inform them about national name brands. In this way, they remedy their deficiencies in social contact or the narrowness of their own shopping horizons.

The kind of advertising which finally motivates such a woman into making a major appliance purchasing decision is often a flyer from one of her favorite stores. It contains the specific price information which is of vital importance to her. For the working class woman, there can hardly be a more favorable configuration of circumstances to move her out of her fundamental pessimism towards dealing successfully in the market place than when she has available a nationally-advertised name brand, a trusted store (preferably one in her neighborhood), and finally a price within her reach. All this, providing, of course, that the tin can is full and the cash is on hand.

*Priorities and Preferences.* This chapter deals with the order of importance assigned to various kinds of expenditures by working class women.

Working class women give the first budget priority to food. However, they reject the idea of food as an item worthy of lavish expenditure. They have a basic concern with meeting what they consider to be minimal nutritive requirements, with a few desserts thrown in, of course; but the idea of spending for food, over and above this level, is a goal that they do not consciously admit.

In distinction to the middle class woman, the working class woman is much more concerned with pleasing herself and her family with the food she prepares than following the dictates of dietary experts or culinary artists. The typical working class wife is not very often worried about whether her meals are getting boring, as long as she knows her husband's and her children's food fancies are being appeased. She is content to continually serve them their favorites so long as these foods remain in favor. She knows her family prefers just plain American cooking. She shows some resistance to foods that are easy to prepare if she feels the result would diminish her family's mealtime pleasure; in some ways, she judges her own performance by the amount of work which went into it.

The equipment within the homes of working class women takes on a higher order of priority than does the external appearance of their house. Working class woman can apparently put up with plain looking houses if the interior of the house is nicely furnished and has all the appliances she desires.

Within the house, they are most devoted to the idea of appliance-rich, modernized kitchens for themselves and attractive bedrooms for their children. These are the rooms a working class wife is most notably concerned with having fixed exactly as she wants. The working class woman envisions a kitchen completely modernized and filled with appliances, all placed in such a way as to make her work handier and more pleasant. This is not done in order to have an escape from the kitchen; instead, it helps her make the kitchen the heart of the home.

The strong interest which a working class mother displays in her children's bedrooms centers around the idea of making these rooms almost dream castles for the children—partially as a means of buying their love, partially to help keep them at home.

Working class women are of two minds over what a living room would be like. Most want the living room "cozy and nice"—a place where the family can gather to spend its spare time and watch television. A few regarded the living room as a public demonstration of the family's efficiency and economic competence; however, these appearance-conscious women are a distinct minority among the working class wives.

All down the line, when it comes to appliances, furnishings and decoration, working class women express a different order of enthusiams or preferences than do middle class women. The working class housewife tends to concentrate on labor-saving devices or appliances which help bring the family together like television; the middle class woman is more interested in esthetics.

The question arises whether working class women exhibit any distinctive or characteristic tastes and, if so, what these are like. Working class housewives do not seem to easily articulate their tastes. They speak of preferences, when they do, for "modern things," by which they usually signify something up-to-date. Their characterization of houses, lamps, sofas as modern are not the same as those by industrial designers or architects. However, there is little or no traditional architecture.

Within the household, working class women completely reject sofas of antique, traditional, or old-fashioned vintage. Thin, wooden-armed sofas, even of modern design are unpopular with them since they do not provide comfort. In general, the bulkier and softer-looking the sofa or chair, the more comfortable it appears to be to a working class woman; thus, the more desirable it is. In contrast, the bulkier a sofa, the more its sturdiness was questioned by middle class housewives.

*Reaching the Working Man's Wife with Advertising.* To summarize the preceding discussion, let us point out that there are five basic goals which activate the consumer behavior of working class housewives. These are: the search for social, economic and physical

security; the desire for a common man level of recognition and respectability; the desire for support and affection from the people important to her; the effort to escape the heavy burden of household labors; and the urge to pretty up her world. Much of what the working class housewife does is directed toward securing herself and her family from real or potential threats to their well-being. This is one of her most deeply rooted motives and one which operates steadily to guide her actions.

Working class women's responses to advertising are clearly influenced by their uncertainty, unsureness and their suspicion of the world around them, their corresponding needs of reassurance about themselves in relation to this world, and their needs for encouragement in the hope that things will go well. Advertising's role is to communicate to these people an image of a gratifying world, a world in which products fit functionally into their drive for a stable and secure life, and are demonstrated to fit constructively and effectively into the daily activities of a housewife working to maintain her family. In doing so, the advertiser must take into account the fact that he is addressing a market where local merchants may use methods which will give the working class consumer a feeling that she has been taken advantage of. The search for the good buy represents one of the main solutions which working class women apply to the problem posed by the desire for goods and services coupled with their tendency to distrust those who provide it. Very often, the national brand serves them as a symbol of the good buy because it means that a solidly established company stands behind it. The advertiser who succeeds in presenting his brand as a well-known and popular product has an advantage with these people. They see it as trustworthy in a market which they believe is full of uncertain values. These housewives are susceptible to the appeal of economy, but they also need assurance that the economy is not only in the purchase price but in the long-term value of the product. To sum up, buying national brands gives the working class wives the feel of economic security of getting a well-known product. Also, the purchase of such products confers upon these women the social security of having done the same thing as millions of other Americans, confirming them in their own private feelings of being accepted in the midst of the common man level.

Typically, the working class family wants to maintain the family's status as modern, respectable and comfortable. They seek a way of life that signalizes mass market respectability and they want to have neighbors like themselves—decent, hard-working people who don't put on airs. In houses, furnishings, clothes, and food, these housewives do not covet the elaborate, ornamental and rich. Their tastes run to the simple, unadorned, and up-to-date.

Advertising can and does facilitate self-identification by the readers as part of the common man group. It does this by relating its product and brand to the good life, as defined by the culture of the average man. Advertising communicates the fact that an object is an expected part of this common life, and also teaches these women how to use the object in that context. Thus, the setting in which a product or brand is advertised has double importance. The setting has the function of making the object seem desirable and also giving the woman a sense of how she might use it and how she might relate it to her own situation. It is important that the advertising not set too high a standard nor give the woman the feeling that the object is beyond her ability to handle comfortably. Since many of these women are uncertain as to their own competence, they need a good deal of assurance from advertising that the object is within their reach socially and psychologically, as well as economically.

Another set of strivings derive from the working class wife's need to constantly secure herself in the affections of others, to reassure herself that her husband and her children love her and that other significant persons do, too. It was pointed out previously that these women tend to feel relatively little security in the affections of others, and in many ways they tend to try to buy this affection. Therefore, this set of attitudes affects their purchasing behavior. The working class housewife's sensitivity to the people in her life, her desire to avoid their criticism and rejection, and to win their love, influences product and brand choice in many ways, and plays a large role in her response to advertising and sales appeals. Advertising which is people-oriented is much more meaningful to her. For example, labor saving devices achieve much more importance when the housewife feels that they can help her to be a better mother and wife; i.e., aid her in caring for and pleasing the people in her life.

Moreover, these women have an extremely personal conception of their homemaking role. These women feel that the personal care one takes for her husband and children is a sign of her love for them, even though she may complain that the task is onerous. Thus, at the same time that advertising offers these women a chance to do their housework with less effort and to feel themselves less burdened down, it must also communicate to them a sense of their worth–a sense of being important and essential to her family. The saving of labor must somehow be compensated for by something which is worthwhile–something which is being done for the family. The implication that products give the housewife time to enjoy herself idly is probably best avoided.

Finally, the working class wife is very much in the market for "pretty things." They like to have their environments a little more pleasant, a little more stimulating. However, they do not like to think of themselves as women who are given to buying fancy objects. It is when they are confronted with something cute for the children that their control over the urge to buy and prettify breaks down most easily. Given these propensities for pretty things, advertising seems to get a better reception when it is something more than factual and practical in its presentation. These women show a strong preference for advertisements in colors because they find the colors themselves stimulating and gratifying. For example, while these women are appliance-hungry and want their kitchens to be the most modern and efficient possible, they also like to spruce the kitchen up with artificial flowers or other spots of color. Since she spends a good deal of her day in the kitchen, the housewife likes it to seem homey and cozy. It would seem worthwhile in advertising items for the kitchen to portray them in a setting which involves some of these more emotionally satisfying images. This would seem to be particularly true of appliances or other articles of kitchen hardware which are in themselves fairly impersonal and work-oriented.

# 22. THE SIGNIFICANCE OF SOCIAL STRATIFICATION IN SELLING

*Richard P. Coleman*

*The concept of social class has been a helpful marketing tool. But the time has come to advance to a more sophisticated application of social class to marketing problems.*

*For example, it is important to recognize that differences as well as similarities exist within each class. This fact explains why some products such as color television, sales of which are not correlated with income generally, enjoy markets in each social class among relatively prosperous or "overprivileged" families.*

*The author points out that social class, like income, may not be a relevant concept in explaining market behavior in some situations. Nevertheless, the fact that social class does not fit all marketing situations is no reason for complete disenchantment with the concept.*

Dating back to the late 1940's, advertisers and marketers have alternately flirted with and cooled on the notion that W. Lloyd Warner's social class concept[1] is an important analytic tool for their profession. The Warnerian idea that six social classes constitute the basic division of American Society has offered many attractions to marketing analysts when they have grown dissatisfied with simple income categories or census-type occupational categories and felt a need for more meaningful classifications, for

[1] See W. Lloyd Warner, Marchia Meeker, and Kenneth Eells, *Social Class in America,* Science Research Associates, Chicago, 1949.

Source: From Martin L. Bell (ed.), *Marketing: A Mature Discipline,* American Marketing Association, Chicago, 1961, Richard P. Coleman, "The Significance of Social Stratification in Selling," pp. 171–184. Richard P. Coleman: Research Manager, Social Research, Inc., Chicago.

categorizations of the citizenry which could prove more relevant to advertising and marketing problems. However, in the course of their attempts to apply the class concept, marketers have not always found it immediately and obviously relevant. Sometimes it has seemed to shed light on advertising and merchandising problems and at other times it hasn't—with the result that many analysts have gone away disenchanted, deciding that social classes are not much more useful than income categories and procedurally far more difficult to employ.

It is the thesis of this writer that the role of social class has too often been misunderstood or oversimplified, and that if the concept is applied in a more sophisticated and realistic fashion, it will shed light on a great many problems to which, at first glance, it has not seemed particularly relevant. What we propose to do here, then, is discuss and illustrate a few of these more subtle, more refined and (it must be acknowledged) more complicated ways of applying social class analyses to marketing and advertising problems. In other words, the purpose of this paper is to clarify *when* and *in what ways* social class concepts are significant in selling, and to suggest when they might not be as significant as other concepts, or at least need to be used in concert with other analytic categories.

## THE WARNERIAN SOCIAL CLASSES

The six social classes which are referred to in this paper are those which W. Lloyd Warner and his associates have observed in their analyses of such diverse communities as Newburyport, Massachusetts,[2] Natchez, Mississippi,[3] Morris, Illinois,[4] Kansas City, Missouri,[5] and Chicago. These social classes are groups of people who are more or less equal to one another in prestige and community status; they are people who readily and regularly interact among themselves in both formal and informal ways; they form a "class" also to the extent that they share the same goals and ways of looking at life. It is this latter fact about social classes which makes them significant to marketers and advertisers.

Briefly characterized, the six classes are as follows, starting from the highest one and going down:[6]

1. The Upper-Upper or "Social Register" Class is composed of locally prominent families, usually with at least second- or third-generation wealth. Almost inevitably,

[2] See W. Lloyd Warner and Paul Lunt, *The Social Life of a Modern Community,* Yale University Press, New Haven, 1941.

[3] See Allison Davis, Burleigh B. Gardner and Mary R. Gardner, *Deep South,* University of Chicago Press, Chicago, 1941.

[4] See W. Lloyd Warner and Associates, *Democracy in Jonesville,* Harper & Brothers, New York, 1949.

[5] The writer's observation on the Kansas City social class system will be included in a forthcoming volume on middle age in Kansas City, currently being prepared for publication by the Committee on Human Development of the University of Chicago.

[6] Some of the phrases and ideas in this characterization have been borrowed from Joseph A. Kahl's excellent synthesizing textbook, *The American Class Structure,* Rinehart & Company, Inc., New York, 1957.

this is the smallest of the six classes—with probably no more than 0.5 per cent of the population able to claim membership in this class. The basic values of these people might be summarized in these phrases: living graciously, upholding the family reputation, reflecting the excellence of one's breeding, and displaying a sense of community responsibility.

2. The Lower-Upper or "Nouveau Riche" Class is made up of the more recently arrived and never-quite-accepted wealthy families. Included in this class are members of each city's "executive elite," as well as founders of large businesses and the newly well-to-do doctors and lawyers. At best only 1.5 per cent of Americans rank at this level—so that all told, no more than 2 per cent of the population can be counted as belonging to one layer or the other of our Upper Class. The goals of people at this particular level are a blend of the Upper-Upper pursuit of gracious living and the Upper-Middle Class's drive for success.

3. In the Upper-Middle Class are moderately successful professional men and women, owners of medium-sized businesses and "organization men" at the managerial level; also included are those younger people in their twenties or very early thirties who are expected to arrive at this occupational status level—and possibly higher—by their middle or late thirties (that is, they are today's "junior executives" and "apprentice professionals" who grew up in such families and/or went to the "better" colleges). Ten per cent of Americans are part of this social class and the great majority of them are college educated.

   The motivating concerns of people in this class are success at career (which is the husband's contribution to the family's status) and tastefully reflecting this success in social participation and home decor (which is the wife's primary responsibility). Cultivating charm and polish, plus a broad range of interests—either civic or cultural, or both—are also goals of the people in this class, just as in the Lower-Upper. For most marketing and advertising purposes, this class and the two above it can be linked together into a single category of "upper status people." The major differences between them—particularly between the Upper-Middle and Lower-Upper—are in degree of "success" and the extent to which this has been translated into gracious living.

4. At the top of the "Average Man World" is the Lower-Middle Class. Approximately 30 per cent or 35 per cent of our citizenry can be considered members of this social class. For the most part they are drawn from the ranks of non-managerial office workers, small business owners, and those highly-paid blue-collar families who are concerned with being accepted and respected in white-collar dominated clubs, churches, and neighborhoods. The key word in understanding the motivations and goals of this class is Respectability, and a second important word is Striving. The men of this class are continually striving, within their limitations, to "do a good job" at their work, and both men and women are determined to be judged "respectable" in their personal behavior by their fellow citizens. Being "respectable" means that they live in well-maintained homes, neatly furnished, in neighborhoods which are more-or-less on the "right side of town." It also means that they will clothe themselves in coats, suits, and dresses from "nice stores" and save for a college education for their children.

5. At the lower half of the "Average Man World" is the Upper-Lower Class, sometimes referred to as "The Ordinary Working Class." Nearly 40 per cent of all Americans are in this class, making it the biggest. The proto-typical member of this class is a semi-skilled worker on one of the nation's assembly lines. Many of these "Ordinary Working Class" people make very good money, but do not bother with using it to become "respectable" in a middle-class way. Whether they just "get by" at work, or moonlight to make extra, Upper-Lowers are oriented more toward enjoying life and living well from day to day than saving for the future or caring what the middle-class world thinks of them. They try to "keep in step with the times" (indeed, one might say the "times" are more important than the "Joneses" to this class), because they want to be at least Modern, if not Middle Class. That is, they try to take advantage of progress to live more comfortably and they work hard enough to keep themselves safely away from a slum level of existence.

6. The Lower-Lower Class of unskilled workers, unassimilated ethnics, and the sporadically employed comprises about 15 per cent of the population, but this class has less than 7 or 8 per cent of the purchasing power, and will not concern us further here. Apathy, fatalism, and a point of view which justifies "getting your kicks whenever you can" characterize the approach toward life, and toward spending money, found among the people of this class.

Now, we do not mean to imply by these characterizations that the members of each class are always homogeneous in behavior. To suggest such would be to exaggerate greatly the meaning of social classes. To properly understand them, it must be recognized that there is a considerable variation in the way individual members of a class realize these class goals and express these values.

For example, within the Upper-Middle and Lower-Upper Class, there is one group—called Upper Bohemians[7] by Russell Lynes—for whom cultural pursuits are more important than belonging to a "good" country club. As a result, the tastes in furniture, housing accommodations, and recreations exhibited by the men and women of this "issues-and-culture set"—leaning toward the *avant garde* and eclectic, as they do—are apt to be very different from those practiced by the more conventional, bourgeois members of these status levels. Nevertheless, to both the Upper Bohemians and the Upper Conventionals, displaying "good taste" is quite important, with the differences between them not so much a question of good-versus-bad taste as one of whose form of good taste is preferred (though, to be sure, the Upper Bohemians are usually quite certain theirs is better).

Other sub-categories can be found in these higher classes and parallel kinds of sub-categories can be found in the Lower-Middle and Upper-Lower Classes. Within the Upper-Lower Class, for instance, there is a large number of people who are quite concerned with their respectability and spend much of their spare time in church trying to do something about it. Their respectability concerns are not quite like those of the Lower-Middle Class, however, for they seem to care more about The Almighty's

[7]See Russell Lynes, *A Surfeit of Honey,* Harper & Brothers, New York, 1957.

view of them than of their fellow man's. Thus, the Upper-Lower Class might, for certain analytic purposes, be sub-divided into Church-Going and Tavern-Hopping segments, although this would by no means exhaust all possibilities of sub-categorization here.

All of this is by way of indicating that the millions of individuals who compose each social class are not necessarily similar or identical in their consumption patterns, even though they are of equal status socially and share a set of goals and points of view which are class-wide. Thus far, the literature on social class in both marketing journals and sociological publications has emphasized the similarities of people within classes and rarely pointed out these variations. This has been necessary, of course, in order to properly introduce the concept and educate social scientists and marketers to its utility, but it has led on occasion to naive misuse of the concept and ultimate disillusion. In my view, it has come time for us to advance into a more sophisticated application of social class to marketing problems, which involves awareness of the differences as well as similarities within each class.

## SOCIAL CLASS VERSUS INCOME

Let us proceed now to stating the basic significance of this class concept for people in the selling field. In the first place, it explains why income categories or divisions of Americans are quite often irrelevant in analyzing product markets, consumers' shopping habits and store preferences, and media consumption. For example, if you take three families, each earning around $8,000 a year, but each from a different social class, a radical difference in their ways of spending money will be observed.

An Upper-Middle Class family in this income bracket, which in this case might be a young lawyer and his wife or perhaps a college professor, is apt to be found spending a relatively large share of its resources on housing (in a "prestige" neighborhood), on rather expensive pieces of furniture, on clothing from quality stores, and on cultural amusements or club memberships. Meanwhile, the Lower-Middle Class family—headed, we will say, by an insurance salesman or a fairly successful grocery store owner, perhaps even a Diesel engineer—probably has a better house, but in not so fancy a neighborhood; it is apt to have as full a wardrobe though not so expensive, and probably more furniture though none by name designers. These people almost certainly have a much bigger savings account in the bank.

Finally, the Working Class family—with a cross-country truck driver or a highly-paid welder as its chief wage-earner—is apt to have less house and less neighborhood than the Lower-Middle or Upper-Middle family; but it will have a bigger, later model car, plus more expensive appliances in its kitchen and a bigger TV set in its living room. This family will spend less on clothing and furniture, but more on food if the number of children is greater, as is likely. One further difference: the man of the house probably spends much more on sports, attending baseball games (for example), going hunting and bowling, and perhaps owning a boat of some description.

The wives in these three families will be quite noticeably different in the kind of department stores they patronize, in the magazines they read, and in the advertising to which they pay attention. The clothing and furniture they select for themselves and their families will differ accordingly, and also because they are seeking quite different goals. This has become very clear in studies Social Research, Inc., has done for the *Chicago Tribune* on the clothing tastes of Chicagoland women, for the Kroehler Company on the place of furniture in American homes, and for MacFadden Publications on the purchasing patterns and motivations of their romance magazines' Working Class readers.[8] (These have been contrasted in turn with the motivations of Middle Class women who read service magazines.)

The Upper-Middle Class wife—even of the struggling young lawyer—usually buys all her public-appearance clothes at specialty shops or in the specialty departments of her community's best department stores; she feels constrained to choose her wardrobe according to rather carefully prescribed standards of appropriateness. In furnishing her home, she thoughtfully considers whether a given piece or a combination of pieces will serve as adequate testament to her aesthetic sensitivities, plus doing credit in turn to her husband's taste in wife-choosing. She pays careful attention to the dictates of the best shelter magazines, the "smart" interior decorators in town, the homes of other women in her class, and maybe that of the boss's wife.

The Lower-Middle Class woman is more single-mindedly concerned with furnishing her home so that it will be "pretty" in a way that suits her and hopefully might win praise from her friends and neighbors. She tires to get ideas from the medium-level shelter and service magazines and is perpetually depressed because her home isn't furnished as much like a dream house as she would like it to be. In this she is quite different from the Upper-Lower wife who is apt to care more about having a full array of expensive, gleaming white appliances in her kitchen than a doll's house of a living room. Where the Lower-Middle housewife usually has a definite style in mind which she's striving to follow, the Upper-Lower woman simply follows the lead of newspaper furniture advertising (and what she sees when window shopping) toward furniture which is "modern-looking," by which she means the "latest thing" that has hit the mass market.

A great many more examples of differences in consumption patterns by class levels could be given, but the principal ones have been well reported already—facetiously by Vance Packard and seriously by Pierre Martineau;[9] for further amplification on this point the latter source is recommended. The significance to merchandisers and advertisers of these findings about motivational differences between classes is fairly obvious, the major idea being that for many products, advertising appeals and merchandising techniques must be differentially geared to the points of view reflected in these three main social classes. Advertising of brands or goods aimed at a specific class must take

[8] This study has been published under the name *Workingman's Wife*, Oceana Press, New York, 1959, by Lee Rainwater, Richard P. Coleman, and Gerald Handel.

[9] See Pierre Martineau, *Motivation in Advertising,* McGraw-Hill Book Company, New York, 1957, and "Social Classes and Spending Behavior," *The Journal of Marketing,* vol. 23, no. 2, October, 1958, pp. 121–130.

into account the motivations of that class, and not try to sell everything as if it were an Upper Class or Upper-Middle status symbol.

Up to now, we've been talking about product areas–clothing, furniture, and residential neighborhoods–where the relationship between social class and quality of goods purchased is highest. In these things the so-called "Quality Market" and the Upper-Middle (and higher) markets coincide. That is, the purchasers of highest quality clothing and highest quality furniture are more nearly from the Upper-Middle and Upper social classes than from the highest income categories, and so on it goes down the hierarchy. The correlation between price of goods purchased and social class is relatively quite high in these product areas while the correlation between price paid and annual income is lower than one might expect.

There is another group of products which are not linked in such a direct way with social class, but neither are they linked with income categories in any obvious relationship. The current car market provides an instructive example of this situation, for the nature of the market cannot be grasped by using one or the other concept exclusively. What is happening in today's car market can only be understood when income categories are placed into a social class framework.

## THE "OVERPRIVILEGED" AS "QUALITY MARKET"

Within each social class group there are families and individuals whose incomes are above average for their class. The Upper-Lower family with an income above $7,000 a year–sometimes a product of both husband and wife working, and sometimes not–is an example of this. So, too, is the Lower-Middle Class business owner or salesman who makes more than $10,000 a year, but has no interest in either the concerts or country clubs of Upper-Middledom and hence is still Lower-Middle Class. The Upper-Middle Class couple with more than $25,000 a year at its disposal but no desire to play the "society game" of subscription balls or private schools is also in this category. These are what might be called the "overprivileged" segments of each class. They are not "overprivileged" in the absolute sense, of course; they are "overprivileged," however, relative to what is required or needed by families in their class. After they have met the basic expectations and standards of their group in the housing, food, furnishing, and clothing areas, they have quite a bit of money left over which is their equivalent of "discretionary income."

In much the same way, each class has its "underprivileged" members; in the Upper-Middle Class these are the younger couples who havent's made the managerial ranks yet, the college professors, the genteel professionals, and a few downwardly mobile people from high-status backgrounds who are trying to hang on to what fragments of status they have left–for the most part these people are below the $12,000-a-year mark and they can barely meet some of the basic requirements of Upper-Middle life, much less experience any of its little luxuries; in the Lower-Middle Class these are the poorly paid bank tellers, the rows of bookkeepers in railroad offices, the school teachers with considerably more status aspiration than income; and in the Upper-Lower Class it is almost any family earning less than $4,500 or $5,000 a year, at today's rates of pay in metropolitan areas.

In the middle of each class's income range are its "average" members, families who are neither underprivileged nor overprivileged by the standards of their class. You might think of this as the Upper-Middle Class family between $12,000 and $20,000 a year, the Lower-Middle family in the $7,000 to $9,000 range, and the Upper-Lower family near $6,000 per annum. However, this word of caution is necessary: a lot of people in the middle income range of their class see themselves as "underprivileged" because they are aspiring to become one of the "overprivileged" in their class or to move on up the ladder to a higher class.

The relevance of all this to the car market is that when you look at this particular market today, you find it is the "average" members of each class, whether Upper-Middle, Lower-Middle, or Upper-Lower, who constitute the heart of the Low-Priced Three's audience; these are the people who are buying Fords and Chevrolets this year and last, and probably next. No longer is the Ford and Chevrolet market just a Lower-Middle income market, or (in class terms) a Lower-Middle or a Lower Class market. Rather, it is recruited from the middle income group *within each* social class. Indeed, the $15,000-a-year Upper-Middle "organization man" is apt to choose a Ford or Chevy from the Impala-Galaxie level or else a top-price station wagon once he ventures into this market, whereas the average-income Lower-Middle man will settle for middle-series Bel Air or Fairlane 500, and the "average-income" Upper Lower guy either splurges for an Impala or "sensibly" contents himself with the spartan Biscayne.

While this has been happening to the Low-Price Three makes the heart of the medium-price car market has relocated in the "overprivileged" segments of each class. Today, rich blue-collar workers are joining prosperous Lower-Middle Class salesmen and well-to-do Upper-Middle Class business owners in buying Pontiacs, Buicks, Oldsmobiles, Chryslers, and even Cadillacs. In fact, what there is left of big-car lust in our society is found at peak strength among the "overprivileged" Upper-Lowers or else among men who have achieved higher status, but grew up as kids in the Upper-Lower class and have not forgotten their wide-eyed envy of the big car owner.

Finally, as you may have guessed by now, the compact car market's heart is to be found in the "underprivileged" segments of each class (here we are speaking of the market for a compact as a first car). The overwhelming majority of Rambler purchasers, Falcon buyers, and foreign economy car owners come from this socio-economic territory. Thus, it is not the really poor who are buying these cheapest, most economical cars–rather it is those who think of themselves as poor relative to their status aspirations and to their needs for a certain level of clothing, furniture, and housing which they could not afford if they bought a more expensive car.

The market for compacts as second cars is somewhat more complicated in its socio-economic geography, being located in the middle range of the Upper-Middle Class, and the "overprivileged" segment of the Lower-Middle. The "overprivileged" Upper-Middle may have one as a third car, but he prefers either a T-Bird, a foreign sports car, a Pontiac convertible, or a beat-up station wagon as his second car, while the "over-privileged" Upper-Lower is apt to go for a used standard if he wants a second car.

If marketers and advertisers had assumed that the market for compacts was going to be the lowest-income or lowest-status members of our society, they would have seriously miscalculated in their merchandising and advertising approach. Rambler, for one, did not make this mistake. American Motors advertised its cars as "bringing sense into the auto market" and thus enabled people who bought one to pride themselves on the high-minded rationality they had displayed. Rambler owners, as they drive down the street, are not ashamed that they couldn't afford better– instead, as the company has told them to be, they are proud that they did not yield, like their neighbors, to base emotional desires for a car bloated in size beyond necessity and loaded in gadgetry beyond reason. Compact car owners have their own form of snobbery–what might be called "sensibility snobbery"–with which to content themselves and justify their purchase.

This analysis of the car market is one example of what I mean by the sophisticated application of social class concepts to marketing and advertising problems. There are many products and many brands which, like cars, are more nearly symbols of high status class within class than symbols of higher status per se. A color television set is such a product, or at least it was two years ago when Social Research, Inc., studied its market. At the time color television manufacturers were puzzled because sales were thinly spread throughout the income scale, without any noticeable increase in concentration until an extremely high level was reached. Furthermore, they were unable to see any particular relationship between social class and color set ownership, since about as many Upper-Lower Class people owned them as did Upper-Middles. However, when the two factors of income and class were put together, in the manner described above, it became clear that the color television market was concentrated among high-income or "overprivileged" members of each social class. Other products which bear this complicated relationship to class and income are the more costly brands and larger sizes of home appliances. Fairly expensive recreational equipment like outboard motor boats also tend to be in this category.

In summary, today's market for quality goods and quality brands is not necessarily drawn from what has historically been described as the "Quality Market" of Upper-Middle and Upper Class people, nor even necessarily from the highest income categories. Rather, in many instances, it is drawn from those people within each social level who have the most discretionary income available for enjoying life's little extras above and beyond the requirements of their class. Every merchandiser and advertiser ought to take a good hard look at what he is selling and ask himself if it bears this particular relationship to the class and income picture. If his product does, and if his brand is one of the more expensive, then he should merchandise it not as if it were just for social climbers or for the upper classes, but rather as part of the Better Life, U.S.A. If, on the other hand, his brand is one of the least expensive, then he is not just selling to the poor, but rather to those in all classes who feel it is only sensible on their part to settle for a brand such as his and save the difference for other things which are more important in their statement of social class aspiration and identity.

## SOCIAL CLASS ISN'T ALWAYS IMPORTANT

Now, to make the picture complete, it must be pointed out that Social Research, Inc., has found some products in which the income factor is all-important and the social class variable is relevant only to the extent that it is correlated with income. Perhaps the most perfect example of this is the market for air conditioners in Southwestern cities. There, everybody–except the sickly and the extremely old-fashioned–agree that air conditioning one's home is imperative if summer is to be survived with any degree of comfort. Consequently the expensiveness of a family's air conditioning equipment–whether centrally installed, or window units to the number of four, three, two, or one–is directly correlated with family income. It is not merely a function of discretionary income–as in our example about purchase of medium-priced cars; it is instead almost completely a function of total annual income. If more Upper-Middles than Upper-Lowers are fully air-conditioned it is only because more of them can afford to be; it is not because Upper-Middles as a group are placing higher priority on the air-conditioned existence.

Undoubtedly air conditioners are not alone in being classless–so that one more thing the marketer who uses social class in a truly sophisticated way needs to understand is that there can be occasions when it is an irrelevant variable. Realizing this, he will not become disenchanted with social class when he finds a marketing problem where it does not shed light or where it does not seem pertinent. Of course, he will want to make sure that in advertising such a product there is indeed no need to take class into account. After all, some apparently classless products are properly sold to the market in a segmental approach, appealing first on one ground to one class, then on other grounds to another.

There are other products–and probably air conditioning is one of them and children's play clothes may be another–where this is not necessary. For such products some factor, such as physical comfort (in the one case) or simple durability (in the other), is so basic in the consumer's consideration that all other motivations pale into insignificance beside it. There are even products, like beer, where the democratic approach–that is, a tone of "let's-all-be-good-fellows-together" is exactly right and segmental appeals or snob stories are all wrong.

Another aspect to the sophisticated employment of social class refers back to the point made earlier that social class groups are not always homogeneous. It must be recognized that at times a product's market is formed by "highbrows" from the Upper-Upper Class on down to the Lower-Middle, or by "suburbanites" and suburban-minded people of all classes–in which case the social class variable may confuse a market analysis more than clarify it.

Particularly must merchandisers and market analysts beware of equating "Class" with "Brow"; for they are not synonymous. For example, the Upper-Middle Class and those above it are mainly middlebrow in taste (veering toward an all-American lower-middlebrow level of preferences in television shows and advertising messages) even though the majority of highbrows are found at this level. At times advertisers have made the mistake of assuming that the Upper-Middle Class should be appealed to in a highly sophisticated fashion—and though this is just fine if the product itself is likely to appeal primarily to the Manhattanized type of Upper-Middle, it is not correct if it is expected to sell to the kind of doctor in Dubuque who enjoys a visit to New York every now and then but would never want to live there.

In short, not only must the sophisticated marketer abandon social class in favor of income categories on occasion in his analysis and interpretation of a market, he must recognize that at times both income and class are superseded in importance by divisions of the public into brow levels, by divisions into "high mobiles" and "low mobiles," innovators and non-innovators, inner-directed and other-directed, urbanites, suburbanites, exurbanites, ruralites, and Floridians, or what have you. Usually, of course, fullest understanding of a market will require that social class be linked in with whichever sub-categorization proves pertinent from among those in the catalogue just recited, much as income and class were linked together for fullest comprehension of the car market.

As a final point, let it be noted that the way of life and the goals of people in each social class are in perpetual flux. Neither the "who" of each class nor "what motivates them" are constants to be assumed without continual re-evaluation. Right now, particularly, it is very clear that our society is changing. Every year the collar-color line is breaking down further. More blue-collar workers are becoming Middle Class as well as middle income and Modern, and a white-collar position is less and less a guarantee of Lower-Middle status. As a consequence of this, the Lower-Middle Class is perhaps somewhat more "materialistic" in outlook and slightly less "respectability" conscious than it was twenty-five years ago, or even eight. Meanwhile, for men and women to achieve Upper-Middle status without college backgrounds is becoming more and more difficult, so that this class is turning much more worldly-wise and well read, much less conventionally bourgeois than it was in the zenith of Babbitt's day.

In short, the form of our society and its division into social classes is not fixed as of Yankee City in 1931, Jonesville in 1944, Kansas City in 1952, or St. Louis in 1960. We won't be able to say exactly the same things about either the classes themselves or their relationships to specific markets by next year at this time. This fact about the American class structure, that it is not static, that it is in the process of change, is in itself important to merchandisers, to advertisers, to anyone in selling. Among other things, it means that undoubtedly they have played a part in past changes and can play a leading role in directing future changes. But of more direct concern here to the marketing analyst it means that if he allows his stratification concept to become dated, his use of it will cease as of that moment to be sophisticated.

# IV

# *Developing the Marketing Plan*

*Once a firm has specified its objectives in terms of the wants and needs of its target segments (as discussed in Section III, "Establishing Marketing Objectives") it must then develop a plan by which it hopes to accomplish them. This section deals with these planning activities.*

*The growing emergence of the marketing concept has contributed to the increased emphasis which management is placing on planning. An understanding of consumer wants and needs and the environmental factors which affect them, plus a realistic appraisal of the firm's resources as compared with those of competitors with respect to the wants and needs of the segments involved, provides a realistic setting for effective marketing planning.*

*Planning has frequently been described as an art, and thus has not been given enough analysis and thought. But for a variety of reasons, most of which have been dealt with in the previous two sections, most management groups are now placing increased emphasis on planning and are constantly seeking more efficient ways of programming the firm's activities over time. Thus, the development of mathematical decision-making models and the availability of high-speed computers have had a decided impact on planning.*

*Optimum planning should take place at several different levels within the organization and must be coordinated carefully in order to maintain the maximum adjustment to the market. Accordingly, management increasingly is turning to specialists from a variety of disciplines to help in formulating what hopefully will be the most effective plan of action.*

*Inevitably the process of planning is a difficult task, for it deals with the future which never can be understood or known with certainty. Nevertheless, planning must go on, and the central problem is how to develop what are believed to be the most efficient combination of strategies. But since the individual marketing strategies—such as those concerned with product, price, channels of distribution, personal selling, physical distribution, and advertising—can be implemented in countless ways, the problem of the most efficient "mix" is a complex one. Since the strategies are essentially marketing strategies, marketing management must play a very important role in the overall planning process.*

# 23. THEORY AND PRACTICE OF MARKET PLANNING

*Wroe Alderson*

*The concept of planning as distinct and separate from the actual planning activities is the subject of this article.*

*The author deals with planning primarily from the time dimension point of view. He stresses planning for a going operation as contrasted with planning for a new or contingent operation.*

Business planning is the linking of two or more executive decisions with the aim of maximizing their joint effectiveness. At least one of the bundle of decisions constituting a plan can be characterized as a strategic decision because of its controlling influence on other decisions. At least one of the remaining decisions may be characterized as a routine or tactical decision because it takes place within the framework established by the choice of strategy.

A strategic decision entails risks of the first magnitude since it defines and limits the range of freedom for more detailed decisions. In the choice of a marketing strategy these risks are complicated by uncertainty as to the counterstrategies of competitors and the not wholly predictable shifts in consumer tastes and preferences. The strategist in marketing creates a plan in order to give coordination and effective impact to marketing effort. He will never be sure whether it is a good plan unless he sticks by it long enough to give it a chance to work. On the other hand, new developments may generate compelling pressures for revising or scrapping the plan. A good marketing strategist like a good military strategist must expect the unexpected, keeping some part of his resources in a fluid reserve to meet contingencies.

Source: From *Cost and Profit Outlook*, vol. II, nos. 7 and 8, July–August, 1958, 6 pp. Wroe Alderson: President, Alderson Associates, Inc., Philadelphia.

Planning is frequently identified not with executive decision-making but with the activities of a staff planner who submits a program for consideration or decision. Since market planning is futile except as it gives direction to action, it should be defined to include activities at both the executive and staff level. At least three phases of the planning process should be distinguished, namely choice of strategy, program design, and adoption and installation of the strategy and program. To discuss planning as an orderly discipline or procedure even more detailed phases of the planning process should be separately identified. The only one that need be mentioned here is the operating audit which should precede even a tentative choice of strategy. The audit is an examination of where a marketing operation is today before trying to decide where it can and should be tomorrow.

## TYPES OF PLANNING PROBLEMS

The network of decisions which constitute a marketing plan must deal with opportunities and obstacles in the market, with values and objectives, with the marketing organization and the resources available to it, and with the times and places at which specified activities are to occur. Each of these elements raises its own special problems as to the most effective relationships among decisions. These are corresponding types of planning or programming, including those with special emphasis on resources, on spatial relations, or on a sequence of activities taking place over time.

The new techniques of linear or mathematical programming are concerned primarily about relationships among resources or inputs into an operating system. They deal with the fundamental economic problem of finding the optimum allocation of resources to achieve a specified result. They enable the analyst to cope with more complex problems of allocation than are involved in the relatively simple illustrations discussed in economic theory. This new analytical framework can embrace the limitations on choice and on flexibility in the use of resources which face the executive in every practical marketing situation. Such are the problems of allocating a total marketing budget to advertising, promotion and personal selling, or determining the relative emphasis on product improvement, price appeal, and increased promotion in expanding the market for a product.

Planning problems which emphasize spatial relationships are common in marketing. These include the determination of sales territories and territorial quotas, the location of stores and warehouses, and the internal layout of a retail store or wholesale warehouse. Specialized procedures, in some cases of a very advanced technical nature, have emerged in these areas of market planning. Location studies for stores and retail developments exhibit a growing affinity for more ambitious studies of spatial relationships such as city and regional planning.

While marketing obviously involves the allocation of resources and decisions concerning spatial relationships, the term "market planning" is commonly associated with an emphasis on the time dimension. A marketing program specifies a sequence of activities to take place over some period of time such as the next fiscal year or the next five years. In special cases a marketing plan may omit reference to calendar time but simply specify what should occur month by month after some initial event has occurred to trigger action. The event establishing "D-day" may be the public announcement of a new product introduction or a move by competition which is anticipated but of uncertain date.

The remainder of this discussion of planning will all be from the viewpoint which emphasizes the time dimension. There are three principal reasons for taking this approach. One is a conviction that techniques are less advanced in this aspect of planning, that the problems are more difficult, and that the need for technical progress in planning is most urgent. The second is that there is a time dimension in the market itself which should be more clearly recognized in planning. A third reason relates to the intriguing and fundamental problems as to the timing and duration of the planning process.

Programming over time, as already indicated, can be divided into two quite different types of situations, one pertaining to planning for a going operation and the other to planning for a new or contingent operation. Some confusion arises in discussions of market planning when some participants in a discussion are thinking in terms of an existing operation and others in terms of a new operation, such as establishing a new company or introducing a new product. The requirements for an adequate plan are not really very different in the two cases, but there are understandable differences of emphasis in the way that written plans would be presented for the two cases. A plan for introducing a new product is more likely to give a fully detailed specification of all of the activities involved. A written plan for a going operation may assume that those who are going to see it are familiar with present activities, so that only the proposed changes need to be specified. On the other hand, a plan for a going operation may be more specific as to the dates on which action is to take place and the individuals who are responsible for these activities. In the case of a new operation the planner may feel that it is sufficient to specify the time required for successive steps or even to go no further than to name the steps in the sequence in which they should occur. So long as no initial date has been established it is not feasible to state a plan for a new operation in terms of calendar time.

The emphasis in this discussion will be on planning for a going operation, partly on the assumption that the bulk of market planning will lie in this area as planning becomes more fully established as a staff function. If planning is being carried on regularly on behalf of the marketing organization, the introduction of a new product may very properly be regarded as a modification in existing operations. There is, of course, the genuine special case of plans concerned with the establishment of an entirely new company which would deserve separate consideration in a comprehensive treatment of the subject.

## THE CASE AGAINST PLANNING

Before proceeding further with the discussion of planning procedures, it should be recognized that the planning movement in business has not evoked universal enthusiasm even though it is making steady progress. There is a case against planning which ranges from the evidence that many firms have been able to get along without it to active opposition stemming from several sources.

Since a marketing plan seeks to relate marketing decisions more effectively and to achieve better coordination of marketing effort, it is interesting to speculate on what has served these purposes where there has been no formal planning. In many cases the factor seems to have been rapid growth in expanding in relatively noncompetitive markets. The momentum of company expansion can force a substantial amount of coordination. The general direction is set by the growth trend and day-to-day decisions are related to the successive adjustments which growth requires. Coordination here is something like the coordination of effort which is brought about by an assembly line in a factory. The basic operation goes relentlessly ahead and the role of the individual is clearly defined in trying to keep up with it. A company which has relied on momentum rather than planning can look very successful one year and very inept the next. When growth levels off or volume actually declines the coordinating effect of momentum is lost and executives may begin to work at cross purposes. This type of disorganization following rapid growth can show up in a moderate-sized company as well as in a large one. The large company, in fact, may have been forced already to adopt at least the rudiments of planning simply because of the growing size and complexity of the operation.

Frequently a company of moderate size appears to get along reasonably well without formal planning because it is still a one-man operation. This one individual may have a clear enough vision of his objectives, a strong enough drive toward achieving them, and sufficient personal force in exacting performance of others to supply all of the coordination which appears to be needed. In situations of this kind coordination breaks down when the company outgrows the man, or where the individual who has been the driving force is no longer able or willing to meet the conditions for the next stage in company progress.

In either type of case described, the argument against planning may stress the rapidity of change and the futility of planning for conditions which do not remain stable long enough for the plan to take effect. This may in part be a mask for the really basic attitude of a strongminded individual who would rather trust his own judgment on the spur of the moment than the more calculated foresight of any staff group. A line executive responsible for decision may be skeptical about any forecast for the future as the basis for planning, about the ability of anyone else to translate facts and forecasts into appropriate plans of action, and he may resist any systematic procedure which poses a potential threat to his own freedom of action. Top management may also have reservations about the planning concept, fearing that some executives may use it as an escape from the risks and responsibilities of prompt decision.

With respect to the introduction of new products, some very large companies are skeptical about the value of detailed planning. They assume that a substantial percentage of all new products will fail and that success lies in the direction of bringing out many new products and then pushing those which gain a foothold. This substitute for planning would appear to be an expensive one even for large companies, and an impossible one for small companies.

The introduction of new products is the one area in which most marketing executives would regard some measure of market planning as absolutely essential. There is real merit, however, in the contention that no market plan for a new product can be fully evaluated aside from an actual market test. Many firms meet this problem by introducing a product in one market after another and learning by its mistakes as the area of distribution is expanded. This procedure is in no way inconsistent with a professional approach to the original program design to avoid useless mistakes or the repetition of the same mistakes on one product after another. Resistance to more thorough market planning for new products arises at least in part from the magnitude of the difficulties. A major difficulty, for example, is in the timing of the introduction of a new product. On the one hand is the need for waiting until the major problems of design and production have been solved. On the other hand, there is the urgency to get started in order to preserve an edge over competitors who may have similar products under development. In the most successful operations product planning and market planning proceed simultaneously, and both are subject to being accelerated or delayed to meet the requirements of the competitive situation.

## PLANNING AS MATCHING MEANS AND ENDS

Despite the plausibility of some of the arguments against planning, every firm and every household engages in planning whether its techniques of planning are rudimentary or advanced. Opposition to formal planning is really an attempt to control the planning function and to keep it within a framework which the particular management finds congenial.

All basic management decisions may be described as the matching of means and ends. Whenever this matching process involves two or more decisions pertaining to activities to take place at different times, the executive is engaged in planning even though he is the type who prefers to call it something else. Take the case of a sales manager for a company selling products with diverse seasonal patterns. If he merely specifies successive areas of concentration for his salesmen in each of the four quarters he is obviously engaged in market planning.

In developing such a plan for deploying his sales force the sales manager is presumably guided by some conception of what he is trying to achieve. It may be a volume figure representing a 10 per cent increase over the preceding year, leveling out of sales volume by months, a shift of volume into more profitable lines, or an opening up of new territories or types of outlets. The matching of means against ends in this relatively simple case is essentially the same process as for more comprehensive forms of market planning which might deal with advertising as well as selling, and with product line and pricing as well as with marketing effort.

But while the relation of means and ends is fundamental to planning it does not follow that decisions as to ends or objectives should always be made first. The staff planner is tempted to adopt the traditional attitude of the economist and to expect management to provide a neat definition of its objectives so that the planner can proceed in orderly fashion to describe the means for attaining objectives. Actually it is quite as appropriate to start with means as to start with ends since the purpose of planning is to achieve a balance between the two. Instead of asking, "Given these objectives what is the best means of achieving them?" it is quite as valid to ask, "Given these means or resources what objectives are appropriate for the operation?"

This point becomes clearer if the problem is described in terms of the inputs and outputs for an operating system. Objectives are the expected outputs which caused the operating system to be created or maintained, or which motivated individuals to attach themselves to the system or to remain with it currently. Means directed toward gaining these ends are applied in the form of inputs into the system. To say that the definition of objectives must come first is equivalent to saying that outputs must be estimated before any attention is given to inputs. Actually it is the matching which is important. Analysis can start with either inputs or outputs. The relationship between the two is progressively clarified in the course of a planning assignment with the ideal aim of finding an optimum balance. An initial situation can be improved upon by increasing the expected outputs, by reducing the inputs, or any combination of changes resulting in a more favorable operating ratio.

The foregoing discussion of objectives may appear to confuse expected and desired outputs. But a desired output has no significance for executive decision unless it is realistically related to a given operating system. Outputs are expected because of the inputs which have been committed to the operation. It is the commitment of resources which gives operational meaning to the notion of desired or expected outputs. After resources have been committed it is quite appropriate for the planner to define appropriate objectives or, in other words, to specify the outputs which can reasonably be expected. When available resources have not yet been committed the planner may start with desired objectives and then specify the resources which must be committed to attain these objectives or expected outputs.

## THE TIME DIMENSION IN MARKET PLANNING

Time is the scarcest and most irrecoverable of all resources. Planning is a way of economizing time. Without planning, crucial dates approach unrecognized, precious time is lost because of lack of estimates of time requirements, and the sequence of events is determined by chance pressures rather than by advance consideration of the most favorable and systematic order. A program provides a road map into the future. Even with the inevitable detours to take account of unforeseen obstructions it is better to use a map than to plunge forward without concern for the character of the terrain.

The time element is especially important in market planning because the market itself has a time dimension. A market is not simply a collection of people or of business firms who may buy our products over some future period. A market grows out of the consuming or producing behavior of these individuals or firms and the way in which our products can fit into these patterns of behavior over a stated operating period. If a given set of prospects do not use our product during 1958 a significant part of our total market has disappeared. The potential market for 1959 and for subsequent years still lies ahead, but the 1958 market is gone forever. What may be even more serious is that the market for 1959 and thereafter is not as large as it ought to be because we did not get started in 1958.

The goals to be attained through a marketing program can usually be specified either in terms of standards of performance for a given operating period or conditions to be achieved by a given date. Performance standards in marketing might be defined in terms of sales and profits. The conditions to be attained might be a certain percentage of market share or a percentage of given type of retail store stocking a product. Quite often both types of goals are sought, one being the major objective and the other regarded as a minimum condition. Thus a firm might seek to obtain a stated market share over the next three years subject to the condition that the percentage of earnings should be maintained or not fall below a stated minimum.

The period to which a plan is to apply is determined by various considerations. For long-range planning the basic factor is what may be called the horizon of predictability. The horizon is the most distant future point for which the planner can realistically foresee the main features of the marketing environment in which the program will have to be carried out. Fortunately the horizon tends to be further away if the planning problem is concerned with the future of a basic product classification than it is when dealing with secondary product features or short-run competitive tactics. Sometimes the horizon is set by some definite consideration such as the expiration date of a patent or franchise or the period required to amortize investment in major equipment.

A very interesting aspect of the time dimension in planning is the question of how much time to allow for the planning function itself. This question arises primarily when a firm is contemplating some basic change in direction and a major program is to be created. Suppose the planning horizon is set for five years ahead. What part of the available time should be allowed for developing a program which will be in effect for the remainder of the five-year period? The more detailed the plan the longer it may take to create it. But the longer the time conserved in planning the shorter the period over which it can be effective. The staff planner will probably push for ample time in which to prepare a valid plan. The line executive who is responsible for getting results under the plan will doubtless press for the earliest possible completion.

Top management may have to decide this issue as to the terminal date for planning on fairly arbitrary grounds. Nevertheless, there is a challenging question here for the theory of planning. In allotting time for planning, management is making an optimizing decision which might be subject to more precise determination. Management wants the best plan possible to go into effect as soon as possible and any choice of a terminal date represents a compromise between these two considerations.

Aside from exploring this intriguing theoretical issue, one avenue for practical progress lies in speeding up the planning process. New mathematical techniques for evaluating marketing strategies offer possibilities of acceleration. Another avenue is that envisaged in this article, namely, offering a road map for market planning to make it a swift and orderly operation. Planning itself is a time consuming activity unless the planner has a well established channel to follow. There are other opportunities for saving time which cannot be covered fully here, involving better coordination of planning and executive action and the partial overlapping of program design and installation.

## MAJOR STEPS IN THE PLANNING PROCESS

For the present purpose of conveying a general conception of the planning process it may be divided into four major steps. At each step the marketing operation is viewed from a particular perspective. The relationship between inputs and outputs is progressively clarified as planning moves through these successive phases. These four steps, as previously enumerated are:

The Market Position Audit
The Generation of Strategies
Design of the Program
Acceptance and Installation

The first stage looks at the firm and its place in the market in much the same way as a field zoologist would look at an animal species in its natural habitat. This step is similar to what is called a situation analysis by many marketing and advertising men. The term "market position audit" is preferred here since the planner is not merely trying to describe a situation but is searching for something. The object of his search is whatever feature distinguishes the firm from all others, what is unique about the niche it occupies in the market or its way of occupying it. The unique matching of a place or opportunity in the market by a differentiated firm as an organized system of marketing effort is what constitutes its market position. The planner examines the firm's position in order to understand the basis for its actual or potential success. Even mere survival in a competitive world is a form of success and cannot be lightly dismissed by the planner in search of a strategy and program to help the firm do better.

The audit takes a functional view of the firm, being concerned with the way the operation functions in the market rather than primarily with the objectives of its participants. Fundamentally the firm must take its marching orders from the market. The first issue as to balance between inputs and outputs pertains to the firm's suppliers and customers and whether the firm provides an effective channel through which they can reach each other. Competitors provide alternative channels for suppliers seeking customers and consumers seeking products. The core of a company's market position consists of those customers and suppliers who have no fully acceptable alternative route to market. All firms get some fringe business from those who are indifferent or use other routes by preference. The growth and stability of a firm, however, depends on preserving or enlarging the core of its position.

A firm's market position is thus defined in terms of customers, suppliers and competition. The relative importance of these factors varies from one situation to another. The market-oriented firm may generally be assumed to be one which recognizes that it owes its continued existence to its customers. But there are numerous cases, as in the marketing of agricultural products and raw materials, in which the firm's position rests primarily on the urgency of suppliers seeking outlets. In general the firm has to function in such a way as to give satisfactory service to both customers and suppliers. Otherwise it may be by-passed because of pressures building up on one side of the market or the other.

Competition, actual or potential, can invade the firm's market position by taking advantage of these pressures. At a given stage in its history a firm is relatively vulnerable or invulnerable to competition. For many a firm the best way to meet competition is to apply itself everlastingly to improving its services to customers and suppliers. This is true in the main for the widely prevalent market situation which economists describe as oligopoly. The chief exceptions are in clear cases of doupoly in which two strong firms divide the market between them or in which a smaller but ambitious firm is trying to match or surpass the leader. Competitive trends and strategies are an essential point of reference in such cases.

The second stage is concerned with the dynamic or strategic view of the marketing operation. Its purpose is to generate strategies for consideration and final selection. The first stage takes the operation as it is but the second is concerned with how it may be changed. The changes which merit evaluation are those which give promise of increasing the outputs of the system either absolutely or relative to inputs. A strategy is a matching of a pattern of inputs against a pattern of outputs. A proposed strategy may modify the existing patterns so substantially as to constitute what amounts to a new operation. In terms of market position the aim of a strategy is to improve performance in the niche the company now occupies, to enhance and enlarge its position, or to accomplish a transition into a new area of operation, merely holding on to its present position or even abandoning it eventually.

The generation of strategies is a fundamental phase of planning since the purpose of a marketing program is to give effect to a strategy. The explicit consideration and acceptance of a strategy may mark the transition to formal planning from a previous reliance on the momentum of growth. The germ of a strategic idea is most likely to spring from intuition tempered by experience. The staff planner provides the material for intuition to work on by listing the possible strategies consistent with the firm's present position or which would provide a transition to an improved position. As one professional planner puts it, a fundamental strategy is a conception of the manner in which the firm wishes to occupy the market. There are usually sharply contrasting alternatives to be considered such as producing a high quality product for an exclusive market as compared to a stripped down product at an economy price. Planning techniques also embrace formal methods for predicting the outcome of alternative strategies.

The third stage is the design of the marketing program to give effect to the chosen strategy. This is the step which tends to be identified with staff planning as narrowly defined or restricted. It is possible but not necessarily desirable for programming to be carried out by an individual or group that had nothing to do with the determination of objectives and strategies. In the best practice these fundamental issues remain open during the programming stage. It may not be prudent to make a final choice of strategies until there has been an opportunity to review the corresponding programs, at least in outline form. It may not be possible to fix on objectives or expected outputs without some test as to what outputs are feasible, given the available inputs.

While programming is discussed here as only one of the four phases of the planning process it has many technical problems of its own. Program design begins by laying out a sequence of activities to take place over a stated period of time. In marketing it will not ordinarily be a simple sequence but a complex of concurrent sequences. Programming offers a severe challenge to the skill of the planner in the systematic construction and coordination of sequences of marketing activities. A budget and a time schedule are essential elements in a fully specified program.

At the programming stage the planner must distinguish between the analytical and the administrative views of the plan. The analytical view utilizes an operating model to decide whether the program effectively expresses a strategy and to evaluate the probabilities of achieving the expected outputs. Analytical models are very helpful in making a final choice of strategies. The administrative view translates the plan into detailed working instructions. It deals with the concrete organization rather than an abstract model. It fixes responsibility as to who will direct particular activities at given times and places. The analytical view gives confidence that the plan will work and the administrative view is the instrument for actually putting it to work.

The final stage of planning is the adoption and installation of a strategy and program. Up to this point the application of the plan is purely hypothetical and planning may have taken place in a vacuum so far as responsibility for action is concerned. The adoption of a plan is the mass production of executive decisions. That is to say, it confirms by a single step the entire network of decisions embodied in the plan. The process of adopting the plan may spread over a considerable period with the executive giving provisional approval to one aspect and then another. In a real sense, however, the adoption of a plan is a single executive action since the essence of planning is the interdependence of these decisions which must be linked together for maximum effect.

The fundamental meaning of the acceptance of a plan lies in the commitment of resources required under the plan to attain the expected outputs. The highest function of the executive is to commit existing resources or to obtain additional resources as needed. He cannot be said to have established official objectives for the firm until he commits the resources which impart some degree of probability to the attainment of expected outputs.

The installation of a plan means presenting it to the organization which is going to carry it out and convincing them of its workability. It further means instructing each participant in his individual role and training him for it if his previous experience is inadequate. The staff planner may or may not share responsibility for the details of installation but he is usually on hand to assist with the presentation. In the best practice installation is well thought out before the plan is completed. Market planning according to this four-step model can greatly enhance the effectiveness of marketing action.

# 24. FRAMEWORK FOR MARKETING STRATEGY

*Harry Allison*

*It is the responsibility of the marketing staff to maximize a firm's total revenue net of selling costs. This calls for statistical as well as sales "know-how," as many factors must be equated and others, such as fixed and variable costs, "juggled" to produce the most advantageous net possible.*

*Outlined here is a framework within which to view marketing situations and strategies that might be helpful in developing an optimal marketing plan.*

The purpose of this paper is to accent both the need for a systematic approach to marketing management decision-making and the need—in each decision-making situation—for a complete consideration of the many variables involved. The emphasis is on how marketing decisions should be made rather than on how they are, in fact, made; yet, it is hoped that the former parallels the latter closely enough that the marketing practitioner does not feel uncomfortable.

The ideas presented are not particularly new. The writer has drawn heavily from an article by P. J. Verdoorn[1] and also from writings by Wroe Alderson,[2] Albert W. Frey,[3] Alfred R. Oxenfeldt,[4] D. M. Phelps,[5] and John A. Howard.[5] Comments of colleagues and students have also contributed to all sections of this article.

[1] P. J. Verdoorn, "Marketing from the Producer's Point of View," *The Journal of Marketing,* vol. XX, 3, January, 1956, pp. 221–235.

[2] Wroe Alderson, *Marketing Behavior and Executive Action,* Richard D. Irwin, Inc., Homewood, Ill., 1957, particularly chap. IV.

Source: From *California Management Review,* vol. 4, Fall, 1961, pp. 75-95.  Harry Allison: Assistant Professor, School of Business Administration, University of California, Berkeley.

Briefly, the framework views the job of the marketing staff as that of identifying all relevant marketing alternatives confronting the firm, of choosing from among these alternatives the particular alternative at each output level which best satisfies the goals of the firm, and of carrying out the marketing side of the firm's final plan of action as efficiently and effectively as possible.

The process of choosing among the relevant alternatives involves the marketing staff in an attempt to maximize long-run total revenue net of selling costs at particular output levels, given the outside-imposed and firm-imposed restrictions on the marketing staff's actions.[6] This requires that optimum use be made of those factors which both affect total revenue net of selling costs and are under the control of the firm.

To achieve optimum use of these firm-controlled factors, the marketing staff must take into account not only the effect of the firm-controlled factors on each other, but also the impact of those factors which affect total revenue net of selling costs and are in some way influenced, but not controlled, by the firm and the effect of those factors which affect total revenue net of selling costs but are neither controlled nor influenced by the firm.

Optimum use of each firm-controlled factor which affects total revenue net of selling costs implies that–within the outside-imposed and firm-imposed restrictions–the marketing staff allocates the firm's marketing efforts in such a way that all expenditures on marketing are put to the best possible use. This, in turn, requires that the marginal effort expended on each controlled factor returns the same marginal revenue net of selling costs per dollar spent and that no better obtainable combined use for the controlled factors exists at the particular levels of output.

The optimum output level for the firm is determined by equating marginal revenue net of selling costs to marginal cost of production. When there are no effective restrictions on the actions of the marketing and production staffs and when the above equalities are

[3] Albert W. Frey, *How Many Dollars for Advertising,* The Ronald Press Company, New York, 1955, particularly chap. 4.

[4] Alfred R. Oxenfeldt, "The Formulation of a Market Strategy" in Eugene J. Kelley and William Lazer, *Managerial Marketing: Perspectives and Viewpoints,* Richard D. Irwin, Inc., Homewood, Ill., 1958, pp. 264–272.

[5] D. M. Phelps, *Sales Management,* Richard D. Irwin, Inc., Homewood, Ill., 1953. Also, John A. Howard, *Marketing Management: Analysis and Decision,* Richard D. Irwin, Inc., Homewood, Ill., 1957, particularly chaps. I and II.

[6] Total relationships are used throughout this paper rather than average relationships, because dealing with totals eliminates the danger of becoming engrossed with increasing profit per unit at the expense of total profits, and also because total relationships are a step closer to the underlying sales and production input data and to the concept of marginal increments than are average relationships. Selling costs are taken to include the costs associated with such activities as advertising, personal selling, physical distribution, and services. While variables such as product design and quality level are considered to be marketing variables in this paper, changes in such variables are treated as defining a new product with new revenue and cost functions. The costs associated with such changes would not be subtracted from total revenue in getting the total-revenue-net-of-selling-costs curve but rather would be handled on the production side through a shift in the total-production-cost curve.

realized, each controlled factor in marketing and production is exploited to the point where the marginal contribution net of all costs—marketing and production costs, including the cost of the factor itself—of the last dollar expended on each factor is zero.

## IDENTIFYING ALTERNATIVES

Selected marketing plans can, of course, be no better than the best of the identified alternatives. Whether the specific group of alternatives under consideration for a particular output level includes the optimum marketing plan for that level depends on the marketing intuition and imaginative reasoning of the individuals involved; on their own past experience; on their observation of current and former practices of the firm, competitors, and firms in other industries; and on the time and resources devoted to devising plans. The availability of both time and resources for use in determining alternatives is frequently limited. Even if not, at some point, the benefits anticipated from any further search for alternatives will no longer justify the cost.

## RESTRICTIONS IMPOSED BY THE FIRM

Firm-imposed restrictions on the marketing staff's freedom to choose among the alternatives it does identify may arise from goals or objectives established for the firm by top management, restrictions set by top management on the manipulation of the firm-controlled factors affecting total revenue net of selling costs, or the past activities of the firm.

*The firm's goals.* The goals or objectives of the firm may range from unqualified short- or long-run profit maximization to goals which by no means need result in either maximum short-run or maximum long-run profits.[7]

Where non-profit-maximizing goals are involved, the marketing staff must first sort the identified marketing alternatives to remove those which do not meet the requirements of the non-profit goals of the firm. Alternatives satisfying the non-profit goals are then sorted by their long-run profit contribution with the marketing staff selecting the plan—for each output level—which seems likely to yield the largest total revenue net of selling costs over the long run.[8]

This view sees the goal of the firm not as maximum long-run profits *per se,* but rather as long-run profits that are as large as possible, given the restricting effect of any and

[7]Examples of the latter are goals to (1) maintain—or increase some stated level—the firm's share of the market, (2) avoid inciting aggressive action from competitors, (3) keep financial control of the firm in the hands of the present ownership, (4) secure some stated rate of sales increase, (5) achieve some particular industrial and/or social power position for the firm's management, (6) maintain some minimum level of employment, (7) continue the firm's position of a leader in new product development or in product quality, or (8) carry out some stated social welfare goal.

[8]The predicted outcome of any plan has a degree of uncertainty, but for some plans the degree of uncertainty is greater than for others; thus, the weighing of alternative plans has to include some element of discounting for uncertainty.

all non-profit goals instituted by the firm's top management. In such context the non-profit goals become simply a part of firm-imposed restrictions on the actions of the marketing and/or production staff. Should the marketing staff find certain non-profit goals too restrictive, it can always appeal to top management to relax the restrictions. However, the marketing staff does not control the final decision on the goals. Therefore, at some point, it must accept the goals established by top management whether it likes them or not.

*Limits on the manipulation of firm-controlled factor.* The dictates of top management with regard to manipulation of firm-controlled factors which affect total revenue net of selling costs may be another restriction on the marketing staff. Such restrictions could be applied through any of the controlled factors cited later in this paper. A few examples of restriction by top management are:

1. setting maximum or minimum prices beyond which the marketing staff cannot go,
2. prescribing or proscribing certain channels of distribution, or
3. insisting that advertising and/or personal selling expenditures not go beyond a certain level.

*Past activities of the firm.* Further firm-imposed restrictions on the actions of the marketing staff arise from past activities of the firm. First, there may be a positive or negative prepossession toward an identified alternative as a result of the firm's previous experience with that alternative or a parallel version of it.

If the firm is reasonably prosperous, its existing marketing policies create a resistance to change simply through their past acceptance and current performance. These existing policies are tried and proven and, as such, hold a degree of attractiveness over the uncertainty of even the most promising of the other alternatives. Likewise, marketing policies which have failed in the past carry a stigma which heavily discounts their current and future consideration, regardless of a change in the conditions involved in their failure.

Secondly, past activities have brought the firm into the current period with a number of commitments which are binding for the present and carry an actual or implied obligation for the future.[9] Such commitments can be changed if there is sufficient time. However, the change may involve absorbing losses on some sunk costs, buying the firm out of certain long-term obligations, and/or accepting some loss of goodwill from those who feel that implied obligations are being disregarded. The situation parallels the production problem of obsolescence in which case the firm finds itself with existing plant and equipment that falls short of the ideal.

[9] The range of commitments affecting marketing activities is quite large, e.g. (1) inventories may be excessive or short; (2) certain facilities and equipment may be owned, while others may be under long-term leases which may include some penalty clause if the agreement is cancelled; (3) critical positions are already staffed and lines of authority and responsibility are established; (4) production licensing agreements may be in existence, and (5) channel agencies may claim certain territorial rights and may hold commitments from the firm involving some degree of specific marketing support.

## OUTSIDE-IMPOSED RESTRICTIONS

The marketing staff finds its range of choice among alternatives limited by forces outside the firm as well as by its own top management. Outside-imposed restrictions may take the form of insufficient time, government regulation, industry environment, and rationing of inputs.

*Insufficient time.* The time restriction has its first impact through limiting the amount of effort the marketing staff can expend in searching for, and in evaluating, alternatives. The result is that fewer alternatives are identified, fewer receive detailed evaluation, and less extensive analyses are given to those that are evaluated.

The other effect of the time restriction is to make some of the identified alternatives unobtainable simply because it is impossible to complete at least one necessary element of those alternatives within the time available. Such situations can best be described by the term "short-run."

*Government regulation.* Various types of local, state, federal, and foreign government regulations restrict the actions of the marketing staff in many and varied ways. Licensing requirements, pricing restrictions, foreign exchange regulations, control of advertising appeals, and restraints on relationships with customers, agents, and competitors, are just a few of the many examples that could be cited here.

*Industry environment.* Various industry practices growing out of the market structure and historical experience of the industry may have acquired sanction through strength of usage, or been adopted through informal or formal agreement. Trade discount structures and channels of distribution often fall into the first category, frequency of model changes and pricing into the second, and advertising copy into the third. While in these cases the firm can adopt marketing alternatives which take it outside the industry pattern, the demands of customers, pressure of competition, and the threat of actual chastisement by industry leaders heavily discount such alternatives.

*Rationing of inputs.* At times the marketing staff may have to set aside otherwise desirable alternatives because the firm, through no fault of its own, is unable to secure the particular inputs needed—such as financing, materials, or personnel, to carry them out.

Some outside-imposed restrictions classed as rationing of inputs might also be viewed as arising from time restrictions. For example, if enough time were available, additional salesmen could be trained to meet the requirements of any proposal. Also, in some cases of material shortages, additional time may be all that is needed for suppliers to expand their plants and equipment to fill the firm's orders for materials without unreasonable delay.

Most outside-imposed restrictions are beyond the control of the influence of the firm's top management, and must, therefore, be accepted by the marketing staff as unmodifiable. The nature of certain industry practices and certain government regulations—particularly those designed specifically for the industry of which the firm is a part—can, however, frequently be influenced by the firm itself. If the firm is in a dominant position within its own industry, it may even control industry acceptance or rejection of particular practices. If nothing else, it is certainly the firm's top management who must decide how closely the firm will adhere to specific industry practices.

## REVENUE NET OF SELLING COSTS

As indicated earlier, the identified alternatives satisfying both firm-imposed and outside-imposed restrictions must be evaluated at each output level in terms of their expected total revenue net of selling costs. Such evaluation requires extensive consideration of all factors affecting total sales and any of the selling costs. This is no small task, as the range of such factors is extremely broad. It seems particularly useful in marketing decision-making to group the many and varied factors affecting revenue and selling costs on the basis of the degree of control held over them by the firm. Such a classification results in the following categories:

1. factors controlled by the firm,
2. factors influenced but not controlled by the firm, and
3. factors neither influenced nor controlled by the firm.

It will be noted that these groupings of factors affecting total revenue net of selling costs include many of the considerations brought up earlier in discussing firm-imposed and outside-imposed restrictions. There, these factors entered only when they were fixed values set by internal or external forces and, as such, were given conditions within the bounds of which the marketing staff had to operate. The present section includes these considerations when they do not have fixed, predetermined values but rather are variables whose value is either under the control of the marketing staff or whose value must be assessed or predicted by the marketing staff as a part of the process of evaluating the impact of alternative marketing programs.

## FIRM-CONTROLLED FACTORS

The firm-controlled factors affecting total revenue net of selling costs are of primary interest because these are factors that the marketing staff can, and does, manipulate in trying to evolve optimum marketing programs for specific levels of output.

They include advertising, assortment, channel(s) of distribution, geographic outreach, group(s) of customers to whom the firm tires to appeal, location(s) for the firm, marketing research, organizational structure and administrative framework for the marketing functions, personal selling, physical distribution, pricing, product design features, quality level, sales promotion including miscellaneous devices, and services.

This list of controlled factors is not intended to be exhaustive or to cite only areas of equivalent importance. Rather, it is intended to point up the primary areas of marketing decision. The controlled factors—and also the factors in the two groupings which follow—have been listed alphabetically in order to avoid the almost impossible task of assigning a ranking of relative importance to each factor.

Each category has a number of subparts. For example, advertising would involve decisions about such things as the total amount to be spent on advertising; copy content; media selection; timing of campaigns; use to be made of cooperative advertisements and promotional allowances; allocation of the advertising budget according to type of final customer, channel agency, and geographic area.

There are many opportunities for disagreement concerning the most appropriate assignment of the subparts. In the case of advertising, the aspect of the geographic allocation might just as well be included under the category of geographic outreach, allocation by type of final customer with the category of the group(s) of customers to whom the firm tries to appeal, and the allocation by channel agency and the use to be made of cooperative advertisements and promotional allowances with the category of channel(s) of distribution. The essential thing is that all subparts are recognized and accounted for, regardless of the category under which they are listed.

Objections may also arise because some readers prefer to take some of the aspects given only sub-category status in the above classification and elevate them to full-category status. Other readers may want to drop certain factors from the listing presented and relegate them to sub-category status. For example, the group of customers to whom the firm tries to appeal could be viewed as the result of decisions on services, quality level, product design features, pricing. Or a decision with regard to customer groups could be viewed as largely predetermining the services, quality level, product design features, pricing, etc.

The position taken here is that none of the listed controlled factors should be relegated to such a subordinate position that its use in a particular marketing program is arrived at without direct consideration. All the cited controlled factors should be recognized as specific areas of decision involved in designing marketing programs, and as such each should be dealt with directly and not piecemeal through the summation of decisions on other controlled factors.

For the purpose of manipulating the firm-controlled factors, it is essential, however, that the interdependence of the controlled factors be recognized—what the marketing staff does with one of these factors affects the performance of the effort expended on the others. Likewise, it needs to be recognized that most of the controlled factors are to some degree a substitute for each other, e.g., a price reduction may be used instead of an increase in advertising or personal selling expenditures or a higher cost location in place of some of the advertising outlays.

## FIRM-INFLUENCED FACTORS

The influenced-but-not-controlled factors encompass all those areas in which the firm's own actions may well create reactions that in turn have an impact on the firm's total sales and its selling costs. Factors influenced but not controlled include such categories as:

- Actions of producers of substitute and complementary goods,
- Cooperation of the independent channel agencies selling the firm's products,
- Number of competitors,
- Performance of the firm's employees,
- Reactions of buyers,
- Technology affecting use of the firm's products.

The most sensitive factor in the above grouping is that of the actions of producers of substitute and complementary goods, in particular the actions of competitors. No marketing alternative can be evaluated without making allowance for the impact of the counterstrategy that the alternative is likely to elicit from competitors. The simplest counterstrategy for competitors frequently is to try to parallel the firm's own actions; however, competitive marketing staffs have at their disposal all the firm-controlled factors mentioned earlier, and may choose to manipulate any one, or any combination, of them in trying to hit upon the most effective counterstrategy.

The category of cooperation of the independent channel agencies selling the firm's products includes such things as compliance with pricing recommendations, participation in promotional campaigns, stocking of minimum inventory, and providing repair service and repair parts. The number of competitors is influenced primarily through the firm's pricing and advertising policies although any of the controlled factors might be manipulated in such a manner as to close out—or make unattractive—opportunities to potential competitors.

The performance of the firm's employees involves such considerations as morale; competence—a result of recruiting policies, training programs, and experience; stimulation of the sales force through leadership and appropriate compensation; proper control and coordination procedures; and lack of disruptions such as strikes.

In regard to the reactions of buyers, the firm, of course, hopes to influence buyers in a positive way toward itself and in a negative way toward competitors. Advertising and personal selling are the most direct factors for realizing this, but actually all the controlled factors are manipulated with the goal of influencing buyer reactions in a manner favorable to the firm.

Technology affecting use of the firm's products is influenced through the firm's own research on additional uses and through what encouragement or discouragement the firm's marketing program creates in regard to research by others either to find additional uses for the product or to create substitute products.

## OUTSIDE FACTORS

A number of factors outside both the influence and the control of the firm have an impact on the absolute and the relative effectiveness of given levels of the firm-controlled factors. These same factors also affect the manner in which the influenced-but-not-controlled factors react to various manipulations of the firm-controlled factors.

Changes in these reactions, in turn, have a secondary impact on the effectiveness of the firm-controlled factors. Thus, in evaluating alternatives, allowance must be made for both primary and secondary effects of the anticipated levels of the neither-influenced-nor-controlled factors. This group includes acts of God, buyer expectations with regard to the future level of economic activity, demand for complementary items and items of which the firm's product is a part, general level of economic activity, government action in foreign policy and in domestic monetary and tax matters, population characteristics including distribution by age, education, ethnic background, geographic area, income, etc., population size, and standard of living.

Droughts, hail storms, or unseasonal frosts may destroy or damage certain crops so that sellers of packing and canning supplies find little market response regardless of how firm-controlled factors are manipulated in the marketing program. Furthermore, under these conditions, the relative effectiveness of increased personal selling versus a price concession may be somewhat different than in a normal crop year.

In addition, the bleak prospects for sales may have a negative impact on the morale of the sales force and, through this, a secondary negative reaction on the effectiveness of the personal selling factor. Likewise, different buyer expectations, such as optimistic versus pessimistic outlooks of industrial, commercial, or household buyers with regard to the future level of economic activity, generally call for different marketing approaches, if a firm's marketing staff is to achieve the maximum feasible total revenue net of selling costs for a given output level.

An example of the impact of the demand for an item of which the firm's product is a part would be the impact of the demand for new housing on the sales of a firm manufacturing bathroom fixtures. The absolute and relative responses to alternative manipulations of the controlled factors might vary considerably with the demand for new housing. Also, changes in the standard of living might progressively shift a firm's product from the category of a luxury toward that of a necessity. Such a change would have repercussions on the effectiveness of the different firm-controlled factors.

## CONDITIONS TO BE MET

In choosing from the various alternative manipulations of firm-controlled marketing factors at a given level of output, the marketing staff should not seek the plan with the lowest selling costs, as such a plan usually produces relatively little total revenue; nor should it seek the plan with the highest total revenue, as such a plan usually has exceptionally high selling costs. The goal, rather, is to sort the feasible alternatives at each output level to determine which alternative yields the maximum total revenue net of selling costs for that output level.

If no one plan satisfies both the lowest selling costs and the highest total revenue criteria for a particular output, it becomes very probable that the plan chosen on the basis of maximum total revenue net of selling costs will be neither the minimum selling costs plan nor the maximum total revenue plan for that output. Of course, once a plan is chosen as the best of the feasible alternatives at a given output level, the marketing staff should be prepared to execute that plan at the lowest possible cost and in a manner which would maximize the total revenue realized from that plan. In short, the marketing staff is responsible for carrying out chosen plans as efficiently and as effectively as possible.

## MARGINAL REVENUE NET

In manipulating the levels of the firm-controlled factors for any particular marketing alternative, the marketing staff should equalize the net return over selling costs to the marginal effort expended on all of the firm-controlled marketing factors. This net return to the marginal effort can be referred to as the marginal revenue net of selling costs and is defined as the change in total revenue minus the change in all selling costs–including changes in the cost of the marketing factor being manipulated–associated with the increasing sales by one unit. If all controlled marketing factors except one are held constant in securing the one unit increase in sales, the marginal revenue net of selling costs from the additional unit of sales can be viewed as the return to the marginal effort expended on a particular controlled marketing factor. Unless the marginal revenues net of selling costs are equal for the last dollars spent on advertising, location, personal selling, services, etc., at a particular level of output, the firm's total revenue net of selling costs–and, therefore, the firm's profits–for that output level can be increased by transferring marginal dollars from the controlled factors yielding the lower marginal return into the controlled factors yielding the higher marginal return.

For example, if the last dollar spent on advertising has a marginal revenue net of selling costs of 50 cents, while the last dollar spent on personal selling returns only 25 cents, total revenue net of selling costs can be increased by taking marginal dollars out of personal selling and applying them to advertising where the net return is higher. As the amount spent on advertising is increased, the marginal revenue net of selling costs of dollars spent on advertising will decline (presumably the richer return areas have already been exploited so that additional expenditures are confronted with declining returns). Conversely, as the amount spent on personal selling is reduced, the marginal revenue net of selling costs of dollars spent on personal selling will increase (the marginal dollars are removed from the least lucrative areas so that the marginal revenue net of selling costs for the remaining dollars is higher).

Conceptually, this transfer of effort from the low-return variables to the high-return variables would pay dividends as long as inequalities remained among the marginal revenues net of selling costs. In actual practice, of course, expenditures on advertising, rent, personal selling, services, etc., would not be made in dollar increments even at the margin but rather would be varied in chunks of lump sum amounts. Thus, at best, the equality condition for marginal revenues net of selling costs could only be approximated.

## SPREADING COSTS AND REVENUES

It should be noted that the period of time used in the calculation of the marginal revenue net of selling costs associated with a specific change should be sufficiently long to give a reasonable spreading out of any one-time marketing costs that may be involved in the change, or else only a realistic part—rather than all—of the one-time costs should be charged against the change.

This same consideration would hold for the revenue data as well. The initial impact on revenue of a specific change may be either extremely light or extremely heavy relative to the longer-run impact. In such situations again, the period of time used in the calculation of the marginal revenue net of selling costs should be long enough to give a reasonable leveling out of the initial reaction, or else the original impact data should be adjusted for the failure to do so.

## BALANCED PROGRAM

While the condition of balanced effort as reflected in the equality of the marginal revenues net of selling costs for all of the firm-controlled factors is a necessary condition for maximizing total revenue net of selling costs at any output level, it is not in itself sufficient to assure that the desired maximum is achieved. Poor marketing programs can be balanced so that the marginal revenues net of selling costs are equal just as in the case of good marketing programs.

Thus, not only should a balanced program be achieved at each output level, but it should be the best possible balanced program for that level of output. In order to maximize total revenue net of selling costs for a particular output level, not only must the condition of equal marginal revenues net of selling costs be attained for all controlled marketing factors, but also it must not be possible to increase the total revenue net of selling costs for that output level by altering the nature of the marketing program through changing any one controlled factor or combination of controlled factors.

## SALES ENGINEERS

From the perspective of what is to follow, the marketing staff is looked upon as a group of sales engineers working with a sales function to produce dollars of revenue net of selling costs just as production engineers are traditionally viewed as working with a production function to produce units of product. The sales inputs are the firm-controlled marketing factors.

These have a cost to the firm just as have production inputs.[10] The marketing staff's performance is measured in dollars of total revenue net of selling costs. It is charged

[10] A price reduction has a cost equal to the amount of the price reduction times the number of units that could have been sold at the higher price and a return equal to the increased number of units sold times the new price. A price increase has a cost equal to the reduction in units sold times the old price and a return equal to the amount of the price increase times the quantity sold at the new

with manipulating the firm-controlled marketing inputs within the context of known marketing techniques in a manner that realizes the maximum long-run revenue net of selling costs at each output level within the restrictions, if any, which are imposed by the outside forces or by the firm itself.

While the task of the marketing staff and its approach to that task seem to parallel the production situation, the marketing side of the firm is not nearly as neat conceptually as the production side. Factors outside the direct control of the firm have a much greater significance for marketing. Furthermore, the impact of the many revenue affecting factors–including the firm-controlled factors–on total revenue net of selling costs can be assessed much less accurately than can the impact of production factors on output and production costs.

## THE SALES FUNCTION

In Figure 1 a number of equal-sales contours representing progressively larger sales have been determined, and the equal-cost lines tangent to each have been inserted, thereby identifying the economically efficient way to sell each of the indicated levels of output.[11] It should be noted that for any one set of contours such as that given in Figure 1, a number of things are taken as being constant at particular levels. They are:

1. all firm-controlled marketing factors, other than the two being manipulated,
2. all of the neither-influenced-nor-controlled marketing factors, and
3. the initial level of all the influenced-but-not-controlled marketing factors.

The impact of any changes induced in the level of the influenced-but-not-controlled factors through manipulating the two controlled factors is incorporated into the estimated values for the sales level contours.

For low levels of sales the equal-sales contours would intersect both of the illustrated axes, as these lower levels could be attained either with relatively large amounts of advertising and no personal selling or with relatively large amounts of personal selling and no advertising.

At high levels of sales where large amounts of advertising and personal selling are being used, the equal-sales contours may begin to turn back on themselves as either extreme

price level. If in the case of a price reduction, the firm must absorb losses on dealer inventories, or if in either case there are costs of changing price lists and catalogues or other costs associated with the price change, such costs would have to be allocated over time and charged against the expected return from the proposed price change.

[11]The equal-cost lines are straight lines since dollars spent on advertising are a perfect substitute for dollars spent on personal selling as far as total expenditures are concerned–i.e., there is a constant dollar cost rate of substitution between advertising and personal selling. Changes in prices of inputs related to the quantity used could be accounted for through departing from straight equal-cost lines or through inserting several sets of straight equal-cost lines with different slopes and relating the equal-sales contours to the set of equal-cost lines appropriate to the quantity of inputs involved.

The equal-sales contours are illustrated as curved in a convex fashion toward the origin because advertising and personal selling are infrequently perfect substitutes for each other in their ability to create sales. For example, as marginal effort is transferred from advertising to personal selling, the marginal performance of the effort in advertising increases while that of personal selling decreases. Thus, if the total sales effectiveness is to be retained–i.e., if the firm is to stay on the same equal-sales contour–it will take larger and larger chunks of personal selling effort to balance reductions in advertising.

**Figure 1**

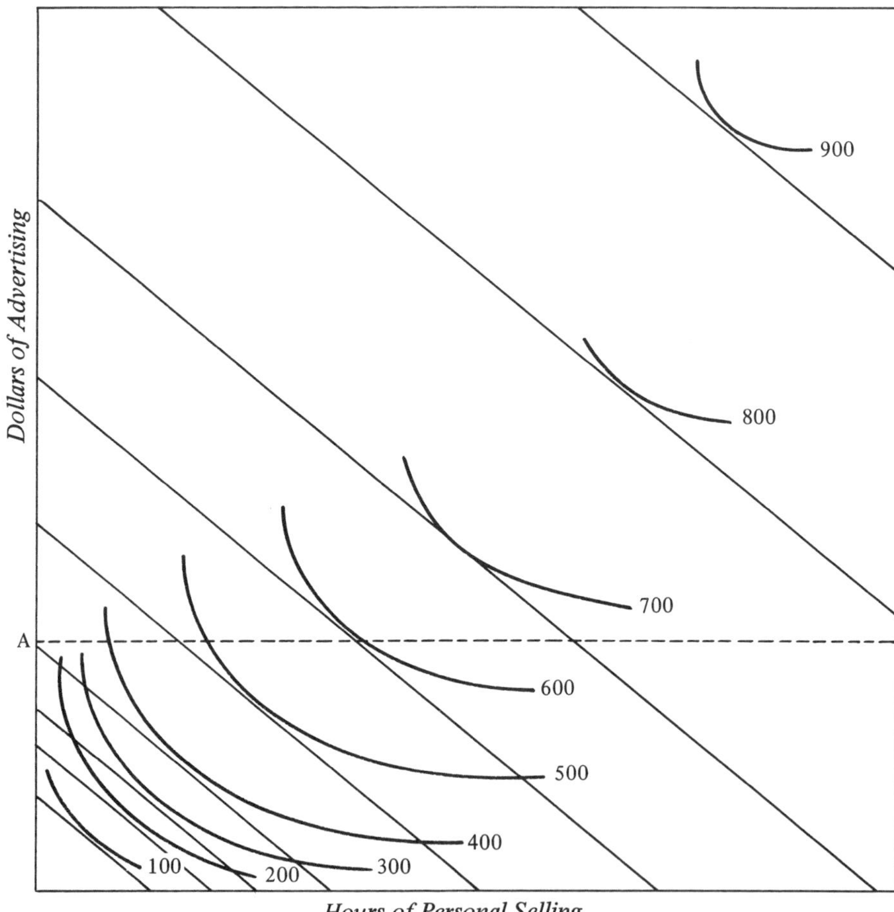


of the contour is approached. For example, the firm's marketing staff might find it had so saturated the market in which it was working with personal selling that it was realizing a negative unit-of-sales return to marginal increases in personal selling effort. Therefore, it would be forced to increase advertising outlays along with increases in the personal selling outlay in order to remain on a given equal-sales contour, that is, in order to overcome the negative impact from the increased calls of the sales force.

Naturally, the marketing staff would not be interested in pushing any controlled marketing factor into the area where marginal increments had a negative return unless it was required to do so by firm-imposed restrictions—for instance, using a certain size of sales force in order to give employment to all of the relatives of top management.

A change in the value of any of the factors assumed to be constant changes the illustrated sales surface. Thus, given the many variables taken to be constant, the realistic range of values they might have, and the resulting numerous possible combinations that might arise, there is literally a multitude of the illustrated advertising and personal selling relationships.

The proportion of such relationships having significance for a particular decision-making situation is usually relatively small, since the marketing staff is only interested in the more promising of the feasible levels for the controlled factors and in the more probable of the possible levels for the influenced-but-not-controlled and the neither-influenced-nor-controlled factors. Taking a relatively small proportion of a multitude of relationships, however, still yields a sizable number of relationships that are relevant to any one particular decision-making situation.

There is some further help in that, even within a particular relationship, ranges of the two observed variables are eliminated from consideration either because such levels are not feasible or because they hold little or no promise.

Furthermore, while the equal-sales contours are drawn as continuous relationships in the theoretical cases, the marketing staff generally finds it sufficient—even within the more promising ranges of the variables—to evaluate a series of discrete points. The latter occurs either because finer gradations are not feasible owing to the imperfect divisibility of one or more of the inputs or because it is sufficiently accurate to use these points as benchmarks and interpolate between them in order to get the continuous curve.

## TOTAL CURVE

The series of tangency points between the equal-sales contours and the equal-cost lines in Figure 1 supply the data for deriving the total-revenue-net-of-selling-costs curve. Each tangency point represents a particular level of sales achieved at some indicated selling cost to the firm. The sales level multiplied by the price per unit—taken as fixed in this example—minus the sum of the cost indicated by the appropriate equal-cost line and the cost of the other selling factors taken as fixed for the two-variable analysis yields the total revenue net of selling costs for that level of output. Repeating the process over the range of sales levels and plotting the resulting dollar data against output produces a curve similar to that shown in Figure 2.

**Figure 2**

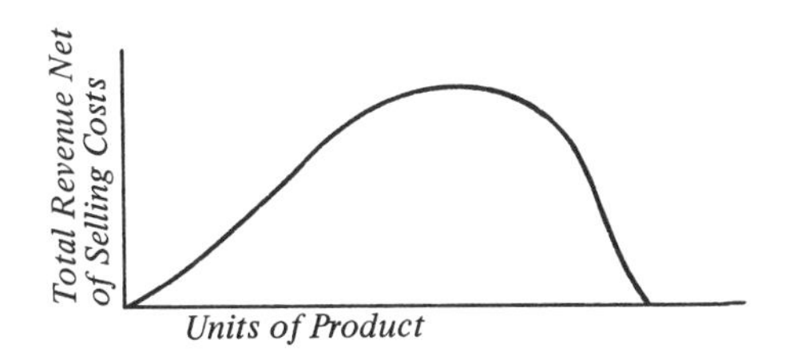

The total-revenue-net-of-selling-costs curve may initially rise at an increasing or decreasing rate depending upon whether increasing returns occur.[12] However, as the sales level increases, the curve eventually begins to rise at a decreasing rate, reaches a peak, and then falls toward—and finally through—zero. Unless firm-imposed restrictions force the marketing staff to do so, it is not going to be interested in plans carrying sales beyond the peak point of this curve, since in the falling range the marginal revenues net of selling costs for the manipulated factors are negative.

## INCORPORATING ADDITIONAL INPUTS

A third firm-controlled marketing input can be graphically accounted for by developing a sales function—like that in Figure 1—for each of the relevant levels of the third input. The tangency points on each of these sales functions can then be reduced to individual total-revenue-net-of-selling-costs curves by the process described above.

These curves can, in turn, all be plotted on the same set of total dollars versus output axes as shown in Figure 3. The highest sections of the resulting family of curves then trace the appropriate total-revenue-net-of-selling-costs curve for the three-input relationship. If fine enough gradations of the third variable are used, the high points of the individual curves should trace a smooth, continuous curve. Otherwise, the curve derived from the high points would have a scalloped effect as shown in Figure 3.

This approach is especially useful with those variables that are particularly difficult or clumsy to treat as one of two manipulated variables generating a sales function such as was done earlier in the example dealing with advertising and personal selling. Price is one of the several variables that fall into this category. Thus, in Figure 3 each total-revenue-net-of-selling-costs curve can be viewed as representing the optimum combinations of advertising and personal selling for selling various quantities of the product at a particular price level.[13]

**Figure 3**

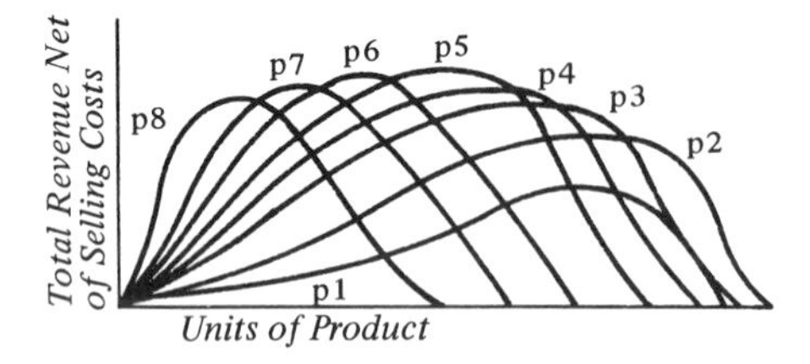


[12] The result here is a function of both the situation and the variable(s) being considered—e.g., in certain situations advertising may have a range in which increasing returns occur.

[13] Owing to the many variables having some effect on total revenue net of selling costs, it is difficult to generalize about just how the total-revenue-net-of-selling-costs curves would appear relative to each other. One would expect, however, to find that the highest segments at the low output levels were associated with relatively high prices while the highest segments at the high output levels were associated with relatively low prices.

A fourth firm-controlled marketing factor can be incorporated by constructing a family of curves such as that shown in Figure 3 for alternative levels of the fourth factor. These several families of total-revenue-net-of-selling-costs curves can then all be plotted on the same diagram with the highest sections of these curves being taken to make up the total-revenue-net-of-selling-costs curve for the four-input case.

An example could be developed using the four inputs, advertising, personal selling, price, and channel of distribution. For each alternative channel a family of total-revenue-net-of-selling-costs curves reflecting varying combinations of advertising, personal selling, and price could be derived as discussed in the three-variable case cited. In most situations the channels of interest are restricted to two or three possibilities so that the task would not be so formidable as it might seem at first thought.

It is just a short step from the above four-variable example to the multi-variable case where, rather than develop the complete sales functions and the resulting families of total-revenue-net-of-selling-costs curves, the marketing staff intensively evaluates only what appear to be the most relevant alternative combinations of the firm-controlled marketing factors.

The total-revenue-net-of-selling-costs curve is then represented by a disconnected series of points, each of which identifies the maximum total-revenue-net-of-selling-costs plan for a specific output level. The basic reasoning patterns of a sales function and its companion total-revenue-net-of-selling-costs curve still apply in such a development. The chosen marketing alternatives lie on a multi-dimensional sales surface at points of tangency between equal-sales and equal-cost relationships with the selection process following the same decision rules as in the less complex examples sketched above.

## PROFITABLE LEVEL OF OUTPUT

If no outside- and firm-imposed restrictions exist, or if, at least, those that do exist are ineffective in the sense that they do not prevent either the marketing or the production staff from reaching desired alternatives, then all points on the total-revenue-net-of-selling-costs curve and on the total-production-cost curve will represent balanced marketing programs and balanced production programs. Given no effective non-profit-maximizing firm-imposed restrictions, top management would then select the output level where marginal revenue net of selling costs equaled the marginal cost of production.[14]

Since, under the above conditions, both the marketing and production programs would be balanced within themselves, the chosen level of output will be a position at which the marginal revenues net of selling costs are equal for all firm-controlled

[14] Here, as throughout this discussion, it is assumed that at least one alternative yielding positive profits exists for the firm.

marketing factors, the marginal costs are equal for all firm-controlled production factors, and the marginal revenues net of selling costs are equal to the marginal costs of production.

At this point, all firm-controlled factors are fully exploited to where the last dollar spent on each just returns a dollar—i.e., for each factor the marginal contribution net of all costs (marketing and production, including the cost of the factor itself) is equal to zero.

When the total-revenue-net-of-selling-costs curve and the total-production-cost curve are both smooth instead of scalloped, the above equality position takes place where the slopes of the two curves are equal. If one or both of the two curves is scalloped instead of smooth, the equality of marginal revenue net of selling costs and marginal cost of production, may occur more than once and, therefore, may not be a sufficient condition in itself. In such cases the profit maximizing solution is at the marginal equality point where the total-revenue-net-of-selling-costs curve lies furthest above the total-production-cost curve.

## MARGINAL EQUALITY POINT

The point of marginal equalities must lie at or before the peak of the total-revenue-net-of-selling-costs curve. After this curve begins to turn down, the firm is confronted with declining total revenue net of selling costs and rising total production cost (average production cost may be falling because of economies of scale, but total production cost would be rising) so that profit declines.

Actually as a result of rising total production cost, the profit maximizing solution is likely to occur at an output level prior to the peak of the total-revenue-net-of-selling-costs curve rather than at the peak itself. Such a solution is presented in Figure 4 for the case of a scalloped total-revenue-net-of-selling-costs curve and a smooth total-production-cost curve.

## THE IMPACT OF RESTRICTIONS

In the examples which follow, it is always assumed that the stated restrictions are the only restrictions on the manipulation of the firm-controlled marketing and production

**Figure 4**

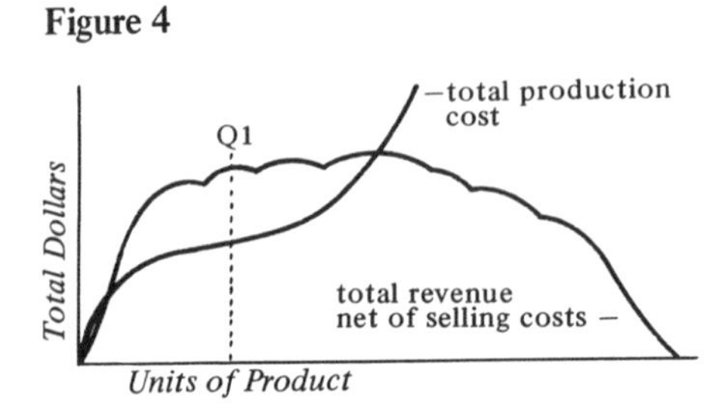

factors. Furthermore, it is assumed that the marketing and production staffs always strive (within the limitations of any restrictions on their actions) to maximize total revenue net of selling costs at each output level and to minimize total costs of production at each output level. Thus, when the discussion centers on the problem of balance within either the marketing or the production program, it is assumed that the discussion of balance refers to balance within the best obtainable marketing or production alternative at a specified level of output.

## BALANCE ISN'T EVERYTHING

As indicated earlier, even poor alternatives can be balanced. Balance, therefore, is not of such high merit that the firm will select a balanced but poor marketing or production alternative over an unbalanced alternative that has a higher total revenue net of selling costs or a lower total cost of production. In effect, the proper derivation of the equal-sales contours in the sales function or of the equal-output contours in the production function should eliminate alternatives that were balanced but inefficient from consideration as these alternatives would lie beyond the specific contour for their sales or output level.

## FIXED PLANT

Plant facilities may be fixed either because of a time restriction or a capital restriction. In either case, the marketing staff is not involved, and there is no effect on the total-revenue-net-of-selling-costs curve. At each output level, the marketing staff can reach the desired programs and can achieve a balancing within those programs in that the marginal revenues net of selling costs can be equated for all of the firm-controlled marketing factors.

The production staff, however, finds that certain desired alternatives are ruled out and that they have to move from a long-run cost function to a short-run relationship where fixed factors are involved. The production staff should balance the variable inputs in the production mix by equating the marginal costs of the variable factors to each other, but only at one output level can these marginal costs be equated to the marginal cost of increasing the plant size.

At low output levels the marginal cost of the plant is higher than that of the variable factors—in such a situation, the production staff would prefer to use less plant and more of the variable factors if it were possible. At high output levels the marginal cost of the plant is lower than that of the variable factors, and here the production staff would prefer to increase the amount of plant in their production mix and reduce the amounts of the variable factors.

In putting marketing and production data together, top management should equate the marginal revenues net of selling costs of the controlled marketing factors to the marginal costs of the controlled production factors which are not fixed. Only if, by chance, this equality occurs at that one point where the marginal cost of the plant equals the marginal costs of the firm-controlled variable production factors, would all of the marginal values be equal.

## FIXED INDIVIDUAL BUDGETS

Situations in which the marketing staff is given a fixed budget for one of the firm-controlled marketing factors are quite parallel in their impact on total revenue net of selling costs to the effect of a fixed plant on the production-cost relationship. A major difference does arise in that, in the case of a fixed plant, it is assumed that the plant size can neither be reduced nor increased, while in the case of fixed marketing budgets, it is generally acceptable to spend less than the fixed budget, if it should be advantageous to the firm to do so.[15]

Thus, at the lower output levels where the budget restriction is ineffective, the marketing staff can balance the marginal revenues net of selling costs for all marketing factors. At output levels where the budget restriction is effective, the marketing staff should equate the marginal values for the variable firm-controlled marketing factors to each other. At such levels, the factor restricted from increased use by the budget limitation has a marginal net revenue that is higher than the other controlled marketing factors. Thus, at these levels of output, the marketing staff would, if permitted, find it desirable to increase the amount of the fixed-budget item and reduce the amounts of the variable items.

For example, if a budget limitation restricted advertising outlays to level A in Figure 1, a horizontal line drawn through A would establish the range of choice open to the marketing staff. Note that once the budget restriction becomes effective, the marketing staff must resort to economically inefficient methods simply because the advertising outlay cannot be increased–i.e., given budget restriction A in Figure 1, 600 units of sales can be reached only by using an economically inefficient combination of advertising and personal selling. Also note that–given the fixed advertising budget and the assumed levels of the other firm-controlled marketing factors–the firm in Figure 1 cannot realize 700 or more units of sales regardless of how much personal selling effort it stands ready to use.

Budget restrictions on marketing factors do not affect the production-cost relationship. When the marketing and production data are brought together by top management, the marginal revenues net of selling costs for all the controlled marketing factors not restricted by budget limitations should be equated to the marginal costs of the controlled production inputs. If this takes place at levels of output where the budget limitations are ineffective, a complete balancing both within and between the firm-controlled marketing and production factors can be achieved.

[15] The marketing staff may, however, decide that it must expend its full budget–even though this means using an inefficient marketing program–in order to protect its long-run interest. For example, an excessive advertising budget may be fully expended simply because failure to do so may have an adverse impact on future requests for funds for advertising.

An expanded example of the budget restriction case is the situation in which the marketing staff is given a fixed total marketing budget with no limitations on how it might be used. Here the budget should be allocated among the controlled marketing factors so that the marginal revenues net of selling costs from all the budget restricted factors are equal. Price would probably be the only controlled marketing factor not affected by the budget restriction.

Thus, after the budget restriction begins to force the firm away from desired marketing alternatives, the marginal revenue net of selling costs for the price factor should be taken out of equality with the marginal values of the other controlled marketing factors. In the output range where the budget restriction is effective, the marginal revenues net of selling costs for the restricted factors should be equal to each other and larger than the marginal revenue net of selling costs for the price variable. Thus, at these output levels, the marketing staff would like to expand the use of the restricted factors and adjust price upward.

In reaching the decision on the level of output for the firm, top management should equate the marginal revenue net of selling costs for price to the marginal costs of the production inputs. If this equality occurs within the range of output where the budget restriction on the marketing staff is ineffective, the marginal revenues net of selling costs for the controlled marketing factors would all be equal to each other and to the marginal costs of the controlled production inputs.

Manipulation of the price factor may be restricted for the marketing staff through top management setting a minimum below which price cannot be lowered, a maximum above which price cannot be raised, or a specific price that can neither be lowered nor raised. The latter case is similar to the fixed plant situation in production.

Given an unchangeable price, the marketing staff should equate the marginal revenues net of selling costs at each output level for all firm-controlled marketing factors other than price. Probably at one output level, at least, the price dictated by top management will be ideal so that, at that output level–or levels–the marginal revenues net of selling costs can be equated for all the firm-controlled marketing factors.

At levels of output below the latter point, the marginal revenue net of selling costs for the price factor is lower than that of the other firm-controlled marketing factors. In selling these outputs, the marketing staff would like to be able to raise price and increase the amounts used of the other controlled marketing factors.

At the levels of output above the point where all the marginal revenues net of selling costs are equal, the situation is just reversed–i.e., the marginal revenue net of selling costs for price is relatively high. Here the marketing staff would like to lower price and reduce the amounts used of the other controlled marketing factors.

The setting of price has no impact on the production-cost relationship. In putting marketing and production data together, top management should select that level of output which equates the marginal revenues net of selling costs for all the firm-controlled marketing factors except price to the marginal costs of all controlled production inputs. Only if this output level is also the point where the marketing program is in complete balance, would the firm be operated where all the marginal values of the firm-controlled factors were equal.

If the price set by top management is merely a minimum or maximum price, rather than an unchangeable price, the marketing staff can achieve balanced marketing programs for all output levels where the ideal price for the output level falls within the unrestricted ranges. If the solution to the level of output for the firm falls within this range of outputs, all firm-controlled factors would be balanced with their marginal revenues net of selling costs being equal to each other and to their marginal costs of production.

## FIXED QUANTITY

Quantity, like price, can be fixed by top management through setting a minimum, a maximum, or a specific unchangeable level. If it is assumed that the fixed quantity level does not grow out of a restriction on any of the firm-controlled marketing or production factors, but rather reflects such desires of top management as:

1. not growing beyond a certain point,
2. realizing some fixed percentage increase in sales,
3. achieving some stated share of the industry market, or
4. growing to some absolute size level,

then the quantity restriction would have no impact on the total revenue net of selling costs relationship or on the production cost relationship. At all levels of output both the marketing and the production staffs would be able to achieve their desired balanced programs.

If output is to be at some unchangeable level, top management will find that the marginal revenues net of selling costs for the controlled marketing factors do not equal the marginal costs of the controlled production factors at the fixed level of output unless, by chance, the fixed level of output falls just at the output level where the total equality occurred. If output is set in the sense of stating a minimum or a maximum quantity, marginal revenues net of selling costs for the controlled marketing factors can be equated to the marginal costs of the controlled production factors only if this equality occurs within the range of accepted quantity levels. If such is not the case, the chosen level of output must fall on the stated minimum or maximum quantity. In these situations, all marginal revenues net of selling costs should be equated for the controlled marketing factors and the marginal costs of production should be equated for the controlled production factors; however, the two groups–marginal revenues net of selling costs and marginal costs of production–would not be equated to each other.

## SUMMARY

Essentially, the marketing staff is viewed as having responsibility for maximizing total revenue net of selling costs for each level of output. Achieving the best possible combination of the controlled marketing factors at a particular output level requires that the revenue net of selling costs realized from the marginal effort expended on each of the controlled factors be equal, and that no feasible change in any one or any group of the controlled factors be able to improve the firm's total revenue net of selling costs for that output level.

Ideally, when top management chooses the particular combination of marketing and production programs for the firm, the marginal values of the firm-controlled factors on both the marketing and production sides of the firm should be equal so that the net contribution of the last dollar spent in any and all areas of the firm would be equal to zero.

Generally, the marketing staff is not given an entirely free hand in carrying out its responsibility, but rather finds itself confronted with restrictions on its choice among alternative marketing plans as a result of outside- and firm-imposed limitations on the actions it can take. Thus, the marketing staff may well find that the above conditions cannot be realized; yet, they are conditions which are to be pursued as far as possible.

If outside- or firm-imposed restrictions prevent either the marketing staff or the production staff from reaching otherwise desired alternatives at particular output levels, top management should pick the marketing and production combination which balances the marginal values for the unrestricted controlled marketing and production factors and which thereby equates the marginal contribution net of all costs for the unrestricted controlled factors to zero.[16]

In the process of evaluating specific manipulations of the firm-controlled marketing factors, allowance must be made for anticipated responses from those factors, influenced but not controlled and for the impact of any such responses, in turn, on the outcome of the original manipulation of the controlled factors.

Furthermore, the marketing staff must incorporate into its evaluation of the alternative manipulations of the controlled factors, both the primary and secondary effects of the expected levels of those total revenue and/or selling cost influencing factors which are neither controlled nor influenced by the firm.

[16] An alternative formulation would be to view the marketing staff as, in effect, the grand strategists of the firm operating within firm-imposed restrictions determined by top management. In such a perspective, the production staff would be required to submit the production cost data to the marketing staff. The marketing staff would then proceed to move directly to the maximum long-run profit strategy consistent with the outside- and firm-imposed restrictions. Here the marketing staff could somewhat restrict the range of output over which it did extensive evaluations of marketing alternatives. It could also by-pass the marginal revenue net of selling costs concept, and move directly to dealing with marginal contribution net of all costs for the controlled marketing factors.

## DATA FOR FRAMEWORK

It is well recognized that much of the data about the impacts and interrelationships of the various factors affecting total revenue net of selling costs are not known to the firm. Furthermore, it is recognized that some of these data cannot be objectively measured, while in the case of others, it is too costly in terms of time and money to measure them for the decision at hand either because the necessary time and money are not available to the firm or because, for the particular situation, the contribution of the objectively measured data is not deemed worth the cost of obtaining it.

What is maintained here is not that the marketing staff will have, or even will be able to secure, all the data demanded by the decision-making situation, but rather that:

1. the decision must be made (if no action is taken, the implication is that it has been decided that inaction is the best course) and that
2. the final decision indirectly assigns a value, or at least a range of values, to all the unquantified variables involved.

Therefore, since the final decision can only be the correct solution under some set of assumed values for the unquantified variables; and since these unquantified variables will receive at best implied values, or ranges of value, through the final decision, it is best to attack the problem of estimating them head on.

The head-on approach has two merits. First, the estimating or "guesstimating" process used in the head-on approach at least rules out obviously impossible and highly improbable values for the unquantified variables, while such values might slip by undetected on an indirect assignment basis if a decision is reached by completely ignoring them.

Second, this approach will more clearly indicate the weaknesses in the quantitative estimates behind the decision so that significance of these weaknesses can be properly assessed in terms of their impact on the probability of a favorable outcome. In short, as its second contribution, the head-on approach makes the decision-maker more aware of when he is about to draw to an inside straight position.

## ROLE OF FRAMEWORK

The role of the developed framework approach presented here is not to supply the answers to marketing problems, but rather to offer a consistent and reasonably inclusive frame of reference within which to search for the answers. The emphasis is on the nature of the problem, the wide range of variables, interrelationships among the variables which must be reckoned with, and the conditions that should be met.

Real-world decision-making situations may fall short of this framework for many reasons; yet, attempting to approximate the framework should result in improved marketing decisions through a more systematic and complete consideration of the variables involved, even though much of the evaluation is still done through executive judgment.

Thus, it is hoped that the presented framework has value as a tool for improving marketing decision-making. Furthermore, it is hoped that it conveys a better understanding of the marketing sector of the firm to individuals outside marketing, thereby fostering a more cooperative relationship between marketing and nonmarketing groups.

Throughout this article an effort has been made to integrate the presented framework with the standard approach to production relationships. It is hoped that this not only makes the framework more palatable to the theorist but also contributes to a better appreciation of the process of making marketing decisions and to a better understanding of the interrelationships among the factors affecting total revenue net of selling costs.

# 25. AN APPROACH TO SUCCESSFUL MARKETING PLANNING

*Andrall E. Pearson*

*One of the most critical parts of a marketing plan is the development of ways by which the plan can be implemented.*

*The author of the following article discusses ways by which plans can be made a way of life in the marketing organization. In addition, he shows the importance of making a realistic appraisal of the firm's strengths and weaknesses, and the need for critical assumptions and for feasible goals.*

Formal marketing planning as it is practiced today in many companies probably represents the biggest single waste of time and money in the entire corporate realm. Most formal marketing plans simply do not produce the results expected of them. By formal marketing planning, we mean a written breakdown of objectives and the methods of reaching them as opposed to informal marketing planning, which is largely verbal.

There is certainly no one cause or any one patented, painless solution for ineffective marketing planning. However, there does appear to be one central ingredient that separates useful marketing planning from the other variety—getting off on the right foot. In other words, the proper approach to the job can greatly increase the chances of doing successful marketing planning.

Far too many companies approach formal marketing planning as if it were either a verbal extension of their sales forecasting and budgeting procedures or a device to record their annual advertising and merchandising programs. In companies where

Source: From *Business Horizons,* Winter 1959, vol. 2, pp. 74–82. Andrall E. Pearson: Management Consultant, McKinsey and Co., Inc., New York.

formal marketing planning is being done successfully, more time is spent by key executives on thinking through their approach to planning in terms of:

1. why they do formal marketing planning,
2. how they decide the scope of their plans, and
3. how they organize to get the job done effectively.

Although busy executives initially may begrudge time given to this planning of their planning, experience shows that the time is well spent.

## BENEFITS OF FORMAL PLAN

Three benefits common to any well-devised formal marketing plan are:

1. improved internal coordination and communication;
2. disciplined thinking on the part of the planners, which comes from having to write down ideas; and
3. a framework to guide day-to-day decisions and to measure progress.

*Improved Communication.* Ideally, a formal marketing plan should improve communication of marketing methods and goals down through the field sales organization; up through the top management; and across the organization to each operating department, including manufacturing, research and development, and engineering.

There are, however, many reasons why formal written plans fall short of being effective communication tools. Most often it is the simple failure to circulate the completed marketing plan throughout the organization. Fragments are routed to selected staffs instead of to all key marketing personnel, with the result that the very groups operating under the plan are not aware of the full range of objectives. Lack of full communication to allied operating elements of the business, such as manufacturing, makes coordination and integration of effort much more difficult, if not impossible.

Another cause of the failure of formal marketing plans as communication tools is the physical make-up of the reports themselves. Sometimes they are exhaustively detailed, which discourages readers; at other times they are scantily outlined, so that salient facts are omitted or obscured. To achieve the desired blend of the practical requirement for brevity with the need to be convincing, the pertinent data can be presented in tables at the end of the plan. Separating the details from the conclusions in this way permits the plan itself to be written in a concise fashion that encourages thorough reading. It also permits the interested reader to delve into background data where necessary to follow a line of reasoning or to accept a conclusion.

*Disciplined Thinking.* One of the greatest advantages of putting formal marketing plans on paper is that the planner is forced to consider all of his problems and opportunities *concurrently,* finding the best solutions instead of the most expedient ones. Studying problems in relationship to each other lends a perspective that enables him to direct his efforts more effectively. However, to be a useful discipline, the format of the formal plan demands specific data, such as financial facts, industry data, and stated action programs required to achieve sales goals.

Writing a formal plan further disciplines the planner by making him concentrate on areas of prime importance. One of the major requirements of successful marketing planning is to select the relatively few areas of marketing that most need to be planned and, by implication, to agree on the many aspects that are not vital to the particular business.

*Measured Progress.* Generally, formal marketing plans are made on an annual basis and updated each quarter. However, one of the prime benefits that a formal plan provides throughout the year is that it serves as a framework for day-to-day decision-making and provides a yardstick for follow-up.

In order to do this, a plan must deal in broad guidelines. For example, a goal of increasing a company's retail volume by 20 per cent must include an explanation of why that figure was chosen and generally how it is to be achieved. Progress can then be reviewed not just in terms of whether the goal was achieved but, more important, whether the program was carried out. This assessment usually discloses that unattained goals can be traced to specific programs that were either ineffective or poorly executed. Thus, problem areas are pinpointed, and corrective action can be taken in terms of specific program readjustments.

## HOW TO PLAN

It is impossible to generalize on what specific points a company's marketing plans should cover. No two companies face exactly the same problems or opportunities. But there are four elements around which any company can build what may be called a comprehensive marketing plan that will lead to the benefits just discussed. These four elements are:

1. an appraisal of the company's or product's strengths and weaknesses in the market place;
2. a definition of the assumptions on which the company's plans have been based;
3. a statement of the goals sought; and
4. a list of the major programs to be employed in achieving the goals.

### Self-Appraisal

Very few marketing plans contain an adequate appraisal of factors from which a sound evaluation of company strengths and limitations can be made. Following are some of the most important factors to study in making this appraisal.

*Industry and general economic trends.* The trends in the national economy and in a particular industry often have even more bearing on company profits than the efforts within a company. Consequently, plans should isolate these external trends and draw conclusions as to their influence on the particular company and its products. While these external trends cannot be changed by the company, it can plan for them and cope with them.

In the grocery business, for example, a skillful producer's marketing plan should consider such key trends as concentration of the retail business in fewer hands, movement toward private labels, increased costs of launching new products, and the dramatic growth of wholesalers. One food company that failed to properly evaluate these trends in its industry environment had historically concentrated on selling directly to the independent grocer, bypassing the wholesaler. After a number of successive years of lower profits and sales, top management started looking for answers outside as well as inside the company. They discovered that their poor performance was related to the rapidly growing trend of the grocery wholesaler's selling to affiliated independents. The company had a very poor standing with these wholesalers as a result of past sales policies. Consequently, they had belatedly begun to step up their selling efforts aimed at these more efficient and very influential wholesalers. The company's executives freely admit that they missed the boat on this trend because they had not been keeping careful track of outside trends.

*Company analysis.* An analysis of the trends that really count in a business, such as share of the market, return on investment, and introduction of new products, is one of the most effective safeguards against the great danger in planning–overoptimism. The practice of putting trends in writing forces management to acknowledge the unpleasant as well as the pleasant.

For example, sales planners frequently include only the past year's sales figures and then forecast impressive annual increases for the next five years. This makes for good reading; but if the product involved has shown six years of decline in share of market, annual gains are unlikely to be achieved until the decline is stemmed and recovery is made. As obvious as this error may sound, it is characteristic of many marketing plans.

*Current competitive conditions.* Every plan should include a carefully written appraisal of what competitors are doing with their product lines, prices, and distribution methods. In addition, there should be an appraisal of the company's own product line, market penetration, distribution methods, and so forth. This means looking at such things as product quality allowances or complaints, the strength of the dealer body, and distribution costs. Such a comparative appraisal is a useful device for isolating problems and opportunities facing a company. For example, if the appraisal of competition shows that smaller competitors are growing, including this evaluation in the plan helps to gain recognition of this threat and ensures that action programs have provided for combating it. Failure to periodically appraise the competition often results in overlooking these forces until long after they have become a serious threat.

The sum of these appraisals of past trends and current conditions should give a realistic picture of a company's strengths and limitations in the marketplace and, consequently, of what it can reasonably hope to achieve. If these analyses are omitted from the plan, those who are responsible for approving it are deprived of an integral part of the thought process behind it. Moreover, if the plan has to be revised later, having these analyses available will make the job of replanning easier and ensure that all of the same facts are considered.

## Defining Assumptions

After completing the self-appraisal, the planner should have enough information to make certain assumptions about future operating conditions. These assumptions will be guidelines for anticipating developments that will influence his ability to reach planned goals. Thus, they should be carefully stated and explained and should be included in the written plan.

To many executives, an assumption is equivalent to a prediction. And practical executives shy away from predictions. However, failure to plan without making or defining assumptions is tantamount to predicting that nothing will change.

A statement of assumptions is important because, in the first place, it reduces the danger of planning in a vacuum. It carries the analyses of trends, discussed earlier, one step further and forces the planners to focus their attention on the future shape and importance of the key external conditions.

Furthermore, defining assumptions provides an excellent means of smoking out differing points of view regarding the future. Once these differences are resolved, management can be confident that everyone throughout the organization is planning his own work on the basis of the same assumptions. Thus, for example, the production department will know that marketing is assuming an industry growth of 15 per cent and will plan its own operations accordingly.

Finally, putting assumptions in writing makes it possible to review them as conditions change and to make sure that plans are adjusted to fit unanticipated developments. In the 1958 business downturn, for instance, many companies were caught short unnecessarily. As a result, having no assumptions about the economy, these companies continued business-as-usual policies and programs long after they had become ineffective and inadequate. If they had made assumptions about the general economy, they would have been reminded to alter their goals and programs when these assumptions proved wrong.

*Selectivity.* Clearly, it is neither necessary nor practical to make assumptions about the entire range of factors that make up the national economy and the company's competitive enviroment. The key factors will vary from one industry to another and even from one company to another. Assumptions about labor strikes, for example, are very important in the steel industry but not in the chemical industry.

Here are some assumptions that might have been extracted from the marketing plan of a leading consumer-goods producer.

With respect to the general economy, we assume that:

1. There will be no major change in the gross national product.
2. There will be no major strike affecting consumer buying practices.
3. There will be a 2 per cent increase in the cost of living during the year.

With respect to our industry competitive climate, we assume that:

1. Present industry overcapacity will grow from 110 to 125 per cent as two new competitive plants come into operation.
2. Price pressures will reduce industry price levels by roughtly 10 per cent across the board.
3. Two new products will be introduced prior to the fourth quarter of the year by our leading competitors.

Of course, these assumptions may or may not be realized. But whichever way the economy and industry move, the planner is prepared. Each month or quarter when the marketing plan is reviewed, the assumptions are also reviewed. If they have not materialized, the plan can be modified accordingly. If they have materialized, there will be no cause for concern because they will have already been factored into the planning.

**Developing Useful Goals**

The third element of a comprehensive marketing plan is a set of goals that are both specific and achievable. If the foregoing steps (analysis of the company's strengths and weaknesses and definition of assumptions) have been carefully carried out, the planner is in a good position to set achievable targets.

*Quantitative.* If targets are to be specific, they must be quantitative. A quantitative goal is easily understood. For example, a goal to lower sales costs by 10 per cent communicates both magnitude and impact far better than just a goal to lower sales costs. Inclusion of the 10 per cent figure reduces confusion and permits two executives to approve the same statement with the same interpretation of it.

A quantitative goal also connotes the strength of the action programs that will be required to achieve it. Thus, an aim of increasing retail distribution from 30 per cent to 55 per cent will call for drastic programs, whereas an increase from 10 to 12 per cent will not.

Finally, a quantitative goal facilitates better measurement of progress as the plan is carried out. It is easy to measure progress toward adding five new products, or twenty-six new distributors, or twenty new salesmen during the year. Often, however, executives merely indicate that new products should be added; distributor coverage should be improved; or sales strength should be increased.

*Qualitative.* The importance of quantitative goals, however, does not imply that qualitative goals are taboo in comprehensive marketing planning. Far from it. One recent, outstanding example of a nonquantitative type was to change the Marlboro cigarette image from a luxury item to a he-man cigarette. This was not a goal that had immediate quantitative implications, but it ultimately led to a major improvement in the product's advertising and selling effectiveness and its share of the market.

*Broad range of goals.* In the past, the marketing department has often confined itself to setting achievement aims within the scope of marketing activities. Increasingly, however, it is becoming standard practice for the marketing department to help establish or at least record in its marketing plan all of the major plans for a particular product. Thus, the marketing plan for a product line might state such nonmarketing goals as lowering product costs by 10 per cent; reducing back orders to 15 per cent; and adding three new products and four product improvements to the line.

This total goal approach offers several advantages in comparison to compartmentalized goal-setting. It encourages integration of effort by the various operating departments such as production, engineering, and research and development. It permits drawing up a total planned profit-and-loss statement for the product line, so that when all of the marketing and major nonmarketing goals are put together, the direction that the product will be taking over the plan period can be seen. Without this total picture, it is impractical to make an accurate product profit-and-loss statement that reflects cost reductions, product additions, and so forth, without raising a swarm of unanswerable questions.

A third major advantage of the total or integrated approach to marketing goal-setting is that it helps to broaden the thinking of the marketing executive. He is forced to consider the plans and problems of other operating departments in relation to his own and is more likely to take a company-wide point of view.

## Formulating Programs

Programs are the fourth element in comprehensive marketing planning. They are the trigger that gets action, the steps that are going to be taken in order to get the job done. Thus, to be useful, programs must be geared to accomplishing specific goals. But they must also be based on a firm grounding of strengths, limitations, and assumptions about the future. Therefore, they cannot be, as is often the case, the place to start planning. Rather, programs must be derived from the other three elements of planning discussed earlier.

*Two types of marketing programs.* Many companies find it useful to set up *general* programs to be used throughout the year and *specific* programs to be used during the next quarter. Basically, there is no difference between these two types of programs. However, it is impractical and unnecessary to be very detailed or specific about programs two or three quarters ahead. Conditions change too rapidly for this in almost any industry. It is desirable, however, to be both specific and detailed about plans for the coming three months. A quarterly program might cover such factors as the objective of the program, how it works, where it will be used or conducted, the cost, expected results, assignment of responsibilities, and deadlines.

A specific program of this kind helps the reader as well as the planner to get a picture of its key details. Moreover, it helps to secure approval of the program from executives in upper echelons because it gives them an adequate basis for deciding whether the program is well conceived and properly focused.

*Deadlines and assignment of responsibility.* One of the most successful devices for securing necessary action in the proper sequence on marketing programs is to insist on the inclusion of deadlines and assignments of responsibility in all written plans. This device forces the planners to think out who must do what in order to ensure action. The written word is a published persuader that stays in the mind of each executive who sees his name in print as being responsible for a certain action.

Deadlines not only prescribe time limits but also establish priorities. In setting deadlines, it is necessary to consider and weigh the importance of each program against all other demands on the time of those involved in carrying out the plan. Finally, a written assignment of responsibility and deadlines provides a specific and inescapable means of follow-up. To demonstrate how this process works, Table 1 describes a program to step up sales to oil company outlets (gas stations).

By scanning such a written program, it is evident that Mr. Murphy missed his deadlines and thereby delayed completion of the final project. Determining first that the deadlines were realistic, Mr. Murphy's boss has sufficient evidence to deal with this problem and to correct Mr. Murphy's misguided sense of priority. Experience clearly indicates

**Table 1. Function of Deadlines in a Marketing Program**

| *Step* | *Responsibility* | *Deadline* | *Completed* |
|---|---|---|---|
| 1. Develop form to analyze capacity of present dealers to sell oil outlets | Jones (market research) | 6/10 | 6/10 |
| 2. Use form to evaluate dealers' ability to sell oil outlets | Murphy (sales manager) | 6/25 | 7/15 |
| 3. Visit all potential oil outlets and determine present as well as potential sources | Each district manager | 6/30 | 6/30 |
| 4. Relate findings of dealer analysis and field visits; establish necessary sales programs for each dealer | Murphy (sales manager) | 7/15 | 8/15 |
| 5. Determine results of sales calls by each dealer on oil company outlets | Jones (market research) | 8/15 | 9/15 |

that without such deadlines *in written form*, it is all too easy to let critical steps fall by the wayside. Setting deadlines and defining responsibility will not automatically produce results; however, it almost invariably improves the batting average, especially if the key marketing executive personally follows up on deadlines.

*Integrating programs with marketing goals.* An obvious requirement of comprehensive marketing planning is to see that every action program is aimed at the accomplishment of a specific goal. The advantage of being able to relate marketing action programs to specific and stated goals is twofold. First, the programs will be helping to accomplish specific, measurable goals rather than merely improving sales or some other vaguely stated purpose. Second, the likelihood of accomplishing the goals can be weighed. That is, when all the programs aimed at one specific goal are added together, they should promise a good chance of reaching that goal.

Nonmarketing programs as well as nonmarketing goals should be included in the body of a formal marketing plan. Even though the responsibility for carrying out the program lies outside the marketing department, it is useful and desirable to summarize in the marketing plan the major programs that will affect the marketing of the product. And here again the secret of success lies in selectivity and brevity.

Failure to include the major nonmarketing programs affecting marketing profits or success often leads to unnecessary confusion and sometimes to cross-purposes. For example, when one product manager listed the research programs applying to his product lines, he discovered that the research department was spending most of its time on products that were of secondary importance in marketing. He called this to the research director's attention, and a change was made in the development program.

## HOW TO ORGANIZE

Organizing for comprehensive marketing planning is no easy job. However, certain organizational principles can help reduce wasted motion. Let us discuss some of these principles.

*Scheduling.* Develop a schedule for completing each phase of the plan and stick to it. Formal planning must become a way of life in the marketing department, supported and carried out by each key marketing executive. The schedule should call for work on the plan for the next year to begin early enough in the current year to permit adequate time for market research and analysis of key data and trends. In addition, the schedule should provide for the early development of a preliminary plan that can be approved or altered in principle. The use of a preliminary plan avoids wasting valuable time in developing finished programs that may not be acceptable to top marketing management.

*Coordinating.* Provide for formal contact among key planning groups during the planning process. Although the various planning groups may make their preliminary plans relatively independent of one another, formal contact among the key groups is essential before final plans are adopted. This formal contact coordinates the efforts of the various planning groups (see Figure 1) by:

1. Reducing duplication of effort,
2. Providing an important means of exchanging information and ideas,
3. Ensuring that the final plans of each group embody the thinking and programs of the various other planning groups.

*Information Gathering.* The company's information-gathering and reporting systems must supply the information needed to do comprehensive planning and to maintain adequate control. On the planning side, it should be possible to determine in advance what kinds of information about the company, its products, industry trends, and other key trends will be needed each year. Many of these requirements can be built into the company's regular reporting system. This planning information will, of course, consist of nonfinancial as well as financial information. For example, data about the general economy, industry distribution trends, and company product acceptance may be required annually. This should then be collected systematically to avoid a last-minute rush as plans are being drawn together.

Control information should be concerned with reporting performance against plans. This concept of information reporting focuses attention where it should be—on how well the company is carrying out its marketing plans. Regular reporting of performance against plan can also contribute to a gradual and steady improvement in the planning

**Figure 1. Stages of successful planning**

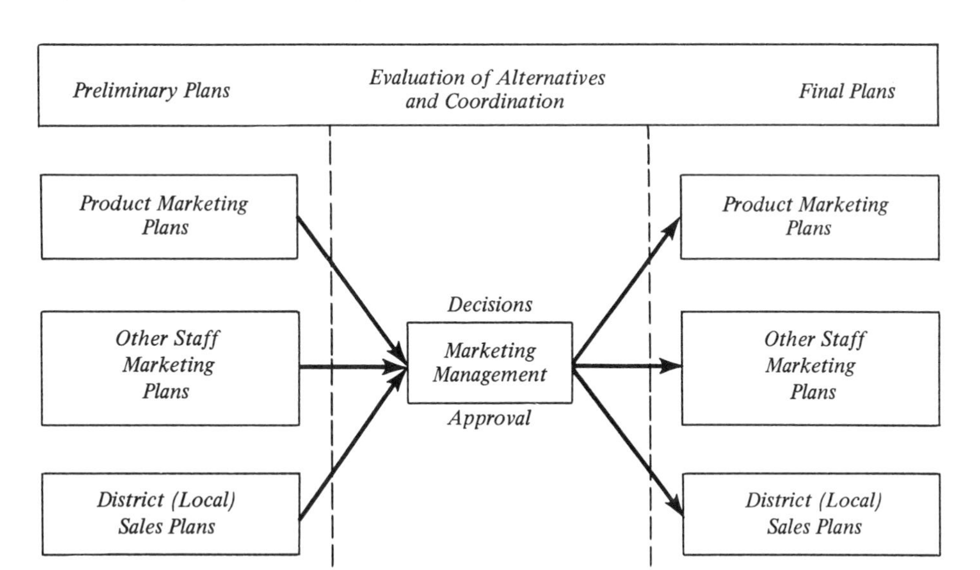

skills of executives, for no one likes to see a low percentage of attainment reported for his department or product line.

*Developing Skills.* Recognize the limitations of people. Planning, like any other element of business activity, requires developed skills as well as natural ability. An untrained planner cannot be expected to develop practical plans any more than an untrained salesman can be entrusted to sell skillfully. This means that top marketing executives must work with their key subordinates throughout the planning process to show them how to plan.

All too often, down-the-line executives are given the assignment to make a marketing plan for a product and bring it to the department head when it is finished. Clearly, this results in a good deal of wasted effort on the part of capable people who simply have never been taught how to make a sound marketing plan. When the plan is finally submitted, there is often too little time for major revisions, and it is adopted with reservations and skepticism.

*Clearing with Top Management.* Top management should be thoroughly committed to the marketing plans. Otherwise, the company is likely to be forced to operate under two sets of objectives—the ones in its formal plan and those imposed informally by top management.

There are no easy answers to this problem. At a minimum, top management must be receptive to the need for formal marketing planning. They should know how the planning job was approached. Above all, they should be exposed to enough details of the plan itself to provide a basis for understanding of its goals and programs. Then, if conditions change or financial goals are missed, the pressure from above to change the plans in midstream is reduced.

Thus, a central requirement for successful formal marketing planning is involvement and understanding on the part of top management. While they do not need to know all of the planning details, top management must have enough knowledge about the plan's contents to ensure its support.

## SUMMARY

Comprehensive marketing planning is no guarantee that goals will be reached. But it does overcome the major weakness of much marketing planning today—spending valuable executive time doing the wrong things. If the planning process starts with an appraisal of strengths and weaknesses, a definition of key assumptions, and a development of useful goals, the company's action programs are very likely to be geared to the key factors governing their success.

Clearly, making the process of formal marketing planning work is more than merely developing sound plans. Once plans are developed, carrying them out must become a way of life in the marketing organization. Under this concept, goals once set are rarely changed. Programs, on the other hand, are revised whenever necessary to achieve the goals. As plans are executed, performance must be measured against plans. When goals are not attained, programs must then be re-evaluated. Barring ineffective execution, if planned programs do not achieve planned goals, the programs, not the goals, must be revised or supplemented.

In this way, the productive effort of the marketing department is directed and harnessed toward chosen goals; it is no longer necessary to settle for results that are achieved by programs that may well be inadequate to begin with.

Companies that utilize comprehensive marketing planning consistently find that it yields at least these five major benefits:

1. Action is coordinated and directed toward a single set of goals throughout the organization.
2. Execution activities are keyed to accomplish important things because the comprehensive plan isolates and emphasizes the key factors for marketing success.
3. Plans are carried into action because specific basis exists for follow-up and control.
4. Planning skills are improved and discrepancies in plans are easy to spot.
5. The reviewing executive can see the basis on which the plans were made; he will not be dependent on verbal fill-ins that are characteristic of less rigorous forms of planning.

# 26. DECISION THEORY AND MARKETING MANAGEMENT

*Robert D. Buzzell and Charles C. Slater*

*This article contains a brief summary of probability decision theory as a tool of marketing management. Through the use of a specific example it is shown how such theory can be implemented.*

*The significance of the following article is not only in the application of decision-models to problem-solving in marketing, but also in the exposition of the assumptions on which the models are based.*

The term "decision theory" refers to a body of methods by which complex problems of decision under uncertainty can, in effect, be reduced to a limited number of simpler problems for purposes of analysis. A more specific term for the method recommended here is *individual decision-making under risk.*[1] By this is meant a formal analysis of decision alternatives and their consequences when the effects of the decision are not known with certainty.

## DECISION THEORY APPROACH

The basic elements of decision-making under risk may be summarized briefly.[2] A decision-maker (person or firm) must choose among several "acts" or "strategies"

[1]Compare Duncan Luce and Howard Raiffa, *Games and Decisions*, John Wiley and Sons, Inc., New York, 1957, pp. 12–15.

[2]See Robert Schlaifer, *Probability and Statistics for Business Decisions,* McGraw-Hill Book Co., Inc., New York, 1959; and Luce and Raiffa, *op. cit.*

Source: From *Journal of Marketing,* vol. 26, July, 1962, pp. 7–16. Robert D. Buzzell: Assistant Professor, Graduate School of Business Administration, Harvard University. Charles C. Slater: Head of Consumer Marketing Services, Arthur D. Little, Inc., Cambridge, Mass.

which we denote as $A_1, A_2 \ldots A_n$. Each act is a well-defined series of actions or procedures; thus, "Act 1" may mean, "Build a new retail outlet at X location with 20,000 square feet of floor space." "Act 2" may represent the reverse, "Build no new retail outlet." Insofar as possible, the sets of acts employed in the analysis should include *all* reasonable possibilities in a given situation. Experience, judgment, and creativity are required to identify the decision possibilities in a marketing problem.

Choice among the various possible acts is difficult because the consequences of an act depend on certain *conditions* which cannot be predicted with certainty. These conditions may be termed "states of nature" and designated $S_1, S_2 \ldots S_m$. The "state of nature" concept includes all factors which determine the effects of a marketing decision (for example, the responses of customers, general business conditions, and competitors' reactions). For example, "State 1" may represent "population in the trading area increases 10 per cent in the next five years, and competitors build three new stores." As in the case of decision possibilities, *all* relevant states of nature should be included in the analysis of a decision, so far as possible. In a literal sense, of course, this can never be attained, so that "complete" optimization is not feasible.

The states affecting the outcome of a decision may *be related to* the particular decision chosen. For example, a decision to use a specific advertising strategy might lead to a defensive response by competitors which could not occur if a different strategy were selected. Consequently, the relevant "states of nature" must be identified for *each* possible act A, although, of course, the same states of nature *may* apply to several or all acts.

Assuming that a given act is selected and that a given state of nature prevails, it is possible to determine the "payoff" to the decision-maker. By "payoff" is meant the monetary and other consequences of the decision. A difficult problem is presented when nonmonetary "payoffs" must be incorporated. In relatively simple problems, it may be possible to assign "cash equivalents" to these consequences. More generally, modern utility theory provides a mechanism for assigning numerical measures to the results of a decision, including monetary and other effects. These payoffs should be estimated on a *net* basis; that is, the costs of carrying out the decision (if any) should be deducted from its estimated revenue.

Determining the payoff of an act under a given state is not an easy task, since a decision of any real importance has far-reaching indirect consequences, in addition to its immediate impact on profits. For example, a decision to market a new product has effects on the long-term sales patterns of existing products, in addition to its own success or failure. Estimation of payoffs is further complicated by the fact that, if they are to be realistic, payoff measures must reflect the particular values of the decision-maker, and these vary among persons. While the treatment of payoffs in this example is straight-forward, it does not imply that the problem is this simple in practice.

Because the outcome of a decision is shrouded in uncertainty, a key element in the analysis of a decision is to assign *probabilities* to the various possible "states of nature."

In some cases, especially those involving *repetitive* decisions such as routine buying and inventory control, it is relatively simple to determine the probabilities of occurrence for various "states" through analysis of quantitative evidence. For example, sales data may reveal that demand for an item is between ten and nineteen units per week 20 per cent of the time, between twenty and twenty-nine units 15 per cent of the time, and so on. These *relative frequencies* may then be used directly as probabilities of occurrence for the various states of demand (assuming, of course, that no basic changes take place in the market, seasonal variations have been accounted for, and so forth).

In most cases involving basic marketing policy problems, however, determination of probabilities for the relevant "states" is not so easy. In most cases, major policy decisions are not repetitive problems, and past experience may provide only a rough and rather ambiguous guide. *Nevertheless, even very crude approximations of probabilities for the various states affecting a decision still are better than none at all.*

The probabilities assigned to the various states represent the decision-maker's "betting odds" as to the probable responses of customers, competitors, and so forth. Admittedly, it is very difficult to assign odds or probabilities to such events. But even in the most informal kind of decision-making, this is precisely what managers *must do.* Any risky decision implies some assessment as to what will ensue from the decision. The real difference between "decision theory" and present management practice is the formalization of this "intuitive" process of choosing among various possibilities. While this may not improve the judgment of the individual decision-maker, it improves his communication with others and facilitates the collection and analysis of further information. More important, it forces an executive to examine his problem in concrete terms, and thus serves as a stimulus to more systematic thinking on his part.

Given the various possibilities, the relevant states of nature and estimates of their probabilities of occurrence, and the payoffs for each act given each state, some act must be selected as the "best" of those available. Several different criteria have been proposed for selection of the "best" or "optimal" act, depending in part on whether or not probabilities are assigned to the states. The one adopted in this analysis is that of selecting the act with the *highest expected payoff.* The expected payoff of an act is defined as the average of its (net) payoffs under all possible states of nature, each weighted by its probability of occurrence.

To illustrate the concept of expected payoff, consider the following simple problem:

| | *Decision possibilities* | | |
|---|---|---|---|
| *States of nature* | *$A_1$: build a new store* | *$A_2$: do not build* | *Probability of state* |
| $s_1$: new subdivision is built | \$1,000,000 | 0 | 0.3 |
| $s_2$: new subdivision is not built | –500,000 | 0 | 0.7 |

Here the payoffs, as previously explained, represent dollar profits to the decision-maker, with future profits discounted to present values. The probabilities are based on management's assessments of such factors as population growth, real estate markets, and zoning. The expected payoff of $A_2$ is obviously zero, since this decision has no payoff regardless of what happens. The expected payoff of $A_1$ may be computed as follows:

$$\$1{,}000{,}000\ (0.3) - \$500{,}000\ (0.7) = \$300{,}000 - 350{,}000 = -\$50{,}000$$

Under this criterion, then, $A_2$ should be chosen, and the new store should not be built. This is equivalent to saying that the chances of success are not good enough to justify the risk.

The logic of selecting the act with the maximum expected payoff is clear-cut in the case of repetitive decisions. Since the decision is repeated over and over, we expect (by definition) the average return per decision to be the expected payoff as computed above. Hence, we should select the act that produces the highest average payoff per decision and the highest total payoff in the long run.

On the other hand, when a decision is to be made only once, the rationale of the expected payoff criterion is not so obvious. This criterion leads to the optimal decision in the sense of yielding a decision consistent with the decision-maker's preferences, as summarized in the payoff table.[3]

## DISTRIBUTION PROBLEMS OF THE BAKING INDUSTRY

Wholesale bakers, in common with many other types of firms, face difficult marketing problems as a result of changes in the character of their markets. These problems arise from substantial excess capacity on the one hand, and concentration of buying power among corporate chains, voluntaries, and cooperatives, on the other hand.

*Development of Marketing Policies.* The present-day marketing policies of wholesale bakers can best be understood in the context of the historical factors underlying their development and modification.

The commerical baking industry emerged during the latter half of the nineteenth century. During this period, as commercial bakers expanded their distribution beyond the immediate neighborhood of their plants, they developed a set of marketing policies geared to the needs of the small independent grocers. Among the more important of these were:[4]

1. Frequent deliveries were made to individual stores.

[3] Luce and Raiffa, *op. cit.*, pp. 20–23; also Schlaifer, *op. cit.*, chap. 2.

[4] William G. Panschar, "Baking in America," vol. 1, *Economic Development*, Northwestern University Press, Evanston, Ill., 1956, pp. 71–84, 93–99.

2. Bakers assumed responsibility for returned stale goods.
3. Retailers customarily stocked several brands.
4. Bakers provided display equipment, stocked displays, and deliberately overstocked shelves in order to increase brand exposure.
5. Price competition was abandoned in view of the oligopolistic character of each retail market. In addition, "flat pricing" became customary; that is, each customer was charged the same unit price regardless of quantities purchased or terms of sale.

These marketing policies, developed for the most part in the early twentieth century, largely comprise the "rules of the game" in the baking industry today. While each policy can be explained as a rational response to market conditions prevailing at the time, many of them have become less and less appropriate as market conditions have changed. The impact of these changes has been made all the more severe because of the inhibiting constraints of labor unions and competitive retaliation in response to change.

*Responses to Changing Market Conditions.* Wholesale bakers in a given market tend to charge identical or nearly identical prices for white bread and other staple bakery products. The explanation lies primarily in the oligopolistic interdependence of the sellers, although illegal price-fixing agreements have been discovered or alleged in some cases.[5] Unit costs are sensitive to changes in output, since fixed production and distribution costs represent a substantial proportion of the total cost for modern bakery plants. Declines in sales in some markets have had the effect of reducing profits substantially. The response of the larger and more efficient competitors has been, in many cases, to *raise* prices and thus hold an "umbrella" over their weaker competitors. Obviously this policy has tended to aggravate the problem of shrinking demand by increasing the cost gap between chain bakeries and purchased baked goods.

An even more important aspect of pricing is the policy of "flat pricing." Typically, no quantity discounts are offered, nor are lower prices available for customers who are willing to forego the traditional store delivery and display services. But chains and other large buyers feel they are entitled to such discounts, and have exerted considerable pressure for them. The evidence is clear that substantial *potential* cost savings are associated with large purchases.

A systems engineering study showed that drivers' product handling rates (units handled per minute of driver time) are directly related to the number of units delivered per route stop.[6] The handling rate was more than 50 per cent greater for stops at which 200 units are delivered than for stops at which 100 units are delivered. *Realized* cost

[5] For example, *Continental Baking Company v. United States,* U.S. Court of Appeals for the Sixth Circuit, No. 13865 (decided July 18, 1960); *Bakers of Washington, Inc., et al.,* FTC Complaint, Docket 8309 (issued March 7, 1961).

[6] *Distribution: The Challenge of the Sixties,* a report prepared for the American Bakers' Association, Arthur D. Little, Inc., Cambridge, Mass., March, 1961.

savings are not this great, since drivers are paid on a commission basis so that improvements in driver efficiency are not reflected in lower unit wage costs. Even under the commission system, however, substantial savings in unit distribution costs are associated with larger drop sizes. (The systems engineering study also revealed that limited-service methods of distribution permit significant reduction in costs.)

Despite evidence that lower costs are associated with quantity sales and limited-service distribution methods, most wholesale bakers have resisted demands for differential pricing. This resistance is based in part on the commission system of compensation typically part of the companies' union agreements. Another factor underlying the resistance to change is the fear that doing so would alienate the small outlets which require full service and which (it is believed) would resent any preferential treatment for their larger competitors, even if justified. Also, it is feared that initiation of quantity or service discounts might lead to chaotic price competition unrelated to any economic justification.

Wholesale bakers have also resisted making private brands for chains or voluntaries because of fear of being boycotted by independents. As a compromise measure, many bakers have developed "secondary" brands of bread which are sold at lower prices than the regular brands, although little difference exists in product characteristics. The price differential is not, however, great enough to equal chain-baked brands, and the main result has been a reduction in average profit for the bakers.

In summary, wholesale bakers have responded to the twin challenges of large-scale retailing and declining per capita bread consumption by attempting to maintain the *status quo.* As output has declined, prices have been raised to maintain the profitability of marginal operators. A uniform local system of pricing and customer services has largely been preserved, despite persistent pressures to deviate from it. Territorial expansion has taken place with the result of higher unit distribution costs. Apart from the general inertia of any established marketing system, several specific factors have tended to impede a more flexible response.

The commission system of driver compensation has discouraged quantity and service discounts. Fear of retaliation by small retail customers has prevented bakers from dealing more realistically with chains. Because of the existence of excess capacity, bakers have feared and sought to avoid the chaotic price competition which might ensue if the traditional ground rules were discarded.

The method of analysis which this article recommends is that of statistical decision theory. The application of this method to a specific bakery marketing policy problem is outlined in the following section.

## DECISION THEORY ANALYSIS APPLIED

For purposes of this exposition, a "model bakery market" has been developed, consisting of three competing wholesale bakers, several retail food chains and voluntary groups, and a number of independent food retailers. For obvious reasons, the other possible acts, appropriate states of nature, and the payoffs must be identified or estimated for a specific firm. Different firms, even in the same local market, might conceive of different acts and states, and almost certainly would have different payoffs for a given decision and state.

In the context of this model market, the analysis is directed to the resolution of a specific decision problem, that of responding to a customer's request for provision of a private brand. Although this analysis is incomplete in the sense that we have not traced the *full* implications of each possible decision, suggestions for a continuation of the analysis are made in a subsequent section.

*The Model Bakery Market.* The hypothetical bakery market was designed to reflect typical market and operating conditions in many metropolitan areas in the United States. In this market there are three wholesale bakers, designated as A, B, and C; and two chain bakeries, those of the Blue Chain and the Red Chain. Wholesale Baker Z, located in a nearby city, is a potential "outside" competitor. The customers served by these bakeries are designated as follows:

Blue, Red, and Green corporate chains,
Retailer cooperatives I and II,
Voluntary chain I,
Independent supermarkets,
Small independent stores,
Sales outside the market to various customers.

The white-pan bread sales of each bakery to each customer are shown in Table 1. Bakery A has the dominant market position, with sales of approximately 400,000 units per week; competitors B and C sell approximately 250,000 units and 100,000 units, respectively. The two chain bakeries produce 250,000 units per week. Thus, the total bread market amounts to about 1,000,000 units per week.

It is assumed that the total market is fixed in the short run and that demand is sufficiently inelastic so that it will not be quickly affected by bakers' marketing decisions. Selling or transfer prices per unit for each bakery are also given in Table 1. It is assumed that each bakery follows the typical industry policy of "flat pricing," with no systematic price differentials for quantities purchased or services required. An average difference of one cent per loaf in *realized* price exists in favor of large customers, primarily on account of their greater utilization of advertising and other allowances.

The cost structure of Bakeries A, B, and C is shown in Table 2. Operating costs are classified as fixed costs (administration, production, and distribution), and variable costs (production and distribution). The relationship of costs to sales volume is a simple linear one:

Total Cost = Fixed Cost + Variable Cost Per Unit (Output in Units)

This equation for bakery operating costs provides a reasonably good approximation to their actual cost structure.

**Table 1. Weekly sales by class of customer, selling or transfer prices per unit, and dollar sales volume for competing bakeries in "Everytown, U. S. A." market**

| | *White Bread Sales in Thousands of Units by Customer and Price per Unit Sales to* | | | | | | | | | | | | |
|---|---|---|---|---|---|---|---|---|---|---|---|---|---|
| *Bakery* | *Yellow chain* | *Blue chain* | *Red chain* | *Green chain* | *Coop. I* | *Coop. II* | *Vol. I* | *Small chains* | *Indep. supers* | *Small indeps.* | *Outside market* | *Total* | *Dollar volume* |
| A | 22@.19 | 50@.19 | 10@.19 | 7@.19 | 114@.19 | 76@.19 | 60@.19 | 22@.20 | 11@.20 | 22@.20 | – | 394 | 75,410 |
| B | 15@.19 | 36@.19 | 8@.19 | 3@.19 | 72@.19 | 48@.19 | 39@.19 | 15@.20 | 8@.20 | 15@.20 | – | 95 | 17,920 |
| C | 3@.19 | 14@.19 | | | 24@.19 | 16@.19 | 11@.19 | 3@.20 | 1@.20 | 3@.20 | 20@.18 | 95 | 17,920 |
| Red chain | | | 162@.155 | | | | | | | | | 162 | 25,110 |
| Green chain | | | | 90@.165 | | | | | | | | 90 | 14,850 |
| Z | | | | | | | | | | | | – | – |
| Total | 40 | 100 | 180 | 100 | 210 | 140 | 110 | 40 | 20 | 40 | 20 | 1,000 | 183,205 |

The assumed fixed and variable costs have been used in Table 2 to compute net profits for each of the three competing wholesale bakers under the "initial market conditions" of Table 1. For example, Baker A has sales of 394,000 units per week. This level of sales results in total weekly variable costs of $54,474, plus fixed costs of $12,662 per week, or a total cost of $67,136.

Hence, net profit before taxes amounts to sales of $75,410 minus operating and fixed costs of $67,136 = $8,274. Profits of Bakeries B and C have been computed in similar fashion in Table 2. While Tables 1 and 2 present a simplified picture of revenues and cost, they are accurate enough for the illustration.

*Analysis of a Decision.* In the context of the "model bakery market" described in Tables 1 and 2, the application of decision theory to a policy problem may now be illustrated. In this analysis the viewpoint of Baker B, the second largest wholesale baker in the market, is taken.

*Let us assume that the Blue Chain asks Baker B to produce a private brand of bread for sale in the Blue Stores.* The problem is, how should Baker B respond to such a request? The decision theory approach may be summarized in six "steps" as follows:

1. *Identification of Different Possibilities.* Baker B has at least five different basic courses of action open to him, in response to the Blue Chain's request:

- $A_1$. Ignore the request; that is, refuse it outright, or delay any response so long as it amounts to a refusal.

**Table 2. Weekly costs, sales, and profits of competing wholesale bakeries in "Everytown, U. S. A." market**

| *Sales, cost, or profit* | *Baker A* | *Baker B* | *Baker C* |
|---|---|---|---|
| Fixed cost–baking | $ 4,310 | $ 3,732 | $ 1,384 |
| Fixed cost–routes | 1,741 | 1,429 | 559 |
| Fixed cost–marketing | 2,277 | 1,743 | 538 |
| Fixed cost–administration | 4,334 | 2,261 | 862 |
| Total fixed costs | $12,662 | $ 9,165 | $ 3,343 |
| Variable cost–baking | $.09641/unit | $.10545/unit | $.11053/unit |
| Variable cost–routes | .03072/unit | .02928/unit | .03007/unit |
| Variable cost–marketing | .01113/unit | .01115/unit | .01122/unit |
| Total variable cost | $.13826/unit | $.14588/unit | $.15182/unit |
| Initial market conditions: | | | |
| Sales | $75,410 | $49,590 | $17,920 |
| Total cost | 67,136 | 46,955 | 17,767 |
| Net profit | $ 8,274 | $ 2,635 | $ 153 |

- $A_2$. Make a counter-offer to produce a "secondary brand" bread to be sold at a lower price than the regular "B Brand" Bread.
- $A_3$. Reduce price on the regular brand.
- $A_4$. Accede to the request of the Blue Chain.
- $A_5$. Institute a system of price differentials based on quantity and service rendered by Baker B. Such price differentials would necessarily (under the law) be offered to all buyers in the market; but in view of the Blue Chain's size and personnel capabilities, this would presumably result in somewhat lower prices to Blue than to most others.

Identification of these possibilities implies a considerable knowledge of the nature of the wholesale bread market and the motivations of the customers therein. It is assumed that the Blue Chain wants a private brand so as to improve its competitive position relative to the Red Chain, which has its own bakery plant. If this is true, the real question is, what possibilities are available to Baker B that might enable the Blue Chain to attain this goal? Possibilities $A_2$, $A_3$, and $A_5$ have little to do with private brands, but all are designed to help the Blue Chain achieve its presumed objective. Perhaps still other possibilities could be identified.

2. *Enumeration of States of Nature.* For each possibility, it is necessary to identify the possible "outcomes" or states of nature governing the effect of the decision. In this problem, the states must take account of the responses of Baker B's customers and competitors to any action he takes.

If Baker B follows possibility $A_1$ and ignores the Blue Chain's request, there are six possible outcomes:

- $S_{11}$ Blue is supplied by outside Baker Z. Having achieved a foothold in the market, Z also supplies private label bread to the Yellow Chain and to Coop I.
- $S_{12}$ Blue is supplied by Z, but Z fails to get any other business.
- $S_{13}$ Blue is supplied by local Bakery A or Bakery C.
- $S_{14}$ Blue acquires its own bakery plant and decreases its purchases from B.
- $S_{15}$ Blue decides to wait; but resentful of B's refusal, adopts minor counter-measures, including reduced display space and less careful maintenance of B's display stocks.
- $S_{16}$ Blue decides to wait and does *not* adopt any counter-measures.

In similar fashion, the possible outcomes of each of B's decision possibilities have been enumerated. Some of these outcomes are common to some or all of the decision possibilities; but in general the relevant "states" or outcomes depend on the particular decision made by B. The whole range of decisions and outcomes is summarized in Table 3.

As was suggested in the general discussion of decision theory, the number and nature of the outcomes differ for the various decision possibilities, since these outcomes consist in part of *responses* to a particular decision. This also implies that the *probabilities* of the various outcomes differ from one possibility to another, even if the possible outcomes themselves are the same.

**Table 3. Decision alternatives and possible outcomes**

| $A_1$ *ignore request* | $A_2$ *offer secondary loaf* | $A_3$ *reduce price* | $A_4$ *accede to request* | $A_5$ *price diff. system* |
|---|---|---|---|---|
| $S_{11}$ Z supplies Blue, Yellow and Coop. I. | $S_{21}$ (same as $S_{11}$) | $S_{31} = S_{11}$ | – | $S_{51} = S_{11}$ (Blue rejects counter-offer) |
| $S_{12}$ Z supplies Blue only | $S_{22}$ (same as $S_{12}$) | $S_{32} = S_{12}$ | – | $S_{52} = S_{12}$ |
| $S_{13}$ A or C supplies Blue | $S_{23}$ (same as $S_{13}$) | $S_{33} = S_{13}$ | – | $S_{53} = S_{13}$ |
| $S_{14}$ Blue acquires own Bakery | $S_{24}$ (same as $S_{14}$) | $S_{34} = S_{14}$ | – | – |
| $S_{15}$ Blue waits, harrasses B | $S_{25}$ (same as $S_{15}$) | – | – | – |
| $S_{16}$ Blue waits | $S_{26}$ (same as $S_{16}$) | – | – | – |
| – | $S_{27}$ Blue accepts offer; A and C follow suit | – | – | – |
| – | – | $S_{38}$ Blue accepts offer; A and C do *not* follow suit | – | – |
| – | – | $S_{39}$ Blue accepts; A and C follow; B retains slight advantage | – | – |
| – | – | $S_{3,10}$ Blue accepts; A and C follow; market returns to original division | – | – |
| – | – | – | $S_{4,11}$ Blue accepts; A and C offer secondary loaf | – |
| – | – | – | $S_{4,12}$ Blue accepts; A and C lower prices; B is forced to meet | – |
| – | – | – | $S_{4,13}$ Blue accepts; A and C offer private labels to Yellow and Coop. I. | – |
| – | – | – | – | $S_{5,14}$ Blue accepts; A and C follow suit |
| – | – | – | – | $S_{5,15}$ Blue accepts; A and C lower prices |

3. *Exploration of Further Possibilities and Outcomes.* The analysis of the decision process usually cannot stop realistically with a single "round" of actions and their outcomes. In order to appraise the consequences of each decision possibility, it is necessary to explore the whole chain of effects and reactions that would ensue from a given action by Baker B.

   For example, suppose B refuses ($A_1$) and Z supplies the Blue Chain as well as the Yellow Chain and Coop I ($S_{11}$). Then B is confronted by a new set of possibilities: he can retaliate by supplying retailers in Z's own market, hoping to drive Z out of the local market; or he can meet Z's competition locally. If he retaliates in Z's market, the outcome will again depend on the "state of nature." The possible outcome, for instance, is that legal action will be taken against B for geographic price discrimination.

   This process can be conceived as a "game" in which the decision-maker takes "turns" with a fictitious opponent ("Nature") representing the whole complex of personal and impersonal market forces bearing on his decisions. An illustrative series of moves is depicted in a tree diagram in Figure 1. In this example we have traced out two "rounds" of the game: first, B makes a move by choosing $A_1$; then Nature "chooses" (in a statistical sense) one of the states or outcomes; then B moves again by choosing an action from a new set of possibilities; and, finally, Nature moves again.

   The game could, of course, be traced out beyond the second round through a third, a fourth, and so on; but if the analysis is ever to be completed and used, it must be cut off somewhere. Also, it is clear that as the analysis is carried further, the estimates of payoffs and probabilities become more and more speculative, so that the value of analyzing further rounds probably diminishes rapidly.

4. *Estimation of Payoffs.* The payoffs for each decision and each applicable outcome have been estimated by tracing through the effects on Baker B's sales, costs, and profits.

   These payoffs are shown for the illustrative moves and countermoves in Figure 1. Consider, for example, the branch of the tree corresponding to the series $A_1$, $S_{11}$, $A'_{111}$, $S'_{1111}$. This represents a decision by B to refuse Blue's request; an invasion of B's market by Z; retaliation by B in Z's market; and legal action against B as a result of the retaliation. It is assumed that this chain of events results in Z attaining a fairly permanent niche in B's market.

   Based on past experience with private brand sales, it is estimated that Blue, Yellow, and Coop I will shift to at least 40 per cent private brand volume, and that B will lose about this same percentage of his former sales to them. This implies a loss of about 52,000 units per week for B; and each unit represents a loss in gross contribution (price minus variable cost) of $.04412. Hence, B's revenue would be reduced by about $2,300 per week. When this weekly loss is converted to its present value, based on a yearly discount of 10 per cent over a five-year period it is equivalent to an outright cash loss of $688,200.

**Figure 1. Illustrative analysis of decision possibilities and outcomes—$A_1$: B refuses Blue's request (payoffs in thousands of dollars)**

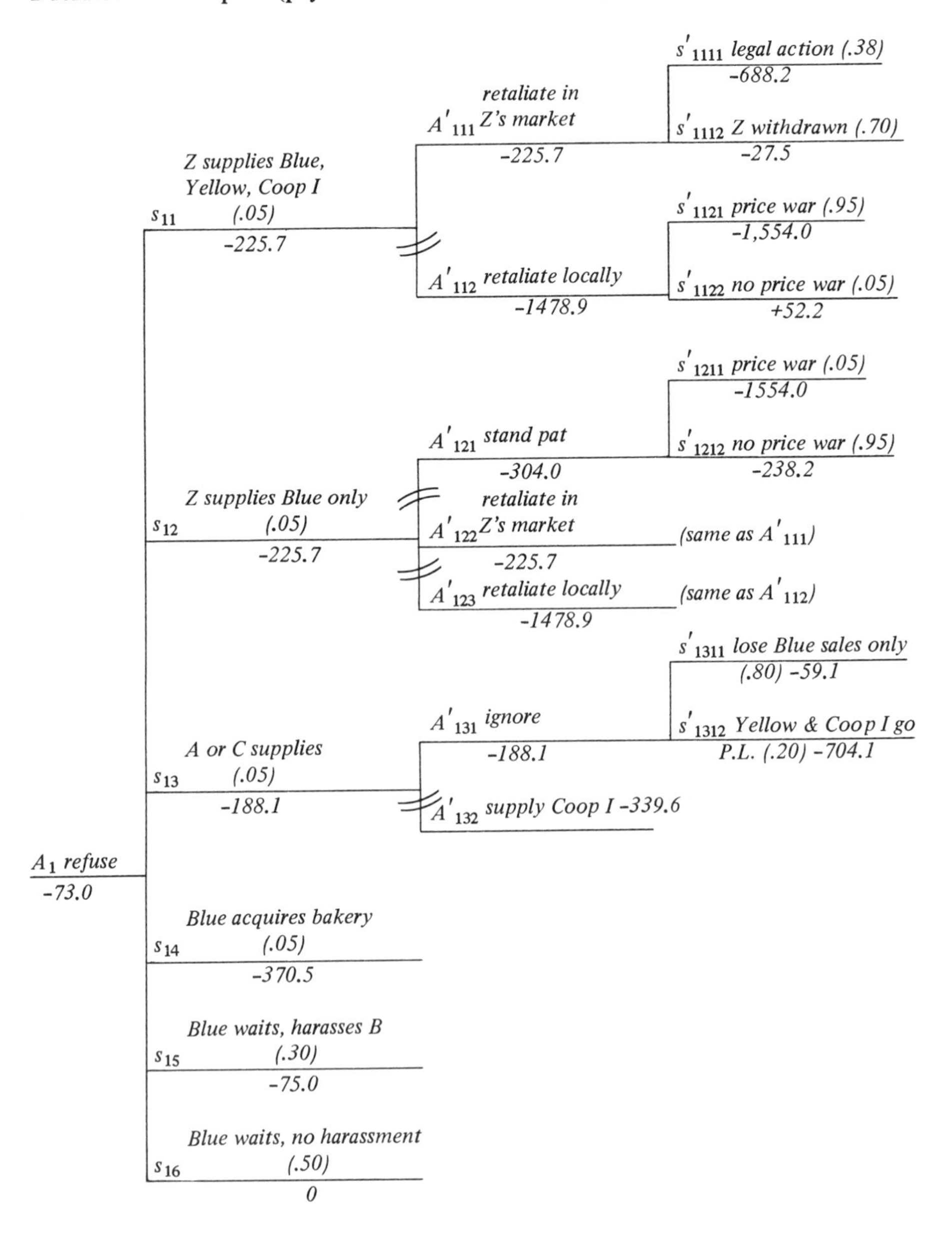


In a similar manner, the payoffs for each possible chain of decisions and outcomes have been estimated and are shown in Figure 1. These estimates are used, together with the estimated probabilities for "Nature's" plays, to derive expected payoffs for each of B's possibilities. Of course, this method of estimating payoffs is oversimplified. In practice, two other factors would have to be considered:

- In addition to the direct effects on revenue and costs, some of the outcomes might involve non-monetary consequences, such as the stigma and the inconveniences of litigation.
- Some of the monetary losses may be so great (for example, the sequence $A_1, S_{11}, A'_{112}, S'_{1121}$) that they imply bankruptcy for B. In such a case, the loss is really greater in relation to less drastic outcomes than is implied by the payoff measures.

5. *Assessment of Probabilities.* Now it is necessary to assign probabilities to each outcome under each possible decision. As suggested previously, this is a very difficult task, but one that must be done at least implicitly in every decision of this kind. The assessments shown in Figure 1 are based on the experience of one of the authors in studying the wholesale bakery market over a number of years, together with conversations with several leading bakery executives.

6. *Computation of Expected Payoff and Choice of Optimal Decision.* Given the individual payoffs and their probabilities, computation of the expected payoff for each decision possibility is a straightforward matter. This is illustrated in Figure 1.

In this analysis, it is necessary to start at the *end* of each chain of acts and outcomes (the extreme right in Figure 1) and work "backward" to the initial set of decision possibilities. Consider, first, the branch corresponding to $A_1, S_{11}, A'_{111}$. If B chooses $A_1$, then $A'_{111}$, there are two possible outcomes: $S'_{1111}$ and $S'_{1112}$. The payoff under $S'_{1111}$ is –\$688,200 and under $S'_{1112}$ it is –\$27,500. The estimated probabilities are 0.30 and 0.70, respectively. Hence, the *expected* payoff at the "fork" representing $A'_{111}$ is .30 (–\$688,200) + .70 (–\$1,554,000) = –\$225,700.

Similarly, the expected payoff for $A'_{112}$ is –\$1,478,900. Obviously $A'_{111}$ is preferred to $A'_{112}$. Hence, in Figure 1 the branch corresponding to $A'_{112}$ has been blocked off; it would never be followed if $A'_{111}$ were available.

It follows that the expected payoff for $S_{11}$ is –\$225,700, the "better" of the two second-round decision possibilities available to B. In similar fashion, the payoffs for $S_{12}, S_{13}$, and so on have been estimated and are shown in Figure 1.

Now the expected payoff for the initial decision Alternative $A_1$ can be computed: it is

.05 (–\$225,700) + .05 (–\$225,700) + . . . + .50 (0) = –\$73,000

The same procedure has also been followed for $A_2, A_3, A_4$, and $A_5$; and the results are summarized in Figure 2. In this diagram the second "round" has been omitted and only the initial choices by B and "Nature" are shown. The figures were derived, however, by an analysis of the second-round payoffs and probabilities as illustrated for $A_1$ in Figure 1.

The analysis shown in Figure 2 suggests clearly that the optimal act for Baker B is $A_5$, the price and service differential system. This does not, of course, imply that this policy is optimal for all wholesale bakers, since it reflects the specific market conditions, cost structure, and payoff-probability estimates of Baker B which may not be valid in another context.

Examination of Figure 2 also sheds some light on the market behavior of wholesale bakers during the postwar period. The most common response, of course, has been "$A_1$" a refusal to produce private brands or to offer acceptable alternatives. While this response has been generally unsuccessful, and wholesale bakers have lost market position, it does have the merit that it avoids any of the possibly disastrous consequences of $A_3$ and $A_4$. The specter of price war has tended to dominate industry thinking. It is difficult to understand the reluctance to establish price and service differentials for large customers. It may be, of course, that bakery executives have feared price war as a possible outcome of this policy as well as of $A_3$ and $A_4$. The restraints imposed by the commission system of driver compensation (which limits the potential savings of limited service) have no doubt also played a part.

*Values of Decision Theory Approach.* Among the most important values of this formal approach to decision problems is that it serves to focus attention on the critical issues involved. In the present example, some of the key questions that naturally arise from the analysis are the following:

1. If a wholesale baker supplies chains with private brands, will other customers retaliate by partial or complete "boycotting?" Is this response permanent or transient? Surveys and limited test markets can answer this.
2. Under what circumstances can a chain (or coop or voluntary chain) "afford" to acquire its own bakery plant through backward integration? If these conditions can be identified, we can assign more meaningful probability estimates to the outcome, "Blue gets own bakery plant," as well as better evaluations of its payoff. Cost analysis and careful assessment of the volume needs of Blue Chain may shed light on this.
3. If a bakery forestalls a request for a private brand by offering a secondary brand in its place, does this diminish the future probability of the chain renewing its request? If a secondary brand is offered for sale, what percentage of former regular brand buyers (ultimate consumers) will shift to the lower-priced brand? How does this depend on the amount and type of advertising and sales promotion, if at all?
4. If price differentials based on quantity and service are established, which customers will be able and willing to take advantage of them? What will the impact on average revenue per unit be?
5. How does a given decision affect possible future courses of action? For example, does the introduction of a secondary brand at one time make the decision to supply private brands in the future more or less feasible? Do secondary brands have any effect on the

**Figure 2. Summary of first round of decision possibilities, outcomes, and payoffs for wholesale bakery private label decision (payoffs in thousands of dollars)**

| Action | Outcome | Payoff |
|---|---|---|
| $A_1$ ignore or refuse – 73.0 | $S_{11}$ Z supplies Blue and others (.05) | – 225.7 |
| | $S_{12}$ Z supplies Blue only (.05) | – 225.7 |
| | $S_{13}$ A or C supplies Blue (.05) | – 188.1 |
| | $S_{14}$ Blue acquires bakery (.05) | – 370.5 |
| | $S_{15}$ Blue waits, harasses B (.30) | – 75.0 |
| | $S_{16}$ Blue waits (.50) | 0 |
| $A_2$ counter offer –265.2 | $S_{21}$ Z supplies Blue and others (.02) | –225.7 |
| | $S_{22}$ Z supplies Blue only (.03) | –225.7 |
| | $S_{23}$ A or C supplies Blue (.01) | –188.1 |
| | $S_{24}$ Blue acquires bakery (.01) | –370.5 |
| | $S_{25}$ Blue waits, harasses B (.01) | – 75.0 |
| | $S_{26}$ Blue waits (.02) | 0 |
| | $S_{27}$ Blue accepts A and C follow suit (.90) | –275.1 |
| $A_3$ reduce price by .02 – 1337.0 | $S_{31}$ Z supplies Blue and others (.03) | – 225.7 |
| | $S_{32}$ Z supplies Blue only (.04) | – 225.7 |
| | $S_{33}$ A or C supplies Blue (.02) | – 188.1 |
| | $S_{34}$ Blue acquires bakery (.01) | – 370.5 |
| | $S_{35}$ Blue accepts, A and C do not meet (.05) | – 456.6 |
| | $S_{36}$ Blue accepts, A and C meet, B retains advan. (.10) | –1249.2 |
| | $S_{37}$ Blue accepts, A and C meet, return to original share (.75) | –1554 |
| $A_4$ accede –260.7 | $S_{41}$ Blue accepts, A and C offer secondary (.70) | – 22.2 |
| | $S_{42}$ Blue accepts, A and C reduce prices (.10) | – 1442.7 |
| | $S_{43}$ Blue accepts, A and C supply Coop I and Yellow (.20) | – 504.3 |
| $A_5$ price differential system + 125.2 | $S_{51}$ Z supplies Blue and others (.05) | – 225.7 |
| | $S_{52}$ Z supplies Blue only (.05) | – 225.7 |
| | $S_{53}$ A or C supplies Blue (.05) | – 188.1 |
| | $S_{54}$ Blue accepts, A and C follow suit (.60) | 0 |
| | $S_{55}$ Blue accepts, A and C reduce prices (.25) | + 628.5 |

assumed "resentment" of independent retailers toward bakers who supply chains with private brands?

Although these questions cannot be answered now, at least partial answers to some of them could be obtained through properly designed research efforts. A major advantage of structuring a problem in formal terms is to indicate the directions that research efforts should take.

It is natural to ask whether or not formal decision theory is "practical." It is feasible to carry out such analyses of marketing problems, and does the use of such an approach offer any advantages over current practice?

In conclusion, there are side benefits. The process need not be time-consuming; however, by preventing a hurried selection of the most obvious conclusion, the way is paved to creative thinking in a manner that fosters dispassionate communication about the problem. There is a strong probability that through such an approach research activities necessary for solution of the problem will be more clearly defined and their application explicitly anticipated.

Finally, the principle advantage of formal decision theory over informal executive judgment is implied by the word "formal." The type of analysis illustrated here requires the decision-maker to *formalize* his thinking regarding a problem—to structure his judgment and to "put it down in black and white." That this is likely to improve the quality of executive judgment seems self-evident. Whenever a decision must be made and its outcome is not known with certainty, some informal equivalent of the decision theory must be employed.

# 27. A MODEL FOR MARKETING PROGRAMMING

*R. P. Willett*

*Although the mix concept is a marketing fact of life, it has not always been the most useful "tool" for the marketing manager.*

*The author questions the usefulness of the conventional mix concept and suggests an alternative approach to marketing program-design.*

Surprisingly few marketing programs—even for new products—are so completely ineffective in producing sales that they are abandoned as total failures. Mediocre marketing programs may be temporarily successful. And unsuccessful marketing programs may appear successful because of the marketing decision-maker's joint problems of calculating expectations of performance, and being able and willing to recognize variance between expectations and performance.

Perhaps there is a "Parkinson's Law" of expectations . . . that expectations contract to conform to market performance.

The apparent success of such programs masks the need for finer measurements of a marketing program's performance and provokes situations where firms are not realizing full value from marketing dollars spent. However, inadequate measurement of performance is only symptomatic of the real problem. A major share of the blame for this underutilization of marketing resources must be directed at the framework used in designing the marketing offering of product, price, channel, and promotion—the concept of the marketing mix. The mix concept is more than just another interesting

Source: From *Journal of Marketing,* vol. 27, January, 1963, pp. 40–45. R. P. Willett: Associate Professor of Marketing, Graduate School of Business, Indiana University.

marketing theory; it is an organic characteristic of any firm's accumulated marketing decisions.

The conventional expression of the marketing mix concept fails in its assumptions when applied to the real world of dynamic markets and competition, and the internal dynamics of the firm. A criterion for a firm's survival in our economy requires that solutions to marketing problems reflect the firm's economic dynamics. Recognition of the firm's dynamic state is not enough; an acceptable framework for marketing planning must also supply a conceptual approach and ultimately operational techniques for marketing decision-making.

The beginnings of an effective conceptual approach to marketing programming are available to the decision-maker who asks the right questions about the impacts of his prospective decisions.

## A CONVENTIONAL SOLUTION

Consider the conventional solution to the problem of designing an effective and internally-consistent marketing program. The real test of the effectiveness of the marketing program is its ability to produce a profit for the firm.

Because the central issue here is the most profitable combination of marketing variables, we can transcend most of the definitional problems by adopting a marginalist approach; whatever the method of expressing the firm's profit objective, the optimum marketing mix is that combination of marketing's product, price, channel, and promotion inputs that produces the closest conformity to the firm's overall profit objective.

Armed with a precise measuring device, the marketing manager is in a position to build a marketing program along the lines suggested by contemporary treatments of the marketing mix concept. The marketing program is put together at one point in time, to produce a desired profit in a stated period. The marketing manager carefully examines all possible combinations of product, price, channel, and promotion strategies, and selects the composite that maximizes the return to the firm. Theoretically, he would continue to vary the values of the inputs in the marketing mix until contributions to profit cease.

Conceptually, a simple static approach to the determination of the optimum marketing mix is both interesting and useful. Selected principles of economics can easily be applied to the solution of marketing problems when treated in this context. But, real difficulties occur when we attempt to apply this conceptual framework to reality. From the point of view of the decision-maker, there is no solution to the mix problem stated in the above manner. Possible combinations of kinds of marketing inputs associated with all possible values of dollar expenditure or sacrifice become infinite. Under such conditions, no executive is in a position to initiate a search for the best possible combination of marketing inputs.

Limitations on the ability to measure marginal costs and revenue contributions also effectively short-circuit the operational potential of the conventional mix concept.

To state profit as a period concept is an inherent part of the logic of the marketing mix; but a static view of profit breaks down when applied to constantly changing consumer-level and channel-level markets, and the dynamics of competitive interaction.

Consider the case of a manufacturer of a particular consumer good in a market that has reached an initial stage of maturity. Consumers have demonstrated an accelerated shift in preferences from nonprice to price elements in firms' marketing offerings. This behavior shift has been coupled with a decay of the effectiveness of selective distribution, a reduction in the average quality level of product, and the entry of additional competitors. Given a static view of profit, the temptation for the firm might be to make individual adjustments of prices, channels, or other variables in the marketing program to maintain the past or existing revenue levels.

Viewed in the context of expected as well as present return, a more creative solution might include consideration of a variety of factors: the realized and as yet unused impact of the firm's own efforts already applied to the market; the current and most efficient scales of operation; the firm's organizational capacities; the firm's ability to innovate; a reconsideration of the entire marketing program; and the interaction of its parts rather than an adjustment of single parts.

These limitations in the static mix concept will certainly evoke no surprise from the marketing manager, and have in general been recognized by the marketing academician. Many of these same criticisms have been raised in a previous issue of the *Journal of Marketing.*[1] But if this whole mix concept is nonoperational, what do marketing practitioners substitute as a workable framework for their decision-making? Obviously judgment is at times substituted for measurement.

More importantly, a variety of subjective questions and answers about the impacts of individual inputs in the mix are traded off against the neat marginal contribution-to-profit measurements implicit in the simple mix concept. But the questions asked are frequently not made explicit and integrated into the formal search and decision process. This sets the stage for substantial underutilization of firms' resources. Properly framed and backed up by assumptions and a framework reflecting a sensitivity to market dynamics, a partially subjective approach to the design of the marketing program is probably an optimum solution at this stage in the development of marketing management.

## DYNAMICS AND THE FIRM

Any firm's composite marketing program represents its offering to a dynamic market operating within a dynamic economy. The firm itself is subject to continuous change and adjustment. Conventionally, the marketing function is tagged as the revenue-producing segment of the firm; but marketing activity, regardless of its scale, has a

[1] P. J. Verdoorn, "Marketing From the Producer's Point of View," *Journal of Marketing,* vol. 20, January, 1956, pp. 221–235.

multidimensional impact on the firm's operating results. Every marketing effort or input has the potential of inducing either directly or indirectly a market response, a competitive response, a cost response within the firm, and an investment response within the firm. Designs of a marketing program must reflect these economic dynamics.

Dynamic models in economics are not a new invention. Currently, the development of modern decision theory introduces dynamics in the form of uncertainty. Developments in techniques of capital budgeting also have their foundation in a dynamic view of our economic behavior.

Borrowing from these points of view, the first adaptation that the marketing executive must make is to recast the profit objective in terms of the future and some consistent sequences in time. Admittedly, there are a variety of objectives that are and have been substituted for profit. But none of the substitutes is a better test of the success or as useful as profit in the rational calculation of payoffs from alternative courses of marketing action.

Furthermore, many of the alternatives to profit may be at least partially calculable in terms of profit. Under such conditions, an appropriate variation of the profit objective might be the maximization of the present value of the enterprise. Rather than being a focus at a point in time, profit becomes a stream, consisting of a cost stream and a revenue stream. Equally important is the capital or investment stream that must accompany or precede the operational business of producing a profit. The concept of the profit stream does no damage to the ability to use whatever modifier of profit the firm feels appropriate. In summary, the firm may still maximize or accept some satisfactory stream of profit discounted to reflect the present value of some future profit position.

Questions that need to be answered begin to multiply. What marketing program will provide the most desirable stream of current asset replacement and additions to capital? In an economy characterized by business fluctuations, what pattern of marketing programming is most appropriate for a given set of expectations about future economic fluctuations? What marketing program will create over time the most effective differential competitive advantage for the firm? Given an operational set of marketing objectives, what composite program will create the desired marketing offering, sales pattern, firm image, and present and future market position?

## ATTRIBUTES OF MARKETING INPUTS

Comprehensive mathematical solutions to the program design problem do not currently exist; consequently, the marketing manager must make the best use of his own decision-making talents and the few scientific tools at his disposal in subjectively assembling the composite program.

The first step and most important requirement in such an approach is simple: the marketing manager must ask the right questions about the impacts of each marketing decision on the market, the firm, and every other decision

Because the problem facing a marketing manager—that of choosing the best possible combination of marketing offerings—is a function of the knowledge of what the impact of each decision will be, both for the firm and in the marketplace, the information he seeks must reflect the kinds of interaction that occur among all the various decisions that make up a representative marketing program. The questions suggested are designed to identify the impacts and interactions among decisions that make up the total marketing program. Supplied with answers, these questions can become a starting point in a more realistic conceptual approach to marketing program design.

## THE RIGHT QUESTIONS

*Productivity Level of Marketing Inputs.* What is the productivity level or dollar return on dollar investment in any single marketing input offered to the market?

Probably the most basic attribute of any resource used in the creation of the firm's offering is the relationship between dollar input and dollar output. Sales dollars received for dollars expended on a particular element of the marketing offering probably differ widely among industries and even among product classes within industries. Rough measurements suggesting the productivity of the various inputs in a total marketing program may be sufficient guides to answer this kind of question. Such rough measurements become in effect first approximations that will be modified and sharpened as the decision-maker continues to explore the effects of a given marketing input.

*Elasticity of Marketing Inputs.* What is the elasticity or rate of market response to changes in any input in the total marketing program over moderate ranges of variation of expenditure on the input?

More precise guidelines for judging the profitability of the market's response to changes in inputs are suggested when some estimate of the elasticity of market response to changes of various marketing inputs is provided, and considered jointly with estimates of the likely productivity levels of the inputs. Price elasticity, promotional elasticity, and other variations of the elasticity concept are well-established principles of economic and marketing behavior that are operative in practice.

*Threshold of Market Response.* At what level of input for any marketing variable is the threshold of effectiveness reached, as evidenced by an increase in the marginal productivity of marketing dollars spent?

The threshold effect appears to be well established as a marketing concept. First of all, certain minimum levels of expenditure on a marketing input are necessary to evoke more than a nominal market response. At this point, the marginal productivity of dollars spent increases sharply, remains constant, or increases gradually for additional increments of input, then may rapidly produce diminishing returns.

Obviously different kinds of marketing inputs will exhibit different patterns of increasing and diminishing returns relative to the levels of expenditure. Some firms have even been able to document this market response pattern in limited experiments. The most obvious example of the threshold effect occurs in the case of various advertising media where certain minimum levels of investment are required to induce any market response at all, but where successive increments of expenditure reduce the marginal productivity of dollars spent.

*Time Lag in Market Response.* How is the impact of a change in an input in the marketing program propagated throughout the market in time; and how much lag time is associated with the input's ability to induce an initial market response?

Although this concept is not well established as a general case it can certainly be seen operating in the so-called product life cycle. The concept of differential time periods for market reaction to inputs should be useful in shorter time periods than the typical product cycle, and also applicable to other inputs in the firm's marketing program.

Time lags, of course, become important when there are substantial differences among the response lags that might be expected from the various components of the program being designed. For example, the differential time rates of market response to advertising placed in different media as a part of a promotional compaign present the marketer with a distinct scheduling problem.

*Economies of Scale.* What are the economies and diseconomies of scale associated with the different kinds of marketing activities to be designed into the total program? At what level of dollar investment in the marketing program do the economies of scale associated with some inputs of the program tend to be canceled by diseconomies of scale associated with others?

Even the most perfectly blended marketing program will encompass individual marketing activities operating at different levels, the overall scale of operation being determined by the aggregate revenue requirements of the firm. In addition, different functions will have differential gains from larger scales of operations. Choice of inputs in the mix and their levels of operation should reflect the balance of economies and diseconomies of scale likely to appear in the marketing cost structure.

The channels and physical distribution dimensions of the marketing program are frequent sources of conflicting scales of operation. To cite a possibility, the lowest average unit cost of warehousing and shipping may be achieved with a limited number of large facilities and shipments, only to be offset by the opportunity costs of not providing prompt customer service.

*Decay Rate of Marketing Inputs.* What is the decay rate of market response to any input in the total marketing offering?

The logic of time lags for market response applies equally well to the concept of a decay of effectiveness for a marketing input. Decay of effectiveness for any input in the marketing program is a function of consumers' learning patterns and reactions to change or innovation.

The concept is illustrated in advertising where market response to particular kinds of advertising may degenerate over a series of time periods. The same pattern probably applies to the full range of marketing offerings, including price. Differential decay rates of elements of a marketing program become significant when posed as determinants of the frequency of change or innovation necessary to maintain market position.

*Substitution of Marketing Inputs.* What inputs in the marketing program can be effectively substituted for one another? Is the substitution of one kind of marketing effort for another a process that tends to be unilateral or bilateral?

The extent to which the individual inputs of a marketing program are effective substitutes for one another plays a major role in the final selection of the most efficient marketing program. Further, the unilateral or bilateral nature of substitution appears to be reasonably well established, at least in economic theory.

Price-nonprice substitutability is a general example of this phenomenon; but attention should be given to other kinds of trade-offs that may be used to produce a more flexible marketing program. Answers are needed to questions about the substituability of channel efficiency for mass promotion, promotion for product quality, product quality for channel effort, and about the productivity of the inverse of these tradeoffs.

*Reinforcement of Marketing Inputs.* What inputs in the total marketing program tend to produce the greatest joint impact in the market, or in effect tend to reinforce each other?

Combination of different kinds of marketing inputs can produce a greater impact on a market than the results of each input taken separately. Equally important is the possibility that various inputs in a marketing program can easily destroy one another's effectiveness. The need for complimentary decisions in the construction of the overall marketing program appears to be a well-established design criterion.

*Competitive Potential to Counter.* What inputs in the total marketing program offer the greatest resistance to competitive ability to counter with a similar or new offering?

One of the most fertile areas for innovating in marketing occurs here. Where there is recognized interaction among firms in a defined market situation, designing a marketing program that is as immune as possible to competition's ability to counteract the firm's impact on the market becomes an important overall marketing strategy.

It is quite likely that the principle of diminishing marginal utility is operative here. A second or third or subsequent number of similar marketing programs or individual strategies has less impact on the market than does the effort of the innovator. Thus, innovation applies not only to cases where technology cannot be duplicated quickly, but also in situations where the special nature of the marketing offering permits a firm to capture a new market position or image.

*Sequence and Timing of Decisions.* What inputs in the total marketing program are linked in sequence so that the greatest effect in the market is attained when a particular pattern of application of efforts in sequence is followed?

Another reasonably well-established marketing principle indicates that marketing activities in definite sequence elicit the greatest market response. Well recognized as a factor in the design of sales promotion activities, this concept is applicable, for example, to problems of new product introduction, or to decisions involved in scheduling the physical distribution function.

The use of sampling prior to the appearance of other promotional devices in the introduction of a new product illustrates one possible sequencing problem. Selection of the sequence for parts of a program's application to the market becomes a part of the scheduling problem for the marketing manager. In addition, timing problems will frequently grow out of changing demands on the marketing program that are a function of business fluctuation or short-term shifts in consumer preferences.

## ORGANIZATIONAL CAPACITY CONSTRAINT

Although organizational capacity is not an attribute of parts of a marketing program in the usual sense, it does become an important constraint in determining whether or not the expected results from marketing effort will be realized.

Normally, organizational behavior and capabilities are treated as a side element in presentations of the mix concept. Failure to equate the proposed scale of marketing operations with the entire firm's organizational capacity may well be more costly than any other type of design error. Revenue and cost impacts of marketing decisions become statistics, and these quantitative dimensions over a long enough time period are readily variable. Human potential and conflict are infinitely harder to establish factually, and to adjust to changing firm conditions. In fact, the decision-maker is probably more sensitive to changes in environment and subject to more uncertainties than the raw materials of his trade.

## FROM QUESTIONS TO MONEY

The conceptual framework suggested here has not been made operational. However, the only real test of the validity of the concepts is their usefulness in increasing the dollar payoff from the firm's marketing strategies. Unfortunately, the "giant step" from concepts to operational solutions to the mix problem requires the use of analytical tools and empirical data not readily available.

One natural advantage of the framework proposed is its suggestions of kinds of data and decision methodology that are relevant in solutions to the marketing programming problem. But suggestions are not enough.

Research is needed in three specific areas if this kind of conceptual framework is to be more than a conversation piece. First, the presence and nature of the market responses suggested need to be empirically measured. Second, these market responses need to be translated into the common denominators of revenue, costs, and investment. Third, the most advanced decision-making logic and tools available need to be adapted to the nuances of marketing program design.

*Empirical Measurement of Impacts.* Marketing has frequently lagged behind other functional areas of business in meaningfully using performance data that are the by-products of their activities. The firm's need for and consequent preoccupation with narrowly defined market potential data are probably responsible for the lack of attention to data reflecting the marketing program's performance. These same factors have hindered meaningful behavioral research, an equally important source of data in the design of marketing strategies.

Many firms could contribute greatly to their own future marketing success by simply recording marketing performance data already being generated. Given existing data processing techniques, the potential return on investment in such data gathering is great. Where marketing performance data are not readily available from the firm's usual recording facilities, the emerging experimental design and quasi-experimental design techniques offer a workable alternative for measuring the effects of marketing efforts.

*Monetary Common Denominators.* To measure effectively the overall impact of a proposed marketing strategy, the marketing decision-maker must be able to add up the multiplicity of impacts suggested. Because the impacts are diverse, operational measurements depend on the use of a common denominator. The pro-forma profit and loss and return on investment models provide a way of assembling the revenue, cost, and investment effects associated with the various impacts of marketing actions. Research is needed here to trace the kinds of dollar-and-cents effects that will be attached to each of the possible kinds of market response.

*Decision-Making Methodology.* The decision-maker himself must share the responsibility for any criticism of marketing program inadequacies. There has been a virtual renaissance in the development of the logic of decision-making that challenges the adequacy of the scientific method. New decision-making logic applicable to marketing management needs to be recognized and applied. The traditional staff research support for marketing decisions needs to be re-evaluated. Finally, the array of quantitative analysis techniques currently being refined in other areas needs to be adapted for marketing's use.

The end result of using concepts and analytical processes similar to those in this article is a greater probability that a firm's final marketing plans will reflect the dynamics of a going concern operating in a market system.

# V

# *Putting the Marketing Plan into Action*

*This section is a logical continuation of the preceding one, "Developing the Marketing Plan."*

*From a realistic point of view, planning of any precise nature should not take place until the planners know a considerable amount about each of the individual strategies to be considered. Much has been written of a descriptive nature about each of the major strategies; and the objective here is to single out the best analytical and conceptual materials dealing with these underlying strategies.*

*The first part of this section is concerned with the strategy of* products and product lines. *It contains readings which deal with such subjects as the product's life cycle, and the time lag in new product development.*

*In the next part of the section, the dynamics of* product brands *is discussed.*

*The subject of* packaging *is then considered from the standpoint of management, and also from the viewpoint of the consumer.*

Pricing *is dealt with from a marketing standpoint, and with a variety of approaches to pricing problems.*

*Next under consideration are* channels of distribution, *which have a considerable effect on other strategies such as pricing, advertising, personal selling, brand policy, and physical distribution.*

*Although the subject of* physical distribution *is rarely discussed to any great extent in most books on marketing, the subject is an important one–from a conceptual point of view and also with respect to specific problems solved.*

*Finally, there are probably no topics in marketing that receive so much attention in print as do* selling *and* advertising; *these are two areas in which management can apply certain concepts from the behavioral sciences, and also use techniques of quantification.*

# 28. TOP MANAGEMENT'S STAKE IN THE PRODUCT LIFE CYCLE

*Arch Patton*

*The concept of life cycle of people is familiar to most students of marketing. In the present article much the same concept is applied to products, including the key parts in the cycle and the implications of each for management decisions.*

It is relatively easy for top management to recognize the profit implications of price reductions, design changes, product obsolescence, and other of the more obvious competitive weapons where a particular product is concerned. But executives have been slower to grasp the importance of a product's position in its life cycle as a basis for planning the strategy of profitable product exploitation. Too often their attention is focused on day-to-day competitive situations, or company-wide problems, rather than on the opportunities to advantageously shape a product's destiny that result from trends inherent in its life cycle.

The life cycle of a product has many points of similarity with the human life cycle; the product is born, grows lustily, attains a dynamic maturity, then enters its declining years. Like the human, a product that has not built up its potential during the formative years is likely to be relatively unsuccessful in its maturity. And just as each of us must manage our financial resources during maturity to take advantage of opportunities or protect ourselves against adversity, so executives who control the destiny of a product must optimize their use of capital resources in the latter stages of the product life cycle.

Source: *The Management Review,* vol. 48, June, 1959, pp. 9–14, 67–71, 76–79. Arch Patton: Principal and Director, McKinsey & Company, Inc., New York.

There are critical differences between the product and the human life cycle. Every person has an average life expectancy—his allotted "three score years and ten." But the life expectancy of a product varies widely. When a dress designer creates the "sack" style, he probably expects that it will have little more than a year of life; the design of a Chippendale chair may be "good" for generations. Aspirin is still aspirin after sixty-five years, but jet-prop engines were virtually obsolete by the time they came off the drawing board.

Although man has fruitlessly sought the elixir that will extend his own span on this planet, product life cycles—or phases of the cycle—have been lengthened or shortened by a variety of causes. When patents on the tubeless tire did not stand up in court, the product moved through the introductory and growth stages to maturity in less than four years. The automobile industry lengthened its maturity period immeasurably by what has come to be called "planned style obsolescence," which made automobiles a symbol of success rather than a means of transportation. (The auto industry's short-cycle model change based largely on styling has been tried in other industries with relatively less success. Perhaps if TV sets, refrigerators, and washing machines were parked in our driveways, the result might have been different.)

## THE LIFE-CYCLE CONCEPT

Essentially, the product life-cycle concept is a simple one. It has three key elements:

1. Products move through the cycle of introduction, growth, maturity, and decline at varying speeds.
2. Unit profits climb sharply in the growth phase and start to decline because of competitive pressures during the maturity phase, while volume continues to rise.
3. The functional emphasis required for successful product exploitation—engineering and research, manufacturing, marketing, and financial control—changes from phase to phase in the cycle as shifts occur in the economics of profitability.

At the risk of oversimplifying the life-cycle concept, Figure 1 gives a view of the profit and volume relationships occurring in each phase of the cycle. The losses of the early introductory phase give way to soaring unit profit margins during the growth phase. Profits turn down—while volume continues to expand—in maturity, and both slump during the decline, or obsolescence, phase.

These profit-volume shifts, in turn, lead to changes in the relative importance of the various functions within a company from phase to phase. This is probably best described by a brief review of the distinguishing environmental characteristics in each segment of the product life cycle.

*The Introductory Phase.* The critical ingredient here is research or engineering skill in product development. However, skill in testing and launching the product ranks high as a factor in its ultimate success. Many a "better mousetrap" never saw the light of

**Figure 1. Profit-volume relationships in the product life cycle**

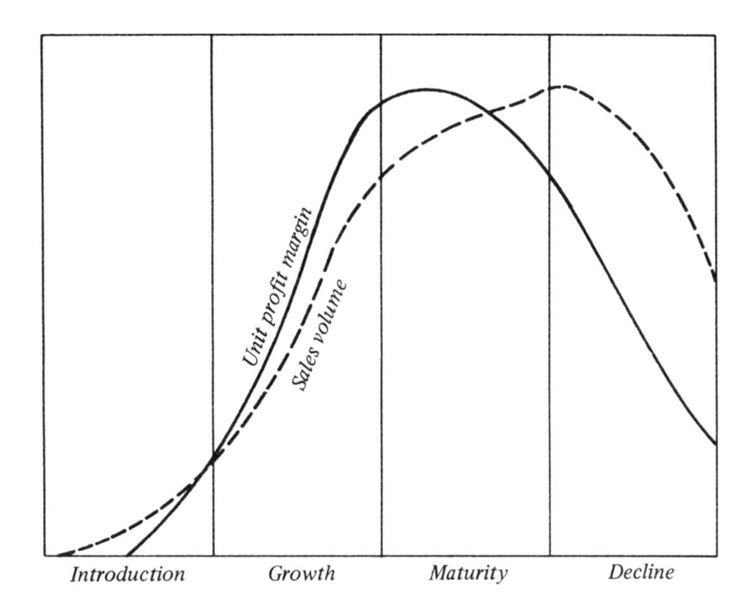


day because consumers did not know which door to beat a path to. Normally, losses are heavy in this period, for volume is too small to yield a profit in the face of high promotional costs.

*The Growth Phase.* The product having survived the introductory phase, the problem becomes one of getting a workable version on the market in sufficient volume to secure a brand franchise. This is of special importance for a consumer product, which must build acceptance at the distribution, retail, and consumer levels.

Thus manufacturing becomes the key function. Many products have died in the growth phase because engineering or research tinkered with product design so long that competitors pre-empted the market by the time production got under way. Indeed, there is evidence that, under certain market conditions, volume is more important than product quality at this stage. The consumer apparently will accept uneven quality in a product's early growth period if he wants the product and has little basis for comparison between products. However, it must be added that the extent to which a product provides real consumer satisfaction at this stage largely establishes the quality climate in which the product will live in later stages of its life cycle.

This is a period of high and sharply rising profits for manufacturer, distributor, and retailer. Risks can be accepted that would be disastrous in a more competitive era, for soaring demand covers a multitude of sins involving hasty or ill-considered actions.

At some point in the growth phase, marketing decisions of great future importance are made. For example, agreeing to market the product through a specific distribution channel, or to sell only to the "quality" market, may become important restrictions on product maneuverability in the next, or maturity, phase.

*The Maturity Phase.* As volume rises and the market becomes increasingly saturated, marketing steps to the center of the stage. Generally speaking, at this point all competitive products are reliable and there is less and less to choose between them. Improvements in the product tend to be small, with "selling features" or style changes dominant.

Profit margins begin to slip during this phase, despite rising volume. This results from each agency in the distribution process–starting with the retailer, moving back to the distributor, and finally reaching the manufacturer–giving up some profit in an effort to maintain or increase volume. This may take the form of one link in the chain absorbing costs that normally are borne by another (distributors handling credit and financing for retailers, manufacturers consigning stock to distributors), or taking over the functions of the other (as when manufacturers set up branches to replace distributors or retail outlets to bypass both distributors and retailers).

Often overlooked in assessing product distribution costs at this juncture are the costs *beyond* the manufacturer's sales force–the profit margins of distributors and retailers. These costs loom large in the total product cost, lie closest to the consumer, and are the first to feel a price squeeze. If the experience of recent years is any criterion, price pressure on a "mature" product at the manufacturer level lags behind retail and distributor price pressures. This tendency underlies the movement among manufacturers to "get closer to the consumer" by establishing branches or retail outlets. Such a step is designed to protect the factory profit by accepting a break-even, or loss, if necessary, at the branch or retail level to move the product in quantity.

Creative selling may develop whole new markets for the product in the maturity phase, despite apparent saturation of the market. Cigarette manufacturers opened the female market when the sales to male smokers approached saturation; and deodorant makers reversed this procedure by turning to the male market after saturating the female market.

*The Decline Phase.* As a product becomes increasingly mature, the pressure to reduce costs in each step of the engineering-manufacturing-distribution process mounts. This results from growing price competition, as the difference between competitive products is reduced to the vanishing point and increasingly sophisticated consumers evaluate price and quality more effectively in their buying. The advantages of the "old" product versus the attractiveness of the "new" products coming on the market also plays a part in the consumer's assessment of product value at this point.

The need for controlling costs, which normally starts while volume is still rising, becomes a matter of survival as the product moves into the decline phase. The few manufacturers of streetcars, steam locomotives, and windmills still in business are the last of a long list of competitors; they survived by withstanding price pressures of the decline phase longer than the others, or by developing other products.

The dominant role of marketing at product maturity gives way in the final phase of the product life cycle to the need for a coordinated control over all product costs: engineering, manufacturing, and marketing. The functional emphasis in a product's decline–and in the late maturity phase–thus becomes one of "managing" product expenditures to optimize the return on each dollar of cost.

The product can no longer afford a marketing, or manufacturing, or engineering-oriented management. It cannot afford, for instance, to have the engineering department spend 90 per cent of its development budget on marginal improvements with little consumer attraction; or to have a manufacturing department "under run" a seasonal product 30 per cent to protect itself against being overstocked at the year end; or to have a sales department overestimate product requirements by 20 per cent to ensure prompt delivery.

Each of the above decisions (they actually occurred) appeared reasonable to the functionally oriented executives who made them, and, had the products involved been in the growth phase, the chances are good that these errors in judgment would have been buried under the rising tide of demand. However, each of the products faced the severe price pressures of late maturity, and company profits were sharply reduced by these unilateral decisions.

As the necessity for "managing" the exploitation of a product grows more acute, financial controls become increasingly important. So do the skill, resourcefulness, and courage of the financial executive. He becomes, in effect, the chief of staff to the executive with over-all profit responsibility, who alone has the authority to insist that functional executives develop a coordinated program to optimize product profitability.

So functional control comes full cycle in the decline phase. The executive with over-all responsibility saw to it that the product was successfully introduced; then he yielded a measure of influence to the manufacturing and marketing executive as the cycle unfolded, only to reassert his authority in the final phase.

## SOME BIG QUESTIONS

There are those who believe that so many exceptions can be found to the product life cycle that it has questionable validity. They point out, for example, that many products of venerable vintage–such as steel, brick, coal, cement, bread, copper, shoes, and window glass–fluctuate with the economy rather than conform to the traditional product life-cycle pattern. Similarly, a broad range of consumer and specialty items appears to be impervious to the normal life-cycle pressures. These include such products as drugs, patent medicines, branded packaged foods, printing presses, roller window shades, drill presses, saws, bicycles, and the like.

Some products appear to be less subject to price competition at maturity than others for reasons that are not always readily explainable. One segment of this fortunate group consists of relatively low-priced products with pleasure- or health-giving properties that people have come to believe in—and have little basis for judging. Products of this type are generally bought emotionally, frequently from habit or simply liking the product, as distinct from purchases that are made after a more or less judicious comparison of the merits of competing products.

The whole range of proprietary and ethical medicines, and certain proprietary specialties—Angostura Bitters and Hershey chocolate, for example—fall in this category. Another segment includes a large group of products that so dominate the market that their manufacturers are in a position to exercise great influence, if not actual control, over prices.

Durable consumer products, which are more subject to price competition than emotionally bought consumer items, appear to have certain life-cycle advantages over products bought by industry. These largely reflect the franchise that a refrigerator, or shoe, or furniture manufacturer has at both the retail and consumer level. The new producer of a durable consumer item (radio, refrigerator) faces the costly prospect of building brand acceptance among retailers and consumers, even with a vastly improved or new product. Industry's hard-headed purchasing agents, on the other hand, are willing to buy a new product—or drop an old one—in short order if the reason is demonstrable. With less emotion involved in the buying decision, the advantage of innovation is quickly lost in an industrial product. Imitators often are ready, willing, and able to copy a successful new development, and buyers will frequently accept the "copy" on the basis of relatively minor price, delivery, or service advantages.

Much of the doubt about the validity of the life-cycle concept appears to stem from two basic sources: the economics of the production-distribution process, and the definition of what constitutes a new product.

For instance, anthracite coal does not exhibit the price weaknesses associated with a product in its decline phase. Yet domestic output of anthracite has been cut 50 per cent during the past fifteen years as a result of the competitive inroads made by oil and gas. The reason coal prices did not decline, of course, lies in rising union-controlled labor rates and the failure of a large number of marginal producers that were forced by declining volume to close down.

In other words, the fact that anthracite coal does not behave like a product in its decline phase results from a combination of economic factors that made it possible to maintain prices, despite a large drop in demand, by curtailing output. A similar economic balancing act seems to occur to many other commodity or commodity-type products in the decline phase.

A substantial number of products that do not follow the typical life-cycle pattern are protected by the economics of their production-distribution process. Patents, a limited number of producers willing to live and let live, heavy brand-advertising expenditures, and a dominant market share by a single producer—all help a product negate the facts of the life cycle.

However, the most complex element to untangle in understanding the life-cycle concept involves the question: What is a new product? For example, are stereo records a new product or simply an improved variation of the conventional monophonic record? How about the steam iron versus the dry iron? Or filter cigarettes versus the original nonfilters? Or fluorescent versus incandescent lamps? Or color television versus black and white TV?

The difficulty of determining under what conditions a new product moves into its own cycle and when it is a variation of an old product that merely fluctuates around the life cycle of the "mother" product is a major factor in doubts regarding the product life cycle.

There appear to be few universally recognized characteristics distinguishing the new product from an improved variation of an old one. Indeed, examination of a good many products indicates there may be several degrees of "newness."

1. *The unquestionably new product.* Stereo records show all the signs of a new product at introduction: high price, severe performance problems, spotty distribution, and the like. As another example, the transistor does certain things better than radio tubes, and at a lower cost.
2. *The partially new product.* The steam iron satisfies a consumer need–for dampening fabric–that the original dry iron cannot. However, the steam iron can do everything the dry iron does, hence competes as a general-use iron with the latter. Another example might be the portable radio, which does everything the table radio does and, in addition, can be readily carried about. The key here appears to be a product that extends the market, but also competes with the old product.
3. *The major product change.* Basic technological changes may yield a new product that becomes a mature product virtually overnight by simply replacing the old product. LP records and tubeless tires are cases in point. The principal manufacturers switched from the old to the new product so quickly that the new product had virtually no life cycle of its own.
4. *The minor product change.* Power steering, remote-control TV tuning, and the like may give the product a short-term competitive edge, but they do not alter the life-cycle pattern of the product.

These examples indicate that a new product can reasonably be described in these terms: "A new product is a product that opens up an entirely new market, replaces an existing product, or significantly broadens the market for an existing product."

Since there are many marginal situations where–even with the advantage of hindsight–it is difficult to distinguish the new product from the variations in an old one, there is obviously considerable risk of error in assessing the future of an existing product. For many years prior to the war, for example, telephone installations fluctuated with building construction and the economic cycle. The telephone showed every characteristic of a mature product during those decades. Yet in the postwar years, telephone installations zoomed and far outstripped new construction.

Why? The answer lies in a change in the promotional philosophy of the telephone company after the war. The gaily colored phones, the advertising about the use of these phones in the den, kitchen, and so on, contributed to an upward push that renewed the growth pattern of what appeared to have become a mature product.

## ECONOMIC FORCES AT WORK

Some industries have found it essential to *count on* relatively short life cycles for their products. Ethical drug and packaged cereal manufacturers discovered that sales of new products normally enter a declining phase in three to five years. Therefore, if product-development programs are not planned around this short life cycle, company profits become unrealistically high for a short period and then slump drastically.

A patent-protected product may stay in the high-margin growth phase for years after an unpatented item of identical vintage has been subjected to profit-slashing price competition in its maturity phase. When the Ronson lighter patents expired a few years ago, the product switched from what appeared to be its growth phase to a highly competitive maturity phase virtually overnight.

Fundamental economic forces are constantly at work changing the life-cycle pattern of products. For example, the farm market is in the process of a major shift from small operators who look at farming as a way of life to large farmer businessmen (and even farm corporations). Such a move is likely to mean that the distribution mechanism for selling the farm market will tend toward fewer and larger outlets. This, in turn, may well speed up the life cycle of farm products as the more aggressive manufacturers sense the opportunity to gain an advantage by stepping up the tempo of marketing change and product development.

This would not be the first time that imaginative engineering has shortened the life cycle of existing products by finding new approaches to better serve customers within industries facing basic changes in their profit climate. Not too many years ago the design of a printing press, or a steam generator, or a machine tool, or a paper-making machine changed relatively infrequently. Today, competitive engineering is forcing constant change in the life-cycle pattern of such products.

Studies of the product life cycle face the problem that the four major phases of the cycle do not divide themselves into clean-cut compartments. At any given point in time, a product may appear to have attained maturity when actually it has merely reached a temporary plateau in the growth phase prior to its next big upsurge, or an economic recession can give a growth-destined product temporary symptoms of maturity. This means that it is frequently difficult to judge with accuracy the phase of the cycle in which the product currently finds itself.

## VALUE OF THE CONCEPT

Despite the many unanswered questions, the life-cycle concept has proved to be a sound planning tool when properly used. An appliance manufacturer was considering an expensive advertising and promotional campaign designed to create a "quality image" for its product. A survey showed that this particular appliance was in the late maturity phase of the life cycle. Competition was keen, and the company's product had spotty distribution (rarely in "quality" outlets); it was considered a "price" item by retailers, and recent models had had serious performance deficiencies. If this product had been in the growth phase, attempting to change a "price" image into a "quality" image might have been practical. The fact that this product was in the maturity phase, however, argued that, in the short term, funds could be used to better advantage in other directions. The reason, of course, was that both the consumer and retailer image of this and competing products had "hardened." Any material change in this image would require a huge advertising and promotional expenditure over many years–and years were too long to wait for improvement.

Another manufacturer was considering eliminating wholly-owned branches in large cities because they were losing money. However, the product was a mature one, and field surveys indicated that gaining tight control of retail distribution in big cities was essential to maintaining volume. This pointed to the need for *more,* not fewer, branches, and led to a careful investigation of the whole distribution process. It was found that:

1. company-owned branches had consistently captured a higher market share than the best independent distributors,
2. the *manufacturing profit* on branch volume easily offset branch losses, and
3. in spite of branch losses or break-even results, the company was generating substantially greater profits in branch markets than distributor markets having similar potentials–enough to make the return on large branch investments very attractive.

In this case, a major decision was reversed because the life-cycle position of the product forced a more intensive study of the problem.

The life-cycle concept has been valuable in planning the future product exploitation strategy of many companies. For example, General Motors' early decision that a strong dealer organization was essential to its future success gave this company an important competitive edge as the automobile attained maturity. The decision of companies like Stewart-Warner, CBS, Raytheon, and Stromberg-Carlson to withdraw from television set production early in this product's maturity phase points to their recognition that life-cycle pressures were working against them.

On the other hand, many companies have made decisions damaging to their product's position in the market, indicating that they did not fully understand the forces at work at various stages in the product's life cycle. Servel decided to switch distribution of its gas refrigerators from local gas companies to the more typical distributor-dealer channels during the product's maturity phase. The loss of sales momentum at this critical juncture in the gas refrigerator's life cycle is regarded as an important factor in the company's ultimate withdrawal from refrigerator production.

## PROFITS AND PERSONNEL

To be sure, much remains to be learned about the economics of the product life cycle. But studies to date have shown that two critical management areas are best understood in terms of this cycle:

1. product profitability, and
2. the personnel requirements of product management.

*Product Profitability.* The fact that product profits are greatly influenced by their life-cycle position points to the wisdom of taking this into account in product-exploitation strategy. Great risks can be taken in the growth phase. Indeed, time is so critical at this juncture that such risks often *must* be accepted. However, a careful husbanding of resources is essential in the later maturity phase, when profit margins are so low that losses become very difficult to recoup.

Underlying any discussion of the product life cycle is the pressing need for management effort to insure the generation of new products to provide stability of company profits. This is particularly vital in industries where product life cycles are characteristically short. The role of the research and development functions and the strategy of merger cannot be underestimated as elements in long-term profitability—or even survival.

*Personnel Strategy.* The perspective that the life-cycle concept provides top management in the development of executive personnel can greatly influence company profits. When General Motors chose Harlow Curtice as its chief executive in 1953, the directors' action undoubtedly reflected the maturity of the automobile itself and the need for a strong marketing executive.

The shifting of the functional job skills that are required in the several phases of the product life cycle makes it possible for top management to assess future personnel needs with some accuracy. Research and engineering are the key in the introductory phase, manufacturing in the growth phase, marketing in the maturity phase, and financial and over-all management judgment in the decline phase.

However, since phases of individual product life cycles are constantly changing and usually overlap phases of other products, there is evidence that a *balanced* group of functional executives is of prime importance. Companies dominated by engineering, manufacturing, marketing, or financial executives seem to have problems in other phases of the cycle or in managing a group of products in different life-cycle stages. A fast growing chemical company, dominated by research-oriented executives, discovered to its surprise that several key products were in the late maturity phase and were not being effectively marketed. Top management considered theirs to be a "growth" business–which, in general, it was–but had not faced up to the problems of the mature products in their line.

The need for a balanced group of functional executives is attested to by the expanding product line of the average company. This means that more and more individual products are likely to be in different phases of the life cycle at a given point. For example, the major TV producers also sell radios and high-fidelity equipment. Each of these products is in a different phase of the life cycle: hi-fi is rapidly growing, TV is at maturity, and table radios are close to the decline phase. Thus each has different problems and opportunities and requires executives with somewhat different talents.

In the long run, since all products get older and the maturity and decline phases constitute the longest portion of the life cycle, a growing demand for executives who can accept full profit responsibility is clearly forecast. How these men are to be identified and trained is one of the problems that many comapnies, with an eye on the life cycle of their products, are wrestling with today.

# 29. THE PSYCHOLOGICAL LABEL ON THE PRODUCT

*Pierre Martineau*

*Every product has a role to fulfill, indeed is created to help consumers to achieve some goals or solve some problems. Thus, consumers assign various psychological values to products, and these values tend to prevail over a long period of time.*

*The author of the following selection deals with this process of psychological "labeling" from several different points of view, and demonstrates that people rarely think of products only in terms of physical characteristics of the products.*

## 1.

An advertising agency asked me to explore the possibility of a study as to how the consumer can prefer one brand of sugar over another when chemically all brands are exactly the same. To them this is a puzzling situation. The housewife continues to choose some one brand with the positive conviction that, "It's better—the quality is superior. I can't explain, but I know it's better." Yet, factually the brands are indistinguishable. The difference exists only in her mind.

Repeatedly we stumble across this same situation, and we usually shake our heads at such unreasonable behavior.

Any number of manufacturers put up house brands for grocery chains, so that their products end up competing with one another under different labels and invariably at tangible price differentials. And the lower-price brand isn't always the largest seller.

Source: From Pierre Mateineau, *Motivation in Advertising,* New York: Copyright © 1957, used by permission of McGraw-Hill Book Co., pp. 40-42. Pierre Martineau: Director of Research and Marketing, *Chicago Tribune.*

In a year's study, twice as many families bought a certain brand of margarine in a Chicago food chain instead of the absolutely identical product under the chain label, even though the latter was cheaper.

It is easier to swallow these apparent violations of common sense if we realize that many other forces besides rationality are involved in perfectly normal human behavior. And it is perfectly normal and human for psychological overtones to become inextricably linked with products, institutions, and places, and in many instances to be the primary determinant of consumer behavior.

I would be the first to grant that functional advantages, quality differences, and price can each be the all-important factor in a buying decision. I am only highlighting the point that in very many instances, however, it is this halo of psychological meanings which is responsible for the popularity or the rejection of the product.

Take the umbrella, for instance. It performs its function in completely satisfactory fashion. There is nothing wrong with its quality or its price. But the reason most people don't buy umbrellas today is that it stamps them as ultraconservatives–old fuddy-duddies. No teen-ager, no "sports-car-butch-haircut" adult, no smart young modern carries an umbrella.

I don't eat oatmeal for the same reason. I can argue with myself it is a highly nutritious, low-cost food. But I still think of it as old-fashioned, plus other notions about horses and oats.

Lots of people buy auto trailers, I guess. But not I. Regardless of the wonders they may offer, I can only think of itinerant laborers, retired brakemen heading for St. Petersburg, and dubious camps at the city's edge. All these impressions, whether based on fact or not, intervene to smother any interest on my part in the auto trailer.

These, of course, happen to be negative associations for me. Obviously, just as many brands and places and institutions have as their most important asset an aura of strongly positive psychological meanings which have actually nothing to do with reality. People generally do justify their choice by insistently citing performance reasons or economic factors, and they obviously believe them. I have heard Cadillac owners spell out the low depreciation, cost of operation, safety features, and so on, of their cars– all of which may be true. But certainly one of the Cadillac's greatest sales assets is its symbolic meaning of achievement and financial success.

We tend so much to think of objects as absolutes. The manufacturer feels that his product will sell because of its innate quality and technical superiorities, as if the consumer can detect these with unfailing accuracy. Production experts, agricultural leaders, economists, and intellectuals generally believe that the task of marketing consists only of offering a good product, which somehow a discriminating public will decide to buy. Not many of these people think about the problem of investing the product with the psychological meanings which are going to play such a considerable part in their life histories.

I have listened to government advisers relate their counsel to the apple growers about offering apple juice to the American family, including a lengthy rigmarole about taste tests. So it is offered, and what happens? Very little—taste tests or not. Prune juice, grape juice, apple juice, cranberry juice: none of these has had any prairie-fire success, because even in the matter of food selection, we pick and choose according to those meanings which are in our minds, not those in the products. None of these particular juices have a sufficiently desirable halo.

The truth of the matter is that, far from being absolutes with fixed sets of qualities, products and institutions and brands have almost entirely subjective definitions.

Even with so basic an item as food, what we choose becomes for the most part a problem of subjective appeals. The constant succession of new products being offered to the American table displaces other products which are seen as less desirable, although their food value, taste, and quality have not changed. Their virtues and their defects to a large extent exist in my mind, not in themselves.

So many people in blindfold tests are unable to distinguish between cigarettes. Yet few things are more personal, excite more loyalty than the individual brand. I might smoke one cigarette of my wife's brand, but not two. She refuses to take any of mine, preferring to scratch around the house in cigarette boxes and coat pockets for just a stray of her own brand. My cigarette is too masculine, too strong, too much "me" in her eyes, although the blend of tobacco is probably indistinguishable from that in her cigarette.

I have argued at length about instant coffee with the die-hards. They insist heatedly it just doesn't taste like real coffee. Time and again I have served the instant coffee in a Silex, so that these people thought they were drinking regular coffee. Then they enjoy it. I have won bets on several occasions when I demonstrated that they couldn't tell the difference in taste.

It is very apparent that their rejection stems from subjective factors which have nothing to do with taste. And it is precisely this negative set of meanings which must be modified before the unconverted start buying it.

As another direction of meaning, at my house we never serve kohlrabi, sauerkraut, cotto salami, or pumpernickel bread, because in our eyes, these are peasant foods. But my wife does offer guests such illogical dainties as vodka punch, shrimp creole, port-wine cheese, even Mexican-sunflower seeds, because these have an air of being *classé* and exotic.

What I have been demonstrating is that every product and service has an aura of subjective meanings over and above its utilitarian meanings which perform a very real function for the individual. Apart from its first purpose of transportation, the automobile serves also to define the individual's social importance, his ideas of his own personality, his notions of care or carelessness toward possessions, his attitude toward the relation of the individual to mechanical objects. Thus each car becomes for the individual not just a physical object costing "x" dollars with various performance qualities but an object defined by a specific aura of psychological attitudes.

Gasoline is something put in cars to make them run, and with regard to its physical properties, most people firmly believe that gasoline is gasoline. And yet they do exhibit consistent buying preference for certain brands, based on their subjective definitions. In addition to performance qualities, the gasoline becomes defined by the appearance and color scheme of the gasoline station and the behavior of the attendants, plus general notions of the moral responsibility of the company selling the product—all of which are attitudes.

A cigar, a perfume, a shaving lotion, a face powder, a lipstick have a minimum of functional use. Millions of people live just as long, are just as happy without ever using them. Physiologically they are completely unnecessary. The product areas and the brands are defined almost completely by their subjective meanings.

## 2.

One of our primary criteria for evaluating automobiles is their appearance. We say with an air of finality that this car definitely is beautiful, that car is reasonably attractive, and another line will sell poorly because it doesn't have real beauty. Here again we are speaking of beauty as if it were an unchanging, eternal reality seen in the same likeness by everyone.

Yet nothing could be more subjective, more temporary, more illusory than car beauty. It most obviously is no fixed and permanent quality. The designs which were unveiled as breathtaking only fifteen years ago now seem ridiculously out of date—just funny. And today's beauties will appear quite as silly fifteen years hence. So this element which is such a key factor in sales success is at best only a kaleidoscopic, ephemeral quality—here today and gone tomorrow.

And in spite of a few agreements, it is actually all things to all people. One man buys a Buick, and as he and his wife admire it, they both say, "It's beautiful." The next-door neighbors are viewing their new Mercury with the same ecstatic words—"It's beautiful." What they mean, of course, is, "We like it." Appearance can exist as an independent factor. But generally it is a broad feeling summation of many, many things that people are trying to convey. We approach cars with a whole set of meanings far beyond the simple fact of how they look. Yet we telescope all these meanings into one shorthand symbol—beauty.

At the present time, we believe that sleekness in body design is expressive of smartness, raciness, power, modernity, high style. When a design, such as Nash, departs from this pattern, then we read a different set of meanings into it. Fullness of body is not the current trend of dress—we know that. A breakaway from sleekness and length might introduce the notion of dumpiness, which we interpret as inferior, not smart, clumsy.

Very often people are not certain exactly what meanings are involved with some departure, and that in itself is disturbing. This is one of the important functions of advertising: to create a set of meanings and to crystallize them so that the symbol is perfectly clear and, of course, desirable.

This whole province of product design and product beauty is almost entirely a realm of subjective meanings.

So is the concept of style, which is not unrelated to beauty. Style and obsolescence are more and more often described as the primary function of goods in our consumption economy, not utility. Almost no one wears clothes or keeps furniture around until they wear out. We get rid of them when we feel they have gone out of style.

Lest we tend to narrow the concept of style to women's clothes and perhaps cars, let me indicate how thoroughly this force has permeated many areas of consumption goods. The forests of new houses mushrooming in ever-spreading suburbia are almost entirely ranch-style and, now, split-level. Wrought-iron furniture, severely modern lamp styles, sectional davenports, and colorful draperies dominate the living rooms in the model homes "now open for exhibition." And the dining room area and dining room furniture are steadily contracting.

The carpeting industry reports more new designs in the past five years than in the previous fifty years. Refrigerators and washers have broken with the rigid tradition of operating-room white and now are paraded in gala pastel colors. Twenty years ago ginger ale was the standard mixer for drinks. Today soda sales are competing in the summer with tonic water, in the winter with the vogue for "on-the-rocks" short drinks.

But what is style?

It exists purely and simply in our minds. It is entirely subjective. No one knows how it starts, how it spreads, or how it is enforced. We used to think of it as something originated by high society, to be different, and then imitated by the lower classes. But characteristic fads for pizza, blue jeans, Dixieland jazz, and men's caps are traveling from the lower class upward.

Yet this completely subjective force that has no tangible existence is recognized as the fulcrum of economic behavior in so many areas.

Without a qualm of conscience about waste or unreasonable extravagance, I consign loads of clothing to my wife's charities because they are out of style. I toss away hats with brims too wide or too narrow, an overcoat inches too short, shirts the wrong color, and suits with lapels too wide. Thousands of workers in automobile factories are thrown out of jobs because the car styling is wrong, jarring the whole economy of such cities as Toledo and Kenosha and South Bend.

The fur industry has been badly buffeted because mink is so oversold as the fur "that leaves you breathless." Many a woman thinks that if she can't have mink, she is out of style to take anything less. And because she can't afford to buy mink, she would rather go without.

**3.**

I hope I have established the point that a significant part of human behavior and buying is involved with purely psychological meanings that have nothing to do with engineering triumphs, chemical discoveries, or the large, economy size. And since this is so, then advertising, which is charged with the responsibility for helping to sell goods, must also concern itself with these psychological meanings.

If this is disturbing to our philosophical and moral notions of thrift and rational behavior, I can only say this is the way people are. This is the reason they buy. They are satisfying psychological "wants" which are just as real as biological wants. This is what they desire from their lives. This is what they hope to find in advertising.

Social scientists point out—and here I could quote the psychoanalyst Freud, the social anthropologist Warner, and the philosopher Langer—that all human behavior which is not purely organic is a form of self-expression.

In our gestures, in our jewelry, in our patterns of speech and dress, in a thousand subtle mannerisms, we are trying to convey to others and to ourselves exactly what we are. We don't want anyone to be mistaken about us. One woman conveys her accentuated femininity with a smart coiffure, much costume jewelry, cosmetics, and exotic cigarettes. Her next-door neighbor wears no make-up and a dowdy haircut, and refuses to smoke. One garbs herself in pirates' costumes and pixie pants, even for her housework; the other restricts herself to drab house dresses. Each is trying to say, not with flamboyant clarity, probably not even consciously, but with recognizable subtlety, exactly what she is.

I, as an individual, don't wear a beard or a beret like some *avantgarde* artist. And, at the other extreme, I avoid the drab brown-suit-brown-tie motif of the ultraconservative. Each and every form of behavior has to be fitting to my age group, to my social clique, and to my particular occupational niche.

In an intelligent, normal person, virtually everything is motivated by subtle reference to the individual's self-ideal—the kind of character ideal he wants to become. No reproach is worse than that you are letting yourself go, losing your self-control, going all to pieces—all of which are different ways of saying that one is not living up to his self-ideal.

When the individual buys anything, he makes the psychological decision, "This is just right." On rare occasions we do lose choice. The article is the only one of its kind, and we have to take it. At other times we do get pressured into accepting something. Then we have growing misgivings that it isn't exactly suitable.

But the purchase that I sense is entirely right fills me with feelings of satisfaction, which is an awareness that it is altogether fitting for me. Of course, there are other elements, like price. However, I wouldn't buy chewing tobacco or a derby for 90 per cent off. Unless the product fits me, unless its psychological meanings jibe with my self-conceptions and with what I want to convey about myself, you couldn't give it to me.

In addition to my practical purposes, I have various psychological goals that I am hopeful of gratifying. A man with thinning hair may grow a mustache and go bare-headed in the worst weather, not for any sensible reason, but to fulfill his own goal of conveying his vigor and potency. What practical difference does it make if he loses his hair? None. But he is concerned lest it be interpreted as a symbol of declining vigor.

We strive to cope with our feelings of inadequacy, our hunger for acceptance by others, our desire for recognition, our strivings for mobility and to break emotional dependencies. All these and a multitude of other motivations establish definite goals which become very real to the individual.

In this yearning for self-expression, we reach for products, for brands, for institutions which will be compatible with our schemes of what we think we are or want to be. Naturally we do require certain things to carry on the business of life. But there is so much latitude in our economy of abundance. We are invariably in position to select on the basis of the secondary meanings attached to the products.

Actually, I have the choice of many forms of transportation in most situations. But I do not ride the public streetcars or a motorcycle or a motor coach. Each of them has many merits. Yet they would all say the incorrect thing about me—my position, my personality, my occupational role.

There is nothing wrong with a motorcycle as a piece of machinery. What stands in my way are the unreal actualities—those eloquent reflectors of my character, of the "me." I am certain that if I drove to work on a motorcycle some bright day, my superiors would consider that I was exposing hitherto unsuspected character weaknesses, inconsistent with my role as a businessman. In your mind and my mind, the layman on a motorcycle is an arrested mental type, an irresponsible exhibitionist, a delivery boy in a silver-studded leather jacket and boots swaggering around hamburger stands.

All this has nothing to do with the piece of machinery *per se.* Yet this cloud of negative attitudes is a tangible, existent reality, as firmly attached to the motorcycle as the seat. The manufacturer who might hope to advertise motorcycles into a better sales position would have to wrestle with this set of negative attitudes.

Again and again in our studies we have turned up situations where similar sets of unfavorable associations were glued to a brand. But the manufacturer's advertising was wandering about in a never-never land. It didn't face up to the subjective meanings which were very significantly interfering with buyer considerations. Why give me demonstrations of smooth smoking if my real objection to cigars is a mental picture of repellent trays of butts or of the airline attitude that cigar smoking is annoying to other people?

Why tell me that "movies are better than ever" when the psychological obstacle that halts my moviegoing is the imagery of uncontrolled rowdy behavior by teen-agers in the suburban theaters?

**4.**

This habit of attaching meanings, attitudes, feelings, even moods to inanimate objects is characteristically human. It is the mental process of symbolization, which is an integral part of the human brain's activity.

We work every day, for instance, not only for the financial returns, which of course are important, but also from numerous other motives. In a recent study, men were asked if they would stop work if it was no longer necessary financially. The great majority said that they would keep on working. Apart from a livelihood, work means friendship and contact with other people; it generates feelings of doing something worthwhile; it wards off isolation and loneliness. As nearly as we can, we choose our occupations for their prestige value, for their opportunities for self-realization, because of our own notions of physical and mental adaptation. The middle-class American wants a white-collar job, not only for its pay scales, but because of his notions of greater social prestige.

Clothing is another commonplace example of our tendency to invest things with meanings which can become active motivations. Completely apart from its functional purposes of protection, modesty, and even decoration, our clothing fulfills an enormous range of both personal and social meanings that we utilize ceaselessly.

The Christmas-necktie situation illustrates how intensely personal our clothing can become. Most of us males regularly receive gift offerings of neckties on Christmas, Father's Day, and birthdays. These are genuine expressions of feeling from our parents, our wives, our children, and our in-laws. We say, "Thank you," and rarely, rarely wear them. Why not? They are expensive enough; they certainly have all the quality that any tie has. But somehow, in some way they say the wrong thing about me. I try to explain my rejection by saying that they are too loud or too dull. Actually, I sense in a very vague but compelling way that they do not capture the subtleties and nuances of the personality that I think I am.

And neither can I grasp the individuality of another person. On occasion I have bought gifts of clothing and costume jewelry for my wife. Then it dawned on me that she seldom wore my selections. I can't imagine any man picking out a hat or a pair of shoes or a handbag for his wife. Because we just simply cannot penetrate the wall around another person's self, we cannot divine precisely the subtleties that he or she is trying to convey with costuming.

We even use clothing to express mood. In the evening I change into loafers and sports coat to imply relaxation and informality. If I get up in the morning feeling especially jaunty and exuberant, pleased with myself because people laughed at my jokes last evening at the party, then I toy with bow ties, high-colored shirts, and flashy handkerchiefs.

I have spoken at conventions held at summer resorts where most of the audience wore sports clothes. But the speakers had to appear in white shirts and darker suits to signify their seriousness of purpose. Driving through small towns in the summer, it is easy to single out the bank cashier or the newspaper editor—the only individual in the sea of overalls and sports shirts who is uncomfortably garbed in a white shirt and necktie.

The businessman's costume is heavily charged with moral symbolism—heavy shoes, padded coat, white shirt, drab-colored suits, constricting neckties: elements that say that he is mature, responsible, serious in purpose, with the highest moral integrity.

The men's-wear industry now hopes that men can be sold the notion of style with the same force as women. But very many retailers and manufacturers in this field cannot bring themselves to dress like style setters. Even though it would be to their financial advantage,they are much more anxious in their own choice of garb to appear as conservative and successful businessmen. The hopes of their industry run squarely into the universal American conviction that something is wrong with the man overly concerned with clothes. He may be effeminate, or conceited—or a shadowy character on the margins of society, like a gambler.

Another recent study indicates how much the meanings attached to men's clothing can influence occupational success. Contrary to the American credo that job performance should be the criterion, there is very real belief that one's mode of dress can affect his opportunities and promotions.

In response to a question asking what would happen if a foreman were promoted to an office position and then failed to dress right, 61 per cent of the men interviewed said that this person would be fired, demoted, or transferred. Another 14 per cent said that the man couldn't be promoted further in the future. And 17 per cent more figured that he would quit his job or accept a demotion. So nine-tenths of the people studied said that failure to dress correctly would have serious consequences on the man's whole future.

## 5.

We generally start our approach to an advertising compaign by talking about sales ideas. We will create a rational, logical sales idea. But the motive force of any idea is determined by its meaning—which is all the associations that the idea represents to the individual. The richer the meaning, the more powerful the idea. And richness includes such associations as feelings, emotions, images, and symbolic meanings.

Every word, every idea can have what is called a "denotative" and a "connotative" value. "Denotative" is comparable to pointing to an object—and that's all. "Connotative" refers to the many associations it stirs up in our minds.

For instance, if I denote a mouse, I simply am saying, "That is a mouse." Period. Nothing more. But on the connotative side, the notion of "mouse" evokes an image of a gray creature running along a pipe in the basement, a memory of an experience while living in the country when you were invaded by field mice, feelings of unpleasantness, filth, curiosity that women should be so frightened about mice, notions about mousey people, wharf rats, and so on and on.

Those happen to be mostly unpleasant associations. Suppose I encounter the name "Myrtle Beach." That's all it is to me—just a name, because I don't know anything about it. It has no connotative meanings. On the other hand, "Coronado Beach" brings up a flood of associations—pleasant feelings, memories of people, beautiful grounds, picturesque old elevators, considerable emotion.

Far too much advertising is narrowly denotative. It merely points to the product and proclaims some restricted range of functional benefits. Actually, in our highly competitive system, few products are able to maintain any technical superiority for long. They must be invested with overtones to individualize them; they must be endowed with richness of associations and imagery; they must have many levels of meaning, if we expect them to be top sellers, if we hope that they will achieve the emotional attachment which shows up as brand loyalty.

Imagery plays a highly significant part in motivating our daily behavior. It is far more vivid and compelling than abstract ideas; it generates many emotional accompaniments which become translated into strong drives.

An overcoat is just an overcoat. But a trench coat conjures imagery of private detectives, foreign intrigue, handsome younger men, adventure, daring, actors, glamorous girls, spies. I want it—not because it's a protective raincoat, but because of all this associated imagery and feeling.

The semblance of truth is far more important in advertising than truth itself. We believe what we want to believe. Actually, this is true about most things. A movie star picks out a romantic name because we worship the illusion rather than the reality. Even when we know that William Holden's name is something funny-sounding and that Kirk Douglas and Cary Grant were born something else, we stubbornly hang on to the illusion. We behave toward the illusion, not the fact.

We know from any marketing experience how much package design and color can boost the sales of a product. But what does a new red package contribute to the quality of the ingredients? Nothing whatever. We aren't going to eat the package or smoke it. Yet it feeds our mental notions that, mysteriously, the product itself has become better, more desirable.

When I put on a pair of dark glasses, I feel that somehow I'm a different person. I'm not, of course, but I think I am. Wearing a homburg hat makes me a different person. A woman luxuriating in her first mink is certain that she has been completely transformed.

The product which has no other meaning except its functional uses is dull and uninteresting. Advertising which conveys only the functional uses—that the product supposedly does only what it is supposed to do—is restrictive and static.

One of the most potent factors in the high desirability of coffee and cigarettes and clothing to Americans is precisely that they do have so many directions of meaning, that they are so self-expressive, and they are so clearly understood, at least on intuitive and implicit levels.

The orthodox traditionalists of advertising insistently advocate a convincing statement of product benefits. But what are product benefits? Who said that the concept of product benefits has to be restricted to physical factors and functional uses? Aren't the psychological meanings included in product benefits if that's what I want from the product?

I didn't choose the modern furniture in my living room just for something to sit on. I most of all want the meanings of sophistication, individuality, *avant-garde* styling. Why aren't these product benefits? I don't wear dark glasses just to keep sun out of my eyes. I'm much more interested in the overtones: being, for the moment, a racer, a movie star, a mountain climber, a skiing champion, an airline pilot. These are by far the most impelling product benefits to me, not some dull mumbo-jumbo about what the glasses are made of.

If style is becoming an all-important criterion in the selection of furniture and homes and automobiles, then it is imperative for advertising to crystallize the style meanings of its products. It would appear downright stupid to spend millions of dollars shouting "double-torsion, superblack picture tubes" or "automatic roto-dollies" when the goods are being rejected because of styling—which is entirely a subjective element.

Style is only one of the meanings which are encompassed in the range of psychological overtones, of course. They can go in a multitude of directions. They can be both positive and negative. They are not absolute elements; they are subjective. They can be molded. They can be crystallized, they can be modified, they can be expanded, or they can be completely submerged by a dominant set of new meanings.

But they cannot be ignored.

## 6.

The advertiser today understands the importance of attractive packaging, attractive labels, giving the product the right name. These factors have nothing whatever to do with the contents of the product, yet all by themselves they can play a vital role in its success or rejection. Entirely by themselves they contribute desirability. Most of all, the manufacturer, or any advertiser, should realize that one of his fundamental objectives in marketing is the psychological "label" on the product or institution.

This psychological label is particularly significant today in view of the standardization of quality and the identity of service which are typically true of our market place. Besides any practical purposes, advertising must help the individual integrate the product with his psychological goals and self-conceptions. How can he use it for self-expression? What inner goals can he satisfy through its psychological overtones? What does it say about his good taste? Does it clearly define his social status? His general prestige? Does it present his personality interestingly? Does it help him to define himself as serious and responsible, as adventurous, as carefree, or as whatever he thinks himself to be?

We say that our economy is controlled by laws of supply and demand. The producer can push up the price for his goods to the limits of demand. But what is "demand"? It means that people want something. It means desirability. And desirability is a subjective factor, not an absolute quality bound up in the nature of the product. Corsets, chewing tobacco, harnesses, buggy whips, high-button shoes no longer have demand, not because of any product weakness but because their subjective desirability has entirely vanished. Demand exists in the consumer's mind, not in the product. The producer in actuality is striving for some favorable share of the consumer's mind. And in this process of building subjective desirability, the psychological label on his products plays the crucial role.

# 30. THE ADOPTION PROCESS

*Foundation for Research on Human Behavior*

*A common problem faced by a business firm introducing new products has to do with the nature and extent of the adoption process. If one could predict with any accuracy who would first adopt a product as well as when, a more effective new-products marketing program could be devised.*

*This article gives some psychological insights into this kind of problem.*

For many products, the process of adoption follows a rather uniform pattern, from the time the new product is developed until it is widely accepted by the ultimate consumers. More is known about the adoption of agricultural products and practices than about others. Rural sociologists have been concerned with the introduction of new practices and with new product adoption in agriculture for a number of years, and they have systematically studied the process by which change takes place. In addition, some studies have been made of other kinds of innovation, including the adoption by doctors of new wonder drugs for treatment,[1] the adoption of new educational practices by school systems,[2] and the adoption of color television.[3] The process of adoption in all these cases has been quite similar. There are exceptions to the pattern; for example, black and white television. The general pattern appears so widely, however, that it is the central theme of this report.

[1] E. Katz, The two-step flow of communications: an up-to-date report on an hypothesis. *Public Opinion Quarterly,* 1957, 21, 61–78. H. Menzel and E. Katz, Social relations and innovation in the medical profession: the epidemiology of a new drug. *Public Opinion Quarterly,* 1955–56, 19, 337–352.

[2] P. R. Mort and T. M. Pierce, *A time scale for measuring the adaptability of school systems.* Metropolitan School Study Council, New York, 1947.

[3] Batten, Barton, Durstine & Osborn. *Colortown.*

Source: From *The Adoption of New Products: Process and Influence,* Ann Arbor, Michigan: Foundation for Research on Human Behavior, 1959, pp. 1–8.

Researchers have charted the course of a new product by determining *when* people adopt it. The curve which results is a simple one, the well known probability curve, in cumulative form.[4] A few people adopt a product at first, then a few more, followed by a rather sharp increase and finally a leveling off when most of the potential consumers have adopted the product.

Such a curve is presented in general form in Figure 1. No scale is given for the time dimension, because this differs from product to product. A number of studies indicate, however, the *form* of the curve remains constant, and therefore that knowledge of the time required for a first relatively small group to adopt a new product will, by establishing the time scale for that product, make possible fairly accurate prediction of the rate of adoption by the rest of the applicable universe.

## THE KIND OF CHANGE

The time it takes from introduction to widespread acceptance depends, in part at least, on the kind of change involved. The adoption of a new product can be viewed as a special case of attitude change. Almost by definition, such a change encounters resistance. The new product or method usually alters or replaces something which is already part of the individual's pattern of thought. If the change under consideration is a really major one, it is quite likely that the attitudes and feelings associated with the old way are strongly held and will account for a great deal of resistance. On the other hand, if the change is trivial, the associated attitudes may be taken on easily. (They may also be cast off easily, of course.) Most new products or practices probably encounter resistance somewhere between these two extremes.

When new products are being adopted, there are different levels of *complexity* of change. The greater the complexity, the more resistance is aroused, and the longer the period required for adoption. Researchers have listed four levels of complexity in the changes usually confronting farmers who are adopting new products or practices.[5]

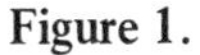

**Figure 1.**

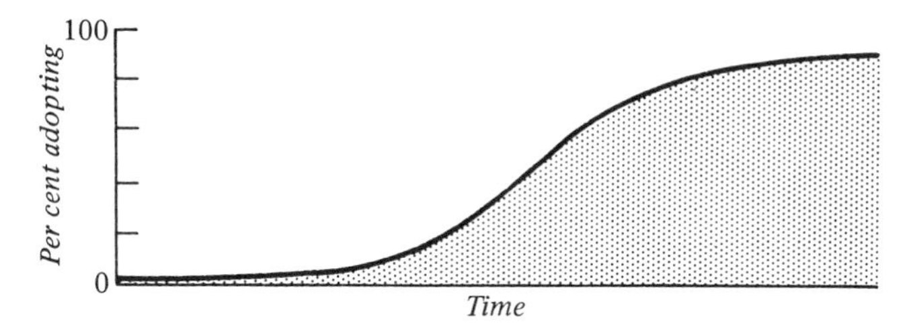


[4] North Central Rural Sociology Committee, Subcommittee for the Study of the Diffusion of Farm Practices. *The diffusion process.* Agriculture Extension Service, Iowa State College, Special Report No. 18, 1957.

[5] *Ibid.* Also, E. A. Wilkening, The role of communicating agents in technological change in agriculture. *Social Forces,* 1956, 34, 361–367.

Least complex is a simple change in materials or equipment. Such a change might be the decision to try another brand of fertilizer or to increase the amount already being used. A change in technique is slightly more complex. The farmer must learn to use the new method and this may involve more risk. An example might be applying fertilizer along planted rows, instead of broadcast over the field. The third level involves both a change in materials and a change in technique. A farmer who has never used fertilizer faces such a change. He must adopt the new material, acquire the equipment to apply it, and learn how to use the equipment. The most complex change is a change of enterprise; for example, a change from cotton growing to dairying.

Obviously there are shadings in complexity among these four types of change, and other kinds of new products may involve a wider range of complexities than do farming practices. However, the level of complexity is an important factor in determining the time it takes for a new product to be adopted. Fifteen years elapsed between the introduction of hybrid seed corn and its adoption by almost 98 per cent of the farmers.[6] Other changes take longer. The adoption of new educational practices by school systems took fifty years.[7] Some changes take place quickly.

It is not always easy to tell how complex a change is involved in a new product. Hybrid corn is one example. Initially, this seemed like a simple change in materials. Actually, it was a far more complex change. Farmers feared the total reliance on commercial sources for seed corn, something they had previously produced for themselves. Furthermore, many farmers took pride in their ability to select good seed corn from their own crop, and they were accorded status for this skill. The new hybrid corn not only made the farmer feel more dependent, it also did away with an important source of prestige. A large majority of farmers had probably adopted hybrid corn within five years of the initial distribution, but it took fifteen years before almost all farmers were using it. Now, when a new hybrid variety of anything is introduced, it is adopted much more quickly. Examples are hybrid chickens and hybrid hogs.

The complexity of the change is only one important factor in determining the time required for adoption. There are others. For instance, *cost* is important. The more costly the item, the longer it takes before it is widely adopted. *Rate of return* and *visibility of return* are also important. A change which has rapid and obvious results is adopted more quickly than a change with slower, less visible results. In the long run, of course, the change which produces slower results may return more, but it still is not adopted as quickly. A new fertilizer is likely to be adopted more quickly, for example, than soil conservation practices.

[6] B. Ryan and N. C. Gross, The diffusion of hybrid seed corn in two Iowa communities. *Rural Sociology,* 1943, 8, 15–24. Also, B. Ryan and N. C. Gross, *Acceptance and diffusion of hybrid seed corn in two Iowa communities,* Iowa Agriculture Experiment Station, Research Bulletin 372, 1950.

[7] Mort and Pierce, *op. cit.*

## THE INDIVIDUAL ADOPTION PROCESS

The decision to adopt a new product is not simply a "yes" or "no" decision, nor is it something that happens all at once. When an individual is confronted with the possibility of change, he goes through several mental stages before he finally makes up his mind to adopt or not to adopt. Five stages in the decision-making process may be distinguished.[8] Farmers readily recognized these stages when questioned regarding their decisions to make changes and adopt new products.

*Awareness* comes first. At this point, the farmer learns about the new product. He knows it exists, but he has only general information about it. The *interest or information* stage follows. If interested, the farmer begins to collect more specific information about the new product. If his interest continues to grow, he wants to know the potentialities of the new product for him, whether or not it will increase his income or contribute to other ends considered by him to be important. The next step is the *mental application or evaluation* stage. The farmer goes through the change mentally and asks himself, "How would I do it? Can I do it? If I do it, will I be better off?" The final stage before adoption is the *trial* stage. At this point the farmer tries the product out on a small scale if this is possible. Many farmers purchased a small can of weed spray and used it on their gardens before they used it on their crops on a large scale. A great many farmers planted six acres of hybrid seed corn the first year, the acreage one bushel of the new seed would sow. Some products cannot be tried out on a small scale, and it seems quite reasonable to expect such products to require a longer adoption time. However, people seem to be quite ingenious at finding ways to try new ideas. Some housewives prepared small amounts of food for freezing, and either rented locker space or used a neighbor's freezer before they gave up traditional canning methods and bought the necessary equipment for themselves. Marketing people have been aware of the value of free trials for many years. The trial stage appears to play a crucial role in the decision-making process. However, the other stages are important too, and probably give meaning to this final step before adoption. They should not be ignored.

The last stage is the *adoption* stage. At this point the farmer decides to adopt the new product and begins using it on a full scale. Presumably he is a "satisfied customer," at least until some other product comes along to replace it and the adoption process starts again.

## ADOPTER CATEGORIES

Obviously, not all people adopt a new product at the same time. The adoption curve illustrates this point and suggests that some people arrive at a decision more quickly than others. Some people adopt very quickly. Others wait a long time before they take up the new product, and still others never adopt. There has been a great deal of interest in these individual differences and a great deal of speculation about "innovators," those who are first in a community to adopt a new product. To these

[8] North Central Rural Sociology Committee, Subcommittee for the Study of the Diffusion of Farm practices, *op. cit.*

individual differences, the Iowa State researchers took the data from a number of independent studies of new product adoption by farmers. They divided people into groups according to time of adoption,[9] and then studied each group. Significant differences appeared among them. These were the groups they distinguished and studied:

| | People adopting | Cumulative total adopting |
|---|---|---|
| • First | 2.5% innovators | 2.5% |
| • Next | 13.5% early adopters | 16.0% |
| • Next | 34.0% early majority | 50.0% |
| • Next | 34.0% late majority | 84.0% |
| • Last | 16.0% laggards | 100.0% |

"Innovators" are arbitrarily defined here as the first 2.5 per cent to adopt the new product. Based on the data compiled, these generalizations appear for farm innovators.[10]

They have larger than average farms, are well educated and usually come from well established families. They usually have a relatively high net worth and—probably more important—a large amount of risk capital. They can afford and do take calculated risks on new products. They are respected for being successful, but ordinarily do not enjoy the highest prestige in the community. Because innovators adopt new ideas so much sooner than the average farmer, they are sometimes ridiculed by their conservative neighbors. This neighborhood group pressure is largely ignored by the innovators, however. The innovators are watched by their neighbors, but they are not followed immediately in new practices.

The activities of innovators often transcend local community boundaries. Rural innovators frequently belong to formal organizations at the county, regional, state, or national level. In addition, they are likely to have many informal contacts outside the community: they may visit with others many miles away who are also trying a new technique or product, or who are technical experts.

The "early adopters" are defined as the next 13.5 per cent of the people who adopt the new product. According to the researchers, early adopter farmers have the following characteristics.

They are younger than the average farmer, but not necessarily younger than the innovators. They also have a higher than average education, and participate more in the formal activities of the community through such organizations as churches, the PTA, and farm organizations. They

[9]For convenience in making comparative studies, researchers used standard deviations of a normal distribution to establish the percentage breaks between categories. People who fall within one standard deviation above the mean are considered in the early majority; people who are between one and two standard deviations above the mean are early adopters. Similarly, people within one standard deviation below the mean are late majority, etc.

[10]North Central Rural Sociology Committee, Subcommittee for the Study of the Diffusion of Farm Practices, *op. cit.* Also, North Central Rural Sociology Committee, Subcommittee on the Diffusion of New Ideas and Farm Practices. *How farm people accept new ideas.* Iowa Agriculture Extension Service, Iowa State College, Special Report No. 15, 1955. Also E. M. Rogers, Categorizing the adopters of agriculture practices, *Rural Sociology,* 1943, 8, 15-24.

participate more than the average in agricultural cooperatives and in government agency programs in the community (such as Extension Service or Soil Conservation). In fact, there is some evidence that this group furnishes a disproportionate amount of the formal leadership (elected officers) in the community. The early adopters are also respected as good sources of new farm information by their neighbors.

The third category of adopters is the "early majority," the 34 per cent of people who bring the total adoption to 50 per cent. The number of adoptions increases rapidly after this group begins to adopt. (See chart.)

The early majority are slightly above average in age, education, and farming experience. They have medium high social and economic status. They are less active in formal groups than innovators or early adopters, but more active than those who adopt later. In many cases they are not formal leaders in the community organizations, but they are active members in these organizations. They also attend Extension meetings and farm demonstrations.

The people in this category are most likely to be informal rather than elected leaders. They have a following insofar as people respect their opinions, their "high morality and sound judgment." They are "just like their following, only more so." They must be sure an idea will work before they adopt it. If the informal leader fails two or three times, his following looks elsewhere for information and guidance. Because the informal leader has more limited resources than the early adopters and innovators, he cannot afford to make poor decisions: the social and economic costs are too high.

These people tend to associate mainly in their own community. When people in the community are asked to name neighbors and friends with whom they talk over ideas, these early majority are named disproportionally frequently. On their part, they value highly the opinions their neighbors and friends hold about them, for this is their main source of status and prestige. The early majority may look to the early adopters for their new farm information.

The "late majority" are the fourth category. These are the 34 per cent of farmers who have adopted the new product after the average farmer is already using it.

Those in this group have less education and are older than the average farmer. While they participate less actively in formal groups, they probably form the bulk of the membership in these formal organizations. Individually they belong to fewer organizations, are less active in organizational work, and take fewer leadership roles than the earlier adopters. They do not participate in as many activities outside the community as do people who adopt earlier.

The last category, the final 16 per cent of those who adopt a new idea, are the "laggards." This group may include the "non-adopters" as well if the new product is not used by everyone.

They have the least education and are the oldest. They participate least in formal organizations, cooperatives, and government agency programs. They have the smallest farms and the least capital. Many are suspicious of county Extension agents and agricultural salesmen.

These are some of the important differences among the adopter categories. They may provide useful guidelines for further exploration. For example, each of these categories plays an important role for the others in the adoption process. Innovators are the pioneers, and early adopters wait to see the innovators' results before trying the new product themselves. The early adopters, in turn, often influence the early majority. In addition, each of these categories seems to rely on different sources of information and influence, other than the sources already described.

# 31. TIME LAG IN NEW PRODUCT DEVELOPMENT

*Lee Adler*

*Here is an analysis of forty-two case histories, showing that product development is considerably more time-consuming than many marketers realize.*

*The question is–how can time allocations be made more realistic?*

New product development is crucial to the success of many companies . . . and likewise the time dimension is crucial to successful new product development.

But this temporal aspect has several facets. Some of these factors are well understood. Marketing executives are aware of the advantages that accrue to the new product that hits the market first. They are also aware of being too late–hitting the downside of a product cycle; becoming the victim of changing consumer habits, tastes and styles; or of having an idea fail because it is ahead of its time.

However, there is one temporal aspect that is often underrated. This is the length of time it takes to develop new products. To put it another way, one of the prime causes of product failure lies in "underestimating the time . . . needed for orderly market development and growth."[1] *The fear of wrong marketing timing leads to faulty development timing.*

[1]Clarence F. Manning, "Principles of Product Strategy," speech before 12th Annual Marketing Conference, National Industrial Conference Board, October 28, 1964.

Source: From *Journal of Marketing,* vol. 30, January, 1966, pp. 17-21. Lee Adler: Vice President for Research and Planning, Pritchard, Wood, Incorporated.

That is, anxiety about timing in the market makes time an enemy in the laboratory. Ironically, the outcome is that time kills the very thing it is designed to save.

The insufficient time allowed for proper development is then expressed in other ways in accounting for the high rate of new product failures. Such explanations as inadequate market analysis, failure to discover product defects until after launching, skipping or glossing over steps in development such as pilot production or market testing—all of these are ways of saying that the felt pressures of market timing resulted in an unfortunate telescoping of development timing.

The fact is that it takes much longer to develop new products than usually is thought to be the case. The conventional rule of thumb about allowing two to three years will be wrong more often than not.

This point is documented by a review of published accounts of new products. This search of literature uncovered forty-two case histories. See the accompanying table; it provides information on *consumer packaged goods, other consumer goods, and industrial goods.*

It would be misleading to average the length of time it took to develop these new products from the time they were a "gleam in the eye" until actual market introduction, simply because of the various possible definitions of a new product. A new product can be new to an individual company but not to the industry. Or it can be a new ingredient, feature, package, strength, flavor, etc. added to an existing product. Or it can be brand new in every sense, for example, the Polaroid camera and Xerox electrostatic reproduction.

In the accompanying table, elapsed time is calculated from the date that development began or that the idea was conceived until test marketing or initial marketing. These elapsed times are approximations for several reasons. As a careful examination of the literature made clear, dates are often vague because company records are poor, recollections foggy, and cases reported unsystematically. Moreover, chronologies are further confused by gaps between birth of idea and beginning of development.

Nonetheless, these cases clearly demonstrate that on the whole product development is more time-consuming than commonly recognized. The range was from six months for Sinclair Power-X gasoline to fifty-five years for television. Many new products took five years, ten years, and even longer to bring to fruition.

Marketers need to allot considerably more time to the development process than most of them do.

**Table 1. New product development time:** *I. CONSUMER PACKAGED GOODS*

| *Product* | *Company* | *Date development started or idea born* | *Test or initial markets* | *Large-scale or national* | *Elapsed time* | *Reference* | *Remarks* |
|---|---|---|---|---|---|---|---|
| Birdseye frozen foods | Birdseye Division, General Foods | 1908 | 1923 | | 15 years | *Printers' Ink,* 5/29/64 | |
| Ban roll-on deodorant | Bristol-Myers | About 1948 | 1954 | March, 1955 | 6 years | *Printers' Ink,* 6/5/59 *Sponsor,* 4/16/56 | Roll-on idea came from an outside inventor, hence presumably predates 1948. Bristol-Myers developed product that failed in test markets in 1951. Company researchers worked on plastics, finally assigned outside company job of making plastic marbles. Consumer-panel studies favorable in fall, 1953. Final test markets, summer, 1954. National advertising, March, 1955. |
| Calm powder deodorant in aerosol can | Alberto-Culver | 1959 | | February, 1964 | 5 years | *Printers' Ink,* 1/24/64 | Non-spray powder deodorants were tried about 1948-50, did not "get off the ground" then. |
| Chlorodent tooth paste | Lever Brothers | 1930s | March, 1951 | Early 1952 | Between 11 and 21 years | *Tide,* 3/28/52 | Idea developed in 1930s; two J. Walter Thompson vice presidents formed a company, Rystan, with a patent for chlorophyll products. Idea subsequently presented to Lever, and Lever licensed to produce tooth paste. |
| Citroid cold compound | Grove Laboratories | 1954-55 | | 1956 | 1 to 2 years | *Advertising Agency,* 10/26/56 | |
| Coldene cold-remedy liquid | Pharma-Craft | 1954 | 1955 | 1956 | 1 year | *Printers' Ink,* 2/7/58 | |

| | | | | | | | |
|---|---|---|---|---|---|---|---|
| Crest fluoride tooth paste | Proctor & Gamble | 1945 | January, 1955 | January, 1956 | 10 years | *Advertising Age,* 8/1/60 | Discovery that stannous fluoride is a preventive against tooth decay first made by Dr. Joseph C. Muhler in 1945, when he was a sophomore at School of Dentistry, University of Indiana. Since P&G had a parallel interest, Dr. Muhler continued to work on the project. |
| Decaf decaffeinated instant coffee | Nestlé | 1947 | 1953 | | 10 years | *Tide,* 1/25/57 Nestlé Company | |
| Flav-R-Straws | Frontier Foods Corp. and others | 1953 | April, 1956 | Early 1957 | 3 years | *Food Business,* 4/57 | Inventor sold idea to Frontier in 1955. By January, 1956, Frontier was in trouble, and product taken over by others. |
| Gerber strained baby foods | Gerber | 1927 | 1928 | | 1 year | *Business Decisions That Changed Our Lives,* Sidney Furst, Milton Sherman (Random House, 1964), p. 167. | |
| Hills Brothers instant coffee | Hills Brothers Coffee | 1934 | 1956 | | 22 years | *New York Times,* 11/16/56 | |
| Johnson liquid shoe polish containers that are also applicators | S. C. Johnson | 1957 | February, 1960 | Early 1961 | 3 years | *Printers' Ink,* 7/14/61 | |
| Lustre Creme liquid shampoo | Colgate-Palmolive | 1950 | | June, 1958 | 8 years | *Drug Trade News,* 5/19/58 | Five years of product tests, three years of consumer research. |
| Marlboro filter cigarettes | Philip Morris | May, 1953 | March, 1955 | | 2 years | *Advertising Age,* 2/28/55 | Marlboro had previously existed as a premium non-filter cigarette; development of filter, hard package, flip-top were new; red ("beauty") tip derived from earlier non-filter product. |

**Table 1. New product development time:** *I. CONSUMER PACKAGED GOODS* **(continued)**

| *Product* | *Company* | *Date development started or idea born* | *Test or initial markets* | *Large-scale or national* | *Elapsed time* | *Reference* | *Remarks* |
|---|---|---|---|---|---|---|---|
| Maxim concentrated instant coffee | General Foods | 1954 | May, 1964 | | 10 years | *Printers' Ink,* 5/1/64 | Preserves flavor and aroma of freshly brewed coffee. Process involves freezing of freshly percolated coffee. To use, crystals are dropped into cup of boiling (or iced) water. |
| Minute Maid frozen orange juice | Minute Maid | 1944 | 1946 | | 2 years | *Sales Management,* 4/1/49 *Advertising Age,* 3/14/49 | Introduced in 1946 under private label; and in 1947 under Minute Maid name. |
| Minute Rice | General Foods | 1931 | | First quarter, 1949 | 18 years | *Food Field Reporter,* 12/13/54 *Advertising Agency,* 11/49 | Idea originally came from member of Afghanistan royal family. GF had plant ready in 1941. World War II interrupted; army used plant. Consumer-tested in spring, 1946. Began national distribution in late 1948. |
| Purina Dog Chow | Ralston-Purina | 1951 | February, 1955 | April, 1957 | 4 years | *Wall Street Journal,* 1/2/58 | Began search for a dry dog food in 1951; developed light aerated feed using new formula in 1953; began testing February, 1955; in four additional test markets in 1955-56; achieved national distribution by April, 1957. |
| Red Kettle dry-soup mixes | Campbell Soup | Before 1943 | | August, 1962 | 19 years plus | *Advertising Age,* 9/24/62 *Food Field Reporter,* 8/28/61 | Campbell first tested dry noodle soup in 1943-44, withdrew product because "we were dissatisfied with the processes and packages available." Resumed testing in 1959. |

| Product | Company | Date development started or idea born | Test or initial markets | Large-scale or national | Elapsed time | Reference | Remarks |
|---|---|---|---|---|---|---|---|
| Stripe tooth paste | Lever Brothers | 1952 | 1957 | Early 1958 | 5½ to 6 years | *New York Times,* 1/15/58 | Inventor spent four years developing the striping device. Took Lever engineers six months to design a production machine. Product then in test markets for 14 months. |
| Wisk liquid detergent | Lever Brothers | 1955 | January, 1956 | | 1 year | *Fortune,* 6/59 | |
| Wrinkle-removing creams | (Many) | | 1963-64 | | | | Protein used in these creams, developed during World War II. |

*II. OTHER CONSUMER GOODS*

| *Product* | *Company* | *Date development started or idea born* | *Test or initial markets* | *Large-scale or national* | *Elapsed time* | *Reference* | *Remarks* |
|---|---|---|---|---|---|---|---|
| Bendix washer/dryer | Bendix | Prior to World War II | | March, 1953 | 12 years plus | *Fortune,* 3/53 | |
| Eversharp "Fountain Ball" ball pen | Eversharp | January, 1958 | September, 1958 | January, 1959 | 8 months | *Sales Management,* 1/2/59 | Eight months in product development; one year in product and market testing. |
| Fairchild Mark IV 8mm. sound projector | Fairchild Camera & Instrument | Late 1961 | August, 1963 | | 2 years | *New Products, New Profits,* American Management Association, 1964 | Fairchild describes as "better than average effort," due to technical advances in dealing with the complexities involved. |
| Floron plastic floor tile | Pabco Products | 1947-48 | | October, 1953 | 5 to 6 years | *Sales Management,* 1/1/55 | |
| GE electric tooth brush | General Electric | 1958-59 | October, 1961 | April, 1962 | 3 to 4 years | *Printers' Ink,* 7/20/62 | Electric tooth brushes available for 30 years; wall-socket recharging, new. |

**Table 1. New Product development time:** *II. OTHER CONSUMER GOODS* **(continued)**

| *Product* | *Company* | *Date development started or idea born* | *Test or initial markets* | *Large-scale or national* | *Elapsed time* | *Reference* | *Remarks* |
|---|---|---|---|---|---|---|---|
| Polaroid Land Camera | Polaroid Corp. | 1945-46 | 1947-48 | | 2 years | *Business Week,* 9/3/49 and 1/19/63 *Printers' Ink,* 5/29/64 *Standard & Poor's Corporate Records,* 1965, p. 9745. | |
| Polaroid Color-pack Camera | Polaroid Corp. | 1948 | January, 1963 | May, 1963 | 15 years plus | *Business Week,* 1/19/63 | |
| Scripto Tilt Tip ball pen | Scripto | 1959 | April, 1961 | Mid-1961 | 2 years | *Advertising Age,* 1/30/61 | |
| Sinclair Power-X gasoline; Extra Duty Motor Oil | Sinclair Oil | Late 1952 | | April, 1953 | 6 months | *Printers' Ink,* 6/18/54 | |
| Smith Corona portable electric typewriter | Smith Corona | 1952 | Early 1957 | | 5 years | *New York Times,* 11/17/57 | |
| Sunbeam electric tooth brush | Sunbeam Corp. | | | | 5 years | *Sales Management,* 9/4/64 | |
| Talon zipper | Corporate predecessor of Talon, Inc. | 1883 | 1913 | 1918 | 30 years | *Business Decisions That Changed Our Lives,* Sidney Furst, Milton Sherman (Random House, 1964), p. 115. | Zippers first thought of as shoe-fastening device in 1883. In 1894, product first developed for use in shoes. First modern zipper concept emerged in 1908. First successful mass production, 1913; and first applications to clothing in 1913-18. In 1918, an ex-GI suggested use of zippers for money belts, and this was really the first commercial success. |

| | | | | | | | |
|---|---|---|---|---|---|---|---|
| Television | (Many) | 1884 | 1939 | 1946-47 | 55 years | Federal Communications Commission, "Broadcast Primer," Bulletin 2-B, 1961. | In 1884, Nipkow, a German, patented a scanning disk for transmitting pictures by wireless–this is credited with being the first development that led |

ultimately to what is now known as television. In 1890 Jenkins began his studies in the U.S. In the 1900s, Rignoux and Fournier conducted "television" experiments in France. In 1915, Marconi predicted a "visible telephone." In 1923, Zworykin applied for patent on the iconoscope, a TV camera-tube. In 1925, Jenkins demonstrated a mechanical television apparatus. In 1927 the first experimental television program from New York to Washington made by Bell Laboratories. In 1928 the first station, WGY, established in Schenectady. In 1930 RCA demonstrated large-screen TV in New York. In 1936 RCA tested outdoor TV pickup in Camden. By 1937, 17 experimental stations in existence. The first commercial program authorized on July 1, 1941 by WNBT–New York, but the first TV sets shown to consumers at New York World's Fair in 1939, and available to consumers in 1939–40.

*III. INDUSTRIAL GOODS*

| *Product* | *Company* | *Date development started or idea born* | *Test or initial markets* | *Large-scale or national* | *Elapsed time* | *Reference* | *Remarks* |
|---|---|---|---|---|---|---|---|
| Dictet portable recording | Dictaphone Corp. | 1954 | Early | | 20 months | *A Critical Look at the Purchasing Function,* Robert F. Logler, American Management Association Bulletin No. 13, 1961, pp. 113-21. | |
| Isothalic chemical component to improve house paints | Oronite Corp. (subsidiary of Standard Oil of California) | 1951 | Late 1957–early 1958 | | 6 to 7 years plus | *Sales Management,* 9/19/58 | Specific development of superior house paint begun in 1951. Oronite began work on Isothalic during World War II. Isothalic reported to be 10 years in development. |
| Krilium soil conditioner | Monsanto | 1939 | May, 1952 | | 12½ years | *Fortune,* 12/52 | 10 years in laboratory; 2½ years in field test. |

Table 1. New product development time: *III. INDUSTRIAL GOODS* (continued)

| *Product* | *Company* | *Date development started or idea born* | *Test or initial markets* | *Large-scale or national* | *Elapsed time* | *Reference* | *Remarks* |
|---|---|---|---|---|---|---|---|
| Page Master selective pocket-paging system | Stromberg Carlson | 1955 | | March, 1957 | 2 years | American Management Association Bulletin No. 13, 1961, pp. 122-41. | |
| Penicillin | (Many) | 1928 | 1943 | | 15 years | *Business Week,* 3/3/45 | Discovered by Sir Alex Fleming. |
| Transistor | Bell Laboratories | 1940 | 1955-56 | | 15 to 16 years | *Business Week,* 3/26/60 | First discovery accidental, in 1940. First laboratory transistor, debut in 1948. Prototype qualities available, 1954. First consumer applications in hearing aids and radios, 1955-56. |
| Xerox electrostatic copying machine | Xerox Corp. | 1935 | 1950 | | 15 years | *Forbes,* 9/15/62 *Fortune,* 7/62 *New York Times,* 12/10/61 *Standard & Poor's Corporate Records,* 1965, p. 4472. | |

# 32. THE DEATH AND BURIAL OF "SICK" PRODUCTS

*R. S. Alexander*

*Products, like men, are mortal. They flourish for a time, then decline and die.*

*While the death of a man is catastrophic in the sense that it occurs at a specific point in time, that of a product tends to be an indefinite process that may continue until its last user forgets that it ever existed and so will no longer try to buy it.*

*The author presents a thoughtful and practical plan for selecting products for elimination; gathering information about them; making decisions about them; and, if necessary, removing the doomed products from the line.*

Euthanasia applied to human beings is criminal; but aging products enjoy or suffer no such legal protection. This is a sad fact of business life.

The word "product" is used here not in its broad economic sense of anything produced—such as wheat, coal, a car, or a chair—but in its narrower meaning of an article made to distinct specifications and intended for sale under a separate brand or catalogue number. In the broader sense of the word, certain products may last as long as industrial civilization endures; in the narrow sense, most of them are playthings of change.

Much has been written about managing the development and marketing of new products, but business literature is largely devoid of material on product deletion.

Source: From *Journal of Marketing,* vol. 28, April, 1964, pp. 1–7. R. S. Alexander: Professor Emeritus of Marketing, Graduate School of Business, Columbia University.

This is not surprising. New products have glamor. Their management is fraught with great risks. Their successful introduction promises growth in sales and profits that may be fantastic.

But putting products to death—or letting them die—is a drab business, and often engenders much of the sadness of a final parting with old and tried friends. "The portable 6-sided, pretzel polisher was the first product The Company ever made. Our line will no longer be our line without it."

But while deletion is an uninspiring and depressing process, in a changing market it is almost as vital as the addition of new products. The old product that is a "football" of competition or has lost much of its market appeal is likely to generate more than its share of small unprofitable orders; to make necessary short, costly production runs; to demand an exorbitant amount of executive attention; and to tie up capital that could be used more profitably in other ventures.

Just as a crust of barnacles on the hold of a ship retards the vessel's movement, so do a number of worn-out items in a company's product mix affect the company's progress.

Most of the costs that result from the lack of an effective deletion system are hidden and become apparent only after careful analysis. As a result, management often overlooks them. The need for examining the product line to discover outworn members, and for analysis to arrive at intelligent decisions to discard or to keep them, very rarely assumes the urgency of a crisis. Too often, management thinks of this as something that should be done but that can wait until tomorrow.

This is why a definite procedure for deletion of products should be set up, and why the authority and responsibility for the various activities involved should be clearly and definitely assigned. This is especially important because this work usually requires the cooperation of several functional groups within the business firm, including at least marketing, production, finance, and sometimes personnel.

Definite responsibility should be assigned for at least the following activities involved in the process:

1. selecting products which are candidates for elimination;
2. gathering information about them and analyzing the information;
3. making decisions about elimination; and
4. if necessary, removing the doomed products from the line.

## SELECTION OF PRODUCTS FOR POSSIBLE ELIMINATION

As a first step, we are not seeking the factors on which the final decision to delete or to retain turns, but merely those which indicate that the product's continuation in the product mix should be considered carefully with elimination as a possibility. Although removal from the product line may seem to be the prime aim, the result is not inevitably deletion from the line; instead, careful analysis may lead to changes in the product itself or in the methods of making or marketing it.

*Sales Trend.* If the trend of a product's sales is downward over a time period that is significant in relation to the normal life of others like it, its continuation in the mix deserves careful examination. There may be many reasons for such a decline that in no way point toward deletion; but when decline continues over a period of time the situation needs to be studied.

*Price Trend.* A downward trend in the price of a new product may be expected if the firm introducing it pursues a skimming-price policy, or if all firms making it realize substantial cost savings as a result of volume production and increased processing know-how. But when the price of an established product whose competitive pattern has been relatively stabilized shows a downward trend over a significant period of time, the future of that product should receive attention.

*Profit Trend.* A declining profit either in dollars or as a per cent of sales or investment should raise questions about a product's continued place in the product line. Such a trend usually is the result of a price-factory cost squeeze, although it may be the outcome of a loss in market appeal or a change in the method of customer purchase which forces higher marketing expenditures.

*Substitute Products.* When a substitute article appears on the market, especially if it represents an improvement over an old product, management must face the question of whether to retain or discard the old product. This is true regardless of who introduces the substitute. The problem is especially difficult when the new product serves the same general purpose as the old one but is not an exact substitute for it.

*Product Effectiveness.* Certain products may lose some of their effectiveness for the purposes they serve. For example, disease germs may develop strains that are resistant to a certain antibiotic. When this happens, the question of whether to keep or delete the drug involves issues not only of the interests of the firm but of the public welfare.

*Executive Time.* A possible tipoff as to the location of "illness" in a product mix lies in a study of the amount of executive time and attention devoted to each of the items in the product line. Sick products, like sick people, demand a lot of care; but one must be careful to distinguish the "growing pains" of a new product from the more serious disorders of one that has matured and is now declining.

The six indicators mentioned do not of themselves provide evidence justifying deletion. But they can help management to single out from a line of products those upon which it can profitably spend time and money in analyzing them, with elimination from the line as a *possibility.*

## ANALYSIS AND DECISION-MAKING ABOUT "SICK" PRODUCTS

Although the work of analyzing a sick or decrepit product is usually done by people other than the management executives who decide what to do about it, the two processes are interdependent. Unless the right factors are chosen for analysis and unless the work is properly done, the decision is not likely to be an intelligent one. Accordingly, these two factors will be discussed together.

What information does a decision-maker need about a product, and what sort of analysis of it should he have in order to render a sound verdict as to its future? The deletion decision should not turn on the sole issue of profitability. Profit is the most important objective of a business; but individual firms often seek to achieve both long-run and short-run objectives other than profit.

So, in any individual case the critical factors and the weights assigned them in making a decision must be chosen in the light of the situation of the firm and the management objectives.

### Profits

Profit management in a firm with a multi-product line (the usual situation in our economy) is not the simple operation generally contemplated in economic theory. Such a firm usually has in its product mix

1. items in various stages of introduction and development, some of which may be fantastically profitable and others deep "in the red";
2. items which are mature but not "superannuated," whose profit rate is likely to be satisfactory; and
3. declining items which may yield a net profit somewhat less than adequate or may show heavy losses.

The task is to manage the whole line or mix so that it will show a satisfactory profit for the company. In this process, two questions are vital; What is a profit? How much profit is satisfactory?

Operating-statement accounting makes it possible to determine with reasonable accuracy the total amount of net profit a company earns on an overall basis. But when the management of a multi-product firm seeks to determine how much of this total is generated by its activities in making and marketing each product in its mix, the process is almost incredibly complex; and the results are almost certain to be conditioned on an issue of assumptions which are so debatable that no management can feel entirely comfortable in basing decisions on them.

This is because such a large portion of the costs of the average multi-product firm are or behave like overhead or joint expense. Almost inevitably several of the items in the product mix are made of common materials, with the same equipment, and by manpower which is interchangeable. Most of the company's marketing efforts and expenses are devoted to selling and distributing the mix or a line within the mix, rather than individual items.

In general, the more varied the product mix of a firm, the greater is the portion of its total expense that must be classified as joint or overhead. In such a company, many types of cost which ordinarily can be considered direct tend to behave like overhead or joint expenses. This is particularly true of marketing costs such as advertising that does not feature specific items; personal selling; order handling; and delivery.

This means that a large part of a company's costs must be assigned to products on some arbitrary basis and that however logical this basis may be, it is subject to considerable reasonable doubt in specific cases. It also means that if one product is removed from the mix, many of these costs remain to be reassigned to the items that stay in the line. As a result, any attempt to "prune" the product mix entirely on the basis of the profit contribution, or lack of it, of specific items is almost certain to be disappointing and in some cases disastrous.

But if a multi-product firm could allocate costs to individual items in the mix on some basis recognized as sound and thus compute product-profit accurately, what standard of profit should be set up as a criterion to justify deletion?

Probably most managements either formally or unconsciously set overall company profit targets. Such targets may be expressed in terms of dollars, although to be most useful in product management they usually must be translated into percentages on investment, or money used. An an example, a company may have as its profit target 15 per cent on investment before taxes.

Certainly *every* product in the mix should not be required to achieve the target, which really amounts to an average. To do so would be to deny the inevitable variations in profit potential among products.

Probably a practical minimum standard can be worked out, below which a product should be eliminated unless other considerations demand its retention. Such a standard can be derived from a balancing out of the profit rates among products in the mix, so as to arrive at the overall company target as an average. The minimum standard then represents a figure that would tip the balance enough to endanger the overall target.

What role, then, should considerations of product profit play in managerial decisions as to deletion or retention?

1. Management probably will be wise to recognize an overall company target profit in dollars or rate on investment, and to set in relation to it a minimum below which the profit on an individual product should not fall without marking that item for deletion (unless other special considerations demand its retention).

2. Management should "cast a bilious eye" on all arguments that a questionable product be kept in the mix because it helps to defray overhead and joint costs. Down that road, at the end of a series of decisions to retain such products, lies a mix entirely

or largely composed of items each busily "sopping up" overhead, but few or none contributing anything to net profit.

3. This does not mean that management should ignore the effect of a product deletion on overhead or joint costs. Decision-makers must be keenly aware of the fact that the total of such costs borne by a sick product must, after it is deleted, be reallocated to other products, and with the result that they may become of doubtful profitability. A detailed examination of the joint or overhead costs charged against an ailing product may indicate that some of them can be eliminated in whole or in part if it is eliminated. Such costs are notoriously "sticky" and difficult to get rid of; but every pretext should be used to try to find ways to reduce them.

4. If a deletion decision involves a product or a group of products responsible for a significant portion of a firm's total sales volume, decision-makers can assess the effects of overhead and joint costs on the problem, by compiling as estimated company operating statement after the deletion and comparing it with the current one. Such a forecasted statement should include expected net income from the use of the capital and facilities released by deletion if an opportunity for their use is readily at hand. Surviving joint and overhead expenses can even be reallocated to the remaining products, in order to arrive at an estimate of the effect that deletion might have, not only on the total company net income but on the profitability of each of the remaining products as well. Obviously such a cost analysis is likely to be expensive, and so is not justified unless the sales volume stakes are high.

**Financial Considerations**

Deletion is likely not only to affect the profit performance of a firm but to modify its financial structure as well.

To make and sell a product, a company must invest some of its capital. In considering its deletion, the decision-makers must estimate what will happen to the capital funds presently used in making and marketing it.

When a product is dropped from the mix, most or all of the circulating capital invested in it—such as inventories of materials, goods in process, and finished goods and accounts receivable—should drain back into the cash account; and if carried out in an orderly fashion, deletion will not disturb this part of the capital structure except to increase the ratio of cash to other assets.

This will be true, unless the deletion decision is deferred until product deterioration has gone so far that the decision assumes the aspect of a crisis and its execution that of a catastrophe.

The funds invested in the equipment and other facilities needed to make and market the "sick" product are a different matter. If the equipment is versatile and standard, it may be diverted to other uses. If the firm has no need of it and if the equipment has been properly depreciated, management may find a market for it at a price approaching or even exceeding its book value.

In either case, the capital structure of the company is not disturbed except by a shift from equipment to cash in the case of sale. In such a case management would be wise, before making a deletion decision, to determine how much cash this action promises to release as well as the chances for its reinvestment.

If the equipment is suited for only one purpose, it is highly unlikely that management can either find another use for it or sell it on favorable terms. If it is old and almost completely depreciated, it can probably be scrapped and its remaining value "written off" without serious impairment of the firm's capital structure.

But if it is only partly depreciated, the decision-makers must weigh the relative desirability of two possible courses of action:

1. to delete immediately, hoping that the ensuing improvement in the firm's operating results will more than offset the impairment in capital structure that deletion will cause; or
2. to seek to recapture as much as possible of its value, by continuing to make and market the product as long as its price is enough to cover out-of-pocket costs and leave something over to apply to depreciation.

This choice depends largely on two things: the relation between the amount of fixed and circulating capital that is involved; and the opportunities available to use the funds, executive abilities, manpower, and transferable facilities released by deletion for making profits in other ventures.

This matter of opportunity costs is a factor in every deletion decision. The dropping of a product is almost certain to release some capital, facilities, manpower skills, and executive abilities. If opportunities can be found in which these assets can be invested without undue risk and with promise of attractice profits, it may be good management to absorb considerable immediate loss in deleting a sick product.

If no such opportunities can be found, it is probably wise to retain the product so long as the cash inflow from its sales covers out-of-pocket costs and contributes something to depreciation and other overhead expenses. In such a case, however, it is the part of good management to seek actively for new ventures which promise satisfactory profits, and to be ready to delete promptly when such an opportunity is found.

## Employee Relations

The effect which product elimination may have on the employees of a firm is often an important factor in decisions either to drop or to retain products.

This is not likely to be a deciding factor if new product projects are under development to which the people employed in making and marketing the doubtful product can be transferred, unless such transfer would deprive them of the earning power of special skills. But when deletion of a product means discharging or transferring unionized employees, the decision-makers must give careful thought to the effect their action is likely to have on company-union relations.

Even in the absence of union pressure, management usually feels a strong sense of responsibility for the people in its employ. Just how far management can go in conserving specific jobs at the expense of deferring or foregoing necessary deletions before it endangers the livelihood of all the employees of the firm is a nice question of balance.

**Marketing Factors**

Many multi-product firms retain in their marketing mixes one or more items which, on the basis of profits and the company financial structure, should be deleted. To continue to make and market a losing product is no managerial crime. It is reprehensible only when management does not know the product is a losing one or, knowing the facts, does not have sound reasons for retaining it. Such reasons are very likely to lie in the marketing area.

Deletions of products are often deferred or neglected because of management's desire to carry a "full line," whatever that means. This desire may be grounded on sound reasons of consumer patronage or on a dubious yearning for the "prestige" that a full line is supposed to engender. But there is no magic about a full line or the prestige that is supposed to flow from it. Both should be evaluated on the basis of their effects on the firm's sales volume, profits, and capacity to survive and grow.

Products are often associated in the marketing process. The sale of one is helped by the presence of another in the product mix.

When elimination of a product forces a customer who buys all or a large part of his requirements of a group of profitable items from the firm to turn to another supplier for his needs of the dropped product, he might shift some or all of his other patronage as well. Accordingly, it is sometimes wise for management to retain in its mix a no-profit item, in order to hold sales volume of highly profitable products. But this should not be done blindly without analysis.

Rarely can management tell ahead of time exactly how much other business will be lost by deleting a product, or in what proportions the losses will fall among the remaining items. But in many cases the amount of sales volume can be computed that will be *hazarded* by such action; what other products will be subject to that hazard; and what portion of their volume will be involved. When this marketing interdependence exists in a deletion problem, the decision-makers should seek to discover the customers who buy the sick product; what other items in the mix they buy; in what quantities; and how much profit they contribute.

The firm using direct marketing channels can do this with precision and at relatively little cost. The firm marketing through indirect channels will find it more difficult, and the information will be less exact; but it still may be worthwhile. If the stakes are high enough, marketing research may be conducted to discover the extent to which the customer purchases of profitable items actually are associated with that of the sick product. Although the results may not be precise, they may supply an order-of-magnitude idea of the interlocking patronage situation.

Product interrelationships in marketing constitute a significant factor in making deletion decisions, but should never be accepted as the deciding factor without careful study to disclose at least the extent of the hazards they involve.

### Other Possibilities

The fact that a product's market is declining or that its profit performance is substandard does not mean that deletion is the *only* remedy.

Profits can be made in a shrinking market. There are things other than elimination of a product that can be done about deteriorating profit performance. They tend to fall into four categories.

1. Costs. A careful study may uncover ways of reducing factory costs. This may result from improved processes that either eliminate manpower or equipment time or else increase yield; or from the elimination of forms or features that once were necessary or worthwhile but are no longer needed. The natural first recourse of allocating joint and overhead costs on a basis that is "kinder" to the doubtful product is not to be viewed with enthusiasm. After reallocation, these costs still remain in the business; and the general profit picture has not been improved in the least.

2. Marketing. Before deleting a product, management will be wise to examine the methods of marketing it, to see if they can be changed to improve its profit picture.

   Can advertising and sales effort be reduced without serious loss of volume? A holding operation requires much less effort and money than a promotional one.

   Are services being given that the product no longer needs?

   Can savings be made in order handling and delivery, even at some loss of customer satisfaction? For example, customers may be buying the product in small orders that are expensive to handle.

   On the other hand, by spending more marketing effort, can volume be increased so as to bring about a reduction in factory cost greater than the added marketing expense? In this attempt, an unexpected "assist" may come from competitors who delete the product and leave more of the field to the firm.

   By remodeling the product, "dressing it up," and using a new marketing approach, can it be brought back to a state of health and profit? Here the decision-makers must be careful not to use funds and facilities that could be more profitably invested in developing and marketing new products.

3. Price. It is natural to assume that the price of a failing product cannot be raised. At least in part, its plight is probably due to the fact that it is "kicked around" by competition, and thus that competition will not allow any increases.

But competitors may be tired of the game, too. One company that tried increasing prices found that wholesalers and retailers did not resent a larger cost-of-goods-sold base on which to apply their customary gross profit rates, and that consumers continued to buy and competitors soon followed suit.

Although a price rise will not usually add to the sum total of user happiness, it may not subtract materially from total purchases. The decision-makers should not ignore the possibility of using a price reduction to gain enough physical volume to bring about a more-than-offsetting decline in unit costs, although at this stage the success of such a gambit is not likely.

4. Cross Production. In the materials field, when small production runs make costs prohibitive, arrangements may sometimes be made for Firm A to make the *entire* supply of Product X for itself and Competitor B. Then B reciprocates with another similar product. Such "trades," for instance, are to be found in the chemical business.

**Summation for Decision**

In solving deletion problems, the decision-makers must draw together into a single pattern the results of the analysis of all the factors bearing on the matter. Although this is probably most often done on an intangible, subjective basis, some firms have experimented with the formula method.

For example, a manufacturer of electric motors included in its formula the following factors:

- Profitability
- Position on growth curve
- Product leadership
- Market position
- Marketing dependence of other products

Each factor was assigned a weight in terms of possible "counts" against the product. For instance, if the doubtful item promised no profits for the next three years, it had a count of fifty points against it, while more promising prospects were assigned lesser counts. A critical total for all factors was set in advance which would automatically doom a product. Such a system can include other factors–such as recapturability of invested capital, alternate available uses of facilities, effects on labor force, or other variables peculiar to the individual case.

The use of a formula lends an aura of precision to the act of decision-making and assures a degree of uniformity in it. But obviously the weights assigned to different factors cannot be the same in all cases. For example, if the deletion of a doubtful product endangers a large volume of sales of other highly profitable items, that alone should probably decide the matter.

The same thing is true if deletion will force so heavy a writeoff of invested funds as to impair the firm's capital structure. Certainly this will be true if all or most of the investment can be recaptured by the depreciation route if the product stays in the mix.

This kind of decision requires that the factors be weighted differently in each case. But when managers are given a formula, they may tend to quit thinking and do too much "weighing."

## THE DELETION OF A PRODUCT

Once the decision to eliminate a product is made, plans must be drawn for its death and burial with the least disturbance of customer relations and of the other operations of the firm.

Such plans must deal with a variety of detailed problems. Probably the most important fall into four categories: timing; parts and replacements; stocks; and holdover demand.

*Timing.* It is desirable that deletion be timed so as to dovetail with the financial, manpower, and facilities needs for new products. As manpower and facilities are released from the dying product and as the capital devoted to it flows back into the cash account, it is ideal if these can be immediately used in a new venture. Although this can never be completely achieved, it may be approximated.

The death of a product should be timed so as to cause the least disturbance to customers. They should be informed about the elimination of the product far enough in advance so they can make arrangements for replacement, if any are available, but not so far in advance that they will switch to new suppliers before the deleting firm's inventories of the product are sold. Deletion at the beginning of a selling season or in the middle of it probably will create maximum customer inconvenience, whereas at the end of the season it will be the least disturbing.

*Parts and Replacements.* If the product to be killed off is a durable one, probably the deleting firm will find it necessary to maintain stocks of repair parts for about the expected life of the units most recently sold. The firm that leaves a trail of uncared-for "orphan" products cannot expect to engender much good will from dealers or users. Provision for the care and maintenance of the orphan is a necessary cost of deletion.

This problem is much more widespread than is commonly understood. The woman who buys a set of china or silverware and finds that she cannot replace broken or lost pieces does not entertain an affectionate regard for the maker. The same sort of thing is true if she installs draperies and later, when one of them is damaged, finds that the pattern is no longer available.

*Stocks.* The deletion plan should provide for clearing out the stocks of the dying product and materials used in its production, so as to recover the maximum amount of the working capital invested in it. This is very largely a matter of timing—the tapering off of purchase, production, and selling activities. However, this objective may conflict with those of minimizing inconvenience to customers and servicing the orphan units in use after deletion.

*Holdover Demand.* However much the demand for a product may decline, it probably will retain some following of devoted users. They are bound to be disturbed by its deletion and are likely to be vocal about it; and usually there is little that management can do to mitigate this situation.

Sometimes a firm can avoid all these difficulties by finding another firm to purchase the product. This should usually be tried before any other deletion steps are taken. A product with a volume too small for a big firm to handle profitably may be a money-maker for a smaller one with less overhead and more flexibility.

## NEGLECT OR ACTION?

The process of product deletion is important. The more dynamic the business, the more important it is.

But it is something that most company executives prefer not to do; and therefore it will not get done unless management establishes definite, clearcut policies to guide it, sets up carefully articulated procedures for doing it, and makes a positive and unmistakable assignment of authority and responsibility for it.

Exactly what these policies should be, what form these procedures should take, and to whom the job should be assigned are matters that must vary with the structure and operating methods of the firm and with its position in the industry and the market.

In any case, though, the need for managerial attention, planning, and supervision of the deletion function cannot be overemphasized. Many business firms are paying dearly for their neglect of this problem, but unfortunately do not realize how much this is costing them.

## *B. Product brands*

# 33. BRANDING POLICIES AND PRACTICES

*Thomas F. Schutte and Victor J. Cook*

*Here are the highlights of a research study on various factors giving rise to the growth and development of private branding. The branding policies and practices of approximately 200 manufacturing and distributing companies were examined.*

In the spring of 1964, the Marketing Science Institute launched a major study designed to identify and evaluate the factors or variables that are taken into account by manufacturers and distributors in determining their branding policies and programs. Some of the questions for which we sought answers include:

Are there identifiable trends in distributor branding that are related to specific kinds of products, specific industries, or types of business organizations?

What are the factors or variables that cause some managements to undertake distributors' brands programs, while others emphasize manufacturers' brands to the exclusion of private labels?

To avoid difficulties in semantics, the terms *private brand* and *distributor's brand* will be used synonymously, as will the terms *manufacturer's brand* and *national brand.* A manufacturer's brand is one sponsored, or owned, by a company whose primary or traditional business is producing the given product line. A distributor's brand is one sponsored, or owned, by a company whose primary or traditional business is distributing the product line.

Source: Raymond M. Haas (ed.), *Science, Technology, and Marketing,* Chicago: American Marketing Association, 1966, pp. 197–213. Thomas F. Schutte: Assistant Professor of Marketing, University of Pennsylvania. Victor J. Cook: Research Associate, Marketing Science Institute, Philadelphia.

The brand policy issue with which this presentation is concerned has relevance to thousands of products and product lines. Therefore, it was necessary to select representative durable, semidurable, and nondurable product categories for the more specific phases of the investigation. The seven product categories selected are as follows:

1. Grocery products (inclusive of paper products and detergents)
2. Drugs and toiletries
3. Shoes
4. Gasoline
5. Tires
6. Household appliances
7. Television receivers

The fieldwork associated with the study was performed in two parts. The first part involved the collection of data necessary for identifying private brand market share and trends for those consumer product categories just mentioned. The market share trend data generally cover the period from 1955 to 1965. The sources of this information include syndicated marketing research services, trade associations, and business firms.

The second major element of the fieldwork involved interviews with executives in approximately two hundred manufacturing, retailing, and other distributing organizations. The manufacturer respondents were selected on the basis of their brand policy position and product category. Distributor respondents included mass merchandisers, traditional department stores, specialty merchandise chains, buying organizations, and independent merchandisers.

## OVERVIEW

At one time or another, management in most companies becomes concerned with the problem of brand policy determination—since it is the very core of the private brand issue.

Manufacturers have often attempted to assess the impact of a new policy. This kind of question may have arisen: "Should we produce private brands or not, and if we do, what happens to our profits and our market standing?" Or, management is concerned frequently about a change in a customer's brand policy: "What do we do now that one of our biggest customers has his own private brands?"

Distributors are often concerned with this problem: "Should we continue with national brands in this product category, or should we move into our own labels?"

The private brand issue may even affect ad agency or media operations. Perhaps these companies have had to decide whether to accept accounts with distributors who want to advertise private brands.

The difficulty of making these assessments is well known to corporate management—especially since the little information has been made available either to help in making policy evaluation, or to explain why the pressures of a given brand policy are different from one industry to another. For example, when looking at a broad range of consumer products, there are wide differences in the amount of private brand penetration.

Using some of the best information available, we found that distributors' brand share runs from an average of approximately 7 per cent in portable appliances, to over 50 per cent in shoes (Figure 1). In between these extremes, distributors' brands have an average of 13 per cent of volume in grocery store products, 16 per cent in gasoline sales, 33 per cent in major appliances, and 36 per cent in tires.

Trends in market composition vary extensively. For one product the private brand share may grow dramatically, while the national brand share declines. For another product the private brand share may gain a strong foothold and then begin to lose ground rapidly.

When looking at business firms we find important differences in brand policies. Sometimes companies—perhaps similar in other respects—may have opposite brand policies. One manufacturer may engage extensively in private label production, while another never does. Some distributors may do most of their volume in a product line with private brands, while others remain with manufacturers' brands.

Why are distributors' brands so strong in some product lines and not in others? Why are trends in private label share so different from one industry to another? What

**Figure 1. Distributors' brand market share by product category (average for measured products)**

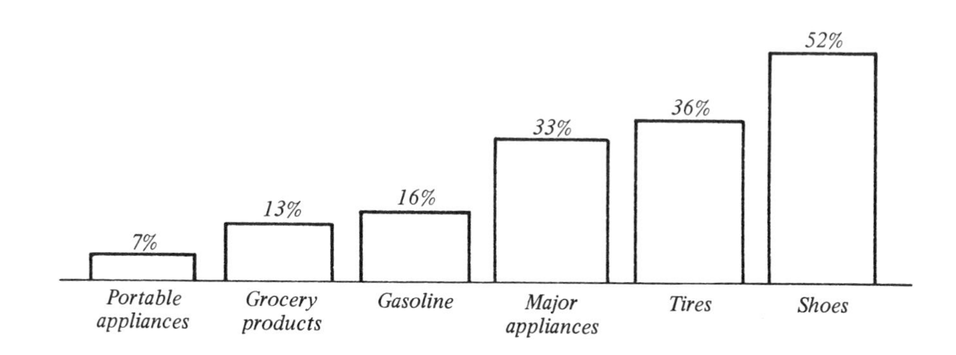

factors lead to a given brand policy? Why are different policies adopted by similar companies? And what are the results when one policy is used over another?

## GENERAL FORCES SHAPING TRENDS IN BRAND OWNERSHIP

Let us look at this question first: "Why are distributors' brands so strong in some product lines and not in others?" We attempted to identify the economic and marketing forces which might shape trends in private brand sales.

One economic force we considered was excess capacity, because it is mentioned frequently as a "cause" of private branding. We found that excess *industry* capacity was not related to distributors' brand share in any consistent fashion. For the industries we examined, those with the highest private brand share were not the ones that had seen the highest or most persistent periods of excess capacity. Furthermore, there was no clear relationship between changes in industry capacity utilization and changes in private brand share. While excess capacity may motivate an *individual* company to change its brand policy, it does not seem to show up on an industrywide basis.

Another force examined was the level of economic activity. We found that changes in general conditions do seem to affect private brand share of market in nondurable goods like grocery products and toiletries. Since purchases on nondurables are repeated many times within periods of change in the general economy, it is *possible* that private label share could decline in good times–*if* consumers switch to national brands when they have more money to spend. Private brand share in a number of nondurable product lines does in fact tend to decline as prosperity increases, but not in durable goods.

Purchases of consumer durables are less frequently repeated during ups and downs in business activity. Where possible, consumers postpone purchases of durables in bad times and tend to increase them in good times. In consumer durables, we found that private brand share increases during high prosperity. In fact, it increased greatly between 1961 and 1966. In this same period, private brand share in many nondurables declined.

Turning now to some structural characteristics of industries, contrary to what one might expect, bigness in manufacturing seems to stimulate private labeling as a competitive strategy, rather than choke it off. We found that private label share seems to increase with the level of concentration in manufacturing–up to a point. Where the top four manufacturers control as much as, say, 90 per cent of total volume, this tendency seems to be cut short. But if private brand production becomes a strong competitive weapon as bigness in manufacturing increases, we might see, even in highly concentrated industries, nonleading manufacturers turning to private brand production as one way to sap the strength of market leaders.

Bigness in branding can also be pinned down, and it is surprisingly uniform in the consumer products we examined. On the average, we found that about 20 per cent of the brands available in a product line capture some 90 per cent of the volume. This dominance in branding pinpoints the difficulty faced by new brands, with either type of ownership, in breaking into a market successfully.

Another thing we found is that bigness in branding is not limited to manufacturers alone. One out of every five market leaders is a distributor's brand and it gets a proportionate share of the volume.

The top ranking manufacturers' and distributors' brands seem to have consolidated their strength over the last decade. In several product lines, the leading brands account for a larger total share of volume today than ten years ago.

We attempted to assess the relationship between private branding and some key marketing forces. One of these was advertising. We found that the dollars spent on national advertising in a given product category tend to *grow* with increases in private brand share—up to a point. This point seems to be reached when private brands obtain about 60 per cent of the volume. At this level of private brand penetration, the amount of money spent on advertising leading national brands tends to decline.

The initial increase is probably due, in part, to advertisers taking steps to head off the inroads being made by private brands. But part of it is probably due to changes in the market itself, as we can see by looking at the product life-cycle concept.

Products with the highest private brand share were in the decline stage of their life cycle; and those with the lowest share, in the introductory stage. But there was a more important relationship between changes in private brand share and the life cycle. Whatever gains private brands make tend to come in the growth stage of a life cycle. Changes in the share of market for both manufacturers' and distributors' brands tend to stabilize by the time products enter the decline and saturation stage of the product life cycle.

Price is another key marketing factor which was examined. As one might expect, large percentage price differentials tend to go with high private brand share, and small percentage price differentials with low private brand share in *nondurable products.* However, there seems to be *no* clear relationship for *durable products.*

When examining price differentials for nondurables over time, we found that the *annual changes* in percentage price differentials for a single product line had little or no relationship to changes in private brand share. Percentage price differentials went up and down from one year to the next without *any* clear effect upon private brand share of product volume.

## FACTORS AFFECTING MANUFACTURERS' BRAND POLICIES

The following questions are relevant to our discussion of manufacturers' brand policies and programs:

1. *Who* produces private brands?

2. *Why* does a firm produce them?
3. Is it *profitable* to produce private brands?
4. *What* are some of the *risks* involved?

There are three alternative brand policies to be considered:

1. *Manufacturers' brand policy*—where the firm does not produce any private brands.
2. *Mixed brand policy*—where the firm produces both its own brands and private brands for distributors.
3. *Distributors' brand policy*—where the manufacturer produces only private brands.

It is possible to generalize about manufacturer behavior on the basis of whether or not the firm produces private brands. For example, distributors' brand policy firms tend to be small and generally under 50 million dollars in sales volume, while manufacturers' and mixed brand policy firms tend to be large and usually over 100 million dollars in sales.

Many distributors' brand firms are not new—many existed prior to World War II and the emergence of a sellers' market and the discount house. In fact, many of these firms were very successful financially in the pre-war era.

Irrespective of product category, the findings show that there is a definite trend toward more mixed brand policy firms. Also, the number of distributors' brand firms has been declining. There are some important reasons for this growth in mixed brand firms and the associate decline in manufacturers' and distributors' brand firms. For example, a number of manufacturers' brand and mixed brand firms are acquiring or merging with distributors' brand firms. Also, some of the present distributors' brand policy firms are facing survival difficulties—managerial problems, insufficient capital financing, or sales declines.

Furthermore, there is evidence to suggest that the trend toward more mixed brand firms will continue. Over half of the manufacturer respondents in our study indicated there is a softening attitude among manufacturers' brand firms toward considering mixed brand programs. An example of this softening attitude may be found in the comments made by a vice president of an over 300-million-dollar grocery products company:

> . . . firms continuously ask us to produce private labels for them at a low price . . . I ask them what they are willing to pay . . . I just wonder if a firm will someday ever offer us a price at which we can afford to produce. . . . *unlike in our past,* we will at least sit down with private label prospects even though the sessions may not be fruitful . . . .

Just what are some of the reasons why a manufacturers' brand policy firm would pursue a mixed brand program?

No producer has safeguards which prevent any one of its manufacturers' brand customers from deciding to establish his own private brand program. If the customer represents an important volume, the manufacturers may find it difficult to refuse his private brand business. Furthermore, the firm may be reluctant to permit a competing producer to secure the distributors' brand business.

Also, manufacturers' brand producers are frequently motivated to create a mixed brand policy in order to accommodate their present customers who currently buy private brands from other suppliers. In return, the customer may be willing to give the manufacturer's brand desirable shelf space or other forms of sales promotion.

A mixed brand policy enables a firm to produce distributors' brands on a short-run basis if there should be a sudden decline in the firm's manufacturers' brand market share; or temporary excess capacity; or period of brand policy formulation. This stop-gap principle is employed particularly by firms producing nondurable products.

Mixed brand policy firms may use similar production and marketing resources to produce their national and private brands. Unlike before, mixed brand manufacturers are *not* producing two entirely different products under the national and private brand generally because of cost considerations. Furthermore, large retailers increasingly require relatively high levels of product quality for their private brands.

Some manufacturers pursue a mixed brand program primarily because of the hope for increased profits of the firm. We found that two distinct costing philosophies existed among manufacturers of private brands:

Either private brands are thought of as "plus business" produced on an incremental cost basis, *or* private brands are considered as an integral part of the business and treated like manufacturers' brands in terms of proportionate cost allocation and profit contribution.

Those firms which produced private brands as "plus business" failed to allocate sufficiently such costs as research and development, administration, factory burden, and marketing services. For example, two-thirds of all the manufacturing firms in our study failed to allocate fully research and development costs to the private brand segment of their business. Over half of all the manufacturer respondents failed to allocate all of the administrative costs associated with their firms' private brands. Most of the firms said that bargaining and negotiation was a major factor in setting the price to private brand customers.

We were able to relate the firm's private brand costing practices to profitability. In other words, mixed brand firms were more successful if they took the matter of private branding seriously.

In general, manufacturers' brand firms are more profitable than mixed brand and distributors' brand firms (see Figure 2). However, when the net profits of mixed brand policy firms were compared with average industry profits, we found that about 40 per cent of these firms were above the industry average (see Figure 3).

Figure 2. Brand policy and profits on sales

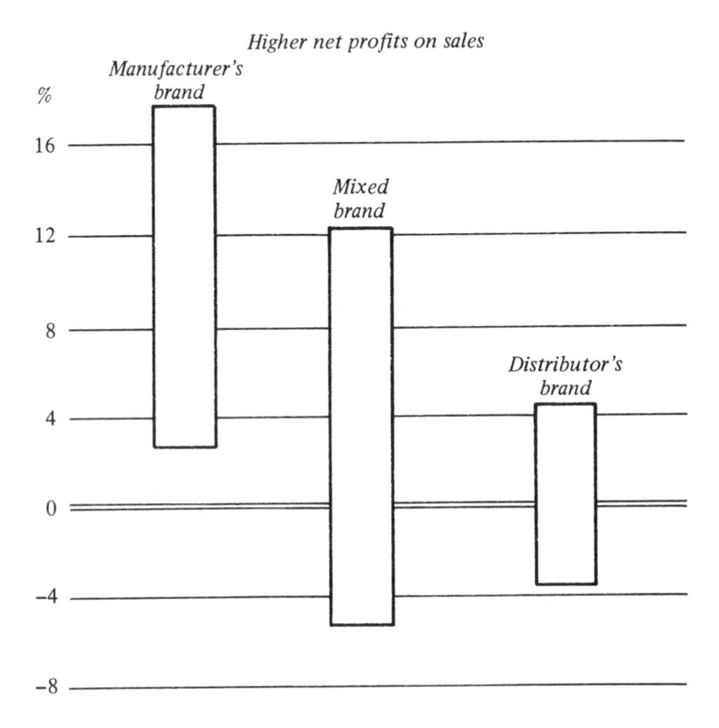


We were able to identify some of the important characteristics of these above average or successful mixed brand firms. For example, these firms have formal policies concerning the production of private brands. The firms are committed to private brand programs.

Generally, the successful firms had private brand administrators which reported to the vice-president of marketing. The administrator coordinated all the activities relating to the firm's private brand activities.

Private brand program planning was a key element among successful mixed brand firms. These firms not only knew why they were involved in a mixed brand program, but had policies and procedures regarding:

- the conditions under which distributors' brand production should increase or decrease as a per cent of output;
- the negotiation and drafting of contracts;
- the servicing of distributors' brand accounts.

Successful companies usually have predetermined criteria for selecting private brand accounts. These firms generally have minimum volume requirements. Long-run (or

Figure 3. Brand policy and industry profits

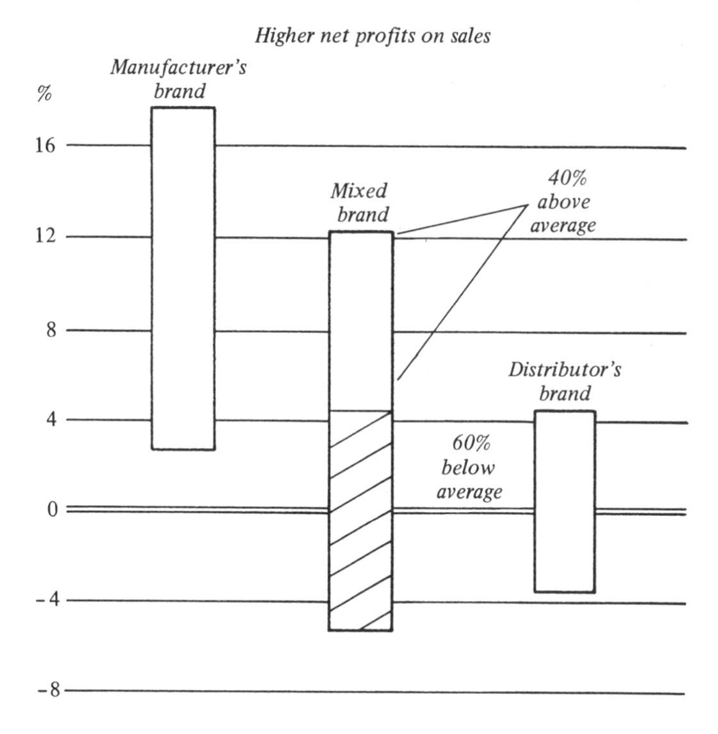


continuous supply) relationships are sought as opposed to "one shot deals." These manufacturers *expect* a profit return and refuse accounts which fail to recognize this.

Mixed brand firms are offering greater services for their private brand accounts. There was evidence that well-developed private brand programs take good advantage of the firm's existing marketing resources such as:

- sales personnel,
- product planning and development facilities,
- inventory control systems,
- promotional capabilities.

With few exceptions, most of the successful mixed brand firms offered similar products to private brand customers. In fact, most firms employ the same production control and testing techniques for both brands. The recognized and acknowledged physical differences were due primarily to product appearance and packaging distinctions.

Both durable and nondurable product manufacturers generally have formalized written contracts with their private brand accounts.

Formal periodic review of private brand programs was a frequent practice among successful mixed brand policy firms. The manufacturer examines the profit contributions made by the private brand program. The effects of the program upon production and marketing are examined.

Also, review of the program from the standpoint of their customers is very important. In fact, several manufacturers indicated that periodic review included inviting the private brand account executives to visit the manufacturer's offices to evaluate present and future supplier-buyer relationships. Future plans of the manufacturer are discussed regarding new products, new building programs, or new research programs.

When examining the reasons why a manufacturers' brand policy producer would embark upon a mixed brand program, a new kind of mixed brand firm emerged. These firms are generally characterized by:

- sales volume of over 200 million dollars;
- inability to achieve a position of market dominance other than the number two or three position in the industry;
- relatively high product differentiation costs, such as personal selling, sales promotion, advertising, and product features;
- relatively good production and marketing capabilities.

You may be interested in an example of a grocery products firm which fit these characteristics and pursued a mixed brand program. This firm:

- had net sales in excess of half a billion dollars;
- began a well-planned program of selling to private branders *after* an extensive two-year research study of private brand marketing.
- prepared a customer's handbook describing the firm's private brand production capabilities, product quality, packaging, promotion, administration, pricing and costing procedures, and minimum order requirements.
- selected several high volume grocery chains as target accounts;
- did not vary the formula or the containers (except for labels) from its manufacturers' brand product;
- in fact, produced the same formula and used the same containers for each of its private brand accounts;
- assisted its accounts with promotional strategies and programs.

Now you may wonder about the success of this firm's selective program of private branding. Some of the results are as follows:

- at retail, the private brand product is offering a challenge to the industry's market leader;
- the retailer's markup on the private label is well above the gross margin on most manufacturers' brands;
- the producer has increased volume and improved profits.

A mixed brand policy program is not without its possible risks to the manufacturer. For example, mixed brand firms face the risk of possible exposure of confidential cost data. More and more distributors are seeking known cost contracts. In fact, some manufacturers stated that a few private brand distributors required access to the firm's cost accounting records. Such confidential cost data could be made available to competing firms, if the distributor should change suppliers.

The practice of "cherry picking" is another risk. This is the practice of a private brand merchandiser's splitting his buying among two or more producers on the basis of getting the very best of each supplier's product–particularly within a given product line. Thus, a supplier may be deprived of expected higher volume accounts. Some suppliers will not generally sell private brands to competing buyers (such as Wards and Sears).

Some manufacturers have been reluctant to produce private brands for fear of criticism from the wholesaler and/or retailer customers who sell the products under the manufacturers' brand.

A private brand program may cause a producer to become so preoccupied with its successful development that the manufacturers' brand program suffers–"the tail wags the dog."

A firm's involvement in producing private brands may produce adverse effects upon the firm's profit position–particularly if the philosophy of "plus business" is adopted. Improper cost accounting and failure to plan a distirbutors' brand program generally result in a firm's continuing to produce private brands without ever knowing that anticipated profits are never realized.

Governmental regulations represent one very important area which may well affect the future success of private brand programs. For example, branding policies may be affected by the results of industry hearings and investigations, pending court cases, and regulatory agency rulings. As many of you know, the Borden case is one of the most current branding issues before government and marketing. The FTC charged the Borden Company with violating Section 2(a) of the Robinson-Patman Act, as a result of selling "like grade and quality" evaporated milk to customers at different prices. The importance of the case to marketers centers around the fact that *private brand* customers bought the product for less than *manufacturers' brand* customers. Although the ten-year-old case has not ended, the Supreme Court has made one significant decision: ". . . labels do not differentiate products for the purpose of determining grade or quality."[1]

It shoudl be stressed that this decision does not mean the end of private branding. There are alternatives for the manufacturer. However, it does appear that the Supreme Court decision opens up another big question which must someday be reconciled by government and marketing: "Given a manufacturer producing both his own and a private brand, what constitutes the minimum or acceptable level of physical product differentiation between the brands for purposes of remaining outside the jurisdiction of Section 2(a) of the Robinson-Patman Act?"

## GUIDELINES FOR EXPLAINING DISTRIBUTORS' BRAND POLICIES

The question we want to consider now is: "What are some of the more important factors that lead a distributor, or retailer, to adopt his own brand?"

[1] U. S. Bureau of National Affairs, Inc., *The United States Law Week,* XXXIV, March 22, 1966, p. 4288.

First, some minimum requirements exist for a distributor to launch a private brand program in any product line. These may be called the "Threshold Volume Requirements." There are wide differences in these requirements from one product category to another. For example, we estimated the threshold volume in a canned food specialty to be $150,000 annually at retail. In contrast, threshold volume in some consumer durables was estimated to be $10 million annually at retail. But while threshold volume limits smaller retailers, it does not explain why a large distributor with volume greater than threshold requirements goes heavily into his own brand in some lines and not at all in others.

One important distinction is that two basic sets of operating conditions cause different factors to come into play in private brand policy determination. Distributors place *emphasis on short-term or tactical considerations* when entry into private branding is relatively easy. Ease of entry is reflected in the following operating conditions:

1. limited dollar commitment to distributors' brands, or threshold volume requirements with brand policy determined on a product-by-product basis;
2. no major changes in normal merchandising operations required by private brand;
3. no after-purchase-service; and
4. short-term supplier contracts.

When *opposite conditions hold,* distributors were found to place *emphasis on longer-term or strategic considerations* in brand policy determination.

Private brand decisions based on tactical factors come into sharpest focus with special merchandise operations, like grocery chains, while the strategic considerations can be viewed most clearly in the case of durable goods marketing by general merchandise chains like Sears and Pennys.

Seven short-term factors emerged in most of the interviews as important considerations in the decision to "go" or "not go" into private labels in a given product category. These are:

1. product category sales volume;
2. profit potential;
3. supply price;
4. strength of leading brands;
5. competitors' success with private brands;
6. nature of the product; and
7. day-to-day merchandising requirements.

We examined these seven factors—the ones that distributors think important in brand policy determination—and looked at how they fit into the branding decisions of several large chains. Although we were able to get only a limited amount of cost and profit data, it was clear that distributors take these considerations very seriously. And from our interpretation of how distributors make brand policy decisions, we came up with a notion that seems useful in explaining situations where tactical factors are emphasized.

It seemed that several of these short-term factors could be summarized in a single measure which we called the "Distributors' Brand Profit Differential."

The Distributors' Brand Profit Differential is based on the idea that a private brand must show an added profit opportunity, above that gained from a sales mix composed entirely of manufacturers' brands. In this way, distributors view their own label as one of several available in a product category. The private brand becomes attractive when it adds more to dollar "product profits," or total profit in the category, than to "product costs," or handling and selling expenses. A private brand's share of costs can be approximated by taking its share of unit volume. This assumes the costs of moving each brand in a category vary directly with unit volume. An initial estimate of the Distributors' Brand Profit Differential becomes the per cent difference between the share of gross profits a private brand earns in the category and the share of costs it generates, as illustrated in Figure 4.

The initial estimate of the Profit Differential may be improved by including assignable costs and revenues which vary by brand. For example, sales promotion and advertising costs may be higher for the distributor's brand. Special administrative time may be needed. Separate quality testing and control may be necessary. On the other side,

**Figure 4. Basis of the distributors' brand profit differential**

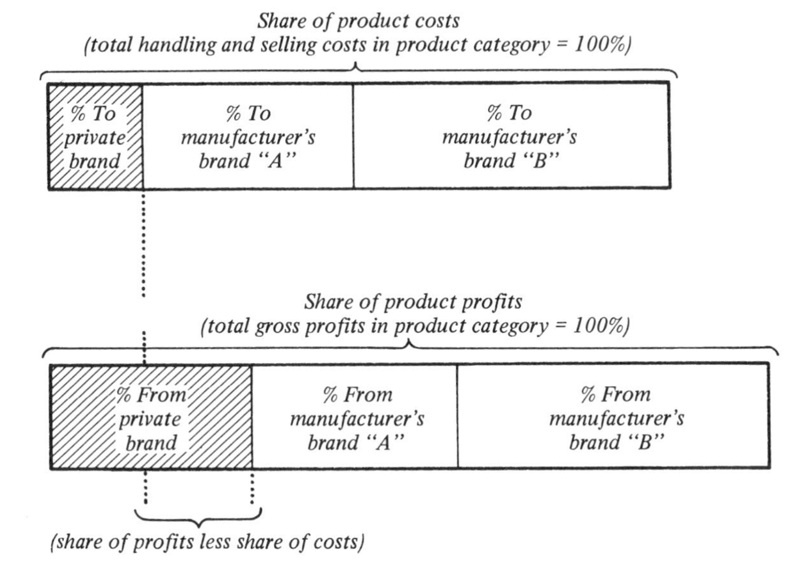

manufacturers' brands sometimes carry special promotional allowances from suppliers not available under the private label. Each of these assignable costs or receipts is included in the estimated Distributors' Brand Profit Differential to give a more realistic picture of profit potential.

If the Distributors' Brand Profit Differential turns out to be negative, as it might when compared with an offering of highly profitable, fast turning manufacturers' brands, the private label probably would not be adopted by the distributor. If the Distributors' Brand Profit Differential is slightly positive, say between 1 and 3 per cent, a profit advantage exists, and the private brand becomes attractive. And as the Profit Differential grows, the advantage in adding a private brand becomes so great there is a tendency for distributors to push their own label to a larger share of product sales volume.

While we did not find distributors using the notion of a Distributors' Brand Profit Differential, the measure reflects fairly well the way they view relative profitability in brand policy determination. In addition, this measure makes use of cost, volume, and profit data normally available to distributors and does not require computer processing.

Two of the short-term factors suggested earlier cannot be worked directly into a profit measure. These are:

1. nature of the product; and
2. day-to-day merchandising needs.

They can have an important effect too. For example, distributors shy away from products that are not easily duplicated under their own brand. These are products with unique recipes or formulas like some prepared foods and toiletry items. On the other hand, some products may be put under the distributors' brand to satisfy a special merchandising need, or to fill out a price line or quality gap. These two factors could alter policies which might be expected on the basis of "high" or "low" short-term profit.

Five basic tactical or short-term factors were found to explain situations where distributors develop private brand programs on a product-by-product basis. The conditions are as follows:

- large dollar sales volume in the product category;
- estimated private brand sales in excess of Threshold Volume Requirements;
- positive Distributors' Brand Profit Differential;
- standardized product, from standpoint of both demand and physical characteristics;
- short-term merchandising need.

The strategic considerations, however, are different. Short-term gains are not sufficient reasons to develop a private brand program when:

1. large dollar commitment, or high threshold volume, is involved;
2. major changes in merchandising programs are required;
3. after-purchase-service is necessary; and
4. long-term supplier contracts are the rule.

Since consumer durable marketing by general merchandise chains offers the best illustration of a situation where strategic factors dominate brand policy determination, let us take a look at these operations now.

Short-term profit is not a big factor in brand policy decision for general merchandise chains. If it were, many of these firms would probably have remained with manufacturers' brands in consumer durables. Most of the executives responsible for private brand programs in durables suggested that prior short-term profit experience with national brands was satisfactory. The decision to develop their own brands was not made because manufacturers' brands were not highly profitable in the short run.

Distributors' brand policies were based on these key strategic factors:

- *control* over marketing planning and performance,
- *selective use* of manufacturers' capabilities,
- *central planning* of merchandise operations without interference from competing brands at store level,
- *store/brand franchise* development.

At some stage in the growth of multi-line, interregional merchandising organizations, programs built around manufacturers' brands in consumer durables are *too inflexible* to meet the organization's changing requirements. This stage is well beyond threshold volume and seems to be reached when a general merchandise chain believes its greatest long-term advantage rests in a program with such key factors as follows:

- centralized purchasing from suppliers,
- product lines tailored to the *distributor's* requirements–not what the supplier feels is best,
- merchandising programs which emphasize local advertising at lower rates,
- in-store promotion,
- desire for a brand which precludes direct comparison shopping and loss-leader price cutting.

Overall, we found that general merchandise chains believe these and other similar strategic factors, taken collectively, make *long-term* growth in product volume and departmental profitability greater under their own brands than with manufacturers' brands.

## CONCLUSIONS

The forces giving rise to private branding, whether environmental or corporate, are varied and complex. One overall impression that emerges from this study is that private branding is no longer marketing's stepchild. The "battle of the brands" has not been won, but has changed in form and dimension. There may be some truth in a statement from a leading merchandising executive: "Yesterday's antagonists have become today's protagonists, and yesterday's battle has become today's competitive coexistence."

# 34. THE FUNCTIONS OF ADVERTISING IN OUR CULTURE

*Irving S. White*

*The viewpoint set forth in the following article is that the role of advertising cannot be understood, nor can it be effective, unless there is an understanding of . . . how the* product *is perceived as part of the culture, how the* brand name *functions as a "short-hand" description of meaning, and how* product-use experience *serves as a feedback to consumers.*

The function of advertising in our culture may be characterized in two theoretical ways.

First, there are those who state the theory within the framework of economic laws, asserting that advertising affects knowledge about the demand for a product.

This article attempts to develop a second orientation. It is that the function of advertising is to help to organize and modify the *basic perceptual processes* of the consumer, so that he is guided toward *seeing* and *feeling* a product in a given predictable way.

*Advertising as a Perceptual Process.* With the recently formed partnership between the social scientist and the marketing professional, some foundation has been laid for a general reorientation toward understanding this influence as a dynamic process between communicators and perceivers. David Ogilvy and other advertising practitioners

Source: From *Journal of Marketing,* vol. 24, July, 1959, pp. 8–14. Irving S. White: Director of Creative Research Associates, Chicago.

have formally incorporated terms such as "brand image" as applied to various advertised products. Journalists such as Martin Mayer have come to see advertising as affecting the "values" of a product.[1]

Yet "images" and "values" have no meaning outside of the experience and outlook of the consumer as a personality and the consumer-market as a social group. Gardner and Levy, influenced by the social psychology of George Herbert Mead, have shown how consumers are swayed toward or against a product because of the way a brand image is perceived.[2] And Martineau's *Motivation in Advertising* is a practical and lucid application of that proposition.[3]

It is a truism that the function of advertising is to inform and sell. But the more basic theoretical question is, how does advertising perform this function?

*The Variables of Consumer Experience.* Most advertisers would agree that advertising should orient the consumer toward a consistent, and usually pleasurable, relationship with their products. Consistency implies a rather stable organization of meanings and values centering around a product as an "object" in one's life. It is this consistency which gives what is often called "character" to a product or service. Cadillacs, for example, have traditionally meant specific mechanical, aesthetic, and social experiences to their adherents. Buying a Cadillac has often meant success and power to the purchaser, and the conviction that in several years from the time of puchase his car would still connote the same qualities. Pleasure merely means that the consumer derives gratifications out of this object-relationship that motivate him toward repeating and reinforcing the experience.

To structure the experience of the potential consumer along lines of consistent and predictable satisfactions requires an understanding of the total source of meanings, the *whole* interaction between the consumer and the product. For any advertiser, there is a certain amount of realistic humility inherent in the knowledge that advertising is only one of the several sources of stimulation that a product contains for the individual in society. The influences of culture and of private sensations modify and intermingle with the stimuli of advertising to achieve the final pattern of relationship between the seller's product (or ideas and services) and the consumer. What perceptions can advertising influence, and what can it not?

Even to begin to answer this question means an investigation of the structure of the product as an "object" in relationship with the individual. After interviewing hundreds of consumers, utilizing techniques of different levels of penetration, getting at "unconscious" and "conscious" attitudes and needs, three sources of meaning about a product have been isolated.

[1] Martin Mayer, *Madison Avenue, U.S.A.*, Harper and Brothers, New York, 1958.

[2] Burleigh B. Gardner and Sidney J. Levy, "The Product and the Brand," *Harvard Business Review*, vol. 33, no. 2, March–April, 1955, pp. 33–39.

[3] Pierre Martineau, *Motivation in Advertising*, McGraw-Hill Book Company, New York, 1957.

The first source is the set of meanings stemming from the *cultural definition of* the product. The second source of meaning comes from the consumer's organized set of notions about the brand, that is, the *brand image.* The third source of meaning is from direct *experience with the product.*

## CULTURAL DEFINITION OF THE PRODUCT

Social psychology and anthropology have dealt with the problem of objects in culture. That is, how do people come to understand and relate in a socially consistent manner to artifacts that are with them from time of birth?

The concept of "object" implies more than just a unidirectional flow of activity from the manipulator to the manipulated. It also implies a set of stimulations and communications in the reverse direction that guide the actions of the user. This means a dynamic relationship between the artifact and the user, wherein the latter perceives and acts upon the former according to the organized meanings that the culture and its subcultures have formulated for it.

The fact that few objects are naturally and intrinsically what they seem to be has been clearly indicated by such thinkers as George Herbert Mead, Jean Piaget, and Heinz Werner. A child growing up within a society begins by viewing an object in a idiosyncratic, self-centered way, and gradually redefines his relationship to it in terms of the broader, adult society. The acculturated individual internalizes the way the general society view the artifact, and sees the product in a setting of needs and values that control his action and attitudes about it. For example, there is nothing intrinsic in a baseball bat toaccount for its relationship to its user; a member of a primitive society could easily mistake it for a weapon.

It is perhaps more accurate to think of culture as involving a "climate of valuations" rather than being a thing apart from people. "Climate" implies the possibility for shift, and "valuations" suggests that the climate is made up of ideas, beliefs, feelings, and actions expressed by people. Yet the word "culture" as an abstraction also implies that the whole is greater than the sum of its parts, and that people learn from and conform to the patterns of people as a whole.

Elvis Presley in his early exposure on television and in popular music was responded to by a host of individual teen-agers who reacted to him with their own private senses. As Presley grew as an ideal, teen-agers were no longer free to accept him or reject him simply as individuals. They had to cope with a new level of values—that of the teen-age *society.*

Sometimes the important patterns of behavior and perception are learned from smaller reference groups, as adolescents, for example, respond to popular records. Sometimes learning is funneled through the larger, common culture, as in the singing of "The Star Spangled Banner." Although adults live in the same culture, they do not see a popular hit in the same light as teen-agers. Nor do non-Americans respond to the national anthem in the same was as Americans. An object or an idea differentiates itself along lines of the implied *membership* behind it.

Culture places the product in a social context and imbues it with meanings that set the broadest limitations on how it is expereinced. A commerical product becomes culturally defined by the broad history of interaction with its market. In particular, the definition is determined by the social, biological, and psychic needs the product fulfills for its user. Thus, when a product achieves a niche in its cultural context, it is an object which denotes *consistent* (*not* unalterable) and *predictable* behavior within the social structure.

The ballpoint pen, for example, is intrinsically nothing but a complex set of tactile and visual sensations. These sensations are selected and modified by its user, according to the cultural definition of a ballpoint pen, and purposively placed in a social setting. That is, the object becomes perceived by the consumer. The result is that the user experiences a handy, easy-to-use, and relatively inexpensive tool for communicating his thoughts.

*Advertising and Culture.* Cultural influence is obvious when one thinks of how a cigarette in the mouth of a woman may be perceived today as compared to how it was perceived thirty or forty years ago. The above-the-ankle skirt might have indicated many qualities about its wearer during the last century that would be fallacious today.

Advertising must take account of the current values and product-definitions of the society (or subsociety) in which it intends to operate. In other words, advertisers must be aware of the role of the object in the life of the consumer. Likewise, advertisers must understand the limits of these broader cultural definitions before trying to amplify the product into a brand image.

For example, the social values implied by the concept "perfume" are such that its users are necessarily considered feminine. Any attempt by advertising to contradict the strong mores inherent in such a cultural definition might backfire as a commercial enterprise. Advertisers of male cosmetics and other self-indulgent items have discovered that they must carefully conceal the femininity and narcissism involved in colognes.

Culturally, then, the function of advertising is to understand, to reflect, and in most instances to accept the value-structure of society before it can go about its creative task of helping to organize in a consistent, gratifying manner the numerous stimulations a product contains for the potential consumer. Advertising can help to select and reinforce certain values and needs inherent in the role of the product. It can operate within the limits of culture to create new expectations for the consumer.

Occasionally an entire society may entertain negative or distorted notions about a product that may be a result of an unfortunate long-standing history between object and consumer. The potential for a limited, positive redefinition on a societal or subsocietal scale may exist in the case of such products.

The reader may think of numerous examples of products and services, the mere mention of which sends a wave of disdain, fear, disgust, discomfort, and other negative reactions through him. Spinach, dentists, hypodermic needles, and long underwear are examples of "objects" with a positive function subordinated to the unfavorable experiences behind them.

In these cases, advertising can embark on the Herculean task of pointing up new avenues of more pleasurable interaction between the product and the consumer, and reformulate aspects of the cultural definitions of a product class. Of course, true reformulation lies in the response by the consumer society to the communicator's message. If the message is consistent with the society's experiences, an advertising-success story may indeed occur in a social movement toward a product. In such instances, reformulation is based on a pleasure-pain principle that promises to take the consumer from an unsatisfying relationship to a gratifying one.

For example, dental care in the mind of the average American is fraught with annoyance and discomfort, on the one hand, or with special precaution, compulsiveness, and concern on the other. Dental care and dentists are too often associated with a conception of teeth as a set of nuisances which nature ordained shall be in one's mouth. The American Dental Association is trying to reorient the client toward conceiving of his teeth and their care in the positive light of self-grooming and social reward in much the manner of the cosmetic industries.[4]

And when the Tea Bureau suggested that tea is the "hefty, hale, and hearty" drink for the average man, it was attempting to counter the stereotyped notions of effeteness, femininity, and snobbishness culturally attributed to the drink.

If the program of redefinition dramatically and effectively brings a product closer to the experience of the consumer, a new cognitive orientation toward the product will take place. Success in changing a popular concept depends upon how intense and stable, how true to experience, is the cultural tradition concerning products, ideas, or services.

Although advertising can help to reorganize some of the social interaction between a consumer and a product, it must be sensitive enough to these patterns to recognize their intensity and stability. An extremely exotic product, perhaps suitable for a small elite group, cannot be converted into a mundane, mass product *merely* by advertising.

## THE BRAND IMAGE AS A SOURCE OF MEANING

The cultural definition of a product is too broad and generalized to allow a consumer to select a brand. It helps to create the initial set of expectations about the product which is then qualified by the second variable in product-consumer interaction, the brand image.

[4] "A Motivational Study of Dental Care: A Pilot Investigation," prepared for the American Dental Association by Social Research, Inc., in the *Journal of the American Dental Association,* serialized in vol. 56, March, April, May, and June, 1958.

The brand image, as a source of meaning, helps the consumer further to select and organize the stimulations of the product, display, and other communications directed to him. Mead's social psychology suggests that an "image" guides one's actions and attitudes toward the object.[5]

It has been further suggested that the *meaning* of any message is the "change which it produces in the (already existing) image" that an individual harbors about the object in question.[6] This means that the message value of a television commerical, for example, lies in the degree and direction of change in a brand image previously held by the viewer. (Reinforcement of an already existing image implies a change in degree.)

Differences among brand images represent much more than literal product differences. A whole different set of notions and actions are inherent in the name "Lincoln" as compared with the name "Jaguar," despite the fact that each make has at least one or two models that are functionally comparable. It is somewhat difficult to imagine the typical Lincoln owner sitting behind the wheel of the typical Jaguar. The difference in the two images is, therefore, more intricate than the simple differences between the two lines of cars.

Tests of consumer reactions to various products and their advertisements indicate that the brand image may undergo change more quickly than the basic cultural definition of the product. Perception of the brand image is more capable of being influenced than is the perception of the general class of the product. This is logical, as the image is formulated within the limits of a culture.

The changes which took place in the brand images of certain filter cigarettes, for example, were fairly swift once the underlying cultural attitudes about filter cigarettes were modified by broader social influences affecting their definition, such as science, medicine, group hysteria. Marlboro could become a *manly* cigarette rather quickly once society relaxed its notions about who might smoke such a cigarette.

The image of the brand appears to be a relatively stable organization of percepts about a product. Once established, a brand image lends the consistency and predictability in the consumer's relationship with the product which allow him to select and experience those aspects of the product he values. Schweppes quinine water must indeed be a different experience to those who have responded to its image than is that of several other brands. The senses become attuned differently, and the social values inherent in the product-consumer interaction are different from brand to brand.

*Advertising and the Brand Image.* The major influence of advertising appears to be felt in the area of consumer perception of the brand. The brand image is the major organizing concept through which the consumer is guided toward perceiving unified patterns of stimulation. This imagery provides the emotional and sensual qualities

[5] George Herbert Mead, *Mind, Self, and Society,* edited by Charles W. Morris, University of Chicago Press, Chicago, 1934.

[6] Kenneth E. Boulding, *The Image,* University of Michigan Press, Ann Arbor, 1956, p. 7.

which distinguish a brand from the general product-class and help the consumer discriminate from brand to brand.

Jello is not just a gelatin dessert, nor are Jello and Royal simply two products united by their common class. For the purchaser of a brand, there is usually a feeling that one has purchased a product distinctly different from another brand. This is probably most obvious in the case of beer and cigarettes.

This is the clue to what is often termed the "irrational" motive of the consumer in purchasing products. Skeptics, classic economists, and behaviorists in market research might demonstrate by blindfold tests how suggestible the average consumer is. They point out that the average consumer cannot distinguish between a Camel or a Philip Morris, or between Schlitz and Miller.

What such a literal understanding of the product-consumer relationship fails to consider is that *the value of a brand and its overall symbolic effects on the consumer cannot be teased apart by tests oriented toward seeing the product in its barest, utilitarian terms.*

Another way of saying this is that the consumer purchases the brand and its cluster of meanings as much as he purchases the literal product. What Vance Packard calls "hidden persuasion" is probably the reference-group and other symbolic values implied in most social communications.[7]

The function of advertising is to create strong subcategories of values and needs within the social structure, and to associate these with the product. Consumers may then select those brands whose sets of implied experiences fit into the sub-group with which he identifies.

The *Chicago Tribune* study on cigarettes and smokers clearly indicated that it is as reasonable to talk about the man who smokes Camels, for example, as having a "Camel personality" as it is to say that the brand itself has a personality.[8] It is reasonable because the two are correlates of each other. To the extent that the consumer perceives the brand image in this stable, predictable (and pleasurable) manner, the brand becomes a need-satisfying monopoly rather than a competitor with other brands. The power of the monopoly is dependent on the degree to which the brand is differentiated from other brands and is pleasurable at the same time.

If this aspect of the function of advertising is recognized, much of the arrogant and sanctimonious tone in some advertising can be relieved and a positive program of distinctive image development put in its place.

This relationship between the consumer and the brand must be understood by the advertiser in the earliest stages of planning if some measure of control and predictability in one's message is to be realized. If it is believed that facial tissue "A" can

[7]Vance Packard, *The Hidden Persuaders,* David McKay Company, Inc., New York, 1957.

[8]*Cigarettes: Their Role and Function, A Study for the Chicago Tribune,* prepared by Social Research, Inc., Chicago, 1953.

appeal to an important part of the market not adequately tapped by facial tissue "B," its advertisers must understand both the expectancies of this market and how advertising might serve to fit in with, reinforce, and organize these sets into a satisfying perceptual whole.

## DIRECT EXPERIENCE WITH THE PRODUCT AS A SOURCE OF MEANING

The third perceptual area is that of direct experience, the *use* which classical theory states determines the *utility* of the product and ultimately its demand. By direct experience with a product, a consumer finally gets his "feedback" in terms of social gratifications and primary sensory experiences that the brand image and cultural definitions have set up for him.

In a sense, the consumer is not fully open to his experiences and is not likely to perceive all the stimuli of a product. His own needs, in conjunction with the social conceptions reinforced by the imagery surrounding the product, emphasize certain aspects of direct experience and weed out others.

In some research on the ballpoint pen, for example, consumers were asked to describe their *writing* experiences with three brands of pens. One of these pens is a brand which stresses efficiency and predictability. The second brand emphasizes a general quality of competence, including prestige and status. The third brand focuses on inexpensiveness and dispensability.

Consumers described their experiences with the pens in terms of the generalized brand image, giving evidence of an awareness of how they were oriented toward the product. It is fairly evident that technical product improvements alone, unless they are highly dramatic or extreme, do not radically alter the consumer's previous ideas about the product. Some outside agent must serve to create a new expectation about the product that will allow the consumer to perceive the difference.

*Advertising and Direct Experience with the Product.* The function of advertising in this third area of consumer perception is to supply the *terms* in which the product is valued. In some ways advertising sets up a "self-fulfilling prophecy."[9] Most researchers are aware that a consumer's reaction to use is channeled in an important way by what he expects to experience. The terms in which the consumer responds to use are, in good part, supplied by advertising. The facets of experience beyond the scope of advertising are the concrete physiological sensations of the consumer.

Nor can broad organizing concepts, such as a cultural definition or a brand image, account for the unpredicted idiosyncrasies of either the consumer or the product. However, by the time the consumer has selected and organized all the communications of the product, he will evaluate the use experience in a fairly patterned manner.

[9] Robert K. Merton, "The Self-Fulfilling Prophecy," in Robert K. Merton, *Social Theory and Social Structure,* The Free Press of Glencoe, New York, 1949.

Too often, the advertiser is so close to competitive aspects of his product that he has personally defined it in a manner that is not of optimum value to the consumer. Competition often causes advertisers to "hop on the current bandwagon" of advertising claims and to shout loudly about values that have little positive meaning to the consumer. In the automobile industry, a complex language of power dynamics has been foisted upon the consumer. Is this the optimum language of use available for him? In filter cigarettes, the language of use among certain competitive brands has been the number of filter-traps contained in the cigarette. Is the filter-cigarette smoker aided in getting gratification out of a cigarette by a terminology that concentrates upon the negatives of smoking?

The advertiser might improve his relationship with the consumer if he realized that his characterization of the consumer's use-experience helps the latter selectively perceive out of the product's numerous stimulations. Direct experience with a product is patterned by the communicable language of the product which has been created or reinforced by advertising.

# *C. Packaging*

# 35. A THEORY OF PACKAGING IN THE MARKETING MIX

*William R. Mason*

*The choice of a product's package ought to represent a reconciliation of a variety of functions, just as is the case in choice of various selling efforts brought to bear on the product. In the following article we learn how each of these functions has potential merit in furthering the sale of the product; but how all of them are, in part at least, mutually exclusive.*

It is axiomatic that the job of packaging is to sell. But after that banality has been voiced, what guides to management judgment–what theories, if you will–influence the choice of a package?

This article is not a checklist of features that should be built into a package, but a rough guide to basic judgments management must bring to bear in its choice of packaging before the particulars of type face, combination of colors, package count, or printing method are up for decision.

The critical judgments that must be made on the packaging choice concern the "mix" of packaging attributes best able to perform, in different degrees, the particular functions of the package that are believed to be important to sales. The basic judgment in choice of packaging is "What jobs should the package do, and how completely should it do each?" The answers to the lesser decisions can fall into place once the "mix" of desirable packaging attributes has been determined, once the assignment of basic functions desired of the package has been made. Frequently, too much effort

Source: From *Business Horizons,* vol. 1, Summer, 1958, pp. 91–95. William R. Mason: Manager, Commercial Development, Nashua Corporation.

and time are devoted to making lesser decisions, usually on questions of graphic art, rather than this basic judgment.

The packager may accept as a guide, when making basic decisions on product "mix," that: *"The major purpose of any package is to influence or control the location of product storage within the marketing channel."* "Storage," as I am using the term, means the holding of goods for future use at any level along the marketing channel, *including the level of the ultimate consumer.* Even at the ultimate consumer level, the product may be stored in several places–sugar, for example, may be stored on a shelf or on the table. The packager is interested in getting the bulk of his product's storage as near as possible to the point of ultimate use.

The functions of the product's package are:

- protecting the product,
- adapting to production line speeds,
- promoting the product,
- increasing product density,[1]
- facilitating the use of the product,
- having re-use value for the consumer.

The performance of a package in the first two of these basic functions is relatively easy to measure through physical testing procedures. And, because it is comparatively easy to evaluate the degrees to which these functions are fulfilled by any package under consideration, such measurement is very common. Today, it must be a rare package that reaches its market without being rated objectively on its degrees of protection and production line adaptability. However, these ratings seem to be applied too often without consideration of the package's ability to fulfill its other possible functions.

There are four other major jobs that the package can do at least partially; these should be assigned priority by company management, but often they seem to be neglected.

All packages have the opportunity to perform, at least partially, each of these functions. But it is an unusual package that performs each to the same degree. That the package gives a superior performance of one function does not necessarily mean that it will give a superior performance of another. Because he needs to choose a package, the packager, whether he recognizes it or not, must assign priorities to the value of each of these functions to further his product's sale and use.

To illustrate, it is usually easy to create a package that has uniquely promotable features quite aside from graphic arts; that is, a package that could eminently perform the promotional function. But something else has to give. Using such a package may require sacrificing a good job in one of the other areas, for example in adaptability to production line speeds or in failure to increase package density. In like fashion, it is

[1] That is, increasing the ratio of product volume to package volume.

frequently possible to build a feature facilitating product use into a package—but not always without sacrificing some measure of product protection.

After all, when a package is criticized as a poor sales—or use—builder, it can be criticized fairly only when its performance of *each* of the basic functions is evaluated. A product may seem "overpackaged" simply because the packager's assignment of priorities differs from the critic's.

## INTERRELATIONSHIPS

Let's examine in a little more detail the way each function impinges on the others:

*Protecting the Product.* Beyond the requirements imposed by various governmental, carrier, and trade practice rulings, there usually are a substantial number of alternatives open to management with regard to product protection—even during the period when the product is in its distribution channel. To illustrate, even though a carrier ruling may require the product's 24-count carton to have a minimum corrugated fiberboard strength of, say, a 100-pound test, a company's management may choose board that meets more severe tests in order to permit higher stacking or use of mechanized materials-handling equipment by certain important handlers at various levels in the product's distribution channel. Accordingly, in such a situation, an opportunity to tailor the product's package to its product-protection job alone is relinquished because of a desire to better the package's performance of its density-increasing and promotional jobs.

But perhaps a more important range of product-protection considerations occurs at the time of product use—especially when the product is partially used. How much protection should the bread wrapper give a partially used load of bread? Will incorporating the use-facilitating features of a pouring spout or a tear tape opening require yielding too much product protection?

*Adapting to Production Line Speeds.* Sometimes the operating speeds of packaging equipment do not match the speeds of other equipment in the production line. Until recently, for instance, the normal operating speeds of wrapping machinery that would handle polyethylene film did not match the normal production line speeds for many products. Two or more wrapping machines were often required in a production line, and the results were poor space utilization, greater capital investment, and sometimes greater labor costs. As an alternative to these wastes, the packager "made do" with other types of film that could be handled by high-speed wrapping equipment but lacked some of polyethylene's protective attributes. New types of wrapping machines have largely corrected this situation. But the point is that the freedom of the packagers to better their packages' protective attributes was limited.

The question of a package's adaptability to production line speeds, however, usually crops up before the package is actually used. The packager's advertising agency or his sales department suggests a new package with striking promise of being able to fulfill the promotional or use-facilitating function better than current packaging; but, upon analysis, the suggested new package is found to require either slow-downs in production line speeds or investment in new packaging equipment. The company's management is then obliged to judge whether or not the suggested package's better performance of the promotional or use-facilitating functions justifies the slower line speed or the different packaging equipment.

*Promoting the Product.* Features may be built into a package which are promotable to consumers, to customers, and to intermediaries in its product's distribution channel. But sometimes a feature desirable for promotion to one of the three is not desirable for one of the others. Features that minimize a retailer's loss or pilferage are, presumably, important to him; but they are not necessarily of any interest to consumers. Features that minimize a consumer's embarrassment at purchase can increase a retailer's stacking or display difficulties and make inventory control more trying.

Even granting a package feature that is promotable regardless of level in its product's distribution or use, incorporation of the feature into the package frequently requires sacrificing some good package performance of one of the other basic package functions. For example, a gift-wrapped set-up box complete with nosegay of artificial flowers is a highly promotable candy package, as is a rigid plastic, resuable package for razors that is large enough to hold a fishing lure. But both packages sacrifice density for better promotion.

*Increasing Product Density.* This seems to be the area where the packager's sales department on the one hand, and his purchasing and production departments on the other, are most often in disagreement about the choice of packaging. Except on those occasions when the sales department recommends yielding a package's higher density in order to improve its promotional value, the sales department is usually advocating increased package density. It improves relations with carriers; it permits better utilization of space throughout the distribution channel, thus encouraging fuller inventory stocks in the pipeline; and it permits more units to be displayed per assigned running foot of self-service display space. But it frequently slows production line speeds and increases per-unit packaging cost.

Usually this issue turns on package shape. The cylinder, for instance, is an efficient package shape for liquids; a given measure of liquid can be packaged cylindrically with less material than is necessary for any rectangular container holding the same amount of liquid. But the normal 12-count (3 X 4 put-up) layer of a 24-count carton will occupy significantly less shelf space if it holds rectangular packages rather than the same number of cylindrical packages with the same amount of liquid.

But bettering a package's performance of its density-increasing function can inhibit good performance in other areas too. The density of many candy packages, for instance, could be improved significantly, but not without loss of their value as items specifically tailored for re-use as sewing baskets or cookie tins. Increasing density could also lessen the package's value as a promotional vehicle or as a promotable item in itself. Package designers seem better able to build points of brand differentiation into a 12-ounce beer bottle than into the higher-density 12-ounce beer can.

*Facilitating the Use of the Product.* Excluding changes in the graphic art of packages, most package changes in recent years have been in facilitating the product's use. All the changes to tear tapes, pouring spouts, squeeze bottles, aerosol cans, and so forth would have to be included here. And, as is obvious to anyone exposed to the mass advertising media, bettering the package's fulfillment of this function has proved to be a means of bettering the package's performance in promotion.

In many cases, however, where the use-facilitiating function of a package has been improved, a case can be built that some degree of product protection has been sacrificed. And, bettering the package's use-facilitating job sometimes means relinquishing some package value as a re-use container for the consumer. The flow of a viscous liquid perhaps can be directed a little more accurately or easily from the mouth of a narrow-necked glass jar than from a tin can, but packaging the liquid in the glass jar means sacrificing the protection against impact provided by the tin can. The tear tape makes a corrugated carton easier to open but, for many purposes, lessens its value as a re-usable container. Some shaker openings make cleanser or spice packages easy to use but, once used, leave the product exposed.

*Having Re-Use Value for the Consumer.* Perhaps the competition of the various functions of the package for recognition by company managements is most apparent in this area. In recent years, according much recognition to this function of the package seems not to have been in vogue. Typically, designing a package to do its other jobs well has meant slighting its re-use value—the previous illustrations of candy and razors notwithstanding. A package's re-use value generally has suffered with successive changes unless its re-usability has been very promotable.

## THE PRINCIPLE, THE COROLLARY, AND RECENT TRENDS

*How does management know whether it is better to sacrifice a measure of product protection for a more promotable package or to build a use-facilitating attribute into the package instead of a density-increasing attribute?*

Assuming that two "mixes" are in conflict or partial conflict, management may find the answer by deciding which will be more likely to push product storage as far from the packager as possible. This is, of course, another way of saying that the basic purpose of a product's package should be as much as possible to maximize product inventory near the point of use or possible use. If neither "mix" holds promise of increasing product inventory at the point of use, does either hold promise of increasing product storage at the next level back from the point of use? If neither "mix" aids in getting the product stored on the dining-room table, does either help in getting more of the product inventoried on the kitchen shelves? If neither helps there, which encourages the greater amount of well-placed open display at retail? If it is a tie between the two package "mixes" at this level, which of the two has promise of encouraging the greater retailer inventory—regardless whether in open display or not?

It foilows, then, that the most successful package changes are those whose impact is greatest at a level in the product's marketing one step forward from the level currently storing the channel's largest share of the product.

Most recent packaging changes can be understood a little better if viewed against the backdrop of these generalizations. Interestingly, they explain current trends in package design that, on the surface, seem to be running in opposite directions. For instance, recently some company managements have been increasing package size or package count. Other managements have unit-packaged, lessened package size, or reduced package count. But both apparently contradictory approaches have the same purpose—*to maximize product inventory as close to a point of use as possible.* Let's examine a few recent package changes in light of these generalizations (I am referring to those changes that typically affect more than just the package's graphic art):

*Changes Involving Package Size or Count.* Proprietary medicine, soap powder or detergent, beverages, and toilet tissue are among those widely distributed consumer products whose recent package changes have included addition of "king" or "giant economy" size packages to their lines. Table salt, facial tissue, crackers, and cereal on the other hand are among the items, distributed in large part through the same marketing channel, which have added smaller-size packages or "unitized" packages to their lines. In each case, promotion turning on "convenience" to the user frequently has accompanied the introduction of the new package size. Where the move has been to increase the package size, packagers are trying to encourage the consumer to maintain inventories of their particular brands far in excess of the consumer's normal needs for the product during any reasonable time span between shopping trips. In effect, the packagers are trying to move a greater share of their channel's total storage function closer to the point of use—from retailer to consumer in this particular illustration. Where the move has been to lessen package size, it is apparent that the packagers are trying to move storage location further forward: to get facial tissues into purses as well as on the vanity; to get brand-identified salt on the dining-room, breakfast, TV, or barbecue table as well as on the pantry shelf; to get half a dozen varieties of cereal in the home rather than in the store in anticipation of a family's vacillating demands. Again, the packagers are trying to move a greater share of the channel's total storage closer to the point of use.

*Changes Involving Package Shape.* Ice cream and milk, in both powdered and liquid forms, are examples of items that have been undergoing changes from cylindrical to space-saving rectangular packages. In part, at least, the change has been precipitated by increased recognition of the marketing channel's limited capacity to store items under refrigeration and of its eagerness to husband its shelf space. In effect, the change permits a greater share of the inventory to be moved forward.

*Changes Involving Packaging Materials.* This is the area where packagers' desires to push storage forward probably have been most apparent. And, incidentally, it is in this area that the lie is put to the belief that a package's prime job is protection of the product. If product protection were the prevailing consideration, few if any of certain kinds of change in packaging materials would ever have taken place. For example:

1. Changes from opaque to transparent materials usually have been represented as irrefutable evidence of the packager's good faith in allowing his customers to see his product. Understandably, the suppliers of transparent packaging materials have done what they could to further this impression. But conversion from opaque to transparent packaging typically has meant something else as well: *It has been a means of obtaining favorable open display shelf space at retail,* where the product could be seen by the consumers. In effect, it has meant moving part of the storage function forward in the channel from concealed storage or low-traffic locations to prominent, high-traffic locations. Small wonder that such a premium has come to be placed on transparency—even for products not especially attractive to the eye.
2. Changes from rigid to flexible materials have almost always meant relinquishing some measure of product protection—and the recent changes from rigid to semirigid or flexible packaging are legion. The changes, while requiring some loss of product-protection value, typically have given the product an especially promotable package, one with conspicuous promise of moving product storage closer to a point of use.

*Changes Involving Addition of "Ease-of-Opening" or "Ease-of-Use" Attributes.* I believe that, where they have been successful, package changes incorporating this kind of feature have tended to move product storage increasingly closer—however slightly—to the point of use. Typically, the movement of storage effected by such "ease-of-opening" package changes has not been at the consumer level in the product's marketing channel; it has been at the retail level. Perhaps it could be argued that the extremely successful rigid flip-top cigarette package has helped move the smoker's storage of his cigarettes a little closer to the point of their use, but the main value of the package with regard to its movement of product storage has been at the retail level. The package, again, was a means of obtaining a good, high-traffic position in open display for the particular brands of cigarette that pioneered this packaging change. It was something distinctively new that could be promoted to the marketing channel itself—quite aside from its being amenable to use in effective promotion to smokers—for brands not having so extensive or complete retail inventories as those enjoyed by more popular brands.

In summary, the choice of a product's package, no less than the choice of the total selling effort brought to bear on the product, has to represent a reconciliation of a variety of functions, each of which has potential merit in furthering the sale of the product, but all of which are, in part at least, mutually exclusive.

The most successful reconciliation will be the one that, to return to our original axiom, produces the most sales. It will emphasize that function which pushes the bulk of product storage one step farther along the marketing channel and one step closer to the ultimate consumer.

# 36. THE MAN IN THE PACKAGE

*Ernest Dichter*

*The trend toward self-service continues, and as it does so, the role of the package as a "salesman" becomes more important.*

*This report attempts to define the characteristics of a well-designed package. From the consumer's point of view it helps to answer the question, "How does design communicate the product's personality?"*

## OUR VANISHING SALESMAN

Aside from the product itself, the most personal contact a manufacturer has with his customers today is the package that contains his product.

This means that the package has a difficult job to do. It must replace the living, breathing salesman as a vital link between the manufacturer and consumer.

More and more, the trend in selling goods is toward self-service. Not only is this true in supermarkets, but also in five-and-dime emporiums, clothing establishments with pipe racks, and an ever growing variety of stores and shops. The salesman simply isn't there any more. And as we get further and further into the era of the Vanishing Salesman, the role of the package *as a salesman* becomes more prominent and more urgent.

Many packaging designers and manufacturers are already aware of the personal character of the package-consumer relationship. At a recent seminar held by the Paraffined

Source: From a booklet published and copyrighted 1957 by The Paraffined Carton Research Council.
Ernest Dichter: President, Institute for Motivational Research, Inc., Croton-on-Hudson, New York.

Carton Research Council, it was evident that designers and makers of the packages are no longer content to view the successful package as one that mainly gives them a feeling of pride about their contributions to the finished article. The successful package was not seen merely as one with an intriguing shape or design, but as one whose over-all design, shape, color, and printed message delivered an impact that resulted in a personal relationship between the consumer and the package on the shelf.

Today the package must come alive at the point of purchase. The salesman may no longer be visible behind the counter, supplying a necessary living element in the selling process. But he is present, just the same.

He has stepped inside the package.

Formerly, a manufacturer had little control over the salesmen who represented his product in retail stores. They were jolly or grumpy, inept or skillful, pleasant or not, courteous or not—depending on the weather or the season or the state of their nerves.

The salesman in the package presents no such problem. He is yours to create and control.

A poorly designed package tells the consumer that the maker of the product does not care. Like an impatient salesman at five minutes before closing time, he is saying "take it or leave it." But a well designed package is proof that the manufacturer really cares about both the customer and the product and is willing to make an extra effort to please. He is employing a friendly, interested salesman.

Just what is a well designed package? According to research, the consumer himself is the measure of a good package.

If you ask him, every consumer has a picture of the ideal package in his head. This is not simply a picture of how the package looks: it is a dramatic visualization of how it feels as he turns it around in his hand, of how it fits into his medicine chest or pantry, and of how easy it is to get at the product inside when he really needs it.

Through his emotional needs, the consumer sets up very demanding standards of good packaging. These may be listed as follows:

1. *Convenience.* Does the package hold enough of the product to satisfy his needs without being too bulky or too heavy?

2. *Adaptability.* How well does the package fit into his freezer, cupboard, glove compartment, or dresser drawer?

3. *Security.* Does he feel assured that you have given him quality? Does the package make him feel it?

4. *Status of prestige.* Does he feel that by buying your package he is expressing something about himself?

5. *Dependability.* Does the package let him feel that he can rely upon you, the manufacturer?

6. *Esthetic satisfaction.* Is he pleased and satisfied by the impact of the design, color, and shape of the package?

Actually these six criteria can be described simply as combining utility, security, and aesthetic appearance. This quotation from the mother of a young perfume purchaser is an example of the practical application of these criteria:

> My daughter has a perfume now that, God bless her, she can use without getting it on the floor or all over her dressing table. She used to have (name of brand) and (name of brand). One she had to shake so hard to get the perfume out that she said it gave her a charley-horse. The other one had such a big hole that whenever she used it she couldn't control it, and it spilled all over, and the whole house smelled. This new kind, now, has just the right kind of hole. And the box is so good-looking, and the bottle is so swanky. You'd think it cost twenty dollars an ounce.

Here a young girl's "dream package" fulfills all the above criteria—with special emphasis on status. The desire for status is a consumer motivation that seems to be as vitally involved in the consumer-package relationship as in the purchase of any product from premium beers to Cadillacs. Status and other factors will be examined at length when we consider the core of all successful packaging: *how well modern packaging meets the emotional and psychological needs of today's consumer,* as expressed in his daily purchasing patterns and his conception of the ideal package.

A good package does not create the personality of a product. Like a good cosmetic on a beautiful girl, the desirable package merely expresses personality in a dramatic, easily recognizable way.

On the other hand, a bad package or design contradicts, underplays, or undermines a product's personality.

These are important considerations, since the personality of a product is an important determinant of brand loyalty. And so this is the place to ask: "Just what is product personality and how is it affected by package design?"

## Two Images of Product Personality

Product personality consists of two parts that we can only isolate on paper. One is the *physical image,* the other is the *personality image.*

Physically a bar of soap is round, square, or octagonal; but in its personality image it may appear boldly masculine or softly feminine, modern or old-hat, of high status or low, light and delicate or heavy and coarse.

Although we have separated the two images here, the consumer never does so. He sees a unified image of the product's personality. And, significant for the package designer, any negative features of either image will affect the total picture in the consumer's head.

For example, some men might reject a bar of soap that was ovoid-shaped, strongly scented, and packaged in a frilly box. Too effeminate, they would say. But they might accept the same soap if it were brick-shaped.

## Other Elements of Packaging Design

Although shape of a product may affect a product's personality all alone, it often shares its influence with other important components of packaging such as color, text, and illustration.

Designers and illustrators of great talent have presented consumers with cake-mix packages in which the illustrated confection seemed so real, virtually dripping with sensory appeals, that the consumer could "taste" the cake when he saw the package on the supermarket shelf. Unfortunately, there are other cake mixes in which the package fails to express the true personality of the cake. Cake is a dessert that signifies abundance to most consumers (ice cream is another), but we often find the illustrated cake cramped on one side of the box, covering not more than 60 per cent of the surface.

In such a case, the best way to revive the cake's true personality is to redesign the package, enlarging the illustration so that it "bleeds off" the box on both edges.

## Design Can Correct Wrong Impression

Sometimes the consumer insists on misinterpreting a product's personality in spite of all a good designer can do.

When this happens, the goal of the packager must be to "change" the product's personality and thus alter the consumer's impression of it.

Tea used to be advertised in a way that reinforced the public's mistaken impression that it was a "weak sister" beverage suitable for sick people and kindly old ladies. Research showed that both the packaging and advertising copy needed to be converted to the masculine gender. This called for stressing the he-man quality of tea, and the use of the color red was recommended—replacing the weak blue previously seen in tea advertising.

In a margarine study, favorable consumer response occurred when the name of the brand was printed against the background of a green leaf while the margarine was represented as the disk of a daisy. This evoked an impression of naturalness, a desirable personality trait for margarine. But consumers formed a mistaken impression of another brand, which showed three pats of margarine encased in a cube of ice. They associated the ice cube with a test tube; the symbol evoked fear (of harmful chemicals) and led to rejection of the product.

Some designs can even prejudice the consumer against the quality of a product. Here is an instance of a Midwestern housewife's response to a margarine package:

> From the point of view of design, I like the (Brand X) box. (Brand Y) is too cluttered, too much to look at. It has more information and is easier to read but only if you're interested. But knowing oleo as I do, I would not stop to read and that's why I'd pick up (Brand X) because the quality seems to be better revealed in the package.

Here the consumer is providing a most direct guide to the designer. Such reactions are the rule rather than the exception, for margarine is a product about which the housewife feels she knows all there is to know.

### Unified Trade Symbol Important

The aims of the most effectively designed package can be defeated if a unified trade symbol is lacking.

In a study of the advertising and promotion problems of a large paper products company, it was found that the use of different trade symbols, including different brand-name designs, for the premium-priced napkins and the lowest-priced napkins made the consumer associate the entire product in all price ranges with the more generally known trade symbol which appeared on the *cheap napkins.* The suggestion of "cheap napkin" was carried over to even the highest priced product. Much of this confusion of product personality was due to the fact that the packaging of the premium item, besides lacking a unified quality trade symbol, did not provide a recognizable *quality differential*–either in color, text, typography, or brand-name design.

### Changing a Product's Personality

People like to say they never judge a book by its cover. *But they do.*

In one study, coffee was served from different coffee makers including the most modern dripolators and the most antique coffee urns. Most of the drinkers said that the coffee poured from the antique urns tasted better. Actually it was the same coffee. This confirmed the fact that modern consumers believe that somehow things were better in the past–more wholesome, purer, etc. But more important, it indicated that the size, style, and shape of the coffee container influenced the drinker's impression of the taste.

This ability of a package or container to modify the personality of a product was further shown in a study for a pharmaceutical company. The so-called potency rating of two different-sized pills was tested. Although the potency of the drug "packaged" in the larger pill was less than that in the smaller one, not only laymen but also many doctors were fooled. The medical men insisted that the larger pill was the more potent!

### Enhancing Status Through Packaging

Size is not always the important factor. Sometimes a new and more tasteful design, high in status value, can alter a product's personality and give it a prestige it never had before. Whiskey decanters designed by artists like Russel Wright and Walter Landor have given a new prestige to some of the cheaper whiskeys. These containers have turned up in the liquor cabinets of persons accustomed to serving only the higher priced whiskeys.

But this kind of "conterfeiting" involves risks that should be taken into account by packaging designers and manufacturers.

One investigation revealed that while, in many cases, the new decanters added prestige to the product, in a significant number of instances the consumer felt that expensive decanters forced manufacturers to "make up the difference" by using cheaper ingredients in the liquor.

However, the positive effects on sales produced by these new decanters should be seriously studied in any consideration of the sales potential that lies in the changing or enhancing of a product's personality.

The proof of the package comes the moment the consumer walks down the aisle of the supermarket. Either the package reaches out to him in a persuasive way, or it lies dead while its nearest and best competitor is chosen for the shopper's basket.

The consumer arrives in the supermarket lost in a fog of competitive claims that have been drummed into his head by newspapers, magazines, radio, TV, and billboards. The similarity of these advertising appeals often arrests the development of a distinctive product personality; this fact is responsible for the widespread lack of brand loyalty among supermarket customers today.

It is up to the package designer, to a large extent, to attract the consumer to the particular product on the shelf. But first he must consider what has happened to the consumer's shopping experience.

## The "New Angle" of Consumer Vision

Today's consumer doesn't see the product on the shelf the way he did ten or fifteen years ago. In the past the product was directly in the line of his vision, straight across the grocer's counter. When he viewed the product in the package, his eyes met it head-on and he could take in all the essentials at a glance. The package presented a clear-cut panel, with its brand name, colors, text, and shape easily visible.

But in today's supermarket, passing among palisades of parallel shelves filled with hundreds of products, the consumer sees mainly a gigantic blur of boxes and cans in which there are no outstanding elements. In this chaos a package must have prominent features of design that catch the eye, hold the attention, and initiate the dramatic interplay between package and patron that makes the package come alive in the customer's hand.

The problem is more complicated than it used to be because the strolling supermarket customer seldom sees many of the packages head-on as he did in the small grocery store. Nowadays his eyes meet the shelf at an angle and he cannot perceive a clear-cut front package panel. One edge of the box and part of one side intrude on the area of vision, breaking and weakening the impact.

In examining the packaging problems arising from this "new angle" of vision, designers and manufacturers might also take into account the phenomenon of *peripheral vision.* Here, in addition to new angles of perception, there is also present the factor of diminished visibility. In peripheral vision, certain colors and designs are barely perceptible. Certain forms and shapes, effective when seen directly by the consumer, become distorted, confused, and weak in impact in the dim light and abnormal angles of peripheral vision.

These visual phenomena suggest new areas for exploration in packaging—in design, typography, color, shape—to assure successful impact from whatever angle the product is viewed by the consumer. Obviously the problem is a complicated one, both technically and psychologically, but many of our major packaging designers are already meeting the challenge of new merchandising techniques.

To be successful a package must accomplish the following things when it is on display:

1. It must achieve a "reaching out" quality.
2. It must provike uninterrupted inspection by the consumer.
3. It must "disappear" and permit the consumer to rehearse the purchase and use of the product.

### The "Reaching Out" Quality

Consider the Cheer detergent box. A design with dynamic action—clean wash flapping in the breeze. A bold color scheme of blue, red, white, and yellow. The result is a package that seems to cry, "Look at me? You can't help yourself? Pick me up and find out what I've got for you?"

It almost reaches out and taps you on the shoulder.

The Log Cabin Syrup can has much the same quality because of its unusual shape. There is no possibility that the supermarket shopper will mistake it for another brand, or fail to find it as his eye scans the shelf.

The package on the shelf must provide tension-producing design factors that cause the consumer to interact with it from a distance. Through its design, color, or some other outstanding feature, it must break through the brand fog created by the many competing products.

Tension-producing design is particularly important for ice cream cartons. The brick shape can be adapted to designs which aid in creating an impression of richness and plenty. Here is where the designer plays a vital role. A design with swirling movements, and a run-over to the sides of the carton, is capable of creating such a psychological illusion of richness and fullness. "X Brand of ice cream comes in that nice square box but it doesn't look like the ordinary box of brick ice cream," said a West Coast mother of four children. "It has a lot of blue and pink polka dots on it, running around all four sides. It makes it look so rich and so full."

This again illustrates that physical form can win consumer acceptance but it must be supplemented with design which projects emotional understanding.

## Uninterrupted Inspection

The package that reaches out to the consumer does not always wind up in the shopping basket. It must have just enough design tension—not too much—to clinch the sale.

Once the package is in the consumer's hand, the interaction between the two should be greatly accelerated. In the case of the Cheer package, the wash flapping in the breeze and the bright colors combine to give movement to the entire package and provide *unity of design.*

This non-static design, with the brand name, copy, and colors creating a directional movement, offers *sequence* and dimension, a natural rhythm and flow from one component to another. It stimulates the shopper's three-dimensional investigation of the package, rather than fixing his attention to any one part.

The Cheer design offers tension to a moderate degree. Research has shown that too much design tension over-excites the consumer so that he cannot "see" the product because of the package. "This hand lotion has a gorgeous package—all tutti-frutti and tinsel," one shopper said. "No, I never tried the lotion. It's probably too rich for my blood."

## A Packaging Paradox

It is clear that a package must not emphasize its own personality to the disadvantage of the product inside. In fact, the effective package must virtually "disappear" at some point in the purchase-and-use process. That is, it must disappear in the psychological sense of fading into the background while the product itself comes forward to become the "figure" that is seen, related to, and remembered by the consumer.

Sometimes, but not always, this means that an effective package should be made of transparent materials. Often the reverse is true. When we buy sausages at a meat department we want the package to fade into the finished product—the hot, crisp, aromatic meat—and not into the cold and greasy food we see through the plastic envelope.

But an opaque Duncan Hines or Betty Crocker cake mix package, with the illustration of the finished cake rich with icing, dominates the package so that within a few moments the design, the colors, the type styles and the shape of the box disappear. What the consumer sees is the luscious cake itself.

Sometimes the package refuses to disappear, and the fault can lie with the personality of the product itself. In the case of a nationally advertised food product, the package was striking, gay, bright, alive with color. But despite the achievement of the designers there was a contradiction between package and product personality.

The package radiated light-hearted gayety and frivolity, a mood that was in stark contrast to the function performed by the product. And so it failed to ring a bell in the mind of the housewife. Or still worse, it generated disbelief and even suspicion by its sharp contrast to the product's personality.

In the case of butter, which must suggest abundance, the matter of design and art for the package assumes paramount importance. As one supermarket shopper, in an Eastern city, remarked:

> I wish they'd show butter in boxes that are not just butter alone. Butter needs to go with something, like pancakes and butter, or baked potatoes and butter. It has to give me the feeling that I'm almost seeing the color of the butter. You know, butter by itself isn't very appetizing, even if it's the most beautiful color. It's when you take butter and combine it with something else that butter has such attraction. Then you can see that wonderful yellow–the richness. It almost makes my mouth water.

What the consumer is saying here is that simply illustrating butter in pats or in quarter-pound sticks, does not provide an appetizing appeal. Butter is a combination product and goes well when it is putting the spice on another food. Thus, she is calling for a pictorial presentation of the uses of butter.

### Rehearsal of Purchase and Use

When a man watches a demonstration of a new car on TV, he imitates the salesman in his own mind. He peeks at the motor under the hood, tries out the automatic shift, raises and lowers the lid of the luggage compartment.

This is a mental rehearsal of the use of the new car. In the same way, mentally, the interested TV viewer rehearses the actual purchase: the bargaining, the signing of the contract, the questions he will ask the dealer, etc. Of course reactions depend greatly on the depth of penetration of the advertising message.

Rehearsal of purchase and use is a psychological factor in the relationship of a consumer to a package, too. The disappearing package brings the product and consumer into a close relationship with no significant barriers to hinder the interaction of the two. "That cake mix looked so good, my mouth watered. I felt like eating the whole thing all up, right there, package and all."

This consumer response is a tribute to the designer's art. But at the same time it emphasizes the paradox of good packaging. Here the package brings the consumer and product together, then steps out of the picture. It disappears without being missed.

### More Traits of a Good Package

*Perpetual Youth.* Like people, packages grow old and tired. But unlike people, they can be renewed. A tired package communicates the personality of a tired product. Today's consumer demands that his favorite products be full of freshness and youth; this calls for a constant renewal of design. Manufacturers of such products as cigarettes and breakfast foods are continually bringing out new package designs to replace those that are old and listless.

*Ever-renewing Involvement of Consumer with Product.* A sale does not end with the purchase of a product. Advertising and promotion continually strive to renew the relationship between consumer and product so as to create an uninterrupted flow of sales. The package on the shelf must perform a similar function—becoming more than a mere receptacle. It must resell itself to the consumer every time he sees it.

*The Pleasure of Handling.* In some products a good package induces exploration with the hands, for example the Marlboro flip-top package.

*Creative Considerateness.* When a car manufacturer designs his windshield to give a better view from the driver's seat, he is exhibiting a concern for the consumer's needs which psychologists call creative considerateness. Consumers expect this attitude to apply to makers and designers of packages, too. Successful examples include the neat carry-home cartons of beer cans or soft drink bottles, and the development of new spouts on milk cartons which eliminate drips and spills. The presence of creative considerateness is an assurance that over-all impact of a package will be greater.

In a packaging test using the techniques of ordinary opinion research, a large number of consumers were asked to indicate their preferences among three different package designs.

The result: 62 per cent chose the most ornate design, 25 per cent the less extravagant one, and 12 per cent the simplest design. The consumer had spoken and it seemed like a green light for ornate design.

But wait. In the real life supermarket situation, away from the questioner who had asked them a direct question about their preferences, 72 per cent bought the package *with the simplest design.*

## How "Yes" Turns into "No"

The average consumer's answer to a direct question may be different from his real answer, as the above switch clearly shows. Does this mean that the consumer must remain unpredictable? That package designers should only design boxes that give themselves satisfaction? Does this indicate that testing must remain essentially a game of chance?

Packaging testing is a gamble only if the wrong techniques are used. For example, in the test discussed above, the following fallacies characteristic of conventional approaches to packaging research are evident:

1. The consumers were forced to answer as "packaging experts" rather than as consumers. They were asked to make a value judgment of the package rather than a consumer's choice.

2. They were presented the package artificially, when in fact consumers can only respond in a psychologically valid way to the package in its competitive environment.

3. All the social pressures of an interview situation are magnified by the direct question. The consumer seeks the most socially acceptable answer—the answer he feels will satisfy the interviewer, enhance his own status, and be in accord with his own self-image.

### The Motivational Answer

Only in a store or supermarket situation can a real test of buyer attitudes be made. Here the consumer is not expected to answer questions; he merely shops in his usual way. By setting up an experimental supermarket, researchers can make valid studies of consumer habits.

In a motivational research laboratory supermarket the consumer is not aware of which package is being tested. He is simply invited by the interviewer to play the "shopping game" and to enter the model store as if he were on a normal shopping trip.

He makes his purchase from among various brands of the same food product, and he has the opportunity to select his favorite brand in the current or the proposed new package—both of which appear in equally favorable positions on the shelves. If he fails to pick either package of the brand being tested, he is invited to "go back and make another purchase" until he has finally chosen one of the packages being tested.

After he has selected one of the packages being tested, he is given an interview by a psychologist who asks him about both packages—the chosen one and the rejected one. There are six steps in these interviews:

1. *Free association.* The consumer is asked to tell everything that comes to his mind as he looks at the packages. On liquid bleach, for example: "It reminds me of an ammonia bottle. I can smell the strong fumes just by looking at it." (Recommendation of the research team: change the shape of the bottle.)
2. *Story.* "Look at this package and make up a story about it," says the psychologist. Such a third-person story permits the consumer to express his true feelings without fear of offending anyone.
3. *Color.* To study colors, the psychologist asks: "How do the colors make you feel?"
4. *Person.* To study the package's personality, the consumer is asked: "When you look at this box, what kind of person are you reminded of?" In one study of deodorants, it was found that the package impressed buyers as feminine, yet the product itself was seen as masculine. This kind of contradiction often hurts sales.
5. *Slogan.* The entire range of associations with the slogan are probed, and its emotional impact is estimated.
6. *Choice imputations.* The consumer is asked to tell how he thinks other consumers will react to the product. Women, for example, are asked which box they think would most likely be chosen by a boy, man, or girl.

## Validation of Laboratory Tests

Finally, packages are tested in actual supermarkets. A special check-out counter is set up by trained interviewers and a board is marked to indicate the reasons for specific purchases. The consumer arranges his purchases on the board according to categories: "reminded by brand," "planned by kind," "substitute," etc.

Depth interviews (that is, extensive and probing interviews) are then conducted in the store by the interviewers.

More valuable information can be obtained from a panel of consumers. Families representing different age, income, education, national, and religious groups are asked to cooperate when a problem requires responses from specific individuals among the consuming population.

On the preceding pages we have examined many of the practical and psychological aspects of the package designer's art. These findings help to tell what makes a package come alive upon contact with the consumer. They form a blueprint for future design and testing.

But this blueprint must be implemented by the skilled designers and craftsmen of the packaging industry. They alone are capable of translating the needs and feelings of the consumer into patterns and planes, colors and type faces that satisfy these needs and feelings.

If designers will continue to add to the three dimensions of their art the vital fourth dimension of consumer motivational psychology, the future of American packaging will seem promising indeed.

# 37. PRICING OBJECTIVES IN LARGE COMPANIES

*Robert F. Lanzillotti*

*Following is an interesting explanation of the processes by which prices are formed in industry. This involves a discussion of company goals and how they provide rationalizations for the setting of prices.*

*Included are analyses of target return on investment, market share, price stabilization, and meeting competition.*

## SCOPE OF PRESENT STUDY

The procedure followed involved the postprandial variety of research. Lengthy interviews were undertaken with officials of twenty companies over periods ranging up to about one week in most cases.[1] A second set of interviews was undertaken several

[1] The companies were selected from among the largest corporations on the basis of the willingness of management to cooperate by permitting extensive interviews with top company officials: Aluminum Company of America, American Can, A & P Tea Company, Du Pont, General Electric, General Foods, General Motors, Goodyear, Gulf, International Harvester, Johns-Manville, Kennecott Copper, Kroger, National Steel, Sears, Standard of Indiana, Standard Oil Company of New Jersey (ESSO), Swift, Union Carbide, and U. S. Steel.

AUTHOR'S NOTE: The Author is indebted to J. B. Dirlam and R. I. Thayer for helpful criticism and many substantive suggestions. This article is an outgrowth of work on a Brookings Institution study on *Pricing in Big Business,* by A. D. H. Kaplan, J. B. Dirlam and R. F. Lanzillotti. The author wishes to acknowledge the generous support of the Brookings Institution. The interpretations and conclusions are those of the author and do not necessarily reflect the views of the Brookings Institution, its staff, or its trustees.

Source: From *American Economic Review,* vol. 48, December, 1958, pp. 923–940. Robert F. Lanzillotti: Associate Professor of Economics, State College of Washington.

years later to fill in gaps in the data and to ascertain if any changes had been made in price policy since the original interviews. Pricing obviously being a sensitive area, some officials did not care to discuss their policies except in general terms, but these persons paved the way to individuals who were more willing and, in some cases, more aware of the practices employed and reasons for them.

The questions were designed to elicit information concerning:

1. whether any formal or informal commercial goals had been adopted by the corporation;
2. the procedures employed for implementing and evaluating the goal;
3. the techniques of price determination (i.e. the mechanics of pricing); and
4. the functions of pricing executives (individuals, committees, special divisions, etc.)–including extent of authority on price matters, kinds of materials utilized by them in setting prices, and relative weights given to various price-influencing factors.

The portion of the informatoin presented in this paper concerns, for each of the twenty companies, the principal and collateral objectives which are regarded as guiding pricing decisions.

The twenty corporations have one feature in common: each of them is among the 200 largest industrial corporations, and over one-half fall within the 100 largest industrials, in terms of assets. But they differ in a wide variety of ways from each other. Some, like Johns-Manville, U. S. Steel, International Harvester, and Union Carbide, dominate a whole industry and are price leaders. At the other extreme, there are companies like Swift and A & P which face so many competitors of various sizes and abilities that in spite of their absolute size they are very far from being able to make decisions for the market, and do not think of competition in terms of actions of one or a few competitors. The other companies fall between these extremes.

## COMPANY GOALS: RATIONALIZATIONS OF PRICING METHODS

It is important to recognize at the outset that a company statement of policy is not necessarily an accurate representation of what that policy is.[2] Also, company rationalizations of pricing do not always represent the first step in planning price policy, and not all pricing of a given company is determined by the general company objective.

In a few cases officials insisted that there was little latitude in selecting a policy. However, for the most part, the prominence of each of the corporations in its respective industry makes most of them masters, to a significant degree, of their fates; hence, they are able to adjust pricing to the company's general goal.

[2] The following analysis is based on the author's interpretations of views expressed orally by officials of the corporations concerned. Of course, neither the companies nor the author wish these views to be interpreted as necessarily the official views of the companies.

Table 1 presents a summary of the principal and collateral pricing goals of the twenty companies as determined from interviews with their respective officials. The most typical pricing objectives cited were:

1. pricing to achieve a target return on investment;
2. stabilization of price and margin;
3. pricing to realize a target market share; and
4. pricing to meet or prevent competition.

In most of the companies, one of the goals predominates, but as the listing of collateral objectives indicates, price-making by any one firm was not always ruled by a single policy objective.[3]

## PRICING TO ACHIEVE A TARGET RETURN ON INVESTMENT

Target return on investment was perhaps the most frequently mentioned of pricing goals.[4] About one-half of the companies explicitly indicated that their pricing policies were based mainly upon the objective of realizing a particular rate of return on investment, in a given year, over the long haul, or both; but in most cases the target was regarded as a long-run objective. The average of the targets mentioned was 14 per cent (after taxes); only one was below 10 per cent; and the highest was 20 per cent.

Under this pricing system both costs and profit goals are based not upon the volume level which is necessarily expected over a short period, but rather on standard volume; and the margins added to standard costs are designed to produce the target profit rate on investment, assuming standard volume to be the long-run average rate of plant

[3] To illustrate, in U. S. Steel, out of a variety of divergent views mentioned, three rationales can be distinguished. 1. The first is the "ideal" price, i.e. pricing that is believed to be "just, fair, and economic," with reference to a general target of about 8 per cent after taxes on stockholders' investment plus long-term debt. This strand is colored by the management's concept of the corporation as the industry leader vested with the responsibilities and subject to the inhibitions of a public utility. In fact, one official said he was "unable to understand or properly describe the Corporation's pricing policy except as something like the approach of the public utilities." 2. The second rationale centers on the difference between the "ideal" system and what officials regard as the "practical exigencies of steel price-making," i.e. limitations imposed upon price policy "by followers who are disloyal and prices of competitive products that get out of hand." 3. A third policy objective is essentially a target market share and is embodied in the motto: "to obtain as a minimum that share of all markets for the product sold, product by product, and territory by territory, to which the corporation's capacity in relation to the industry as the whole entitles it, and to accomplish this participation ratio through the exercise of judgment so as to insure the maximum continuing return on investment to the Corporation."

[4] Target-return pricing is defined as the building up of a price structure designed to provide such a return on capital employed for specific products, product groups, and divisions, as to yield a predetermined corporate average return. In most cases managements referred to stockholders' equity (net worth) plus long-term debt. Usually a standard cost system is used as a means of allocating fixed cost to various product divisions, with the standards premised on an assumed rate of production, typically about 70 per cent to 80 per cent of capacity, and an assumed product-mix as "normal."

**Table 1. Pricing goals of twenty large industrial corporations**

| Company | Principal Pricing Goal | Collateral Pricing Goals | *Rate of Return on Investment (After Taxes) 1947–1955*[a] | | Average Market Share[b] |
|---|---|---|---|---|---|
| | | | *Avg.* | *Range* | |
| Alcoa | 20% on investment (before taxes); higher on new products [about 10% effective rate after taxes] | (a) "Promotive" policy on new products<br>(b) Price stabilization | 13.8 | 7.8–18.7 | Pig & ingot, 37%; sheet, 46%; other fabrications, 62%[c] |
| American Can | Maintenance of market share | (a) "Meeting" competition (using cost of substitute product to determine price)<br>(b) Price stabilization | 11.6 | 9.6–14.7 | Approx. 55% of all types of cans[d] |
| A & P | Increasing market share | "General promotive" (low-margin policy) | 13.0 | 9.7–18.8 | n.a. |
| Du Pont | Target return on investment–no specific figure given | (a) Charging what traffic will bear over long run<br>(b) Maximum return for new products–"life cycle" pricing | 25.9 | 19.6–34.1 | n.a. |
| Esso (Standard Oil of N.J.) | "Fair-return" target–no specific figure given | (a) Maintaining market share<br>(b) Price stabilization | 16.0 | 12.0–18.9 | n.a. |
| General Electric | 20% on investment (after taxes); 7% on sales (after taxes) | (a) Promotive policy on new products<br>(b) Price stabilization on nationally advertised products | 21.4 | 18.4–26.6 | –[e] |
| General Foods | 33-1/3% gross margin: ("1/3 to make, 1/3 to sell, and 1/3 for profit"); expectation of realizing target only on new products | (a) Full line of food products and novelties<br>(b) Maintaining market share | 12.2 | 8.9–15.7 | n.a. |
| General Motors | 20% on investment (after taxes) | Maintaining market share | 26.0 | 19.9–37.0 | 50% of passenger automobiles[f] |

| | | | | | |
|---|---|---|---|---|---|
| Goodyear | "Meeting competitors" | (a) Maintain "position"<br>(b) Price stabilization | 13.3 | 9.2–16.1 | n.a. |
| Gulf | Follow price of most important marketer in each area | (a) Maintain market share<br>(b) Price stabilization | 12.6 | 10.7–16.7 | n.a. |
| International Harvester | 10% on investment (after taxes) | Market share: ceiling of "less than a dominant share of any market" | 8.9 | 4.9–11.9 | Farm tractors, 28–30%; combines, cornpickers, tractor plows, cultivators, mowers, 20–30%; cotton pickers, 65%; light & light-heavy trucks, 5–18%; medium-heavy to heavy-heavy, 12–30% |
| Johns–Manville | Return on investment greater than last 15-year average (about 15% after taxes); higher target for new products | (a) Market share not greater than 20%<br>(b) Stabilization of prices | 14.9 | 10.7–19.6 | n.a. |
| Kennecott | Stabilization of prices | | 16.0 | 9.3–20.9 | n.a. |
| Kroger | Maintaining market share | Target return of 20% on investment before taxes[g] | 12.1 | 9.7–16.1 | n.a. |
| National Steel | Matching the market-price follower | Increase market share | 12.1 | 7.0–17.4 | 5% |
| Sears Roebuck | Increasing market share (8–10% regarded as satisfactory share) | (a) Realization of traditional return on investment of 10–15% (after taxes)<br>(b) General promotive (low margin) policy | 5.4 | 1.6–10.7 | 5–10% average (twice as large a share in hard goods v. soft goods) |
| Standard Oil (Indiana) | Maintain market share | (a) Stabilize prices<br>(b) Target-return on investment (none specified) | 10.4 | 7.9–14.4 | n.a. |
| Swift | Maintenance of market share in livestock buying and meat packing | | 6.9 | 3.9–11.1 | Approximately 10% nationally[h] |
| Union Carbide | Target return on investment[i] | Promotive policy on new products; "life cycle" pricing on chemicals generally | 19.2 | 13.5–24.3 | –[j] |
| U. S. Steel | 8% on investment (after taxes) | (a) Target market share of 30%<br>(b) Stable price<br>(c) Stable margin | 10.3 | 7.6–14.8 | Ingots and steel, 30%; blast furnaces, 34%; finished hot-rolled products, 35%; other steel mill products, 37%[k] |

**Table 1. Pricing goals of twenty large industrial corporations (continued)**

[a]Federal Trade Commission, *Rates of Return (After Taxes) for Identical Companies in Selected Manufacturing Industries, 1940, 1947–55,* Washington [1957], pp. 28–30, except for the following companies whose rates were computed by the author using the methods outlined in the Commission Report: A & P, General Foods, Gulf, International Harvester, Kroger, National Steel, Sears Roebuck, and Swift.

[b]As of 1955, unless otherwise indicated. Source of data is company mentioned unless noted otherwise.

[c]*U. S. v. Alcoa et al.,* "Stipulation Concerning Extension of Tables III-X," dated May 31, 1956, U. S. District Court for the Southern District of New York.

[d]As of 1939. U. S. Department of Justice, *Western Steel Plants and the Tin Plate Industry,* 79th Cong., 1st Sess., Doc. No. 95, p. L 1.

[e]The company states that on the average it aims at not more than 22 to 25 per cent of any given market. Percentages for individual markets or products were not made available, but it is estimated that in some markets, e.g. electrical turbines, General Electric has 60 per cent of the total market. *Cf.* Standard and Poor's, *Industry Surveys,* "Electrical-Electronic-Basic Analysis," Aug. 9, 1956, p. E 21.

[f]Federal Trade Commission, *Industrial Concentration and Product Diversification in the 1000 Largest Manufacturing Companies: 1950*, Washington, Jan. 1957, p. 113.

[g]Target return on investment evidently characterizes company policy as much as target market share. In making investment decisions the company is quoted as follows: "The Kroger Co. normally expected a return on investment of at least 20% before taxes." See McNair, Burnham, and Hersum, *Cases in Retail Management,* New York, 1957, pp. 205 ff.

[h]This represents the average share of total industry shipments of the four largest firms in 1954. *Cf. Concentration in American Industry,* Report of Subcommittee on the Judiciary, U. S. Senate, 85th Cong., 1st Sess., Washington, 1957, p. 315.

[i]In discussions with management officials various prifit-return figures were mentioned, with considerable variation among divisions of the company. No official profit target percentage was given, but the author estimates the *average* profit objective for the corporation to be approximately 35% before taxes, or an effective rate after taxes of about 18 per cent.

[j]Chemicals account for 30 per cent of Carbide's sales, most of which are petro-chemicals, a field that the company opened thirty years ago and still dominates; plastics account for 18 per cent–the company sells 40 per cent of the two most important plastics (vinyl and polyethylene); alloys and metals account for 26 per cent of sales–top U. S. supplier of ferroalloys (e.g. chrome, silicon, manganese), and the biggest U. S. titanium producer; gases account for 14 per cent of sales–estimated to sell 50 per cent of oxygen in the U. S.; carbon, electrodes, and batteries account for 12 per cent of sales–leading U. S. producer of electrodes, refractory carbon, and flashlights and batteries; and miscellaneous–leading operator of atomic energy plants, a leading producer of uranium, the largest U. S. producer of tungsten, and a major supplier of vanadium. *Cf.* "Union Carbide Enriches the Formula," *Fortune,* Feb. 1957, pp. 123 ff.; Standard and Poor's *Industry Surveys,* "Chemicals-Basic Analysis," Dec. 20, 1956, p. C 44; and "Annual Report for 1955 of the Union Carbide and Carbon Corporation."

[k]The range of the corporation's capacity as a percentage of total industry capacity varies from 15 to 54 per cent, as of January 1957. For more detail see *Administered Prices, Hearings Before the Subcommittee on Antitrust and Monopoly of the Senate Committee on the Judiciary,* 85th Cong., 1st Sess., Pt. 2, *Steel,* Washington, 1958, pp. 335–36.

utilization. In effect, the procedure is designed to prevent cyclical or shorter-run changes in volume or product-mix from unduly affecting price, with the expectation that the averaging of fluctuations in cost and demand over the business cycle will produce a particular rate of return on investment.

Firms that were conscious of shooting for a particular target return on investment in their price policies were those that sold products in a market or markets more or less protected and in which the companies were leaders in their respective industries. In Alcoa, Du Pont, Esso, General Electric, General Motors, International Harvester, Johns-Manville, Union Carbide, and U. S. Steel, the pricing of many products was hinged to this particular objective, and with the expectation of being able to reach the target return. Target-return pricing was usually tied in with a long-run view of prices, especially on new products where an "orderly" stepping down ("cascading") of prices was followed by Du Pont, Union Carbide, and Alcoa.

A distinction should be made, however, between those companies that use target return on investment as a rigid and primary guide to pricing and those to whom it is more useful as a benchmark in an area where prices otherwise might be subject to wide and dangerous variations.[5]

Columns 4 and 5 of Table 1 show the average and range of the profit rates realized by the twenty companies over the 1947–1955 period. It will be noted that the target figures are *less* than the actual returns: for the nine-year period, the target-return companies earned on the average slightly more to substantially more than their indicated profit objective (International Harvester being the only exception). Also, there is a rather wide range in the profit rates for each company.[6]

The actual profit rates may be higher than the targets for several possible reasons:

1. The targets may only be nominal or minimal goals (which is suggested by footnote 6).

[5] To illustrate, the use of rate-of-return pricing by U. S. Steel (likened by its officials to a public utility's "fair return"), apparently has not always been consistently followed. Under market pressure, U. S. Steel has at times had to accept much less than this return; when desperate for business, as in 1938, its competitors offered substantial concessions below published prices on almost every type of business. A very different situation shows up in the discussions of the target return by officials of General Motors. Instead of vainly attempting to realize its target in good years and bad, General Motors takes a long-run view and has sufficient assurance of its retention of a minimum market share to accept a diminished profit note in years when diminished output bears a heavy unallocated overhead. Du Pont seems to assume its ability to realize a target return, especially in connection with new products. The same could be said for Union Carbide, the other chemical producer in the sample. International Harvester, although as vulnerable as U. S. Steel to wide swings in volume of business, appeared to be less worried by competitors' ability to jeopardize its prices based on long-run normal cost and return. Harvester was not able to maintain its prices during the great depression, and there is no evidence that such reductions as it made correspond merely to changes in direct cost. But in spite of frank admission by Harvester's management that the company was faced by tough competition, company officials appeared to be much more independent in their pricing policy than U. S. Steel.

[6] If the lowest figure for each firm is omitted, however, the low side of the range of returns approximates the target figure. This is especially true of Alcoa, Du Pont, Johns-Manville, Union Carbide, and U. S. Steel.

2. The generally prosperous nature of the period in question in which company operations exceeded "normal" or average percentage of capacity upon which costs and prices were determined.

3. Some of the companies have found that pricing on an historical-cost basis using the company's traditional objective does not provide adequate capital for replacement and expansion at current costs, and accordingly have made allowance for this factor in their pricing formulas.[7]

Thus, if actual profit rates were "adjusted" for changes in the price level, the actual profits would more closely approximate the stated targets.

Whichever of the foregoing may be the most plausible explanation of the differences between actual and target profit rates, the findings indicate that a distinction must be made between year-to-year and secular profits objectives. The evidence on actual profit rates, taken in conjunction with the targets mentioned, raises serious questions whether these companies are attempting to "maximize" profits on a year-to-year basis. Moreover, to construe the actual profit rates (as against target rates) as evidence of a long-run maximization policy would require the demonstration that the prices charged were based not upon the targets but on what the firms believed they could get as a maximum. In any event, for this sample of firms and for this time period, there are limitations upon profit maximization as an adequate explanation of the relationships between profit targets and actual profit rates.

It is perhaps significant that there has been an increasing tendency in recent years for the companies in the sample to adopt some form of target-return pricing, either across-the-board or at least for particular products. In a few cases it was found that managements had developed a target-return policy between the time of the first interviews with the company and subsequent interviews several years later. The reasons for this movement toward greater use of a target-return approach are varied, but the major influences seem to have been:

1. an increasing awareness of and concern by managements for profit-capital-investment planning and capital budgeting, especially in the conglomerate company within which there is keen competition for capital funds by many units;

2. the desire for a good common denominator for evaluating the performance of divisions and product groups;

3. the wartime experiences of most of the companies with "cost-plus," "cost plus fixed fee," and other contractual arrangements with the government which focused attention on the return on investment; and

[7]When U. S. Steel, for example, announces an increase in its base prices, it usually justifies its action in terms of increased direct costs, especially labor costs. But that rising capital costs have also influenced the prices set in recent years is suggested by President Hood's announcement in connection with the $8.50 increase in 1956: "The new prices do not provide a solution to the problem that United States Steel faces with respect to inadequate depreciation allowances for the replacement of obsolete and outworn facilities, nor do they attempt to provide a solution to the many problems attending the expansion program upon which United States Steel is currently engaged." *New York Times,* August 7, 1956, p. 10.

4. the emulation, by competitors and others, of successful large companies which have followed a target-return policy for many years (several companies in the sample mentioned that they had patterned their general target-return policy after that of Du Pont or General Motors).

It is not surprising that new products above all are singled out for target-return pricing. Since they have no close rivals, new products are usually expected to produce a predetermined level of profit return on the investment represented.[8] No rigid length of time after the introductoin of the product was mentioned in which the target is supposed to be achieved. However, the time horizon is more short range *vis-á-vis* established products in the sense that the target payout is delineated from the start.[9] Accordingly, pricing may take the form of "skimming" the market by exploiting the inelasticity of demand in different markets (maintaining a selected price as long as actual or potential competition permits), or a "penetration" price policy designed to develop mass markets via relatively low prices, provided a rapid expansion of the market and higher-returns may be obtained later. This approach is most typical of Du Pont, Union Carbide, Alcoa, International Harvester, and General Foods. The prescribed target for new products is usually higher than on established products, at least initially. But the target approach is not limited to unique products; it is also typical of low-unit-profit high-volume commodities (e.g. steel, aluminum, and chemicals).

[8] A good example of the kinds of data utilized in determining which new products will be added or which existing facilities will be expanded is one company's procedure for capital investment decisions. The request by a division for new funds shows: 1. estimated new commitment (new fixed investment, working capital, and noncapital expenditures; 2. estimated total utilized investment (the new investment plus transfer of existing investment); 3. estimated annual operating income (i.e. income before depreciation, amortization, depletion, other income and income taxes); and 4. estimated return on investment income, which is shown both as a ratio to the new commitment and the total utilized investment. No figure was mentioned as a minimum return; normally new products were expected to return better than the corporate average, but expansions of existing facilities have been made on a projected return of no greater than 20 to 25 per cent before taxes.

An elaborate check-off list is designed to insure attention to various aspects of projected demand, supply, costs, and competition. Of particular interest are such items as: capacities, captive requirements and future expansion plans of competitors; company's estimated market share before and after expansion; degree of diversity of customers; extent to which success of venture depends upon short- or long-term contracts; the effects of changes in tariff rates on competition from abroad; selling prices used for sales to other units of the company; shape of short-run unit cost curve; comparative cost position of competitors; the degree to which an alternative exists of either making or buying important intermediates; flexibility of proposed facilities for production of other products; the probabilities of obsolescence of the process or products; and the relative position of the company with respect to research and development, technical knowledge, labor supply, patents, and raw materials.

[9] The problem here is not simply one of the target return and target payout period, but rather one of balancing the desire to recoup development and other investment costs as rapidly as possible against the desire to prolong the period from distinctiveness to obsolescence by discouraging potential competitors with a relatively low-price or low-profits policy. The most rapid recovery of investment mentioned was one year, with two years not infrequently mentioned, especially where the innovative monopoly was not expected to last long or process secrecy was not secure. Also, there did not appear to be any consistent relationship between the presence of patent protection and the payout period.

Minimum target profit figures also are used by most of the companies as a basis for sloughing off products and in arriving at "make-or-buy" decisions. An exact minimum target figure was rarely mentioned, but good justifications were required of operating divisions or product departments when returns consistently fell below the corporate average. Not infrequently, officers made statements along the following lines: "If the average corporate return were, say, 20 per cent and the return on investment for a particular item kept falling below 10 per cent, it would be dropped unless

1. a good customer needs it in order to keep a full line, or
2. it is a by-product anyhow, and anything it brings in is really gravy."

A variety of explanations was given by the companies to justify the particular size of the profit target used as a guide in pricing decisions. The most frequently mentioned rationalizations included:

1. fair or reasonable return,
2. the traditional industry concept of fair return in relation to risk factors,
3. desire to equal or better the corporation average return over a recent period,
4. what the company felt it could get as a long-run matter, and
5. use of a specific profit target as a means of stabilizing industry prices.

At least one of the foregoing, and most frequently the first, was mentioned by the companies interviewed, and in a few cases the entire list was offered as justification for the company profit goal.

This reinforces the observation made earlier that no one single objective or policy rules all price-making in any given company. In fact, in many companies a close interrelationship exists among target-return pricing, desire to stabilize prices, and target market-share (either a minimum or maximum objective); this is especially true of U. S. Steel, Union Carbide, and Johns-Manville. It would seem, however, that a target-return approach is ordinarily incompatible with a market-share policy; that is, if a company desires to expand its share of the market, it will be inclined to place less emphasis on rigid adherence to a predetermined target.

## STABILIZATION OF PRICE AND MARGIN

The drive for stabilized prices by companies like U. S. Steel, Alcoa, International Harvester, Johns-Manville, Du Pont, and Union Carbide involves both expectation of proper reward for duty done, i.e. "proper" prices, and a sense of *noblesse oblige.* Having earned what is necessary during poor times to provide an adequate return, they will refrain from upping the price as high as the traffic will bear in prosperity. Likewise, in pricing different items in the product line, there will be an effort (sustained in individual cases by the pricing executive's conscience) to refrain from exploiting any item beyond the limit set by cost-plus.

The distinction between target return on investment as a pricing philosophy and cost-plus pricing in the companies surveyed is difficult to define. Some of the companies that clearly employ the target-return-on-investment procedure in pricing new products—the area of most frequent use of target-return pricing—use cost-plus pricing for other products. The difference between the two rationalizations lies in the extent to which the company is willing to push beyond the limits of a pricing method to some average-return philosophy. According to a General Motors executive, the target plays a prominent role in the formulation of the cost-plus method.[10] But in the case of International Harvester, U. S. Steel, A & P, Johns-Manville, Alcoa, or Union Carbide, it seems fair to say that the pricing executive set the prices of many products on a cost-plus basis (except where competition precludes such action) without questioning the appropriateness of the traditional mark-up.

Cost-plus, therefore, may be viewed as one step on the road to return-on-investment as a guide, or precept for price policy. But some firms never go any farther. The standard can be accepted as self-sufficient, just as the target-return perhaps needs no modification to make it accord with profit maximization (with all the necessary qualifications). Pricing executives seldom look beyond the particular formula with which they are accustomed to justify their decisions. They differentiate between price policies according to the degree of control they exercise; but not by the gap between the price policy and an ideal of profit maximization. They appear as ready to accept cost-plus at a reasonable volume as an ultimate standard for pricing as any other principle.

## TARGET MARKET-SHARE

A maximum or minimum share of the market as a determinant of pricing policy was listed almost as frequently, and seemed to govern policy almost to the same extent as target-return on investment. Share of the market was ordinarily thought of in terms of a maximum, bearing witness to the power of the corporations interviewed. Being giants, they were careful to limit themselves; they apparently did not wish to gobble up any market they entered, unless it was one which they had created, like nylon, asbestos pipe, aluminum screen wire, cable products, or some synthetic chemical.

Hence, the target share of the market as a guide to pricing tended to be used for those products in which the firm did not, at the outset, enjoy a patent or innovative monopoly. Du Pont made no mention of shooting for a given share of the cellophane or nylon market, nor did Union Carbide in the Prestone market; Johns-Manville set no limit to its market share in specialized insulation materials; American Can was not thinking in terms of winning against stiff competition a moderate share of the market

[10]See Donaldson Brown, "Pricing in Relation to Financial Control," *Management and Administration,* Feb. 1924, 7, pp. 195–98, 283–86, 417–22. This may seem to be a rather old reference, but General Motors officials cited it so frequently as an accurate representation of their present-day pricing that it warrants emphasis.

for vacuum packed cans; nor was Alcoa in the wire and cable market. But a General Electric official spoke at length of the company's policy of not exceeding 50 per cent of any given market because it then would become too vulnerable to competition.[11] Johns-Manville officials likewise indicated that product and sales development are geared to attaining a given percentage of the market for a product line. The company endeavors, executives indicated, to maintain the offensive, rather than to be subject to attack because of their large product share. The company felt strongly that 20 per cent of competitive markets was the maximum share in which it was interested. This policy ruled in those areas where Johns-Manville was *not* the price leader. It stresses sales, service, and superior quality of its product in order to maintain its prices somewhat above those of its competitors. Apparently the program of reaching no more than a given market-share and of moving ahead against competition does not find expression in price reductions.

It is not possible to reach any general conclusions from comparisons of target market-shares and actual share of business realized by the companies mentioning this as a policy for pricing purposes. This is due on the one hand to the unwillingness of the companies to specify in detail particular target-share percentages, and on the other to the lack of sufficiently detailed information for the companies in question, especially for the highly diversified firms. Patently, most of these companies have very significant proportions of national markets.[12]

## "MEETING OR MATCHING COMPETITION"

To some of the officials interviewed, the requirement that the product price "meet competition" appeared, at first glance, to preclude the existence of any pricing

[11] He stated, "The company would rather be pushing to expand a 25 per cent share than defending a 50 per cent share." As a matter of fact, he indicated, there were few instances where GE had more than 22 to 25 per cent of a market. In substance, this means that when GE enters an appliance field with a new product, it will price to match its competitors. The company believes that it has been a downward price leader on appliances generally, however, and that both its postwar attempt to lead in price reductions and its long-term reduction in margins (its over-all margins were said to be only 58 per cent as high as in 1940) demonstrate that it has not been content merely to follow the ruling price after moving into a field.

[12] One interesting example of the connection between pricing (livestock bidding), market share, and investment policy is found in Swift. An analysis of livestock buying raises the question whether there is something of an understanding by the major packers of what constitutes their "normal share" of the animals sold in given public stockyards, which was the essence of the Department of Justice's complaint (1948) against Armour, Swift, Cadahy, and Wilson (since dismissed). It would seem that the relative constancy of the proportions of livestock purchased by the principal meat packers is traceable in large part to the short-run fixity of plant capacity, the desire to keep that plant operating at least up to a specific minimum level of utilization (governed partly by labor commitments), and the ever present threat that another packer may secure a larger share of the animals and the market for dressed meats. In view of these considerations, the percentages of animals purchased by the major packers would logically evidence substantial constancy over periods of weeks or months in given markets. But, unless this same approach is carried over into the planning of plant sizes in new locations (or enlargement of established plants), as well as the rate of utilization of these facilities, this would seem to be an insufficient explanation for the long-run stability of shares.

policy at all. Meeting competition according to their view cannot be regarded as a rationalization of action; it is the action itself.

The rationalization of this policy of meeting competition is far from elaborate; at first blush it is perhaps unnecessary. How can "meeting competition" be dignified as one out of several alternative guides to action? In chemicals, Du Pont seems to apply a rule of thumb of adopting the going price in the markets for many standardized products where it never had or else had lost the leadership—e.g. carbon tetrachloride, hydrogen peroxide, disodium phosphate, nitric acid, hydrochloric acid, and various rubber chemicals. Moreover, in the case of many products selling on a freight-equalization basis, prices were not set at a high executive level; the pricing in many cases had not been reviewed for years, having been established beyond the ken of anyone now in the organization. Yet, even here there is perhaps more discretion than the officials are willing or accustomed to admit. In the pricing of neozone, Du Pont was forced—though it had introduced the chemical—to change its price policy because of the tactics of competitors, who shifted the basing point. But need the matter have stopped there? Was there not a decision by Du Pont to go no further than matching the Akron-based price? In many other cases Du Pont undoubtedly, if it chose, could have altered the basing points or other features of the marketing of chemicals of which it produced more than an inconsequential market share.

In many cases the policy of meeting competition appears to be materially influenced by market-share psychology. Esso Standard, while going to great lengths to devise a cost-plus theory, has modified it when and where it seemed necessary or desirable. Standard of Indiana was even more specific in basing its policies on "meeting"—or forestalling—competition. Esso and, to a much lesser extent, Standard of Indiana refrained from publishing or trying to reduce to definiteness the details of the policy. A number of questions related to the companies' rationalizations are basic to understanding the functioning of the policy, for clearly neither company changed prices instantaneously when facing "competition": Did they meet the exact price charged, at the refinery or to the retail dealer? How long did a substandard price have to prevail before it could undermine a cost-plus price? Whose competitive price brought action? How were competitors rated in effectiveness? Answers to these questions are basic to an understanding of the policy. But the oil companies have not divulged the facts that would permit full and consistent treatment of the theory of "meeting competition" as seen by their managements.

It seems also that in some cases the companies are not simply meeting competition—they are preventing it. This appears to have been the purpose of A & P in localizing price cuts to make matters difficult for a competitive store on its opening day, or General Foods in reducing the price of Certo and Sure-Jell in the Northwest where rival pectins were strong.[13] Standard of Indiana, a dominant seller not overfond of price wars, may easily justify meeting competition locally on the basis that the policy offers a permanent threat to potential price-cutters.

In other cases, the companies are aware of specific competitive products whose prices must be matched by their own if volume is to be expanded. Union Carbide knew that its synthetic organic chemicals, like the various alchohols, had to meet or undersell the price of the natural products if the investment was ever to be returned. In other cases, where a standardized commodity–e.g. bakery flour, livestock, feeds, and frozen fish sold by General Foods, flour by General Mills, or wholesale meat by Swift–is simply marketed at a price over which no firm, or even small group of firms, can have control, then pricing policy ceases to have meaning. The phrase "meeting competition" is either inapplicable or inaccurate, since there is no specific competition to meet–only the market price.

## OTHER RATIONALIZATIONS

There are other pegs on which managements hang pricing decisions. In view of American Can's undisputed (at least until 1954) leadership in the metal container industry, and its bargaining power *vis-á-vis* both its suppliers and customers, it is somewhat surprising that the company should not have set out an explicit pricing goal in terms of return on investment. The management seems to be more concerned with the assurance of funds for innovating research than any particular target return on investment, although the maintenance of its market share through its closing-machine leasing policy indirectly accomplishes the same objective. The company's pricing policy could be construed as "marginal" in the sense that it automatically (via its contracts) transmits to its customers increases or decreases in costs of materials (tin plate) or labor in the can factories. In turn, this adjustability in price seems to have had the effect of stabilizing American Can's margin, the price of its services as the owner of can-closing equipment and engineering services, and, at the same time, the price of cans throughout the canning season.

The companies cited many instances involving the need for resolution of conflicts of interest between integrated and nonintegrated firms, and between established giants and newcomers, which displaced the usual bases for their pricing decisions. The Robinson-Patman and Sherman Acts, even when they have not been the basis for actions against the companies, were used as fundamental rationalizations of policy.

[13] This information was not provided by the companies when interviewed, but is based on statements in the A & P antitrust case and the General Foods F. T. C. case made by officials of the respective companies. An A & P official of the Atlantic Division, for example, said, "It might be necessary for us to operate unprofitably for several weeks . . . reducing our line of [sic] 10% several weeks prior to the time the competitor plans to open so that people in the community will be impressed with our low prices. . . ." *U. S. v. New York Great Atlantic and Pacific Tea Co., Inc.,* 67 F. Supp. 626 (1946), p. 668; see also *ibid.*, pp. 667, 669, and Government Brief, pp. 909, 931; and General Foods, F. T. C. Docket No. 5675, Complaint, July 7, 1949.

## A COMPOSITE VIEW OF PRICING OBJECTIVES

Because it is big the large firm envisages itself as a part of a socially integrated group, with responsibilities for the whole pipeline and production (including full-line offerings) and associated distribution. They see themselves in a continuing relationship not only with their own distributors, but even with dealers and ultimate customers, and with their suppliers—even when the latter lacked, or especially when they lacked, the bargaining power of a larger firm. The market, in effect, is regarded as a creature of the firm, and the firm has the responsibility for preserving these relationships and perpetuating its own position.

The size of these firms also makes them an obvious target for antitrust suits, legislation, Congressional investigation, and similar restraining forces. To a certain extent, size thus entails a vulnerability and generates a sense of *noblesse oblige.* This is reinforced by the disposition of the government and the community generally to look on and appeal to these firms as "pattern-setters" for industry generally; and in pricing they are expected to avoid taking full advantage of immediate profit opportunities. This attitude is perhaps most clearly expressed in the *Economic Report of the President* of January 1957, which stated:

> Specifically, business and labor leadership have the responsibility to reach agreements on wages and other labor benefits that are fair to the rest of the community as well as to those persons immediately involved. . . . *And business must recognize the broad public interest in price set on their products and services.* (p. 3, italics added.)

From this point, it is an easy step to the position taken by the typical large firm that it is entitled to a "just price" and "fair return" on investment. In the case of some companies, like U. S. Steel, the resolution of conflicts of interest between integrated and nonintegrated firms, between established giants and newcomers, and between the pattern-setter and the community generally, has modified company price policy to a point where even the managements have come to refer to it as akin to that of a public utility. This may be a logical development in cases where unpleasant experiences of cutthroat competition—especially in fairly standardized products like steel, copper, gasoline, and aluminum—have generated a disposition by management to avoid price changes except through periodic, thoroughly considered, and well-publicized alterations in recognized base prices. By relating price revisions to changes in direct costs (especially increases in wage costs), the firm avoids the annoyance to itself and its customers (who they claim vastly prefer stable prices) of frequent changes in price structure.

This desire for stabilized pricing, oftentimes described with a blanket adjective as "administered," usually implies that the company or companies set some kind of target to which their price policies conform. The price, according to this view, is under the control of one firm acting as the price leader or a group of firms that make policy for the industry. The contention of the business executives themselves is that an administered price, like the tank-wagon price of gasoline, far from being an independent creation of the price leader, is merely a device for approximating a market equilibrium. According to this view, there are so many possibilities of substitution of one product for another, or an offbrand for a name brand, that the limits of discretion are much narrower than is generally supposed. Administration of prices, officials contend, thus merely avoids the decision to use cutthroat competition—which itself would be another form of administered pricing; it also avoids temporary exploitation of shortages. Refraining from raising prices when a higher price is necessary to equate supply with demand, is also justified by management on the grounds that over the long run higher prices would disturb equilibrium by bringing unneeded capacity into the industry. But it is impossible to accept the conventional justification for leadership. It can masquerade as resulting in a genuine "equilibrium" only if the word is made equivalent to whatever is the decision of the leading firms.

The foregoing data, above all, make it clear that management's approach to pricing is based upon *planned* profits. The company proceeds on the assumption of the need for a certain amount of capital to undertake the investment in plant expansion and new factilties which are envisaged for the long haul in order to maintain and/or improve market position. In some cases, quite in contrast to the thinking of management before the second world war, this desire to hold position and to penetrate wider markets requires that capital investment should be planned with built-in excess capacity (this is best illustrated at a rate of 75 or 80 per cent of capacity, which is assumed to be the long-run normal). In deciding upon which products and productive facilities will be added or expanded, the top-level corporation appropriations committee relies upon estimates of returns on utilized investment. The only way in which price policy can be viewed in such companies as these, with their wide variety of products and selling in a large number of different markets, is in terms of profits-investment ratios. This criterion serves as an effective guide for pricing decisions at divisional and departmental levels. If we are to speak of "administered" decisions in the large firm, it is perhaps more accurate to speak of administered *profits* rather than administered *prices.*

## CONCLUSIONS

The principal purpose of this paper has been to contribute to our knowledge of the actual process by which prices are formed in industry, with the expectation that the data will help in constructing a more realistic theory of the firm capable of yielding useful predictions of industrial price behavior. The general hypothesis which emerges is that

1. the large company has a fairly well-defined pricing goal that is related to a long-range profit horizon;
2. its management seeks—especially in multiproduct multimarket operations—a simultaneous decision with respect to price, cost, and product characteristics; and

3. its pricing formulas are handy devices for checking the internal consistency of the separate decisions as against the general company objective.

Under this hypothesis no single theory of the firm—and certainly no single motivational hypothesis such as profit-maximization—is likely to impose an unambiguous course of action for the firm for any given situation; nor will it provide a satisfactory basis for valid and useful predictions of price behavior.

In pursuit of price policies that will yield the maximum satisfaction of the company's community of interests, the findings show that one company will prefer stability, another will seek to expand its market share, or to engage in continuous discovery and pre-emption of new fields, while others will be content to meet competition, to satisfy a set target, or to aim at combinations and variations of these goals. It seems reasonable to conclude that the pricing policies are in almost every case equivalent to a company policy that represents an order of priorities and choice from among competing objectives rather than policies tested by any simple concept of profits maximization. Managerial specialists down the line are given a framework of requirements that must be met, while managers at the top, of course, are free to and do change these requirements to meet particular situations.[14]

Another relevant aspect of the data for theoretical analysis is the conception of the market held by managements of large corporations. Individual products, markets, and pricing are not considered in isolation; the unit of decision-making is the enterprise, and pricing and marketing strategies are viewed in this global context. Because of the tremendously complex joint-cost problems and the lack of knowledge of actual relationships between costs and output or sales, on the one hand, and the joint-revenue aspects of multiproduct companies, on the other, pricing is frequently done for product groups with an eye to the over-all profit position of the company. This means that costing of products ends up as a result of price policy rather than the reverse. In view of the various external pressures on the company and the nature of the strategy of the enterprise, however, it is doubtful if prices would bear any closer relationship to actual costs were detailed cost data available to management. The incentive to realize target rates of profits for the long haul better suits the objectives of management-controlled companies than any desire to profiteer or to seek windfall profits.

It might appear that there are conflicts between the objectives of price leaders and price followers, e.g. between such companies as U. S. Steel and National Steel. Actually, however, it is a matter of leaders having fairly well-defined target objectives, whereas price followers evidently do not have independent targets. Their objective, especially where undifferentiated products make up the bulk of the product line, will be determined by the target set by the price leader. If the target is acceptable, the follower is content to hold a market share and will adjust price policy accordingly.

[14]The managerial philosophy not only calls into question the assumption of profit maximization as a workable description of entrepreneurial behavior, but denies the institutional basis of the classical profit motivation." E. S. Mason, "The Apologetics of 'Managerialism'," *Journal of Business,* Jan. 1958, vol. 31, p. 6.

In more general cases, including differentiated product markets as well as undifferentiated, the extent to which companies—with the dimensions and diversification of those under discussion—serve as leaders or followers on individual products or product groups depends upon the profit-importance of a particular product in a given company's line, the nature of the product—whether a producer or a consumer good—and the size and degree of diversification of companies with which there are product overlaps. Moreover, the manner in which interfirm policies will be coordinated will depend upon the above factors as they bear upon particular products, plus the over-all objectives of the enterprise as a unit and its general market strategy.

A further implication of the findings for the theory of the firm is the relationship found between price and investment decisions. The information on this aspect is limited, but nevertheless the setting of and attempt to follow specific target returns on investment are manifest at two separate levels of operations: short-run pricing and investment decisions. The investment decision presupposes a price (and usually a market-share) assumption, which, in turn, determines short-run price decisions thereafter. Thus, investment decisions in effect are themselves a form of pricing decision, and over time become an inherent part of price policy.

Finally, the general approach of these large corporations to price policy, and the attendant price behavior, raise some important issues for public policy. Their very size—both absolutely and relatively—permits the managements to select from among various alternative courses of action. This is a fairly clear manifestation of economic or market power. In partial reflection of this power, plus a variety of other reasons related to their size, vulnerability to public criticism, and potential antitrust action, these corporations tend to behave more and more like public utilities, especially the target-return-minded companies. To complicate the issue further, target-return pricing implies a policy of stable or rigid pricing, even though exceptions are found with particular product lines.

A crucial question raised by these facets of policy is: What is the net impact on economic growth and stability? More specifically, do target-return pricing, profits planning, and the attendant price behavior, tend to promote or inhibit stability and growth? Much more adequate empirical data on corporation objectives and detailed study of individual company pricing, profits, and investment planning over the course of economic fluctuations are needed before answers can be given to this question.

# 38. THE NATURE OF PRICES AND PRICING

*Donald V. Harper*

*Pricing policy is the business administrator's most intimate contact with economics; and perhaps for this reason the true nature of pricing and its various implications for the firm are difficult to conceptualize and to implement in actual price-decision-making.*

*In the selection that follows, the author reviews briefly the nature of a price offer and four descriptive economic models. A sophisticated appreciation of price cannot be gained without a grasp of the concepts set forth here.*

Prices determine how resources are to be used. They are also the means by which products and services that are in limited supply are rationed among buyers. The price system of the United States is a very complex network composed of the prices of all the products bought and sold in the economy as well as those of a myriad of services, including labor, professional, transportation, and public-utility services, and others ranging from dry cleaning to lawn-mower repair. The interrelationships of all these prices make up the "system" of prices. The price of any particular product or service is not an isolated thing. Each price is linked to a broad, complicated system of prices in which everything seems to depend more or less upon everything else.

If one were to ask a group of randomly selected individuals to define "price," many would reply that price is an amount of money paid by the buyer to the seller of a product or service or, in other words, that price is the money value of a product or service as agreed upon in a market transaction. This definition is, of course, valid as far as it goes. For a complete understanding of a price in any particular transaction,

Source: From *Price Policy and Procedure,* Harcourt, Brace & World, Inc., New York, 1966, pp. 1–26.
Donald V. Harper: Professor of Marketing, University of Minnesota.

much more than the amount of money involved must be known. Both the buyer and the seller should be familiar with not only the money amount, but with the amount and quality of the product or service to be exchanged, the time and place at which the exchange will take place and payment will be made, the form of money to be used, the credit terms and discounts that apply to the transaction, guarantees of the product or service, delivery terms, return privileges, and other factors. In other words, both buyer and seller should be fully aware of all the factors that comprise the total "package" being exchanged for the asked-for amount of money in order that they may evaluate a given price.

The "true" price of a product or service changes whenever any of the associated elements in the package change, as well as when the money amount to be exchanged is altered. For example, if a department store discontinues return privileges on certain articles, or if a manufacturer of industrial machinery reduces the period during which interest will not be charged on credit transactions, the true price has been changed. The money price has not changed, but the package has.

This tends to complicate comparisons of prices on specific products or services over time. The difficulty lies in the frequency with which the conditions or factors change. For example, for many products changes in quality have been substantial over time, thereby rendering any price comparisons somewhat meaningless. Home appliances and automobiles fall into this classification.

Another source of difficulty in comparing prices over time is the fact that the "published," "quoted," "announced," or "list" price of a product or service may, in reality, not be the price actually paid. Various kinds of concealed price concessions may be given to some or all buyers. In such cases, the quoted price is not the "true" price.[1]

## THE CONTRIBUTION OF ECONOMIC THEORY TO PRICE MAKING

### What is Price Theory?

A large proportion of the literature on economic theory is devoted to explaining the pricing mechanism. Price theory, or microeconomics, is concerned with the economic activities of individual economic units, such as consumers, resource owners, and business firms. It deals with the flow of products and services from business firms to consumers, the composition of the flow, and the evaluation or pricing of the component parts of the flow. Similarly, it examines the flow of productive resources (or their services) from resource owners to business firms, their evaluation, and their allocation among alternative uses.[2] In short, one of the main objectives of price theory is to explain by means of abstract analysis how prices are determined under various kinds of market structures.

[1] For a discussion of departures from list prices, see "Discounts That Don't Show," *Business Week,* March 2, 1963, p. 23.

[2] Richard H. Leftwich, *The Price System and Resource Allocation,* rev. ed., Holt, Rinehart and Winston, New York, 1963, p. 8.

Students of marketing and practitioners in the field should be familiar with the basic elements of price theory and its usefulness in the price-making process, but a brief review of price theory and its contribution to price-making may be helpful.

## Cost and Demand Concepts

In order to discuss price theory it is essential that we have a clear understanding of the definitions of certain basic concepts of cost and demand.

Thus, to review briefly, *average total cost* (ATC) is the average cost per unit and is derived by dividing total costs (which include a "normal" return on invested capital) by the number of units of product or service sold.

*Marginal cost* (MC), in contrast, is the change in total costs that results from producing an additional unit of product or service. In other words, it is the extra or additional cost incurred in the production of another unit.

*Average revenue* (AR) is the average revenue per unit sold and is derived by dividing total revenue by the number of units of product or service sold.

*Marginal revenue* (MR) is the change in total revenue that results from the sale of an additional unit of product or service. In other words, it is the additional revenue received from the sale of another unit.

*Price elasticity of demand* is a measure of the responsiveness of the quantity sold to price changes. Specifically, it is the ratio of the percentage response of the quantity sold to a percentage change in price. The demand for a product or service is said to be *elastic* if the total revenue increases as the price is reduced. Demand is *inelastic* if the total revenue decreases when the price is reduced. If there is no change in the total revenue when prices are changed, demand is said to display *unitary elasticity.* Thus, the more sensitive that the quantity demanded is to price changes, the more elastic is the demand for the offering. In graphic terms, a perfectly elastic demand is illustrated by a perfectly horizontal line, a perfectly inelastic demand is illustrated by a perfectly vertical line.

## Kinds of Market Structures

Several kinds of market structures have been isolated by economists in an attempt to explain how prices are determined in a free enterprise economy. The market structure in which a firm operates is determined by three basic elements: the number of firms in the industry, the size of the firms in the industry, and the nature of the product or service sold, in terms of the degree of product differentiation. In discussing these market structures, the economist assumes that the business firm attempts to maximize profits and that the business executive knows what the firm's cost and demand characteristics are.

*Pricing under pure competition.* In a situation of pure competition the following assumptions apply:

1. There is a large number of buyers and sellers, each of whom enjoys so small a share of the market that no single individual or firm has any influence on price.
2. There is complete freedom to enter and leave the industry.
3. The products and services sold are homogeneous (or standardized), so that the offerings of one seller of a given product or service are identical to those of all other sellers of that product or service.
4. There is full knowledge on the part of both buyers and sellers as to the terms and conditions of sale.
5. All factors of production in the economy are fully employed.

Under such circumstances, a firm has no need for a price policy; it sells at a price over which it has no control. The market itself fixes a price that equates the quantities sellers are willing to sell with the quantities buyers are willing to buy. As a consequence, the demand for the output of any particular firm is perfectly elastic; if the firm raised the price on its product above the established price, it would reduce demand to zero, whereas it can sell any amount of the product at the market-determined price. These factors produce a perfectly horizontal demand curve as shown in Figure 1. (Notice that in pure competition the demand curve is also the average-revenue [AR] curve and the marginal-revenue [MR] curve.) The only decisions required of a firm under such circumstances are whether to sell at all and, if so, how much to produce. The firm would maximize its profits by producing the quantity at which marginal cost (MC) is equal to marginal revenue or price. Up to that point, an increase in output adds more to revenue than to cost; beyond that point, an increase in output adds more to cost than to revenue.

Thus in Figure 1, the firm would maximize profits by producing a quantity 0*A*, the price of which would be 0*B*. Here the firm is earning excess profits, that is, profits in excess of a normal return on invested capital or in excess of what the capital would earn in an alternative use. Such excess profits are equal to the rectangle *CDEB*–the

**Figure 1. Pure competition–short run**

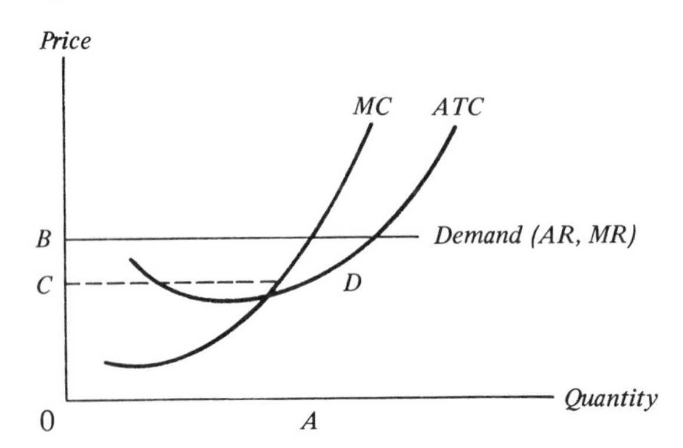

difference between price and average total cost (ATC). Excess profits can exist in the short run, but, under pure competition, in the long run excess profits attract additional firms into the industry and encourage existing firms to expand, thereby causing a downward pressure on price. Therefore, in the long run, price tends to be equal to the minimum average cost of each firm. This produces equilibrium, in which there is no incentive for firms to enter or leave the industry—neither excess profits nor losses are being incurred. Figure 2 illustrates a typical long-run equilibrium situation for the individual firm.

*Pricing under pure monopoly.* Pure monopoly is the reverse of pure competition. In a pure monopoly, the seller has complete control over the output of a product for which there is no substitute so similar that the monopolist's sales are affected by price changes in the substitute product. Consequently, the demand curve for the monopolist's product is equivalent to the demand curve for the entire industry. This, in turn, means that as the monopolist lowers prices he will sell more units of his product or service, and that as he raises prices he will sell fewer units. The demand curve slopes downward to the right, unlike the perfectly horizontal demand curve faced by the seller under pure competition. Hence, the monopolist looks for a combination of price and output that provides him with the greatest total difference between cost and revenue, or the greatest total profit.

In both the short run and the long run the monopolist can maximize profits by equating marginal cost and marginal revenue. In Figure 3, for example, the firm would maximize profits at output 0*A* and price 0*B*, for this is the point at which marginal cost equals marginal revenue. The basic kind of adjustment that the pure monopolist needs to make to maintain the profit-maximizing position in the long run is that of changing the scale of plant.

*Pricing under monopolistic competition.* In monopolistic competition, it is also assumed that there is a large number of buyers and sellers, but, unlike pure competition,

**Figure 2. Pure competition—long run**

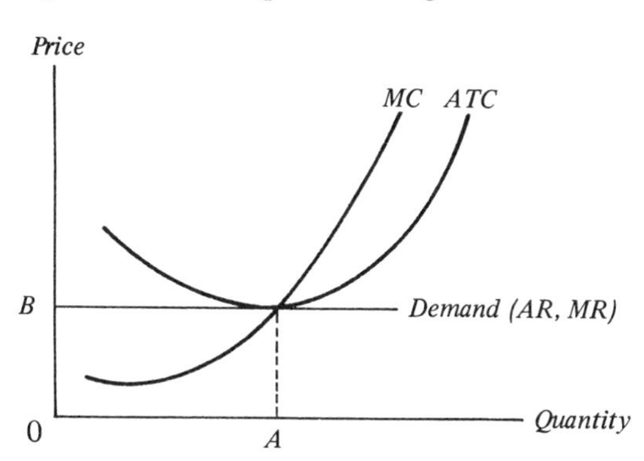

**Figure 3. Pure monopoly**

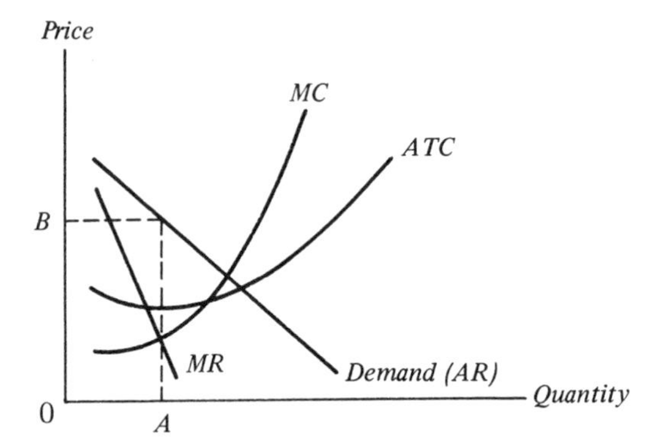


there is product differentiation; that is, the offerings of competing firms are not identical in the eyes of the buyer. However, in monopolistic competition, as in pure competition, the actions of one seller have no perceptible effect upon the other sellers because there is a large number of competitors. Product differentiation accounts for the fact that the demand curve faced by a firm under monopolistic competition is not perfectly elastic but, instead, is somewhat inelastic and slopes downward to the right. Furthermore, because of the competition from close substitutes, the demand curve will not usually have a very steep slope. The short-run pricing situation faced by a firm under monopolistic competition is depicted in Figure 4.

Here we see that in the short run the firm will produce 0*A* units and sell at price 0*B*, thus earning a total excess profit of *CDEB*. With marginal cost equal to marginal revenue at this point, profits are being maximized for the firm. Notice that this does not mean that all firms in the industry will be charging identical prices if they are all maximizing profits since, by definition, firms in monopolistic competition do not

**Figure 4. Monopolistic competition–short run**

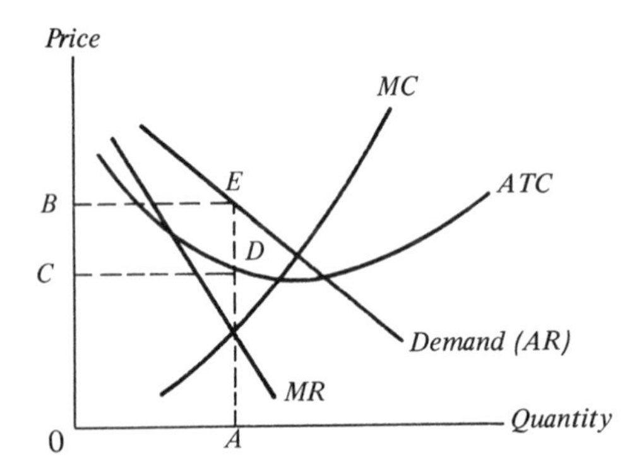

produce homogeneous products or services, and each firm attempts to equate its own marginal cost and marginal revenue. However, the competition from many close substitutes may cause the prices to be relatively close together.

As in pure competition, the presence of excess profits in the short run will attract new competitors and cause existing competitors to expand, thereby producing a long-run tendency for excess profits to diminish. The resultant shift of the demand curve facing the firm, downward and to the left, may eliminate the excess profits, as shown in Figure 5. The theory of monopolistic competition recognizes that the demand curve may not be pushed to actual tangency with the average-total-cost curve, however, since special advantages of branding, trademarks, and patents cannot be removed completely by competition because perfect substitutes cannot be produced. Thus it is possible that the demand curve will not be tangent to the average-total-cost curve in the long run. In any event, in both the short run and the long run, to maximize profits the firm under monopolistic competition attempts to equate marginal cost and marginal revenue.

*Pricing under oligopoly.* Another departure from pure competition is called oligopoly. It exists when there are so few sellers of a particular product or service that the market activities (including pricing) of one seller have an important effect on the other sellers. In such a situation each seller is aware that the competing firms in the industry are interdependent and that in changing his prices or engaging in other market activities he must take into account the probable reactions of the other sellers. Under pure competition, pure monopoly, and monopolistic competition, the seller faces a definite predictable demand situation that can be identified by the firm, at least conceptually. This is not true in an oligopoly situation, however, as long as there is no collusion between the competing sellers. An independent price change by one seller may be

**Figure 5. Monopolistic competition–long run**

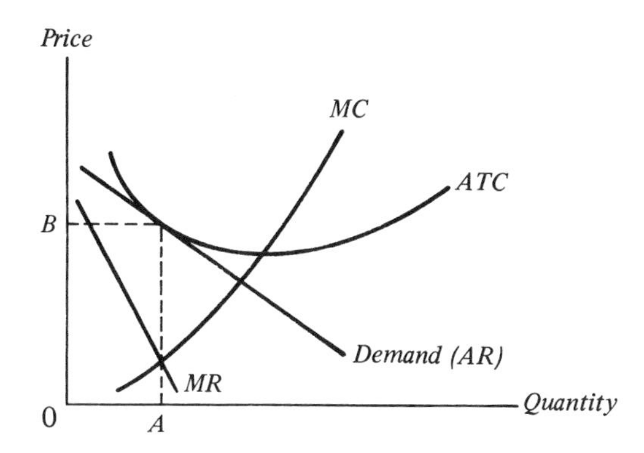

expected to lead to a chain of repercussions that have no definite or predictable outcome. Thus the oligopolist often cannot be sure what will happen if he decides to initiate a unilateral price or output change.

Because there are many different kinds of oligopolies, it is impossible to construct a general theory that will adequately explain all conceivable obligopolistic situations. Consequently, the analysis of oligopoly tends to be less specific than that of other market structures. Some of the characteristics that vary from case to case in an oligopoly, and that make generalizations difficult, are the degree of product differentiation, the ease of entry into the industry, and the ability of a firm to predict with certainty what competing firms will do, particularly their reaction to an action that it proposes to take in the marketplace. To some extent this last characteristic is a function of the presence or lack of collusion.

In an oligopoly, as in the other competitive situations we have discussed, a firm will attempt to equate marginal cost and marginal revenue in order to maximize profits. A thorough survey of the various theories of oligopoly may be found in any text on microeconomic theory. It may be helpful, however, to make a distinction between two kinds of oligopolistic situations. The first is referred to as *pure* or *homogeneous oligopoly* and the second as *differentiated oligopoly.*

In a pure or homogeneous oligopoly there is a small number of firms in the industry, and they sell a homogeneous product or service. All sellers generally are compelled to ask the same price since the purchase decision is predominantly influenced by price when a homogeneous product or service is involved. Furthermore, because there are only a few sellers, each seller must consider what effect his prices will have on pricing by competitors, and each must expect retaliation if he reduces prices. Thus, a firm in an oligopoly will reduce prices only if it thinks it can benefit from the decrease even though competitors should match the lower price.

By way of contrast, in a differentiated oligopoly a seller is not compelled to price at the same level as his competitors since in the eyes of the purchaser, there is some real or imagined product differentiation. Hence prices vary among firms in the oligopoly, and they vary in direct proportion to the differences in the degree of product differentiation among the offerings of the competing firms.

Short-run price behavior in oligopolistic industries is sometimes depicted by a "kinked" demand curve, which can be used to describe either pure oligopoly or differentiated oligopoly, although it is more appropriate for the former. Basically, the kinked demand curve is used to describe a situation in which

1. an acceptable price or cluster of prices has been well established in the industry;
2. if one firm lowers its price, other firms will follow that price or undercut the new price in order to retain their market shares, so that a unilateral price reduction by one firm has the effect of leaving market-share distribution about where it was before or reducing it for the firm that initiated the price reductions; and

3. if one firm increases its price, competing firms will not follow the price increase, thereby causing customers of the firm to shift their patronage to other firms that offer lower prices and causing the firm that initiated the price increase to lose all or part of its share of the market.

Such a kinked demand curve is shown in Figure 6.

In Figure 6 we assume that the established price for the firm is *0B*. If the firm should adjust price downward to *0D*, the other firms will probably follow. As a result, the firm succeeds only in keeping the same share of the market that it had before (or possibly losing some of that share) while decreasing its total revenue. If the firm should increase price to *0E*, other firms will probably not follow the price change, and as a consequence the firm will lose a considerable share of the market to other firms. For this reason the demand curve above point *G* is shown to be considerably more elastic than it is below point *G*.

Given the situation described by the kinked demand curve, the firm tends to avoid price changes in either direction since downward adjustments only decrease total revenue, and upward adjustments reduce market share substantially or eliminate it entirely.

It must be kept in mind, of course, that the kinked demand curve is only one of several possible situations that can exist under oligopoly and is appropriate only when the situation in question possesses characteristics similar to those listed above.

## Usefulness of Price Theory to the Price Maker

Bridging the gap between price theory and the practice of setting prices is difficult. The basic problem is that, to a great extent, conventional price theory does not describe the "real world" in that the assumptions upon which it rests are unrealistic.

One common assumption underlying all traditional theories of price is that the entrepreneur, or businessman, carefully weighs and measures the gains and losses that

**Figure 6. Oligopoly–kinked demand curve**

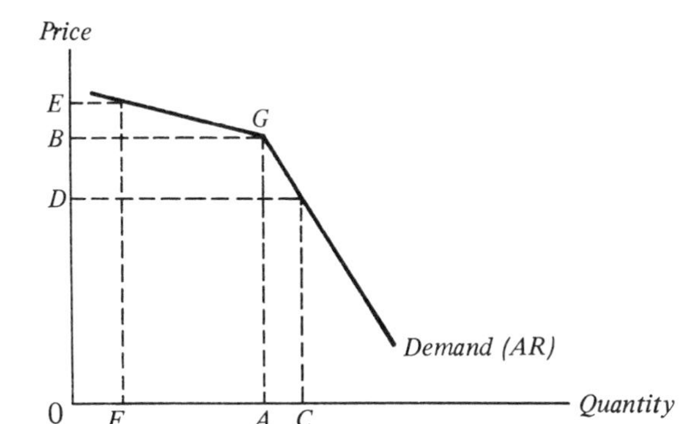

accrue as a result of price decisions that he makes. In theory the price-maker is assumed to be a rational person who is capable of analyzing the implications of his decisions and deciding accordingly. This is not a realistic assumption, however, because human beings are not as rational in their economic behavior as it supposes and because information concerning costs and demand is often not available to them in the form or to the degree that is assumed in price theory. There is, in fact, a great deal of uncertainty regarding both costs and demand in the real world.

Another assumption common to all types of price theory is that the firm and the price-maker attempt to maximize profits. In practice, however, price-makers and other business executives may be guided, at least in the short run, by motives other than, or in addition to, profit maximization.

Price theory is also limited in its usefulness in that it assumes that the firm is a single-product or a single-service firm. In the real world, most firms are involved in selling several different products or services, and the fact that a firm has a multiproduct line has a great impact on its pricing decisions.[3]

Because of these restrictive assumptions, theories of price are simplifications. The following considerations are contrary to the special assumptions that underlie the theory of pure competition.

1. Many industries have a limited number of buyers or sellers, some of whom are quite large in size.
2. Large capital requirements often make it difficult to enter an industry, and the fixed nature of some investments sometimes makes it difficult to leave an industry.
3. Products are rarely homogeneous–instead, product differentiation is the rule, whether these differences are based solely on brand names or whether there are substantial physical differences as well in the products and services offered by competing sellers.
4. Full knowledge is generally lacking, especially on the buyers' side.
5. Many industries, furthermore, often do not operate at full capacity.

Because of these considerations pure competition, as rigorously defined in theory, has never existed in practice, and it never will.

Another problem encountered in attempting to apply price theory is that in practice some market situations contain a number of rival sellers that is neither large nor small, but somewhere in between. In such cases sellers are sometimes concerned about the actions of competitors and sometimes not. This means that in theoretical terms it is impossible to designate such industries as either oligopolies or as examples of monopolistic competition. They simply do not fit into a neat theoretical category.

[3] Donald V. Harper, *Price Policy and Procedure,* Harcourt, Brace & World, Inc., New York, 1966, chaps. 6 and 7.

Thus it is apparent that in practice business decisions involve much more than a mechanical equating of marginal cost and marginal revenue for the purpose of determining production levels and prices, as price theory may seem to suggest. Of course it is impossible for price theory to take into account all the economic factors and data in the real world. Abstract theory must single out what appear to be the most important or most relevant variables, and from these build a general theory of how the price system operates. If this were not the case, theoretical analysis would not be manageable or meaningful.

Price theory has been developed primarily for use in the analysis of the effects of broad economic changes and the evaluation of social controls. It is too much to expect that the tools that are useful for social economics would also be useful in the same degree for the price-maker.[4]

Nevertheless, in the analysis of how an individual firm sets its prices, price theory is helpful to the extent that it sets forth the general forces that affect pricing and offers some explanation of why these forces affect pricing. In addition, price theory permits the isolation of separate influences on prices where there are many influences operating simultaneously, and it brings to light a number of questions that the price-maker should take into account.

Price theory also provides a useful standardized terminology for the discussion of cost and demand concepts. Furthermore, the several kinds of market situations described by price theory, although they are themselves somewhat unrealistic, provide a benchmark against which a "real" pricing situation may be compared. In this regard, for example, price theory points up the necessity of considering the degree of product differentiation and the number of sellers in an industry in any pricing decision.[5]

Finally, price theory is relevant for price-making in that it points out some broad social and economic implications of different pricing policies. Such implications are important not only to government officials and others concerned with public policy matters but to the price-maker as well.

For these reasons, price theory is basic to an understanding of price policy and price procedure and, in fact, to most marketing activities. Certainly, no marketing executive should attempt to assume the responsibilities of price-making without first having a sound knowledge of the basic elements of price theory.

## KINDS OF PRICES AND PRICE-MAKING

It is possible to make use of the terminology and the various market structures set forth in traditional price theory when describing the several kinds of price-making practiced in the economy of the United States today. These types of price-making have

[4] William W. Haynes, *Managerial Economics: Analysis and Cases,* Dorsey Press, Homewood, Ill., 1963, p. 347.

[5] Edward R. Hawkins relates the theory of monopolistic competition to marketing price policies in "Price Policies and Theory," *Journal of Marketing,* January, 1954. He states on p. 233 that most pricing behavior is quite consistent with the general theory of monopolistic competition.

been described by Jules Backman as market pricing, administered or business-controlled pricing, and government-controlled pricing.[6]

## Market Pricing

According to Backman, market pricing exists whenever the seller has no control over the price he receives in the marketplace. In such a situation, price is determined solely by the free play of the forces of supply and demand. The seller either accepts the price determined by this mechanism or he refuses to sell. He cannot sell at a price higher than that established in the market. Notice that market pricing conforms closely to the model of pure competition. Obviously, where there is market pricing the seller makes no price decisions and needs no price policy.

Examples of true market pricing are very rare and are confined mainly to the organized commodity exchanges (such as those where grain, cotton, and other products are traded), some other agricultural markets, and the security exchanges.

## Administered or Business-Controlled Pricing[7]

Administered, or business-controlled, prices are prices that are established by business firms at their own discretion. The seller sets the price and buyers buy or do not buy as they wish. Here prices are not fixed automatically by the impersonal forces of the marketplace but rather are the result of policies and decisions made by sellers. The free play of the forces of supply and demand, along with other factors, are important in influencing pricing decisions, but they do not actually establish the price, as in market pricing. Administered pricing, then, is a broad concept that embraces any situation in which there is some degree of inelasticity in the firm's demand curve, such as under monopolistic competition, oligopoly, and pure monopoly.

Because the seller takes the initiative in price-making instead of receiving a price from the market, administered pricing is sometimes referred to as reversed or "inverted" price-making. Where there is administered pricing, pricing decisions and a price policy are obviously required. As Roland S. Vaile, E. T. Grether, and Reavis Cox have pointed out:

> Price policy and administered pricing assume that there is some discretionary latitude in pricing, within which meaningful decisions are made by the enterprise individually or by groups of enterprises. In almost all business pricing, except for some segments of the primary industries, there is at least a narrow zone of choice among alternatives. Even when sellers are numerous, product differentiation and heterogeneity and the chain linking of products and of types of enterprises

[6] *Price Practices and Price Policies,* Ronald Press, New York, 1953, pp. 3–4.

[7] Some confusion surrounds the term "administered pricing." In this text the term is being used to denote all situations in which prices are established by business firms at their own discretion. Some writers have used it to designate a kind of price behavior (usually undesirable) rather than a method of arriving at or determining a price. Other writers use the term to identify price-making in heavily concentrated industries only. The confusion surrounding the term accounts for part of the criticism of administered pricing.

may create conditions favorable to and opportunities for the exercise of discretion in pricing by individual firms.[8]

Most prices in the American economy are administered prices in this sense of the term, and they are found in all areas of business activity from the corner grocery store to United States Steel or Du Pont. The degree of discretion, or the amount of control, that the seller has over the price of his product or service varies considerably, basically because of variations in the degree of product differentiation and also because of differences in the size of the firm and the number of competitors in the industry. Administered pricing is found in many market-structure situations; there may be a large number of sellers and very little product differentiation, or there may be only two or three firms in an industry and high product differentiation. For example, the manager of gasoline service station A, who sells a "major" brand of gasoline, exercises administrative control over the prices he charges. He sets a price, and potential buyers either pay it or not. However, because gasoline (at least within the broad categories of "major" and "independent" brands) is considered by many, if not most, purchasers of gasoline to be a homogeneous or standardized product (except for the brand-name differences), many buyers of gasoline are quite sensitive to price differences. Thus, if station manager B reduces his price by several cents per gallon while his competitors who also sell major brands do not, he will enjoy increased business because many buyers feel that "gasoline is gasoline" and will patronize the station with the lowest price. Manager A, if he is a competitor of B, then must either suffer a reduction in sales volume or lower his price to be competitive with manager B. If he decides to lower his price, as is often the case, another gasoline price war may begin.[9] Such price wars tend to occur in industries where a product lacks differentiation in the eyes of many buyers, thereby making price the most important factor in the purchase decision. This means that the demand curve faced by the individual seller is highly elastic. For this reason, although the manager of a gasoline service station may exercise administrative control over the prices he charges, his degree of discretion is very much limited by the forces of competition and the nature of demand for the product he sells–barring collusive activity among the gasoline retailers.

In contrast, a seller of a highly differentiated product, such as a manufacturer of a camera that has an exclusive picture-developing feature or a musical instrument with an established, prestigious reputation, is not so limited as to the price at which he can sell his product, nor does he find it so necessary to maintain the same prices as his competitors. Since there is substantial product differentiation, price loses some of its significance to the buyer, and seller A does not have to charge the same price as seller B in order to remain in business. Because his product or service is different from that of his competitors, and because it offers certain features that are not offered by competing products or services, a certain number of buyers may be willing to pay prices

[8] *Marketing in the American Economy,* Ronald Press, New York, 1952, p. 403.

[9] Price competition in gasoline at the retail level is complicated by the existence of "major" and "independent" brands and the accepted differential in price between the two categories. In other words, price warfare in the above example may be not only between retailers of major brands but also between them and those who sell independent brands.

above those asked by competitors in order to obrain these unique product features. In such a situation the demand curve faced by the individual seller is to some degree inelastic. The greater the product differentiation is—whether physical, or psychological, or both—the more control the seller has over the price.

Other important factors that influence the amount of control the seller has over the price of his product or service are the size of the firm and the number of competing sellers. Thus, there are some industries, such as steel manufacturing, where despite the fact that the product is essentially homogeneous, or standardized (except for brand names), the largest firm has been able to exercise a considerable amount of control over price. In this case the other firms in the industry, which is composed of a relatively small number of firms, have been willing to follow its lead, for a number of reasons. This industry approaches pure oligopoly.[10]

Other industries are characterized by considerable product differentiation and are composed of a small number of large firms, as in differentiated oligopoly. The automobile industry is an example. Here the ability to control price is relatively great although, of course, individual firms do not enjoy anything like complete freedom to set prices without regard for the nature of competition and demand, as is pointed out in later chapters.

Thus, the term "administered pricing" is used to designate a catch-all category that includes most pricing environments in the United States and many different degrees of control over price. In fact, one could theoretically set up a scale of values for this category in which industries or firms with very little control over their prices are listed at one end and industries or firms with near monopoly power over prices are shown at the other end.

### Government-Controlled Pricing

The prices of some goods and services produced by private business are set directly by government—federal, state, or local. Consider, for example, government regulation of the rates or prices in the transportation and public-utilities industries, agricultural price programs, and wartime or other emergency price controls. In such cases public administration of prices has replaced or works in conjunction with privately administered prices or market prices. In the case of the traditionally regulated industries—transportation and public utilities—the usual practice is for the regulated companies to make use of their administrative authority to set prices with the understanding that such prices are subject to review and possible adjustment or rejection by the government regulatory agency involved. Thus, in industries such as these, public administration works with and on occasion replaces private administration of prices. In the case of emergency price controls, such as those imposed in wartime, price fixing is done entirely by the government.

In addition to the situations in which government regulates pricing in private industry by means of a formal system of regulation, it should be noted that government is

[10]Price leadership is discussed more fully in Harper, *op. cit.,* chap. 3.

playing an increasingly important role in price-making in other ways as well. For example, government participation in price-making by private business is found in the defense industry and other industries where private business firms supply goods or services to government. In such cases government influences price just as any buyer would. Sometimes government is the only possible buyer (monopsony), and it then exerts a decisive influence on pricing decisions.

Governments also set prices on products or services they provide to the public, such as postal rates, rates for electric power sold by the Tennessee Valley Authority, water rates set by municipally owned companies, and charges for street, sewer, and other improvements made by local governments (monopoly situations).

The scope of government participation in the pricing process of American business is not limited to such overt examples as those cited above. Much of the pricing in the private sector of the economy is subject to influence by government as exerted through pressures from high government officials and Congressional committees (nonstatutory influences) or through legislation such as the Sherman Act, the Robinson-Patman Act, the Federal Trade Commission Act, patent laws, tariff laws, and resale price maintenance laws.

### Kind of Pricing to be Discussed

In this text we shall be concerned chiefly with administered or business-controlled pricing since the vast majority of pricing decisions in the American economy falls into this category. Because market pricing occurs relatively infrequently and involves no price decisions or price policies, it will not be considered further. The role of government in pricing will be discussed in Chapter 4,[11] primarily in connection with the legal environment in which pricing decisions are made and with some nonstatutory government influences on pricing. Direct government regulation of pricing, such as that found in transportation and some other industries, is not covered in this text.[12]

## CRITICISMS OF ADMINISTERED PRICING

Administered pricing has been subjected to criticism from various sources and has been investigated by the federal government. The criticisms are that there is a lack of competition in administered pricing, that administered prices are those of big business, that they are too inflexible, and that they contribute to inflation.

### Lack of Competition in Administered Pricing

One criticism that is sometimes made of administered pricing is that there is much less competition in an industry in which administered pricing exists than would be the case

[11] *Ibid.*

[12] There is extensive literature available on direct government regulation of pricing in the traditionally regulated industries such as transportation in public utilities. For example, an excellent source of information on government regulation of pricing in the transportation industry is D. Philip Locklin, *Economics of Transportation,* 6th ed., Richard D. Irwin, Inc., Homewood, Ill., 1966.

if market pricing prevailed. It has been said that administered prices are "noncompetitive" or "monopoly" prices since the forces of supply and demand do not determine prices, as would be the case under market pricing. It is charged that under administered pricing, competition is reduced or eliminated and that the price-maker has considerable power to charge the price that will be most profitable for his firm.[13]

As we have seen, however, actual examples of market pricing are hard to find in the American economy. The reason for the general absence of market pricing is simple—the conditions necessary for its existence are usually not found in the real world. Market pricing, as we have defined it, approximates pure competition, yet as we pointed out earlier in this chapter, very few market structures in the real world approach the theoretical concept of pure competition in every respect.[14] Instead of pure competition we find various forms of monopolistic competition or oligopoly, which are characterized by product differentiation, small numbers of sellers in some industries, large firms as well as small firms, and lack of complete knowledge.

Despite these elementary flaws in their arguments, critics of administered pricing insist on comparing administered pricing with market pricing or, in other words, pure competition is undesirable. Indeed, the very terms "monopolistic competition" and "imperfect competition" that have been used to designate such departures in price theory seem to imply that there is something unnatural about these forms of competition. It is true, of course, that pure competition, if it existed, would in the long run result in prices equal to minimum average costs and that there would be no sales promotion expenditures and no profits for firms beyond the minimum required to keep them in the business. This is partially responsible for its attractiveness as a standard. Another important reason is that economic theory prior to the 1930s put heavy emphasis on pure competition, so that as new theories developed in later years, they tended to be looked upon as departures from the "norm" of pure competition.

As we have seen, pure competition is generally unattainable in the real world because of its artificial, unrealistic assumptions. Therefore, it is unreasonable to use pure competition as a standard by which to judge the existing competitive system. The theory of pure competition provides a useful model that illustrates in simplified form the general pressures or forces that influence prices. Nonetheless, pure competition, as it is rigorously defined, has never existed and never will exist, although there are isolated examples, such as commodity exchanges, that closely approximate it. Furthermore, it is interesting to note that we probably would not like pure competition even if we could have it. It is doubtful that we would want a situation in which all products of a given type were identical even though they were produced by different firms all of which were small.

[13]For example, the following statement has been attributed to the late Senator Estes Kefauver: "Administered prices are those which, in contrast to competitive prices determined by market supply and demand, are arbitrarily set and held constant, or on occasion even increased despite a fall in demand." See "The Fruits of Price Investigation," *The Progressive,* July, 1961, p. 12.

[14]For a discussion of this point, see Backman, *op. cit.,* pp. 4–6, and *Pricing: Policies and Practices,* National Industrial Conference Board, New York, 1961, pp. 9–12.

What, then, is the role of competition in the real world of administered pricing and less than perfect markets? Is competition any more or less an effective force than would be the case under market pricing or pure competition? It is, of course, difficult to make a general statement as to the role that competition plays in the business world today, since, as we have mentioned, such a wide variety of industries is involved. Competition is certainly more potent in some than in others. It is impossible to measure objectively the degree of competition that exists in any given industry, however. Under administered pricing, competition can be and often is very vigorous. This competition usually revolves around a number of factors in addition to (sometimes instead of) price. These are the host of variables, including personal selling effort, advertising, product development, delivery services, and credit terms, which are referred to as non-price competition. Certainly, in many industries competition is keen although the industries are characterized by administered pricing. In such cases the price-maker does not merely set a price for his product or service arbitrarily. Instead, there are a number of factors that he must take into account, of which competition and competitors' prices are among the more important. He must also consider the nature of demand, costs, the characteristics of the product or service, and various legal aspects. In short, administered pricing is not clearly inconsistent with active competition.[15]

To summarize, administered pricing may in some cases be associated with situations in which active competition does not exist to any great degree, but it is also associated with countless situations in which competition is very active. Properly defined, the term refers to a method of price-making, which in itself does not indicate a lack of vigorous competition.

### Administered Prices—The Prices of Big Business

The claim is sometimes made that administered prices are the prices of "big business" and that small business firms use some other kind of price-making. This is, of course, false since, as we have seen, most prices in the United States are administered, and all kinds and sizes of industries and firms make use of administered pricing. The small retailer, wholesaler, or manufacturer practices price administration just as surely as does Standard Oil of New Jersey or General Motors. Indeed, even when the American economy was characterized chiefly by small business firms, administered pricing prevailed as it does today.

### Inflexibility of Administered Prices

Market prices are usually thought to be highly flexible in nature; that is, they change very often, perhaps every few seconds, in response to changes in the forces affecting them. Administered prices, on the other hand, are said to be more inflexible in that the seller arbitrarily holds them at some given level for some length of time. Actually,

[15] Joel Dean points out that the same set of facts can indicate to some people that a competitive situation exists and to others that a competitive situation does not exist. See "Competition as Seen by the Businessman and the Economist," in Harvey W. Huegy, ed., *The Role and Nature of Competition in Our Marketing Economy,* Bureau of Economic and Business Research, University of Illinois, Urbana, Ill., 1954

whether or not a given price is flexible depends not so much on whether it is a market price or an administered price, but rather on a number of factors that affect the behavior of prices over time. These would include the characteristics of the product or service, the nature of demand for the product or service, the nature of costs in the firm or industry, various legal considerations, the structure of the industry, custom and habit, and many other factors.[16] Today the economic effect of so-called inflexible administered prices is of much less concern than was the case in the 1930s.[17]

One criticism that was prevalent in the 1930s was that inflexible administered prices tended to prevent prices from adjusting automatically to changes in market and production conditions, so that when a recession or depression occurred, the failure of inflexible administered prices to be lowered with sufficient speed to adjust to the new conditions resulted in a sharper reduction in sales volume than would have been the case if the adjustment had been made more rapidly. Thus, it was said, the downswing of the 1930s was worse in that production fell further than it would have if automatic price adjustments had been made. The chief proponent of the idea was Gardner C. Means.[18] Indeed, it is not surprising that Means' definition of an administered price is closely related to the idea of inflexibility since it was he who coined the term originally to mean a price that is set by administrative action and held constant for a period of time.

A number of studies have been made on the topic since then, and all seem to refute the idea that inflexible administered prices actually increased unemployment and reduced production in the depressed 1930s. These studies and those of later recessions indicate that inflexible administered prices are not necessarily accompanied by drastically reduced production during an economic downswing.[19] They indicate that while price is often an important factor, other factors must also be considered in order to explain the changes in production that occur in such periods. However, although the studies provide no factual support for the generalization that declining production and rising

[16]The causes of inflexibility are discussed by Backman in *Price Practices and Price Policies,* chap. 3, and by Dean in *Managerial Economics,* Prentice-Hall, Inc., Englewood Cliffs, N.J., 1951, pp. 458–60.

[17]The term "inflexible" in itself carries a bad connotation. There perhaps would be a different reaction to inflexibility of prices if, instead of the terms "inflexible" and "flexible," the terms "stable" and "unstable" were used.

[18]See his *Industrial Prices and Their Relative Inflexibility,* 74th Cong., 1st sess., Senate Document 13, Government Printing Office, Washington, D.C., 1935.

[19]See Backman, "Price Inflexibility and Changes in Production," *American Economic Review,* September, 1939: "Price Flexibility and Changes in Production," *Conference Board Bulletin,* National Industrial Conference Board, New York, 1939; "Administered Prices," in United States Steel Corporation, *Steel and Inflation: Fact vs. Fiction,* United States Steel Corporation, New York, 1958, pp. 234–54; Backman and Marvin Levine, "Price and Production Behavior in Recession," *Current Economic Comment,* August, 1958; Ernest M. Doblin, "Some Aspects of Price Flexibility," *Review of Economic Statistics,* November, 1940; Alfred C. Neal, *Industrial Concentration and Price Inflexibility,* Public Affairs Press, Washington, D.C., 1942; Saul Nelson and Walter G. Keim, "Price Behavior and Business Policy," *TNEC Monograph 1,* Temporary National Economic Committee, Washington, D.C., 1940; and Willard J. Thorpe and Walter F. Crowder, "The Structure of Industry," *TNEC Monograph 27,* Temporary National Economic Committee, Washington, D.C. 1941.

unemployment during a recession or depression are attributable to price administration, it should be kept in mind that price comparisons over time can be misleading because of qualitative changes in the product and changes in the conditions surrounding the sale of the product.

It is probably true that price inflexibility *can* in *some* instances contribute to low production and high unemployment although, as we have said, such an effect of price inflexibility has been very much exaggerated. Today this problem is thought to be of only minor importance. Commenting on the controversy surrounding administered prices in the 1930s, George J. Stigler remarked: "Toward the end of the decade the literature on rigid prices displayed growing anemia; it is fair to say that economists abandoned the close study of the subject, less because its lack of scientific import was established than because it had become boring."[20]

## Administered Prices and Inflation

In more recent times administered pricing, particularly in concentrated industries, has been accused of having contributed to inflation in the United States.[21] The Senate Subcommittee on Antitrust and Monopoly, under the chairmanship of the late Senator Estes Kefauver, was very much concerned with this question. Testimony before this subcommittee by Means and others to the effect that administered prices were a major cause of the inflation of the 1950s led to various proposals for federal legislation, all of which were unsuccessful.[22]

The charge that price administration has contributed to inflation has been refuted by various studies made of price movements in the 1950s. Backman's analysis of price changes between 1955 and 1957,[23] for example, illustrates that there is no simple or certain relationship between concentration of production capacity and market share in the hands of a few firms and price administration, on the one hand, and the direction or magnitude of price change on the other. Backman found that some of the products sold by concentrated industries bore administered prices and had larger than average price increases, but he also found that in many concentrated industries administered prices showed only small changes. Prices in industries with low concentration and administered prices showed similar disparity. Backman concluded that it is difficult to understand how price administration *per se* could be held responsible for

[20] "Administered Prices and Oligopolistic Inflation," *The Journal of Business,* January, 1962, p. 1.

[21] Thus we have the rather strange situation in which the same kind of pricing is accused of causing depression (deflation) on the one hand and inflation on the other.

[22] In a recent book in which Means attacks administered pricing power in concentrated industries, he argues that such pricing is inflationary. See *Pricing and the Public Interest,* Harper & Brothers, New York, 1962. For a critical discussion of Means' book, see William H. Peterson, "Divergent Views on Pricing Policy," *Harvard Business Review,* March–April, 1963. In a discussion of the problem of concentrated economic power, Carl A. Auerbach concludes that some form of statutory price and wage regulation is needed to attain high employment, steadily increasing output, and stable prices. See "Administered Prices and Concentration of Economic Power," *Minnesota Law Review,* December, 1963.

[23] "Administered Prices," *op. cit.,* pp. 216–28, and "Administered Prices: Their Nature and Behavior," *Current Economic Comment,* November, 1957.

the general price rise from 1955 to 1957. Where other conditions, particularly those affecting demand or costs, either favored or compelled the price rise, administered prices rose. Where these conditions did not favor or compel a price rise, administered prices failed to rise. Market-determined prices, he pointed out, exhibited similar responsiveness. Thus, for Backman: "The primary pressures and responsibilities for price behavior, therefore, are found in these factors [those affecting demand or cost], not in the fact of price administration."[24] Stigler comes to the same conclusion: "The attribution of inflation to monopoly power of enterprises is . . . lacking both a theoretical rationale and an empirical basis."[25]

Thus, despite the difficulties in making price comparisons over time, one must conclude that price administration does not necessarily contribute to inflation. Many administered prices have not increased; in fact, many have declined, while the general price level has risen. It is true that some administered prices have increased along with the increase in the general level of prices and that some of these administered prices have increased at a more rapid rate than the average of all other prices. But some market prices have also increased more than the general price level. In short, empirical evidence shows that it is impossible to generalize on the topic by saying that administered prices do or do not contribute to inflation.

### Conclusions on Criticisms of Administered Pricing

Properly defined, the term "administered pricing" describes a *method* of price-making. It implies nothing about whether the prices set through administrative action are too high or too low, too flexible or too inflexible, whether competition exists or does not exist, or whether such prices contribute to depression or to inflation.

Price administration, or the power of business firms to set a price on their products or services, has been the natural result of the characteristics of the American economy and is found today in all sectors of American economic life. Although it has sometimes been abused, this general method of price-making could not be eliminated without drastically changing the entire economic system—probably for the worse. Thus, we must accept the fact that administered pricing exists and that the term "administered pricing" does not *per se* imply criticism of the pricing process.

[24] "Administered Prices," *op. cit.*, p. 228.

[25] Stigler, *op. cit.*, p. 9. Criticisms of the idea that administered prices contribute to inflation are also found in Horace J. DePodwin and Richard T. Selden, "Business Pricing Policies and Inflation," *Journal of Political Economy*, April, 1963, and in the testimony of Walter D. Fackler and Padraic P. Frucht in the Kefauver hearings. See *Hearings before the Senate Subcommittee on Antitrust and Monopoly*, Part II (Washington, D.C.: U.S. Government Printing Office, 1959, pp. 5221–342.

# 39. PRICING POLICIES FOR NEW PRODUCTS

*Joel Dean*

*How to price a new product is a top-management puzzle that is too often solved by cost-theology and hunch. This article suggests a pricing policy geared to the dynamic nature of a new product's competitive status. Today's high rate of innovation makes the economic evolution of a new product a strategic guide to practical pricing.*

*Joel Dean suggests that most products go through a cycle ranging from protected distinctiveness to maturity and that continual adjustments in price policy are necessary as the product moves through the cycle.*

## MARKET BEHAVIOR

New products have a protected distinctiveness which is doomed to progressive degeneration from competitive inroads. The invention of a new marketable specialty is usually followed by a period of patent protection when markets are still hesitant and unexplored and when product design is fluid. Then comes a period of rapid expansion of sales as market acceptance is gained. Next the product becomes a target for competitive encroachment. New competitors enter the field, and innovations narrow the gap of distinctiveness between the product and its substitutes. The

AUTHOR'S NOTE: For major assistance in preparing this article, I am indebted to Stephen Taylor of Joel Dean Associates. Professors James Bonbright and Carl Shoup and Mr. Samuel Richman of the Graduate School of Business, Columbia University, were kind enough to read the manuscript and make helpful suggestions.

Source: From *Harvard Business Review,* vol. 28, November–December, 1950, pp. 28–36. Joel Dean: Professor of Business Economics, Columbia University.

seller's zone of pricing discretion narrows as his distinctive "specialty" fades into a pedestrian "commodity" which is so little differentiated from other products that the seller has limited independence in pricing, even if rivals are few.

Throughout the cycle, continual changes occur in promotional and price elasticity and in costs of production and distribution. These changes call for adjustments in price policy.

*Elements of Cycle.* Appropriate pricing over the cycle depends on the development of three different aspects of maturity, which usually move in approximately parallel time paths:

1. technical maturity, indicated by declining rate of product development, increasing standardization among brands, and increasing stability of manufacturing processes and knowledge about them;
2. market maturity, indicated by consumer acceptance of the basic service idea, by widespread belief that the products of most manufacturers will perform satisfactorily, and by enough familiarity and sophistication to permit consumers to compare brands competently; and
3. competitive maturity, indicated by increasing stability of market shares and price structures.

Of course, interaction among these components tends to make them move together. That is, intrusion by new competitors helps to develop the market, but entrance is most tempting when the new product appears to be establishing market acceptance.

*Speed of Degeneration.* The rate at which the cycle of degeneration progresses varies widely among products. What are the factors that set its pace? An overriding determinant is technical—the extent to which the economic environment must be reorganized to use the innovation effectively. The scale of plant investment and technical research called forth by the telephone, electric power, the automobile, or air transport makes for a long gestation period, as compared with even such major innovations as cellophane or frozen foods. Development comes fastest when the new gadget fills a new vacuum made to order for it. Electric stoves, as one example, have risen to 50 per cent market saturation in the fast-growing Pacific Northwest, where electric power has become the lowest cost energy. Products still in early developmental stages also provide rich opportunities for product differentiation, which with heavy research costs hold off competitive degeneration.

But aside from technical factors, the rate of degeneration is controlled by economic forces that can be subsumed under

1. rate of market acceptance, and
2. ease of competitive entry.

By *market acceptance* is meant the extent to which buyers consider the product a serious alternative to other ways of performing the same service. Market acceptance is a frictional factor. The effect of cultural lags may endure for some time after quality and costs make products technically useful. The slow catch-on of the "electric pig" (garbage-disposal unit) is an example. On the other hand, the attitude of acceptance may exist long before any workable model can be developed; then the final appearance of the product will produce an explosive growth curve in sales. The antihistamine cold tablet, a spectacular example, reflects the national faith in chemistry's ability to vanquish the common cold. And, of course, low unit price may speed market acceptance of an innovation; ball-point pens and all-steel houses started at about the same time, but look at the difference in their sales curves.

*Ease of Competitive Entry* is a major determinant of the speed of degeneration of a specialty. An illustration is found in the washing machine business before the war, where with little basic patent protection the Maytag position was quickly eroded by small manufacturers who performed essentially an assembly operation. The ball-point pen cascaded from a $12 novelty to a 49-cent "price football," partly because entry barriers of patents and techniques were ineffective. Frozen orange juice, which started as a protected specialty of Minute Maid, is speeding through its competitive cycle, with competing brands now crowding into the market.

At the outset the innovator can control the rate of competitive deterioration to an important degree by nonprice as well as by price strategies. Through successful research in product improvement he can protect his specialty position both by extending the life if his basic patent and by keeping ahead of competitors in product development. The record of the International Business Machines punch-card equipment illustrates this potentiality. Ease of entry is also affected by a policy of stay-out pricing (so low as to make the prospects look uninviting), which under some circumstances may slow down the process of competitive encroachment.

## STEPS IN PIONEER PRICING

Pricing problems start when a company finds a product that is a radical departure from existing ways of performing a service and that is temporarily protected from competition by patents, secrets of production, control at the point of a scarce resource, or by other barriers. The seller here has a wide range of pricing discretion resulting from extreme product differentiation.

A good example of pricing latitude conferred by protected superiority of product is provided by the McGraw Electric Company's "Toastmaster," which, both initially and over a period of years, was able to command a very substantial price premium over competitive toasters. Apparently this advantage resulted from

1. a good product that was distinctive and superior, and
2. substantial and skillful sales promotion.

Similarly, Sunbeam priced its electric iron $2 above comparable models of major firms with considerable success. And Sunbeam courageously priced its new metal coffee-maker at $32, much above competitive makes of glass coffee-makers, but it was highly successful.

To get a picture of how a manufacturer should go about setting his price in the pioneer stage, let me describe the main steps of the process (of course the classification is arbitrary and the steps are interrelated):

1. estimate of demand,
2. decision on market targets,
3. design of promotional strategy, and
4. choice of channels of distribution.

*Estimate of Demand.* The problem at the pioneer stage differs from that in a relatively stable monopoly because the product is beyond the experience of buyers and because the perishability of its distinctiveness must be reckoned with. How can demand for new products be explored? How can we find out how much people will pay for a product that has never before been seen or used? There are several levels of refinement to this analysis.

The initial problem of estimating demand for a new product can be broken into a series of subproblems:

1. whether the product will go at all (assuming price is in a competitive range);
2. what range of price will make the product economically attractive to buyers;
3. what sales volumes can be expected at various points in this price range; and
4. what reaction will price produce in manufacturers and sellers of displaced substitutes.

The first step is an exploration of the *preferences and educability of consumers,* always of course in the light of the technical feasibility of the new product. How many potential buyers are there? Is the product a practical device for meeting their needs? How can it be improved to meet their needs better? What proportion of the potential buyers would prefer, or could be induced to prefer, this product to already existing products (prices being equal)?

Sometimes it is feasible to start with the assumption that all vulnerable substitutes will be fully displaced. For example, to get some idea of the maximum limits of demand for a new type of reflecting-sign material, a company started with estimates of the aggregate number and area of auto license plates, highway markers, railroad operational signs, and name signs for streets and homes. Next, the proportion of each category needing night-light reflection was guessed. For example, it was assumed that only rural and suburban homes could benefit by this kind of name sign, and the estimate of need in this category was made accordingly.

It is not uncommon and possibly not unrealistic for a manufacturer to make the blithe assumption at this stage that the product price will be "within a competitive range" without having much idea of what that range is. For example, in developing a new type of camera equipment, one of the electrical companies judged its acceptability to professional photographers by technical performance without making any inquiry into its economic value. When the equipment was later placed in an economic setting, the indications were that sales would be negligible.

The second step is marking out this *competitive range of price*. Vicarious pricing experience can be secured by interviewing selected distributors who have enough comparative knowledge of customers' alternatives and preferences to judge what price range would make the new product "a good value." Direct discussions with representative experienced industrial users have produced reliable estimates of the "practical" range of prices. Manufacturers of electrical equipment often explore the economic as well as the technical feasibility of a new product by sending engineers with blueprints and models to see customers, such as technical and operating executives.

In guessing the price range of a radically new consumers' product of small unit value, the concept of barter equivalent can be a useful research guide. For example, a manufacturer of paper specialties tested a dramatic new product in the following fashion:

> A wide variety of consumer products totally unlike the new product were purchased and spread out on a big table. Consumers selected the products they would swap for the new product. By finding out whether the product would trade even for a dish pan, a towel, or a hairpin, the executives got a rough idea of what range of prices might strike the typical consumer as reasonable in the light of the values she could get for her money in totally different kinds of expenditures.

But asking prospective consumers how much they think they would be willing to pay for a new product, even by such indirect or disguised methods, may often fail to give a reliable indication of the demand schedule. Most times people just do not know what they would pay. It depends partly on their income and on future alternatives. Early in the postwar period a manufacturer of television sets tried this method and got highly erratic and obviously unreliable results because the distortion of war shortages kept prospects from fully visualizing the multiple alternative ways of spending their money. Another deficiency, which may, however, be less serious than it appears, is that responses are biased by the consumer's confused notion that he is bargaining for a good price. Not until techniques of depth interviewing are more refined than they are now can this crude and direct method of exploring a new product's demand schedule hold much promise of being accurate.

One appliance manufacturer tried out new products on a sample of employees by selling to them at deep discounts, with the stipulation that they could if they wished return the products at the end of the experiment period and get a refund of their low purchase price. Demand for frozen orange juice was tested by placing it in several markets at three different prices, ranging around the price of fresh fruit; the result showed rather low price elasticity.

While inquiries of this sort are often much too short-run to give any real indication of consumer tastes, the relevant point here is that even such rough probing often yields broad impressions of price elasticity, particularly in relation to product variations such as styling, placing of controls, and use of automatic features. It may show, for example, that $5 of cost put into streamlining of chromium stripping can add $50 to the price.

The third step, a more definite inquiry into the *probable sales from several possible prices,* starts with an investigation of the prices of substitutes. Usually the buyer has a choice of existing ways of having the same service performed; an analysis of the costs of these alternatives serves as a guide in setting the price for a new way.

Comparisons are easy and significant for industrial customers who have a costing system to tell them the exact value, say, of a fork-lift truck in terms of warehouse labor saved. Indeed, chemical companies setting up a research project to displace an existing material often know from the start the top price that can be charged for the new substitute in terms of cost of the present material.

But in most cases the comparison is obfuscated by the presence of quality differences that may be important bases for price premiums. This is most true of household appliances, where the alternative is an unknown amount of labor of a mysterious value. In pricing a cargo parachute the alternatives are:

1. free fall in a padded box from a plane flown close to the ground,
2. landing the plane,
3. back shipment by land from the next air terminal, or
4. land shipment all the way.

These alternatives differ widely in their service value and are not very useful pricing guides.

Thus, it is particularly hard to know how much good will be done by making the new product cheaper than the old by various amounts, or how much the market will be restricted by making the new product more expensive. The answers usually come from experiment or research.

The fourth step in estimating demand is to consider the *possibility of retaliation by manufacturers of displaced substitutes* in the form of price cutting. This development may not occur at all if the new product displaces only a small market segment. If old industries do fight it out, however, their incremental costs provide a floor to the resulting price competition and should be brought into price plans. For example, a manufacturer of black-and-white sensitized paper studied the possibility that lowering his price would displace blueprint paper substantially. Not only did he investigate the prices of blueprint paper, but he also felt it necessary to estimate the out-of-pocket cost of making blueprint paper because of the probability that manufacturers already in the market would fight back by reducing prices toward the level of their incremental costs.

*Decision on Market Targets.* When the company has developed some idea of the range of demand and the range of prices that are feasible for the new product, it is in a position to make some basic strategic decisions on market targets and promotional plans. To decide on market objectives requires answers to several questions: What ultimate market share is wanted for the new product? How does it fit into the present product line? What about production methods? What are the possible distribution channels? These are questions of joint costs in production and distribution, of plant expansion outlays, and of potential competition. If entry is easy, the company may not be eager to disrupt its present production and selling operations to capture and hold a large slice of the new market. But if the prospective profits shape up to a substantial new income source, it will be worthwhile to make the capital expenditures on plant needed to reap the full harvest.

A basic factor in answering all these questions is the expected behavior of production and distribution costs. The relevant data here are all the production outlays that will be made after the decision day—the capital expenditures as well as the variable costs. A go-ahead decision will hardly be made without some assurance that these costs can be recovered before the product becomes a football in the market. Many different projections of costs will be made, depending on the alternative scales of output, rate of market expansion, threats of potential competition, and measures to meet that competition that are under consideration. But these factors and the decision that is made on promotional strategy are interdependent. The fact is that this is a circular problem that in theory can only be solved by simultaneous equations.

Fortunately, it is possible to make some approximations that can break the circle. Scale economies become significantly different only with broad changes in the size of plant and the type of production methods. This narrows the range of cost projections to workable proportions. The effects of using different distribution channels can be guessed fairly well without meshing the alternatives in with all the production and selling possibilities. The most vulnerable point of the circle is probably the decision on promotional strategy. The alternatives here are broad and produce a variety of results. The next step in the pricing process is therefore a plan for promotion.

*Design of Promotional Strategy.* Initial promotion outlays are an investment in the product that cannot be recovered until some kind of market has been established. The innovator shoulders the burden of creating a market—educating consumers to the existence and uses of the product. Later imitators will never have to do this job; so, if the innovator does not want to be simply a benefactor to his future competitors, he must make pricing plans to recover his initial outlays before his pricing discretion evaporates.

His basic strategic problem is to find the right mixture of price and promotion to maximize his long-run profits. He can choose a relatively high price in pioneering stages, together with extravagant advertising and dealer discounts, and plan to get his promotion costs back early; or he can use low prices and lean margins from the very outset, in order to discourage potential competition when the barriers of patents, distribution channels, or production techniques become inadequate. This question is discussed further below.

*Choice of Channels of Distribution.* Estimation of the costs of moving the new product through the channels of distribution to the final consumer must enter into the pricing procedure, since these costs govern the factory price that will result in a specified consumer price, and since it is the consumer price that matters for volume. Distributive margins are partly pure promotional costs and partly physical distribution costs. Margins must at least cover the distributors' costs of warehousing, handling, and order taking. These costs are similar to factory production costs in being related to physical capacity and its utilization, i.e. fluctuations in production or sales volume. Hence these set a floor to trade-channel discounts. But distributors usually also contribute promotional effort—in point-of-sale pushing, local advertising, and display—when it is made worth their while.

These pure promotional costs are more optional. Unlike physical handling costs they have no necessary functional relation to sales volume. An added layer of margin in trade discounts to produce this localized sales effort (with retail price fixed) is an optional way for the manufacturer to spend his prospecting money in putting over a new product.

In establishing promotional costs, the manufacturer must decide on the extent to which the selling effort will be delegated to members of the distribution chain. Indeed, some distribution channels, such as house-to-house selling and retail store selling supplemented by home demonstrators, represent a substantial delegation of the manufacturer's promotional job, and these usually involve much higher distribution-channel costs that do conventional methods. Rich distributor margins are an appropriate use of promotional funds only when the producer thinks a high price plus promotion is a better expansion policy on the specialty than low price by itself. Thus there is an intimate interaction between the pricing of a new product and the costs and the problems of floating it down the distribution channels to the final consumer.

## POLICIES FOR PIONEER PRICING

The strategic decision in pricing a new product is the choice between

1. a policy of high initial prices that skim the cream of demand, and
2. a policy of low prices from the outset serving as an active agent for market penetration.

Although the actual range of choice is much wider than this, a sharp dichotomy clarifies the issues for consideration.

*Skimming Price.* For products that represent a drastic departure from accepted ways of performing a service, a policy of relatively high prices coupled with heavy promotional expenditures in the early stages of market development (and lower prices at later stages) has proved successful for many products. There are several reasons for the success of this policy:

1. Demand is likely to be more inelastic with respect to price in the early stages than it is when the product is fully grown. This is particularly true for consumers' goods. A novel product, such as the electric blanket or the electric pig, is not yet accepted as a part of the expenditure pattern. Consumers are still ignorant about its value as compared with the value of conventional alternatives. Moreover, at least in the early stages, the product has so few close rivals that cross-elasticity of demand is low. Promotional elasticity is, on the other hand, quite high, particularly for products with high unit prices such as television sets. Since it is difficult for the customer to value the service of the product in a way to price it intelligently, he is by default principally interested in how well it will work.

2. Launching a new product with a high price is an efficient device for breaking the market up into segments that differ in price elasticity of demand. The initial high price serves to skim the cream of the market that is relatively insensitive to price. Subsequent price reductions tap successively more elastic sectors of the market. This pricing strategy is exemplified by the systematic succession of editions of a book, sometimes starting with a $50 limited personal edition and ending up with a 25-cent pocket book.

3. This policy is safer, or at least appears so. Facing an unknown elasticity of demand, a high initial price serves as a "refusal" price during the stage of exploration. How much costs can be reduced as the market expands and as the design of the product is improved by increasing production efficiency with new techniques is difficult to predict. One of the electrical companies recently introduced a new lamp bulb at a comparatively high initial price, but with the announcement that the price would be reduced as the company found ways of cutting its costs.

4. Many companies are not in a position to finance the product flotation out of distant future revenues. High cash outlays in the early stages result from heavy costs of production and distributor organizing, in addition to the promotional investment in the pioneer product. High prices are a reasonable financing technique for shouldering these burdens in the light of the many uncertainties about the future.

*Penetration Price.* The alternative policy is to use low prices as the principal instrument for penetrating mass markets early. This policy is the reverse of the skimming policy in which the price is lowered only as short-run competition forces it. The passive skimming policy has the virtue of safeguarding some profits at every stage of market penetration. But it prevents quick sales to the many buyers who are at the lower end of the income scale or the lower end of the preference scale and who therefore are unwilling to pay any substantial premium for product or reputation superiority. The active approach in probing possibilities for market expansion by early penetration pricing requires research, forecasting, and courage.

A decision of price for market expansion can be reached at various stages in a product's life cycle: before birth, at birth, in childhood, in adulthood, or in senescence.

The chances for large-volume sales should at least be explored in the early stages of product development research, even before the pilot stage, perhaps with a more definitive exploration when the product goes into production and the price and distribution plans are decided upon. And the question of pricing to expand the market, if not answered earlier, will probably arise once more after the product has established an elite market.

Quite a few products have been rescued from premature senescence by pricing them low enough to tap new markets. The reissues of important books in the 25-cent pocket-book category illustrate this point particularly well. These have produced not only commercial but intellectual renascence as well to many authors. The pattern of sales growth of a product that had reached stability in a high-price market has been known to undergo sharp changes when it was suddenly priced low enough to tap new markets. A contrasting illustration of passive policy is the recent pricing experience of the airlines. Although safety considerations and differences in equipment and service cloud the picture, it is pretty clear that the bargain-rate coach fares of scheduled airlines were adopted in reaction to the cut rates of nonscheduled airlines. This competitive response has apparently established a new pattern of traffic growth for the scheduled airlines.

An example of penetration pricing at the initial stage of the product's market life, again from the book field, is Simon & Schuster's recently adopted policy of bringing out new titles in a $1, paper-bound edition simultaneously with the conventional higher priced, cloth-bound edition.

What conditions warrant aggressive pricing for market penetration? This question cannot be answered categorically, but it may be helpful to generalize that the following conditions indicate the desirability of an early low-price policy:

1. a high price-elasticity of demand in the short run, i.e. a high degree of responsiveness of sales to reductions in price;
2. substantial savings in production costs as the result of greater volume—not a necessary condition, however, since if elasticity of demand is high enough, pricing for market expansion may be profitable without realizing production economies;
3. product characteristics such that it will not seem bizarre when it is first fitted into the consumers' expenditure pattern;
4. a strong threat of potential competition.

This threat of potential competition is a highly persuasive reason for penetration pricing. One of the major objectives of most low-pricing policies in the pioneering stages of market development is to raise entry barriers to prospective competitiors. This is appropriate when entrants must make large-scale investments to reach minimum costs and they cannot slip into an established market by selling at substantial discounts.

In many industries, however, the important potential competitor is a large, multiple-product firm operating as well in other fields as in that represented by the product in question. For such a firm, the most important consideration for entry is not existing margins but the prospect of large and growing volume of sales. Present margins over costs are not the dominant consideration because such firms are normally confident that they can get their costs down as low as competitors' costs if the volume of production is large. Therefore, when total industry sales are not expected to amount to much, a high-margin policy can be followed because entry is improbable in view of the expectation of low volume and because it does not matter too much to potential competitors if the new product is introduced.

The fact remains that for products whose market potential appears big, a policy of stay-out pricing from the outset makes much more sense. When a leading soap manufacturer developed an additive that whitened clothes and enhanced the brilliance of colors, the company chose to take its gains in a larger share of the market rather than in a temporary price premium. Such a decision was sound, since the company's competitors could be expected to match or better the product improvement fairly promptly. Under these circumstances, the price premium would have been short-lived, whereas the gains in market share were more likely to be retained.

Of course, any decision to start out with lower prices must take into account the fact that if the new product calls for capital recovery over a long period, the risk may be great that later entrants will be able to exploit new production techniques which can undercut the pioneer's original cost structure. In such cases, the low-price pattern should be adopted with a view to long-run rather than to short-run profits, with the recognition that it usually takes time to attain the volume potentialities of the market.

It is sound to calculate profits in dollar terms rather than in percentage margins and to think in terms of percentage return on the investment required to produce and sell the expanded volume rather than in terms of percentage mark-up. Profit calculation should also recognize the contributions that market-development pricing can make to the sale of other products and to the long-run future of the company. Often a decision to use development pricing will turn on these considerations of long-term impacts upon the firm's total operation strategy rather than on the profits directly attributable to the individual product.

An example of market-expansion pricing is found in the experience of a producer of asbestos shingles, which have a limited sale in the high-price house market. The company wanted to broaden the market in order to compete effectively with other roofing products for the inexpensive home. It tried to find the price of asphalt shingles that would make the annual cost per unit of roof over a period of years as low as the cheaper roofing that currently commanded the mass market. Indications were that the price would have to be at least this low before volume sales would come. Next, the company explored the relationship between production costs and volume, far beyond the range of its own volume experience. Variable costs and overhead costs were estimated separately, and the possibilities of a different organization of production were explored. Calculating in terms of anticipated dollars of profit rather than in terms of percentage margin, the company reduced the price of asbestos shingles and brought the annual cost down close to the cost of the cheapest asphalt roof. This reduction produced a greatly expanded volume and secured a substantial share of the mass market.

## PRICING IN MATURITY

To determine what pricing policies are appropriate for later stages in the cycle of market and competitive maturity, the manufacturer must be able to tell when a product is approaching maturity. Some of the symptoms of degeneration of competitive status toward the commodity level are:

1. *Weakening in brand preference*–this may be evidenced by a higher cross-elasticity of demand among leading products, the leading brand not being able to continue demanding as much price premium as initially without losing position;
2. *Narrowing physical variation among products as the best designs are developed and standardized*–this has been dramatically demonstrated in automobiles and is still in process in television receivers;
3. *The entry in force of private-label competitors*–this is exemplified by the mail-order houses' sale of own-label refrigerators and paint sprayers;
4. *Market saturation*–the ratio of replacement sales to new equipment sales serves as an indicator of the competitive degeneration of durable goods, but in general it must be kept in mind that both market size and degree of saturation are hard to define (e.g. saturation of the radio market, which was initially thought to be one radio per home and later had to be expanded to one radio per room);
5. *The stabilization of production methods*–a dramatic innovation that slashes costs (e.g. prefabricated houses) may disrupt what appears to be a well-stabilized oligopoly market.

The first step for the manufacturer whose specialty is about to slip into the commodity category is to reduce real prices promptly as soon as symptoms of deterioration appear. This step is essential if he is to forestall the entry of private-label competitors. Examples of failure to make such a reduction are abundant. By and large, private-label competition has speeded up the inevitable evolution of high specialties into commodities and has tended to force margins down by making price reductions more open and more universal than they would otherwise be. From one standpoint, the rapid growth of the private-label share in the market is a symptom of unwise pricing on the part of the national-brand sector of the industry.

This does not mean that the manufacturer should declare open price war in the industry. When he moves into mature competitive stages, he enters oligopoly relationships where price slashing is peculiarly dangerous and unpopular. But, with active competition in prices precluded, competitive efforts may move in other directions, particularly toward product improvement and market segmentation. Product improvement at this stage, where most of the important developments have been put into all brands, practically amounts to market segmentation. For it means adding refinements and quality extras that put the brand in the elite category, with an appeal only to the top-income brackets. This is a common tactic in food marketing, and in the tire industry it was the response of the General Tire Company to the competitive conditions of the 1930s.

As the product matures and as its distinctiveness narrows, a choice must sometimes be made by the company concerning the rung of the competitive price ladder it should occupy—roughly, the choice between a low and a not-so-low relative price.

A price at the low end of the array of the industry's real prices is usually associated with a product mixture showing a lean element of services and reputation (the product being physically similar to competitive brands, however) and a company having a lower gross margin than the other industry members (although not necessarily a lower net margin). The choice of such a low-price policy may be dictated by technical or market inferiorities of the product, or it may be adopted because the company has faith in the long-run price elasticity of demand and the ability of low prices to penetrate an important segment of the market not tapped by higher prices. The classic example is Henry Ford's pricing decision in the 1920s.

## SUMMARY

In pricing products of perishable distinctiveness, a company must study the cycle of competitive degeneration in order to determine its major causes, its probable speed, and the chances of slowing it down. Pricing in the pioneering stage of the cycle involves difficult problems of projecting potential demand and of guessing the relation of price to sales. The first step in this process is to explore consumer preferences and to establish the feasibility of the product, in order to get a rough idea of whether demand will warrant further exploration. The second step is to mark out a range of prices that will make the product economically attractive to buyers. The third step is to estimate the probable sales that will result from alternative prices.

If these initial explorations are encouraging, the next move is to make decisions on promotional strategy and distribution channels. The policy of relatively high prices in the pioneering stage has much to commend it, particularly when sales seem to be comparatively unresponsive to price but quite responsive to educational promotion. On the other hand, the policy of relatively low prices in the pioneering stage, in anticipation of the cost savings resulting from an expanding market, has been strikingly successful under the right conditions. Low prices look to long-run rather than short-run profits and discourage potential competitors.

Pricing in the mature stages of a product's life cycle requires a technique for recognizing when a product is approaching maturity. Pricing problems in this stage border closely on those of oligopoly.

# 40. ATTITUDES AND PRICING

*Alfred Oxenfeldt, David Miller, Abraham Shuchman,*

*and Charles Winick*

*Pricing policy undoubtedly is one of the more difficult decision areas; and to date we have known little about how prices are perceived by the target audiences.*

*However, some insights as to how consumers view the price of an item and how they react to the price can be gleaned from some of the literature of the behavioral sciences. In the selection that follows there is a discussion of some of this literature, with suggestions of ways in which certain concepts may prove helpful to decision-makers.*

Physical scientists have often had to posit the existence of something which was not directly accessible to inquiry and which only subsequently was shown to exist; similarly, social psychologists have postulated the existence of attitudes to explain many facets of human perception and behavior. An attitude is difficult to define precisely, because nobody has ever seen one, although many social scientists have studied, measured, and reported the *effects* of attitudes. For purposes of discussion, an attitude can be defined as a *predisposition to behavior.* The possession of one attitude rather than another, then, disposes a person to behave in a particular way. Although this concept of the attitude, as something underlying behavior, is quite abstract, it is possible to study and measure attitudes fairly accurately.

Source: From Alfred Oxenfeldt, David Miller, Abraham Shuchman, and Charles Winick, *Insights Into Pricing from Operations Research and Behavioral Science,* Wadsworth Publishing Company, Belmont, California, ©1961, pp. 85–101. Reprinted by permission of the publisher; Alfred Oxenfeldt: Professor of Marketing, Graduate School of Business, Columbia University. David Miller: Associate Professor of Statistics, Graduate School of Business, Columbia University. Charles Winick: Marketing Consultant, New York. Abraham Shuchman: Associate Professor of Marketing, Graduate School of Business, Columbia University.

Most of us are not aware of our specific attitudes on any given subject until we are specifically asked about them, even though those attitudes may strongly affect our behavior. Attitudes are not necessarily unconscious, however, even though we cannot state them explicitly without some prodding. Most of us have little occasion to take stock of our various attitudes; but when asked about our attitudes on specific subjects, we generally can express what they are.

The enormous range of attitudes that any individual holds can be seen in compilations like that of Cantril and Strunk,[1] who reported on the literally thousands of attitude surveys that have been made since the 1930s. Not only are attitudes toward traditional subjects like the tariff and capital punishment included in such compilations, but also attitudes toward matters like the current rate of income tax, sexual behavior, and the allowance that a ten-year-old child should get. Newspaper reports of attitude surveys, like those conducted by George Gallup or Elmo Roper, often convey a mistaken impression. The precise percentages in which they give the proportion of the public which holds a given attitude imply that attitudes can be measured precisely and are quite consistent. Actually, the same individual's attitudes on related subjects may be incompatible with one another. A person might believe simultaneously that school taxes should be lowered and that we should have better schools and more highly qualified teachers, even though taxes clearly would have to be increased if schools are to be improved. In a referendum on whether there should be an increase in taxes to pay for better schools, a person holding such views would have to resolve the inconsistency in one way or the other. For the most part, persons can hold contradictory attitudes without ever being forced to face their inconsistency.

Just as our endocrine glands maintain the body's internal equilibrium, by a process which physiologists call homeostasis, everyone apparently has an inner balancing mechanism that keeps disparate attitudes in harmony. In the body, one gland will increase or decrease its flow in response to an increase or decrease in the flow of another gland. Similarly, if a political figure whom a person admires takes a position which the same person dislikes, then the person will modify his attitudes in one direction or the other. He may think less of the candidate or he may modify his opinion on the issue. Some reconciliation of the two opinions, in all probability, will be attempted by the person's homeostatic-like attitude-balancing mechanism.

In some situations, behavior may be inconsistent with attitudes, but these generally are situations in which we lack complete control over our behavior. For example, the 1954 Supreme Court decision on desegregation meant that many southern white students would commingle with Negro students even though the white students might be opposed to such commingling. However, this kind of discrepancy between attitude and behavior is unusual. The apparent conflict between the white students' attitudes and behavior toward Negro students can be explained by the consistency between the students' behavior and their attitudes toward observing laws.

[1] Hadley Cantril and Mildred Strunk, *Public Opinion 1935–1946,* Princeton University Press, Princeton, 1947.

Attitudes are only partial determinants of behavior. Behavior is also affected by temperament, moods, opinions, physical states, and other factors, which are not always easy to distinguish from attitudes. *Temperament* is the expression of the person's activity level and is largely a reflection of basal metabolism and endocrine balance. It is mainly temperament that determines whether a person bounds cheerfully out of bed or requires three cups of coffee to awaken. A *mood* is a condition of temperament—happy, elated, sad, ebullient—which provides a framework for the expression of attitudes. A particular mood is not likely to change attitudes but will alter their expression and cause behavior to be somewhat inconsistent.[2] It is obvious that a shopper's mood when she enters a department store will influence her expressed attitudes toward specific products and her buying behavior.

An *opinion* is the expression of an attitude on a relatively concrete and narrow subject—e.g. Do you think tariffs should be raised on imported bicycles? An opinion may reflect more than one attitude, and an attitude will generally be father to hundreds of specific opinions, just as it is responsible for many feelings and convictions.

Although the concept of the attitude is relatively complicated, its effect on human behavior in many practical situations is such that it is perhaps the most important single area of study and research in social psychology. If we are interested in how people will respond to a traffic light or whether they will buy a product, we must consider their attitudes. These will affect not only their behavior but their values and perceptions, and their interpretation of the behavior of others.

## FORMATION OF ATTITUDES

The process of acquiring an attitude is very subtle; rarely can a person expalin accurately how any of his attitudes were acquired. Allport has suggested that there are four processes by which attitudes are likely to be formed:

1. integrating a number of similar experiences,
2. differentiating from general to specific situations,
3. unusual experiences, or
4. adopting attitudes from others.[3]

*Integration of similar experiences.* As an example of the first of these processes, an American soldier might have gone overseas in World War II without any specific attitudes toward Germans. As his unit moved into Germany and he met the natives, he would inevitably have specific experiences with them. Gradually, he would put together these experiences into an attitude toward Germans.

[2] Patricia Kendall, *Mood and Affect,* The Free Press of Glencoe, New York, 1956.

[3] Gordon W. Allport, "Attitudes," in Carl Murchison (ed.), *Handbook of Social Psychology,* Clark University Press, Worcester, Mass., 1935, pp. 798–844.

*Differentiating from general to specific situations.* Inferences from broad attitudes already held—the second of Allport's processes—account for most of our narrow attitudes. Thus, if a person is asked his attitude toward women drivers, his answer may unconsciously reflect an underlying attitude that women in general are less competent or more careful then men. Someone else may dislike anything foreign and, when asked about the existentialist school of philosophy, will particularize this dislike and express negative attitudes toward existentialism because it is foreign. But the process by which the specific attitude individuates itself into awareness is not likely to be conscious, so that an individual is likely to respond to the specific question without consciously recalling the general underlying attitude that is parent to his answer.

*Unusual experience.* Unusual experiences constitute a third source of formation of attitudes. Reports of the collision between the liners *Andrea Doria* and *Stockholm* off Nantucket in the summer of 1956, for example, suggest that many passengers who had no specific attitudes toward Italians, or who had thought Italians were lazy and incompetent, developed very positive attitudes toward them based on the heroic behavior of the Italian crewmen of the *Andrea Doria.*[4] If experiences involve outstanding examples of success or failure, they are particularly likely to create or alter attitudes.

*Identification.* The adoption of attitudes from others whom we admire or with whom we identify is a fourth and frequent basis of attitude formation. By *identification* we mean the desire of the individual to be like another person and the molding of his ego in line with this desire. One sees examples of this process in the elementary school students who adopt the attitudes of their teachers and sometimes begin to ape their teachers' costumes. Similarly, the high morale of the German troops, even after losing World War II, has been attributed mainly to their identification with their officers.[5] It has been shown the the political affiliations of people, by and large, are similar to those of their parents. Not only political but many other kinds of attitudes derive from parents, because of the great extent to which the growing child identifies with parents.

*Personality.* Another basis of attitude formation, not mentioned by Allport, is the incorporation of attitudes that make one's *personality* feel comfortable. Some attitudes are much more compatible with a person's personality than others. Indeed, to a great extent, our attitudes *are* our personality. Thus, individuals may have needs that make it important, in terms of their "personality economy," to hold particular attitudes. One study, for example, showed that the maintenance of specific attitudes toward the Soviet Union served a variety of very valuable purposes for the

[4]Paul Friedman and Louis Linn, "Some Psychiatric Notes on the *Andrea Doria* Disaster," *American Journal of Psychiatry,* 114: 426–432, 1957.

[5]Edward A. Shils and Morris Janowitz, "Cohesion and Disintegration in the Wehrmacht," *Public Opinion Quarterly,* 12: 300–315, 1948.

personalities of the individuals studied.[6] A number of studies have established this dimension of the "personal significance" of attitudes and have included such subjects as: Why do rumors spread?[7] Why did people believe the Orson Welles "Invasion from Mars" broadcast?[8] What is the "personal significance" of product categories like cigarettes and automobiles?[9] These studies have shown that a person's attitudes help to establish his identity. If one knows a person's predispositions to behavior—his attitudes—one knows a great deal about him and how he will behave. Similarly, if one knows the basic personality structure of an individual, he can forecast quite accurately the attitudes that individual will hold.

*Social factors.* Another major influence on attitudes is the general *social class* or group to which the individual belongs. Jews' attitudes toward eating food that is not "kosher" are derived from their social group.[10] Attitudes that are profoundly anchored in a social group are likely to be very meaningful to the individual. Kinsey has established that our attitudes toward even so central a phenomenon as sex are partially a function of our social class.[11] Perhaps the most poignant story in all of Kinsey's work is that of the lower-class prostitute who told the interviewer, after discussing a whole series of perversions in which she regularly engaged, that she did have one very embarrassing confession to make; it was that she slept "with no clothes on." In the lower-class circles from which she came, sleeping in the nude was simply not done, whereas it is very common in the upper classes. The class and social structure into which a person is born is, then, likely to create a variety of relatively specific and deep-rooted attitudes.

## DIMENSIONS OF ATTITUDES

Attitudes have several dimensions by which they may be measured and described. These dimensions include direction, degree or intensity, salience, and the degree of public or private expression of the attitudes.

*Direction.* The direction of an attitude refers to whether one is for or against a fact, person, or situation. Are the emotional connotations of the attitude positive or negative? Will the individual tend to vote for or against a particular amendment? Will he tend to be friendly or unfriendly toward the new migrants? Does he or does he not like the New York Yankees? This dimension of attitude is easiest to measure and assess.

[6] Jerome S. Bruner, Robert W. White, and M. B. Smith, *Opinions and Personality,* John Wiley & Sons, Inc., New York, 1955.

[7] Leon Festinger *et al.,* "A Study of a Rumor," *Human Relations,* 1: 464–486, 1948.

[8] Hadley Cantril, *The Invasion from Mars,* Princeton University Press, Princeton, N.J., 1940.

[9] *Cigarettes and Automobiles, What They Mean to Americans,* The Chicago Tribune, Chicago, 1954.

[10] The Joseph Jacobs Organization (342 Madison Ave., New York) has published a number of phamphlets that give the details of kosher food taboos.

[11] Alfred C. Kinsey *et al., Sexual Behavior in the Human Female,* W. B. Saunders Company, Philadelphia, 1953.

*Degree.* Another dimension of attitudes is the degree of intensity with which a person holds an attitude. Researchers usually measure this dimension by asking a respondent to rate how strongly he feels about a problem: e.g. "How strongly do you hold this opinion—very strongly, fairly strongly, or don't you care much one way or the other?" Two people, for instance, might want the New York Yankees to win the professional baseball pennant, but they might hold this attitude with different degrees of intensity. Two people may have negative attitudes about Communism, but one may be a Marxist Socialist and the other a right-wing Republican. The Socialist's attitudes toward the economic doctrines of Communism are likely to be much less harsh than those of the right-wing Republican. When an attitude is strongly held, it can be called a conviction.

*Salience.* The salience of an attitude describes how central or peripheral a given attitude is to a person; it indicates the importance of an attitude to an individual. One's most salient ideas, as has been noted, *are* his personality, and are therefore relatively difficult to change—although almost all can be changed under extreme circumstances. For example, attitudes toward parents, money, the opposite sex, and religion are likely to be far more salient than attitudes toward television commercials or traffic regulations.

*Degree of public expression.* The circumstances under which a person is willing to express an attitude may be considered a separate dimension. People will be willing to express some of their opinions publicly but will make others known only in confidence; also, in their public statements they may actually misrepresent their attitudes, because they may feel obliged, for whatever reason, to conceal their true views.

## CHANGING ATTITUDES

Students of attitudes are especially concerned with how they can be changed and modified. Some attitudes may not be consonant with our objectives; consequently, it is of the greatest importance to know whether and how such attitudes can be altered.

Some kinds of attitudes are not likely to change. Attitudes that have a relatively high degree of salience are difficult to change. People who identify strongly with a group—athletes, "beatniks," Ivy Leaguers, etc.—are not likely to adopt attitudes that conflict with the group's norms. Similarly, attitudes that have been expressed publicly are not as changeable as those held in private.

Some kinds of attitudes are amenable to change. An attitude is more likely to be changed if the stimuli making for change are repeated. It is also more likely to be changed if whatever lies behind the attitude is modified, whether the underlying substratum of the attitude be some factual information or some component of the individual's personality, or of his culture or society. An attitude is relatively likely to be changed if those who are persuading the individual to change it seem to share other attitudes with him.

Attitudes can be changed in a number of ways, many of which are similar to the procedures by which the attitudes were acquired in the first place:

- Integration of similar experiences.
- Differentiating from general to specific situations.
- Unusual experiences.
- Identification.
- Personality consonance with the attitudes.
- Social factors.

Specifically designed attitude-changing communications may also be responsible for a change.

Even relatively salient attitudes are subject to change. Within one generation, our attitudes toward the Japanese people have changed sharply. After Pearl Harbor and during World War II, the Japanese were regarded as wily, cruel, and cunning adversaries. After 1945, they were generally believed to be meek and docile. By the late 1950s they were seen as forceful equals of Americans. Each of these attitude changes was related to some shift in American-Japanese relations. Another well-known example of attitude change is found in America's attitude toward the Russians. Before World War II, they were believed to be hostile and unfriendly and relatively backward technologically. During World War II, they were regarded as friendly, although their mastery of modern technology was still believed to be quite poor. With the cold war of the post-1945 period, they were once again regarded as unfriendly. With Sputnik, the Russians were no longer believed to be technologically backward. These attitude changes were facilitated by changing international events, even though, as in the case of the Japanese, each attitude was salient at the time it was held.

There is general agreement that an attitude in a state of flux, or on a subject about which there is little previous information or experience, is the easiest to change.[12] Thus, we might expect that it would be easier to change attitudes toward Martians or lemmings than toward Frenchmen or women. This principle was illustrated in one study of attitudes toward the two candidates for governor of New York in 1958.[13] It was found that voters' attitudes toward Nelson Rockefeller shifted substantially after they had seen him on television, whereas attitudes toward Governor Averell Harriman did not shift much after his television appearances. This was explained on the basis of Harriman's being a familiar personality toward whom attitudes had already formed; whereas, because there were less specific attitudes toward Rockefeller, they could be easily swayed.

*Influence of group membership on attitude change.* World War II supplied much invaluable data about attitude change. The army's research program on attitude change

[12] Charles Winick, "How People Perceived 'The Mad Bomber,' " *Public Opinion Quarterly,* 25, 1961, in press.

[13] *Television and the Political Candidate,* a study conducted by the Cunningham and Walsh Company, 260 Madison Avenue, New York, 1959.

in soldiers was a massive effort.[14] It sharpened our knowledge of the effects of media on attitudes and the role of reference groups in attitude change. *Reference groups* are groups with which a person identifies or aspires to identify. The army research program afforded unparalleled opportunities for experimentation with different approaches to modifying attitudes. It yielded data on the persistence of attitude change. Other opportunities for research during the war occurred when the federal government became interested in getting women to buy more of the generally ignored kinds of animal organs, like brains and kidneys.[15] As a series of experiments clearly demonstrated, it was easier to change the attitudes of women toward the unfamiliar food when they discussed the pros and cons among themselves and decided, on the basis of group discussion, to try the food than when experts in nutrition gave them well documented lectures on the desirability of using the newer foods. This experience supports the conclusion that a group decision is likely to be relatively more effective in activating attitude change than is a decision handed down by an authority figure.

The power of group membership in achieving attitude change, even in the face of considerable resistance to change, can be seen in the development of Alcoholics Anonymous. The feeling of belonging to a larger group is perhaps the major therapeutic agent that Alcoholics Anonymous contributes toward a change in the individual's attitude toward drinking. Membership in Alcoholics Anonymous has helped many problem drinkers to stop drinking, after all other methods have proved unsuccessful.

Even an attitude toward something as personal as one's choice of alcoholic beverage may shift when an individual changes his work-group affiliations. A hobo, sitting on a park bench sipping sherry from a demijohn in a brown paper bag, is likely to modify his attitudes and begin drinking beer when he becomes a workman. Promoted to be an office worker, he may begin to prefer rye whiskey. Once he becomes a junior executive, he may again modify his attitudes and begin drinking Scotch. If he is promoted to top management, his attitudes are likely to be further modified, and he may again be drinking sherry—although doubtless a brand different from the hobo's. The individual's attitude toward drinking will not change automatically with the assumption of each of these social roles. Rather, there will be a process of identification with each new group; and the resulting pattern of behavior requires a shift in attitude. In each group, the person's new friends have attitudes to which he must adapt himself; and such factors, along with the new group identification, make the attitude shift easier to achieve.

*Prestige suggestion as a method of modifying attitudes.* During the 1930s and 1940s a major direction of research in attitude change was the study of prestige suggestion, or the effect of knowing that a particular person holds a specific attitude or has created a particular work of art. In one classical study, Sherif asked his subjects to rank various

[14] Samuel A. Stouffer *et al., The American Soldier,* 4 vol., Princeton University Press, Princeton, N.J., 1948–1950.

[15] *The Problem of Changing Food Habits: Report of the Committee on Food Habits, 1941–1943,* National Research Council, Washington, D. C., 1943.

writers: Conrad, Dickens, Poe, Scott, and Stevenson.[16] Some weeks later, he gave the subjects various literary passages, each attributed to a different member of this group of writers, and asked the subjects to rank the literary merit of the passages. The subjects' ranking of the passages generally coincided with their previously expressed ranking of the authors—although all the passages were actually by the same writer (Stevenson). Clearly, the subjects had evaluated the passages in terms of their underlying attitudes toward their favorite and not-so-favorite authors.

In other studies, students' attitudes toward various current issues and political leaders were established.[17] Some time later, they were shown statements that the political leaders had made on the issues in question. After a period of time, the students were again asked the same questions that had been used to determine their original attitudes. In general, the principle of prestige suggestion operated relatively clearly: the subjects had modified their attitudes so that they corresponded with the attitudes attributed to the political leaders whom they admired.

In the last ten years, numerous studies of prestige suggestion have concentrated on the role of the opinion leader (the person in a group to whom others look for advice on a particular issue) as a major factor in changing attitudes and behavior. This opinion leader has also been called an "influential."[18] He has been shown to influence doctors in selecting prescription drugs;[19] farmers in learning new procedures of agriculture;[20] women in selecting stores to buy in, movies to see, and dresses to buy; and in many other situations.[21] Such studies have demonstrated that prestige suggestion can operate from members of one's own social circle or work group. In addition, they have underscored the importance of the means whereby one receives an attitude-changing communication: it is more likely to be successful if it comes from an opinion leader in one's own group than if it comes from media. A group of Yale psychologists have extensively demonstrated that attitude change is partially a function of the credibility and perceived motivations of the communicator.[22]

## APPLICATION OF BEHAVIORAL SCIENCE MATERIALS ON ATTITUDES TO PRICING

Applications to pricing of the concepts and findings reviewed will now be explored. An exhaustive list of applications will not be attempted; instead, a few prevalent attitudes, some held by those who set price and others held by customers, will be discussed

[16] Muzafer Sherif, "An Experimental Study of Stereotypes," *Journal of Abnormal and Social Psychology,* 29: 371–375, 1935.

[17] Solomon E. Asch, "The Doctrine of Suggestion, Prestige, and Imitation in Social Psychology," *Psychological Review,* 55: 5–20, 1948.

[18] *The Influentials,* Saturday Evening Post, Philadelphia, 1956.

[19] Herbert Menzel and Elihu Katz, "Social Relation and Innovation in the Medical Profession: The Epidemiology of a New Drug," *Public Opinion Quarterly,* 19: 337–352, 1955–1956.

[20] *How Farm People Accept New Ideas,* Iowa State College, Agricultural Extension Service, Ames, Nov. 1955, Special Report No. 15.

[21] Elihu Katz and Paul F. Lazarfeld, *Personal Influence,* The Free Press of Glencoe, New York, 1955.

[22] Carl I. Hovland, Irving L. Janis, and Harold H. Kelley, *Communication and Persuasion,* Yale University Press, New Haven, Conn., 1953.

to indicate how an understanding of attitudes can be of genuine value for all who establish price or who wish to understand the pricing process.

## Attitudes Prevalent Among Price-Setters

What attitudes are held by most business executives that are likely to affect their price decisions? What is the effect of these attitudes? Do they militate for or against price changes? Do they lead executives to charge more or less than they otherwise would? Since such attitudes are often unconscious, do they impair the ability of these executives to make efficient price decisions?

No systematic formal study has been made of attitudes which are shared by executives and influence their pricing decisions. Consequently, it is necessary to make inferences based on the extant literature and personal experience. Two attitudes that apparently affect many price decisions will be discussed briefly, for purposes of illustration, in order to explore whether most price decisions are substantially different than they would be if executives did not hold these attitudes.

First of all, most price-setters seem to believe that *prices should move parallel to costs.* This attitude represents almost a pricing formula. Indeed, according to studies that have been made of industrial pricing methods, the most commonly employed method of establishing price maintains a constant margin between some *base* cost and price.[23] This method is variously termed *cost-plus* or *average-cost* pricing.

Cost-plus pricing prevails despite the demonstrable fact that it rarely will yield maximum profit for the firm and is incompatible with the widely cited "law of supply and demand." This cost method of pricing ignores demand considerations altogether! It probably is employed, despite its inconsistency with economic doctrine, at least partly because of the power of the attitude that prices should be based upon cost alone.

It is easy to explain much anomalous price behavior by this attitude. For example, some businesses raise prices during recession, despite a decline in sales of their product. Sometimes the rise in price is associated with an increase in wage rates won in a labor negotiation, or with a rise in raw-material prices, or with a rise in overhead costs per unit due to a decline in the firm's rate of capacity utilization.

Conversely, in innumerable cases businessmen have maintained prices despite a rise in replacement cost. It is still almost the rule for firms selling at retail not to mark up merchandise on their shelves, when the price of the merchandise has risen, until they themselves purchase new merchandise at the higher price. Their behavior seems to reflect the attitude that prices should move parallel to costs—rather than that they be set in order to obtain a maximum long-run profit for the enterprise.

This attitude is not held by business executives alone. Consumers share it; consequently, they seem to accept—almost cheerfully—increases in price associated with higher costs

[23] National Industrial Conference Board, "Pricing Practices of American Enterprise," *Business Record,* Sept. 1958.

to the producer. Similarly, government officials in public pronouncements imply that businessmen are ignoring their civic responsibility if they raise prices beyond the rise in their costs, but have every right to recover all increases in price that they must pay.

As a result, it is practically impossible to explain price behavior or to predict the behavior of one's competitors and regulatory agencies unless one recognizes and attaches heavy weight to this attitude. Similarly, one cannot understand the operations of the United States economy (and most other industrial economies, where similar attitudes prevail) without taking this dominant attitude into account.

The attitude that prices should vary directly with costs has spawned many related and widespread attitudes. One holds that each item in a firm's entire line of products should "stand on its own feet" and "carry its own weight." As a result of this attitude, items that do not cover their "accounting" costs are dropped—even though they may greatly enhance the attractiveness of the entire line, contribute to convering overhead, and add to total profit. Also, this attitude militates against setting prices in a way that increases the profitability of an entire product line by accepting a very low price for one or a few selected items in the line.

Another significant and prevalent attitude, which is closely related to the attitude that prices should move parallel to costs, is what might be termed "public-utility-type thinking." This is the orientation that businessmen are entitled only to a "reasonable return on their investment"; consequently, even when they have an opportunity to command a very high price—because of a shortage, exceptional product features, or the like—they should not "take advantage of the situation" to demand a high price. Indeed, this attitude, as held by many businessmen and consumers alike, dictates that sellers should add a fairly uniform margin to all products they sell and that this margin should not be changed markedly over time. Many otherwise strange price phenomena—particularly "grey markets"—can be understood more readily if one takes account of attitudes like these, which may underlie the decisions of executive responsible for setting price.

A second major attitude prevalent among price setters is that *management should "do something!" when sales decline.* Business executives, like most other groups, have a conception of their jobs and of themselves to which they attempt to adhere. Among the ingredients likely to be found in an executive's self-image is the attitude that he should be a man of action and deal quickly with difficulties as they arise; he should be resolute and prepared to take the consequences of his decisions. With this kind of general attitude among executives, one is likely to find price behavior that cannot be explained as a rational pursuit of self-interest or maximum profit for the firm.

There are many situations in which businessmen take price action when inaction would clearly be a wiser course. Such examples are especially plentiful during periods of declining sales. When sales fall throughout a market, due to broad economic forces that affect all rival firms more or less equally, it would rarely benefit any one firm to reduce its prices if all of its rivals would follow suit: all the firms would ordinarily sell essentially the same amount they would have sold had they retained the higher price, but would receive less for their product; and, when demand revived, they would have difficulty in raising prices back to their previous levels. Nevertheless, price reductions are extremely common under such circumstances—even in industries where customers, who have been offered a price reduction by a source they do not patronize regularly, are able to obtain a similar price reduction from their present supplier. It is very difficult to explain this behavior without taking account of the tendency of executives to regard inaction—especially with regard to price—as perhaps the most difficult course of action for them.[24]

### Attitudes Among Customers

To understand the source and power of most customer attitudes toward price, it is necessary to understand their attitudes toward money itself. The strongest attitudes that customers carry to the purchase situation probably relate to money itself. Their attitudes toward particular numerical prices, differentials in price for different brands of the same product, changes in price, etc., are often the major explanation for customer behavior; these, however, seem less salient than their attitudes toward money and ordinarily reflect those attitudes quite directly.

*Attitudes toward money.* Since virtually everyone beyond early childhood buys some things, when one speaks of "customer attitudes" he is discussing the attitudes of almost everyone in the society under consideration. In the United States, and almost certainly in all other highly industrialized economies, most persons have extremely strong feelings about money.

Psychoanalysts have helped us to understand the great strength of most people's feelings about money and of the attitudes that reflect these feelings.[25] The salience and strength of these feelings and attitudes partially derive from their having been formed in very early childhood. Certainly, the average person's first contact with money often comes when he learns that money is one reason for his not being able to gratify his whims or desires. It generally takes place at an extremely early age—long before he is capable of understanding the realistic significance of money. In even the most prosperous households, money considerations are cited to the very young child as a major reason for his not wasting or destroying things and as one reason for his not having everything that takes his fancy. Thus, at a very early age, the child comes to regard money as something that is even bigger and more powerful than his parents and something that has almost as much capacity as they do to satisfy his wants.

Another reason for money's importance is that it is frequently used as a reward for children by adults. Especially in the minds of young children, who do not understand

[24] For a fairly detailed consideration of this phenomenon in the steel industry, see Alfred R. Oxenfeldt, *Industrial Pricing and Market Practices,* Englewood Cliffs, N.J.: Prentice-Hall, 1957, pp. 526–528.

[25] Otto Fenichel, *Psychoanalytic Theory of Neurosis,* W. W. Norton & Company, Inc., New York, 1945, pp. 281–283.

the true significance of money, its status as both a reward and a goal gives it great emotional impact and accentuates its power.

Money generates attitudes of great strength for yet other reasons. In many homes, it is a source of tension that is ill disguised from even young children and is often consciously communicated to older ones. This tension may arise because the family income is limited or the income-earner's employment is insecure; or it may result from the divergent standards of expenditure of the individual parents. These circumstances combine to accentuate the emotionalism which parents feel toward money, and which they communicate to their children.

Despite the rough similarity in the circumstances under which most individuals form their earliest attitudes toward money, there is very great divergence in the specific content of those attitudes. For example, some individuals are miserly and other are extravagant; some make a fetish of careful management and accounting for expenditure, while others value greatly the ability to be casual about expenditure. However, despite wide individual differences in fundamental attitudes toward money, there are very few people whose attitudes toward money lack great salience. One can distinguish some attitudes that strongly affect very large numbers of customers and are quite relevant to their reactions toward price, price differentials, and price changes. Other attitudes—such as the attitude toward money as the best index of "success" or "brains"—are no doubt extremely important in explaining human behavior, but are less directly relevant to an understanding of consumer behavior with respect to price. A few of these attitudes will be mentioned and described briefly in order to indicate their relevance to price and to demonstrate that it is not possible to explain consumer behavior fully or set prices effectively without taking cognizance of their content and their power.

*Attitude toward transactions as "battles of wits."* The author of Ecclesiastes in the Old Testament may have gone a bit too far when he exclaimed "Vanity of vanities; all is vanity," but it is obvious that almost everyone usually desires to convey a good impression of himself. Almost everyone has a homeostatic attitudinal balancing mechanism, which enables him to hold as high an opinion of himself as possible. Adults, and more especially parents, must recognize the purchase function as one of their important roles in the family; to make ill-advised purchases, or to pay substantially more than was necessary, thus represents ineptitude—and may even inflict injury on other members of the family. Even more important perhaps, it may signify personal "failure" and may damage one's self-esteem.

If challenged, most people become very "defensive" about their purchases. They are likely to resist the implication that they overpaid or misjudged the quality of their purchase. If they have clearly obtained poor value, they may seek a scapegoat. Generally they blame the seller, accusing him of misrepresenting, acting in poor faith, or something similar. They consider good purchasing (and thus obtaining good value for their money) to be "a matter of principle" and "an end in itself"; their purchase behavior cannot, therefore, be viewed solely in realistic and substantive terms. On substantive grounds, it may not appear to be sufficiently important for a customer of moderate income to walk several blocks to save 11 cents on a $1 purchase. However, as a symbol of "success" and as a mark of virtue, the extra effort will seem warranted to many and actually obligatory to some.

Little differences in price are likely to seem major items to most consumers, for the reasons discussed. Where product quality is demonstrably the same (as where the same model of the same brand of the same product sold at two stores is in question), a great barrier exists for most consumers if price differs even slightly. They require a justification for paying the higher price—and, for the large majority, it does not seem to suffice that they will save themselves some time or effort by paying the higher price. One finds many extreme examples of unrealistic behavior that can be explained only by highly salient attitudes toward money, combined with the attitude that a person reveals his intelligence and diligence by the way he makes purchases. Wealthy women who drive their limousines thirty miles through heavy traffic to save 79 cents (although they are likely to speak of it as 25 per cent) are not freaks by any means. They, and less extreme types, make up a sizable proportion of those who patronize discount houses and who patronize "regular sales" at all retail shops.

*Attitude that waste is shameful, if not sinful.* The United States is identified by many Europeans as a nation of waste. Thus, although Europeans have long regarded it as "wrong" to leave food on a plate when one has finished eating, in the United States only "crude" ill-mannered persons leave their plates absolutely bare. Indeed, the acceleration of waste has come to be viewed as a major American social contribution; and some marketing specialists proclaim that it is a virtual necessity for the continued prosperity of many industries, if not the entire economy. Vance Packard, who has been highly critical of those who influence the consumer to buy more or different things, has hit this problem head-on and inspired further discussion of the subject in his *The Waste Makers.*[26] Nonetheless, most persons in the United States absorb some ascetic and "puritanical" attitudes that are most inhospitable to waste. To destroy property or to use much when little would suffice is regarded as categorically wrong in the attitude systems of most adults in the United States. Similarly, to spend more than one needs to spend may also be regarded as a categorical wrong and an unnecessary waste. Thus, the stigma attaching to waste, reinforcing the attitude that purchases involve a battle of wits, makes most consumers sensitive to the "fairness" of their purchase price; in particular, they are extremely sensitive to differences in price for the same brand of item in different retail shops.

Price assumes particular importance in an economy where brands, especially national ones, assure consumers that quality is uniform among different items of the same brand. Even though service and convenience should realistically figure in their calculations, many consumers tend to think and say that they are getting the same thing when they obtain the same brand and model of a given item. As a result, they tend to measure the "success" of any purchase by comparing the price they paid with what other

[26] Vance Packard, *The Waste Makers,* David McKay Company, Inc., New York, 1960.

customers pay or what other stores charge for the same item, rather than how the item compares in value *for them* with other things they might have purchased with those funds or with the value to them of holding those extra funds. In other words, consumers need assurance that they cannot buy the same item for less elsewhere—far more than they must be assured they need that item more than any other of equal cost. The consumer is not very vulnerable to being proved "wasteful" or foolish if he buys what he could very well have done without.

## CONCLUSIONS

As we survey these applications of behavioral science material on attitudes, what have we said that is new? What conclusions for action can be drawn that are different from those already accepted by market practitioners and teachers?

Cost-plus pricing has been a recognized fact for centuries; and price theorists, most of them very reluctantly, have acknowledged its existence. Some writers have even associated its prevalence with an attitude held by the public at large. Similarly, almost every seller recognizes the sensitivity of his customers to being overcharged, and all claim to charge a "fair price"; indeed, most retailers actively or implicitly match the prices charged by competitors. Thus, behavioral science does not tell us anything about what happens that we did not know before. It does, however, explain why these things happen and it provides suggestions about what must be done.

Since cost-plus pricing rests upon a strongly held attitude, the practice will not be changed without first changing the attitude. Even if it were possible to destroy cost-plus pricing itself, the same results would be achieved by a different route as long as the basic attitude remains. Therefore, the only way to depart from cost-plus pricing would be to vest responsibility for pricing with persons whose biases run counter to these attitudes. Specifically, one might divest accountants and controllers of pricing responsibility and place it in the hands of sales persons who are not likely to ignore demand considerations.

Similarly, the strength of most customers' attitudes about money, and the expression of these attitudes in their reactions to price, contain implied suggestions for action. When a seller encounters an attitude that is so firmly held and deeply rooted, he cannot hope to change it; he must adapt to it. He must claim to provide good value and to change prices in line with other vendors' prices. He cannot hope to persuade many customers to pay him a premium for the added convenience of not seeking out the source charging the lowest price. This is not to say that retailers cannot attract a tiny group of customers by almost any appeal, but a seller takes on a large and unnecessary burden when he fights against rather than reconciles himself to such a strong attitude system.

# 41. BAYESIAN DECISION THEORY IN PRICING STRATEGY

*Paul E. Green*

*This article discusses how Bayesian statistics can be a potentially powerful tool for systematically working with management judgments.*

*Particular emphasis is placed on showing how this type of approach can be used in the area of pricing analysis.*

Since the publication of Robert Schlaifer's pioneering work, *Probability and Statistics for Business Decisions,*[1] the Bayesian approach to decision-making under uncertainty has received much comment, pro and con, by theoretical and applied statisticians alike.

However, in contrast to the large number of theoretical contributions being made to decision theory in general and Bayesian statistics in particular, reported applications of these procedures to real-world problem situations have been rather meager. Applications appear especially lacking in the marketing field.

[1] Robert Schlaifer, *Probability and Statistics for Business Decisions,* McGraw-Hill Book Company, New York, 1959. In addition two excellent general articles dealing with the Bayesian approach are: Harry V. Roberts, "The New Business Statistics," *Journal of Business,* vol. 33, January, 1960, pp. 21–30 and Jack Hirshleifer, "The Bayesian Approach to Statistical Decision–An Exposition," *Journal of Business,* vol. 31, October, 1961, pp. 471–489.

Source: From *Journal of Marketing,* vol. 27, January. 1963, pp. 5–14. Paul E. Green: Market planning and marketing research activities, Textile Fibers Department, E. I. du Pont de Nemours & Co., Inc.

In highly oversimplified terms, the Bayesian approach to decision-making under uncertainty provides a framework for explicitly working with the economic costs of alternative courses of action, the prior knowledge or judgments of the decision maker, and formal modification of these judgments as additional data are introduced into the problem.

In the Du Pont Company, the decision theory approach, often augmented by computer simulation, has been used experimentally over the past few years in a variety of market planning applications, ranging from capacity expansion problems to questions concerning the introduction of new products and long-range price and promotional strategy. The application to follow concerns the use of Bayesian theory in the selection of a "best" pricing policy for a firm in an oligopolistic industry where such factors as demand elasticity, competitive retaliation, threat of future price weakness, and potential entry of new competitors influence the effectiveness of the firm's courses of action. Although the content of this case is apocryphal, its structure has been compounded from actual situations.

No attempt will be made to describe even superficially all of the many facets of the Bayesian approach to decision-making under uncertainty. The content of this article is focused on only two main considerations.

First, in dealing with actual marketing situations, for example, pricing problems, the opportunity to obtain field information may be nonexistent. Second, in dealing with actual marketing problems, the complexity of the situation may force the analyst to develop a problem structure in much greater detail than has been described in the literature.

## AN ILLUSTRATIVE APPLICATION

Since early 1955, the Everclear Plastics Company had been producing a resin called Kromel, basically designed for certain industrial markets. In addition to Everclear, three other firms were producing Kromel resin. Prices among all four suppliers (called here the Kromel industry) were identical: and product quality and service among producers were comparable. Everclear's current share of Kromel industry sales amounted to 10 per cent.

Four industrial end uses comprised the principal marketing area for the Kromel industry. These market segments will be labeled A, B, C, and D. Three of the four segments (B, C, and D) were functionally dependent on segment A in the sense that Kromel's *ultimate* market position and rate of approach to this level in each of these three segments was predicated on the resin's making substantial inroads in segment A.

The Kromel industry's only competition in these four segments consisted of another resin called Verlon, which was produced by six other firms. Shares of the total Verlon-Kromel market (weighted sums over all four segments) currently stood at 70 per cent Verlon industry, and 30 per cent Kromel industry. Since its introduction in 1955, the superior functional characteristics per dollar cost of Kromel had enabled this newer product to displace fairly large poundages of Verlon in market segments B, C, and D.

On the other hand, the functional superiority per dollar cost of Kromel had not been sufficiently high to interest segment A consumers. While past price decreases in Kromel had been made, the cumulative effect of these reductions had still been insufficient to accomplish Kromel sales penetration in segment A. (Sales penetration is defined as a market share exceeding zero.)

In the early fall of 1960, it appeared to Everclear's management that future weakness in Kromel price might be in the offing. The anticipated capacity increases on the part of the firm's Kromel competitors suggested that in the next year or two potential industry supply of this resin might significantly exceed demand, if no substantial market participation for the Kromel industry were established in segment A. In addition, it appeared likely that potential Kromel competitors might enter the business, thus adding to the threat of oversupply in later years.

Segment A, of course, constituted the key factor. If substantial inroads could be made in this segment, it appeared likely that Kromel industry sales growth in the other segments not only could be speeded up, but that ultimate market share levels for this resin could be markedly increased from those anticipated in the absence of segment A penetration. To Everclear's sales management, a price reduction in Kromel still appeared to represent a feasible means to achieve this objective, and (even assuming similar price reductions on the part of Kromel competitors) perhaps could still be profitable to Everclear.

However, a large degree of uncertainty surrounded both the overall attractiveness of this alternative, and under this alternative the amount of the price reduction which would enable Kromel to penetrate market segment A.

## PROBLEM STRUCTURING AND DEVELOPMENT OF THE MODEL

Formulation of the problem required a certain amount of artistry and compromise toward achieving a reasonably adequate description of the problem. But it was also necessary to keep the structure simple enough so that the nature of each input would be comprehensible to the personnel responsible for supplying data for the study.

Problem components had to be formulated, such as:

1. length of planning period;
2. number and nature of courses of action;
3. payoff functions; and
4. states of nature covering future growth of the total Verlon-Kromel market, inter-industry (Kromel vs. Verlon) and intra-Kromel industry effects of a Kromel price

change, implications on Everclear's share of the total Kromel industry, and Everclear's production costs.

Initial discussions with sales management indicated that a planning period of five years should be considered in the study. While the selection of five years was somewhat arbitrary, sales personnel believed that some repercussions of a current price reduction might well extend over several years into the future.

A search for possible courses of action indicated that four pricing alternatives covered the range of actions under consideration:

1. maintenance of status quo on Kromel price, which was $1.00 per pound;
2. a price reduction to $.93 per pound within the next three months;
3. a price reduction to $.85 per pound within the next three months;
4. a price reduction to $.80 per pound within the next three months.

Inasmuch as each price action would be expected to produce a different time pattern in the flow of revenues and costs, and since no added investment in production facilities was contemplated, it was agreed that cumulative, compounded net profits over the five-year planning period would constitute a relevant payoff function. In the absence of any unanimity as to the "correct" opportunity cost of capital, it was decided to use two interest rates of 6 and 10 per cent annually in order to test the sensitivity of outcomes to the cost of the capital variable.

Another consideration came to light during initial problem discussions. Total market growth (for the Kromel or Verlon industry) over the next five years in each market segment constituted a "state of nature" which could impinge on Everclear's profit position. Accordingly, it was agreed to consider three separate forecasts of total market growth, a "most probable," "optimistic," and "pessimistic" forecast.

From these assumptions a base case was then formulated. This main case would first consider the pricing problem under the most probable forecast of total Verlon-Kromel year-by-year sales potential in each segment, using an opportunity cost of capital of 6 per cent annually. The two other total market forecasts and the other cost of capital were then to be treated as subcases, in order to test the sensitivity of the base case outcomes to variations in these particular states of nature.

However, inter- and intra-industry alternative states of nature literally abounded in the Kromel resin problem. Sales management at Everclear had to consider such factors as:

1. The possibility that Kromel resin could effect penetration of market segment A if no price decrease were made;
2. If a price decrease were made, the extent of Verlon retaliation to be anticipated;

3. Given a particular type of Verlon price retaliation, its possible impact on Kromel's penetration of segment A;
4. If segment A were penetrated, the possible market share which the Kromel industry could gain in segment A;
5. If segment A were penetrated, the possible side effects of this event on speeding up Kromel's participation in market segments B, C, and D;
6. If segment A were not penetrated, the impact which the price reduction could still have on speeding up Kromel's participation in segments B, C, and D;
7. If segment A were not penetrated, the possibility that existing Kromel competitors would initiate price reductions a year hence;
8. The possible impact of a current Kromel price reduction on the decisions of existing or potential Kromel producers to increase capacity or enter the industry.

While courses of action, length of planning period, and the payoff measure (cumulative, compounded net profits) for the base case had been fairly quickly agreed upon, the large number of inter- and intra-Kromel industry states of nature deemed relevant to the problem would require rather lengthy discussion with Everclear's sales personnel.

Accordingly, introductory sessions were held with Everclear's sales management, in order to develop a set of states of nature large enough to represent an adequate description of the real problem, yet small enough to be comprehended by the participating sales personnel. Next, separate interview sessions were held with two groups of Everclear's sales personnel; subjective probabilities regarding the occurrence of alternative states of nature under each course of action were developed in these sessions. A final session was held with all contributing personnel in attendance; each projection and/or subjective probability was gone over in detail, and a final set of ground rules for the study was agreed upon. A description of these ground rules appears in Table I.

## USE OF TREE DIAGRAMS

The large number of alternative states of nature which were associated with inter- and intra-industry factors necessitated the construction of "tree diagrams" for each pricing alternative. These diagrams enabled sales management to trace the implications of their assumptions. Figure 1 shows a portion of one such tree diagram.

A word of explanation concerning interpretation of the probability tree is in order. The two principal branches underneath the *$1.00 case* refer to the event of whether or not Kromel penetrates segment A in the first year of the planning period. Sales personnel felt that a 5 per cent chance existed for penetration, hence the figure .05000 under A.

However, if A were penetrated, four market participations were deemed possible: 25, 50, 75 and 100 per cent carrying the conditional probabilities of .15, .35, .40 and .10 respectively.

**Table 1. Subjective probabilities and data estimates associated with Everclear's pricing problem**

1. If Kromel price remained at $1.00/pound and market segment A were not penetrated, what market share pattern for Kromel industry sales pounds would obtain in segments B, C, and D?

*Base assumptions–Kromel industry share*

| | *Segment B* | *Segment C* | *Segment D* |
|---|---|---|---|
| 1961 | 57.0% | 40.0% | 42.0% |
| 1962 | 65.0 | 50.0 | 44.0 |
| 1963 | 75.0 | 80.0 | 46.0 |
| 1964 | 76.0 | 84.0 | 48.0 |
| 1965 | 76.0 | 84.0 | 50.0 |

2. If Kromel price remained at $1.00/pound, what is the probability that Kromel would still penetrate market segment A?

*Probability of penetration–segment A*

| | |
|---|---|
| 1961 | .05 |
| 1962 | .10 |
| 1963 | .20 |
| 1964 | .25 |
| 1965 | .40 |

3. Under price strategies $.93/pound, $.85/pound, and $.80/pound, what is the probability of Verlon industry price retaliation; and given the particular retaliation (shown below), what is the probability that Kromel would still penetrate market segment A?

*Pricing case (entries are probabilities)*

| *Verlon industry retaliation* | *$.93 case* | *$.85 case* | *$.80 case* |
|---|---|---|---|
| Full match of Kromel price reduction | .05 | .15 | .38 |
| Half match of Kromel price reduction | .60 | .75 | .60 |
| Stand pat on price | .35 | .10 | .02 |

*Given a particular Verlon retaliatory action, the probability that Kromel would still penetrate segment A*

| | *$.93 case* | | | *$.85 case* | | | *$.80 case* | | |
|---|---|---|---|---|---|---|---|---|---|
| | *Full match* | *half match* | *Stand pat* | *Full match* | *half match* | *Stand pat* | *Full match* | *half match* | *Stand pat* |
| 1961 | .15 | .20 | .35 | .20 | .40 | .80 | .75 | .80 | .90 |
| 1962 | .25 | .30 | .60 | .30 | .60 | .90 | .80 | .85 | .95 |
| 1963 | .35 | .40 | .65 | .40 | .65 | .95 | .85 | .90 | 1.00 |
| 1964 | .60 | .65 | .75 | .70 | .75 | .98 | .90 | .95 | 1.00 |
| 1965 | .65 | .70 | .80 | .75 | .80 | .98 | .95 | .98 | 1.00 |

4. If penetration in market segment A were effected, what is the probability that Kromel would obtain the specific share of this segment (a) during the first year of penetration, and (b) during the second year of participation?

| *Share* | *First year* | *Second year* |
|---|---|---|
| 25% | .15 | .00 |
| 50 | .35 | .00 |
| 75 | .40 | .00 |
| 100 | .10 | 1.00 |

5. If Kromel penetration of market segment A were effected, what impact would this event have on speeding up Kromel industry participation in segments B, C, and D?

   Segment B–Would speed up market participation one year from base assumption shown under point 1 of this Table.

   Segment C–Would speed up market participation one year from base assumption shown under point 1 of this Table.

   Segment D–Kromel would move up to 85% of the market in the following year, and would obtain 100% of the market in the second year following penetration of segment A.

6. Under the price reduction strategies, if Kromel penetration of market segment A were *not* accomplished, what is the probability that Kromel industry participation in segments B, C, and D (considered as a group) would still be speeded up one year from the base assumption shown under point 1 of this Table?

| | *Probability of speedup* |
|---|---|
| $.93 case | .45 |
| $.85 case | .60 |
| $.80 case | .80 |

7. If Kromel price at the end of any given year were $1.00/pound, $.93/pound, $.85/pound, or $.80/pound respectively, *and* if market segment A were not penetrated, what is the probability that present competitive Kromel producers would take the specific price action shown below?

| *If Kromel price* | *Action* | *Probability* |
|---|---|---|
| @ $1.00/pound | $1.00/pound | .15 |
| | .93 | .80 |
| | .85 | .05 |
| | .80 | .00 |
| @ $.93/pound | .93 | .80 |
| | .85 | .20 |
| | .80 | .00 |
| @ $.85/pound | .85 | 1.00 |
| | .80 | .00 |
| @ $.80/pound | .80 | 1.00 |

8. Under each of the four price strategies, what is the probability that competitive (present or potential) Kromel producers would add to or initiate capacity (as related to the price prevailing in mid-1961) in the years 1963 and 1964? (No capacity changes were assumed in 1965.)

| *Competitor* | *$1.00/pound* | *$.93/pound* | *$.85/pound* | *$.80/pound* |
|---|---|---|---|---|
| R | .50 | .20 | .05 | .00 |
| S | .90 | .75 | .50 | .20 |
| T | .40 | .10 | .05 | .00 |
| U | .70 | .50 | .25 | .00 |
| V | .70 | .50 | .25 | .00 |

*Timing and amount available beginning of year*

| *Competitor* | *1963* | *1964* |
|---|---|---|
| R | 10 million pounds | 20 million pounds |
| S | 12 | 20 |
| T | 12 | 20 |
| U | 6 | 12 |
| V | 6 | 6 |

**Figure 1. Portion of a "tree diagram"; Kromel price simulation**

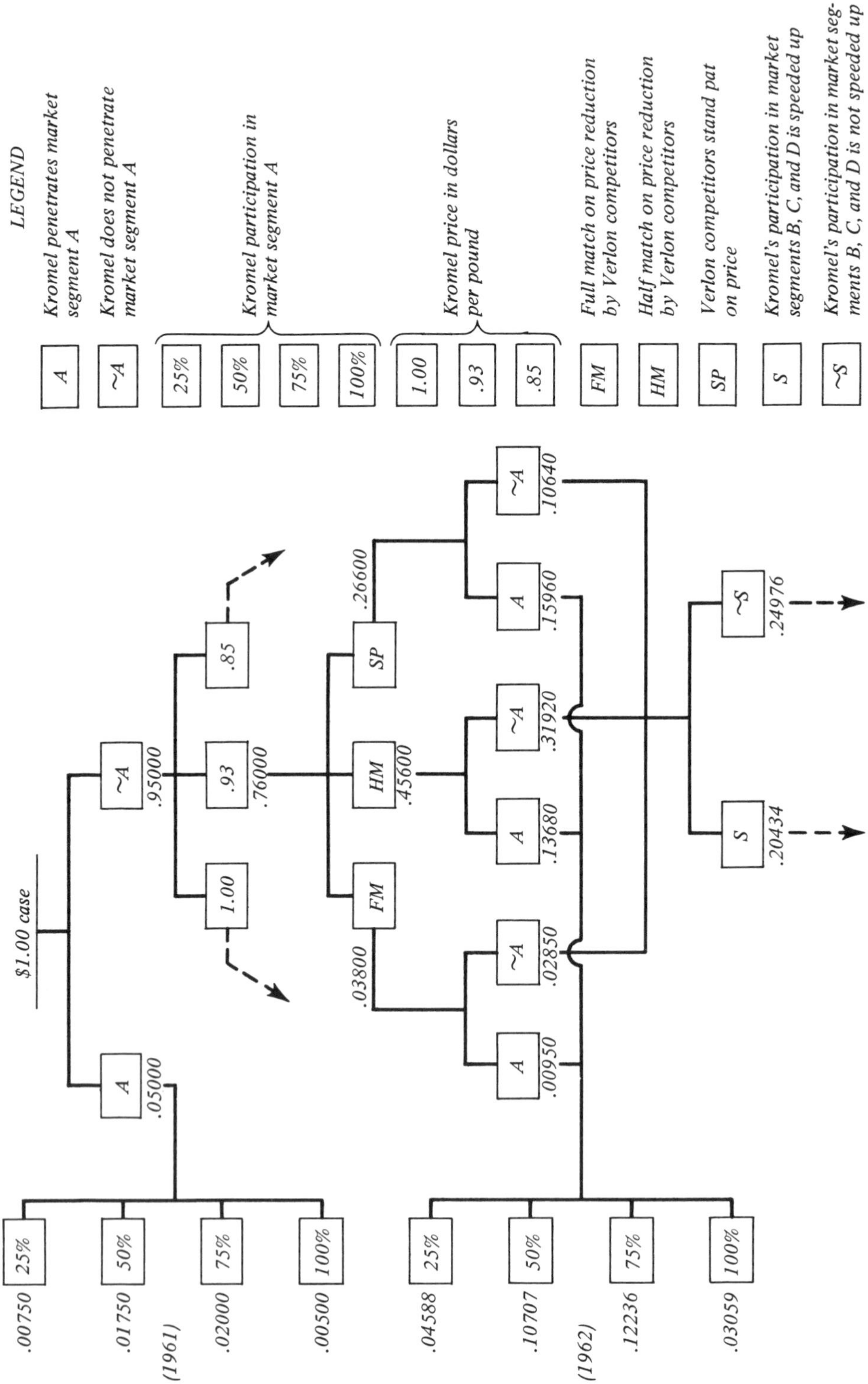

$1.00 case

A .05000
~A .95000

1.00
.93 .76000
.85

.03800 FM
HM .45600
SP .26600

A .00950
~A .02850
A .13680
~A .31920
A .15960
~A .10640

S .20434
~S .24976

(1961)
.00750 25%
.01750 50%
.02000 75%
.00500 100%

(1962)
.04588 25%
.10707 50%
.12236 75%
.03059 100%

LEGEND

|  |  |
|---|---|
| A | Kromel penetrates market segment A |
| ~A | Kromel does not penetrate market segment A |
| 25%, 50%, 75%, 100% | Kromel participation in market segment A |
| 1.00, .93, .85 | Kromel price in dollars per pound |
| FM | Full match on price reduction by Verlon competitors |
| HM | Half match on price reduction by Verlon competitors |
| SP | Verlon competitors stand pat on price |
| S | Kromel's participation in market segments B, C, and D is speeded up |
| ~S | Kromel's participation in market segments B, C, and D is not speeded up |

Multiplication of each conditional probability, in turn, by the .05 marginal probability leads to the four joint probabilities noted in the upper left portion of the chart.

Next, if Kromel did not penetrate segment A during the first year, a probability of .80 was attached to the event that competitive Kromel producers would reduce price to $.93 per pound. Multiplying the conditional probability of .80 by .95 results in the .76000 probability assigned to the joint event, "did not penetrate segment A and Kromel price was reduced to $.93 per pound."

However, if Kromel price were reduced to $.93 per pound, Verlon retaliation had to be considered, leading to the joint probabilities assigned to the next set of tree branches. In this way probabilities were built up for each of the over-400 possible outcomes of the study by appropriate application of the ground rules noted in Table 1.

A mathematical model was next constructed for determining the expected value of Everclear's cumulative, compounded net profits under each price strategy. See Table 2.

This model was then programed for an electronic computer. The simulation was first carried out for the base case assumptions regarding total Verlon-Kromel market growth and cost of capital. Additional runs were made in which these assumptions were varied.

**Table 2. Kromel model–expected value of cumulative, compounded net profits**

The mathematical model used to determine the expected values of Everclear's cumulative, compounded net profits was as follows:

$$CCN\ (X_k) = \sum_{j=1}^{n} p_j \cdot \sum_{i=1}^{m} \left[(1+r)^{m-i}\, T\left\{(D_{ij} - Z_{ij})(K_{ij}M_{ij})\right\}\right]$$

$$Z_{ij} = \phi\ (K_{ij}M_{ij})$$

$CCN\ (X_k)$ = Expected value of Everclear's cumulative, compounded net profits under each $X_k$ price strategy ($k = 1, \ldots, 4$).

$p_j$ = Probability assigned to the j th outcome ($j = 1, 2, \ldots, n$).

$r$ = Interest rate per annum, expressed decimally.

$T$ = Ratio of net to gross profits of Everclear's Kromel operation (assumed constant in the study).

$D_{ij}$ = Kromel price in $/pound in the i th year ($i = 1, 2, \ldots, m$) for the j th outcome.

$Z_{ij}$ = Cost in $/pound of Everclear's Kromel resin in the i th year for the j th outcome. (This cost is a function of the amount of Kromel pounds sold by Everclear.)

$\phi$ = Function of.

$K_{ij}$ = Everclear's overall market share of Kromel Industry sales (in pounds) in the i th year for the j th outcome (expressed decimally).

$M_{ij}$ = Kromel Industry poundage (summed over all four market segments) in the i th year for the j th outcome.

## RESULTS OF THE COMPUTER SIMULATIONS

The computer run for the base case showed some interesting results for the relevant variables affecting Everclear's cumulative, compounded net profits position at the end of the planning period. These results are portrayed in Figures 2 through 4.

Figure 2 summarizes the cumulative probability of Kromel's penetration of market segment A (the critical factor in the study) as a function of time, under each pricing strategy. As would be expected, the lowest price strategy, the *$.80 case,* carried the highest probability of market penetration. However, the cumulative probability approached 1, that *all* price strategies would eventually effect penetration of market segment A by the end of the simulation period. This behavior stems from the impact of price decreases assumed to be initiated by Kromel *competitors* (if penetration were

**Figure 2. Cumulative probability of Kromel's penetration of market segment A (as a function of time and initial price)**

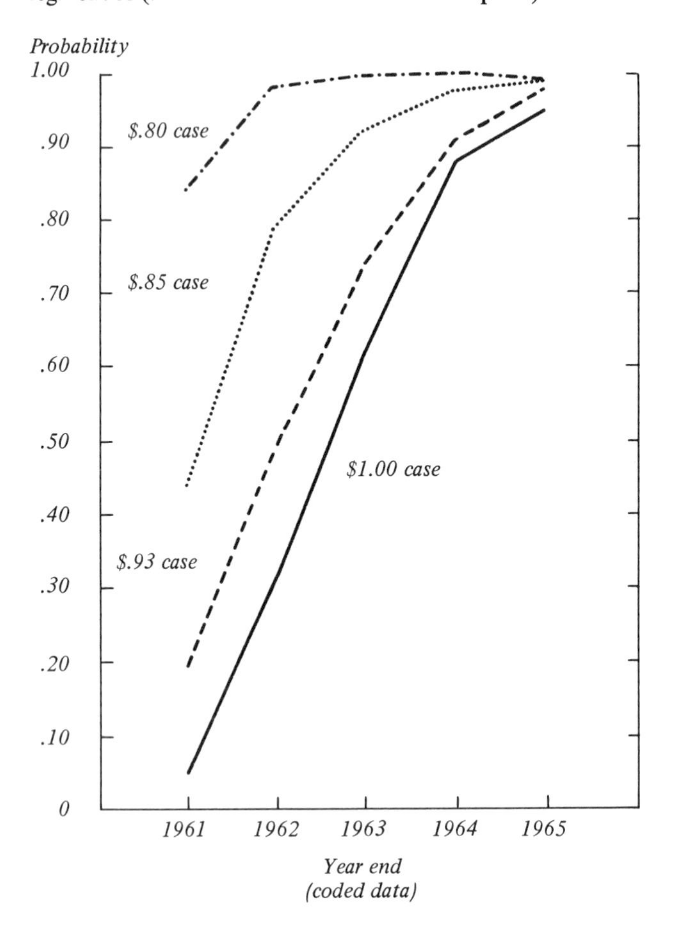

not initially effected under the original price strategies) which in turn changed the probability of Kromel's penetration of segment A in later years, since this probability was related to price.

Figure 3 shows the expected incremental sales dollars (obtained by subtracting the expected outcomes of the *$1.00 case,* used as a reference base, from the expected outcomes of each of the other three cases respectively) generated for Everclear under each price strategy. While some tapering off in average sales dollars generated from the price reduction cases compared to the *$1.00 case* can be noted near the end of the simulation period, this tapering off is less pronounced than that which would be experienced by the total Kromel industry.

The reason for this different pattern is that the price reduction strategies (by reducing the probability of future capacity expansion on the part of existing and potential

**Figure 3. Kromel sales volume–Everclear Plastics Co. (Incremental sales dollars generated over $1.00 case)**

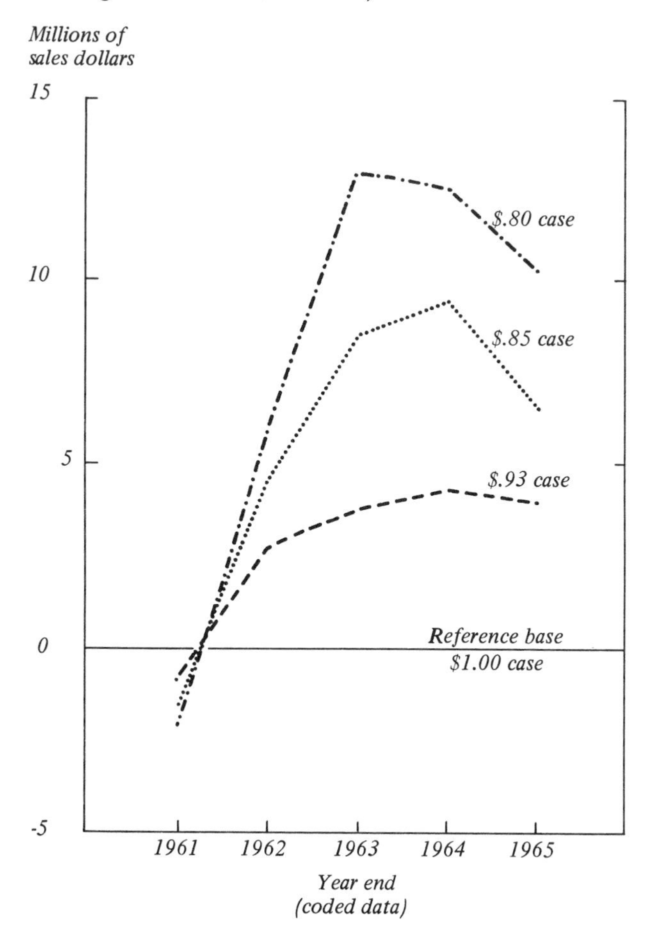

Kromel competitors) led to gains in Everclear's market share, relative to market share under the *$1.00 case.* These increases in Everclear's market share, under the price reduction strategies, partially offset the decline in incremental sales dollar gains (experienced by the Kromel industry near the end of the period) and thus explain the difference in sales patterns that would be observed between Everclear and the Kromel industry.

Figure 4 summarizes the behavior of Everclear's average, year-by-year (compounded) net profits performance again on an incremental basis compared to the *$1.00 case.* As would be expected, time lags in the penetration of segment A, under the price reduction strategies, result in an early profit penalty compared to the *$1.00 case.* This penalty is later overbalanced by the additional sales dollars accruing from earlier (on the average) penetration of segment A under the price reduction strategies versus the *status quo* price case.

**Figure 4. Compounded year-by-year net profits of Everclear Plastics Co. (Compound rate equals 6% annually)**

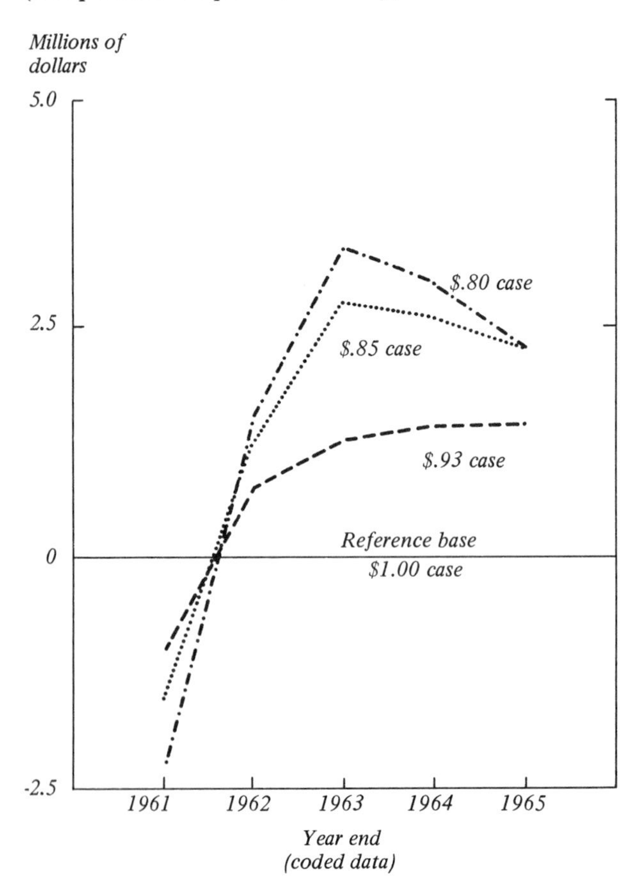

The overall performance of each pricing strategy on Everclear's cumulative, compounded net profits position (expected value basis) at the *end* of the five-year planning period is shown in Table 3. These values were obtained by application of the formula shown in Table 2.

**Table 3. Cumulative, compounded net profits– Everclear Plastics Co. (1961-65)**

| *Price strategy* | *End of period profit position* |
|---|---|
| $1.00 case | $26.5 million |
| .93 case | 30.3 million |
| .85 case | 33.9 million |
| .80 case | 34.9 million |

Table 3 shows that all of the price reduction strategies yield expected payoffs which exceed the *$1.00 case.* These additional profits stem from two principal sources:

1. the higher profits generated in the middle portion of the planning period, as a function of the increased probability of effecting penetration of market segment A, and its associated effect on Kromel industry sales in market segments B, C, and D; and
2. the higher market share for Everclear, resulting from the influence of the price reduction strategies on lowering the probability of capacity expansion and/or entry by Kromel competitors (existing or potential). These combined factors overbalance the lower profit margins per pound associated with the price reduction strategies compared to the *$1.00 case.*

However, a relevant question arose concerning the influence of the more favorable market share factor (under the price reduction cases) on the outcomes of these strategies vs. the *$1.00 case.* Suppose that no favorable difference in market share were obtained under the price reduction strategies compared to the no-price reduction case. That is, suppose the probability that lower Kromel price would discourage future competitive expansion of Kromel industry capacity in the 1963–64 period were zero. How would this affect Everclear's profit position?

In order to test the impact of this variable on Everclear's cumulative, compounded net profits, the market share factor was held constant at the trend level estimated under the no-price reduction, or *$1.00 case* over the simulation period. This analysis resulted in the information given in Table 4.

It is clear from Table 4 that the market share factor is important in producing Everclear's higher profit position as associated with the price reduction

**Table 4. Profit position–market share held constant (Everclear's cumulative, compounded net profits; 1961–65)**

| *Price strategy* | *End of period profit position* |
|---|---|
| $1.00 case | $26.5 million |
| .93 case | 26.9 million |
| .85 case | 27.4 million |
| .80 case | 25.2 million |

alternatives noted in Table 3. If increased share for Everclear were *not* obtained in the 1963–65 period (relative to the share expected under the *$1.00 case*), all strategies would yield close to equal payoffs. That is, over the planning period, the increased sales volume resulting from earlier (on the average) penetration of segment A under the price reduction strategies just about balances the less favorable profit margins associated with these strategies.

However, beyond the planning period, all strategies have for all practical purposes accomplished penetration of segment A. The impact of *higher market share* for Everclear thus assumes an important role toward maintaining higher payoffs for the price reduction cases versus the *$1.00 case.*

When computer run results were analyzed for the sub-cases (varying the total market forecast and cost of capital variables), it was found that the study outcomes were not sensitive to these factors. Although the absolute levels of all payoffs changed, no appreciable change was noted in their relative standing.

*In Summary.* This illustration has shown two principal findings regarding the expected payoffs associated with the alternative courses of action formulated by Everclear:

1. All price reduction strategies result in higher expected payoffs than that associated with the *status quo* pricing case and of these, the *$.80 case* leads to the largest expected value.
2. The higher payoffs associated with the price reduction strategies are quite sensitive to the assumption that Everclear's future market share would be favorably influenced by reductions in Kromel price.

Everclear's management is now at least in a position to appraise the *financial implications* of its marketing assumptions in order to arrive at a reasoned selection among alternative choices.

## IMPLICATIONS

The preceding illustration indicates the extent of problem detail which can be (and frequently must be) introduced to reflect adequately the characteristics of real market situations. Nevertheless, this illustration omits some important features of Bayesian decision theory.

First, payoffs were expressed in monetary terms (cumulative, compounded net profits) rather than utility, in the von Neumann-Morgenstern sense, as discussed by Schlaifer.[2] One assumes implicitly, then, that utility is linear with money. As tempting as this assumption may be, some small-scale studies at Du Pont in which attempts were made to construct empirical utility functions raise some questions regarding the assumption of linearity. However, this feature of the Bayesian approach may well take many years of further education and development before it may find regular application on the industrial scene.

Second, while a plethora of Bayesian prior probabilities were used in this problem, no mention was made of analyzing sample data and calculating *posterior* probabilities. How does one investigate states of nature in problems of this type? Certainly the problems of conducting meaningful experiments are hardly trivial in pricing problems, or the general area of market planning.

Third, just how detailed a structure can be warranted, particularly when the inputs to the problem are largely subjective in character? One may obviously over-structure as well as under-structure a problem. This *caveat,* however, applies to all model building. While sensitivity analysis may be used to shed light on which variables "make a difference," the fact remains that the model-building process is still based largely on the builder's intuitive grasp of problem essentials and the interplay between analyst and decision-maker. The structure of the problem discussed in this article turned out to be complex precisely because the variables included *were* deemed important by the decision-maker(s). And part of the analyst's job is thus to examine the impact of supposedly important variables on the relevant payoff junction and then feed back his findings to the decision-maker.

Finally, in conducting this study, realistic problems have a way of generating quite a lot of arithmetic detail, for example, a multi-stage set of alternative states of nature and payoffs. Implementation of the Bayesian approach must, therefore, frequently be aided by recourse to a high-speed computing device. Moreover, a computer model also facilitates the task of running sensitivity analyses concerning either changes in the payoff values related to any particular combination of state of nature and course of action.

Our experience has indicated that the Bayesian approach, even coupled with the ancillary techniques of computer simulation and sensitivity analysis, does not offer any foolproof procedure for "solving" market planning problems. Still, it would seem that this method *does* offer definite advantage over the more traditional techniques usually associated with market planning. Traditional techniques rarely consider *alternative* states of nature, let alone assigning

[2] Schlaifer, *op. cit.,* chap. 2.

prior probabilities to their occurrence. Moreover, traditional market planning techniques seldom provide for testing the sensitivity of the study's outcomes to departures in the basic assumptions.

At the very least, the Bayesian model forces a more rigorous approach to market planning problems and offers a useful device for quickly finding the financial implications of assumptions about the occurrence of alternative states of nature. In time, this procedure coupled with a more sophisticated approach to the design, collection, and interpretation of field data appears capable of providing an up-to-date and flexible means to meet the more stringent demands of dynamic decision situations, so typical in the problems faced by the marketing manager.

# 42. RETAIL STRATEGY AND THE CLASSIFICATION OF CONSUMER GOODS

*Louis P. Bucklin*

*What guides are available to aid the retailer in developing his marketing strategy?*

*The author shows how the traditional concepts of shopping, convenience, and specialty goods may be updated and integrated with the idea of patronage motives and how they provide the retailer with a new means of evaluating his strategy.*

When Melvin T. Copeland published his famous discussion of the classification of consumer goods, shopping, convenience, and specialty goods, his intent was clearly to create a guide for the development of marketing strategies by manufacturers.[1] Although his discussion involved retailers and retailing, his purpose was to show how consumer buying habits affected the type of channel of distribution and promotional strategy that a manufacturer should adopt. Despite the controversy which still surrounds his classification, his success in creating such a guide may be judged by the fact that through the years few marketing texts have failed to make use of his ideas.

The purpose of this article is to attempt to clarify some of the issues that exist with respect to the classification, and to extend the concept to include the retailer and the study of retail strategy.

[1]Melvin T. Copeland, "Relation of Consumers' Buying Habits to Marketing Methods," *Harvard Business Review,* vol. 1, April, 1923, pp. 282–289.

Source: From *Journal of Marketing,* vol. 27, January, 1963, pp. 51–56. Louis P. Bucklin: Assistant Professor of Business Administration, University of California, Berkeley.

## CONTROVERSY OVER THE CLASSIFICATION SYSTEM

The starting point for the discussion lies with the definitions adopted by the American Marketing Association's Committee on Definitions for the classification system in 1948[2]. These are:

- *Convenience Goods:* Those consumers' goods which the customer purchases frequently, immediately, and with the minimum of effort.
- *Shopping Goods:* Those consumers' goods which the customer in the process of selection and purchase characteristically compares on such bases as suitability, quality, price and style.
- *Specialty Goods:* Those consumers' goods on which a significant group of buyers are habitually willing to make a special purchasing effort.

This set of definitions was retained in virtually the same form by the Committee on Definitions in its latest publication.[3]

Opposing these accepted definitions stands a critique by Richard H. Holton.[4] Finding the Committee's definitions too imprecise to be able to measure consumer buying behavior, he suggested that the following definitions not only would represent the essence of Copeland's original idea, but be operationally more useful as well.

- *Convenience Goods:* Those goods for which the consumer regards the probable gain from making price and quality comparisons as small compared to the cost of making such comparisons.
- *Shopping Goods:* Those goods for which the consumer regards the probable gain from making price and quality comparisons as large relative to the cost of making such comparisons.
- *Specialty Goods:* Those convenience or shopping goods which have such a limited market as to require the consumer to make a special effort to purchase them.

Holton's definitions have particular merit because they make explicit the underlying conditions that control the extent of a consumer's shopping activities. They show that a consumer's buying behavior will be determined not only by the strength of his desire to secure some good, but by his perception of the cost of shopping to obtain it. In other words, the consumer continues to shop *for all goods* so long as he feels that the additional satisfactions from further comparisons are at least equal to the cost of making the additional effort. The distinction between shopping and convenience goods lies principally in the degree of satisfaction to be secured from further comparisons.

*The Specialty Good Issue.* While Holton's conceptualization makes an important contribution, he has sacrificed some of the richness of Copeland's original ideas. This is

[2]Definitions Committee, American Marketing Association, "Report of the Definitions Committee," *Journal of Marketing,* vol. 13, October, 1948, pp. 202–217, at pp. 206 and 215.

[3]Definitions Committee, American Marketing Association, *Marketing Definitions,* American Marketing Association, Chicago, 1960, pp. 11, 21–22.

[4]Richard H. Holton, "The Distinction Between Convenience Goods, Shopping Goods, and Specialty Goods," *Journal of Marketing,* vol. 23, July, 1958, pp. 53–56.

essentially David J. Luck's complaint in a criticism of Holton's proposal.[5] Luck objected the the abandonment of the *willingness* of consumers to make a special effort to buy as the rationale for the concept of specialty goods. He regarded this type of consumer behavior as based upon unique consumer attitudes toward certain goods and not the density of distribution of those goods. Holton, in a reply, rejected Luck's point; he remained convinced that the real meaning of specialty goods could be derived from his convenience goods, shopping goods continuum, and market conditions.[6]

The root of the matter appears to be that insufficient attention has been paid to the fact that the consumer, once embarked upon some buying expedition, may have only one of two possible objectives in mind. A discussion of this aspect of consumer behavior will make possible a closer synthesis of Holton's contribution with the more traditional point of view.

*A Forgotten Idea.* The basis for this discussion is afforded by certain statements, which the marketing profession has largely ignored over the years, in Copeland's original presentation of his ideas. These have regard to the extent of the consumer's awareness of the precise nature of the item he wishes to buy, *before* he starts his shopping trip. Copeland stated that the consumer, in both the case of convenience goods and specialty goods, has full knowledge of the particular good, or its acceptable substitutes, that he will buy before he commences his buying trip. The consumer, however, lacks this knowledge in the case of a shopping good.[7] This means that the buying trip must not only serve the objective of purchasing the good, but must enable the consumer to discover which item he wants to buy.

The behavior of the consumer during any shopping expedition may, as a result, be regarded as heavily dependent upon the state of his decision as to what he wants to buy. If the consumer knows precisely what he wants, he needs only to undertake communication activities sufficient to take title to the desired product. He may also undertake ancillary physical activities involving the handling of the product and delivery. If the consumer is uncertain as to what he wants to buy, then an additional activity will have to be performed. This involves the work of making comparisons between possible alternative purchases, or simply search.

There would be little point, with respect to the problem of classifying consumer goods, in distinguishing between the activity of search and that of making a commitment to buy, if a consumer always performed both before purchasing a good. The crucial point is that he does not. While most of the items that a consumer buys have probably been subjected to comparison at some point in his life, he does not make a search before each purchase. Instead, a past solution to the need is frequently remembered and, if

[5] David J. Luck, "On the Nature of Specialty Goods," *Journal of Marketing,* vol. 24, July, 1959, pp. 61–64.

[6] Richard H. Holton, "What is Really Meant by 'Specialty' Goods?" *Journal of Marketing,* vol. 24, July, 1959, pp. 64–67.

[7] Copeland, *op. cit.,* pp. 283–284.

satisfactory, is implemented.[8] Use of these past decisions for many products quickly moves the consumer past any perceived necessity of undertaking new comparisons and leaves only the task of exchange to be discharged.

## REDEFINITION OF THE SYSTEM

Use of this concept of problem solving permits one to classify consumer buying efforts into two broad categories which may be called shopping and nonshopping goods.

*Shopping Goods.* Shopping goods are those for which the consumer *regularly* formulates a new solution to his need each time it is aroused. They are goods whose suitability is determined through search before the consumer commits himself to each purchase.

The motivation behind this behavior stems from circumstances which tend to perpetuate a lack of complete consumer knowledge about the nature of the product that he would like to buy.[9] Frequent changes in price, style, or product technology cause consumer information to become obsolete. The greater the time lapse between purchases, the more obsolete will his information be. The consumer's needs are also subject to change, or he may seek variety in his purchases as an actual goal. These forces will tend to make past information inappropriate. New search, due to forces internal and external to the consumer, is continuously required for products with purchase determinants which the consumer regards as both important and subject to change.[10]

The number of comparisons that the consumer will make in purchasing a shopping good may be determined by use of Holton's hypothesis on effort. The consumer, in other words, will undertake search for a product until the perceived value to be secured through additional comparisons is less than the estimated cost of making those comparisons. Thus, shopping effort will vary according to the intensity of the desire of the consumer to find the right product, the type of product and the availability of retail facilities. Whether the consumer searches diligently, superficially, or even buys at the first opportunity, however, does not alter the shopping nature of the product.

*Nonshopping Goods.* Turning now to nonshopping goods, one may define these as products for which the consumer is both willing and able to use stored solutions to the problem of finding a product to answer a need. From the remarks on shopping goods it may be generalized that nonshopping goods have purchase determinants which do not change, or which are perceived as changing inconsequentially, between purchases.[11] The consumer, for example, may assume that price for some product never changes or that price is unimportant. It may be unimportant because either the price is low, or the consumer is very wealthy.

[8] George Katona, *Psychological Analysis of Economic Behavior,* McGraw-Hill Book Company, New York, 1951, p. 47.

[9] *Ibid.,* pp. 67–68.

[10] George Katona and Eva Mueller, "A Study of Purchase Decisions in Consumer Behavior," in Lincoln Clark (ed.), *Consumer Behavior,* University Press, New York, 1954, pp. 30–87.

[11] Katona, *op. cit.,* p. 68.

Nonshopping goods may be divided into convenience and specialty goods by means of the concept of a preference map. Bayton introduces this concept as the means to show how the consumer stores information about products.[12] It is a rough ranking of the relative desirability of the different kinds of products that the consumer sees as possible satisfiers for his needs. For present purposes, two basic types of preference maps may be envisaged. One type ranks all known product alternatives equally in terms of desirability. The other ranks one particular product as so superior to all others that the consumer, in effect, believes this product is the only answer to his need.

*Distinguishing the Specialty Good.* This distinction in preference maps creates the basis for discriminating between a convenience good and a specialty good. Clearly, where the consumer is indifferent to the precise item among a number of substitutes which he could buy, he will purchase the most accessible one and look no further. This is a convenience good. On the other hand, where the consumer recognizes only one brand of a product as capable of satisfying his needs, he will be willing to bypass more readily accessible substitutes in order to secure the wanted item. This is a specialty good.

However, most nonshopping goods will probably fall in between these two polar extremes. Preference maps will exist where the differences between the relative desirability of substitutes may range from the slim to the well marked. In order to distinguish between convenience goods and specialty goods in these cases, Holton's hypothesis regarding consumer effort may be employed again. A convenience good, in these terms, becomes one for which the consumer has such little preference among his perceived choices that he buys the item which is most readily available. A specialty good is one for which consumer preference is so strong that he bypasses, or would be willing to bypass, the purchase of more accessible substitutes in order to secure his most wanted item.

It should be noted that this decision on the part of the consumer as to how much effort he should expend takes place under somewhat different conditions than the one for shopping goods. In the nonshopping good instance the consumer has a reasonably good estimate of the additional value to be achieved by purchasing his preferred item. The estimate of the additional cost required to make this purchase may also be made fairly accurately. Consequently, the consumer will be in a much better position to justify the expenditure of additional effort here than in the case of shopping goods where much uncertainty must exist with regard to both of these factors.

*The New Classification.* The classification of consumer goods that results from the analysis is as follows:

- *Convenience Goods:* Those goods for which the consumer, before his need arises, possesses a preference map that indicates a willingness to purchase any of a number of known substitutes rather than to make the additional effort required to buy a particular item.

[12] James A. Bayton, "Motivation, Cognition, Learning–Basic Factors in Consumer Behavior," *Journal of Marketing,* vol. 22, January, 1958, pp. 282–289, at p. 287.

- *Shopping Goods:* Those goods for which the consumer has not developed a complete preference map before the need arises, requiring him to undertake search to construct such a map before purchase.
- *Specialty Goods:* Those goods for which the consumer, before his need arises, possesses a preference map that indicates a willingness to expend the additional effort required to purchase the most preferred item rather than to buy a more readily accessible substitute.

## EXTENSION TO RETAILING

The classification of the goods concept develpped above may now be extended to retailing. As the concept now stands, it is derived from consumer attitudes or motives toward a *product.* These attitudes, or product motives, are based upon the consumer's interpretation of a product's styling, special features, quality, and social status of its brand name, if any. Occasionally the price may also be closely associated with the product by the consumer.

*Classification of Patronage Motives.* The extension of the concept to retailing may be made through the notion of patronage motives, a term long used in marketing. Patronage motives are derived from consumer attitudes concerning the retail establishment. They are related to factors which the consumer is likely to regard as controlled by the retailer. These will include assortment, credit, service, guarantee, shopping ease and enjoyment, and usually price. Patronage motives, however, have never been systematically categorized. It is proposed that the procedure developed above to discriminate among product motives be used to classify consumer buying motives with respect to retail stores as well.

This will provide the basis for the consideration of retail marketing strategy and will aid in clearing up certain ambiguities that would otherwise exist if consumer buying motives were solely classified by product factors. These ambiguities appear, for example, when the consumer has a strong affinity for some particular brand of a product, but little interest in where he buys it. The manufacturer of the product, as a result, would be correct in defining the product as a specialty item if the consumer's preferences were so strong as to cause him to eschew more readily available substitutes. The retailer may regard it as a convenience good, however, since the consumer will make no special effort to purchase the good from any particular store. This problem is clearly avoided by separately classifying product and patronage motives.

The categorization of patronage motives by the above procedure results in the following three definitions. These are:

- *Convenience Stores:* Those stores for which the consumer, before his need for some product arises, possesses a preference map that indicates a willingness to buy from the most accessible store.
- *Shopping Stores:* Those stores for which the consumer has not developed a complete preference map relative to the product he wishes to buy, requiring him to undertake a search to construct such a map before purchase.

- *Specialty Stores:* Those stores for which the consumer, before his need for some product arises, possesses a preference map that indicates a willingness to buy the item from a particular establishment even though it may not be the most accessible.

*The Product-Patronage Matrix.* Although this basis will now afford the retailer a means to consider alternative strategies, a finer classification system may be obtained by relating consumer product motives to consumer patronage motives. By cross-classifying each product motive with each patronage motive, one creates a three-by-three matrix, representing nine possible types of consumer buying behavior. Each of the nine cells in the matrix may be described as follows:

1. *Convenience Store–Convenience Good:* The consumer represented by this category prefers to buy the most readily available brand of product at the most accessible store.
2. *Convenience Store–Shopping Good:* The consumer selects his purchase from among the assortment carried by the most accessible store.
3. *Convenience Store–Specialty Good:* The consumer purchases his favored brand from the most accessible store which has the item in stock.
4. *Shopping Store–Convenience Good:* The consumer is indifferent to the brand of product he buys, but shops among different stores in order to secure better retail service and/or lower retail price.
5. *Shopping Store–Shopping Good:* The consumer makes comparisons among both retail controlled factors and factors associated with the product (brand).
6. *Shopping Store–Specialty Good:* The consumer has a strong preference with respect to the brand of the product, but shops among a number of stores in order to secure the best retail service and/or price for this brand.
7. *Specialty Store–Convenience Good:* The consumer prefers to trade at a specific store, but is indifferent to the brand of product purchased.
8. *Specialty Store–Shopping Good:* The consumer prefers to trade at a certain store, but is uncertain as to which product he wishes to buy and examines the store's assortment for the best purchase.
9. *Specialty Store–Specialty Good:* The consumer has both a preference for a particular store and a specific brand.

Conceivably, each of these nine types of behavior might characterize the buying patterns of some consumers for a given product. It seems more likely, however, that the behavior of consumers toward a product could be represented by only three or four of the categories. The remaining cells would be empty, indicating that no consumers bought the product by these methods. Different cells, of course, would be empty for different products.

## THE FORMATION OF RETAIL STRATEGY

The extended classification system developed above clearly provides additional information important to the manufacturer in the planning of his marketing strategy. Of principal interest here, however, is the means by which the retailer might use the classification system in planning his marketing strategy.

*Three Basic Steps.* The procedure involves three steps. The first is the classification of the retailer's potential customers for some product by market segment, using the nine categories in the consumer buying habit matrix to define the principal segments. The second requires the retailer to determine the nature of the marketing strategies necessary to appeal to each market segment. The final step is the retailer's selection of the market segment, and the strategy associated with it, to which he will sell. A simplified, hypothetical example may help to clarify this process. (See Table 1.)

**Table 1. Proportion of potential dress market in each matrix cell**

| *Buying habit* | *% of market* |
|---|---|
| Convenience store–convenience good | 0 |
| Convenience store–shopping good | 3 |
| Convenience store–specialty good | 20 |
| Shopping store–convenience good | 0 |
| Shopping store–shopping good | 35 |
| Shopping store–specialty good | 2 |
| Specialty store–convenience good | 0 |
| Specialty store–shopping good | 25 |
| Specialty store–specialty good | 15 |
| | 100 |

A former buyer of dresses for a department store decided to open her own dress shop. She rented a small store in the downtown area of a city of 50,000, ten miles distant from a metropolitan center of several hundred thousand population. In contemplating her marketing strategy, she was certain that the different incomes, educational backgrounds, and tastes of the potential customers in her city meant that various groups of these women were using sharply different buying methods for dresses. Her initial problem was to determine, by use of the consumer buying habit matrix, what proportion of her potential market bought dresses in what manner.

By drawing on her own experience, discussions with other retailers in the area, census and other market data, the former buyer estimated that her potential market was divided, according to the matrix, in the following proportions.

This analysis revealed four market segments that she believed were worth further consideration. (In an actual situation, each of these four should be further divided into submarket segments according to other possible factors such as age, income, dress size required, location of residence, etc.) Her next task was to determine the type of marketing mix which would most effectively appeal to each of these segments. The information for these decisions was derived from the characteristics of consumer behavior associated with each of the defined segments. The following is a brief description of her assessment of how elements of the marketing mix ought to be weighted in order to formulate a strategy for each segment.

*A Strategy for Each Segment.* To appeal to the convenience store-specialty good segment she felt that the two most important elements in the mix should be a highly accessible location and a selection of widely-accepted brand merchandise. Of somewhat lesser importance, she found, were depth of assortment, personal selling, and price. Minimal emphasis should be given to store promotion and facilities.

She reasoned that the shopping store-shopping good requires a good central location, emphasis on price, and a broad assortment. She ranked store promotion, accepted brand names and personal selling as secondary. Store facilities would, once again, receive minor emphasis.

The specialty store-shopping good market would, she believed, have to be catered to with an exceptionally strong assortment, a high level of personal selling and more elaborate store facilities. Less emphasis would be needed upon prominent brand names, store promotions, and price. Location was of minor importance.

The specialty store-specialty good category, she thought, would require a marketing mix heavily emphasizing personal selling and highly elaborate store facilities and services. She also felt that prominent brand names would be required, but that these would probably have to include the top names in fashion, including labels from Paris. Depth of assortment would be secondary, while least emphasis would be placed upon store promotion, price, and location.

*Evaluation of Alternatives.* The final step in the analysis required the former dress buyer to assess her abilities to implement any one of these strategies, given the degree of competition existing in each segment. Her considerations were as follows. With regard to the specialty store-specialty good market, she was unprepared to make the investment in store facilities and services that she felt would be necessary. She also thought, since a considerable period of time would probably be required for her to build up the necessary reputation, that this strategy involved substantial risk. Lastly, she believed that her experience in buying high fashion was somewhat limited and that trips to European fashion centers would prove burdensome.

She also doubted her ability to cater to the specialty store-shopping good market, principally because she knew that her store would not be large enough to carry the necessary assortment depth. She felt that this same factor would limit her in attempting to sell to the shopping store-shopping good market as well. Despite the presence of the large market in this segment, she believed that she would not be able to create sufficient volume in her proposed quarters to enable her to compete effectively with the local department store and several large department stores in the neighboring city.

The former buyer believed her best opportunity was in selling to the convenience store-specialty good segment. While there were already two other stores in her city which were serving this segment, she believed that a number of important brands were still not represented. Her past contacts with resources led her to believe that she would stand an excellent chance of securing a number of these lines. By stocking these brands, she thought that she could capture a considerable number of local customers who currently were purchasing them in the large city. In this way, she believed, she would avoid the full force of local competition.

*Decision.* The conclusion of the former buyer to use her store to appeal to the convenience store-specialty good segment represents the culmination to the process of analysis suggested here. It shows how the use of the three-by-three matrix of consumer buying habits may aid the retailer in developing his marketing strategy. It is a device which can isolate the important market segments. It provides further help in enabling the retailer to associate the various types of consumer behavior with those elements of the marketing mix to which they are sensitive. Finally, the analysis forces the retailer to assess the probability of his success in attempting to use the necessary strategy in order to sell each possible market.

# 43. ARE CHANNELS OF DISTRIBUTION WHAT THE TEXTBOOKS SAY?

*Phillip McVey*

*The author maintains that the role of the middleman is obscured by oversimplified treatment in marketing literature and census data.*

*In this article he examines channel-building from the standpoint of the middleman's relative freedom to make choices, while serving as a purchasing agent for his customers.*

Perhaps Wroe Alderson said as much as is safe to say when he described a marketing channel as a group of firms which "constitute a loose coalition engaged in exploiting joint opportunity in the market."[1]

## THEORY AND ACTUALITY

Certainly too much is said about channel relationships in many published textbooks for businessmen and students, if one is to look for proof in current marketing practice. The picture usually given is one of long lists of various types of middlemen and facilitating agencies, which differ minutely but precisely in functions performed. Alignments of particular types are presented as "right" or "customary" for a given commodity or type of producer. Furthermore, it is often implied that

[1] Wroe Alderson, "The Development of Marketing Channels," in Richard M. Clewett (ed.), *Marketing Channels for Manufactured Products,* Richard D. Irwin, Inc., Homewood, Ill., 1954, p. 30.

Source: From *Journal of Marketing,* vol. 24, January, 1960, pp. 61–65. Phillip McVey: Associate Professor of Marketing, University of Nebraska.

it is the producer who selects all the links in the channel and establishes the working arrangements with them, down to and including the outlet which sells his goods to the final user.

Several popular college textbooks in marketing illustrate this manufacturer-oriented approach to channel planning.[2] One reason for fairly standard treatment of channel-building is that the growth of marketing knowledge has proceeded from a description of the activities of existing business firms, leaning heavily on data provided by the U.S. Censuses of Wholesale and Retail Trade. The framework appears orderly and well planned. But little recognition is given to the probability that some channel sequences "just grew" like Topsy, without direction or intent of known parents.

The Census method of counting, whereby each separate establishment is assigned to a single traditional category on the basis of a *major-portion-of-dollar-volume* rule, tends to produce more orderliness in the picture than probably exists. It tends to obscure a great deal of "promiscuous distribution" and channel-jumping. The Census rule, like the Procrustean bed of Greek mythology, effectively reduces the number of categories into which firms are sorted, and avoids hybrid, nondescript classifications.

Yet hybridity is too common among marketing firms to be ignored. For example, almost any wholesaler will do some business at retail; similarly, it is not uncommon for a broker to find himself holding title to a given lot of goods, thus becoming temporarily a merchant middleman. A realistic classification may require the use of relative terms to identify types of operation, according to a range of variables—for example, the *degree* to which a firm caters to a given customer group, or the *frequency* with which a function is performed.

Further study of marketing textbooks may lead a reader to conclude that:

1. middlemen of many types are available to any manufacturer in any market to which he wishes to sell, and within each type there is an ample selection of individual firms;
2. the manufacturer habitually controls the selection and operation of individual firms in his channel; and
3. middlemen respond willingly as *selling agents* for the manufacturer rather than as *purchasing agents* for a coveted group of customers to whom the middlemen sell.

Yet none of these conclusions is entirely valid.

In a product line such as fashion apparel, a garment maker may have an extremely limited choice of types of middlemen: the selling agent, the broker, the direct-buying retailer, or the chain store buying office. The general absence of service wholesalers from this line of trade is not correctable by manufacturers' *fiat.*

[2] Examples are found in: T. N. Beckman, H. H. Maynard, and W. R. Davidson, *Principles of Marketing,* 6th ed., The Ronald Press Company, New York, 1957, pp. 44–45; C. F. Phillips and D. J. Duncan, *Marketing Principles and Methods,* 3d ed., Richard D. Irwin, Inc., Homewood, Ill., 1956, p. 562; M. P. McNair, M. P. Brown, D. S. R. Leighton, and W. B. England, *Problems in Marketing,* 2d ed., McGraw-Hill Book Company, New York, 1957, p. 66.

In a particular market area, the choice may be even more limited. Of individual firms of a given type, there may be no choice at all. These limitations arise, of course, because of the free choices made by the middlemen as to locations, customer groups, and product assortments they elect to sell.

## IS THE "CHANNEL" AN ACADEMIC CONCEPT?

Integrated action up and down a channel is a rare luxury in marketing. Why? It may be that the "channel of distribution" is a concept that is principally academic in usage and unfamiliar to many firms selling to and through these channels.

Instead of a channel, a businessman is likely to concern himself merely with suppliers and customers. His dealings are not with all of the links in the channel but only with those immediately adjacent to him, from which he buys and to which he sells. He may little know nor care what becomes of his products after they leave the hands of some merchant middleman who has paid him for them and released him to return to problems involving his special functions. A manufacturer may not even consider himself as standing at the head of a channel, but only as occupying a link in a channel that begins with his suppliers.

*Policies.* Choice of a channel is not open to any firm unless it has considerable freedom of action in matters of marketing policy. Other areas of policy seem to be treated with more respect. For example, it is well recognized that a *price* policy is an authoritarian privilege open only to those sellers who possess power to withhold goods from the market in considerable quantities, or who have the choice of alternative markets and the means to solicit them. Usually a differentiated product is necessary. Therefore, a wheat farmer can seldom have anything resembling a price policy.

Likewise, a *design* policy is meaningful only when variations in product characteristics have been understood and accepted by customers to be of significance. Manufacturers of semi-finished or component parts, or of textile "gray goods" cannot enjoy this luxury in most cases.

Similarly, the selection of a multi-stage channel is not the prerogative of a manufacturer unless his franchise is coveted by the middlemen he seeks, as being more valuable to them than their franchise would be to him.

Names such as Sears, Roebuck & Company, Macy's, or Kroger mean a great deal more to the customers of these retailers than do the brand names of most of the items sold in their stores. These firms control the channels for many products, even to the point of bringing into existence some manufacturing firms needed to fill gaps in their assortments. In the same manner some national wholesalers, holding the reins of a huge distributive system, are more powerful than either their suppliers or their customers. In such extreme cases the power position is obvious. The big company, regardless of its position in the channel, tries to make its plans and policies effective by taking the initiative for coordinated action.

## UNCERTAINTY AMONG SMALLER FIRMS

As to the many thousands of middle-size and small companies that truly characterize American marketing, the power position is speculative, vacillating, and ephemeral. Strength in certain market areas, the temporary success of a product, ability to perform a certain needed type of financing or promotional effort—these and similar factors enable companies to assume power.

On the other hand, financial reverses, an unfortunate sales campaign, or even the lack of accurate market news—these factors can shift power elsewhere, possibly to another link in the channel or to another firm in the same link. In any case, the opportunity of any firm is contingent upon the willingness of others to use it as a link in the channel.

*Comparison with Advertising Media.* Selection of middlemen has been likened to the selection of advertising media. In both instances the task is to find a vehicle which has an existing coverage (or circulation) which coincides with the market desired. A region blanketed with a neat mosaic of distributors' territories will appear on a map much like the same region covered by television stations.

However, there is an important difference. Seldom does an advertising medium restrict its availability. The advertiser's product need not be sold first to the medium on the grounds of self-interest. Only occasionally will a middleman accept any product he is offered. The requirement that he invest his own money and effort forces him to be selective in terms of probable outcome or profit. No seller can afford to neglect the task of selling *to* the middlemen he seeks, as well as *through* them. Nearly every comprehensive campaign of consumer advertising allots substantial effort to dealer promotion and distributor promotion. Indeed, much consumer advertising is undertaken primarily for the stimulating effect it will have upon middlemen.

*Middlemen's Reactions.* Middlemen's reactions to new-product offerings probably deserve more attention from manufacturers than usual. Wholesalers and retailers, as well as agent middlemen, enjoy an excellent position from which to make keen judgments of a product's probable successes within local markets. Free from the manufacturer's proclivity to "fall in love with the product," but not primarily concerned with its ultimate usage characteristics, middlemen who are alert merchandisers can look at the product with an eye to saleability alone.

Yet it is common practice for manufacturers to force acceptance with a heavy barrage of consumer advertising, introductory high-markup offers, free merchandise, combination deals, cooperative advertising schemes, and the like. These may have the effect of "mesmerizing" middlemen, and of clouding the issue of the product's own rate of initial acceptance.

Lack of effective vertical communication in most channels is a serious deterrent. Possibly no other proof of the weakness of manufacturers' control over channels is so convincing as their inability to obtain facts from their own ultimate and intermediate markets. Information that could be used in product development, pricing, packaging, or promotion-planning is buried in nonstandard records of middlemen, and sometimes purposely secreted from suppliers.

Channel research is one of the most frustrating areas of marketing investigation, since it requires access to data collected by firms which are independent, remotely situated, and suspicious. Unless given incentive to do so, middlemen will not maintain separate sales records by brands sold. Extracting the needed figures by preferred units of measure is often a hopeless task. To get such data, one producer of pipe tools adopted a device commonly used with electric appliances: a "warranty registration" questionnaire attached to the tools. Ostensibly designed to validate users' damage claims, its true purpose was to discover where, when, how, and by whom the tools had been sold.

Communication downward from the manufacturer is also faulty, placing in doubt the claim that all links in the channel are bound together by common objectives. For example, it is seldom practical to disclose a forthcoming promotional plan in all its details and to ask the middlemen whether the plan will be timely, acceptable, and supportable by their efforts. To do so would jeopardize the advantage of surprise, usually a significant competitive stratagem. Yet the value of synchronized, coordinated action of any new plan by all firms in the channel is obvious.

## MIDDLEMEN'S VIEWS

*Channel Building.* To the extent that any middleman can do so, he should think of himself primarily as a purchasing agent for his customers, and only secondarily as a selling agent for his suppliers. The planning of his product line will proceed from an analysis of a finite customer group in which he is interested . . . to the selection of goods capable of satisfying those needs . . . and then to the choice of available suppliers who can provide those goods. Of course, he may actually begin his assortment with one or more basic products, chosen by him as a way of defining the area of customer needs in which he elects to deal.

From that point on, however, his chief stock in trade becomes not the franchises of important suppliers, but rather his customer group. He is interested in selling any product which these customers desire to buy from him. The attractiveness of any new offering by a supplier is not to be judged by the size of the markup or commission, nor the unusual nature of the product, nor details of its manufacture, nor the promises of manufacturer's advertising support.

The key question is: Does it fit the line? That is, does it complement the other products that he sells, in terms of saleability to precisely the same group of buyers? His list of customers is probably less subject to intentional revision than are many other aspects of his business. Is it not at this point, then, that channel building starts?

Some unusual product combinations may result from this approach. A manufacturers' agent selling baby garments in the Southwest took on a line of printed business forms, which the small retailers on whom he called were seeking. An Omaha wholesaler successfully added grocery products to his liquor business. A Cleveland distributor of welding equipment rejected a portable farm welder offered by his principal supplier, since he had no contact with farmers, but was interested in carrying a line of warehouse tractors and lift trucks.

*Approach to New Prospects.* In some cases a middleman may deem it worthwhile to shift from his current customer group to a new list of prospects, in order to find a market for a particularly promising new product. In the main, however, he will not do so. His approach to new prospects is based on their close similarity to those now on his customer list. To all these persons he attempts to become known as a helpful specialist in a well-defined set of recurring needs. The scope of his line, and the interrelation of products in it, must be known to the bulk of his customers. Scrambled merchandising, or stocking of unrelated items, will tend to split his market into many small groups.

*Assortment Sales.* Furthermore, the middleman attempts to weld all of his offerings into a family of items which he can sell in combination, as a packaged assortment, to individual customers. His selling efforts are directed primarily at obtaining orders for the assortment, rather than for individual items. Naturally the greatest *numbers* of his transactions will seldom be made in this way; but often his greatest volume and more profitable sales to "blue-chip" accounts will be assortment sales.

Catering to assortment sales has considerable significance to channel operation, because the kind of sales service which a middleman can offer a single-product supplier is affected thereby. Since he is relatively disinterested in pushing individual items, the middleman is criticized for failure to stress a given brand, or for the poor quality of his salesmen's product knowledge, his disuse of suppliers' advertising materials, his neglect of certain customers (who may be good prospects for individual items but not for the assortment), and even for his unrefined systems of record keeping, in which brand designations may be lost.

## THE MIDDLEMAN AS AN INDEPENDENT MARKET

The middleman is not a hired link in a chain forged by a manufacturer, but rather an independent market, the focus of a large group of customers for whom he buys. Subsequent to some market analysis of his own, he selects products and suppliers, thereby setting at least one link in the channel.

After some experimentation, he settles upon a method of operation, performing those functions he deems inescapable in the light of his own objectives, forming policies for himself wherever he has freedom to do so. Perhaps these methods and policies conform closely to those of a Census category of middleman, but perhaps they do not.

It is true that his choices are in many instances tentative proposals. He is subject to much influence from competitors, from aggressive suppliers, from inadequate finances and faulty information, as well as from habit. Nonetheless, many of his choices are independent.

As he grows and builds a following, he may find that his prestige in his market is greater than that of the suppliers whose goods he sells. In some instances his local strength is so great that a manufacturer is virtually unable to tap that market, except through him. In such a case the manufacturer can have no channel policy with respect to that market.

# 44. THE WHEEL OF RETAILING

*Stanley C. Hollander*

*New types of retailing frequently start off with crude facilities, little prestige, and a reputation for cutting prices and margins. As they mature, they often acquire more expensive buildings, provide more elaborate services, impose higher margins, and become vulnerable to new competition.*

*The author examines the history of numerous retail institutions to determine if this process really constitutes a "natural law of retailing."*

"The wheel of retailing" is the name Professor Malcolm P. McNair has suggested for a major hypothesis concerning patterns of retail development. This hypothesis holds that new types of retailers usually enter the market as low-status, low-margin, low-price operators. Gradually they acquire more elaborate establishments and facilities, with both increased investments and higher operating costs. Finally they mature as high-cost, high-price merchants, vulnerable to newer types who, in turn, go through the same pattern. Department-store merchants, who originally appeared as vigorous competitors to the smaller retailers and who now become vulnerable to discount house and supermarket competition, are often cited as prime examples of the wheel pattern.[1]

[1] M. P. McNair, "Significant Trends and Developments in the Postwar Period," in A. B. Smith, (ed.), *Competitive Distribution in a Free, High-Level Economy and Its Implications for the University,* University of Pittsburgh Press, Pittsburgh, 1958, pp. 1–25 at pp. 17–18.

Source: From *Journal of Marketing,* vol. 25, July, 1960, pp. 37–42, Stanley C. Hollander: Professor of Business Administration, Michigan State University.

Many examples of conformity to this pattern can be found. Nevertheless, we may ask:

1. Is this hypothesis valid for all retailing under all conditions?
2. How accurately does it describe total American retail development?
3. What factors cause wheel-pattern changes in retail institutions?

The following discussion assembles some of the slender empirical evidence available that might shed some light on these three questions. In attempting to answer the third question, a number of hypotheses should be considered that marketing students have advanced concerning the forces that have shaped retail development.

## TENTATIVE EXPLANATIONS OF THE WHEEL

*Retail Personalities.* New types of retail institutions are often established by highly aggressive, cost-conscious entrepreneurs who make every penny count and who have no interest in unprofitable frills. But, as P. D. Converse has suggested, these men may relax their vigilance and control over costs as they acquire age and wealth. Their successors may be less competent. Either the innovators or their successors may be unwilling, or unable, to adjust to changing conditions. Consequently, according to this view, deterioration in management causes movement along the wheel.[2]

*Misguidance.* Hermann Levy has advanced the ingenious, if implausible, explanation that retail trade journals, seduced by profitable advertising from the store equipment and supply industry, coax merchants into superfluous "modernization" and into the installation of overly elaborate facilities.[3]

*Imperfect Competition.* Although retail trade is often cited as the one type of business that approaches the Adam Smith concept of perfect competition, some economists have argued that retailing actually is a good example of imperfect competition. These economists believe that most retailers avoid direct price competition because of several forces, including resale price maintenance, trade association rules in some countries, and, most important, the fear of immediate retaliation. Contrariwise, the same retailers feel that service improvements, including improvements in location, are not susceptible to direct retaliation by competitors. Hence, through a ratchet process, merchants in any established branch of trade tend to provide increasingly elaborate services at increasingly higher margins.[4]

[2] P. D. Converse, "Mediocrity in Retailing," *Journal of Marketing,* vol. 23, April, 1959, pp. 419–420.
[3] Hermann Levy, *The Shops of Britain,* Kegan Paul, Trench, Trubner & Co., London, 1947, pp. 210–211.
[4] D. L. Shawver, *The Development of Theories of Retail Price Determination,* University of Illinois Press, Urbana, 1956, p. 92.

*Excess Capacity.* McNair attributes much of the wheel effect to the development of excess capacity, as more and more dealers enter any branch of retail trade.[5] This hypothesis rests upon an imperfect competition assumption, since, under perfect competition excess capacity would simply reduce margins until the excess vendors were eliminated.

*Secular Trend.* J. B. Jefferys has pointed out that a general, but uneven, long-run increase in the British standard of living provided established merchants with profitable opportunities for trading up. Jefferys thus credits adjustments to changing and wealthier market segments as causing some movement along the wheel. At the same time, pockets of opportunity have remained for new, low-margin operations because of the uneven distribution of living-standard increases.[6]

*Illusion.* Professor B. Holdren has suggested in a recent letter that present tendencies toward scrambled merchandising may create totally illusory impressions of the wheel phenomenon. Store-wide average margins may increase as new, high-markup lines are added to the product mix, even though the margins charged on the original components of that mix remain unchanged.

## DIFFICULTIES OF ANALYSIS

An examination of the actual development of retail institutions here and abroad does shed some light on both the wheel hypothesis and its various explanations. However, a number of significant difficulties hinders the process.

1. Statements concerning changes in retail margins and expenses are the central core of the wheel hypothesis. Yet valid information on historical retail expense rates is very scarce. Long-run changes in percentage margins probably do furnish fairly reliable clues to expense changes, but this is not true over short or intermediate periods. For example, 1957 furniture-store expense rates were about 5 percentage points higher than their 1949–1951 average, yet gross margins actually declined slightly over the same period.[7]
2. Historical margin data are somewhat more plentiful, but these also have to be dredged up from fragmentary sources.[8]
3. Available series on both expenses and margins merely note changes in retailers' outlays and receipts. They do not indicate what caused those changes and they do not report changes in the costs borne by suppliers, consumers, or the community at large.

[5] McNair, *op. cit.*

J. B. Jefferys, *Retail Trading in Great Britain, 1850–1950,* Cambridge University Press, Cambridge, 1954, p. 96, *et passim.*

[7] Cited in Fabian Linden, "Department Store Operations," *Conference Board Business Record,* vol. 14, October, 1958, pp. 410–414, at p. 411.

[8] See Harold Barger, *Distribution's Place in the American Economy Since 1869,* Princeton University Press, Princeton, 1955.

4. Margin data are usually published as averages that may, and frequently do, mask highly divergent tendencies.

5. A conceptual difficulty presents an even more serious problem than the paucity of statistics. When we talk about "types" of retailers, we think of classifications based upon ways of doing business and upon differences in price policy. Yet census categories and other systems for reporting retail statistics are usually based upon major differences in commodity lines. For example, the "pineboard" druggists who appeared in the 1930s are a "type" of retailing for our purposes. Those dealers had cruder fixtures, charged lower prices, carried smaller assortments, gave more attention to turnover, and had less interest in prescriptions than did conventional druggists. Yet census reports for drugstores necessarily included all of the pineboards that maintained any sort of prescription department.

   Discount houses provide another example of an important, but amorphous, category not reflected in census classifications. The label "discount house" covers a variety of retailers. Some carry stocks, others do not. Some have conventional store facilities, whereas others operate in office buildings, lofts, and warehouses. Some feature electrical appliances and hard goods, while others emphasize soft goods. Some pose as wholesalers, and others are practically indistinguishable from all other popular priced retailers in their fields. Consequently discount dealers' operating figures are likely to be merged into the statistics reported for other appliance, hardware, or apparel merchants.

## EXAMPLES OF CONFORMITY

*British.* British retailing provides several examples of conformity to the wheel pattern. The grocery trade has gone through several wheel-like evolutions, according to a detailed analysis made by F. G. Pennance and B. S. Yamey.[9] Established firms did initiate some changes and some margin reductions, so that the pattern is obscured by many cross currents. But the major changes seem to have been due to the appearance and then the maturation, first, of department-store food counters; then, of chain stores; and finally, of cut-price cash-and-carry stores. Now supermarkets seem to be carrying the pattern through another evolution.[10]

Jefferys also has noted a general long-run upgrading in both British department stores and chains.[11] Vague complaints in the cooperative press and a decline in consumer dividend rates suggest that wheel-like changes may have occurred in the British cooperative movement.[12]

[9] F. G. Pennance, and B. S. Yamey, "Competition in the Retail Grocery Trade, 1850–1939," *Economica,* vol. 22, March, 1955, pp. 303–317.

[10] "La Methode Americaine," *Time,* vol. 74, November 16, 1959, pp. 105–106.

[11] Jefferys, *op. cit.*

[12] "Battle of the Dividend," *Co-operative Review,* vol. 36, August, 1956, p. 183; "Independent Commission's Report," *Co-operative Review,* vol. 38, April, 1958, pp. 84–89; "£52 Million Dividend in 1957," *Co-operative Review,* vol. 38, August, 1958, pp. 171–172.

*American.* Very little is known about retail margins in this country before the Civil War. Our early retail history seems to have involved the appearance, first of hawkers, walkers, and peddlers; then, of general stores; next, of specialty stores; and finally, of department stores. Each of these types apparently came in as a lower-margin, lower-price competitor to the established outlets, and thus was consistent with the wheel pattern. We do not know, however, whether there was simply a long-run decline in retail margins through successive improvements in retail efficiency from one type to another (contrary to the wheel pattern), or whether each of the early types was started on a low-margin basis, gradually "up-graded," and so provided room for the next entrant (in accordance with the pattern).

The trends toward increasing margins can be more easily discerned in many branches of retailing after the Civil War. Barger has described increases over the years 1869–1947 among important retail segments, including department stores, mail-order firms, variety stores, and jewelry dealers. He attributes much of the pre-World War I rise in department-store margins to the absorption of wholesaling functions. Changes in merchandise mix, such as the addition of soda fountains and cafeterias to variety stores and the upgrading of mail-order merchandise, seem to have caused some of the other increases. Finally, he believes changes in customer services have been a major force in raising margins.[13] Fabian Linden has extended Barger's observations to note similar 1949–1957 margin increases for department stores, variety chains, and appliance dealers.[14]

Some other examples of at least partial conformity to the wheel pattern may be cited. Many observers feel that both discount-house services and margins have increased substantially in recent years.[15] One major discount-house operator has stated that he has been able to keep his average markup below 12 per cent in spite of considerable expansion in his facilities and commodity mix.[16] However, the consensus seems to be that this probably is an exception to the general rule.

A study of gasoline pricing has pointed out how many of the so-called "off-brand" outlets have changed from the "trackside" stations of pre-war days. The trackside dealers typically maintained unattractive and poorly equipped installations, at out-of-the-way locations where unbranded gasoline was sold on a price basis. Today many of them sell well-promoted regional and local brands, maintain attractive, efficient stations, and provide prompt and courteous service. Some still offer cut prices, but many have raised their prices and margins up to or above national brand levels.[17] Over time, many of the pineboard druggists also seem to have become converted to fairly conventional operations.[18]

[13] Barger, *op. cit.*, p. 82.

[14] Linden, *op. cit.*

[15] D. A. Leohwing, "Resourceful Merchants," *Barron's*, vol. 38, November 17, 1958, p. 3.

[16] S. Masters, quoted in "Three Concepts of Retail Service," *Stores*, vol. 41, July-August, 1959, pp. 18–21.

[17] S. M. Livingston and T. Levitt, "Competition and Retail Gasoline Prices," *The Review of Economics and Statistics*, vol. 41, May, 1959, pp. 119–132 at p. 132.

[18] Paul C. Olsen, *The Marketing of Drug Products*, Rutgers University Press, New Brunswick, 1948, pp. 130–132.

## NON-CONFORMING EXAMPLES

*Foreign.* In underdeveloped countries, the relatively small middle- and upper-income groups have formed the major markets for "modern" types of retailing. Supermarkets and other modern stores have been introduced in those countries largely at the top of the social and price scales, contrary to the wheel pattern.[19] Some nonconforming examples may also be found in somewhat more industrialized environments. The vigorous price competition that developed among Japanese department stores during the first three decades of this century seems directly contrary to the wheel hypothesis.[20] B. S. Yamey's history of resale price maintenance also reports some price-cutting by traditional, well-established British merchants who departed from the wheel pattern in the 1880s and 1890s.[21] Unfortunately, our ignorance of foreign retail history hinders any judgment of the representativeness of these examples.

*American.* Automatic merchandising, perhaps the most "modern" of all American retail institutions, departed from the wheel pattern by starting as a high-cost, high-margin, high-convenience type of retailing.[22] The department-store branch movement and the concomitant rise of planned shopping centers also has progressed directly contrary to the wheel pattern. The early department-store branches consisted of a few stores in exclusive suburbs and some equally high-fashion college and resort shops.

Only in relatively recent years have the branches been adjusted to the changing and more democratic characteristics of the contemporary dormitory suburbs. Suburban shopping centers, too, seem to have appeared first as "Manhasset Miracle Miles" and "Admores" before reaching out to the popular-price customers. In fact, complaints are still heard that the regional shopping centers have displayed excessive resistance to the entry of really aggressive, low-margin outlets.[23] E. R. A. Seligman and R. A. Love's study of retail pricing in the 1930s suggests that pressures on prices and margins were generated by all types of retailers. The mass retailing institutions, such as the department and chain stores, that had existed as types for many decades were responsible for a goodly portion of the price

[19] H. S. Hettinger, "Marketing in Persia," *Journal of Marketing,* vol. 15, January, 1951, pp. 289–297; H. W. Boyd, Jr., R. M. Clewett and R. L. Westfall, "The Marketing Structure of Venezuela," *Journal of Marketing,* vol. 22, April, 1958, pp. 391–397; D. A. Taylor, "Retailing in Brazil," *Journal of Marketing,* vol. 24, July, 1959, pp. 54–58; J. K. Galbraith and R. Holton, *Marketing Efficiency in Puerto Rico,* Harvard University Press, Cambridge, 1955, p. 35.

[20] G. Fukami, "Japanese Department Stores," *Journal of Marketing,* vol. 18, July, 1953, pp. 41–49 at p. 42.

[21] "The Origins of Resale Price Maintenance," *The Economic Journal,* vol. 62, September, 1952, pp. 522–545.

[22] W. S. Fishman, "Sense Makes Dollars," *1959 Directory of Automatic Merchandising,* National Automatic Merchandising Association, Chicago, 1959, p. 52; M. V. Marshall, *Automatic Merchandising,* Graduate School of Business Administration, Harvard University, Boston, 1954, pp. 108–109, 122.

[23] P. E. Smith, *Shopping Centers,* National Retail Merchants' Association, New York, 1956, pp. 11–12; M. L. Sweet, "Tenant-Selection Policies of Regional Shopping Centers," *Journal of Marketing,* vol. 23, April, 1959, pp. 399–404.

cutting.[24] As McNair has pointed out, the wheel operated very slowly in the case of department stores.

Finally, Harold Barger has described the remarkable stability of overall distributive margins during the years 1919–1947.[25] Some shifting of distributive work from wholesalers to retailers apparently affected their relative share of the total margins during this period, but this is not the type of change contemplated by the wheel pattern. Of course, the stability Barger notes conceivably could have been the result of a perfectly smooth functioning of the pattern, with the entrance of low-margin innovators providing exactly the right balance for the upcreep of margins in the longer-established types. But economic changes do not come in smooth and synchronized fashion, and Barger's data probably should indicate considerably wider oscillations if the wheel really set the mold for all retailing in the post-war period.

## CONCLUSIONS

The number of nonconforming examples suggests that the wheel hypothesis is not valid for all retailing. The hypothesis, however, does seem to describe a fairly common pattern in industrialized, expanding economies. Moreover, the wheel is not simply an illusion created by scrambled merchandising, as Holdren suggests. Undoubtedly some of the recent "upcreep" in supermarket average margins is due to the addition of nonfood and other high margin lines. But in recent years the wheel pattern has also been characteristic of department-store retailing, a field that has been relatively unreceptive to new commodity groups.[26]

In some ways, Jefferys' secular trend explanation appears most reasonable. The tendency of many established retailers to reduce prices and margins during depressions suggests also that increases may be a result of generally prospering environments. This explanation helps to resolve an apparent paradox inherent in the wheel concept. Why should reasonably skilled businessmen make decisions that consistently lead their firms along seemingly profitable routes to positions of vulnerability? Jefferys sees movement along the wheel as the result of sensible, businesslike decisions to change with prospering market segments and to leave the poorer customers to low-margin innovators. His explanation is supported by the fact that the vulnerability contemplated by the wheel hypothesis usually means only a loss of market share, not a loss of absolute volume. At least in the United States, though, this explanation is partially contradicted by studies showing that prosperous consumers are especially prone to patronize discount houses. Also they are equally as likely to shop in supermarkets as are poorer consumers.[27]

[24] E. R. A. Seligman and R. A. Love, *Price Cutting and Price Maintenance,* Harper & Brothers, New York, 1932.

[25] Barger, *op. cit.,* pp. ix–x.

[26] R. D. Entenberg, *The Changing Competitive Position of Department Stores in the United States by Merchandise Lines,* University of Pittsburgh Press, Pittsburgh, 1957, p. 52.

[27] R. Holton, *The Supply and Demand Structure of Food Retailing Services, A Case Study,* Harvard University Press, Cambridge, 1954.

The imperfect competition and excess capacity hypotheses also appear highly plausible. Considerably more investigation is needed before their validity can be appraised properly. The wheel pattern developed very slowly, and very recently in the department-store field. Yet market imperfections in that field probably were greater before the automobile gave the consumer shopping mobility. Major portions of the supermarket growth in food retailing and discount-house growth in appliance distribution occurred during periods of vastly expanding consumption, when excess capacity probably was at relatively low levels. At the moment there is little evidence to suggest any clear-cut correlation between the degree of market imperfection and the appearance of the wheel pattern. However, this lack may well be the result of the scarcity of empirical studies of retail competition.

Managerial deterioration certainly must explain some manifestations of the wheel, but not all. Empires rise and fall with changes in the quality of their leadership, and the same thing seems true in business. But the wheel hypothesis is a hypothesis concerning types of retailing and not merely individual firms. Consequently, the managerial-deterioration explanation holds true only if it is assumed that new people entering any established type of retailing as the heads of both old and new companies are consistently less competent than the first generation. Again, the fact that the wheel has operated very slowly in some field suggests that several successive managerial generations can avoid wheel-like maturation and decay.

# 45. THE MANY FACES AND FACETS OF THE MARKETING REVOLUTION

*E. B. Weiss*

*Innovative planning in marketing includes more than predicting new product successes and style changes; it also involves recognizing new merchandising opportunities.*

*Today, more than ever before, the innovative marketer who exploits technological advances and appeals to consumers' increasing sophistication will develop considerable profits. As E. B. Weiss says, nothing is permanent in the new marketing revolution except change itself.*

Marketing revolutions start with the *shopper.*

Since retailers are closest to the shopper, they are usually first to spot the broad, and sometimes violent, shifts in shopper habits.

Yet, even retailers tend to view the clearly apparent changes in shopping habits with a combination of doubt and dismay that results in heel-dragging reaction to the inevitable.

Thus, starting in the 1950s, the shopper clearly indicated that she wanted to shop out in the suburbs. Our major retailers began their trek out to the suburbs most reluctantly. Typically, department stores insisted that any volume they did in the suburbs would be drained away from their downtown main stores.

Source: From *Management and the Marketing Revolution: Merchandising Strategies for the New Era.* New York: Copyright © 1964, used by permission of McGraw-Hill Book Company, pp. 1-17. E. B. Weiss: Vice-President and Director of Special Merchandising Service, Doyle Dane Bernbach Inc., New York.

Again, starting in the 1950s, the shopper clearly indicated that she wanted to do more shopping nocturnally, for a variety of reasons. Established retailers fought night hours—fought night hours bitterly.

Once more, starting in the 1950s, shoppers clearly indicated a growing willingness to shop for a spreading variety of merchandise by self-service; they expected lower prices. Traditional retailers of general merchandise—department stores, variety chains, drug chains, hardware and appliance chains—insisted that general merchandise simply could not be retailed self-service. And when, finally, they reluctantly moved into self-service, they continued to take their traditional hefty margins, thus holding open a big door for the discount retailer.

The list of changes in shopping habits and preferences either fought or subtly resisted by established retailers in the 1950s could easily be extended. But while retailers may have attempted to roadblock the indicated changes, they were at least aware that these changes were in the air, even though their awareness may have been rather dim.

Moreover, even though retailers may have moved reluctantly and with dragging heels in the direction indicated by shopper preferences, they did, in time, make the required shifts.

But manufacturers, generally speaking, tended to be totally unaware of these 1950 to 1960 changes in shopping habits at their inception. What is more, manufacturers tended to be equally unaware of the retailer's belated reactions to these changes until the new retail trends were quite firmly established. Indeed, even when the new trends were reasonably well marked out, many manufacturers *continued* to resist planned reaction—witness the rapid growth of the discount chains which most manufacturers of established brands chose either to ignore, or to resist, for almost ten years—and then belatedly rushed in to capitalize.

Marketing revolution was obviously in the air in the 1950s. The shopper was changing more drastically, and more rapidly, in the decade of the 1950s than in any two or three previous decades. Yet, few brand marketers established rational programs designed to chart these vast shopper changes early enough and then to blueprint the marketing changes that would be required to capitalize them.

Now, in the 1960s, however, I detect a *growing willingness* on the part of manufacturing management, and on the part of manufacturing marketing executives, to accept accelerating shopper changes *as the order of the day.* Instead of ignoring or resisting these shopper changes (hoping that they will disappear), marketing men now tend to try to forecast these changes, to measure their scope, to analyze their potentialities—and then to blueprint marketing programs capable of putting these new market trends to work for the growth of the corporation.

I am more hopeful, therefore, than I was a few years ago that the analytical forecasts of impending marketing changes (some in their infancy) . . . will be accepted by marketing men as practical eventualities, not as a marketing man's version of science fiction, and that these executives will reappraise their marketing program accordingly.

(And let us always remember that science fiction has, time and again, preceded the theoretical scientist in that imaginative leap into the unknown that is man's greatest achievement.)

A few years ago I brought together my first book of then impending marketing trends.[1] Since then, the pace of change at the market place has so accelerated that a *larger* number of new market trends than those covered in the first volume are reported and analyzed here. Moreover, these trends not only are larger in number, but, in potential impact on the world of marketing, will make the marketing revolution of the 1950s seem, by comparison, to be a rather modest disturbance.

I have stated that marketing revolutions for presold brands start with the shopper and are, therefore, first felt and first reacted to by the retailer. It is this reaction of the retailer to the shopper's changing moods, and even whims, that sets the pattern ultimately for the new marketing programs for manufacturers. It is appropriate, therefore, in this . . . chapter to bring into quick review some currently *small* trends in retailing that promise to play *major* roles in the marketing programs of most manufacturers of consumer merchandise of every description. . . . I would like to present, in some detail, two important retail trends which are just beginning to become evident and which show every promise of compelling substantial readjustments in the marketing programs of many presold brands.

The first of these two major retail trends involves the coming expansion of retail volume done *off* the retail floor. For a number of years, I have been predicting that mass retailers would ultimately use every logical means for *reaching out* to the shopper, rather than concentrating exclusively on transactions on the store floor. Sears, Roebuck has been, of course, the chief exponent of this concept, and by far the most successful.

This trend directly reflects the demand by millions of shoppers for shopping facilities that will save them time, effort, and car travel costs, and provide other advantages. It will compel new marketing concepts by manufacturers, as it already has, for example, in the floor-coverings industry.

Lately, a variety of giant retailers have begun to make moves in this direction. Perhaps the most ambitious program designed to this end is the program put together in 1963 by J. C. Penney. Formerly almost exclusively an in-store operation, Penney is now heavily involved in mail order (the first general Penney mail-order catalog was issued in 1963, and it is a hugely ambitious job). Penney also plans mail-order desks in its stores, vastly improved telephone-order facilities, in-home selling crews for certain departments, plus several other innovations that will put Penney in position to tap the shopper wherever and whenever she may be, or may be induced to be, in a shopping mood.

Whether this trend will ever assume proportions that will result in some major retailers rolling up a larger dollar volume *away* from the store floor than *on* the store floor is not a totally farfetched speculation. Such a development would be more likely if the

[1] E. B. Weiss, *Merchandising for Tomorrow,* McGraw-Hill Book Company, New York, 1961.

sale of services were included as well as the sale of merchandise, because many services will be sold away from the retail floor.

Certainly in some departments or merchandise classifications total off-the-floor volume will exceed on-floor volume. (As a matter of fact, some furniture, floor-covering, and appliance stores right now trace a larger part of their total volume to sales made in the home than to sales made on the store floor; and this trend continues.)

This whole retail concept of reaching out to the shopper is in a stage of explosive growth. (At Sears, it has been developed in the mail-order end to a point where the traditional label of "mail order" is no longer properly descriptive: Sears's so-called mail-order business is now more telephone- than traditional mail-order, and Sears is moving away from using the mail-order label.) Yet marketing executives at the manufacturing level have rarely developed specific programs planned to move along with this vast trend among our major retailers toward off-floor retailing. Some manufacturers whose retailers are now heavily involved in in-home selling have developed special programs designed to guide their retailers in more effective in-home selling techniques. Other manufacturers have merely chipped in with allowances for mail-order catalogs, and have let it go at that.

If off-floor retail volume, in a rapidly spreading variety of merchandise classifications, is in a stage of dynamic growth—*and it most assuredly is*—then it surely behooves at least some marketing men to plan as assiduously for this source of retail volume as they do for volume done on the retail floor. But habits are always difficult to break. Marketing men, for decades, have planned merchandising and promotional programs premised on on-floor use. Too few have even begun to give adequate attention to planning merchandising and promotional programs for off-the-floor retail volume.

One decidedly interesting consequence of this trend toward off-the-floor retailing is that it throws into a cocked hat that traditional retail measuring rod of inventory performance dollars per square foot. This is a fascinating development.

For decades, retailers have tended to worship dollars-per-square-foot statistics. The National Retail Merchants Association and the Controllers Congress, as examples, have for years compiled elaborate statistics on dollar-volume-per-square-foot of selling space. While these statistics have represented extremely broad averages, and therefore have incorporated all of the statistical weaknesses of broad average figures, department stores in this instance have tended to base major merchandising decisions on these mathematical compilations. And what is true of department stores is equally true of most other types of mass retailers.

Manufacturers have found, time and again, that store decisions affecting their lines in major outlets have been premised on dollars-per-square-foot of selling space. Where a manufacturer has compaigned for additional floor space, he has all too often been put into reverse by square-foot figures which presumably raised doubts about the space now made available to his line! Moreover, innumerable presentations by manufacturers' salesmen to retailers have been premised on square-foot statistics.

Now, however, merchandising arithmetic is destined for a revolution—yes, believe it or not, retailing faces *still another* revolution. This revolution will, in time, tend to shove square-foot statistics into the discard.

What will take their place?

*Square-mile statistics!*

And what *are* square-mile statistics?

For a lucid explanation I quote from an editorial contribution to an internal Sears publication (*East Wind*) by a Sears vice-president. He writes as follows (and I consider this "must" reading for most marketing men):

> For the past several years, those who feel that the retail business can be run by formulas have talked about dollars per square foot. Supposedly, each square foot of selling space returns a certain number of dollars each year.
>
> This formula may have meant something when it first came out. *Today, however, it is obsolete.* It is obsolete because it leads us to think our business all comes only from people who come *inside* our stores.
>
> Today this is no longer true. Our metropolitan and suburban areas are growing too fast. We can't build stores fast enough to keep them within walking distance of every potential customer. We can't even build them fast enough to make them convenient for every driving customer. Today, we can't wait for business to come to us. *We must go out for it.*
>
> That's why it is much more realistic to consider today's selling, especially in the big ticket departments, not by the square foot but by the *square mile.*
>
> In an average city in our territory, population density averages about 13,000 persons to each square mile (although Manhattan runs as high as 77,000). This potential group of customers is available to us without adding another brick or stone to our building program, if we go out after them.
>
> To the big ticket division manager this represents a challenge. If he chooses just one square mile surrounding his store and launches an all-out attack on that area, he immediately finds himself dealing with thousands of potential new customers. If he uses his sales aids and his outside selling force well, he increases his scale tremendously with no increase in expensive selling space or inventory. Such a well-planned attack brings tremendous satisfaction to any division manager.
>
> But this square-mile attack is not just for big ticket departments. Through our telephone programs, through cards mailed to customers' homes, through our catalogs and in other new and exciting ways we will continue to go after the maximum number of customers from every square mile, and we will get them for every department in the company.

Note particularly the statement in the last paragraph that Sears will broaden its square-mile attack "in new and exciting ways." This conjures up some fascinating new ways of reaching out to the shopper—of selling the shopper *off* the retail floor.

Does it portend a plan that finally will put television to work in the home as a new form of retailing? This has been predicted for years; I made this prophecy at least ten years ago (it is one of many in which my timing was way, way off!).

Apparently this is no longer completely farfetched, because a very down-to-earth retailer was contemplating testing precisely such a plan in 1963. I refer to Unimart, the well-organized, well-run nine-unit membership discount department store chain on the West Coast. Fairchild News Service reports that "marketing through television is a prospect being considered by Unimart according to a Unimart spokesman." The news report goes on to state:

> If this consideration becomes a reality, it will commence experimentally in San Diego, where Unimart has three stores and the most loyal membership. It was noted this operation would supplement in-store shopping. The general public would view merchandise on television commercials, order by phone, and await delivery.
>
> The Unimart official contended this type of operation, if used in place of a conventional store, could lower retail costs, since overhead on warehouse and delivery personnel and facilities, coupled with extensive television advertising, would be lower. Since all merchandise could not be advertised on television, a supplementary catalog probably would be necessary, he noted.
>
> The considered program would handle everyday necessities, not just high-ticket, one-shot merchandise, the spokesman noted. No specific plans have been made toward such an operation, it was learned, but the setup is under serious consideration.
>
> Some Unimart officials reportedly believe telemarts may eventually outdate some discount stores.

In this connection, it is more than merely mental exercise to deploy one's imagination over the off-the-floor retail potentials of some of the fascinating new developments that lie ahead in the rapidly developing art of communication. For example, the major manufacturers in television are quite feverishly at work on a device that will make it possible to insert a tape cartridge into the home television set which will play back, through sound and vision, a recorded program. This development may not only outmode present-day phonograph records; it is entirely conceivable that, some day, a tape cartridge may record a merchandise catalog that can then be played back in the home through the home TV receiver, in color and, of course, with sound.

Could that be one of the "new and exciting ways" that Sears foresees with respect to retailing away from the store floor? I don't profess to know; but I firmly believe it is entirely within the range of potentials.

I believe it can be accepted as basic that:

1. A rapidly increasing percentage of total retail volume, in most merchandise classifications, will be done *off* the retail floor.
2. This in-home retail volume will be done not only through refinements of present techniques—catalogs, telephone, in-home selling crews—but through new marvels of communications yet to come.

The end result will be:

1. To make a shambles of traditional square-foot figures of all types;
2. To bring about a requirement for a new measuring rod to take the place of square-foot statistics;

3. To compel marketing men at the manufacturing level to develop completely new types of marketing, merchandising, and particularly promotional programs that will rationally tie in with and capitalize the opportunities inherent in retailing done *off* the retail floor.

The second retail trend that I propose covering here in some detail revolves around new locations for retail outlets. It is astonishing, when one looks back to 1946–less than twenty years ago–to note the remarkable shift in retail store locations. These shifts in store locations are, of course, in direct response to indicated changes in shopping habits.

The shopping center has, obviously, represented the major shift in store location. There are estimates that shopping centers of all types now account for roughtly 25 per cent of total retail volume (excluding automobiles, lumber and other building supplies, etc.). In some important merchandise categories, shopping centers may now account for 35 per cent of total retail volume–for example, in infants wear, garden supplies, etc.

But the shopping center has been only one of an amazing variety of new types of retail store locations that have emerged largely, if not entirely, since the end of World War II. These would include motels, hotels, marinas, bowling alleys, mass transportation terminals (including the airline and bus terminal), motion picture theaters, highway locations of infinite variety, expressway intersection locations.

It is probable that if total retail volume done in all of the store locations that have sprung up primarily since 1946 (again excluding autos, building supplies, etc.) were totaled up, it would be found that *at least 35 per cent of total retail* now passes through stores in these new locations! Never before in retailing's long history did store location change to such a vast degree in less than two decades. Now, what is apt to happen with respect to store location over the next decade? In particular, what will be some of the newer types of store locations?

I would say that foremost in new store locations will be the gas station. This is a prediction I began to make something over five years ago; it is now actually taking place. Some fifty thousand gas stations will emerge, within the coming decade, as a major outlet for a wide variety of nonautomotive merchandise classifications. Perhaps this qualifies more as a new type of outlet rather than a new store location; but since the gas station tends to be situated in locations quite different from typical or traditional retail store locations, I think it may properly be included in a listing of new types of store locations.

Then, the giant apartment house is destined to emerge as an important new retail store location. In several cities and suburban towns, automatic vendors have already achieved a substantial volume, on food especially. It should be understood that, starting about two years ago, apartment house building–particularly in the suburbs–leaped into a remarkable boom. This apartment house building boom promises to continue for some years to come. A growing percentage of these new apartment houses will include retail store facilities.

Now this is not really a brand new store locational concept. Actually, apartment houses–especially in lower-income neighborhoods–have had stores at the street level for years. But the newer apartment houses I am referring to are not necessarily for low-income families; on the contrary, many qualify as luxury apartment houses occupied by families with incomes ranging from middle to fairly high. Moreover, the store installations are of a new type, including automatic vending installations.

In this connection I am reminded of a book written at least thirty years ago by the founder of the Gillette razor business. In that book, Mr. Gillette envisioned the population of entire cities compressed into a limited number of huge apartment houses. Each apartment house complex would be self-contained and would include not only medical and drug facilities, play facilities, entertainment facilities (including movies), but also retail store facilities.

The fact of the matter is that, in some parts of the nation, we have today apartment house complexes that translate into practical living what was called at that time "a Jules Verne concept by the razor wizard." In these giant apartment houses, residents have available most of their basic requirements in food, drugs, medical service, entertainment, general merchandise.

As part of this same concept, at least one of the great builders of shopping centers is planning several shopping centers that will include huge adjoining apartment houses. It is anticipated that a major part of the volume of many stores in these shopping centers will come from walk-in traffic consisting of residents of the adjoining apartment houses. In fact, the concept is described as furnishing a shopping center with a "captive shopulation."

This is a decidedly interesting development, because it involves a reversal of the vast trend toward shopper mobility. Clearly, shoppers have become mobile as never before: the distances shoppers travel to get to certain stores or shopping centers would have been considered totally incredible only a few years ago. Moreover, shoppers display a vast tendency to spread their patronage over a growing number of shopping centers, neighborhood stores, and downtown stores (not to mention shopping by mail, by telephone, etc.).

Does this mean that shoppers will refuse to be turned into "captives"? Some shoppers–yes. Other shoppers–no.

It is vitally important, in marketing, always to accept the premise that nothing is permanent *except change!* It is also vitally important to remember that every vast trek in one direction inevitably sets up counterforces moving in precisely the *opposite* direction. Thus, it is entirely probable that, just as the wide-open, picture-window house is now giving way to the closed-in, patio-type of house, just as services may be becoming more of a status symbol than the possession of merchandise, just so a growing number of mobile shoppers may now be on the verge of *tiring of their mobility!* When this happens, several types of store locations will come into being, of which I have mentioned so far just two.

Another new type of store location that I believe promises to become of considerable importance really breaks down into two types. I am referring to giant office buildings and to the larger industrial parks. The office building is destined to become a sizable retail outlet for plant workers. The industrial park is destined to become a sizable retail outlet for plant workers.

The office building, years ago, limited its retailing to the so-called cigar stand in the lobby. Then the cigar stand diversified into additional merchandise classifications. Then, in some of the huge office buildings, stores of other types opened up on the lobby floor. An example would be the proliferation of stores in the several giant buildings that comprise Radio City in New York.

Now some retailers are beginning to plan store locations for *upper* floors of office buildings. At least one department store has had such an outlet for several years. Tiffany's is planning a chain of such locations. (Doctors and other professionals have long taken space in office buildings; now retailers will follow them into this location.) Banks (which are a form of retailing) now locate in office buildings.

Interestingly, the appeal of industrial parks and office buildings for shopping stems from essentially the same factors that lead to nocturnal hours for stores, to Sunday shopping, to the pickup in mail-order and telephone shopping, and to in-home selling. In other words, basically we have a situation that makes less shopping time available to shoppers (women at work clearly have less time for shopping). Also, more and more millions want to spend less and less time for shopping, particularly in shopping for necessities and borderline necessities. (Other social and economic factors also cut into shopping time; I enumerated them in detail years ago when I pleaded with retailers to consider nocturnal store hours.) The consequence is that it is becoming increasingly appealing to workers in office buildings and in huge industrial plants and industrial parks to be able to shop at these locations, especially at the noon hour and after quitting time.

I think that the explosion of the market for services of infinite variety will lead to new store locations for retailers offering these services. Clearly, services need not necessarily, or exclusively, be sold in traditoinal store locations or in stores of traditional architecture.

It seems to me that the time must come when millions of people will shop from their cars. I have reference not only to drive-in stores in new locations but also to the probability that a combination of car telephone and radio will permit motorists to shop while driving. We spend more and still more time in our cars. We now use the radio on a huge scale while driving; I believe the total number of hours spent listening to the radio in autos may now approach (if it doesn't already exceed) the total number of hours spent listening to the radio at home. Surely, with a combination of car telephone and car radio, it would be possible to shop for at least some basics from cars in motion. I dare say that, in a tiny way, this has already happened with cars equipped with two-way telephones and radio.

*Maybe in-car shopping will some day equal in-home shopping in volume!* Why not? Millions spend almost as much waking time in their cars as in their home!

That, in turn, may make it possible for stores to locate in out-of-the-way areas rather than in high-traffic areas. In fact, these may not be stores at all in the traditional sense; they may merely be warehouses. (And if home TV ever achieves its oft-predicted destiny and becomes part of in-home shopping, as it can and should, then this, too, will lead to warehouse-type stores in new locations.)

As the entire family uses golf club facilities, it may be that the "pro" shop will emerge as an outlet for a multiplying variety of merchandise. Certainly many more women spend vastly more time at their golf clubs; and where and when women congregate, shopping cannot be far behind.

I gather that billiards and pool may become as popular as did bowling. If so, these establishments may become outlets for merchandise exactly as did the modern bowling alley.

The ski resort has yet to be developed as a retail outlet to the same degree true of summer resorts. Yet skiing has now become the sport of millions.

I am sure this summary of potential new locations for retailing is a mere starter. But it serves to underscore the fluidity of store location. And store location, in time, must be reflected in phases of the marketing programs of manufacturers.

Most of our giant retailers have decided that the shopper is becoming increasingly irritated with rigid departmentalizing. As a consequence, there is a growing trend toward breaking down departmental rigidities. This involved so-called "outposts"; it also involves shelf extenders which contain one or more related items–as an example, coffee percolators in the coffee section of the food supermarket; and in the hosiery department of department stores it now involves adding a wide variety of foot accessories formerly sold exclusively in other departments.

As part of this shopper irritation with departmental rigidities in giant store units, there is also a growing feeling on the part of many shoppers that some stores have simply become too big, and that they present both time problems and physical problems that the shopper is finding less and less alluring. For this reason, as well as from other changes in shopping habits, it is becoming clear to many retailers that a rising percentage of shoppers will welcome new forms of small specialty stores. There is, therefore, a very definite specialty store revolution in the offing–and surely it is obvious that a return to specialty stores by our large retailers will profoundly affect the marketing programs of innumerable manufacturers.

Then the shopper has shown a clear-cut desire to shop on Sunday. Here, too, marketing programs will have to be reshaped, just as nocturnal shopping compelled manufacturers to recast parts of their marketing programs.

More and more millions of shoppers are becoming increasingly sophisticated. As part of this remarkable trend toward sophistication—which stems, of course, from our fantastic cultural revolution—there is now becoming evident a mounting desire among millions of shoppers for merchandise that affords greater latitude in exercising individual taste. It is ironic that in this age of automation, with its implication of new heights in mass-produced, uniform merchandise, there should arrive simultaneously this new desire for merchandise representing individual taste and, therefore, individual choice. Maybe this is not so ironic after all; it is still true that every reaction must, in time, bring its own reaction, and the enormous progress of merchandise produced by automation inevitably had to produce a reaction in the shape and form of custom-made merchandise.

Be that as it may, there is no question that the cultural revolution that is self-evident in our nation is bringing along with it a rapidly rising tide of demand among shoppers for merchandise that enables them to express their individuality. Retailers are, therefore, adding to their exclusive lines—their semi-custom-made lines—and they are more willing than has been the case for years to consider true custom-made lines. Here, again, we see how a change in the mores of the shopper brings with it a compulsion for change on the part of manufacturers.

As our society entered an advanced stage of luxury, it was to be expected that shoppers would show a developing inclination to buy services as well as to buy merchandise. As a matter of fact, there is some reason to believe that the acquisition of services may be on the verge of representing a new form of status symbol. In any event, the share of the shopper's dollar being paid out for services is jumping ahead at an extraordinary pace and without doubt will, within a few years, top the shopper's expenditures for merchandise, especially with respect to disposable income.

Retailers, with their ears so close to the ground, are reacting promptly to this new demand of the shopper for services. We find department stores, the mail-order chains, the variety chains, etc., all promoting new services, ranging from insurance and travel to home building and home renovation services.

Just as an example of how a shift in shopper demand will, in turn, spark a new retail development that, in its turn, will spark new marketing programs by manufacturers, consider the impending entrance of major retailers into home-building and home-renovating programs. This trend will compel the huge home-building supply industry to revamp its marketing program. Not only will the traditional "lumber yard" become a modernized type of self-service building supply outlet, but giant retailers who formerly moved only a minor percentage of building supplies (such as department stores, variety and food chains) will now become major outlets. Some building supply manufacturers who never called on department stores, for example, will now have to include department stores in their marketing scheme.

As part of this trend toward services, and perhaps also as part of a trend away from the acquisition of merchandise as the exclusive status symbol, shoppers are showing a growing willingness to rent a bewildering variety of merchandise. Retailers reacted to this new trend with remarkable promptness; by 1963 practically every major retailer was committed to an expanding program of merchandise rentals. This, in turn, has compelled a number of manufacturers to develop special merchandise lines for rental to the public and, of course, has also compelled manufacturers to develop not only special rental departments within their organizations but also special rental marketing programs.

The shopper is showing additional evidence of objecting to incomplete merchandise assortments in many stores and objecting even more to delayed deliveries. Thus, in the furniture field, the shopper in 1963 was clearly displaying mounting resentment over delivery promises running six to eight weeks after purchase (which were not always kept!).

Several major marketing developments are cropping up as a direct result of this new attitude on the part of shoppers. One reaction by manufacturers involves the development of marketing programs that assure placement on the retail floor of the manufacturer's full line. A second reaction by manufacturers brings with it programs under which the manufacturer ships the shopper's purchases directly to the shopper's home. These are two true marketing revolutions, and they can be attributed directly to new shopper moods.

A growing army of women began to display in the 1960s a resentment of the time involved in getting gas at the typical gas station—and also a resentment at the masculine atmosphere that continues to dominate most gas stations. They began to indicate a preference for having their cars serviced while they shopped for food, for example, or while they shopped in a department store. They also felt "more at home" in these outlets.

The consequence has been that the food chains, the department stores, the variety chains, and even the drug chains have begun to move in on automobile servicing and on the sale of a wide range of automotive products. This, in turn, has compelled the gas station to reappraise its marketing position, and the gas station is now tending in the direction of adding nonautomotive lines and of dressing itself up for more feminine appeal. Here, too, we have a marketing revolution of vast scope.

In addition to the over-all marketing revolution directly attributable to changes in attitudes and preferences among shoppers, there are marketing revolutions that start in other ways. For example, our giant retailers began, in 1962 and 1963, to develop a growing sophistication in their uses of electronic data processing. This has already produced some changes at retail of major proportions. For instance, the more sophisticated and broader uses of EDP by giant retailers have downgraded the importance of the store buyer. The store buyer continues to make buying motions, but he is clearly becoming more of a detail clerk than a decision-maker. His buying functions are, obviously, being taken over by buying committees, and usually the buyer does not even sit on the buying committee.

A General Foods marketing executive, in a public address on this subject, developed the point that their salesmen are now called "account men," and when he outlined the functions of a General Foods account man during a typical day, he stressed the fact that the General Foods account man spends only a minimum amount of time with the food chain buyer. He also brought out the fact that these changes in organizational procedure by the food chain, which are being brought about by EDP and related developments, have made it advisable for General Foods to have some of its account men spend all their time with just one food chain.

Obviously, this one development—the age of EDP in retailing and, of course, also the coming of automation in retailing—is bound to revolutionize the marketing practices of practically all consumer goods manufacturers.

It is decidedly significant to note in this connection that the more sophisticated uses of EDP by retailers and by manufacturers in their marketing functions have suggested the wisdom of new areas of marketing cooperation between manufacturers, wholesalers, and retailers. Thus, in the food industry, starting in 1962, manufacturers, wholesalers, and retailers arranged to sit down periodically to study jointly their mutual problems. This led to the emergence of broad new areas of cooperation between the food producers and their distributors—wholesale and retail. Similar developments will undoubtedly take place in other fields; and where and when this happens, manufacturers' marketing programs will, in time, be profoundly affected.

Marketing has, of course, always been in a state of flux. However, starting in the 1950s and becoming even more self-evident in the present decade of the 1960s are two major marketing developments:

1. A growing awareness among marketing men that the pace of change in marketing is constantly accelerating;
2. A growing awareness that manufacturers' marketing programs must, therefore, be kept under constant review, under constant reappraisal—that shifts in moods and whims of the shopper, shifts in retailing policies and practices, and other changes in our economic and social society must be more promptly and more astutely reflected in manufacturers' marketing programs.

It is the object of this book to place before manufacturers of presold brands the whole complex of changing trends at the marketplace, and to suggest, where this is feasible, how manufacturers will have to react in order most effectively to cope with, and to capitalize on, these developing trends.

*F. Physical distribution*

# 46. THE TOTAL COST APPROACH TO DISTRIBUTION

*Raymond Le Kashman and John F. Stolle*

*Pruning of distribution costs requires more than just studying obvious expenditures, such as warehousing and transportation. Additional costs are scattered throughout the firm's operations, and thus in a sense are hidden—and often neglected because they do not fall within any single executive's purview.*

*The authors discuss the nature of these "other costs" and the total cost methodology of choosing alternative distribution strategies. They stress that responsibility for a total cost approach lies with top management, because all company operations must be analyzed as a whole.*

The more management focuses the company's efforts on cutting distribution costs, the less successful it is likely to be in reducing the real costs of distribution. This apparent paradox is no abstract or armchair play on phrases. It explains why so many companies have diligently pruned distribution costs—in the warehouse and in inventory, in order processing and in transportation—only to find that these hard-earned savings are somehow not translated into improved profit margins. They have been watered down or actually washed out by increases in other costs scattered throughout the company.

Authors' Note: Harold Wolff of Booz-Allen & Hamilton, Inc., helped develop this article and prepared the material for publication.

Source: From *Business Horizons,* vol. 8, Winter, 1965, pp. 33–46. Raymond Le Kashman and John F. Stolle, both Vice-Presidents of Booz-Allen & Hamilton, Inc., management consulting firm.

It is these "other costs," motley and miscellaneous as they first seem, that turn out on closer analysis to be the *real* cost of distribution. (See Figure 1.) They never appear as distribution costs on any financial or operating report, but show up unidentified and unexplained at different times and in assorted places—in purchasing, in production, in paper-work processing—anywhere and everywhere in the business. When the gremlin-like costs are traced to their roots, however, one finds that they are, in fact, all intimately interrelated, linked together by one common bond. They all result from the way the company distributes its products.

It is this aggregation of distribution-related costs—rather than what managements usually mean when they complain about the cost of distribution—that represents the

**Figure 1. The real cost of distribution**

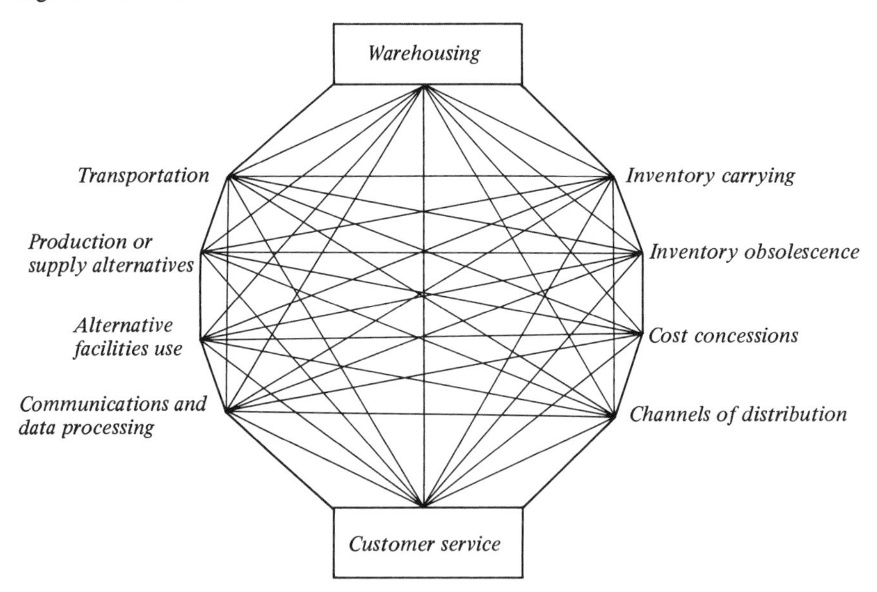


The real cost of distribution includes much more than what most companies consider when they attempt to deal with distribution costs. In a sense, any major distribution decision can affect every cost in the business and each cost is related to all the others. Our experience indicates that the following ten cost elements and interrelationships are the ones that are most likely to prove critical in evaluating the impact of alternative distribution approaches on total costs and total profits.

*Warehousing.* To provide service through the company's chosen channels of distribution, some warehousing is required, involving from one in-plant warehouse to a multiple-unit network dispersed across the country. Service usually becomes better as the number of warehouses is increased, at least up to a point. However, as the number of warehouses increases, their average size decreases; this will begin to reduce the efficiency of service to customers. Also, costs increase. Thus, any change in the three variables—number, type, or location of warehouses—will affect both service and costs.

*Inventory carrying.* The ownership of inventory gives rise to costs for money, insurance, occupancy, pilferage losses and custodial services, and sometimes inventory taxes. Depending on the business involved, this group of costs may range from 10 per cent to 30 per cent of average annual inventory value. Customer service will be improved by keeping inventory at many storage points important and increasing drain of distribution on earnings. These are the costs—rather than those usually defined and dealt with as distribution costs—that have eluded even the most earnest cost-cutting drives. Because of its size and its elusiveness, this cost complex remains for many companies a promising profit-improvement potential.

## THE TOTAL COST APPROACH

*When to Use It.* For earnings-minded managements, the dimensions of this profit potential, and a practical technique for tapping it, have now been tested and proved. A handful of companies have faced up to the across-the-board impact of distribution on

---

in the field near to customers, but this will increase total inventory and the cost for carrying that inventory. Thus, inventory carrying cost is closely linked to warehousing cost and customer service.

*Inventory obsolescence.* If (at a given level of sales) total inventory is increased to provide better customer service, then inventory turnover is decreased. Also, the greater the "pipeline fill" in the distribution system, the slower the inventory turnover. This automatically exposes the owner to greater risks of obsolescence and inventory write-down. This is a particularly important cost for companies having frequent model changeovers, style changes or product perishability.

*Production or supply alternatives.* Production costs vary among plants and vary with the volume produced at each individual plant. Plants have different fixed costs and different unit variable costs as volume is increased. The decision of which plant should serve which customers must give weight not only to transportation and warehousing costs, but also to production and supply costs; these will vary significantly with the volume allocated to each plant.

*Cost concessions.* A special aspect of production or supply alternatives arises from the fact that distribution decisions can affect costs otherwise incurred by suppliers or customers. For example, when a retailer creates his own warehouses, this may free suppliers from packing and shipping small quantities or from maintaining small local warehouses in the field. A retailer who establishes his own warehouse network may be able to recoup some of these costs by negotiation with the supplier.

*Channels of distribution.* The choice of distribution channels profoundly affects the nature and costs of a company's sales organization, its selling price and gross margin structure, its commitment to physical distribution facilities. These in turn will affect production and supply costs.

*Transportation.* Changing the number or location of warehouses changes transportation costs, sometimes in unanticipated and complex ways. For example, an increase in the number of warehouses may initially reduce total transportation costs; but past some determinable point, the cost trend may reverse because of the decreasing ratio of carload to less-than-carload tonnage.

*Communications and data processing.* These costs vary with the complexity of the distribution system and with the level of service provided, including costs for order processing, inventory control, payables, receivables and shipping documents. These costs rise as more distribution points are added to the system. Additionally, as the cycle time or response time of the communications and data processing system is shortened, costs of this service are increased.

*Alternative facilities use.* Changes in inventory requirements or in other aspects of the distribution operation will change space requirements and utilization in a plant-warehouse facility or a retail store. Space used for distribution may be convertible to selling space which yields incremental sales and profits. In the case of retail business, this is actually a variation of the customer service factor since it increases the availability of goods with which to fill customer requirements.

*Customer service.* Stock-outs, excess delivery time, or excess variability of delivery time all result in lost sales. Any change in the distribution sytem will influence these elements of customer service, and therefore must either gain or lose sales for the company. These effects, while difficult to measure, must be considered part of the real cost of distribution.

costs and profits. They have accomplished this by applying an approach—we call it the "total cost approach"—that is designed to convert these intangible and intricate cost interrelationships into tangible dollars-and-cents improvements in profit margins.

A major food manufacturer, after applying effectively an assortment of rigid cost-cutting techniques, has found that this new approach is enabling the company to add 1.7 per cent to its margin on sales.

A major merchandiser, already enjoying the benefits of advanced distribution techniques, found that this same new approach could cut from its corporate costs an additional $7.5 million—3 per cent of the sales value of its products—while at the same time significantly improving service to customers.

At Du Pont, a company well known for its general management excellence, this same new approach underlies the announcement that programs recently instituted are expected to cut $30 million from its total cost, a 10 per cent reduction of the costs attributed to distribution.

These success stories shed some light on how distribution drains profits—and on what can be done about it:

*The real impact of distribution on profits is much greater than most managements think.* In companies in which distribution-connected costs have been studied, they turned out to be significantly greater than management estimated—as much as from a third to a half of the selling price of the product.

*This untapped profit-improvement potential exists because these costs lie in a managerial no-man's land, where they can increase because they are outside the scope of responsibility or control of any operating executive.* These distribution-related costs are not strictly the responsibility of the man in charge of distribution, because they are costs of purchasing, manufacturing, or some other function of the business. But they cannot be dealt with effectively by the executive in charge of these other functions because they are actually caused by distribution decisions, for which only the man in charge of distribution has any responsibility. They are the result of complex interrelationships involving all of the functions of the business. Distribution lies at the crossroad of these complex interactions, and that is what is so different about distribution. In no other function of the business can decisions made at the operating level look so right and be so wrong.

*These costs will not respond to the usual cost-cutting approaches.* Management has achieved near miracles in cutting costs in one function of the business after another, including costs within the distribution function, notably in warehousing, transportation, and order-filling. But conventional cost-cutting approaches are limited to costs that fall within any one operation of the business; for cutting these costs, management can hold some executive responsible. Distribution-related costs are organizational orphans, beyond the reach of even the most diligent, skillful cost-minded executives.

*These costs will respond only to a high level across-the-board re-examination of how distribution affects the total costs and total profits of the business, and of what management action is necessary to tap this profit opportunity.*

Thus the problem and the opportunity are deposited squarely on the desk of the chief executive. The pursuit of these added profits has to get its start, its support, and its sanctions at the top management level. With this high-level effort, even companies that have tightened and tidied their distribution operations can greatly increase earnings by a frontal attack on the basic framework of their distribution decisions and practices.

This broad, basic approach has a continuing payoff, for once the most profitable pattern of distribution has been defined for the present operations of the business, management has in its hands a yardstick for measuring the impact on total profits of any proposed management move. This makes it possible to define the impact on total profits of a new plant or a new product, or a cluster of new customers, and so makes it possible to determine what changes in distribution—if any—will ensure peak profits from these new ventures.

What is this total cost approach? What is new about it? Why have we not heard more about it?

*The Approach Simply Stated.* This approach sounds simple. First, analyze the distribution impact on each cost of the business, and select for more detailed study those activities the cost of which is significantly affected by distribution policies and practices. *Second,* develop the data necessary to measure the profit impact that alternative distribution decisions would have on each of these activities. *Finally,* determine which distribution decision will maximize profits.

Obviously, if it were as simple as it sounds, more companies would long ago have beaten a path to this better mousetrap. Three sets of facts explain why this has not been so:

1. The impact of distribution on costs is more difficult to unravel than is the effect of other business decisions. All functions of a business are somewhat interrelated, but distribution is more complexly intertwined with each. And it is these interrelationships—rather than the costs of the distribution functions *per se*—that are the cause of high distribution costs and the key to understanding and reducing these costs.

2. Because corporate accounting has historically been oriented to finance and production, rather than to marketing or distribution, the operating reports that guide managerial action do not tot up in any one place the full impact of distribution on costs. The real cost of distribution never stares management in the face.

3. Even where managements have become aware of these costs and their impacts on profits, there was until recently very little that anyone could do about the pervasive effects of distribution. Even a relatively simple problem in distribution system design can involve hundreds of bits of information that interact in thousands of ways. So there was no way of dealing with the distribution cost complex until techniques were developed to manipulate this mass of material as a single integrated entity.

This last is, in fact, the major reason why these distribution-related costs have continued to rise and to depress profits margins throughout our economy. And for that same reason the total cost concept remained until recently a topic for textbook discussion, theoretically provocative but of little practical use. But techniques have been developed to deal with information in these quantities and with interrelationships of such complexity. They have converted this sound but previously unworkable concept into a practical management approach.

The examples that follow are composites of a number of companies. The relevant facts and figures have thus been disguised without in any way changing the practical significance of the results. The first example traces the step-by-step process involved in the analysis of the factors that enter into the application of the total cost approach in a business engaged primarily in the retail distribution of a wide range of consumer products; the second shows how this complex array of informaton is analyzed and manipulated to provide management with profitable answers to some familiar distribution problems.

## WHAT MAKES DISTRIBUTION DIFFERENT

Consider the problem facing the management of a large company whose business consists of a widely dispersed chain of retail stores and a few factories that produce some of the merchandise sold in these stores. This company has shipped directly from its suppliers and its factories to its stores, but wants to determine whether there would be any profit advantage in shifting to a national system of field warehouses.

When this company looked at the combined cost of warehousing and of transportation that would result from introducing various combinations of field warehouses, it appeared, as shown in Figure 2, that the lowest cost system was one with six warehouses. But this would *increase* its distribution costs by $12.9 million. Thus, on the basis of apparent distribution costs alone, there was no profit advantage in any field warehouse system.

However, when this study investigated how alternative distribution networks would affect other costs in the company, the answer was quite different. As shown in Figure 3, the most efficient warehouse system turned out to be one with five, rather than six, field warehouses. And this five-warehouse system would cut the total costs of the company by $7.7 million; an increase of 1.4 per cent on sales.

Looking at distribution from a standpoint of total costs, this company discovered an opportunity to increase its profits that it could not have identified or taken advantage of in any other way. What explains the difference? What legerdemain turned up this handsome profit potential that represented a 22.4 per cent return on the investment required to design and install this field warehouse system? The answer, in this case as in other similar corporate experiences, involves following through the various steps of the total cost approach—that is, to determine the total cost of the present operation and then compare it with the total costs that would follow from alternative distribution systems.

**Figure 2. Distribution cost solution**

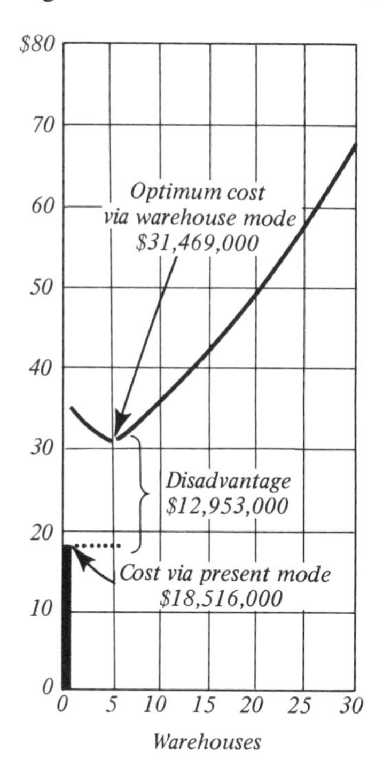


**Figure 3. Total cost solution**

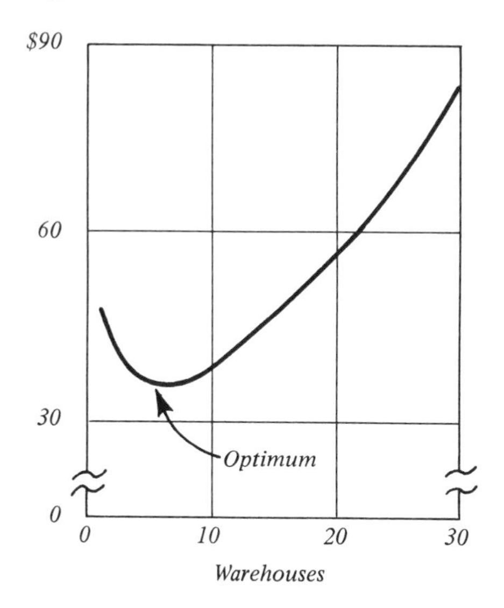

At its very inception, the total cost approach is different in a number of ways from the traditional functional approach to distribution management. In the first place, it deals with the impact of distribution decisions on business costs wherever these costs appear. Secondly, many important cost factors and many critical relationships between distribution and other parts of the business are not usually translatable to quantitive terms. Customer service is a classic example.

The first step was to determine what distribution-related factors contribute significantly to total costs, trace the interrelationships of these factors, and then quantify both the factors and the interrelationships. This process has to be repeated anew for each company because of the important differences from industry to industry and even from one company to another in the same industry.

Then each of these have to be translated into a common denominator, so they can be measured and compared. If impact is measured in dollars, a unit that meets these requirements, it is possible to reduce all of the cost and profit considerations and all of these intricate interrelationships to one final total dollar cost for each alternative course of action.

The significance of this for management is seen in Figure 4; graphs show, for each major activity affected, the impact of different field warehouse systems (indicated by the numbers along the base of each graph) on the total cost of this operation. These graphs clearly show that for each factor of costs, a certain number of warehouses would yield the lowest costs and the maximum profit. Because each of these factors has its own built-in logic, each curve takes on its own configuration. The sum of all of these curves–each with its own optimum–is one final curve that defines the total cost. That in turn defines the optimum number of warehouses for this operation, when all considerations are taken into account. Except by chance coincidence, this point will differ from the optimum of each of the component curves. Obviously, a piecemeal approach to cost reduction will not yield the maximum profit impact achieved by this total cost approach.

These graphs show that even though one or several elements of distribution cost are cut to their lowest practical level, total costs may actually increase, and dealing with these costs one at a time will not produce the best result. They show the pitfalls of considering these various factors as single and static, instead of as interrelated and dynamic. The first and second graphs in the series make apparent the process whereby the consideration of distribution costs alone–the cost of warehouse plus the cost of transportation–led to the conclusion that no change in distribution could add to the profitability of the business. Only the final graph, summing up all of the interacting factors involved, demonstrates unmistakably that a shift to the five-warehouse system would be a very profitable move for this management.

Actually, in this case as in so many others, a reduction in warehouse and transportation could in fact lead to increases in other distribution-related costs, with the result that total costs would be increased and this significant profit opportunity missed. Only by increasing these distribution costs could total expenses be cut and total

**Figure 4. Total cost approach**

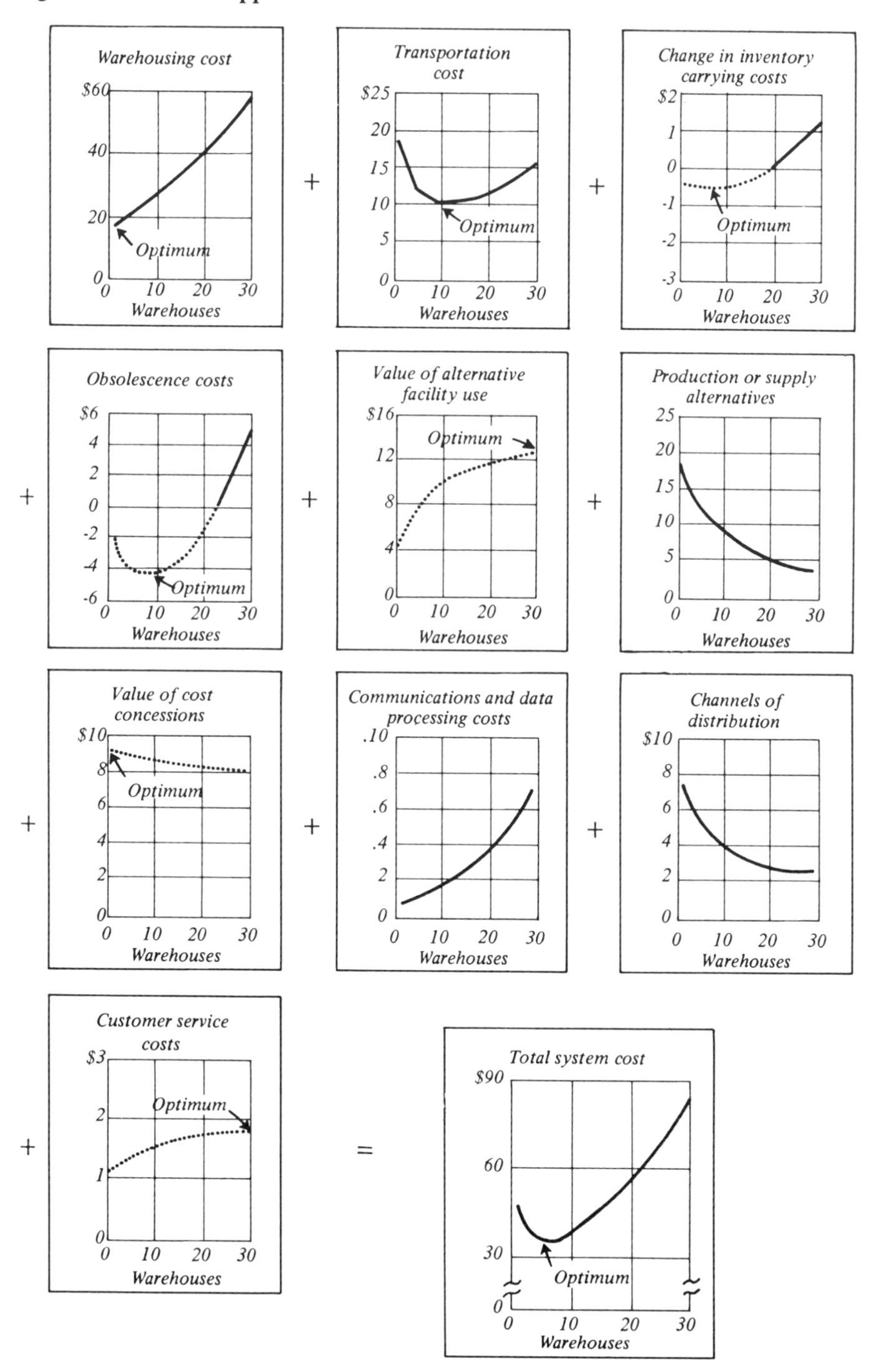

earnings increased in this company. By this kind of trade-off the total cost approach brings a company closer to achieving its maximum potential profit. The actual figures from this company's calculations for the five-warehouse system are shown in Table 1.

It is difficult to conceive of a distribution problem in a company of any substantial size that could not show near-term benefits from this kind of analytical approach; the approach does much more than offer a one-time solution to what is actually a perennial problem. Because this company distributes mostly through its own retail outlets, the channels of distribution are not currently an important variable. They involve only the small amount of its product that it makes in its own factories but sells to other customers. The availability of field warehouses, however, would make it possible to sell and ship more of the output of these plants direct to customers rather than through local jobbers. As it turned out, the $200,000 it added to profitability was just about what it cost to design and engineer this whole new distribution system.

In this case, the company had good reason for considering the significance of distribution channels. Looking ahead, it could see the possibility of integrating backwards, then becoming more heavily involved in manufacturing. In that case, alternative channels of distribution might become more important. The point is that in this kind of analytical exercise it is essential to consider all possible directions for company growth. Otherwise, a new distribution system, however profitable it may be under present conditions, might freeze the company into a set of cost factors that would preclude an otherwise profitable growth opportunity. The total cost approach offers management this built-in flexibility in assessing alternatives.

**Table 1. Profit impact of distribution–gains (losses)** *(in millions of dollars)*

| | |
|---|---|
| Warehousing | (14.4) |
| Transportation | 0.5 |
| **Total distribution costs** | **(13.9)** |
| Inventory | |
| Carrying costs | 1.4 |
| Obsolescence costs | 4.3 |
| Value of alternative use of facilities | 7.8 |
| | **13.5** |
| Production and purchasing | |
| Production and raw materials costs | 0.2 |
| Reduced cost of purchased finished goods | 6.7 |
| | **6.9** |
| Data processing | **(0.2)** |
| Marketing | |
| Channels of distribution | 0.2 |
| Customer service | 1.4 |
| | **1.6** |
| **Total profit impact of distribution-related items** | **21.8** |
| Pretax Profit Increase | 7.9 |

Every time management makes a decision of any magnitude, it ought to be in a position to get an answer to the question, "How will it affect distribution costs throughout the company?" The total cost approach puts the company in a position to make continuing gains by applying a rigid yardstick to any proposed corporate venture. Whenever manufacturing management designs a new plant, develops a new production process, or turns to a new source of raw materials, the pattern of distribution-related costs will be changed throughout the business. Similar far-flung changes will take place whenever marketing management adds a new product or a promising new group of customers. The total cost approach enables management to define how these changes will interact with distribution to affect the company's total cost and its total profits. It tells management what distribution decisions need to be made to avoid the loss of potential profits, or to add to them. So both short-term and long-term benefits result from management's recognition of these complex cost and profit relationships.

## FROM DATA TO DECISION

How these complex interrelationships and the mass of related data enable management to put a dollar value on alternative courses of action can be seen quite readily in the following case. The total cost approach was used by a division of a large manufacturing company. This division does an annual business of about $45 million, with over 3,000 customers located in every state. It has manufacturers and warehouses at five points across the country, shipping to customers via both rail and truck.

The profit problems this management posed have a familiar ring; some are long-range problems.

Without any major investment, can we increase our profits by changing our distribution system?

Can total costs be reduced by shifting some of our available equipment from one factory to another?

Can we further reduce costs and increase profits by changing our marketing approach?

Is there any profit advantage in changing the capacity of one or more of our present plants, or perhaps building a new facility at another location?

Could we further improve profitability by changing our warehouse capacities or locations?

An analysis of this company's business showed quite readily what factors and what interactions determined the total profit of the product delivered to the customer.

*Finding Relevant Facts.* Every distribution study has to start with a definition of where the customers are located and what requirements they impose on their suppliers. In this case, some customers requested that products be shipped to them by rail, and others stipulated that they be served by truck. Some buy f.o.b., others at a delivered price. Options, consolidation requirements, or other ingredients of the customer service package are often relevant.

Different companies will have differing requirements for details. In this case, it was important that the data be broken down by sales districts. Therefore, it was determined for 160 sales districts what percentages of sales came into each district by rail and by truck, and percentages were found in each sales district for f.o.b. and delivered prices.

The company then knew where the products were going and how they were going to get there. Next, information was needed that would help determine from which of the five plants and warehouses each sales district should be supplied. This involved an in-depth analysis of the cost of production and warehousing per unit in each of the plants and warehouses for various volume levels.

Figure 5 shows the total plant and warehouse cost for the Indiana installation of this division, for amounts from 0 to 2,100,000 hundredweight. The total plant cost is built up by analyzing the cost for varying production volume of materials, inbound freight, direct labor, and plant overhead. Each of these cost elements will, of course, differ at each plant, even within the same company. Total warehouse costs over this same volume range were similarly analyzed. The same calculations were made for each of the company's five facilities.

Figure 6 shows these total cost curves for all of the plants and warehouses. These costs are, of course, different for each facility at each point on the curve. Not only does each curve start at a different point, reflecting different overhead costs, but the rate of

**Figure 5. Total plant and warehousing cost, Indiana plant**

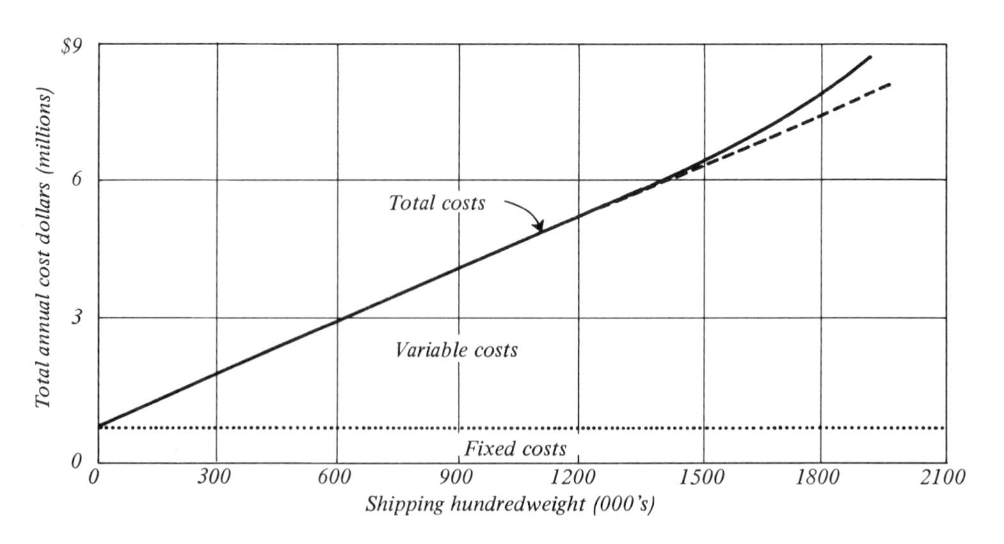

Figure 6. Total plant and warehousing cost, five plants

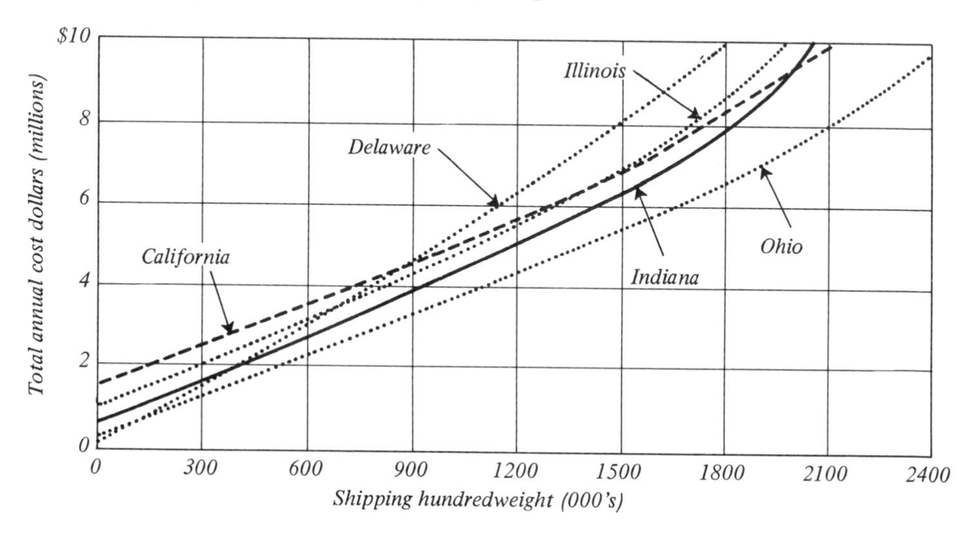


increase is also different, reflecting different variable cost factors at increasing volumes for each installation. These cost differences play an important role in the calculations. It then became necessary to know the cost of shipping from each warehouse to each sales district, by train and by truck. This information is readily available, though gathering it is often a time-consuming chore. Any other factors influencing profitability have to be studied similarly, in relation to each of the other cost factors. In this case, management, as a matter of policy, eliminated from consideration any changes in data processing, customer service, and channels of distribution, so these were held as constants. Under other circumstances these factors might have been evaluated as significant variables. Similarly, in other company situations, other cost factors might have required analysis so that their impact could be introduced into the final decision.

*Manipulating the Data.* At this point, available information showed for each unit of product and for each customer the profit contribution under all possible combinations of production and distribution. The problem that remained was to put all these possibilities together into a single solution that would maximize the company's total earnings.

While this could be done by a series of pencil and paper calculations in which each combination of factors could be worked out and the profitability of each pattern determined, it would represent an enormous and costly chore. That, of course, is the reason why the total cost concept has not found its way into management thinking until recently. To make the process practical requires a computer to process the data. And to introduce this data into the computer calls for a range of mathematical techniques known as nonlinear programing and simulation modeling. The technical aspects of these techniques are not important for their managerial implications. What is significant is that they do exist, that they do work, and that once the computer program has been written, this kind of distribution problem can be solved in a matter of minutes.

Concerning the questions confronting the management of this company, the total cost approach was able to provide a very precise answer to each of them:

1. By rearranging the company's distribution pattern and making appropriate shifts in production and warehousing loads, it was possible without any change in facilities to increase this company's profits by $492,000 a year. The largest ingredient in this change would come from reduced materials cost at $126,000, with warehouse savings contributing $138,000, direct labor saving in the plants adding $57,000, and plant overhead $27,000. Transportation, so often overstressed in distribution decisions, contributed only $54,000 to this total profit improvement package.
2. Additional savings of $180,000 could be effected by shifting equipment from one plant to another at minor cost. To determine this, it was necessary to develop new production cost curves for alternative arrangements of equipment and run these through the computer, comparing them with the most profitable way of using the equipment as presently located.
3. Further savings of $447,000 a year would result if about half of the customers could be persuaded to shift from truck to rail delivery. These reduced costs could be added to earnings or passed on to the customer, thus giving the company a competitively significant price advantage.
4. It was determined that there was no plant addition that would provide an acceptable return on investment. Although building a new plant in Michigan would result in lower production and warehousing costs amounting to $225,000, the return on the investments would be only 2 per cent, and the "other costs" discussed above more than offset any possible gains, so that this investment would not be a wise one.
5. On the other hand, an addition to the capacity of the warehouse at the Delaware plant would add $75,000 a year to profits and represent a sound investment. This was determined by setting up new warehousing cost schedules and running them through the computer alongside the costs under existing conditions. The comparison showed that the investment in the added Delaware warehouse capacity would return almost 25 per cent a year.

The total addition to profits adds up to almost $750,000 a year, from changes in distribution and facilities, that were well within the company's capabilities. These would add 1.7 per cent to this company's margin on sales. The important point is this: these profits could not have been generated by decisions based on the insight or the experience of the most competent line executive. Only the total cost approach could have established, for example, that the earnings of this business could be increased by supplying its customers in the Dakotas from a plant in Ohio rather than from a much nearer facility in Illinois. Yet when total profits were calculated, this turned out to be an element in the most profitable use of the existing facilities of this company.

Similarly, only a total cost calculation could provide the background for estimating the return on investment that could be expected from building a new facility in Michigan. Actually, that new plant would have reduced production and warehousing costs by an appreciable figure. However, other costs would be incurred in serving customers from this facility rather than from the present plant in Illinois; these other costs substantially reduced the potential savings and made the investment an unsound one. This ability to put precise price and profit tags on each pattern of alternatives makes the total cost approach a particularly effective management tool.

## MAKING THE TOTAL COST APPROACH WORK

The successful applications of the total cost approach illustrated by these examples leave no doubt that this approach can, for many companies, uncover profit opportunities previously obscured by established ways of looking at distribution costs and by existing methods of managing distribution functions. But the experience of the successful companies also serves as a warning to those who are tempted to use the term "total cost" lightly. Understanding of many factors is required in order to undertake the kind of analysis required to define what all these costs are and what they really amount to, to develop a way to recover the profits they represent, and then to translate that solution into actual practice.

Though experience shows that the approach works out differently in every practical application, the sequence of steps that management has to take is always the same and it always involves the same inexorable logic:

*To succeed, the total cost approach must have the active endorsement of top management.* The total cost concept can be initiated at any place in the company, but unless it receives strong support from the top, it will not progress successfully, for the simple reason that only top management can insist that the real cost and profit impact of distribution be defined and measured, and at regular intervals. Only top management can see to it that there is a senior executive actively concerned with doing something about this impact of distribution on costs and on profitability. And only top management can assign to this executive the authority necessary to tackle this problem across organizational lines, in order to identify and take advantage of this profit opportunity.

*Only a carefully conceived feasibility study can determine whether or not a restructuring of the distribution system is likely to be profitable.* This thorough kind of study requires a wide range of technical and managerial skills. The team that can do such a study has to include transportation, production, and materials handling specialists, warehousing and logistics experts, as well as analysts with backgrounds in economics, mathematical decision making and operations research.

Some companies have found it appropriate to assemble these skills within the company, while others have preferred to bring the necessary talent in from outside; this is a decision that management must make. But one fact cannot be avoided: this kind of study involves a much wider range of talents than is usually brought to bear on distribution problems, as well as a broad experience in the application of these capabilities to these total cost problems.

*A more substantial and more time-consuming study is then required to determine in detail what changes are indicated, what profits can validly be expected from alternative ways of effecting these changes and what improvement in profits can be anticipated from the most practical solution.*

To succeed in this effort the firm must develop quantitative information on the variables that affect each cost factor and the interrelationships among the various factors. Much of this information may be available in company records, and some of what is not available can usually be derived from existing reports. In most cases, it will be necessary to generate additional data.

Then, all of the significant interrelationships must be traced through the operation, the significant correlations defined and quantified, and all of this data subjected to mathematical analysis.

Next, the appropriate mathematical models must be constructed and then tested against past experience to validate their effectiveness. Then, alternative solutions to present and foreseeable problems have to be developed, and these studied by putting them through the model. This puts dollar values against each alternative and defines the optimum solution–the one that is most practical and most profitable.

Finally, the business implications of this solution need to be checked against organizational requirements, implications for competitive strategy, and ultimately for practicality in terms of timing and return on investment.

*The final stage in the application of the total cost approach is the actual implementation of the solution.* Initially, this involves putting into place the distribution system that matches the company's existing needs and its requirements for the short-term future. Since the business itself and its external environment are both changing inevitably with the passage of time, with changes in product and in marketing policies and practices, as well as in response to changes in competitive forces and stragegies, it is likely to prove profitable to rerun the problem at regular intervals. This process will redefine optimum distribution decisions and adjust plant loads and shipping schedules.

The companies that have been successful in using this approach have found that along with this restructuring of their distribution system, certain additional steps are likely to be critical. The assignment of responsibility for distribution has to be clarified. An information system has to be developed that will provide data on distribution costs and performance to whomever is responsible for controlling these activities. The company's data-gathering and data-processing system must be adapted so that it will pick up routinely the necessary informational input. Procedures must also be established to feed into the information system intelligence concerning conditions in the marketplace, and notably a continuing reassessment of prevailing customer service levels.

Thus the accumulated experience not only confirms the practicality and profitability of the total cost approach, but it also defines some clear-cut guidelines for managements who propose to put this approach to work. Experience in applying this approach suggests, too, that a number of additional considerations need to be clarified.

The fact that this substantial profit opportunity exists in a company is no implicit criticism of its operating management. No traffic manager or transportation specialist can be expected to deal with a problem the roots of which extend far beyond his sphere into manufacturing and marketing. Nor can the best warehouse manager be expected to come up with solutions to problems the causes and conditions of which extend from purchasing and supplier relationships at one extreme, to customer service considerations at the other. Even those companies that have centralized distribution responsibility in the hands of a single high-level executive rarely can provide this executive with the wide range of supporting capabilities and in-depth experience necessary to deal with this profit potential.

Nor does the fact that the necessary action requires top management support mean that the chief executive has to become an expert in the complexities of the mathematical tools involved, any more than he has to become knowledgeable in computer technology or the relative merits of the hardware and software. No one intends to suggest that management has to do or know anything specific or technical about distribution. What is required is management's insistence that something be done, by someone with the appropriate capabilities and experience.

In this sense, the challenge of the total cost approach has another interesting management meaning. The relentless and increasing impact of distribution on profits is one of a growing category of management problems that are not going to be solved satisfactorily within the framework of traditional organizational and decision-making approaches. The most effective solution to any company's distribution problem requires looking at the company as a whole and dealing with the profitability of the entity. More and more, management is being faced with problems requiring this kind of across-the-board attention.

At the same time new concepts, new techniques, and new technology are becoming available that are peculiarly able to cope with this very kind of problem. The more we learn about the computer and about such techniques as simulation, the more apparent it is that they are used to fullest advantage when they are used to deal with problems like these for which no other problem-solving technique is truly appropriate.

There is every reason to believe that with the increasing complexity of modern businesses and the mounting competitive pressures in their environment, the ability of companies to forge ahead and to grow profitably may have a direct relationship to the ability of management to put these new tools and their vast new capabilities to work. In the days ahead, competition between companies may in large measure reflect the skill with which competing managements take advantage of these new management tools.

# 47. NEW REASONING IN CHOOSING A WAREHOUSE LOCATION

*Irvin R. Whiteman*

*Should a company in need of additional warehouse space expand in already crowded quarters or pack up and move to more copious surroundings? Optimum solution of such a problem involves candid appraisal of the present and wise prediction of future needs.*

*That such a decision cannot be made by hunch or crystal ball is apparent. But how should it be made? In this article, the author shows how a Los Angeles distributor assigned values to various warehouse location considerations to work out the expansion problem.*

Problems of outer space make headlines every day; but problems of space on earth constitute the day-to-day challenges.

Consider, for example, the decisions faced by the Milford Company of California, a wholesale liquor distributor which holds exclusives with a number of leading distilleries. Its growth over the years has been a steady one. In 1961 the sales volume was approximately $22,000,000 per year. Having already exhausted any further expansion possibilities at existing facilities in Beverly Hills, management was confronted with the familiar problem of selecting a new site.

Source: From *Journal of Marketing,* vol. 28, January, 1964, pp. 38–43. Irvin R. Whiteman: Director of Operation Research, Computer Concepts, Inc., Los Angeles.

A study covering the selection of warehouse sites in the time period 1965 to 1975 was conducted; both single and multiple warehouse arrangements were considered. As a result of the study, a site was selected and ground broken on a plot of 4.3 acres. The building, completed in July, 1962, covers 71,400 square feet, of which 60,000 is occupied by the warehouse and the remainder by offices. Sufficient land is available to expand the facilities by 50 per cent.

## THE STUDY

The selection of a site, typical of problems of management, is one clouded with uncertainties. In problems of time-phasing, there is real ambiguity in deciding dollar costs. Business is not executed in a single instant of time; it is built up over a number of years and is expected to have a continuous existence in the future.

What are the costs of using facilities which are already in use, and what will be the salvage value in future years of any expenditures made this year? If something new is being procured or developed, no real experience upon which to base cost estimates may exist. It is surprising, in practice, how inaccurate even careful estimates of future costs have proved to be. Careless estimates tend to be "out of this world."

Of the expenses borne by the company, some are applicable to the selection of a warehouse site, whereas others are not. Clearly, wherever the warehouse is located, the internal arrangement and the operation of the warehouse must be conducted efficiently; this is true regardless of location. Also essentially independent of the location is the type of warehouse, provided sufficient acreage is available.

Those costs deemed applicable to the selection of the warehouse site were broken down into the following three primary categories:

1. Distribution costs
2. Real estate costs
3. Processing costs–differential additional data processing costs between a multiwarehouse complex and a single warehouse.

## DISTRIBUTION COSTS

Preliminary investigations showed that of the three primary expenses–(1) distribution, (2) real estate, and (3) processing–those of distribution were major.

Costs such as inventory, internal warehouse operation, and type of warehouse were omitted from consideration, inasmuch as they remain essentially independent of the ultimate warehouse location.

To obtain that warehouse site associated with minimal distribution costs, the cost of distribution associated with a warehouse located in each of the forty-four existing sales districts was determined. A comparison of all possible locations showed that area associated with minimal distribution costs.

For pictorial purposes, topographical maps were prepared for the 1960 and 1970 time periods. These maps (see Figures 1 through 4), consist of a Los Angeles background upon which contour lines of equal distribution cost have been superimposed.

The areas of minimal cost are fairly large and flat, with relatively little change in shape between the two time periods. This indicates that the warehouse location is not dramatically affected by the expected changes of population growth and sales posture in the next decade. The variation of distribution costs in the minimal areas is very slight and, hence, other considerations–such as real estate costs, railroad sidings and zone limitations–prove to be overriding.

*Procedure.* The distribution cost of any given warehouse location was computed as follows:

1. Locations of sales districts were laid out on a large oversized map, geographical centers of each district estimated, and aerial distances between centers determined.

**Figure 1. Distribution costs–1960 single warehouse**

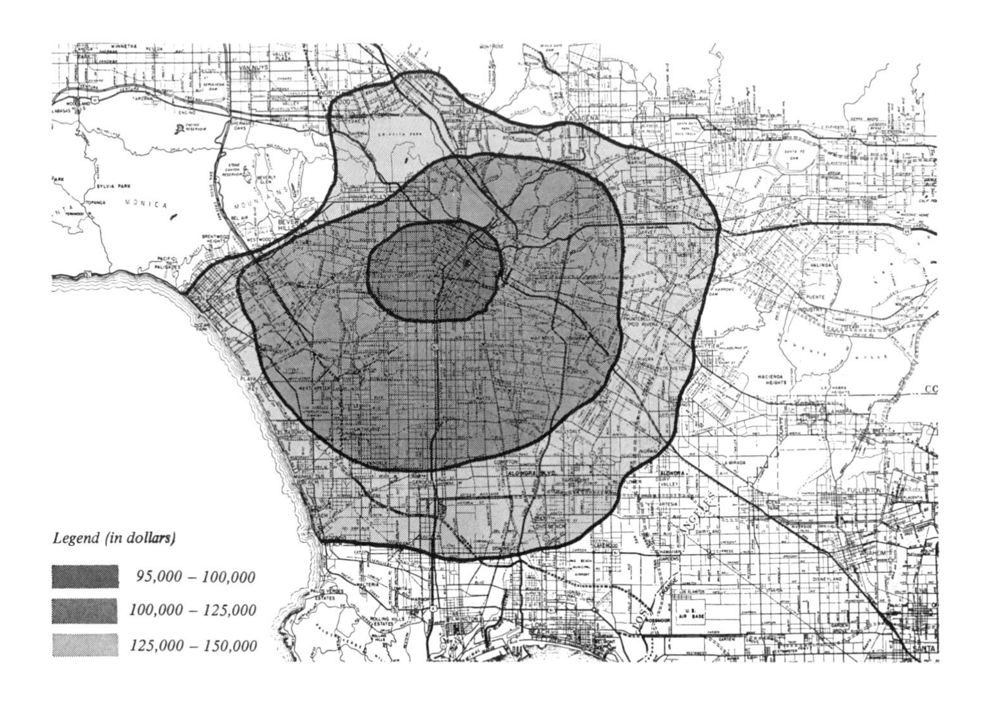

Figure 2. Distribution costs–1970 single warehouse

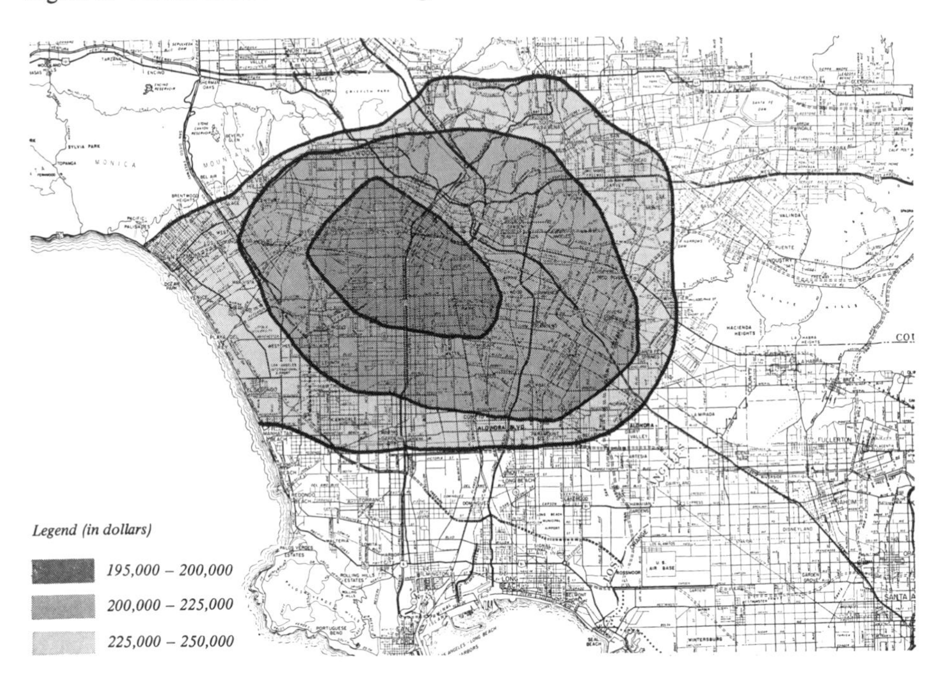


Figure 3. Distribution costs–1960 two-warehouse complex

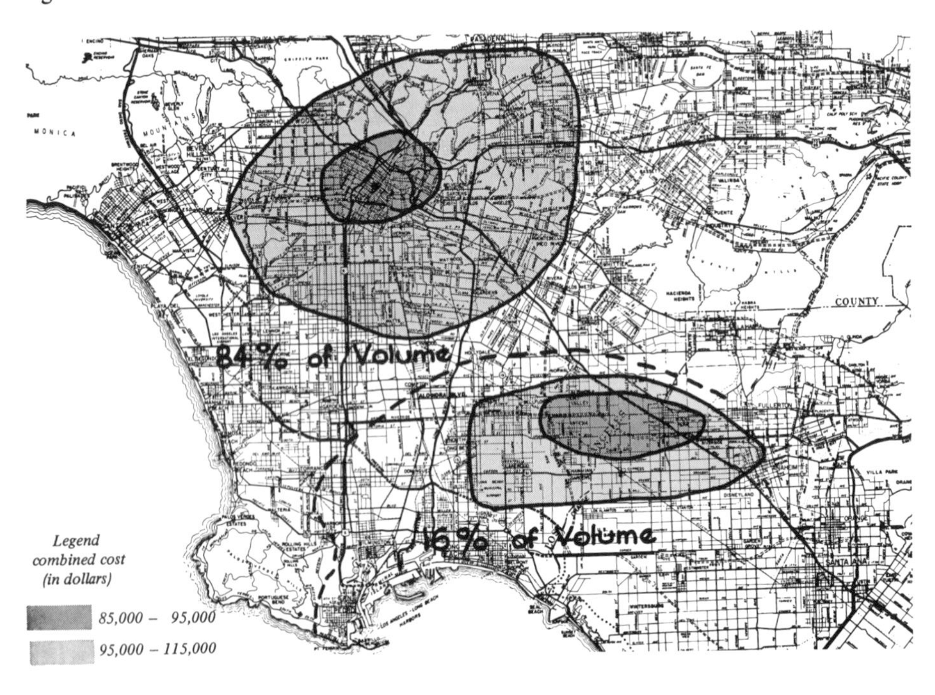

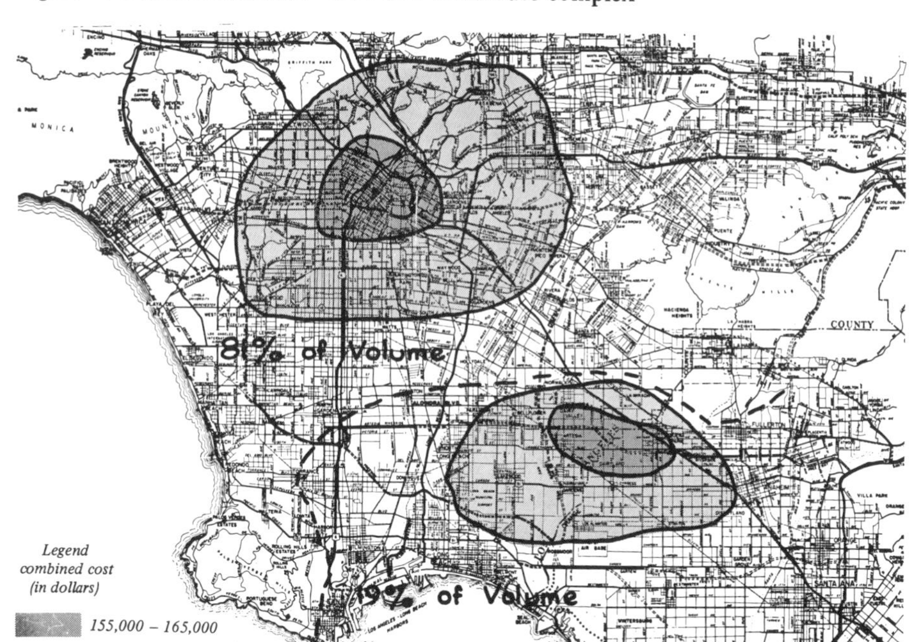


**Figure 4. Distribution costs–1970 two-warehouse complex**

2. Since aerial distances understate ground traveling distances, a sample of ground mileage distance was taken and found to differ from aerial distance by a factor of approximately 0.3. All aerial mileage was converted to ground mileage by multiplying by 1.3. To obtain a round-trip distance, a multiplier of 2 was subsequently used.

3. To obtain the number of truck trips necessary to serve any given sales district, the annual sales total for each district was converted to cases of liquor. Dividing this number by the average truck-load capacity provided the annual number of truck trips necessary to supply the district.

4. The cost of servicing a given district was obtained as the product of the number of trips per year, the length of trip, and the average mileage cost of truck operation.

5. The cost of warehouse operation in any given district is the summation of distribution costs to every other district.

*1970 Estimates.* Essential to the selection of a suitable warehouse site was a prediction of sales for Milford Liquor in the decade ahead, around 1970. The predictions were based upon the premises that sales volume is closely correlated with population and that newly-formed sales districts grow faster than old, well-established districts.

1. Estimates on population growth rates were formulated from Census data for the years 1950 and 1960, complemented by estimates of the Los Angeles City Planning

Commission. Based upon the expected growth rate in each sales district and upon whether the district was new or well established, the district sales volumes for the year 1970 were adjusted by factors of 1.5, 2, or 3. Study of sales growth indicated that these factors were reasonable.

2. Some of the recently created sales districts were adjusted by factors of 2 or 3. With intensified sales effort, it is reasonable to believe that these districts should, on the whole, increase at a greater rate than the older, already well-established districts. Those new districts, located in areas which were expected to experience a high population growth, were given the higher rating.

3. Based upon expected 1970 sales, distribution costs were obtained as before.

## REAL ESTATE COSTS

The figures on transportation costs for the years 1960 and 1970 indicate that the area of minimal distribution cost is large and relatively shallow. Since the differences in distribution costs within this area are slight and not significant in the face of future uncertainties, the specific location was determined by the additional considerations of real estate costs, taxes, railroad sidings, and zoning. That area which best met the requirements of minimal cost was found to be the City of Commerce.

Real estate costs were based upon a lease-back arrangement. That is, Milford would purchase the property, sell it to an interested financial party, and then lease the building from this party. The yearly lease-back price was assumed to be 10 per cent of the original cost of the property. The cost of the warehouse was not included as a consideration, because this cost would remain essentially invariant with respect to location.

## WAREHOUSE CONSIDERATIONS

The cost associated with a two-warehouse policy was examined. Two considerations are of prime importance:

1. the location of the respective warehouses; and
2. the amount of volume each should share.

As to the location of the warehouses, it is possible, in terms of the Milford area sales distribution, to consider the Los Angeles area in terms of an ellipse extending from San Fernando Valley to Orange County. Clearly the two warehouses should be located in the proximity of the major axis.

In examining the actual sales breakdown, the lowest cost was found to be one in which the main warehouse carries approximately 80 per cent of the load, and the second warehouse approximately 20 per cent.

Splitting the Los Angeles environs into two separate areas decreases the sensitivity of warehouse location to transportation costs. Each warehouse has less overall area to cover.

Hence, the specific location of each warehouse is not quite so critical in that the effects of the longest trips have been eliminated. Referring to Figures 3 and 4, it can be seen that the individual contours are very "shallow" and that a great deal of flexibility exists with respect to warehouse location in these areas. Within the proximity of these areas, other overriding features predominate.

## COMPARISON OF A SINGLE WAREHOUSE WITH A TWO-WAREHOUSE COMPLEX

Single warehouse costs were calculated for different locations for the years 1960 and 1970. These costs are shown in Tables 1 and 2.

Comparisons of several selected two-warehouse combinations for the years 1960 and 1970 are shown in Tables 3 and 4.

For both time periods, it is seen that the combination 1–City of Commerce and Buena Park–show a savings of $1,162 and $16,472 respectively annually. As indicated

**Table 1. Distribution and total operating costs–single warehouse–1960**

| *Location* | *Distribution costs* | *Real estate costs* | *Total* |
|---|---|---|---|
| Los Angeles | $ 94,733 | $55,000 | $149,733 |
| *City of Commerce* | *103,659* | *6,250* | *109,909* |
| Vernon | 97,137 | 40,000 | 137,137 |
| South Gate | 103,535 | 20,000 | 123,535 |
| Huntington Park | 96,170 | 32,500 | 128,670 |

**Table 2. Distribution and total operating costs–single warehouse–1970**

| *Location* | *Distribution costs* | *Real estate costs* | *Total* |
|---|---|---|---|
| Los Angeles | $193,760 | $55,000 | $248,760 |
| *City of Commerce* | *200,083* | *6,250* | *206,333* |
| Vernon | 196,452 | 40,000 | 236,452 |
| South Gate | 203,300 | 20,000 | 223,300 |
| Huntington Park | 195,395 | 32,500 | 227,895 |

**Table 3. Distribution and total operating costs–two-warehouse case–1960**

| *Locations of warehouse combination* | *Distribution costs–each warehouse* | *Total distri-bution costs* | *Optimum volume division* | *Real estate costs–each plant* | *Total real estate costs* | *Commu-nication costs* | *Total operat-ing costs* | *Gain over one ware-house in optimum location* |
|---|---|---|---|---|---|---|---|---|
| 1. City of Commerce | $81,411 | $95,897 | 84% | $ 5,000 | $ 9,250 | $3,600 | $108,747 | $ 1,162 |
| Buena Park | 14,486 | | 16% | 4,250 | | | | |
| 2. Los Angeles | 59,834 | 79,113 | 81% | 44,000 | 48,250 | 3,600 | 130,963 | -21,054 |
| Buena Park | 19,230 | | 19% | 4,250 | | | | |
| 3. Vernon | 63,659 | 84,599 | 80% | 24,000 | 28,250 | 3,600 | 116,449 | -6,540 |
| Buena Park | 20,940 | | 20% | 4,250 | | | | |

**Table 4. Distribution and total operating costs–two-warehouse case–1970**

| *Locations of warehouse combination* | *Distribution costs–each warehouse* | *Total distri-bution costs* | *Optimum volume division* | *Real estate costs–each plant* | *Total real estate costs* | *Commu-nication costs* | *Total operat-ing costs* | *Gain over one ware-house in optimum location* |
|---|---|---|---|---|---|---|---|---|
| 1. City of Commerse | $133,918 | $175,611 | 81% | $ 5,000 | $ 9,250 | $5,000 | $189,861 | $16,472 |
| Buena Park | 41,693 | | 19% | 4,250 | | | | |
| 2. Los Angeles | 106,238 | 153,496 | 75% | 44,000 | 48,250 | 5,000 | 206,746 | -413 |
| Buena Park | 47,258 | | 25% | 4,250 | | | | |
| 3. Vernon | 117,075 | 160,924 | 77% | 24,000 | 28,250 | 5,000 | 194,174 | 12,159 |
| Buena Park | 43,849 | | 23% | 4,250 | | | | |

previously, a great deal of latitude exists in the actual combinations of locations chosen with respect to distribution costs; hence, the combinations chosen reflect realistic considerations.

Based upon the optimum volume distribution, real estate acreage was apportioned between the two warehouse locations. In the single-warehouse case, real estate costs were based upon a lot size of five acres. In the two-warehouse case, it was felt that an apportionment of 20 per cent to 80 per cent (1 to 4 acres) was not entirely realistic because, even though the warehouse might be proportionately reduced, the surrounding land requirements would not.

As a basis for real estate costs, a minimum of 2.5 acres was chosen for the smaller warehouse, and the figure of 4 acres for the larger. The assessment of these costs is shown in the columns of the tabular breakdown. One item of interest is the column entitled "Communication Costs." Clearly there is a major difference between the single warehouse and the two-warehouse complex in the processing of invoices.

Two possible situations exist. First, each of the two different warehouses may function as autonomous units. Second, one warehouse may act as the "master" warehouse, in which all administrative functions are performed, and the other as a "satellite."

Each of these possibilities poses some cost penalty. In the case of two separate independent units, those savings which accrue by being able to warrant a large single central processing unit are lost. In the second case, in which the master warehouse processes all invoices and transmits this information to the satellite warehouse via some data link, there is the additional cost of communication.

However, the master-satellite combination appeared to be less costly—approximately $300 per month. This cost was taken to be additive to the cost of the two-warehouse operation.

Again, even with this additional cost, the savings intrinsic in the lowering of distribution costs result in an overall lower total operating cost; that is, the cost of operating two warehouses is less than the cost of operating one warehouse.

It is difficult to tell whether these savings are real, in that they are based on predictions of business and community growth in the next ten years. Regardless of whether a single-warehouse or a two-warehouse policy is chosen, however, the location of the main warehouse should be near the "centroid" of the Los Angeles area, that is, the City of Commerce.

As shown in the two-warehouse case, a fair amount of flexibility exists with respect to the actual locations; no penalty is associated with keeping the main warehouse in the City of Commerce. This is based upon the knowledge that if a warehouse is to be self-sustaining, it should be located in the heart of the area it serves.

## ACTION TAKEN

Since the location of the main warehouse is essentially independent of whether it is the sole warehouse or a master warehouse supporting a satellite, a step-by-step expansion was advocated. It was recommended that a single warehouse be established in the environs of the City of Commerce, and that within the next five years or so a decision based upon sales figures of that date be made as to the establishment of a warehouse in the heart of the new area.

# 48. MODERN METHODS FOR LOCAL DELIVERY ROUTE DESIGN

*Richard B. Maffei*

*Improving the design of routes and thereby reducing delivery costs is a major marketing problem.*

*Here is a practical case study in which hundreds of trucks and thousands of customers were involved, and with interesting results.*

A vice-president of a large milk company, recognizing that local delivery operations accounted for a large part of his budget, raised several questions:

- Are we making the most effective use of our wholesale delivery trucks?
- Are our routes laid out in the best possible way?
- Is there any way to estimate what our budget would be if we added accounts, dropped accounts, increased our volume, decreased our volume, and so on?
- Is there any way to estimate the irregularity of day-to-day loads on individual routes?
- Can we devise ways to make it easy to redesign routes so that our good route men can always work to their maximum capacity and earn additional money?

These questions might well have been asked by any number of managers in different fields. The milk-delivery problem is not unlike the problem of delivering bread, or soft drinks, or beer, or cookies and crackers, or gasoline, or fuel oil, or packages, or

Source: From *Journal of Marketing,* vol. 29, July, 1965, pp. 13–18. Richard B. Maffei: Independent industrial consultant, Boston.

mail. Each industry has special problems that must be dealt with in special ways, but the fundamental fact is that logical procedures are the same.

Several dominant similarities exist:

- Trucks are loaded either at a plant or an outlying station.
- The routeman drives to some initial point on his route.
- From this point he visits other customers on his route, perhaps making both regular stops and callbacks as the situation warrants.
- During the course of the day he may stop for breakfast or lunch.
- When he makes his last stop and delivers his goods he returns to the point from which he started.
- Finally he goes to some central place, deposits money, puts his notes and books in order, places orders, and prepares his delivery plan for the next working day.

There are, of course, many variations. For example, in the gasoline delivery field a truck may load up two or three times at the distribution station during any one shift. In the bread business the pickup of stale products may complicate the problem of estimating customer time. Biscuit company salesmen may be on a weekly or biweekly cycle rather than on a day-to-day delivery pattern. Companies such as Railway Express and United Parcel pick up and deliver at different points. Such characteristics are endless in their specific qualities, but all are representable in some logical format.

## REPRESENTING THE DELIVERY SYSTEM

By looking down from an airplane onto a densely populated metropolitan area, one can imagine stores distributed along main arteries and clustered into blocks. At a low enough altitude one can see trucks moving along streets, halting at stop lights and in front of stores or customer points. A schematic version of routes is shown in Figure 1.

Early in the morning a truck leaves P, the plant point.

Loaded with its daily quota of milk and milk products, it heads toward the first customer on the route. When the truck arrives, the routeman goes through a typical work sequence, returns to the truck, and heads toward his second stop. He continues in this way until he delivers to all customers on the route who want delivery on that day. He finally returns to the plant to plan for the next day's work.

With this pattern of work as a base, it is possible to evolve requirements for developing a simulation, or model, of activities for the total operational procedure.

1. Define the route by one of two methods:
   - Enclose the area by a set of straight lines and define them by two vertices each (that is, a starting and ending point).
   - Specify a "line" route which means nothing more than a collection of customers. One might think of this as a route serving only very large customers.

Figure 1. Diagram of routes in a delivery area

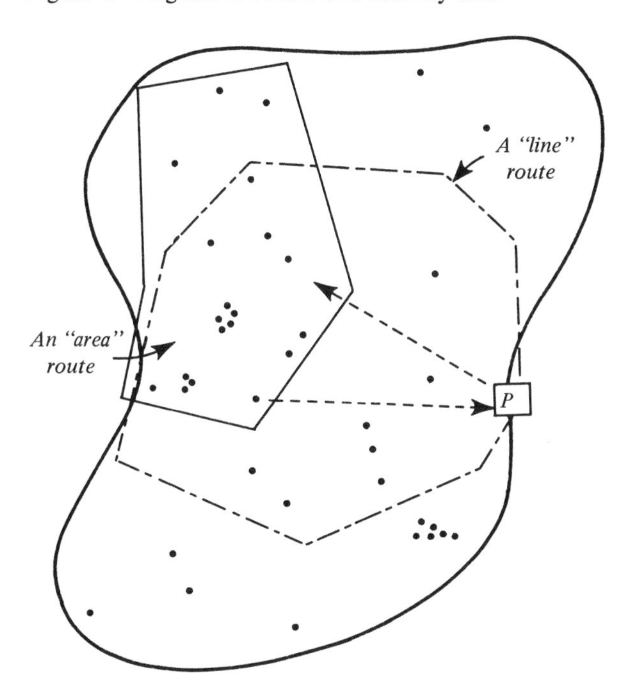


2. Represent customers as points on a gridded map.
3. Develop ways to measure the time spent at each customer point.
4. Develop ways to estimate the distance and time spent to, from, and on the route.
5. Develop a reporting system that will bring together all the essential information for review by the management decision-maker.

## A SIMPLE ILLUSTRATION

Doing all of these things might or might not require the facilities of a computer. Actually, a spectrum of methods has been developed ranging from simple mapping to complete computerization for multiple routes. A description of the complete logic of these methods can be shown by a simple illustration.

In Figure 2, four customer points have been plotted. The task for the routeman is to leave from plant P, enter into his route, service all four customers, and return to plant P.

Under certain conditions, total servicing time (that is, time spent in such activities as bringing goods from truck into store, getting paid, or taking orders) does *not* depend

Figure 2. A simple route

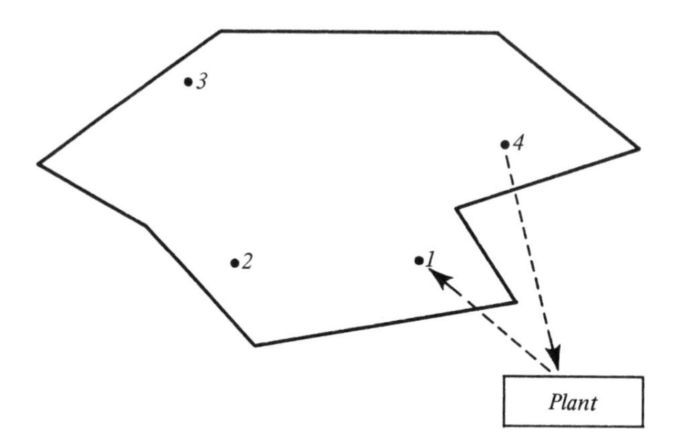


upon the order in which the customers are visited. For purposes of this illustration it can be assumed that total service time is 200 minutes.

There are many paths by which the customers can be visited. To facilitate this search, a travel-time table (see Table 1) has been constructed. Thus, to go from plant P to customer 1 takes 34 minutes; from customer 1 to 2, 17 minutes; and so on. To traverse the route in the following way: P 1 2 3 4 P, which also can be written (P, 1, 2, 3, 4, P) would take 34 + 17 + 26 + 31 + 48 = 156 minutes.

With the addition of the 200 minutes for servicing customers, and an assumed 45 minutes for plant work and allowances, a total of 401 minutes results.

Table 2 includes information about some of the other paths by which the customers can be visited. There are 24 possibilities for these four customers. The times to traverse the route, starting and ending at the plant P, range from a low of 156 minutes to a high of 205 minutes. It appears, therefore, in this example that a poor sequence of visits could result in 50 minutes more time than is necessary.

This illustration was designed to point out the manner in which it is possible to find out how "best" to find the proper sequence. Theoretically, one can always search and

Table 1. Travel-time table (minutes) for Figure 2

| | | | *To* | | |
|---|---|---|---|---|---|
| *From* | *1* | *2* | *3* | *4* | *P* |
| 1 | 0 | 17 | 34 | 23 | 34 |
| 2 | 17 | 0 | 26 | 34 | 47 |
| 3 | 34 | 26 | 0 | 31 | 67 |
| 4 | 23 | 34 | 31 | 0 | 48 |
| P | 34 | 47 | 67 | 48 | 0 |

**Table 2. Selected visiting patterns and total estimated time (minutes) for Figure 2**

| *Visiting pattern sequence* | *Time to, from, on route* | *Time serving* | *Plant time* | *Total time* |
|---|---|---|---|---|
| P, 1, 2, 3, 4, P | 156 | 200 | 45 | 401 |
| P, 2, 3, 4, 1, P | 161 | 200 | 45 | 406 |
| P, 3, 2, 1, 4, P | 181 | 200 | 45 | 426 |
| P, 4, 3, 2, 1, P | 156 | 200 | 45 | 445 |
| P, 4, 2, 1, 3, P | 200 | 200 | 45 | 450 |
| P, 2, 4, 1, 3, P | 205 | 200 | 45 | 450 |
| P, 1, 4, 2, 3, P | 184 | 200 | 45 | 429 |

evaluate all possibilities; but clearly this approach becomes impractical as the number of customers increases.

The problem of route reblocking can now be formulated. In the case of the milk company previously mentioned, management wanted to know how much time would be spent servicing any arbitrary collection of customers, either within certain route boundaries, or "strung out" in any sort of a line. That is, they wanted to have the capability to redesign routes almost at will.

For example, if the routes in Figure 1 were changed arbitrarily from one grouping or shape to another, would total time servicing all routes increase, stay the same, or decrease? Simulations to answer this question can be designed.

## THE SPECTRUM OF ANALYTIC METHODS

It would serve no useful purpose to describe in detail all the various manual and computer techniques developed to handle this complex problem for the milk company. A brief description of each major method will suffice.

*First Method.* A potent mapping routine was written. Base maps for the appropriate metropolitan areas, obtained from the United States Department of the Interior, were mounted with a permanent plastic face. All maps were gridded first into 150 ft. × 150 ft. squares. All customers were located with reference to these base maps and were assigned a 10-digit code that uniquely located a customer point within one of the squares.

Detailed customer information was maintained on punched cards. Relevant information included location data, class of trade, average weekly volume, daily delivery pattern requirements, dollar sales, and special characteristics. With this information and special mapping routines it was possible to generate overlay maps. For example, it was possible to plot location of big customers, of dollar volume, of Tuesday customers, and so on.

With the use of accurately scaled overlay maps with base maps, excellent visual ideas about required routing were obtained, lending an invaluable assist to the dispatcher. See Figure 3.

*Second Method.* The mapping routine could not generate summarized data for an individual route or a collection of routes. For this reason a second set of procedures was developed.

A dispatcher utilizing these procedures had available initially a set of preprocessed cards showing daily estimated customer service time. Preparation of these cards was based on special automatic forecasting methods. The dispatcher took the cards directly to a sorter and sorted out those that he wanted one routeman to service "tomorrow." He took these cards to a specially wired IBM 407 Printer, fed them through, and received a report that gave him (1) estimated time on the road; (2) estimated time servicing customers; (3) plant and allowance time; and (4) total. See Table 3.

If the dispatcher found that he had overscheduled a driver (for example, total time exceeded 8 hours), he could eliminate a few customer cards and try again; if he had

**Figure 3. A base map showing the number of customers and locations**

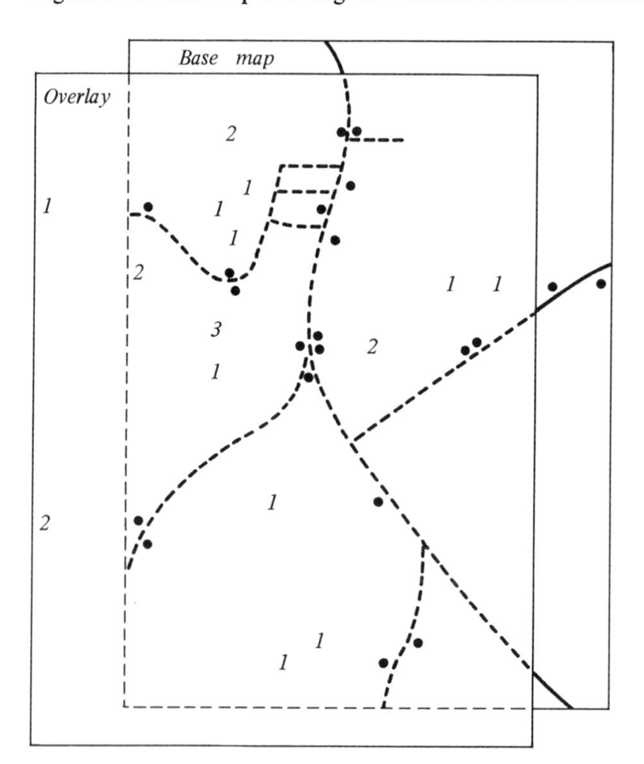

**Table 3. Volume and time analysis of one route**

| Route No. 123 | Distance from previous customer | Daily volume (case equivalents) M | Tu | W | Th | F | S | Time (minutes) M | Tu | W | Th | F | S | Total hours |
|---|---|---|---|---|---|---|---|---|---|---|---|---|---|---|
| Howard Johnson | - | 17 | 18 | 20 | 22 | 25 | 28 | 18 | 18 | 19 | 19 | 19 | 17 | |
| AAA Bakery | 3.2 | 2 | 2 | 4 | 3 | 4 | 5 | 6 | 6 | 7 | 7 | 7 | 7 | |
| Hartwell Farms | 5.1 | 5 | 7 | 4 | 3 | 9 | 6 | 6 | 6 | 5 | 4 | 7 | 6 | |
| Concord Dairy | 4.2 | 1 | 1 | 2 | 4 | 7 | 6 | 3 | 3 | 3 | 4 | 5 | 4 | |
| Radio | 1.6 | 1 | | | | | | | | | | | | |
| (and so forth) | | | | | | | | | | | | | | |

underscheduled, he could add cards. In this way he got an idea of his load requirements for days or even weeks ahead, depending on the accuracy of the forecasted demand. In other words, the dispatcher had within his control the ability to analyze route characteristics intelligently and quickly.

*Third Method.* A third method was an extension of the second and was designed to seek out a near optimal visiting sequence. In the hypothetical illustration previously given, the total time to service four customers on a route could vary from a low, or optimal, of 401 minutes to a high of 450 minutes.

In the previous set of formal procedures or "mode," as they are usually referred to in computer application language, the dispatcher decided upon the order to visit customers on the basis of judgment and experience, and obtained his estimates.

For the present mode being discussed, the computer was programed to seek out a near-optimal solution. No simple and efficient mathematical solution to the so-called "traveling-salesmen problem" was then or is yet available. Two or three fairly good methods were found. Results with one of these, that was both simple to conceive and easy to program, seemed satisfactory.

In this mode the dispatcher could have done one of two things:

1. He could have fed the computer a set of cards representing customers that he said were all in the route.
2. He could have fed the computer a set of customer cards and a set of route vertex cards (a route being defined as the area enclosed by a set of straight lines with vertex end points).

In the first case the computer searched until it found a near-optimal sequence, and then it printed a report. In the second case the computer first found out which customers were within the boundaries of the route. Then it obtained the near-optimal sequence and printed a report. In these submodes one route was dealt with at a time.

Finally, there was a mode which was not fully programed in which multiple routes were dealt with simultaneously. The reports that were to have been printed gave detailed information of many routes combined and each route separately. This mode was not programed automatically to revise route boundaries. Revisions of routes were to have been accomplished outside the structure of the formal program by persons familiar with the problems of routing. The formal analysis by computer methods would have provided managers with the ability to search for good solutions rapidly.

## BACKGROUND STUDIES

An idea of the preparation and effort involved in setting up these systems can be had by noting some of the data requirements.

All customers had to be located on the base map grid system. This was not a time-consuming task. A few clerk-months of time were invested and the job was handled most efficiently. Four thousand customer points were involved.

Analyses of time to service customers by size of delivery had to be made. This part of the problem was facilitated by the fact that excellent time study data on travel operations were available. It was necessary to process the data by use of statistical techniques and computers. After much refinement of data, equations of the form

$$T = A + BV + CV^2 + DV^3$$

were derived for 12 different customer classifications.

Here T stands for total customer time, and V stands for delivery volume on the given day. In all cases within the range of the real data, average total costs per unit decreased as volume delivery increased; costs at the same level of volume varied among customer classes. These derived functional relations were based on many thousands of time-study observations. See Figure 4.

**Figure 4. A typical time-to-deliver and volume-delivered curve**

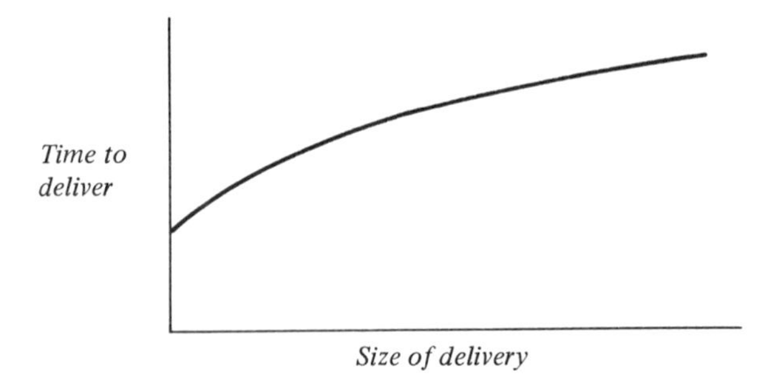

Customer-delivery patterns had to be developed for each customer in the system. For example, some wanted daily delivery, some wanted every-other-day delivery, and so on.

In this simulation there was no need to assume that a customer should have had deliveries made in a specified way. For example, if one wanted to see what would have happened if small customers who were currently receiving delivery every day went on to a three-day cycle, it would have been exceedingly easy to study the economic importance of such a projected change. The economics of actual and assumed patterns were studied in the same manner.

All customer data were developed from field visits and records; all customers were studied. The results of these studies were useful beyond the scope of the simulation, in that changes in the basic design of the customer data accounting system were brought about.

## QUESTIONS AND ANSWERS

Management found that many studies of interest could be undertaken with the analytic methods devised. They felt that reblocking should be done route by route, and therefore emphasized the uses of the program modes that had to do with single routes, rather than with total system redesign.

Quantitative studies involving some of the major routes in the system brought out interesting facts. It should be remembered that the following discussion involves wholesale milk routes in which the ratio of traveling time to service time ranged from 1 : 5 to 1 : 6. For situations in which travel time is a more substantial proportion of total time, many conclusions would be quite different.

On the average, good use was being made of wholesale route trucks. However, there were strong indications that day-to-day use varied widely. Light use of trucks was made early in the week; heavy use, later in the week. This pattern was generated by consumer purchase habits and store delivery requirements. If either or both could have been changed, better use could have been made of equipment.

Route layouts might have been improved in some cases, but greater gains seemed realizable by better sequencing of customer visits.

The simulations seemed to have their greatest potential use in the study of how estimated costs and profits–changed under various *assumed* route conditions. For example, it was possible to estimate how many delivery hours could have been saved if the small customers were required to go to a less frequent delivery schedule. Small customers were dropped from routes where there was clear evidence of an actual loss connected with delivery to them. Hosts of "what if" questions were answerable using the developed customer data and the simulations.

Day-to-day patterns of delivery-time requirements were irregular (that is, low at start of week; high at end of week) in almost every case that was analyzed. Furthermore, evidence in almost all the dozen or so classes of trade studied showed that this pattern persisted. Two notable examples of rather regular patterns were schools and hospitals. This meant that route specialization by class of trade would not help to eliminate the pattern that results in a very uneven work load.

One of the more important results stemmed from the fact that rapid redesign of routes was possible when accurate data were combined with the simulation. In fact, it was possible to think in terms of redesign on a weekly or biweekly period.

This posed major policy problems for management. Did they have sufficient control over the size of their work force to change it as required? Could labor be absorbed into other jobs when demand was down and released from these jobs onto trucks when demand was up? Could and should customer delivery patterns be modified to suit the best interests of the milk company? Could loads be balanced? Should a man be allowed to take on as much work as he was able and thereby create wide discrepancies in take-home pay between the normal and the highly productive routeman? What should the characteristics of an incentive plan be?

It was the considered opinion of the consultants involved that there would be no real difficulty in the development of simulators that could be used as devices to create daily dispatching plans. The major technical problem was one of designing good data systems rather than good simulators. The minimum number of trucks on the road each day that would simultaneously guarantee good customer service and maximum wages for those workers who work constantly could be determined. One problem was how to provide for those workers who were needed in peak periods and not needed as drivers in other periods. Perhaps the policy answer is simple. It does not appear so.

This hard fact remains: it is possible to design a low-cost delivery system. Implementation depends upon factors involving labor-management-customer relationships.

*G. Selling*

# 49. SALES AS A PART OF MARKETING

*Hector Lazo and Arnold Corbin*

*The marketing concept has greatly affected the organization of the marketing department. One of the most important changes has to do with the personal selling function.*

*This excerpt deals with the changing responsibilities of sales managers and the impact of these changes on the organization of the sales function.*

## THE "NEW" AND THE "OLD" SALES DEPARTMENTS

In the early stages of development of the marketing management concept, sales managers expressed much fear that, in effect, the sales department was being abolished or greatly reduced in importance. But experience has proved the contention of some of the advance advocates of the concept that, although changed, the sales manager's position actually was being broadened and enhanced.

Under the "old" concept, the sales manager was primarily responsible for "getting the orders." His was the job of day-to-day selling, of hiring and training salesmen to sell; order-getting was his job, his life, and his responsibility.

Under the "new" marketing management concept, the sales manager is still responsible for these activities, *but in addition,* he has the responsibility of transmitting to, and imbuing the men on the selling front with, the new company and management

Source: From *Management in Marketing: Text and Cases,* New York: McGraw-Hill Book Company, copyright © 1961, pp. 231–240. Used by permission of McGraw-Hill Book Company. Hector Lazo: Chairman, Marketing Area, and Professor of Marketing, Graduate School of Business Administration, New York University. Arnold Corbin: Professor of Marketing, Graduate School of Business Administration, New York University.

philosophy and thinking. Salesmen today must be profit- as well as volume-conscious. They must know—and it is the job of the sales manager to see that they do know—how the sales function fits into the total marketing operation and the contribution that it makes to the health and welfare of the entire company.

To be sure, day-to-day supervision is still important and must go on. But there is far more to modern selling under the marketing concept than just "getting the orders." Hence the new sales manager needs to develop much more accurate methods of appraisal of sales performance, based on territorial and manpower potentials. This means that the new sales manager must give as much attention to marketing research, territorial analysis, manpower analysis, motivation, and communication, as he does to day-to-day management of the field activities of the sales force. He can no longer direct its selling effort on a solo basis; he must know what the advertising and sales promotion managers are planning so that he can inform his own men of these plans and programs and thereby ensure a unified, integrated total marketing effort based upon close coordination with other members of the marketing team.

Further, the new sales manager needs to develop both a new philosophy of training based upon the total marketing concept and the training procedures to implement it. Fortunately, the new sales manager has access to many new training methods and techniques to accomplish this objective; these he must use effectively if he is to get the most out of his manpower. For example, he might employ some of the newer developments in improving meetings with his salesmen. Emphasis is not only on audience participation but on the development of audience selling techniques by actual demonstration and participation in the meeting. This, in effect, uses the principle of learning by doing, but it is done under the supervision of the sales executive so that weaknesses and strengths can be pointed out immediately.

Another technique makes use of some of the more recently introduced principles of personnel development and improvement. Personal counseling and guidance, the techniques of "listening" advocated in the development of proper communications, and the newer methods of evaluation through the encouragement of self-appraisal, these are all techniques borrowed from modern personnel administration and management. The new sales manager makes use of these principles, devoting considerable time to planning and preparation for such conferences with his men.

Perhaps the most important change in the scope and nature of the sales manager's job under marketing management is that he must become a *planner,* a strategy developer, as well as an operator. He therefore needs to know a lot more about marketing research and its uses in helping to produce better and more effective sales efforts. He needs to know a lot more about motivation and the uses of the social sciences in developing effective marketing programs. The new sales manager will participate as a staff planner with the other staff assistants of the marketing director in the development of marketing objectives, policies, and plans. He will therefore develop into a combination of both staff and line operator; his specialized knowledge of selling and the field requirements of the market will give him a larger voice in the counsels of the company with respect to both long- and short-range planning. In the execution of these plans, once approved, he will still be the primary directing force. He will now, perhaps for the first time, have an adequate team of cooperators to back his effort, since virtually all will have had a hand in formulating the program and a vested interest in its successful execution.[1]

## CHANGES IN THE ORGANIZATION OF THE SALES FUNCTION

As might be expected, these changes will be reflected to some extent in the organizational setup of the sales function.

Traditionally, most companies have adopted one or some combination of four basic types of sales department organization at headquarters: the *functional,* the *product,* the *regional,* and the *market* (or *customer*).

*The Functional Type of Organization.* Under the functional type, the functions which assisted sales were organized as a kind of general staff, came under the jurisdiction of sales, and hence were responsible to sales (see Figure 1). But under the marketing management concept, several of these departments are now raised to an equal level with sales. Before the adoption of the concept, the internal conflicts that often resulted from such a diverse functional grouping under the sales manager often resulted in rather loose organization and failure to achieve effective integration. Thus, although the partnership of sales and advertising was generally recognized, advertising, in effect, often operated independently of sales, and this led to much confusion, overlapping, and lack of coordination of effort. Similarly, although sales promotion was considered a natural partner of sales, considerable friction developed in some organizations between the order getter and the "idea man" who developed sales promotion material. Functionally, sales promotion may have been responsible to sales, but actually it often worked at cross-purposes.

With the full-scale adoption of the marketing management concept, this functional type of sales headquarters organization would seem to be on the way out. The organization of the marketing department into two well-recognized areas of services and operations . . . obviates the necessity for a functional type of organization.

*The Product Type of Organization.* Some modifications may also be expected in the product setup (see Figure 2). Typically here, the director of sales or general sales manager had a sales manager for product A, a sales manager for product B, etc. Under these product sales managers there generally developed staffs of varying size, depending upon the importance of the division (and the aggressiveness of the product sales manager), which formed a kind of planning "wall" between the sales manager and the

[1] For a thoughtful analysis of how the marketing concept *should* affect sales management and the field sales force, as well as what the modern sales department *should* contribute to its company's success, see Eugene J. Kelley and William Lazer, "Basic Duties of the Modern Sales Department," *Industrial Marketing,* April, 1960, p. 68 ff.

**Figure 1. Functional-type organization (rubber products manufacturer)**

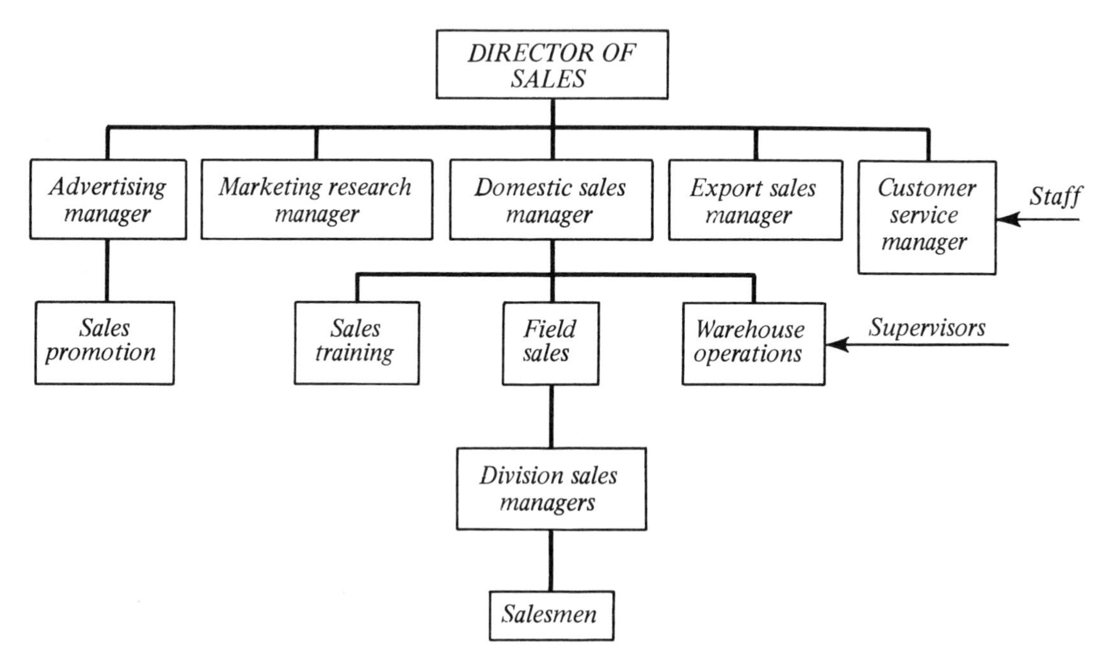


*Source: From* Charting the Company Organization Structure, *Studies in Personnel Policy 168, National Industrial Conference Board, Inc., New York, 1959; and American Management Association Marketing Course, New York, 1958.*

field sales force. The development of two new types of marketing executives, the product manager and the pooled or central staff assistant to the marketing director, would seem to obviate the need for such staffs for product sales managers in the future.

It is to be noted that the position of product manager is not clear in business today. In some companies, such a product manager is in fact the sales manager; in others, the product sales manager; in still others, he would be more correctly described as the product general manager or commodity manager. But in most cases he is a staff officer, although his exact position in the organization is not fixed: he may be at the corporate level, he may be a staff assistant to the director of marketing, and in some cases, staff to the sales manager. He is a fairly recent addition to most company staffs and a natural by-product of the ever-increasing diversification of the product mix. The growth of product technology, the growing use of marketing research as a tool for marketing, and the increased reliance of successful business on long-term planning have also contributed to the development of the specific type of staff coordinator known as the "product manager."

In some larger companies where the product manager in effect becomes the general manager of a product division, he basically is a line executive and is held responsible

**Figure 2. Product-type organization (office machines manufacturer)**

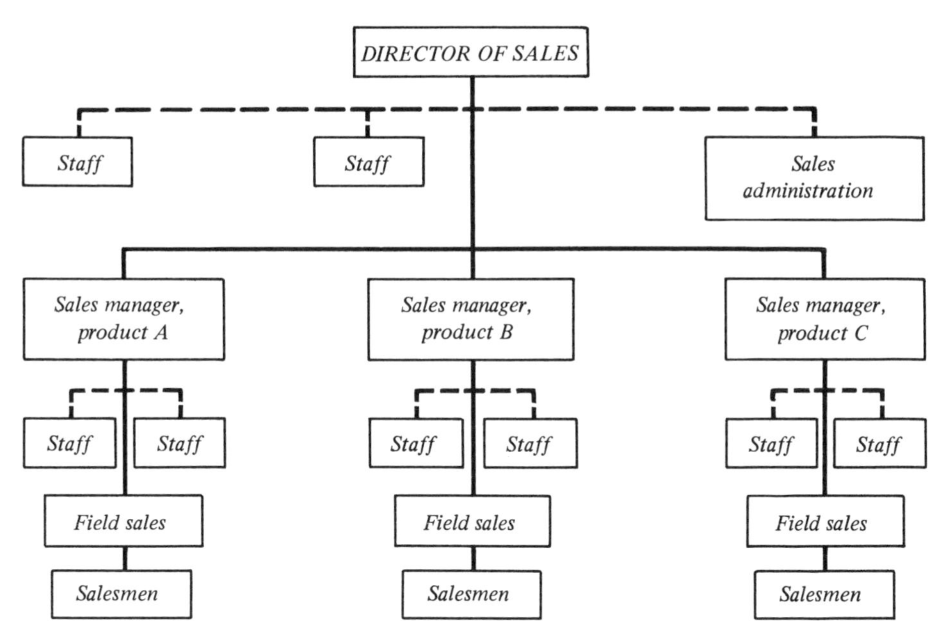


*Source: From* Charting the Company Organization Structure, *Studies in Personnel Policy 168, National Industrial Conference Board, Inc., New York, 1959; and American Management Association Marketing Course, New York, 1958.*

for the profitable operation of his division and the coordination of its activities. In other companies, he may be the long-range planner, making forecasts, recommending pricing policies, investigating potentials, and formulating marketing policies for the consideration of the director of marketing. His chief contribution lies in the realm of ideas, although it is requisite that he should have sales ability and sales sense. Experience in sales, familiarity with research, preferably also with production and technology, seem to be the ideal background for such a staff official. But his position, as a *staff* man removes him from the field of operations to a large extent. The position of product sales manager is therefore likely to undergo substantial change as more and more companies adopt the marketing concept.

Similarly, the development of the pooled, or central, service idea under the director of marketing will undoubtedly modify the product sales manager's position. Some organizations provide for pooled staff services for all operating divisions. This would free the product sales manager of responsibility for planning, policy development, research, and similar duties and convert him almost entirely into an operating sales manager specializing on one product or a group of products. In certain types of organizations, this indeed seems the likely development, in spite of the current emphasis in other firms on the staff nature of the product manager's duties.

*The Regional and Market Types of Organization.* The two other fundamental types of organization of the sales function are the regional—where selling operations are organized geographically by regions or areas (see Figure 3)—and the market type—where the organizational units correspond to the different kinds of customers who buy the product of the particular company (see Figure 4).

Thus, for example, the Sunshine Biscuit Company of New York, with a vice-president for sales located in New York City, has eleven "areas," roughly corresponding to territories served by different bakeries. Even where some of the bakeries, as such, have been discontinued, the regional sales setup has been maintained, and the sales division is called by the name of the existing or former bakery city. Specifically, the New England sales division is known as "Newton Highlands," although, in this instance, it is so named less because of the former bakery, which was closed some years ago, than because of the present large warehouse from which the sales force operates, and which serves as headquarters for the New England operations of the company. The Kansas City "area," however, is the one served primarily by the Kansas City bakery. In any event, convenience of serving the area in question is a major consideration in the sales organization of this company.

**Figure 3. Regional-type organization (large food manufacturer)**

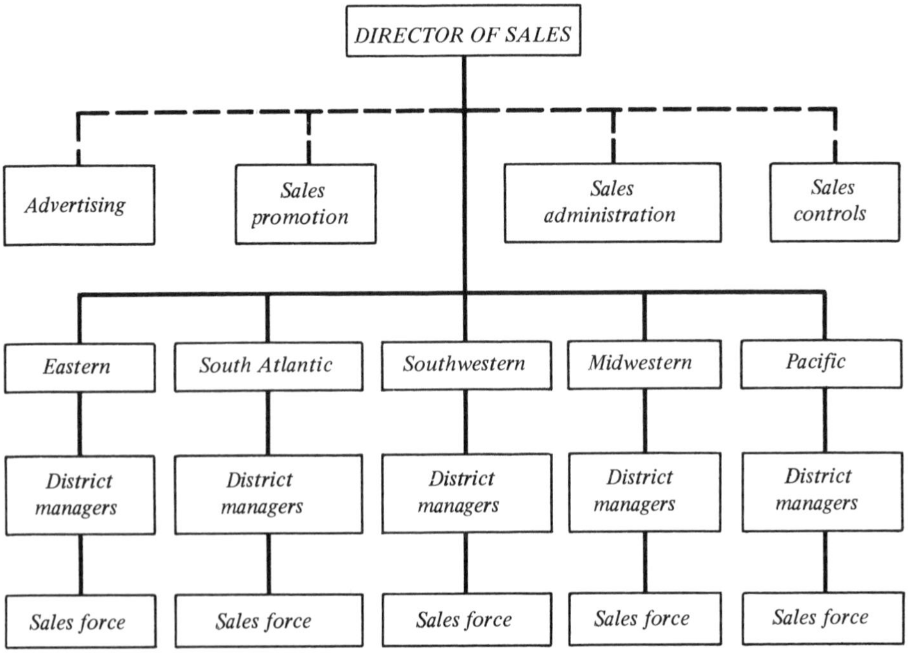

*DIRECTOR OF SALES*

*Advertising* | *Sales promotion* | *Sales administration* | *Sales controls*

*Eastern* | *South Atlantic* | *Southwestern* | *Midwestern* | *Pacific*

*District managers* | *District managers* | *District managers* | *District managers* | *District managers*

*Sales force* | *Sales force* | *Sales force* | *Sales force* | *Sales force*

*Source: From* Charting the Company Organization Structure, *Studies in Personnel Policy 168, National Industrial Conference Board, Inc., New York, 1959; and American Management Association Marketing Course. New York, 1958.*

**Figure 4. Market-type organization (packaging machinery manufacturer)**

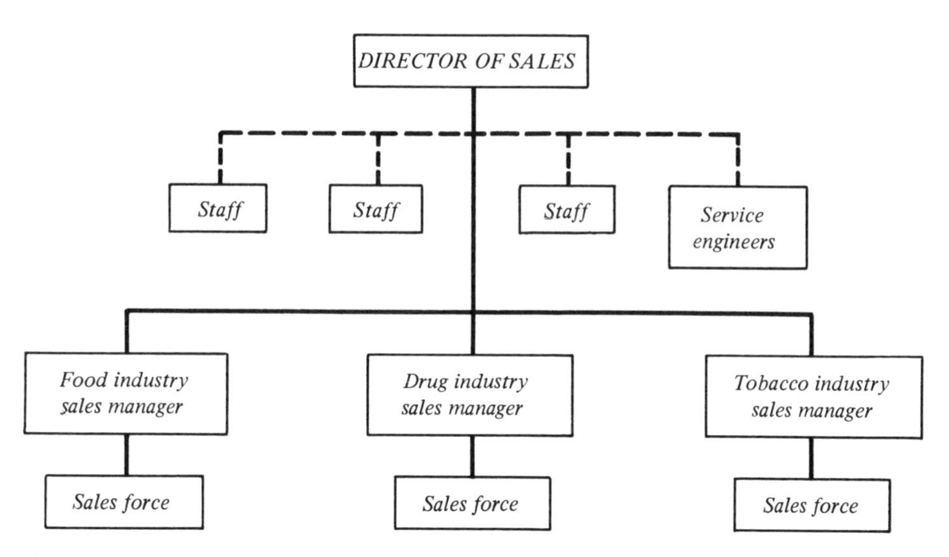


*Source: From* Charting the Company Organization Structure, *Studies in Personnel Policy 168, National Industrial Conference Board, Inc., New York, 1959; and American Management Marketing Course, New York, 1958.*

In the market type of organization, on the other hand, divisions are set up according to the type of customer who buys the product. Thus, the manufacturer of packaging machinery might well have a food division, drug division, tobacco division, etc., each in the charge of an *industry* sales manager. Here the major consideration is the type of customer, his needs, and wants; the sales manager becomes a specialist in the customer needs of a specific industry. The food division sales manager knows every major packaged food manufacturer, how many machines he needs or can use, where, what capacity, how he buys, who the major purchasing influence is, where this influence is located, and so on. In soliciting business from the Sunshine Biscuit Company, for example, the food division sales manager would know that the machinery specifications are likely to be set by the chief engineer and the vice-president for manufacturing at the company's headquarters in Long Island City, New York. The sales manager or his assistant may travel wherever necessary to install the machinery, but sales are made by contacting the principal buying influence, in this case, at company headquarters. Very often, this market type of sales organization calls for technological experts, "service engineers" or the like, who supply technical knowledge and assistance to the sales force and generally operate from headquarters. The Lukens Steel Company mentioned elsewhere is a case in point.

*Combination-type Organizations.* With the increased focus on customer requirements under marketing management, it might be expected that the market or customer type of sales organization might be the one to prevail. However, not every product mix lends itself to such an organizational structure, although combinations of regional and market types, and even combinations of all four types (see Figure 5), sometimes occur. Thus, for example, a national food company organized primarily along regional lines might also have a separate chain store division, specializing in selling to large chain buyers. Some drug and pharmaceutical houses maintain regional sales organizations, but within these regional departments there may be a chain store division, a wholesale division, etc. A prominent manufacturer of women's house dresses, located in Baltimore, Maryland, with three regional sales departments, Eastern, Southern, and Middle Western, has these three regional departments further subdivided into syndicate sales, department store sales, and independents. Such firms as Sears, Roebuck, Montgomery Ward, J. C. Penney, and others are served by the first division; department stores by the second; but the many small "women's specialty shops" would be handled by the third division exclusively.

**Figure 5. Combination-type organization: functional, product, regional, and market (chemical products manufacturer)**

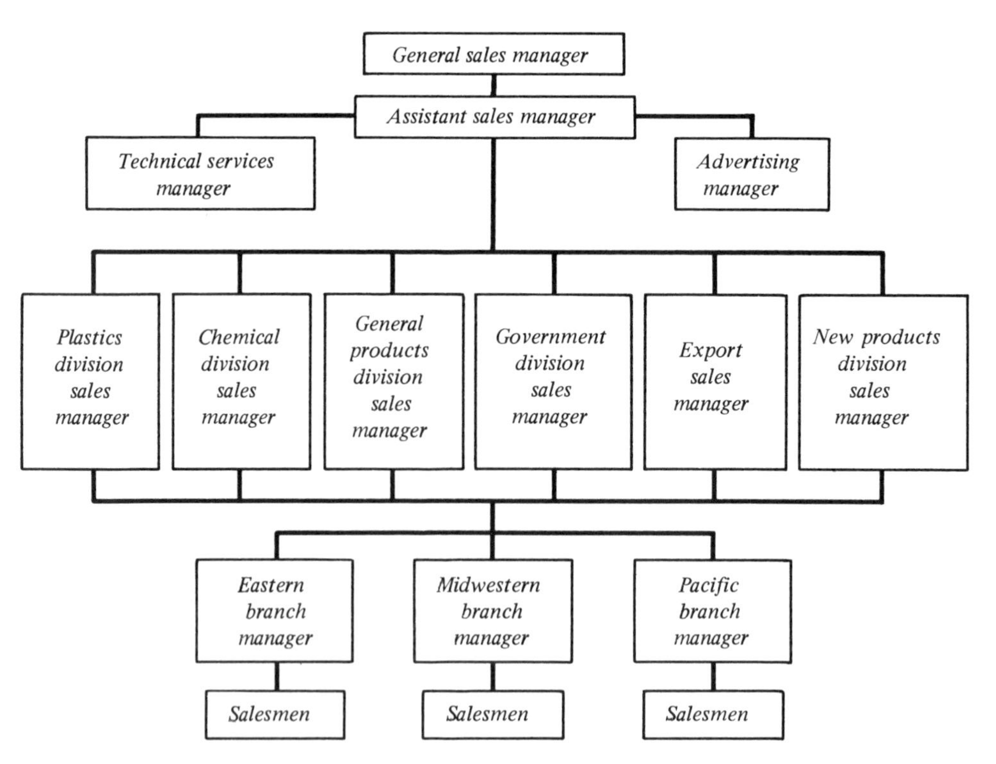


*Source: From* Charting the Company Organization Structure, *Studies in Personnel Policy 168, National Industrial Conference Board, Inc., New York, 1959; and American Management Association Marketing Course, New York, 1958.*

It is not yet clear what the most efficient type of sales organization may be under fully developed marketing management. As has been repeatedly pointed out, the entire concept is still in process of evolution and is likely to be so for many years to come. Each company must, in the end, organize its own sales function according to its own requirements, facilities, capabilities, and marketing philosophy, as well as the needs of its customers.

It does seem clear, however, that what we have heretofore considered as fundamental types of organization for the sales function will undergo considerable change in the years ahead. This is not entirely strange, since, as we have seen, the only fundamental law in marketing is *change.* In a dynamic economy, it would be difficult to imagine any major phase of operations remaining static. The organization of sales, no less than the organization of advertising, of product planning, of marketing research, will change; in fact, it has indeed already changed. But in contrast with such new functions as product planning it seems likely that the sales organization of the future will *evolve* out of the generally accepted basic types of organization shown in Figures 1 through 4.

# 50. THE APPLICATION OF SOCIAL SCIENCE FINDINGS TO SELLING AND THE SALESMAN

*Samuel N. Stevens*

*In the following discussion an industrial psychologist shows how information from the behavioral sciences applies to sales activities.*

*He states findings on the sociopsychological characteristics of salesmen and the sociopsychological nature of the sales environment that need careful consideration by marketing management.*

In one of the most penetrating studies of America as a civilization, Max Lerner defines the distinguishing characteristic of our American tradition as "the emphasis placed on dynamism." "This dynamism," he observes, "cannot be chastely selective, with its elements chosen or rejected on the basis of class outlook and political belief. . . . The fact is that the American experience has operated in every area. There has been the dynamism of the pioneer and the mechanic, the independent farmer and the trade-union worker; of the toolmaker, the inventor, the financier. There has been the dynamism of the 'company men'–the managers, the factory organizers, the salesmen who have made the irrepressible practical imagination of Americans world-famous."[1]

The psychologist, the sociologist, and the economist have all recognized that the saga of American success is vested in the willingness of men of vision to dare to dream, and

[1] Max Lerner, *America as a Civilization*, Simon and Schuster, Inc., New York, 1957.

Source: From *Aspects of Modern Marketing, AMA Management Report no. 15,* New York: American Management Association, Inc., 1958, pp. 85–94. Samuel N. Stevens: President, Stevens, Thurow and Associates, Inc., Chicago.

of hard-headed entrepreneurs to take the calculated risk. At the center of our business enterprise has been the man who sold the products of our mines, rivers, forests, and factories. Since the early days of the twentieth century, when the American people began to develop needs beyond the most primitive, it has been the peddler, wandering over the countryside with his cart of wares; the drummer, traveling by horse and buggy to visit the general stores along the highways and byways of our country; and the fast-talking, lone-wolf specialty salesman who, even as they sold their goods, created expanding needs and opened up ever larger markets. It is no exaggeration to say that, from an economic point of view, selling has been the most dramatic symbol of American dynamism. And the salesman has been called the last but most enduring social symbol of a restless, hungry, growing American culture.

## A HISTORICAL PERSPECTIVE

In the early years of the twentieth century, the psychologist and the economist were the social scientists most interested in selling as a social phenomenon and the salesman as an economic factor in modern society. From 1900 to 1925, the psychologist's interest in these areas was focused primarily upon three problems:

1. The selection of men who would succeed as salesmen.
2. The psychological nature of selling as a form of behavior.
3. The training and supervision of the salesmen as aspects of learning and motivation.

During these years, advertising, sales promotion, and what there was of market research were thought of primarily as supporting mechanisms for the payoff work of the face-to-face salesman. In 1907 Walter Dill Scott[2] published the first systematic analysis of the problems of advertising and selling from the psychological point of view. From that time until the present, the books and articles written on the subject have been legion. The fact that much of this literature has been superficial, trite, and sterile need not cause us to overlook the important facts which underlie the problems as they were defined by both the psychologist and the economist.

The first important research in the selection of salesmen was carried on by Walter Dill Scott for the American Tobacco Company. Scott's search for important differences in the psychological characteristics of good and poor salesmen and of salesmen and non-salesmen was a pioneering effort. The fact that no significant results were achieved should surprise no one with any time perspective, for instruments capable of the precise measurement of individual differences in areas of sales significance did not then exist. Since that time, of course, the persistent quest for psychological understanding in this area has met with more success. Gradually we have developed a valid analytic concept of the sales environment and reliable instruments for the measurement of most of the important differences which distinguish the persuasive, hyperkinetic individual

[2] Walter Dill Scott, *The Psychology of Advertising,* Small, Maynard & Co., Boston, 1907.

who can sell from the more analytical, less aggressive person who will find more stable occupational patterns more congenial.

The interest of psychologists in the problems of training and motivation began to be expressed in research form after World War I. The impressive psychological instruments and the greater understanding of the psychology of learning developed through research on military problems during the war led both professional and business men to be overly optimistic about the successful application of these tools and insights to the sales training situation. Yet continued research in the field of communication has since produced a body of technical and scientific knowledge which has taken most of the guesswork out of the organization of materials for sales training purposes. And the growth of clinical psychology, with its intensive studies of the personalities and social motivations of individuals, has made the supervision of salesmen a much more creative management function than it had been possible to achieve through the purely statistical and analytical approach taken prior to World War I.

## SOCIO-PSYCHOLOGICAL CHARACTERISTICS OF SALESMEN

At this point, let us consider, in rather general terms, the major conclusions which social scientists have reached in regard to the social and psychological characteristics of salesmen; later, we shall deal in the same manner with conclusions reached in regard to the sales environment.

1. *There is no significant relationship between intelligence-test scores and sales success.* The requirements for ability to learn, to solve problems, and to adjust quickly to the sales situation obviously differ widely in practice, depending upon the nature of the product, the type of selling involved, the competitive nature of the market, and many other such factors. Specialty selling and engineering selling, for example, make such different demands of the salesman that they can hardly be classified as being of the same order of experience.

2. *No significant relationship has been found between independent measures of personality traits and sales success.* Many of our "classical" notions of what makes a salesman do not appear to have any validity when put to psychological test. As selling has become more professional, the successful salesman has become less of a stereotype.

3. *No correlation exists between age and sales success.* Many research studies have revealed that, in companies which have established fairly rigid age ranges for the selection of salesmen, these standards have been almost as frequently ignored by the field sales managers as they have been recognized. The simple fact is that age, although theoretically related to maturity, is not absolutely correlated with it. In short, many young men are more mature than older men.

4. *There is no correlation between measurable character traits and sales success.* Many "typical" character traits ascribed to salesmen since the early days of the hard sell have been found to have little basis in reality. We find that the traits which make for

success in selling are the same as those which win the approval of employers in other occupations.

5. *There is no significant correlation between level of education and sales success.* Respect for education as an important tool in selling has grown by leaps and bounds. There has, in fact, been a tendency to set artificial levels of educational achievement for many sales positions. Yet careful statistical analysis of the educational backgrounds of individuals who are succeeding as salesmen reveals no such firm relationship between the amount of formal learning and the strict educational requirements for success in a given sales job. This does not mean that education is of no importance; it simply re-emphasizes the fact that there are many factors other than education which ultimately determine the success or failure of the salesman.

6. *No significant correlation exists between level of sales activity and sales success among individual salesmen.* This finding may be very difficult for many sales managers to accept. By tradition as well as by inclination there has been an understandable tendency for managers to believe that increased day-to-day activity will more or less inevitably produce increased sales volume. Theoretically, this is, of course, correct: A given man with a given selling method will produce more through sustained activity. Yet the fact is that attempts to increase the level of sales activity generally contribute less to increased sales volume than an equal amount of attention directed toward improving the selling method. Research clearly indicates that better selling techniques applied to carefully selected prospects are more likely to produce results.

7. *Each of the above factors has significance when studied in relation to all of the others in individual salesmen.* While no one of the factors cited above—age, education, personality, level of activity, and the rest—seems to have predictive significance, research indicates that when such social and psychological variables are studied in relation to one another the resulting profiles are valid guides for the selection of men who are likely to become successful salesmen. It was not until a very large number of important psychological instruments had been developed and more sophisticated statistical methods for the treatment of data had come into being that we were able to secure significantly useful results from our research in the evaluation of sales potential. Today it is possible to combine the social and psychological factors in such a way as to determine with considerable accuracy, in advance of employment, the likelihood of success in selling.

8. *Such study as that indicated in point 7 above can provide a useful tool for selection and development.* When, on the basis of research which compares the successful with the unsuccessful salesmen, a profile is built which reflects the unique characteristics of the successful men, it becomes possible to upgrade the sales force progressively through the use of the profile as a critical standard for the selection of new men.

9. *Salesmen are more likely to succeed when chosen with regard to the kinds of customers they will deal with than in terms of the types of products sold.* We must recognize that the salesman does not operate in a vacuum. He works in a sales environment in which he and the potential customer are important factors. When the salesman is compatible

with his customer, he has a much greater chance of success than when he is not. Therefore, an important part of the analysis upon which a sales profile is based should be a study of the kinds of customers the potential or prospective salesman will deal with.

10. *Salesmen differ from non-salesmen in four important ways:*

- Salesmen are persuasive rather than critical.
- Salesmen are intuitive rather than analytical.
- Salesmen have higher average energy levels (expressed in activity).
- Salesmen are more strongly motivated by the desire for prestige, power, and material gain than by a service ideal or the need for security.

11. *Salesmen's interests cluster around a dominantly persuasive common core.* Almost all of the important research into the interests of salesmen and marketing people substantiates this finding. The role of secondary interests varies with the nature of the product sold and the peculiarities of the sales environment itself. For instance, people engaged in technical and scientific selling almost always have a secondary interest that is either engineering or scientific, or both, while a man who is successful as a feed salesman will have a range of interests of relatively minor strength compared with his persuasive interest. In both cases the product and the sales environment give validity to the interest pattern.

These points represent the major findings of research on the socio-psychological characteristics of salesmen. The extent to which a manager of salesmen can creatively and imaginatively apply this knowledge in finding and developing men who can sell is the measure of his managerial success.

## NATURE OF THE SALES ENVIRONMENT

Turning our attention now to the environment in which the salesman works, let us consider those environmental characteristics which psychological research indicates contribute most strongly to successful selling.

1. *An atmosphere of mutual compatibility must be achieved.* As we have already indicated, it is wise to select the salesman with primary consideration for the kind of customer he will deal with. When this is done, one of the most important aspects of natural environmental compatibility is realized. When the salesman knowingly plans his call to meet the convenience of the customer and makes his presentation in terms of known customer needs, a further development of a compatible environment takes place. Finally, the achievement of a mutually agreed-upon sales decision involves the realization by both the customer and the salesman of an increased sense of personal worth. Compatibility therefore begins with a sense of community between salesman and customer based on congenial personality factors; it develops as a skilled salesman

molds the sales enviroment; and it achieves its climax through the experience of a heightened sense of personal worth as a sales decision is mutually arrived at.

2. *The customer's attention must be focused on the salesman and his message.* The psychological factors involved in the making of a sale have long been recognized. The structuring of the sales environment so that the salesman and his message become the focal points for the attention of the prospective customer is one of the most widely acknowledged fundamentals of sales training.

3. *An atmosphere of permissiveness must be established by evoking a felt need on the part of the customer.* Successful selling results when the sales environment is permissive rather than hostile or indifferent. Usually, such a positive, permissive environment is achieved as a direct result of felt need on the part of the customer.

4. *The natural aggressiveness of the salesman must be channeled to enhance the customer's ego; it should not be allowed to express itself in self-assertion, dominance, or hostility.* We must recognize that in any sales situation there is an element of psychological competition and a striving for ego-dominance on the part of both the salesman and the customer. That salesman is most likely to be successful who is able to achieve control by enhancing the ego of the customer rather than by asserting his own dominance.

5. *An atmosphere conducive to decision and action toward the resolution of the customer's felt need must be established through the development of feelings of satisfaction and profit.* The closing of a sale has long been considered the central problem in sales training. A great deal of research has been devoted to determining the most effective techniques by which the customer can be led to sign on the dotted line. Whatever the techniques recommended by the professional experts in the field, one essential psychological condition must be achieved. This may be described as the resolution of felt need through the development of feelings of satisfaction and profit. The psychological as well as the economic benefits of affirmative action in line with the desires and recommendations of the salesman become compelling conditioning factors to direct action.

The good salesman is aware, implicity, of these things. He has an intuitive feel for them. A subtle aspect of sales training is the development of an *explicit* understanding of these factors, so that the salesman can manipulate the sales enviroment with more sureness and awareness.

## BASIC SELLING TOOLS

There are a number of basic tools with which the salesman must be equipped in order to implement the social science findings described above in the way that will be most productive for his particular company and its particular products. In general, these basic tools are of three major types, as described below.

1. *Technical product knowledge.* Tangible and concrete information concerning his company's products, processes, and services constitutes the salesman's basic tool. This type of knowledge can be effectively communicated to salesmen in groups by means of

demonstrations and discussion, or individually by means of well-prepared brochures, booklets, and the like. Adequacy and correctness of product knowledge must be constantly checked and evaluated by the sales supervisor. Research has revealed that many times the failure of the salesman is the result of inadequate or incorrect product knowledge. It cannot be assumed that because a salesman is told once he will remember forever.

2. *Administrative techniques* (organization of territory, development of call pattern, record keeping, etc.). Good sales management today attempts to develop wisdom and know-how in this area through extremely concentrated training and close face-to-face supervision. It is not natural for a salesman to consistently reorganize his detailed knowledge of territory changes; neither will he readily accept the discipline of highly structured call patterns; and he simply is not temperamentally suited to the correct maintenance of a large number of records. The better the man is as a salesman, in fact, the less congenial he is likely to find the necessity for close and constant record keeping. Management, therefore, must develop a number of highly effective motivational methods to secure the kind of cooperation from the salesman that good sales control requires.

3. *Group training* (face-to-face sales strategy and motivation, demonstration, directed practice, side-by-side field practice). Many studies have been carried on to determine the relative effectiveness of field demonstration and role playing in teaching selling strategy. The consensus at the present time is that both of these methods are highly effective. In view of the central psychological principles we have discussed, it is clear that the salesman must *do* in order to learn. Listening and observing are, of course, forms of doing, yet they do not have the same efficiency-producing effect as actual field performance under observation. It does not seem likely that there will ever be an effective substitute for side-by-side field practice carried on sympathetically by the sales manager and his salesman.

## CHANGING TIMES, CHANGING NEEDS

Today, only a small segment of the total sales environment presents a congenial condition for direct selling. The needs and wants of the consuming public are being predetermined through the use of advertising and sales promotion in magazines and on radio and television. In the consumer area, for example, the sales merchandiser no longer deals directly with a customer; instead, he deals with a buyer or a buying panel. His problem is not to influence the ultimate consumer to buy, but rather to convince the professional buyer that the other functions of marketing have already created a demand for the product, and that he can profitably make precious shelf space available. This situation presents the consumer salesman with an entirely different challenge, to meet which he requires an entirely different selling approach. He must be able to talk technically in terms of frontages, shelf space, product movement, supporting promotions, the economic effects of couponing, the secondary services which the manufacturer will render the distributor, and the influence of displays on the impulse buyer.

In the industrial field the same kind of problem exists, although it has a slightly different psychological context. The industrial salesman must sell to a professional purchasing agent who has received his product specifications from some other company official. As a result, the industrial salesman must establish friendly relations with management users in order that they will specify his product when requisitioning through the purchasing office. With regard to the psychology of selling, this means that the industrial salesman must be a good public relations man and a good service engineer far in advance of the occasion of actual felt need on the part of the business.

It becomes obvious that today's salesmen are not entrepreneurs, but professional communicators, working within the framework of a fairly rigid management system. Thus, they are not wholly dependent on individual performance or productivity for income or economic advantage. The psychological problems, therefore, not only continue to be related to the selection of the kind of man who will accept the challenge of professional persuasiveness in a highly structured situation but also have to do with the development of techniques by which the use of incentives and internal and external motivations can be rationalized and made effective. The salesman must be able not only to understand his product and his customer but to relate this understanding to the economics of marketing and to such institutional problems as pricing and profit.

The typical problems which interest the psychologist and the sociologist today derive from an appreciation of the dynamic elements which comprise the marketing complex. "Motivation research" is a phrase symbolic of the new focus of interest. Projective techniques, as applied to both the salesman and the customer, are new devices. The nature of the corporate image, the power of the brand name, and the maintenance of a consumer franchise are all attracting the research time and interest of the social scientist. Morale studies, as they reveal the attitudes of salesmen toward the sales process and the company product, are assuming new and increased significance. The professionalization of sales training–with its highly operational definitions, its use of double and sometimes triple stimuli as learning facilitators, and its dynamic implementation of other incentives than money alone–is of increasing socio-psychological importance.

Hovering over these more highly individualistic problems are many which have to do with the sheer economics of distribution. The costs of doing business today threaten to eat up the ever-narrowing margin of profitability. Basic and applied research on products, packaging, and production techniques take an increasing toll from the consumer's dollar. Fringe benefits, pensions, and unemployment compensation involve added administrative costs which throw the traditional corporate concepts of doing business out of balance. These considerations cannot fail to affect the salesman and his selling effort.

## TOWARD A PSYCHOLOGY OF MARKETING

Clearly, great changes have occurred in our economy during the past fifteen years. The impact of these changes must be appreciated if sales management is to meet the challenge. The economic and social character of the mid-twentieth-century marketplace is the direct result of the fact that American dynamism has continued to work steadily toward the adaptation of our capitalistic, competitive society to the increasing complexities of a world-wide revolution. The more complex our economic society becomes, the more unstable it is. The greater our economic resources to meet our expanding needs are, the more fierce competition becomes and the more critical the role of selling appears to be in the marketing complex.

Free enterprise, symbolized by the freewheeling entrepreneur of an earlier day, has been subject to many social and political controls. Government has assumed the role of the father-protector of the consumer. Sheer economic power is no longer looked upon with approval by many highly placed government officials. Efforts to place limitations on competition through the use of arbitrary economic power have been most vigorous at the very time when competition itself has been most bitter. The very tentative and uncertain balance between demonstrated need and capacity to produce is in constant danger of being lost. We observe, with a growing sense of frustration and concern, a spiraling gross national product and a tightening margin of gross profit.

It is in the light of these dynamic changes that mid-century selling has been forced to become an integral part of a larger and more complex economic process. We call this larger process "marketing." In an earlier day, advertising, sales promotion, credit and deferred-payment plans, and product development were supplementary aids to direct selling. Today these functions of marketing are themselves aspects of a total sales effort, and face-to-face selling is no longer the dominant causative factor in the distribution of goods.

This transformation is not entirely accepted by salesmen and their sales managers. Many of the frustrations now being experienced are the direct result of the failure of sales management realistically to adjust the role of the salesman to the changing patterns of modern marketing. Unless new insights are quickly gained, we may find ourselves in a declining economy. We may see a depression in the midst of plenty—a "profitless prosperity," as some have ominously called it.

Because selling has become marketing and because the entrepreneur salesman has of necessity become a professional, the need for more exact and more discriminating selection of sales personnel has become more pressing than ever. Our research into the characteristic of the "new" mid-twentieth-century sales-marketer has produced results which are most encouraging. The selection profiles which we have developed, in both the consumer and the industrial fields, reflect the changes in the sales job and in the characteristics of the successful salesman.

We are sure that, at most levels of selling, the sales-marketer must be more educable and have a higher intelligence potential than the salesman of the past. He must be less of an individualist and more of a team player. He must be as strongly motivated for personal success as salesmen ever were. He must be a more disciplined person, with greater control over his energy output. He must be more of a student, using his fund of marketing and sales knowledge with greater intuitional skill. He must be capable of more precise analysis of the marketing variables which affect his sales effort, and he must acquire additional skills in organizing, planning, and scheduling his sales work.

It will be obvious to all thoughtful sales managers that this type of salesman will require more guidance and will profit more from well-scheduled training. His economic requirements will be greater. His chances for professional growth will have to be more carefully spelled out. Sales supervision will require a higher degree of real managerial leadership. From every point of view it is reasonable to suggest that, *as selling becomes marketing, it also comes of age.* An expanding economy and an enlarged opportunity for personal financial achievement go hand in hand.

The psychologist and the sociologist may become true servants of management as they assist it, through research and consultation, in achieving increased understanding of the nature of the marketing process and the role of the salesman in it.

# 51. WHAT MAKES A GOOD SALESMAN

*David Mayer and Herbert M. Greenberg*

*Everyone who screens and hires salesmen for his company has developed some ideas as to what makes a good salesman. The beliefs are many; but the thesis of the following article is that the psychological characteristics of empathy and ego-drive are the two central qualities in any and all successful salesmen.*

*It is posited that hiring fails to consider the most important qualities of the man, but instead dwells on superficial trivia. To substantiate their conclusions, the authors tested scores of salesmen in several industries; and they found that empathy and ego-drive, measurable through psychological tests, correlated highly with sales success.*

More than thirty-five years ago, the insurance industry embarked on an intensive program to solve the problem of costly, wasteful turnover among its agents. Estimates at that time indicated that there was a turnover of better than 50 per cent within the first year and almost 80 per cent within the first three years. After the expenditure of millions of dollars and thirty-five years of research, the turnover in the insurance industry remains approximately 50 per cent within the first year and 80 per cent within the first three years.

What is the cost of this turnover? Nearly incalculable. Consider:

- The substantial sums paid new salesmen as salary, draw on commission, expense accounts, and so on, which are wasted when those salesmen fail to sell.

Source: From *Harvard Business Review,* vol. 42, July–August, 1964, pp. 119–125. David Mayer and Herbert M. Greenberg: Principal officers of the Marketing Survey and Research Corporation, New York.

- The staggering company costs, in time, money, and energy, of recruiting, selecting, training, and supervising men who inherently do not have the ability to succeed.
- The vast costs caused by lost sales, dropouts, reduced company reputation, poor morale, permanently burned territory, and the like.

What accounts for this expensive inefficiency? Basically this: companies have simply not known what makes one man able to sell and another not. As Robert N. McMurry has observed:

"A very high proportion of those engaged in selling cannot sell. . . . If American sales efficiency is to be maximized and the appalling waste of money and manpower which exists today is to be minimized, a constructive analysis must be made of what selling really is and how its effectiveness can be enhanced. . . . We must look a good deal further–into the mysteries of personality and psychology–if we want real answers."[1]

It was the obvious need for a better method of sales selection that led us to embark on seven years of field research in this area. The article which follows is based on the insights we gained as to the basic characteristics necessary for a salesman to be able to sell successfully. Confirming the fact that we are on the right track is the predictive power of the selection instrument (battery of tests) that we developed out of the same research. (See Table 1.)

## TWO ESSENTIALS

Our basic theory is that a good salesman must have at least two basic qualities: empathy and ego-drive.

*Ability to Feel. Empathy,* the important central ability to *feel* as the other fellow does in order to be able to sell him a product or service, must be possessed in large measure. Having empathy does not necessarily mean being sympathetic. One can know what the other fellow feels without agreeing with that feeling. But a salesman simply cannot sell well without the invaluable and irreplaceable ability to get a powerful feedback from his client through empathy.

A parallel might be drawn in this connection between the old antiaircraft weapons and the new heat-attracted missiles. With the old type of ballistic weapon, the gunner would take aim at an airplane, correcting as best he could for windage and driftage, and then fire. If the shell missed by just a few inches because of a slight error in calculation or because the plane took evasive action, the miss might just as well have been by hundreds of yards for all the good it did.

*This is the salesman with poor empathy. He aims at the target as best he can and proceeds along his sales track; but if his target–the customer–fails to perform as predicted, the sale is missed.*

[1] Robert N. McMurry, "The Mystique of Super-Salesmanship," *Harvard Business Review,* April, 1961, p. 113.

**Table 1. Three examples of predictive results from selection instrument based on empathy and ego-drive**

| *Number of men predicted for each group** | | *Data at end of (months)* | *Actual sales performance (number of men who reached each quarter of sales force)* — *Top half* | | *Bottom half* | | *Quit or fired* |
|---|---|---|---|---|---|---|---|
| | | | *Top/quarter* | *2nd/quarter* | *3rd/quarter* | *Bottom/quarter* | |
| | | | In the retail automobile industry | | | | |
| A | 34 | 6 mos. | 17 | 13 | 1 | 0 | 3 |
| | | 18 | 19 | 9 | 0 | 0 | 6 |
| B | 49 | 6 | 9 | 23 | 8 | 2 | 7 |
| | | 18 | 10 | 19 | 8 | 0 | 12 |
| C | 60 | 6 | 0 | 9 | 20 | 14 | 17 |
| | | 18 | 0 | 2 | 21 | 8 | 29 |
| D | 52 | 6 | 0 | 0 | 10 | 18 | 24 |
| | | 18 | 0 | 0 | 9 | 7 | 36 |
| | | | In the insurance industry | | | | |
| A | 22 | 6 mos. | 13 | 4 | 1 | 0 | 4 |
| | | 14 | 13 | 4 | 0 | 0 | 5 |
| B | 55 | 6 | 7 | 23 | 11 | 2 | 12 |
| | | 14 | 11 | 20 | 7 | 1 | 16 |
| C | 56 | 6 | 1 | 5 | 19 | 12 | 19 |
| | | 14 | 1 | 4 | 11 | 5 | 35 |
| D | 48 | 6 | 0 | 0 | 4 | 10 | 34 |
| | | 14 | 0 | 0 | 3 | 4 | 41 |
| | | | In the mutual funds industry | | | | |
| A | 11 | 6 mos. | 5 | 4 | 1 | 0 | 1 |
| B | 20 | 6 | 4 | 9 | 3 | 0 | 4 |
| C | 49 | 6 | 0 | 4 | 15 | 12 | 18 |
| D | 34 | 6 | 0 | 1 | 7 | 10 | 16 |

*Predictions made on basis of test, without seeing men or any records:
- A means outstanding, top potential as a salesman, almost certain to succeed with high productivity.
- B means recommended, good productivity, and can sometimes be designated as developable into an A.
- C means not recommended, even though a C can under the right circumstances edge into becoming a low B.
- D means absolutely not recommended; the applicant concerned has virtually no possibility of success.

On the other hand, the new missiles, if they are anywhere near the target, become attracted to the heat of the target's engine, and regardless of its evasive action, they finally home in and hit their mark.

*This is the salesman with good empathy. He senses the reactions of the customer and is able to adjust to these reactions. He is not simply bound by a prepared sales track, but he functions in terms of the real interaction between himself and the customer. Sensing what the customer is feeling, he is able to change pace, double back on his track, and make whatever creative modifications might be necessary to home in on the target and close the sale.*

*Need to Conquer.* The second of the basic qualities absolutely needed by a good salesman is a particular kind of *ego-drive* which makes him want and need to make the sale in a personal or ego way, not merely for the money to be gained. His feeling must be that he *has* to make the sale; the customer is there to help him fulfill his personal need. In effect, to the top salesman, the sale–the conquest–provides a powerful means of enhancing his ego. His self-picture improves dramatically by virtue of conquest, and diminishes with failure.

Because of the nature of all selling, the salesman will fail to sell more often than he will succeed. Thus, since failure tends to diminish his self-picture, his ego cannot be so weak that the poor self-picture continues for too long a time. Rather, the failure must act as a trigger–as a motivation toward greater efforts–which with success will bring the ego enhancement he seeks. A subtle balance must be found between (a) an ego partially weakened in precisely the right way to need a great deal of enhancement (the sale) and (b) an ego sufficiently strong to be motivated by failure but not to be shattered by it.

*The salesman's empathy, coupled with his intense ego-drive, enables him to home in on the target effectively and make the sale. He has the drive, the need to make the sale, and his empathy gives him the connecting tool with which to do it.*

## SYNERGISTIC EFFECTS

In this discussion of the relationship of empathy and ego-drive to successful selling, we will treat these dynamic factors as separate characteristics. Indeed, they are separate in that someone can have a great deal of empathy and any level of ego-drive–extremely strong to extremely weak. Someone with poor empathy can also have any level of ego-drive. Yet, as determinants of sales ability, empathy and ego-drive act on and, in fact, reinforce each other.

The person with strong ego-drive has maximum motivation to fully utilize whatever empathy he possesses. Needing the sale, he is not likely to let his empathy spill over and become sympathy. His ego need for the conquest is not likely to allow him to side with the customer; instead, it spurs him on to use his knowledge of the customer fully to make the sale.

On the other hand, the person with little or no ego-drive is hardly likely to use his empathy in a persuasive manner. He understands people and may know perfectly well what things he might say to close the sale effectively, but his understanding is apt to become sympathy. If he does not need the conquest, his very knowledge of the real needs of the potential customer may tell him that the customer in fact should not buy. Since he does not need the sale in an inner personal sense, he then may not persuade the customer to buy. So we frequently say in our evaluations of potential salesmen, "This man has fine empathy, but he is not likely to use it persuasively—he will not use it to close."

Thus, there is a dynamic relationship between empathy and ego-drive. It takes a combination of the two, each working to reinforce the other—each enabling the other to be fully utilized—to make the successful salesman.

*Need for Balance.* It calls for a very special, balanced ego to need the sale intensely and yet allow the salesman to look closely at the customer and fully benefit from an empathic perception of the customer's reactions and needs.

Thus, there are a number of possible permutations of empathy and drive. A man may have a high degree of both empathy and drive (*ED*), or little of either (*ed*), or two kinds of combinations in between (*Ed* and *eD*). For example:

*ED*—A salesman who has a great deal of both empathy and strong inner sales drive will be at or near the top of the sales force.

*Ed*—A salesman with fine empathy but too little drive may be a splendid person but will be unable to close his deal effectively. This is the "nice guy." Everyone likes him, and from all appearances he should turn out to be one of the best men on the force. He somehow "doesn't make it." People end up liking him, but buying from the company down the street. He is often hired because he does have such fine personal qualities. Yet his closing ability is weak. He will get along with the customer, understand him, and bring him near the close; but he does not have that inner hunger to move the customer that final one foot to the actual sale. It is this last element of the sale—the close—which empathy alone cannot achieve, and where the assertive quality of ego-drive becomes the all-important essential.

*eD*—A salesman with much drive but too little empathy will bulldoze his way through to some sales, but he will miss a great many and will hurt his employer through his lack of understanding of people.

*ed*—A salesman without much empathy or drive should not actually be a salesman, although a great many present salesmen fall into this group. An employer would avoid much grief by finding this out in advance, before so much effort is spent in trying to hire, train, and spoon-feed a man who does not have within him the basic dynamics to be successful.

## FAILURE OF TESTS

Since the selection of top salesmen is potentially of such enormous value, why, it might be asked, has there been so little success to date in developing methods to preselect effectively?

For at least fifty years, psychologists have been working very hard in the area of testing. Almost every aspect of human personality, behavior, attitude, and ability has at one time or another come under the scrutiny of the tester. There have been some notable successes in testing, most especially perhaps in the IQ and mechanical-ability areas. Of late, personality testing, especially with the increasing use of projective techniques, has gained a certain level of sophistication. The area which has been to date most barren of real scientific success has been aptitude testing, where the aptitude consists of personality dynamics rather than simple mechanical abilities.

*Four Reasons.* The ability to sell, an exceedingly human and totally nonmechanical aptitude, has resisted attempts to measure it effectively. The reasons for this failure up until now are many, but there appear to be four basic causes for sales aptitude test failure.

1. *Tests have been looking for interest, not ability.* The concept that a man's interest is equatable to his ability is perhaps the single largest cause of test failure. Thus, tests have been developed through asking questions of successful salesmen or successful people in other fields, with the assumption that if an applicant expresses the same kind of interest pattern as an established salesman, he too will be a successful salesman.

   This assumption is wrong on its face. Psychologically, interest does not equal aptitude. Even if someone is interested in exactly the same specific things as Mickey Mantle or Willie Mays, this of course does not in any way indicate the possession of a similar baseball skill. Equally, the fact that an individual might have the same interest pattern as a successful salesman does not mean that he can sell. Even if he wants to sell, it does not mean that he *can* sell.

2. *Tests have been eminently "fakable."* When an individual is applying for a job, he obviously will attempt to tell the potential employer whatever he thinks the employer wants to hear. Given a certain amount of intelligence, the applicant will know that he should say he would "rather be a salesman than a librarian," regardless of his real preference. He knows that he should say he would "rather be with people than at home reading a good book," that he "prefers talking to a P.T.A. group to listening to good music," or that he would "rather lead a group discussion than be a forest ranger."

   There are manuals on the market on how to beat sales aptitude tests, but, even without such a manual, the average intelligent person can quickly see what is sought and then give the tester what the tester wants. Thus, the tests may simply succeed in negatively screening those who are so unintelligent that they are unable to see the particular response pattern sought. In other words, since they are too dull to fake, they may be screened out. The perceptive interviewer, however, is likely to notice this kind of stupidity even more quickly than the tests do, and he can probably do a better job of this negative screening than the average fakable test.

3. *Tests have favored group conformity, not individual creativity.* Recent critics of psychological testing decry the testers who are seeking conformity and the standardized ways in which they judge applicants for sales and other occupations. This criticism is all too valid. The creative thinker, the impulsive, free spirit, the original, imaginative, hard-driving individual is often screened out by tests which demand rigid adherence to convention–an adherence, in fact, that borders on a passive acceptance of authority, a fear of anything that might in any way upset the applecart of bureaucratic order. Paradoxically, this fearful, cautious, authoritarian conformist, although he might make

a good civil servant, or even a fair controller or paperwork administrative executive, would never make a successful salesman.

Many of these tests not only fail to select good salesmen, but they may actually screen out the really top producers because of their creativity, impulsiveness, or originality—characteristics which most tests downgrade as strangeness or weakness. We discovered a situation of this type recently in working with a client:

A company in the Southwest embarked on an intensive recruiting effort for salesmen. We began receiving the tests of a number of applicants. These tests all appeared to follow a certain pattern. The men were not quite recommendable, and all for about the same reason—a definite lack of ego-drive. For the most part, they had some empathy, and without exception they had good verbal ability, but none had the intense inner need for the sale that we look for in a productive salesman.

After about twenty such tests came through our office, we questioned the sales manager as to what criteria he was using for screening the men who took the test. We found that before he gave the men our test, he had them take the sales aptitude test which had been developed by his company some years before. Those men who scored high on that test were given our test.

We had previously analyzed that company's test and found it to be a fairly good verbal abilities measure, and to some extent a measure of intelligence and insight. Men with strong ego-drive could not as a rule score near the top of that test. And so the very men with the quality we were seeking—strong ego drive—were actually screened out. We then asked the sales manager not to use that test but to screen only for credit reference and general appearance, and to give our test to those who passed this simple screening. After that we began seeing the expected number of "A" and "B" recommendable applicants—about one man in every five.

4. *Tests have tried to isolate fractional traits rather than to reveal the whole dynamics of the man.* Most personality and aptitude tests are totally traitological in their construction and approach. They see personality as a series or "bundle" of piecemeal traits. Thus, someone may be high in "sociability" while being low in "self-sufficiency" and "dominance." Someone else may be high in "personal relations," but low in "co-operativeness." Somehow, the whole (or the *Gestalt*) gets lost. The dynamic interaction that is personality, as viewed by most modern-day psychologists, is buried in a series of fractionalized, mathematically separable traits.

Thus, it is said that the salesman, somewhat like the Boy Scout, should be very "sociable," "dominant," "friendly," "responsible," "honest," and "loyal." The totality—the dynamics within the person that will permit him to sell successfully—is really lost sight of. Clearly, someone may be "sociable," "responsible," and so on, but still be a very poor salesman.

In our research we attempted to bypass traits and to go directly to the central dynamisms that we believed were basic to sales ability: empathy and ego-drive. By seeking these deeper, more central, characteristics, we immediately reduced the possibility of faking, since the respondent would find it extremely difficult to determine what *in fact* was being sought. Needless to say, the importance of interest as a variable has been reduced sharply, and the conformity factor has been completely subordinated to the basic central characteristics being measured. Thus, rather than starting with the question, "How do salesmen collectively answer certain items?" we began with the question, "What makes a really fine salesman?" and then, "How do you discover these human characteristics?"

This use of central dynamics rather than traits, with its corollary implications, has produced what we believe to be a positive method of predicting sales success that is advanced beyond what has been done to date.

## FALLACY OF EXPERIENCE

Many sales executives feel that the type of selling in their industry (and even in their particular company) is somehow completely special and unique. This is true to an extent. There is no question that a data-processing equipment salesman needs somewhat different training and background than does an automobile salesman. Differences in requirements are obvious, and whether or not the applicant meets the special qualifications for a particular job can easily be seen in the applicant's biography or readily measured. What is not so easily seen, however, are the basic sales dynamics we have been discussing, which permit an individual to sell successfully, almost regardless of what he is selling.

To date, we have gained experience with more than 7,000 salesmen of tangibles as well as intangibles, in wholesale as well as retail selling, big-ticket and little-ticket items. And the dynamics of success remain approximately the same in all cases. Sales ability is fundamental, more so than the product being sold. Long before he comes to know the product, mostly during his childhood and growing-up experience, the future successful salesman is developing the human qualities essential for selling. Thus, when emphasis is placed on experience, and experience counts more than such essentials as empathy and drive, what is accomplished can only be called the *inbreeding of mediocrity.*

We have found that the experienced person who is pirated from a competitor is most often piratable simply because he is not succeeding well with that competitor. He feels that somehow he can magically do better with the new company. This is rarely true. He remains what he is, mediocre, or worse. What companies need is a greater willingness to seek individuals with basic sales potential in the general marketplace. Experience is more or less easily gained, but real sales ability is not at all so easily gained.

Among butchers, coal miners, steelworkers, and even the unemployed there are many—*perhaps one in ten*—who, whether they themselves know it or not, possess ability to be an "A," top-producing salesman; and at least one in five would be on a "B" or better level for most types of selling. Many of these are potentially far better salesmen than some who have accumulated many years of experience. The case of "Big Jim," as we shall call him, is a good example:

All we knew about Jim at first was that he had walked into the showroom of one of our automobile clients in response to its ad and had taken our test. We reported that he was the only "A" in the group, and strongly recommended that he be hired. There was shocked silence at the other end of the telephone. We were then told that his test had been included as a joke.

As it was described to us, he had ambled into the showroom one morning wearing dungarees, an old polo shirt, and sneakers. He had then gone on to proclaim, "I sure do hanker to sell them there cars." The dealer had included his test just to get a laugh, or perhaps to see if we were sufficiently alert to weed him out. The man had never sold a car or anything else in his life, and had neither the appearance nor the background which would indicate that he ever could sell anything.

Today he is one of the dealer's best salesmen. Soon after he started working, he "hankered to see that there Seattle World's Fair," and sold enough cars in the first week of the month to give him money to get there and spend two weeks. On his return he made enough money in the last week of the month to equal the staff's monthly average.

Obviously, most men down from the hills wearing dungarees and sneakers are not going to be top salesmen. Some, however, may be, and their lack of experience in no way reduces the possibility that they have the inner dynamics of which fine top producers are made. It is equally obvious that a great many men who present a fine appearance, a "good front," do not turn out to be top salesmen. The real question—and always the first question—is, "Does this man have the basic inner dynamics to sell successfully?"

*Background Blindness.* Putting emphasis on experience often works in another way to reduce sales effectiveness. A company grows used to seeing its men in various job "slots," in certain departments, limited to special kinds of experience. Such men may be doing a satisfactory job where they are. But it frequently happens that the blind habit of "special experience" has kept the company from using the man in a more effective and appropriate way. For instance:

A western company in the leasing business wanted us to evaluate a branch employing forty-two men to determine why there had been a mediocre level of sales activity, why there had been some difficulties among the men, and whether some of the forty-two should possibly be let go. After looking at the test of each man, we did an "X-ray" of the branch; that is, following the table of organization, we evaluated the staff, department by department, especially in terms of who was working with, over, and under whom, pointing out the strengths and weaknesses of each department.

Virtually all the men on the staff were found to be worth keeping on, but a good third were suggested for job shifts to other departments. Thus, the man with greatest sales ability, together with a great deal of managerial ability (by no means the same thing), was found in the accounting department. But that job did not completely satisfy him. He has since become the new branch sales manager, a more appropriate use of his considerable abilities.

One of the older men, though rated an adequate "B" salesman, was evaluated as an "A" office manager. He had good empathy, but not the strongest ego-drive, which was why he was a "B" rather than an "A" salesman. But on the managerial side, he had the ability to handle details, relatively rare for a salesman; he was able to delegate authority and make decisions fairly rapidly and well. These qualities, plus his good empathy, gave him excellent potential as a manager, but not as sales manager, for his only moderate drive would have hurt him in the latter position. As office-administrative manager, the position he was moved up into, he has performed solidly.

The former office-administrative manager, a man well able to handle details reliably and responsibly, but with little empathy (and thus unable to deal understandingly with his office staff), was moved laterally into the accounting department, an area in which he had had some previous experience, and where he could carefully deal with and manage details rather than people.

Thus, what counts more than experience is the man's basic inner abilities. Each present employee, as well as each new applicant, should be placed in the area where he can be most creative and productive.

## ROLE OF TRAINING

The steelworker, the coal miner, the displaced textile worker, or for that matter even "Big Jim," regardless of how much real sales ability each possesses, cannot suddenly start selling insurance, mutual funds, electronics equipment, or automobiles. Each one will need training. Companies have spent very large sums of money in developing effective training programs. When they are working with a man with potential, these training programs can and do bring out this potential and develop an excellent salesman. Without sound training, even "A" level salesmen are seriously limited.

Yet how often have men gone through long and expensive training programs only to fail totally when put out into the field? When this happens, the trainer, and perhaps the training program itself, is blamed, and sometimes even discarded. But most often it is neither the trainer nor the training program that is at fault; rather it is the fact that they were given the impossible task of turning a sow's ear into a silk purse. The most skilled diamond polisher, given a piece of coal, can only succeed in creating a highly polished piece of coal; but given the roughest type of uncut diamond, he can indeed turn it into the most precious stone. Here is a case in point:

About three years ago, a company in the Northeast installed an especially fine training program, in which a great deal of money was invested. At the end of two years, the results of this program were appraised. It was found that sales had not increased beyond what might normally be expected in that industry during that period of time. The investment in the training program seemed to have been a total waste. The entire training program was therefore dropped. Six months later, we were asked by management to test and evaluate the present sales force and to try to determine why the training program, so highly recommended, had failed so badly.

The reason was immediately apparent. Out of a sales force of eighteen men, there was only one rating "A," and his sales actually had improved after the training program. Two other men were "B" level salesmen, and they too had improved to some extent with training. The remaining fifteen men were "C" and "D" salesmen who should not have been selling in the first place. They simply did not have the potential of good salesmen. They were rigid, opinionated, and for the most part seriously lacking in empathy. This type of man rarely responds to training, no matter how thoroughgoing the program. This was an obvious case of trying to make silk purses out of fifteen assorted sow's ears.

The role of training is clear. It is vital. In today's highly competitive market it is most important to bring every employee up to his maximum potential of productivity. Efficiency in training, using the best of modern methods, is necessary to do this. But training can succeed only if selection succeeds. Good raw silk must be provided first, before the training department can be expected to produce the silk purses. Just as few manufacturers would allow their products to be produced on the basis of rough estimates of size and weight, but would demand scientific control of these basic characteristics, so too must the process of selection be made more scientific and accurate.

The role of the salesman is so vital to the success of a company that it is amazing to these writers how little stress industry has placed on selecting the best raw material. To sell effectively in the U.S. market of today, a salesman needs to have empathy. To sell effectively in the foreign market, crossing cultural lines, requires even more empathy. And marketing goods and services anywhere calls for a great deal of ego-drive. The U.S. Department of Commerce recently stated that American industry has no problem with its production. Its main problem is distribution. Effective salesmen are the key to distribution, and proper selection is the key to finding, using, and profiting from salesmen of good quality.

## CONCLUSION

Industry must improve its ability to select top salesmen. Failure to date has stemmed from such errors as: the belief that interest equals aptitude; the fakability of aptitude tests; the crippling emphasis on conformity rather than creativity; and the subdivision of a man into piecemeal traits, rather than understanding him as a whole person. Experience appears to be less important than a man's possession of the two central characteristics of empathy and ego-drive, which he must have to permit him to sell successfully. Training can only succeed when the raw material is present.

Selecting men with empathy and ego-drive should contribute in some degree to helping industry meet one of its most pressing problems: reducing the high cost of turnover and selecting genuinely better salesmen.

# 52. NEW PATTERNS IN SALES MANAGEMENT

*Rensis Likert*

*Two broadly different systems of sales management are available. One system is founded on traditional theories of management. The other is a newer system, based on the principles and practices of those who are the highest-producing sales managers.*

*Following is an explanation of the development of this newer system, including the data on which it is based, and information about its practical use.*

Some three or four centuries ago a powerful problem-solving process, called the scientific method, was developed. Quantitative scientific research began to be applied in the physical and engineering sciences at that time. Since then, these sciences have progressed at an ever-accelerating rate, until today we successfully launch guided missiles, we fly around the world in outer space, and we talk of putting a man on the moon in a year or two—of all sorts of things that were inconceivable even fifty years ago.

Application of this problem-solving process was later extended to the fields of biology and medicine. The vaccines for polio are but one example of the important and rapid progress which has since been made in these fields.

Only recently have quantitative scientific research methods been applied to the social sciences. As yet, only a relatively small amount of the total funds spent nationally for

Source: From Martin A. Warshaw (ed.), *Changing Perspectives in Marketing: Sixth Annual Conference on Marketing Management,* Ann Arbor, Michigan: Bureau of Business Research, Graduate School of Business Administration, The University of Michigan, 1962, pp. 1–25. Rensis Likert: Director, Institute for Social Research, and Professor of Psychology and of Sociology, The University of Michigan.

research is available for use in the social sciences. This year, according to reports of the National Science Foundation, the total expenditure in the United States for research and development will be about fifteen or sixteen billion dollars. Less than 2 per cent of this will be spent in the social sicences, and included in this 2 per cent will be less than one-quarter of 1 per cent which will go to the field of human organization. Despite the slow start, however, quantitative research in the social sciences is growing and, with financial support from both government and industry, growing at an impressive rate and yielding important findings. These findings will have widespread implications for the management of marketing.

At the Institute for Social Research, which is composed of the Survey Research Center and the Research Center for Group Dynamics, we have been engaged, since 1947, on an extensive program of scientific research on the problems of leadership and organizational performance. We have conducted about ninety different studies in some thirty different industries. These studies have been concerned with widely divergent kinds of human activity, from the most routine repetitive task to the complex one of the scientist doing research in an industrial or governmental health laboratory.

Our studies have dealt with entire organizations, including the company president, the people reporting directly to him, various levels of management, and nonsupervisory employees.

In our research, we use the same kind of rigorous procedures that have always characterized the scientific method. Personal judgment or wisdom is of interest to us only to the extent that it may give us clues as to what to measure. A fundamental research design which we have used frequently is to seek situations which provide measurable differences in performance not attributable to differences in technology or aptitude. Such situations are not easy to find.

In clerical and some other operations, however, we have found parallel departments employing identical technology and staffed with persons of comparable aptitudes. In such situations, differences in performance are clearly attributable to the differences in leadership and supervision from department to department. In instances where we have not been able to find comparable units using identical technologies, we have been compelled to employ less powerful research designs. These include evaluating performance in terms of time standards and the occasional use of judgmental ratings.

Once a research site has been selected, we obtain measurements of the causal variables such as the organizational structure, the managerial philosophy of management, and the behavior of managers and supervisors. We also obtain measurements of the intervening variables—the attitudinal, motivational, and communication variables—and the end-result variables, such as sales volume, production, waste, and earnings. We then analyze the data by relating the measurements of the causal variables to those of the intervening and end-result variables to discover the relationships between such variables as leadership behavior, employee motivation, and financial success.

The completion of a number of studies using the over-all approach which I have just described gave us data showing the principles and practices used by the highest-producing managers. This knowledge enabled us to conduct experiments to see whether performance is improved when managers are helped to apply in their own management the principles used by the highest-producing managers. Other studies employing an experimental design are now in preparation.

Our research studies are conducted in such a way that we, or others, can repeat the study in other situations to test the general applicability of our findings. By this process of replication, we can determine whether a specific finding was merely a function of a specific situation or has a more general and broader applicability upon which we can confidently build a body of knowledge.

From our research, and from the research going on at Ohio State, Yale, Cornell, California, M.I.T., and other places, there is steadily emerging a clearer and clearer pattern of the differences in the management principles and practices used by the high-producing and low-producing managers. The evidence demonstrates that the high-producing managers in American industry are gradually evolving a more effective—and also more complex—system of management. These high-producing managers are deviating in important ways, too, from the underlying assumptions upon which the standard operating procedures of their companies are based.

It is possible to integrate the principles used, on the average, by the highest-producing managers into an over-all system of management which I call the *newer theory—or system—of management.* This theory and the research findings upon which it is based are described in *New Patterns of Management.*[1]

I shall summarize some of the important operating characteristics of the newer system of management. Then I shall examine some research findings that test the extent to which this newer system appears to be applicable to sales management. After this, I shall discuss briefly some of the principles and practices which the theory calls for when applied to the management of a sales organization.

The general pattern of the high-producing managers differs significantly from that of the low-producing managers. The high producers are achieving higher performance and lower costs with less feeling of hierarchical, or unreasonable, pressure on the part of their subordinates. The subordinates have more freedom to pace themselves in their jobs. They are more enthusiastic about their work. There is better teamwork among the subordinates, less anxiety, less conflict, and less stress.

That the high-producing managers are creating a more powerful social system can be seen from the data shown in Figure 1. These data are from a service operation and involve thirty-one different departments located in five major metropolitan areas. The departments vary in size from about twenty to seventy-five employees. The nonsupervisory employees belong to a union.

The data shown in Figure 1 deal with the men's perception of how much influence their manager has on what goes on in the department—his capacity to exercise control

[1] Rensis Likert, *New Patterns of Management,* McGraw-Hill Book Company, New York, 1961.

**Figure 1. Relation of department productivity to average amount of influence actually exercised by various hierarchical levels (as seen by nonsupervisory employees)**

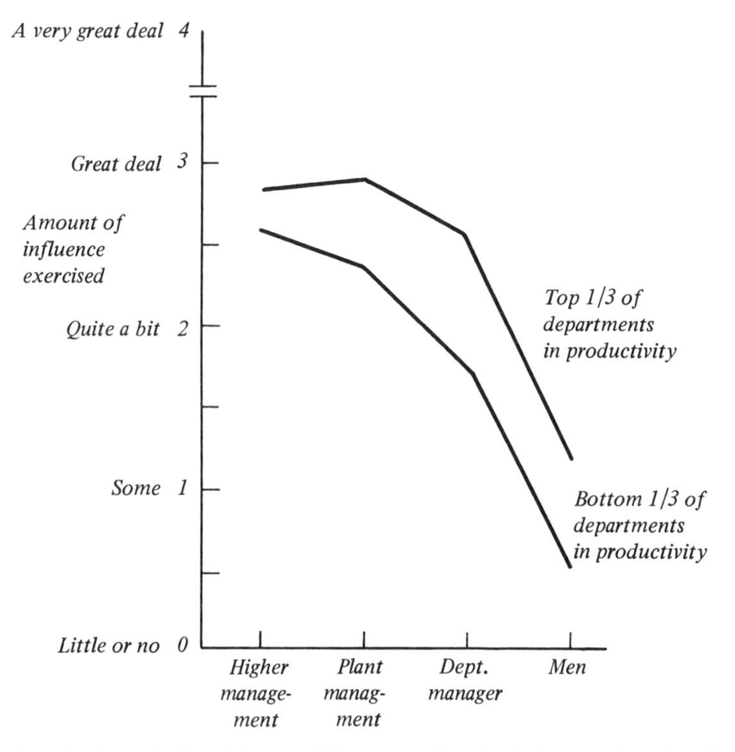


*Source: Part of a figure in* New Patterns of Management *by Rensis Likert. Copyright 1961. McGraw-Hill Book Co., Inc. Used by permission.*

or influence. To obtain these data we asked the men the following questions: "In general, how much say or influence do the men have as to what goes on in the department? How much does the manager have? The plant management? Higher management?" To each question the men could answer, "Little or no influence," "Some," "Quite a bit," "Great deal," or "A very great deal." Figure 1 gives the composite scores for the ten most productive departments and the ten least productive departments of the thirty-one departments.

The same question was asked of the managers, and their answers yielded the same general pattern and conclusions as the men's. The only appreciable difference was that the managers saw themselves as having more influence than any other hierarchical level.

The data in Figure 1 show that the high-producing managers have created a more powerful social system in which they have a greater capacity to exercise influence and coordination than is the case with the low-producing managers. An important characteristic of this social system created by the high-producing managers is that *everyone* can exert more influence than can the people in the less-productive social system. The managers have more influence but so, too, do the men; there is greater capacity for upward, as well as downward, influence. In support of this important finding, we have data which show that high-producing managers are far more effective in communicating upward to higher management such information as problems of equipment, material, and scheduling, ideas for improving the operation, complaints, and grievances. These high-producing managers are also more effective in getting constructive action from their superiors on these and similar problems than are the low-producing managers. Both communication and the exercise of influence are performed more effectively.

Let's ask ourselves, then, what kind of organization the high-producing manager is building. What characterizes this more effective system of management with its better communication, better decision-making based on more accurate information, more cooperative motivation, and greater coordination?

An essential characteristic of this more effective system of management is that it harnesses human motives so that their forces are mutually reinforcing rather than being blunted because different motives are calling for conflicting behavior. This newer system taps the noneconomic motives so that they reinforce and increase the motivational forces arising from the economic motives. This is in contrast to the traditional systems of management where the motivational forces from the noneconomic motives are often in opposition to those forces from the economic motives and as a consequence reduce the effectiveness of the economic motives. This occurs, for example, when direct hierarchical pressure for increased production or cost reduction creates hostile attitudes and resentful behavior which in turn leads to restriction of output, slowdowns, or wildcat strikes.

The high-producing managers realize that merely buying a man's time and issuing instructions does not yield the best results. Similarly, they realize that relying on economic motives alone will not achieve the best performance.

If these same general principles hold in the case of selling, then reliance on economic motives alone should yield less satisfactory results than when the noneconomic motives are used to reinforce the economic. This, as we shall see, is the case. The highest motivation and the best sales performance occur when powerful noneconomic motives reinforce the economic.

It is now possible to assist the top management of any company to build its organization into a newer kind of management system in which the noneconomic motives reinforce the economic. Such a development requires many steps, but one which is fundamental is to apply throughout the organization the *principle of supportive relationships.* This principle should be used to derive appropriate operating procedures and practices and to serve as a general guide to the day-to-day operation of the system. This principle can be stated as follows: *The leadership and other processes of the organization must be such as to ensure a maximum probability that in all interactions and all relationships with the organization each member will, in the light of his background, values, and expectations, view the experience as supportive and one which builds and maintains his sense of personal worth and importance.*

In applying this principle to company operations it is well to keep in mind that the relationship between the superior and subordinate is crucial. This relationship should, as the principle specifies, be one which is supportive and ego-building. At times circumstances may prevent a superior from behaving in a supportive manner but such behavior should be held to the absolute minimum; the more often the behavior is ego-building rather than ego-deflating the better will be its effect on organization performance. It is essential also in applying this principle to keep in mind that the interactions between the leader and the subordinates must be viewed in the light of the subordinate's background, his values, and his expectations. The subordinate's perception of the situation rather than the supervisor's perception determines whether or not the experience is supportive. The superior's behavior and the situation must be such that the subordinate, in the light of his background and expectations, sees the experience as one which contributes to his sense of personal worth and importance, one which increases and maintains his sense of significance and human dignity.

You can test whether the superior's behavior is seen as supportive by asking such questions as the following. If the principle of supportive relationships is being applied well, a subordinate will answer each question with a reaction favorable to the superior:

1. To what extent does your superior try to understand your problems and do something about them?

2. How much is your superior really interested in helping you with your personal and family problems?

3. How much help do you get from your superior in doing your work?

a. How much is he interested in training you and helping you learn better ways of doing your work?
b. How much does he help you solve your problems constructively—not tell you the answers but help you think through your problems?

4. To what extent is he interested in helping you get the training which will assist you in being promoted?

5. To what extent does your superior try to keep you informed about matters related to your job?

6. How fully does your superior share information with you about the company, its financial condition, earnings, etc., or does he keep such information to himself?

7. How much confidence and trust do you have in your superior? How much do you feel he has in you?

8. Does your superior ask your opinion when a problem comes up which involves your work?

a. Does he value your ideas and seek them and endeavor to use them?
b. How well does he listen to you?

9. Does he hold group meetings of his subordinates and are such meetings worthwhile?

a. Does he help the group develop its skill in reaching sound solutions?
b. Does he help the group develop its skills in effective interaction, in becoming a well-knit team rather than hostile subfactions?
c. Does he use the ideas and solutions which emerge, and does he also help the group to apply its solutions?

10. To what extent does your boss convey to you a feeling of confidence that you can do your job successfully? Does he expect the "impossible" and fully believe you can and will do it?

11. To what extent is he interested in helping you to achieve and maintain a good income?

12. Is he friendly and easily approached?

It is a sobering experience to ask a subordinate these questions and independently to ask his superior to estimate the subordinate's answers and then to compare the two sets of answers. The discrepancies between the two sets of answers all too often are so great as to make one think that the superior and the subordinate cannot be reacting to the same situation. There are important forces[2] causing the subordinate not to reveal to his superior many of his reactions. Nevertheless, to apply effectively the principle of supportive relationships, the superior must be able to estimate with reasonable accuracy the subordinate's reactions and perceptions.[3]

From the principle of supportive relationships an important derivation can be made having direct applicability to building a management system in which the noneconomic motives reinforce the economic motives. This derivation states that full use of the potential present in the manpower resources of an organization will occur only when the organization consists of overlapping, highly effective work groups with each group having high group loyalty and high performance goals.

The traditional organizational structure does not use this group form of organization but consists of a man-to-man model—superior to individual subordinate model (Figure 2a). In this model the president has full authority and responsibility. He delegates to each vice-president specific authority and responsibility and holds each accountable. Each vice-president in turn does the same with each of his subordinates. The entire process—stating policy, issuing orders, following up, checking, etc.—involves man-to-man interaction.

[2] See Likert, *op. cit.*, pp. 52–55.

[3] *Ibid.*, chap. 13 for suggestions on how to obtain accurate information on the subordinate's reactions and perceptions.

**Figure 2. Man-to-man and group patterns of organization**

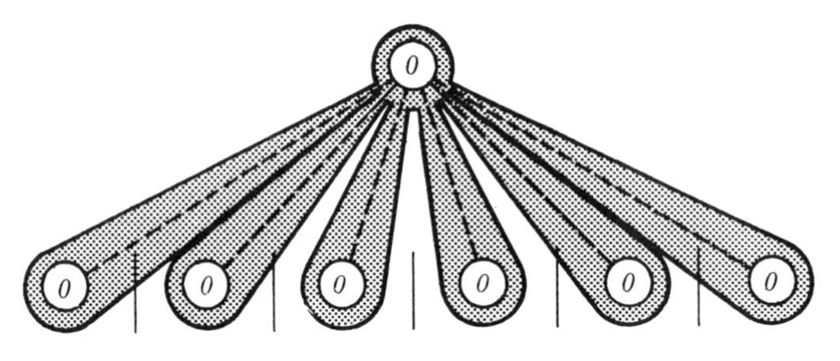

*(a) Man-to-man pattern of organization*

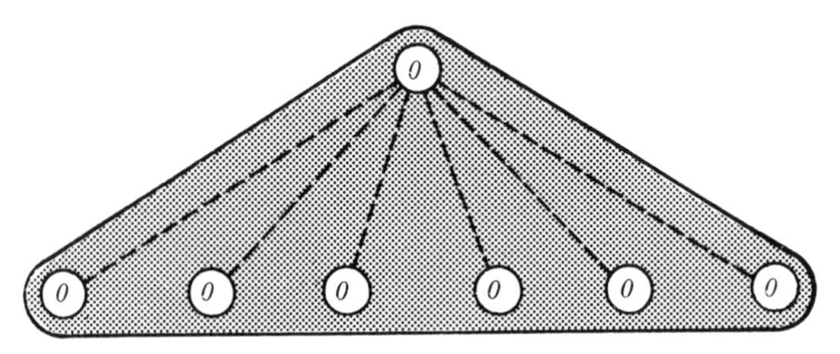

*(b) Group pattern of organization*

*Source: From* New Patterns of Management *by Rensis Likert. Copyright 1961. McGraw-Hill Book Co., Inc. Used by permission.*

The newer system of management in applying the derivation from the principle of supportive relationships calls for an overlapping group form of structure (Figure 2b). When the group process of supervision is used properly, clear-cut responsibilities are established, decisions are arrived at, and functions performed rapidly and productively. Problems are solved in an efficient fashion, with focused discussion and a minimum of idle talk. There is confidence and trust, full but succinct communication adequately understood. Important issues are recognized and dealt with.

I want to emphasize that when I talk about the group method of supervision I am not talking about the "wishy-washy," "common denominator" sort of committee, about which the superior can say, "Well, the group made this decision and I couldn't do a thing about it." Quite the contrary! The group method of supervision requires the superior to be fully responsible for decisions and for building his subordinates into a group which makes the best decisions. *The superior is fully responsible for the decisions that emerge and for the results accomplished.*[4]

[4] *Ibid.,* chaps. 8, 9, 11, and 12 for a discussion of the multiple overlapping group form of management system.

The overlapping group form of organization is structured so that the superior of one group is a subordinate in the next higher group, thus forming a "linking pin" between hierarchical levels, as shown in Figure 3. We have clear-cut evidence that if a manager is going to do a competent job of leadership at his own level, he must be able to influence the decisions of his peers and his superior. Without sideward and upward influence, downward effectiveness is seriously handicapped.

The application of the principal of supportive relationships and the multiple overlapping group form of organization are two essential characteristics of the newer system of management in which the noneconomic motives are mobilized so as to reinforce the economic. Another important characteristic is that managers and supervisors have high performance goals and feel a reciprocal responsibility to the total organization as well as to their own men. There are other important characteristics but we do not have time to consider them today.

Let us turn now to the questions: Is this newer system applicable to sales management? Can it be used to help sales managers improve sales performance significantly?

Sales managers quite generally are saying to us in our interviews with them that the most important problem they face is how to motivate salesmen. When we ask managers to compare their best salesman with their poorest, time and again they say that their poorest salesman knows just as much about the technical aspects of the job, e.g. markets, products, etc., as does their best salesman, but the poorer salesman just does not get out and call on prospects; he does not make sales presentations. What calls he

**Figure 3. The linking pin**

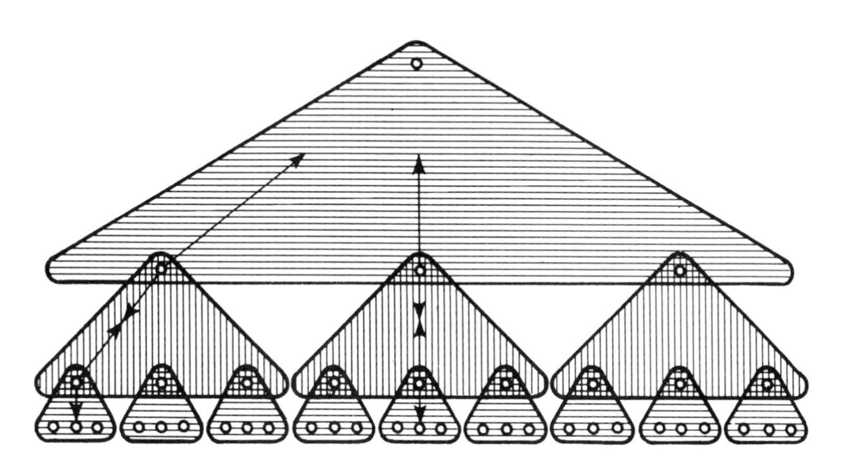

*(The arrows indicate the linking pin function)*

*Source: From* New Patterns of Management *by Rensis Likert. Copyright 1961. McGraw-Hill Book Co., Inc. Used by permission.*

does make are often on poorer prospects. He makes fewer closings on poorer prospects and so gets appreciably less business.

What sales managers are saying, in essence, is that if they had some way of spurring their salesmen on, of tapping the noneconomic motives so that these motives reinforced the economic, they would get significantly better results. This, of course, is precisely what the newer theory of organization makes possible.

Let us look at the motivational consequences and the results achieved when different systems of management are used. What happens when a sales manager uses the traditional system of management and relies on direct hierarchical pressure, or only upon economic motives in the form, for example, of commissions? What happens when the manager uses the newer system and applies the principle of supportive relationships and the overlapping group form of organization?

Presented in Figure 4a are data from an operation involving forty different independent sales units under relatively independent management but all part of a large company which operates nationally. Geographically these units are widely scattered throughout the nation. They vary in size from eight salesmen to some fifty salesmen, with a supporting staff of clerical and supervisory personnel.

These forty units consist of twenty pairs of units picked from a total of approximately one hundred such units in the company. One unit of each pair comes from the best units in the company. The top sales management of the company selected these units on the basis of such criteria as sales volume, costs, quality of business sold, and development of manpower. Each of these units was matched by size and type of market with another unit which was not among the top twenty. Some of these other matching units were about average; some were below average. In Figure 4a the twenty superior units, which we shall refer to as "better units," are indicated by a large black dot, and the "poorer units" are shown by a vertical bar.

The two axes in Figure 4a deal with measurements based on information obtained from the salesmen. The vertical axis reflects the extent to which the men feel that their sales manager has a well-organized sales plan which he tries to get his men to follow and the level of sales goals he has for his unit. Since the extent to which a manager has a well-organized sales plan and the level of his sales goals were found to be highly correlated for these sales managers, I have combined them into a single index called *Sales Managers' Performance Goals.* This will simplify our presentation and save time.

The horizontal axis shows comparable measurements as to the extent to which the men feel that the *men* in the unit have a well-organized plan of work and have high sales goals. As with the managers, these two variables are highly correlated for the men and have been combined into a single index. The mean (average) score for all of the men in a sales unit is shown in Figure 4a and is called the *Salesmen's Performance Goals.*

The numbers assigned to the two axes shown in Figure 4a are comparable since identical questions were used to obtain the men's reactions to the job organization and sales

Figure 4a. Salesmen's performance goals vs. sales managers' performance goals

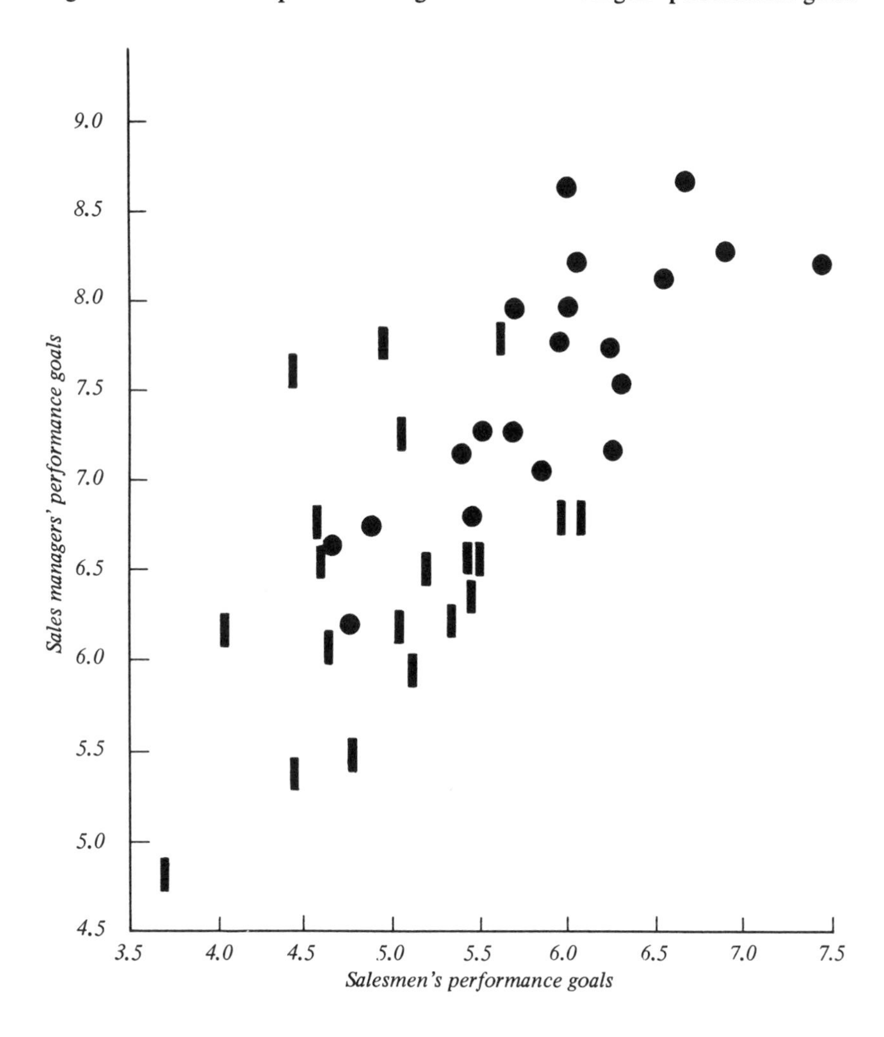


goals of their manager on the one hand and to the job organization and sales goals of their colleagues on the other.

An examination of Figure 4a reveals many important facts. There is a marked relationship between the performance goal scores of the managers and those of the men in their unit. The higher the performance goals of the manager, the higher in general are the performance goals of the men in the sales unit. There is not a single unit in which the manager has low performance goals and the men have high performance goals.

On the average, the performance goals of the men in a unit are appreciably lower than those of their manager. As Figure 4a shows, the mean performance goals score of the men in a sales unit is about one to one and one-half points lower than the performance goal score of the manager of that unit.

These results demonstrate that it is necessary for a sales manager to have high performance goals if the men in his sales unit are to have high goals. The manager's goals and job organization are very important in determining the goals and job organization of his men. Moreover, it is necessary for the manager to have higher goals on this combined dimension than those he seeks for the men. This is shown by the fact that although the men's scores tend to be high if the manager's is high, and low if his is low, the average score for the men in a sales unit is *lower in every sales unit* than that of the manager of the unit.

A fundamental finding revealed by Figure 4a is that the better units (black dots) are overwhelmingly in the upper right-hand part of the figure and the poorer units (vertical bars) are in the lower left-hand portion. If a sales unit is to achieve outstanding performance, it is necessary for *both* its manager and its men to have high performance goals. Both manager and men need to have a well-organized plan of operation and high sales goals. As Figure 4a shows, it is *not* sufficient for the manager alone to score high on job organization and performance goals.

There are three sales units in Figure 4a where the managers have high performance scores but the men have below average scores, and all three are poorer units. These results raise the question: What must a manager do, in addition to having high performance goals himself, to create high performance goals on the part of his men? How does a manager assist his men to develop well-organized plans of work and to establish high sales goals in addition to having them himself?

The results in Figure 4b help to answer the question. Figure 4b is exactly the same as Figure 4a except for the added dotted lines, rectangle, and circles. The dotted lines in Figure 4b mark off the upper-right quadrant of the figure. The managers in the sales units marked off in this manner are behaving differently from the rest of the sales managers. Every one of the sales managers in the units in this upper-right quadrant, except one, are using group methods of supervision in managing their sales organization. The one exception is the poorer unit enclosed in the rectangle. Of the nineteen units in which the manager uses group methods of supervision, seventeen are better units; only two are poorer.

The management practices of the other twenty units contrast sharply with the practices used by the managers of the twenty units which we have just examined. None of the managers of these other units, namely, those not in the upper-right quadrant, uses group methods of supervision. It is significant that these other units are characterized by having lower salesmen's performance goals and by being predominantly poorer sales units. Seventeen of these twenty units are poorer units.

It may be well to describe briefly what is meant by "group methods of supervision." The exact process varies appreciably from unit to unit but typically is likely to be about as follows. The salesmen meet regularly in group meetings. The number of men varies depending upon the number in the territory but usually does not exceed twelve or

Figure 4b. Salesmen's performance goals vs. sales managers' performance goals with reference to specific units

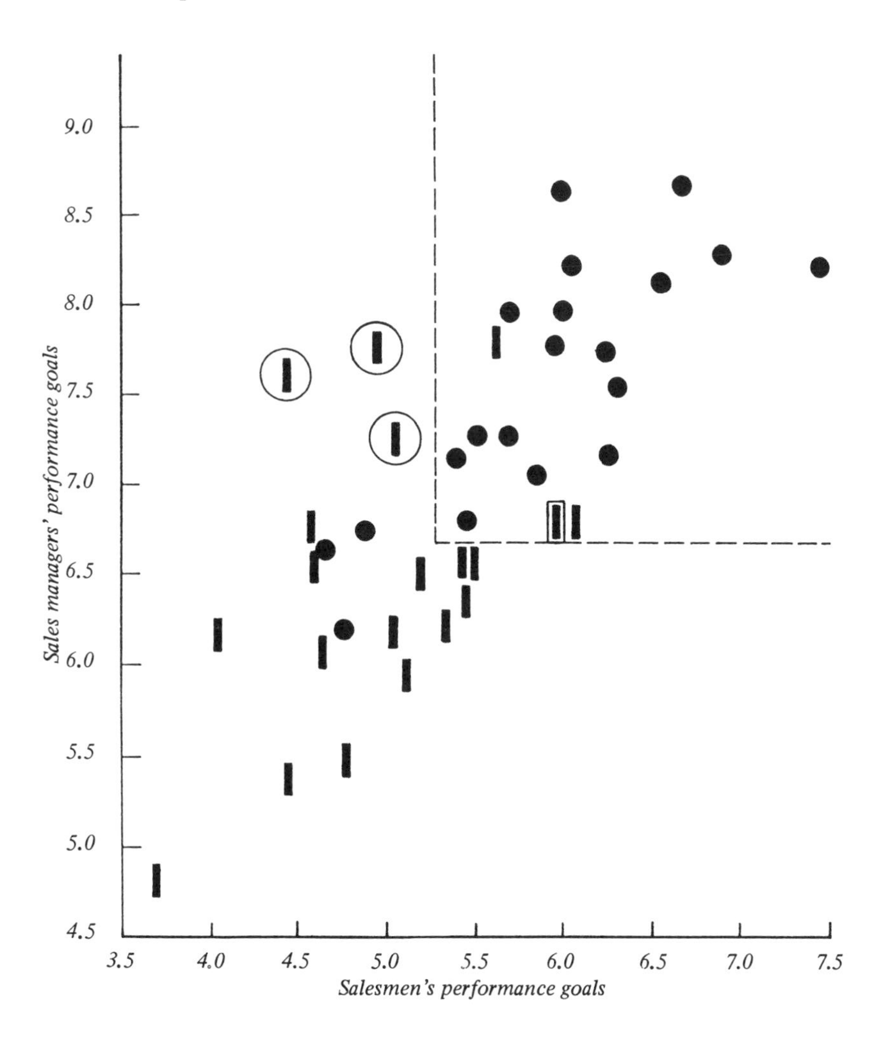


fifteen. They are likely to meet at regular intervals every two weeks or every month. As a rule, the sales manager or one of his sales supervisors presides. Each salesman, in turn, presents to the group a report of his activity for the period since the last meeting of the group. He describes such things as the number and kinds of prospects he has obtained, the calls he has made, the nature of the sales presentations he has used, the closings he has attempted, the number of sales achieved, and the volume and quality of his total sales. The other men in the group analyze the salesman's efforts, methods, and results. Suggestions from their experience and know-how are offered. The outcome is a valuable coaching session. For example, if sales results can be improved through better prospecting, this is made clear, and the steps and methods to achieve this improvement are spelled out.

After this analysis by the group, each man with the advice and assistance of the group sets goals for himself concerning the work he will do and the results he will achieve before the next meeting of the group.

The manager or supervisor acts as chairman of the group but the analyses and interactions are among the men. The chairman keeps the orientation of the group on a helpful, constructive, problem-solving basis. He sees that the tone is helpful and supportive, not ego-deflating as a result of negative criticisms and comments.

Each salesman, as a consequence of the group meeting, feels a commitment to the group to do the work and achieve the results which he has set for himself. His motivation is often stimulated by having members of the group remind him in a friendly and even forceful way of his goals and commitments if they see him lagging. Moreover, because of the group loyalty created by the meetings, a salesman can, if he needs it, obtain coaching on some problem or assistance on a case not only from his supervisor but also from the other salesmen who had discussed the problem or offered a relevant suggestion in the previous meeting. Each salesman has available to assist him the technical know-how of his supervisor or manager and also that of his colleagues. Salesmen derive two important benefits from effective group meetings: they set and strive to achieve higher sales goals—goals which more nearly reflect their own potentiality—and they receive more technical assistance in selling, obtaining help from both their superior and their peers.

These group meetings are effective when the manager (or supervisor) does a competent job of presiding over the interactions among the men. The results are generally disappointing and are largely a waste of time whenever the manager uses the meeting only for personal interaction between himself and each man individually. This occurs when the manager, himself, analyzes each man's performance and results and sets goals for him. Such meetings, dominated by the manager, do not create group loyalty and are likely to have an adverse rather than a favorable impact upon the salesman's motivation. Moreover, the sales know-how among the salesmen is not used.

The group method of supervision was used unitially in this company only for the new salesmen, men with less than three years with the company. In many sales units, however, the advantages of the group process were recognized by the established salesmen, and at their request it was extended to include them. The most successful sales units, i.e. those with largest volume and lowest costs, are now using group processes of supervision for both their new salesmen and their established salesmen. As a rule, each of the different groups within a sales unit consists only of new salesmen or established men. This has proved desirable since many of the problems of new salesmen are different from the problems of established salesmen.

The salesmen in the forty units represented in Figure 4b are paid on a commission basis. The plan of compensation seeks to use the economic motive in the most effective way possible. But as the results in Figure 4b demonstrate, adding the power of the noneconomic motives significantly improves performance over that achieved when economic motives alone are tapped.

Among the most powerful of the noneconomic motives is the desire to achieve and maintain a sense of personal worth and importance. It can be used in many different ways as a source of motivational forces. Some ways are appreciably better than others in using more of the total potential motivational forces available and using these forces more constructively. Procedures such as contests, or the manager's giving recognition for outstanding sales performance, appear to harness less of the available motivational forces and of the know-how possessed by the sales organization than when group forces are mobilized through the use of group methods of supervision. Competitive procedures, such as contests, pit salesman against salesman and reward him for keeping his know-how to himself. This stimulates each salesman to keep to himself all that he learns about how better to promote his own product, to sell successfully against competing products, and to achieve high levels of sales volume. The sharing of know-how, which the group supervision method encourages, can be an important factor in enabling an entire sales organization to attain outstanding performance, rather than having a limited number of salesmen do so.

Managers of the sales units in the upper-right quadrant of Figure 4b are behaving consistently in their efforts to harness the full power of noneconomic motives. They use group methods of supervision and they apply well the principle of supportive relationships. Both of these general principles and their related procedures appear important in the success of the managers. These two general principles both derive their fundamental motivational force from the desire to achieve and maintain a sense of personal worth and importance.

As seen by their men, the managers who use group methods of supervision are doing a significantly better job of applying the principle of supportive relationships and score appreciably higher in supportive behavior than do the managers who are not using group methods of supervision.

In contrast to the sales units in the upper-right quadrant, the *men* in the three sales units in Figure 4b which are circled have relatively low performance goals. The managers of these three units are similar to the managers of units in the upper-right quadrant in having high performance goals, but, unlike the latter, these three managers have not been successful in encouraging the men in their units to set high performance goals for themselves. The men in these three units are rejecting the high performance goals of their managers. As might be expected, there are substantial differences in the management principles employed by these three managers in comparison with the managers of the units in the upper-right quadrant.

The managers of the three circled sales units are not employing group methods of supervision. Their methods of management involve man-to-man interaction and dominance. Moreover, these three managers are not applying the principle of supportive relationships. Much of the behavior of these managers violates this principle. This is shown by the poor score of these three units with regard to the managers' application of this principle; they rank thirty-three, thirty-seven, and thirty-eight, out of forty.

In these three circled units the men not only reject high performance goals for themselves but they also feel to a greater extent than do the men in the other units that their sales managers are putting unreasonable pressure on them to produce. Direct managerial pressure for high performance and high performance goals quite consistently evokes this feeling on the part of the men.

In the light of all these facts, it is not surprising that these three circled units are, as Figure 4b shows, among the poorer sales units.

In contrast to these three circled sales units is the one at the extreme right of Figure 4b. This is the unit in which the men have the highest performance goals of any unit. As might be expected from the preceding discussion, the manager of this unit applies the principle of supportive relationships well and, in comparison with the other managers, places the greatest emphasis on teamwork and group methods of supervision. He strives hard to build a sales unit whose members pull together toward commonly accepted goals. The men respond by setting and achieving high goals for themselves. This is one of the better units.

There is a substantial body of research findings which demonstrates that the greater the loyalty of the members of a group toward the group, the greater is the motivation among the members to achieve the goals of the group and the greater is the probability that the group will achieve its goals. If the goals of such groups are low, they will restrict production; if the goals are high, they will achieve outstanding performance.

These findings suggest that it is important for a sales manager to know how to develop high group loyalty among his men as well as to know how to assist them to establish performance goals commensurate with their potentiality. How, then, can a manager proceed so as to develop high group loyalty in his organization?

The results shown in Figure 5 shed important light on this problem. The loyalty of the men in a unit toward each other was measured and is called *peer group loyalty score.* This score is plotted along the vertical axis of Figure 5. The forty sales units were divided into four groups of ten each on the basis of the extent to which the sales manager is applying the principle of supportive relationships *(Salesmanagers' Supportive Behavior Score).* The four bars in Figure 5 present data for these four groups of ten sales units each.

The bar on the right in Figure 5 shows the mean (average) peer group loyalty score for the ten sales units whose sales managers are doing the best job of applying the principle of supportive relationships. The left-hand bar in Figure 5 shows the results for the ten units whose managers score lowest on applying the principle of supportive relationships. The intermediate bars show average peer group loyalty scores for the two intermediate groups of ten sales units.

Figure 5 shows the marked differences in peer group loyalty scores in relationship to the managers' supportive behavior. In units whose managers are applying the principle

**Figure 5. Relationship between sales managers' supportive behavior and salesmen's peer group loyalty**

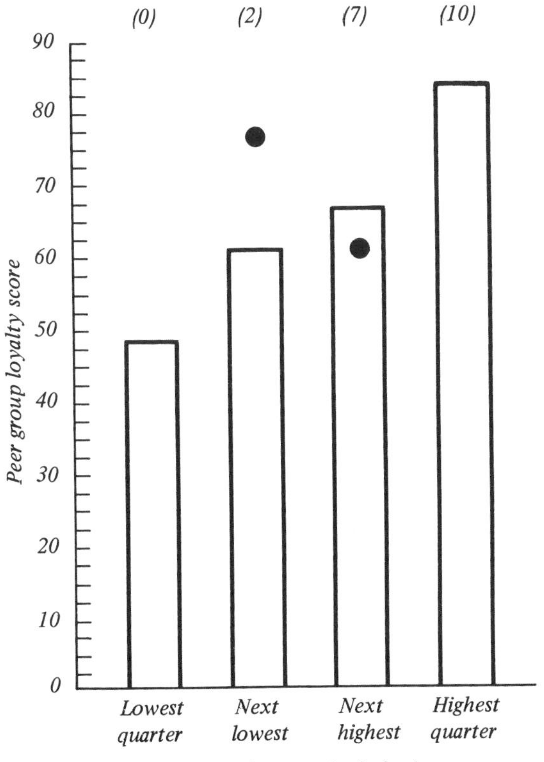


of supportive relationships most effectively, the peer group loyalty scores are appreciably higher than in the units whose managers achieve a low supportive behavior score.

The number in parentheses above each bar shows the extent to which the managers in each group of ten units are using group methods of supervision. In the right-hand bar, ten of the ten units are using group methods of supervision, in the next group seven of the ten, in the next two of the ten, and in the left bar group none of the ten.

In the bar under the number (7), i.e. next to the bar on the right, there is a large dot opposite a peer group loyalty score of sixty-one. This is the mean (average) peer group loyalty score for the three sales units in that cluster of ten whose managers do *not* use group methods of supervision. Under the number (2) and above the second bar from the left there is another large black dot opposite a peer group loyalty score of seventy-six. This is the mean peer group loyalty score for the two sales units whose managers *do* use group methods of supervision. In both bars in the center of the chart, that is, the one under (7) and the one under (2), the managers who use group methods of supervision achieve higher levels of peer group loyalty than the managers who do not. This is consistent with the data shown by the bars on the right and the left.

As the data in Figure 5 show, managers who use group methods of supervision and also effectively apply the principle of supportive relationships are much more likely to have high peer group loyalty among the men in their units than are the managers who do not follow these principles and practices of management. Both group methods of supervision and the effective use of the principle of supportive relationships are required since neither one alone produces as good results as the combination.

As might be expected from the preceding discussion, managers who apply well the principle of supportive relationships and also have high performance goal scores are much more likely to have better sales units than are the managers who display the opposite behavior. This is shown in Figure 6. As will be observed, all of the sales units

**Figure 6. Sales managers' performance goals vs. sales managers' supportive behavior score**

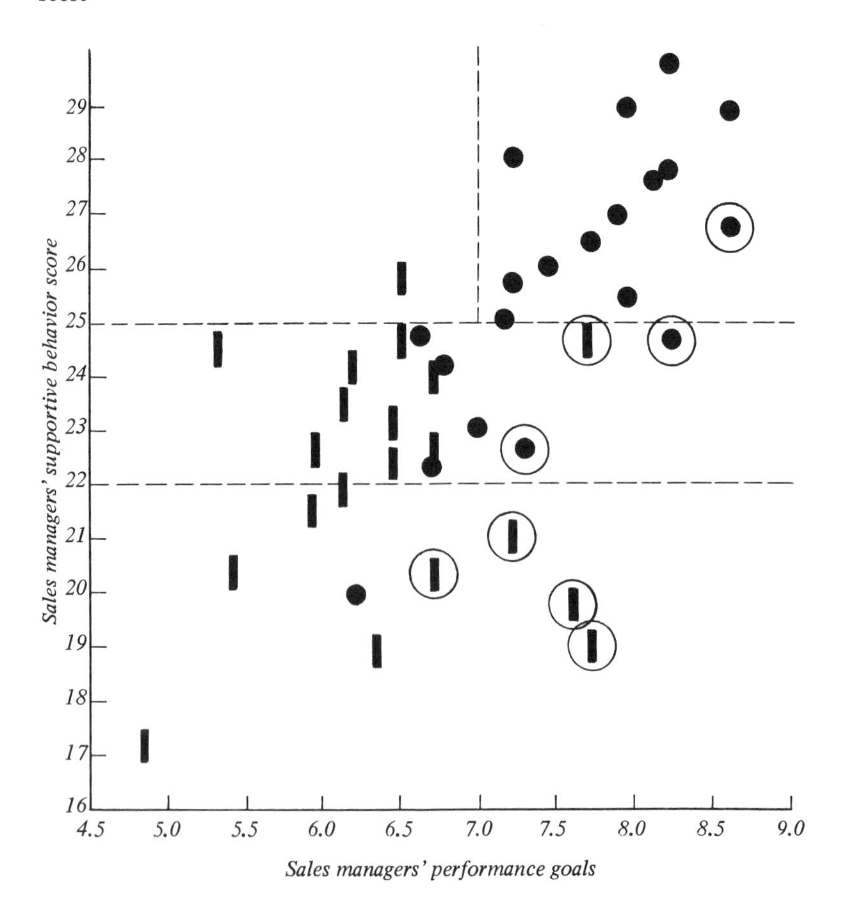

whose managers' supportive behavior score is above twenty-five and whose managers' performance goals are above seven are better performing units (shown by black dots). Moreover, every one of the managers of these sales units is using group methods of supervision. All of the units except one, whose manager's supportive behavior score is below twenty-two, are poorer performing units (shown by vertical bars). None of these sales units have managers who are using group methods of supervision. Again, as would be expected, all of the mean (average) peer group loyalty scores of the salesmen in the former group of units (i.e. above twenty-five) are higher than the highest for the ten sales units whose managers' supportive behavior scores are less than twenty-two.

The eight sales units with circles around them in Figure 6 fall in the top ten of all the units with regard to the extent to which the men feel the manager is putting unreasonable pressure on them to produce. These units tend, in relation to the other units, to be toward the lower-right part of the figure. These are, therefore, units whose managers have relatively high performance goals in comparison with the extent to which they are applying effectively the principle of supportive relationships. These data demonstrate that direct, hierarchical managerial pressure for production produces a feeling of unreasonable pressure in the men and fails to yield the high levels of sales performance which the managers who apply the pressure desire.

The results presented in Figures 4a, 4b, 5, and 6 point to a fundamental conclusion: sales managers who, as seen by their men, have well-organized plans of operation, high sales goals, use group methods of supervision, and apply the principle of supportive relationships are appreciably more likely to have better sales units under their direction than are the managers who, as seen by their men, display the opposite pattern of behavior. The latter are much more likely to be in charge of poorer sales units.

I started this presentation by briefly describing a newer system of management based on the principles and practices used by the managers who are achieving the highest productivity and lowest costs in American business. I then mentioned a few of the basic characteristics of this newer system. As we have seen, the results from a major study of sales management show, as do data from other studies of sales management, that the fundamental principles of this newer system are applicable to the management of sales organizations.

Sales managers, consequently, have available to them today two broadly different systems of management. One, of course, is the system in general use today based on traditional theories of management. The other is the newer system of management based on the principles and practices of the highest-producing managers. This newer system is available because of the creativity of the higher-producing managers and the contribution of quantitative social science research, which is making clear the nature of the principles used by these high-producing managers.

Figure 7 schematically presents the two contrasting courses of action open to a sales manager. There are, of course, intermediate courses of action which also are likely to yield intermediate results so far as sales volume, costs, and over-all performance are concerned.

**Figure 7. Well-organized plan of operation via traditional systems and new management system**

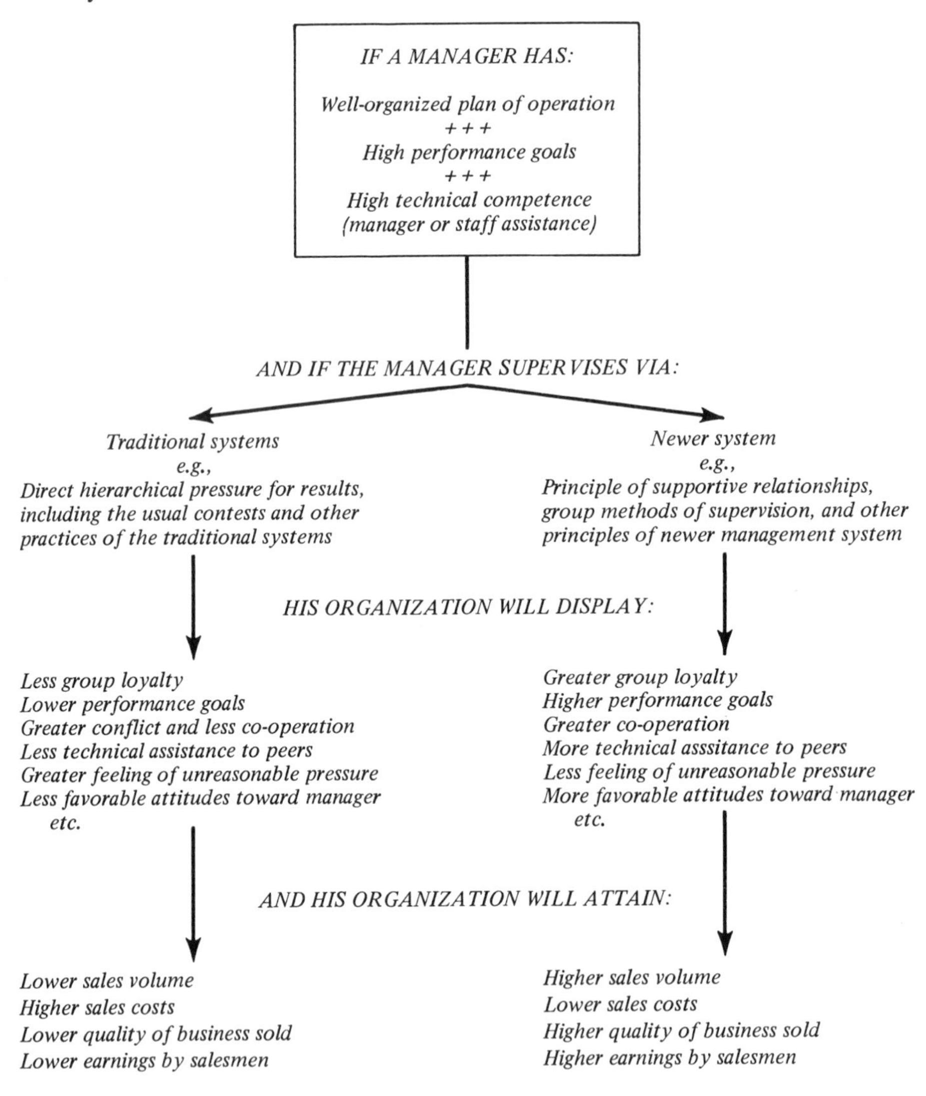


This newer system of management has been applied in a regional sales organization involving about three hundred people and within two years dramatically demonstrated its superiority over the traditional systems.

# 53. THE FAIL-SAFE SALESMAN

*William H. Reynolds*

*One of the sales manager's thorniest problems is that of controlling, from the home office, the performance of the field force. Of course, companies attempt to secure high sales performance by selective hiring procedures and training courses for salesmen.*

*Borrowing the techniques of reliability engineering presently applied to complex component systems of, say, missiles, the author discusses the "real" level of salesman reliability. Team-selling and salesman back-up personnel are elements of redundancy similar to those found in reliability engineering.*

*The following selection represents a look at sales management from a new perspective. Even though reliability engineering as found in production is not directly applicable to sales management, his sales performance in a sense is a mathematical function of his strengths and weaknesses.*

The central and distinguishing feature of sales management is its management by remote control. Contrast the sales manager supervising salesmen in the field with the chief clerk supervising a bullpen of accountants. The chief clerk can observe work in progress and can provide help, praise, or censure, as needed. Mistakes can be corrected as they occur. The chief clerk, to use an aerospace term, operates in real time; he and his men have immediate feedback.

Source: From *Business Horizons,* vol. 9, Summer, 1966, pp. 19–26. William H. Reynolds: Associate Professor of Marketing, University of California at Los Angeles.

The sales manager, on the other hand, has no way of knowing—immediately, at least—whether all of his men are on the job. He may have ways of getting this information sooner or later, but it will always be after the fact. Delayed feedback characterizes his relationship with the men he supervises.

An extreme case of management by remote control (action at a distance) is the problem faced by aerospace engineers in designing an object to be hurled several hundred miles into space. It is rarely practical to fix anything that goes wrong with a "bird" once it has been boosted from a launching pad at Cape Kennedy. Somewhat the same is true of salesmen. Once they are out in the territory and on their own, it is hard to remedy any serious mistake they might make.

## RELIABILITY ENGINEERING

*Development of Theory.* In the case of the missile, the answer that has been developed to this problem is the relatively new discipline of reliability engineering. Reliability engineering aims at the "fail-safe system" and is now applied widely as an adjunct to conventional quality control throughout the aerospace-defense industry. It has also crept into industrial and consumer goods fields; Ford Motor Company, for instance, has a reliability program for its passenger cars, which is directed by a former missile engineer.

This method for deriving the reliability of a system from the individual reliabilities of its components was first developed during World War II by German scientists and technicians working on the V-1 flying bomb:

> Robert Lusser, one of the reliability pioneers, narrates how he and his colleagues, while working with Wernher von Braun on the V-1 missile, met with the reliability problem. The first approach they took towards V-1 reliability was that a chain cannot be stronger than its weakest link. Thus, the missile will be as reliable as this weakest link can be made, or as strong. Although the V-1 was a comparatively simple system, they experienced failure after failure because some component failed in each trial. The missile was 100 per cent unreliable at the beginning in spite of the great efforts made in selecting the components. From the weakest-link concept, which was obviously wrong, they proceeded to the concept that all components must somehow be involved in system reliability, because in some trials it happened that good components, considered to be the strong links in the system, failed and caused system failure. Thus the philosophy emerged that system reliability somehow equals the average of the reliabilities of all the components in the system. But the system was still very much worse than the average component reliability, as found in component tests. No progress was made until one day a mathematician, Erich Pieruschka, who worked with the von Braun team on other problems, was consulted and gave the surprising answer that if the probability of survival of one component is $1/x$, the probability of survival of a system of n such components is $1/(x)^n$. . . .
>
> From Dr. Pieruschka's advice the reliability formula for series systems emerged which is often called Lusser's product law of reliabilities,
>
> $$R_{system} = R_1 R_2 R_3 \ldots R_n$$
>
> and which showed that the reliability of the individual components must be very much higher than the system reliability. Therefore, new components of much higher reliabilities were designed and built, and the result was that the V-1 achieved a 75 per cent reliability.[1]

[1] Igor Bazovsky, *Reliability Theory and Practice,* Prentice-Hall, Inc., Englewood Cliffs, N.J., 1961, pp. 275–76. This paper draws heavily upon Bazovsky.

*The 90 Per Cent Salesman.* The principles of reliability engineering can also be applied to evaluating salesmen, and to their selection and training. The foregoing explanation of reliability engineering suggests that it is *not* sufficient to consider only their weakest points or to average their strengths and weaknesses. The latter mistake is very common; sales managers–and managers in general–live in hope, despite constant disappointments, that a man's strength in one area will counterbalance his weakness in another. That this hope is vain can be seen by considering the case of a salesman with a reliability of 90 per cent in one essential component of his job and 20 per cent in another. His over-all reliability, considering only these two components, is only 18 per cent. He is, in fact, weaker than his weakest link.

Imagine a man we might call a 90 per cent salesman, not A or A+, but a good B, possibly even a B+. He would get a 90 per cent score across the board if graded on each of the various aspects of his job–his personal relationships with customers, his knowledge of the product line, his pricing and negotiation strategies, his attention to business, and his follow-up of leads. Nine times out of ten, he will avoid mistakes in each of these areas. He is, all in all, a pretty good man.

These five aspects of the salesman's job might be called components of his total *system* of competences. Any sales manager, familiar with his own industry, could add to the list, but five seems a reasonable number of areas in which a salesman should be competent. Suppose now that a mistake by a salesman in any one of the assumed five components of his job would be enough to kill a sale. What probability of success does the 90 per cent salesman have in completing any particular sale?

With a 90 per cent probability of avoiding mistakes in two job components, the probability of error-free performance in *both* is the product of the two, $.90 \times .90$, or 81 per cent. With five areas to consider, the probability of error-free performance is $(.90)^5$ or 59 per cent. Despite a high reliability of 90 per cent in each component of his job, the reliability of the 90 per cent salesman as a total system for producing sales is low enough that he will obtain only slightly more than half the sales he ought to get.

The 70 per cent salesman–and there are a great many of them–is not, as might be supposed, only a little less reliable than the 90 per cent salesman, but is drastically less reliable. Instead of an over-all system reliability of 59 per cent, his probability of error-free performance in five different job components–$(.70)^5$–is only 16.8 per cent.

Total system reliability is the *product* rather than the *average* of the reliabilities of the components making up the system. The implication is that the test profile of a salesman might be evaluated better by multiplying his scores on individual items than by computing an average score. This method would differentiate more sharply between good and bad salesmen, as in the comparison made above of the 90 per cent and 70 per cent salesmen. Also, weaknesses would not be masked by strengths but would be given full weight. (Efforts are being made to develop a rating scheme embodying this idea.)

## THE CERTAINTY OF FAILURE

Reliability engineers have two maxims, which will be recognized as valid by any experienced sales manager:

*Maxim I.* If anything can go wrong, it will.

*Maxim II.* If nothing can go wrong, something will go wrong anyway.

Reliability engineers, in effect, accept the certainty of failure, and go on from there to seek ways to make failure less disastrous. Aerospace engineers are not an exceptionally gloomy lot. They deal with systems consisting of thousands of components. They know every time they count down to zero that at least one component in these systems will fail, even if each has a reliability of 0.999 or higher. Reliability to three or four nines is still not enough.

Accepting the inevitability of component failure, the problem changes. Instead of seeking impossible reliabilities in individual components, the designer asks himself: How can system failure be prevented even if component failures occur? What steps can I take to ensure that components, if they fail, will fail-safe, and the system will continue to operate?

Some sales managers similarly recognize that their salesmen are certain to fail in some aspects of their job. For example, the design of earth-moving and construction equipment has become very complex in the past decade or so, and many equipment distributors have seen the number of items in their lines double or quadruple. A major and increasingly critical problem in the industry is the failure of salesmen to keep up with the product knowledge required for effective selling. The old-time equipment salesman was an expert whose advice was solicited by his customers. Because this situation is less true of the new breed, some distributors see only an instance of a general decline in competence–"Salesmen today aren't like they were in my time." They use rewards and penalties to try to induce salesmen to perform at a higher level.

Other distributors, perhaps more enlightened, see the problem as primarily one of selection and training. They employ higher caliber men, put them through formal product courses, and equip them with field handbooks. These distributors might be said to be attempting to improve component reliability.

A few distributors have come to feel that even the best salesman cannot really be expected nowadays to have the broad product knowledge of his predecessors. Accordingly, they backstop the salesman with applications engineers and service and maintenance experts. These distributors are applying one of the central concepts of reliability engineering. They accept the fact that the salesman, even if highly qualified and superbly trained, will often fail to have the product knowledge necessary to deal with some customers.

## REDUNDANCY IN THE SALES JOB

Redundant design is one of the techniques used by the aerospace engineer to improve the reliability of a system. Automobiles offer several examples of redundant fail-safe engineering. If the power brakes fail, the driver can still work them by sheer foot power. Some tires have other tires inside them, which will take over the job of keeping the car on the road if a blowout occurs.

Some readers may have noticed that less-than-crucial mistakes—such as forgetting a customer's name momentarily—were not discussed in the case of the 90 per cent salesman. A sale will not ordinarily be lost if this type of mistake happens, unless it happens often enough to cause real irritation. Mistakes of this kind do not cause total system failure, mainly because of a built-in redundancy in the complex set of activities necessary to produce a sale. G. J. Levenback has commented that several light bulbs can go out in the Times Square news sign (which consists of 13,000 light bulbs) without affecting the readability of the sign:

> In the case of the light bulb sign, redundancy is presented by the combination of sign, reader, and language: several bulbs or even letters could be missing from the intended display and the reader would still be able to understand the message. . . . On the other hand, if we consider a missile or a satellite, there might be a set of critical components such that, if one fails, the whole system is dead.[2]

A salesman's job is at least as complex as that of a Times Square billboard, and it is not necessary for him to be error free in the 13,000 or more separable activities he performs daily. We are concerned only with the mistakes he might make that are serious enough or repeated often enough to cause failure in one of the critical components of his job. Deliberate redundancy is one way to avoid system failure when critical components fail.

Redundant design can enormously improve the reliability of a system. Suppose that a transducer in a missile system has a reliability of 0.999 or only one chance in a thousand of failing. If backstopped by another transducer of the same reliability, the probability that *both* will fail becomes one in a million. The reliability of the system has been improved by three orders of magnitude.

The idea is that the two components are in a *parallel* rather than in a series hookup, as in the case of the component systems discussed earlier. Lusser's Law applies to series hookups, and the failure of *either* component will cause the system to fail. *Both* components must fail if they are arranged in parallel. (See Figure 1.)

Redundancy in managing the sales force can take two forms. First, as in the case of the equipment distributors, the salesman can be backstopped by experts at the home offices.

[2] G. J. Levenback, "Systems Reliability and Engineering Statistical Aspects," *American Scientist,* LIII, September, 1965, pp. 378–79.

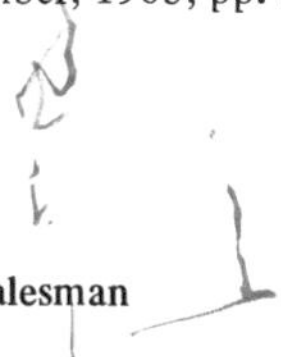

**Figure 1. Reliability: series and parallel components**

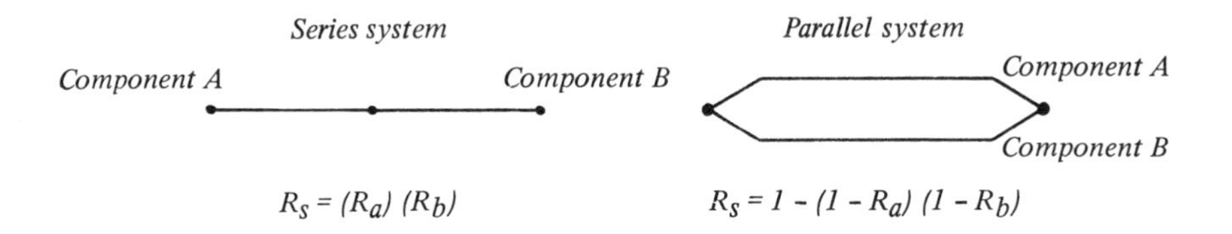


Second, team selling can be used to avoid putting too much reliance on a single salesman in a sales situation.

Both these solutions look upon the salesman as a component that might fail and whose task can be shifted to the redundant components if failure occurs. In the first case, the redundant components are "stand-by," to be called in as needed; in the second, the redundant components are "operating," ready to take over the job immediately.

*The Switching Problem.* The use of standby components raises a new problem; if a standby transducer is to be introduced whenever an operating transducer fails, some kind of switching arrangement is required. The switch must note the fact of failure and turn on the standby transducer. The switch, however, is an extra component and is also subject to failure. The reliability of the switch thus becomes part of the overall reliability of the system, and switch failure can cause failure of the system.

In fact, this situation is what appears to happen when salesmen are supported by home office specialists. Some switching arrangement is needed to "turn on" these people when they are needed in the sales situation. But the "switch" cannot be counted upon to operate routinely and automatically. Salesmen complain bitterly that service and repair men do not respond promptly and efficiently. Applications engineers complain that salesmen do not use their skills appropriately. Credit managers are notoriously often bypassed by salesmen.

These instances all describe switch failure and explain why the expected increased reliability from home office backstop personnel often fails to materialize. Good sales management will give an inordinate amount of attention to switch reliability.

The important thing to realize, returning to the concept of management by remote control, is that most of the time it is the salesman himself who must operate the switch. Sometimes, by the equivalent of telemetry[3] in missile engineering, the sales manager can detect that something is wrong in the field and dispatch help. The response of the sales manager, however, even with the best reporting system in the world, will always be delayed. For immediate, real time response, the salesman must be trained to know when he needs help, what kind of help he needs, how to ask for it, and how to use it. Rotation of personnel, frequent sales meetings, and other devices must be used to

[3]Measurement at a distance.

foster what amounts to a sales management attitude in the salesman. The compensation plan should take cognizance of how well the salesman performs this aspect of his job.

*Team Selling.* Team selling avoids the switch problem. The applications engineer and the salesman, working together, both in contact with the customer, increase system reliability without the complication of the switch. The redundant component is operating. Aerospace firms, because of the complexity and high technological content of the products they sell, have been forced into a kind of team selling. The salesman, or field representative, in fact does little if any selling himself. His main task is to feed information about the customer back to the home office and to coordinate the efforts of the selling team. Other firms might look into the feasibility of this approach for their own sales efforts. The problem is that it is expensive, and the firm must consider whether the additional reliability in the percentage of completed sales is worth the added sales expense.

A point to be emphasized is that the salesmen in a sales team must be hooked up in parallel rather than in series for the advantages of redundant design to be gained. Having one salesman on the team a specialist in customer relations and another a specialist in the product will improve the reliability of the total system only by improving *component* reliability. Adding the extra specialist salesman conceivably could even cause a decline in the reliability of the system. For example, the product ignorance of the customer specialist might alienate technically minded buyers, and the product specialist might make a mistake in customer relations too serious for the customer specialist to overcome.

Both of the salesmen in this hypothetical team must be trained in the other's specialty for true redundancy to be achieved. Customer contact men must be given training courses in the product, and application engineers must receive training in customer relations. Both will end up as relatively high-powered men, and the salaries they will demand is one reason why team selling is expensive.

## SALESMAN SELECTION AND STRESS REDUCTION

Estimates of the reliability of particular components are developed by testing to destruction a large enough sample of the components to compute the mean time of failure and the distribution of failures under certain stress levels. A hundred components might be tested in this way to determine the expected reliability of the single component, which is eventually installed in the final over-all system.

Environmental testing is an important part of this process, and many aerospace companies have environmental laboratories that can simulate, for example, the environments a missile might encounter in space or during re-entry. A component might have a certain reliability under some environmental conditions (stresses) and another reliability under another.

Salesman selection procedures should similarly take into account the kinds of stresses the salesman will be exposed to in the field. This is simply another way of stating the commonplace that selection procedures should be based upon the demands of the job. But how many companies have actually examined salesman failures in an effort to identify crucial stresses? How many firms used environmental testing to screen salesmen compared to the number of firms who still rely on interviews and pencil-and-paper tests?

Various forms of environmental tests are available. One of the simplest is previous experience. A salesman who has demonstrated his ability in other sales jobs is a better bet than one who has not. In fact, previous sales success is one of our best predictors of future success. (The same, incidentally, is true of many electronic components. A transistor "off the shelf" has a lower reliability than one that has been operating for a time.)

Experienced salesmen cost money, and alternative environmental tests can be used by the firm that raises its own salesmen. Role-playing sessions, for instance, can be used for screening and selection as well as for training. Field tryouts could be used more extensively before a commitment is made. The employment interview decried above could be structured into a stressful situation; in some firms, the prospective employee might be taken to lunch and plied with martinis. One ploy to test how a candidate handles failure–an important ingredient in sales success–is to tell him bluntly that he has failed the selection tests and observe his behavior. The stresses built into the selection procedure must, of course, duplicate to the extent possible the stresses in the actual sales environment.

The relationship of reliability to stress suggests that salesman reliability can be improved by designing the job and selecting the salesman so that he is working at less than capacity. This is a special case of redundancy, in which redundant competence is used to ensure that the salesman will not fail at the level of stress anticipated.

## FAILURES AND CHECK-OUTS

The foregoing has been concerned mainly with chance failures and how they can be controlled by redundant design and selection procedures related to expected stress. Two other kinds of failure need to be considered by the reliability engineer and the sales manager–early failure and wear-out failure.

Early failures occur when the component is first placed in service. Some components may fail immediately, but, if they work at all, are good for thousands of hours. All of us are familiar with this kind of failure in our do-it-yourself jobs around the house. We put up a picture hook and hang a picture; if the hook stays fixed and the picture does not fall to the floor, we walk away fairly confident that the nail-hook-picture system has sufficient reliability for our purpose.

Early failures are controlled by "burn-in," trying the component out in actual operation, and by "debugging," fixing whatever goes wrong with the component when it is first operated. The sales manager must similarly watch for signs of early failure in his new recruits as they are burned-in and he must use some kind of coaching system for debugging. The amount of effort he puts into the prevention of early failure will depend on recruitment costs. If salesmen can be hired easily, and little training is required, a sales manager might look upon his salesmen as replaceable components and accept a high rate of early failure. Some automobile dealers, for example, will hire almost anyone who walks in off the street. If the new salesman works out, he stays; if he does not, he leaves. No serious costs are incurred in spite of the high early failure rate.

Few sales managers can take this attitude, however, and minimizing early failures can be rewarding. Once over the hump the new recruit can be a long-term valuable employee. Parallel redundancy during a recruit's novitiate is more important than at any other time. An old timer accompanying a new man on his first few excursions into the field can protect a firm against costly early failures in addition to providing valuable coaching.

Wear-out failures are controlled by preventive maintenance, which means the replacement of components well within their expected useful life. Ethical considerations make this a difficult policy to follow with salesmen, and, in any case, human beings do not wear out in quite the same way electronic equipment does.

Another point to consider is that prevention of wear-out failure by replacing components increases the probability of early failures. Organizations with high turnover suffer more from early failures than from chance or wear-out failures. This fact seems to be intuitively recognized by the apparently overly tolerant sales manager who puts up with unsatisfactory employees. He accepts chance and wear-out failures to minimize early failures. The hard-nosed sales manager follows an opposite tack.

This distinction between random, early, and wear-out failures suggests that a firm might make some effort to determine the kinds of failures it is encountering. Each kind of failure has a different solution, and inappropriate corrective action can worsen failure rates rather than improve them. Salesmen are replaced as failures occur, and, since failures occur at different times, a sales force soon comes to consist of salesmen varying greatly with respect to time in job. Disentangling kinds of failure under these circumstances is difficult, but, nevertheless, imperative.

## CHECK-OUT PROCEDURES

Check-out prior to failure is a device used to improve component and system reliability. It is especially applicable to stand-by systems, which may have failed without any external indication. It is also applicable to operating systems that have not yet encountered a particular task for which they were designed. A missile in a silo is an example of the former; a warning system to detect enemy missiles is an example of the latter. Readiness is the objective sought.[4]

[4] Milton Kamins, *Determining Checkout Intervals for Systems Subject to Random Failures,* Research Memorandum RM–2578, RAND Corporation, Santa Monica, Calif., June 15, 1960, p. 5.

Salesmen and sales support personnel must also be checked out periodically. Many firms recognize this need with programs for refresher training or executive field tours to observe salesmen in action. Customer contact—bypassing the salesman—is sometimes initiated to check out his performance.

Check-out procedures can *cause* failures as well as prevent them. A system may be in good operating condition until it is torn down, inspected, and reassembled. In the same way, repeated check-outs of salesmen can damage morale and cause more failures than they prevent. A good sales manager will often suffer insomniac agonies over reports that one of his salesmen is drinking or otherwise on the verge of failure. Attempts to verify the report might destroy the effectiveness of the salesman altogether. Check-outs can also cause failures simply by being wrong. A good salesman in a random slump might mistakenly be discarded and a new salesman of unknown reliability installed in his place.

Check-out procedures are nevertheless essential. Failure can occur in many aspects of the salesman's job and not be detectable until considerably later. The sales manager cannot rely on neat expense and call reports and the fact that a salesman is currently up to quota. He must have a clear idea of the things his salesman must do to produce sales and check to be sure they are being done. He should be aware, however, of the risks involved in too frequent or too onerous check-out.

## IN SUMMARY

This article has attempted to point out some analogies between reliability engineering and sales management. Its intention has been heuristic—to look at the problems of the sales manager in a somewhat novel way in the hope of suggesting new solutions to old problems.

The key concept is that reliability depends upon redundancy. Redundant personnel and redundant competence are costly, and they can easily look more like fat than bone to an aggressive sales manager trying to build a hard-hitting streamlined organization. His attempts to improve efficiency can increase failure rates. He should ask himself what contribution, if any, this redundant and apparently unnecessary function or job makes to the over-all reliability of the system.

Robert K. Merton, the distinguished sociologist and student of organization, has commented:

> The newer, more differentiated concept of redundancy is relative and statistical. It recognizes that efficiency increases the prospect of error, that redundancy (or reduced efficiency) makes for safety from error. It leads us to think of, and then, in certain cases, to measure a functionally optimum amount of redundancy among specified conditions: that amount which will approximate a maximum probability of achieving the wanted outcome but not so large an amount that the last increment will fail appreciably to enlarge that probability.[5]

[5] Robert K. Merton, "The Environment of the Innovating Organization: Some Conjectures and Proposals," in Gary A Steiner (ed.), *The Creative Organization,* The University of Chicago Press, Chicago, 1965, p. 61.

Redundancy is useless, however, unless the organization switch system has a high degree of reliability. Proper coordination between the field and the home office is really the main task of the sales manager. Redundant home office specialists who can be "switched on" promptly when needed are the essential elements in a fail-safe sales force. To accomplish this goal, less attention might be given to telemetry in the form of reporting systems, and more attention to building a sales management attitude in the salesman.

# 54. HOW COMMUNICATION WORKS

*Wilbur Schramm*

*Communication is not just a simple type of interaction, but is comprised of a number of critical parts.*

*The author describes the process and then analyzes how it works. He emphasizes the dynamic nature of the process, as well as the interdependency of the parts.*

## THE PROCESS

It will be easier to see how mass communication works if we first look at the communication process in general.

*Communication* comes from the Latin *communis,* common. When we communicate we are trying to establish a "commonness" with someone. That is, we are trying to share information, an idea, or an attitude. At this moment I am trying to communicate to you the idea that the essence of communication is getting the receiver and the sender "tuned" together for a particular message. At this same moment, someone somewhere is excitedly phoning the fire department that the house is on fire. Somewhere else a young man in a parked automobile is trying to convey the understanding that he is moon-eyed because he loves the young lady. Somewhere else a newspaper is trying to persuade its readers to believe as it does about the Republican Party. All these are forms of communication, and the process in each case is essentially the same.

Source: From Wilbur Schramm (ed.), *The Process and Effects of Mass Communication,* Urbana: University of Illinois Press, 1955, pp. 3–26. Wilbur Schramm: Director of the Institute of Communications Research, and Research Professor, University of Illinois.

Communication always requires at least three elements—the source, the message, and the destination. A *source* may be an individual (speaking, writing, drawing, gesturing) or a communication organization (like a newspaper, publishing house, television station or motion picture studio). The *message* may be in the form of ink on paper, sound waves in the air, impulses in an electric current, a wave of the hand, a flag in the air, or any other signal capable of being interpreted meaningfully. The *destination* may be an *individual* listening, watching, or reading; or a member of a *group*, such as a discussion group, a lecture audience, a football crowd, or a mob; or an individual member of the particular group we call the *mass audience,* such as the reader of a newspaper or a viewer of television.

Now what happens when the source tries to build up this "commonness" with his intended receiver? First, the source encodes his message. That is, he takes the information or feeling he wants to share and puts it into a form that can be transmitted. The "pictures in our heads" can't be transmitted until they are coded. When they are coded into spoken words, they can be transmitted easily and effectively, but they can't travel very far unless radio carries them. If they are coded into written words, they go more slowly than spoken words, but they go farther and last longer. Indeed, some messages long outlive their senders—the *Iliad,* for instance; the Gettysburg address; Chartres cathedral. Once coded and sent, a message is quite free of its sender, and what it does is beyond the power of the sender to change. Every writer feels a sense of helplessness when he finally commits his story or his poem to print; you doubtless feel the same way when you mail an important letter. Will it reach the right person? Will he understand it as you intend him to? Will he respond as you want him to? For in order to complete the act of communication the message must be decoded. And there is good reason, as we shall see, for the sender to wonder whether his receiver will really be in tune with him, whether the message will be interpreted without distortion, whether the "picture in the head" of the receiver will bear any resemblance to that in the head of the sender.

We are talking about something very like a radio or telephone circuit. In fact, it is perfectly possible to draw a picture of the human communication system that way:

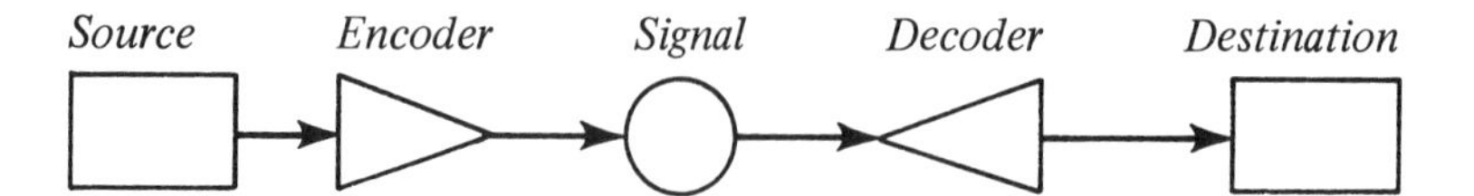


Substitute "microphone" for encoder, and "earphone" for decoder and you are talking about electronic communication. Consider that the "source" and "encoder" are one person, "decoder" and "destination" are another, and the signal is language, and you are talking about human communication.

Now it is perfectly possible by looking at these diagrams to predict how such a system will work. For one thing, such a system can be no stronger than its weakest link. In engineering terms, there may be filtering or distortion at any stage. In human terms, if the source does not have adequate or clear information; if the message is not encoded fully, accurately, effectively in transmittible signs; if these are not transmitted fast enough and accurately enough, despite interference and competition, to the desired receiver; if the message is not decoded in a pattern that corresponds to the encoding; and finally, if the destination is unable to handle the decoded message so as to produce the desired response—then, obviously, the system is working at less than top efficiency. When we realize that *all* these steps must be accomplished with relatively high efficiency if any communication is to be successful, the everyday act of explaining something to a stranger, or writing a letter, seems a minor miracle.

A system like this will have a maximum capacity for handling information and this will depend on the separate capacities of each unit on the chain—for example, the capacity of the channel (how fast can one talk?) or the capacity of the encoder (can your student understand something explained quickly?). If the coding is good (for example, no unnecessary words) the capacity of the channel can be approached, but it can never be exceeded. You can readily see that one of the great skills of communication will lie in knowing how near capacity to operate a channel.

This is partly determined for us by the nature of the language. English, like every other language, has its sequences of words and sounds governed by certain probabilities. If it were organized so that no set of probabilities governed the likelihood that certain words would follow certain other words (for example, that a noun would follow an adjective, or that "States" or "Nations" would follow "United") then we would have nonsense. As a matter of fact, we can calculate the relative amount of freedom open to us in writing any language. For English, the freedom is about 50 per cent. (Incidentally, this is about the required amount of freedom to enable us to construct interesting crossword puzzles. Shannon has estimated that if we had about 70 per cent freedom, we could construct three-dimensional crossword puzzles. If we had only 20 per cent, crossword puzzle making would not be worthwhile.)

So much for language *redundancy,* as communication theorists call it, meaning the percentage of the message which is not open to free choice. But there is also the communicator's redundancy, and this is an important aspect of constructing a message. For if we think our audience may have a hard time understanding the message, we can deliberately introduce more redundancy; we can repeat (just as the radio operator on a ship may send "SOS" over and over again to make sure it is heard and decoded), or we can give examples and analogies. In other words, we always have to choose between transmitting more information in a given time, or transmitting less and repeating more in the hope of being better understood. And as you know, it is often a delicate choice, because too slow a rate will bore an audience, whereas too fast a rate may confuse it.

Perhaps the most important thing about such a system is one we have been talking about all too glibly—the fact that receiver and sender must be in tune. This is clear enough in the case of a radio transmitter and receiver, but somewhat more complicated when it means that a human receiver must be able to understand a human sender.

Let us redraw our diagram in very simple form, like this:

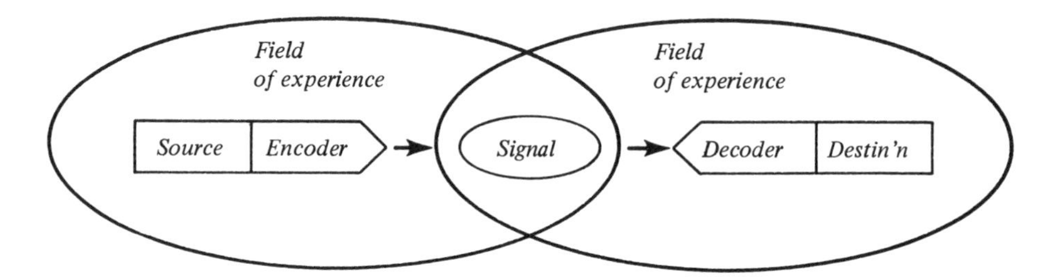


Think of those circles as the accumulated experience of the two individuals trying to communicate. The source can encode, and the destination can decode, only in terms of the experience each has had. If we have never learned any Russian, we can neither code nor decode in that language. If an African tribesman has never seen or heard of an airplane, he can only decode the sight of a plane in terms of whatever experience he has had. The plane may seem to him to be a bird, and the aviator a god borne on wings. If the circles have a large area in common, then communication is easy. If the circles do not meet—if there has been no common experience—then communication is impossible. If the circles have only a small area in common—that is, if the experiences of source and destination have been strikingly unlike—then it is going to be very difficult to get an intended meaning across from one to the other. This is the difficulty we face when a non-science-trained person tries to read Einstein, or when we try to communicate with another culture much different from ours.

The source, then, tries to encode in such a way as to make it easy for the destination to tune in the message—to relate it to parts of his experience which are much like those of the source. What does he have to work with?

Messages are made up of signs. A sign is a signal that stands for something in experience. The word "dog" is a sign that stands for our generalized experience with dogs. The word would be meaningless to a person who came from a dog-less island and had never read of or heard of a dog. But most of us have learned that word by association, just as we learn most signs. Someone called our attention to an animal, and said "dog." When we learned the word, it produced in us much the same response as the object it stood for. That is, when we heard "dog" we could recall the appearance of dogs, their sound, their feel, perhaps their smell. But there is an important difference between the sign and the object: the sign always represents the object at a reduced level of cues. By this we mean simply that the sign will not call forth all the responses that the object itself will call forth. The sign "dog," for example, will probably not call forth in us the same wariness or attention a strange dog might attract if it wandered into our presence. This is the price we pay for portability in language. We have a sign system that we can use in place of the less portable originals (for example, Margaret Mitchell could re-create the burning of Atlanta in a novel, and a photograph could transport world-wide the appearance of a bursting atomic bomb), but our sign system is merely a kind of shorthand. The coder has to be able to write the shorthand, the decoder to read it. And no two persons have learned exactly the same system. For example, a person who has known only Arctic huskies will not have learned exactly the same meaning for the shorthand sign "dog" as will a person who comes from a city where he has known only pekes and poms.

We have come now to a point where we need to tinker a little more with our diagram of the communication process. It is obvious that each person in the communication process is both an encoder and a decoder. He receives and transmits. He must be able to write readable shorthand, and to read other people's shorthand. Therefore, it is possible to describe either sender or receiver in a human communication system thus:

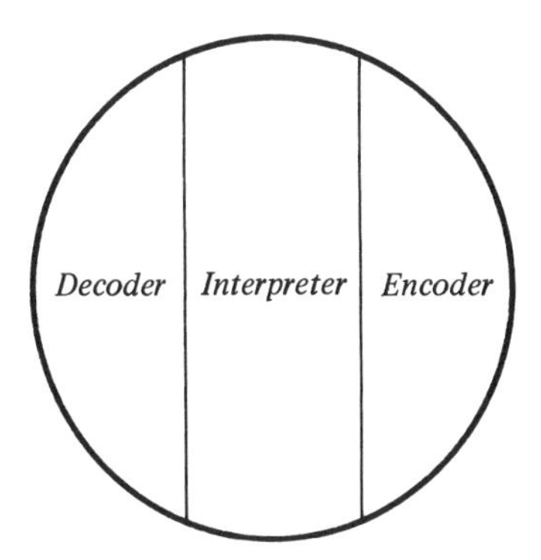


What happens when a signal comes to you? Remember that it comes in the form of a sign. If you have learned the sign, you have learned certain responses with it. We can call these mediatory responses, because they mediate what happens to the message in your nervous system. These responses are the *meaning* the sign has for you. They are learned from experience, as we said, but they are affected by the state of your organism at the moment. For example, if you are hungry, a picture of a steak may not arouse exactly the same response in you as when you are overfed.

But subject to these effects, the mediatory responses will then determine what you do about the sign. For you have learned other sets of reactions connected to the mediatory responses. A sign that means a certain thing to you will start certain other processes in your nerves and muscles. A sign that means "fire," for example, will certainly trigger off some activity in you. A sign that means you are in danger may start the process in your nerves and muscles that makes you say "help!" In other words, the meaning that results from your decoding of a sign will start you *en*coding. Exactly *what* you encode will depend on your choice of the responses available in the situation and connected with the meaning.

Whether this encoding actually results in some overt communication or action depends partly on the barriers in the way. You may think it better to keep silent. And if an action does occur, the nature of the action will also depend on the avenues for action available to you and the barriers in your way. The code of your group may not sanction the action you want to take. The meaning of a sign may make you want to hit the person who has said it, but he may be too big, or you may be in the wrong social situation. You may merely ignore him, or "look murder at him," or say something nasty about him to someone else.

But whatever the exact result, this is the process in which you are constantly engaged. You are constantly decoding signs from your environment, interpreting these signs, and encoding something as a result. In fact, it is misleading to think of the communication process as starting somewhere and ending somewhere. It is really endless. We are little switchboard centers handling and rerouting the great endless current of communication. We can accurately think of communication as passing through us—changed, to be sure, by our interpretations, our habits, our abilities and capabilities, but the input still being reflected in the output.

We need now to add another element to our description of the communication process. Consider what happens in a conversation between two people. One is constantly communicating back to the other, thus:

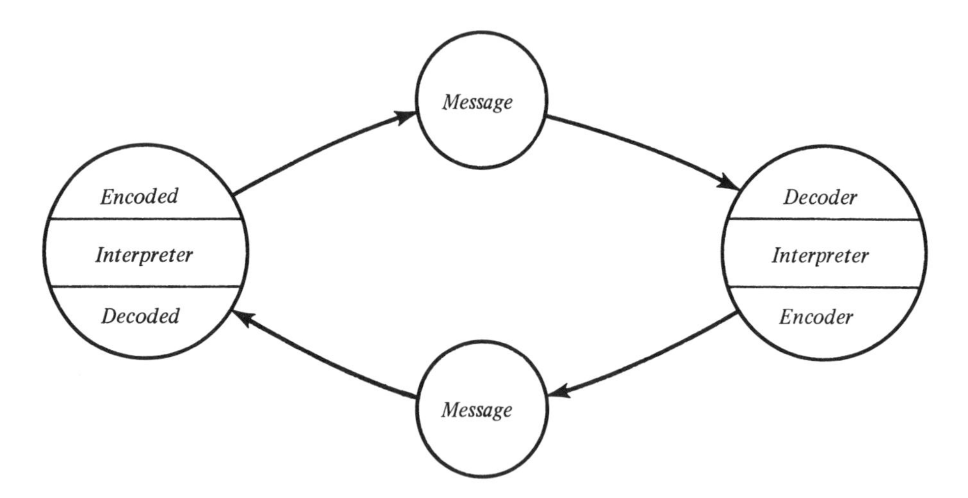


The return process is called *feedback,* and plays a very important part in communication because it tells us how our messages are being interpreted. Does the hearer say, "Yes, yes, that's right," as we try to persuade him? Does he nod his head in agreement? Does a puzzled frown appear on his forehead? Does he look away as though he were losing interest? All these are feedback. So is a letter to the editor of a newspaper, protesting an editorial. So is an answer to a letter. So is the applause of a lecture audience. An experienced communicator is attentive to feedback, and constantly modifies his messages in light of what he observes in or hears from his audience.

At least one other example of feedback, also, is familiar to all of us. We get feedback from our own messages. That is, we hear our own voices and can correct mispronunciations. We see the words we have written on paper, and can correct misspellings or change the style. When we do that, here is what is happening:

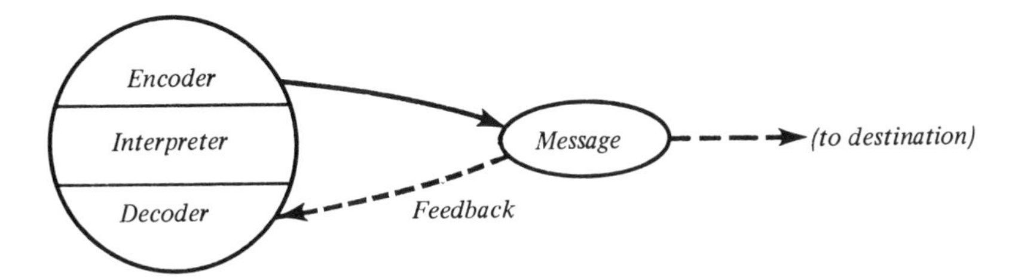


It is clear that in any kind of communication we rarely send out messages in a single channel, and this is the final element we must add to our account of the communication process. When you speak to me, the sound waves from your voice are the primary message. But there are others: the expression on your face, your gestures, the relation of a given message to past messages. Even the primary message conveys information on several levels. It gives me words to decode. It emphasizes certain words above others. It presents the words in a pattern of intonation and timing which contribute to the total meaning. The quality of your voice (deep, high, shrill, rasping, rich, thin, loud, soft), itself, carries information about you and what you are saying.

This multiple channel situation exists even in printed mass communication, where the channels are perhaps most restricted. Meaning is conveyed, not only by the words in a news item, but also by the size of the headline, the position on the page and the page in the paper, the association with pictures, the use of boldface and other typographical devices. All these tell us something about the item. Thus we can visualize the typical channel of communication, not as a simple telegraph circuit, in which current does or does not flow, but rather as a sort of coaxial cable in which many signals flow in parallel from source toward the destination.

These parallel relationships are complex, but you can see their general pattern. A communicator can emphasize a point by adding as many parallel messages as he feels are deserved. If he is communicating by speaking, he can stress a word, pause just before it, say it with a rising inflection, gesture while he says it, look earnestly at his audience. Or he can keep all the signals parallel—except *one.* He can speak solemnly, but wink, as Lowell Thomas sometimes does. He can stress a word in a way that makes it mean something else—for example: "That's a *fine* job you did!" And by so doing he conveys secondary meanings of sarcasm or humor or doubt.

The same thing can be done with printed prose, with broadcast, with television or films. The secondary channels of the sight-sound media are especially rich. I am reminded of a skillful but deadly job done entirely with secondary channels on a certain political candidate. A sidewalk interview program was filmed to run in local theaters. Ostensibly it was a completely impartial program. An equal number of followers of each candidate were interviewed—first, one who favored Candidate A, then one who favored Candidate B, and so on. They were asked exactly the same questions, and said about the same things, although on opposite sides of the political fence, of course. But there was one interesting difference. Whereas the supporters of Candidate A were ordinary folks, not outstandingly attractive or impressive, the followers of Candidate B who were chosen to be interviewed invariably had something slightly wrong with them.

They looked wildeyed, or they stuttered, or they wore unpressed suits. The extra meaning was communicated. Need I say which candidate won?

But this is the process by which communication works, whether it is mass communication, or communication in a group, or communication between individuals.

## COMMUNICATION IN TERMS OF LEARNING THEORY

So far we have avoided talking about this complicated process in what may seem to you to be the obvious way to talk about it—in the terminology and symbols of learning theory.[1] We have done so for the sake of simplicity. Now in order to fill in the picture it seems desirable to sketch the diagram of how communication looks to a psychologist of learning. If psychological diagrams bother you, you can skip to section 3.

Let's start with the diagram, then explain it.

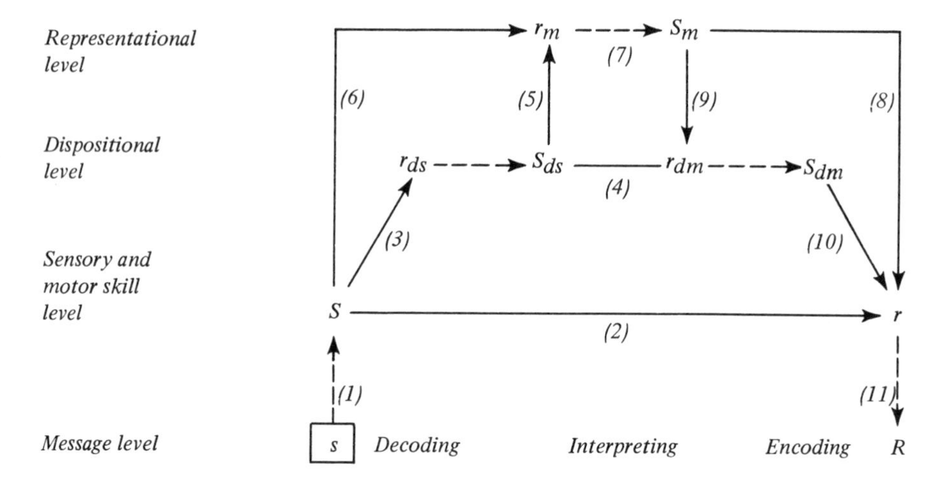


The diagram isn't as complicated as it looks. Remember that time in the diagram moves from left to right, and then follow the numbers and you won't get far off the road.

Begin with (1). This is input. At the message level we have a collection of objectively measurable signs [S]. These come to your sense organs, where they constitute a stimulus for action. This stimulus we call S. When the process gets as far as S, you are paying attention. The message has been accepted. It may not have been accepted as intended; S may not equal [S]; the sensory mechanism may have seen or heard it incompletely. But everything else that happens as a result of the message in that particular destination will now necessarily be the result of the stimulus accepted by your sense organs.

[1] For the model in the following pages the author is indebted to his colleague, Dr. Charles E. Osgood. Dr. Osgood has since published the model in a more advanced form.

Now look at number (2). The message may not have to go to any other level in order to bring about a response. If a man waves his fist near your nose, you may dodge. If he squeezes your hand, you may say "ouch!" These are learned, almost automatic, responses on the sensory and motor skill level.

But the stimulus may also bring about other kinds of activity within your nervous system. Look at number (3). The stimulus S may be translated into a grammatical response on your dispositional level—by which we mean the level of learned integrations (attitudes, values, sets, etc.) which make it so easy for you to dispose of the variety of stimuli that come to you in the course of a day. These are what we call the intervening variables. Suppose the stimulus stirs up activity in this area of intervening variables. Two things may happen. Look at number (4). The response may be so well learned that it doesn't even have to go to the level of thinking. You hear a line of a poem, and almost automatically say the second line. In that case the activity is through numbers (4) and (10).

More often, however, the activity goes through number (5). Here the original stimulus has been decoded into grammar, fed through the intervening variables, and sent up to the representational level of the central nervous system, where meanings are assigned and ideas considered. Occasionally a stimulus comes to that level without going through the intervening variables—as in number (6). These stimuli create activity in the central nervous system ($r_m$) which is the terminus of the decoding part of the process. This is equivalent to the meaning or significance of the signs Ⓢ. What happens in number (7), then, is what we have been referring to as interpretation. The response $r_m$ which we call meaning becomes in turn a stimulus which sets the encoding process in action, so that (7) is both the terminus of decoding and the start of encoding. We learn to associate meanings with desired responses. And so the encoding process moves through (8) or (9). That is, we give certain orders which either pass directly to the neuromuscular system (through 8) or are passed through the intervening variables (through 9 and 10). In any case, all this activity of the nervous system finally results in a response on the motor skill level (r), which results in output (number 11). If the output is an overt response (R), then we have another message, which may offer itself as a collection of signs Ⓢ and be accepted by still another person as a stimulus (S).

This is what we believe happens when someone says to you, "cigarette?" and you answer "yes, please," or "no, thanks." If you are interested in doing so, you can translate all that is said about the communication process in this paper into the psychological symbols we have just been using. But to make the account simpler, we are going to shift gears at this point and talk about communication effects and mass communication in the terms we used in the first section of this article.

## HOW COMMUNICATION HAS AN EFFECT

The chief reason we study this process is to learn something about how it achieves effects. We want to know what a given kind of communication does to people. Given a certain message content, we should like to be able to predict what effect that content will have on its receivers.

Every time we insert an advertisement in a newspaper, put up a sign, explain something to a class, scold a child, write a letter, or put our political candidate on radio or television, we are making a prediction about the effect communication will have. I am predicting now that what I am writing will help you understand the common everyday miracle of communication. Perhaps I am wrong. Certainly many political parties have been proved wrong in their predictions about the effects of their candidates' radio speeches. Some ads sell goods; others don't. Some class teaching "goes over"; some does not. For it is apparent to you, from what you have read so far, that there is no such thing as a simple and easily predictable relationship between message content and effect.

Nevertheless, it is possible to describe simply what might be called the conditions of success in communication—by which we mean the conditions that must be fulfilled if the message is to arouse its intended response. Let us set them down here briefly, and then talk about them:

1. *The message must be so designed and delivered as to gain the attention of the intended destination.*

2. *The message must employ signs which refer to experience common to source and destination, so as to "get the meaning across."*
3. *The message must arouse personality needs in the destination and suggest some ways to meet those needs.*
4. *The message must suggest a way to meet those needs which is appropriate to the group situation in which the destination finds himself at the time when he is moved to make the desired response.*

You can see, by looking at these requirements, why the expert communicator usually begins by finding out as much as he can about his intended destination, and why "know your audience" is the first rule of practical mass communication. For it is important to know the right timing for a message, the kind of language one must use to be understood, the attitudes and values one must appeal to in order to be effective, and the group standards in which the desired action will have to take place. This is relatively easy in face-to-face communication, more difficult in mass communication. In either case, it is necessary.

Let us talk about these four requirements.

1. *The message must be so designed and delivered as to gain the attention of the intended destination.* This is not so easy as it sounds. For one thing, the message must be made available. There will be no communication if we don't talk loudly enough to be heard, or if our letter is not delivered, or if we smile at the right person when she isn't looking. And even if the message is available, it may not be selected. Each of us has

available far more communication than we can possibly accept or decode. We therefore scan our environment in much the same way as we scan newspaper headlines or read a table of contents. We choose messages according to our impression of their general characteristics—whether they fit our needs and interests. We choose usually on the basis of an impression we get from one cue in the message, which may be a headline, a name in a radio news story, a picture, a patch of color, or a sound. If that cue does not appeal to us, we may never open our senses to the message. In different situations, of course, we choose differently among these cues. For example, if you are speaking to me at a time when I am relaxed and unbusy, or when I am waiting for the kind of message you have (for instance, that my friends have come to take me fishing), then you are more likely to get good attention than if you address me when noise blots out what you say, or when all my attention is given to some competing message, or when I am too sleepy to pay attention, or when I am thinking about something else and have simply "tuned out." (How many times have you finished speaking and realized that your intended receiver had simply not heard a word you said?) The designing of a message for attention, then, involves timing, and placing, and equipping it with cues which will appeal to the receiver's interests.

2. *The message must employ signs which refer to experience common to both source and destination, in order to "get the meaning across."* We have already talked about this problem of getting the receiver in tune with the sender. Let us add now that as our experience with environment grows, we tend to classify and catalog experience in terms of how it relates to other experience and to our needs and interests. As we grow older that catalog system grows harder and firmer. It tends to reject messages that do not fit its structure, or distort them so that they do fit. It will reject Einstein, perhaps, because it feels it can't understand him. If an airplane is a completely new experience, but a bird is not, it may, as we have said, interpret the plane as a large, noisy bird. If it is Republican it will tend to reject Democratic radio speeches or to recall only the parts that can be made into pro-Republican arguments; this is one of the things we have found out about voting behavior. Therefore, in designing a message we have to be sure not only that we speak the "same language" as the receiver, and that we don't "write over his head," but also that we don't conflict too directly with the way he sees and catalogs the world. There are some circumstances, true, in which it works well to conflict directly, but for the most part these are the circumstances in which our understandings and attitudes are not yet firm or fixed, and they are relatively few and far between. In communicating, as in flying an airplane, the rule is that when a stiff wind is blowing, one doesn't land cross-wind unless he has to.

3. *The message must arouse personality needs in the destination and suggest some way to meet those needs.* We take action because of need and toward goals. In certain simple situations, the action response is quite automatic. When our nerves signal "pain-heat-finger" we jerk our fingers back from the hot pan. When our optic nerve signals "red traffic light" we stop the car. In more complicated situations we usually have more freedom of choice, and we choose the action which, in the given situation, will come closest to meeting our needs or goals. The first requisite of an effective message, therefore (as every advertising man knows), is that it relate itself to one of our

personality needs—the needs for security, status, belongingness, understanding, freedom from constraint, love, freedom from anxiety, and so forth. It must arouse a drive. It must make the individual feel a need or a tension which he can satisfy by action. Then the message can try to control the resulting action by suggesting what action to take. Thus an advertisement usually tells you to buy, what, and where. Propaganda to enemy troops usually suggests a specific action, such as surrender, subversion, or malingering. The suggested action, of course, is not always the one taken. If an easier, cheaper, or otherwise more acceptable action leading to the same goal is seen, that will probably be selected instead. For instance, it may be that the receiver is not the kind of person to take vigorous action, even though that seems called for. The person's values may inhibit him from doing what is suggested. Or his group role and membership may control what action he takes, and it is this control we must talk about now.

4. *The message must suggest a way to meet those needs which is appropriate to the group situation in which the destination finds himself at the time when he is moved to make the desired response.* We live in groups. We get our first education in the primary group of our family. We learn most of our standards and values from groups. We learn roles in groups, because those roles give us the most orderly and satisfying routine of life. We make most of our communication responses in groups. And if communication is going to bring about change in our behavior, the first place we look for approval of this new behavior is to the group. We are scarcely aware of the great importance our group involvements have for us, or of the loyalties we develop toward our several groups and institutions, until our place in the group or the group itself is threatened. But yet if our groups do not sanction the response we are inclined to make to communication, then we are very unlikely to make it. On the other hand, if our group strongly approves of a certain kind of action, that is the one we are likely to select out of several otherwise even choices.

You can see how this works in practical situations. The Jewish culture does not approve the eating of pork; the Indian culture does not approve the slaughter of cows, and the eating of beef. Therefore, it is highly unlikely that even the most eloquent advertisement will persuade an orthodox Jewish family to go contrary to its group sanctions, and buy pork; or an orthodox Hindu family, to buy beef. Or take the very simple communication situation of a young man and a young woman in a parked automobile. The young man communicates the idea that he wants a kiss. There isn't much likelihood of his not gaining attention for that communication or of its not being understood. But how the young woman responds will depend on a number of factors, partly individual, partly group. Does she want to be kissed at that moment? Does she want to be kissed by that young man? Is the situation at the moment—a moon, soft music from the radio, a convertible—conducive to the response the young man wants? But then, how about the group customs under which the girl lives? If this is a first date, is it "done" to kiss a boy on a first date? Is petting condoned in the case of a girl her age? What has she learned from her parents and her friends about these things? Of course, she won't knowingly have a little debate with herself such as we have suggested here, but all these elements and more will enter into the decision as to whether she tilts up her chin or says, "No, Jerry. Let's go home."

There are two things we can say with confidence about predicting communication effects. One is that a message is much more likely to succeed if it fits the patterns of understandings, attitudes, values and goals that a receiver has; or at least if it starts with this pattern and tries to reshape it slightly. Communication research men call this latter process "canalizing," meaning that the sender provides a channel to direct the already existing motives in the receiver. Advertising men and propagandists say it more bluntly; they say that a communicator must "start where the audience is." You can see why this is. Our personalities—our patterns of habits, attitudes, drives, values, and so forth—grow very slowly but firmly. I have elsewhere compared the process to the slow, sure, ponderous growth of a stalagmite on a cave floor. The stalagmite builds up from the calcareous residue of the water dripping on it from the cave roof. Each drop leaves only a tiny residue, and it is very seldom that we can detect the residue of any single drop, or that any single drop will make a fundamental change in the shape or appearance of the stalagmite. Yet together all these drops do build the stalagmite, and over the years it changes considerably in size and somewhat in shape. This is the way our environment drips into us, drop by drop, each drop leaving a little residue, each tending to follow the existing pattern. This personality pattern we are talking about is, of course, an active thing—not passive, like the stalagmite—but still the similarity is there. When we introduce one drop of communication into a person where millions of drops have already fallen and left their residue, we can hardly expect to reshape the personality fundamentally by that one drop. If we are communicating to a child, it is easier, because the situation is not so firmly fixed. If we are communicating in an area where ideas and values are not yet determined—if our drop of communication falls where not many have fallen before—then we may be able to see a change as a result of our communication.

But in general we must admit that the best thing we can do is to build on what already exists. If we take advantage of the existing pattern of understanding, drives, and attitudes, to gain acceptance for our message, then we may hope to divert the pattern slightly in the direction we want to move it. Let's go back to elections again for an example. It is very hard to change the minds of convinced Republicans or Democrats through communication, or even to get them to listen to the arguments of the opposing party. On the other hand, it is possible to start with a Republican or Democratic viewpoint and slightly modify the existing party viewpoints in one way or other. If this process goes on for long enough, it may even be possible to get confirmed partymen to reverse their voting pattern. This is what the Republicans were trying to do in the 1952 election by stressing "the mess in Washington," "time for a change," "the mistakes in Korea," and "the threat of Communism," and apparently they were successful in getting some ordinarily Democratic votes. But in 1952, as in every compaign, the real objectives of the campaigning were the new voters and the undecided voters.

The second thing we can say with confidence about communication effects is that they are resultants of a number of forces, of which the communicator can really control only one. The sender, that is, can shape his message and can decide when and where to introduce it. But the message is only one of at least four important elements that determine what response occurs. The other three are the situation in which the communication is received and in which the response, if any, must occur; the personality state of the receiver; and his group relationships and standards. This is why it is so dangerous to try to predict exactly what will be the effect of any message except the simplest one in the simplest situation.

Let us take an example. In Korea, in the first year of the war there, I was interviewing a North Korean prisoner of war who had recently surrendered with one of our surrender leaflets on his person. It looked like an open and shut case: the man had picked up the leaflet, thought it over, and decided to surrender. But I was interviewing him anyway, trying to see just how the leaflet had its effect. This is what he told me.

He said that when he picked up the leaflet, it actually made him fight harder. It rather irritated him, and he didn't like the idea of having to surrender. He wasn't exactly a warlike man; he had been a clerk, and was quiet and rather slow; but the message actually aroused a lot of aggression in him. Then the situation deteriorated. His division was hit hard and thrown back, and he lost contact with the command post. He had no food, except what he could find in the fields, and little ammunition. What was left of his company was isolated by itself in a rocky valley. Even then, he said, the morale was good, and there was no talk of surrendering. As a matter of fact, he said, the others would have shot him if he had tried to surrender. But then a couple of our planes spotted them, shot up their hideout, and dropped some napalm. When it was over, he found himself alone, a half mile from where he had been, with half his jacket burned off, and no sign of any of his company. A couple of hours later some of our tanks came along. And only then did the leaflet have an effect. He remembered it had told him to surrender with his hands up, and he did so.

In other words, the communication had no effect (even had an opposite effect from the one intended) so long as the situation, the personality, and the group norms were not favorable. When the situation deteriorated, the group influence was removed, and the personality aggression was burned up, then finally the message had an effect. I tell you this story hoping it will teach you what it taught me: that it is dangerous to assume any simple and direct relationship between a message and its effect without knowing all the other elements in the process.

## THE NATURE OF MASS COMMUNICATION

Now let us look at mass communication in the light of what we have already said about communication in general.

The process is exactly what we have described, but the elements in the process are not the same.

The chief source, in mass communication, is a communication organization or an institutionalized person. By a communication organization we mean a newspaper, a broadcasting network or station, a film studio, a book or magazine publishing house. By an institutionalized person we mean such a person as the editor of a newspaper, who speaks in his editorial columns through the facilities of the institution and with more voice and prestige than he would have if he were speaking without the institution.

The organization works exactly as the individual communicator does. It operates as decoder, interpreter, and encoder. On a newspaper, for example, the input to be decoded flows in through the news wires and the reporters. It is evaluated, checked, amplified where necessary, written into a story, assigned headline and position, printed, distributed. This is the same process as goes on within an individual communicator, but it is carried out by a group of persons rather than by one individual. The quality of organization required to get a group of reporters, editors, and printers working together as a smooth communication unit, decoding, interpreting, and encoding so that the whole operation and product has an individual quality, is a quite remarkable thing. We have become so used to this performance that we have forgotten how remarkable it is.

Another difference between the communication organization and the individual communicator is that the organization has a very high ratio of output to input. Individuals vary, of course, in their output-input ratios. Persons who are in the business of communicating (preachers or teachers, for example) ordinarily have higher ratios than others, and so do naturally talkative persons who are not professional communicators. Very quiet persons have relatively higher input. But the communication institution is so designed as to be able to encode thousands–sometimes millions–of identical messages at the same time. To carry these, intricate and efficient channels must be provided. There have to be provisions for printing and delivering thousands of newspapers, magazines, or books, for making prints of a film and showing them in hundreds or thousands of theaters, for translating sound waves into electricity and distributing it through wires and through the air to millions of receiving sets.

The *destinations* of mass communication are individuals at the ends of these channels–individuals reading the evening paper, looking through the new magazine, reading the new book, sitting in the motion picture theater, turning the dial on the radio set. This receiving situation is much different from that which pertains in face-to-face communication, for one thing, because there is very little direct *feedback* from the receivers to the sender. The destination who, in a face-to-face situation, will nod his head and smile or frown while the sender is speaking, and then encode a reply himself, will very seldom talk back to the radio network or write a letter to the editor. Indeed, the kind of feedback that comes to a mass communication organization is a kind of inferential expression–receivers stop buying the publication, or no longer listen to the program, or cease to buy the product advertised. Only in rare instances do these organizations have an opportunity to see, more directly than that, how their messages are going over. That is one reason why mass communication conducts so much audience research, to find out what programs are being listened to, what stories are being read, what ads attended to. It is one of their few substitutes for the feedback which makes interpersonal communication so relatively easy to plan and control.

There are other discussions about the audiences of the different media, and we need not discuss them in any detail here. These audiences cluster, not only around a newspaper, magazine, or television station, but also around certain stories in the paper, certain parts of the magazine, certain television or radio programs. For example, Station A will not have the same audience at 8:00 as it had at 7:00, because some of these listeners will have moved to Stations B or C, and some of the listeners from B and C will have moved to A. Newspaper D will not have the same audience on its sports pages as on its society pages, although there will be some overlap. What determines which offering of mass communication will be selected by any given individual? Perhaps the easiest way to put it is to say that choice is determined by the Fraction of Selection–

$$\frac{\text{Expectation of reward}}{\text{Effort required}}$$

You can increase the value of that fraction either by increasing the numerator or decreasing the denominator, which is to say that an individual is more likely to select a certain communication if it promises him more reward or requires less effort than comparable communications. You can see how this works in your own experience. You are much more likely to read the newspaper or magazine at hand than to walk six blocks to the newstand to buy a bigger newspaper or magazine. You are more likely to listen to a station which has a loud clear signal than to one which is faint and fading and requires constant effort from you to hear at all. But if the big game of the week is on that faint station, or if your favorite author is in the magazine at the newsstand, then there is more likelihood that you will make the additional effort. If you were a member of the underground in occupied France during World War II, you probably risked your life to hear news from the forbidden Allied radio. You aren't likely to stay up until 2 A.M. simply to hear a radio program, but if by staying up that long you can find out how the Normandy invasion is coming or who has won the Presidential election–then you will probably make the extra effort just as most of the rest of us did. It is hardly necessary to point out that no two receivers may have exactly the same fraction of selection. One of them may expect more reward from Milton Berle than will the other. One of them may consider it less effort to walk six blocks to the newsstand than does the other. But according to how this fraction looks to individuals in any given situation, the audience of mass communication is determined.

Unlike lecture audiences and small groups, mass communication audiences (with the exception of the people in a motion picture theater at the same time) have very little contact with each other. People in one house listening to Jack Benny don't know whether anybody in the next house is listening to him or not. A person reading an editorial in the New York *Times* has little group feeling for the other people in this country who read editorials in the New York *Times.* These audiences are individuals, rather than groups. But each individual is connected with a group or groups–his family, his close friends, his occupational or school group–and this is a very important thing to remember about mass communication. The more we study it, the more we are coming to think that the great effects of mass communication are gained by feeding ideas and information into small groups through individual receivers. In some groups, as you well know, it is a sign of status to be familiar with some part of mass communication (for example, in the teen-age group to hear the currently screamable crooner, or in some business groups to read the *Wall Street Journal*). In many a group, it is a news story from the radio, or an editorial from the *Tribune,* or an article from the *Times,* or an article from one of the big magazines, that furnishes the subject of conversation on a given day. The story, or article, or editorial, is then re-interpreted by the group, and the result is encoded in group opinion and perhaps in group action. Thus it may well be that the chief influence of mass communication on individuals is really a kind of secondary influence, reflected to the group and back again.

We are ready now to draw a diagram of mass communication, and to talk about the kinds of messages this sort of system requires and what we know about predicting their effects. This is the way mass communication seems to work:

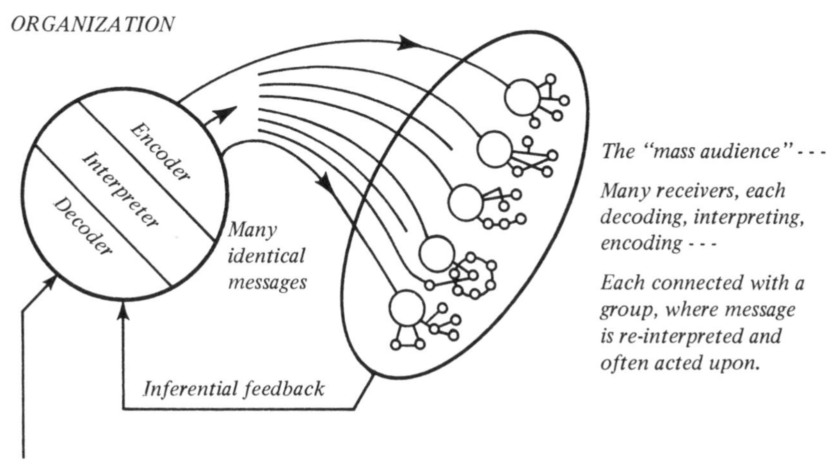


Now it is easy to see that there will be certain restrictions on the kinds of program which can be carried over these identical circuits to these little-known and changing audiences. The communication organization knows it is dealing with individuals, yet does not know them as individuals. Its audience research classifies, rather than individualizes, the audience. Audience research, that is, says that so many people are listening at a given time, or that so many men and so many women are likely to read a given kind of article, or that the readers of a given magazine are in the upper economic bracket and have had on the average twelve years of schooling. Whereas the individual communicator is dealing with individuals and able to watch the way his message is received and modify it if necessary, the organization is dealing only with averages and classes. It must pitch its reading level somewhere below the estimated average of its audience, in order not to cut off too many of the lower half of the audience. It must choose its content according to the best estimate it can make of what the broadest classes of receivers want and need. Whereas the individual communicator is free to experiment because he can instantly correct any mistake, the organization is loath to experiment. When it finds an apparently successful formula, it keeps on that way. Or it changes the details but not the essentials. If one organization makes a great success with a given kind of message, others tend to copy it—not because of any lack of originality, but because this is one of the few kinds of feedback available from the mass audience. That is why we have so much sameness on the radio, why one successful comic strip tends to be followed by others of the same kind, one successful news or digest magazine by others, one kind of comedy program by others of the same kind, and so forth.

What can we say about the effects of these mass communication messages? For one thing, mass communication has pervasive effect because in many respects it has taken over the function of *society communicating*. Our society, like any other communication unit, functions as decoder, interpreter, and encoder. It decodes our environment for us, watches the horizon for danger and promise and entertainment. It then operates to interpret what it has decoded, arrives at a consensus so that it can put policy into effect, keeps the ordinary interactions of communal life going, and helps its members enjoy life.

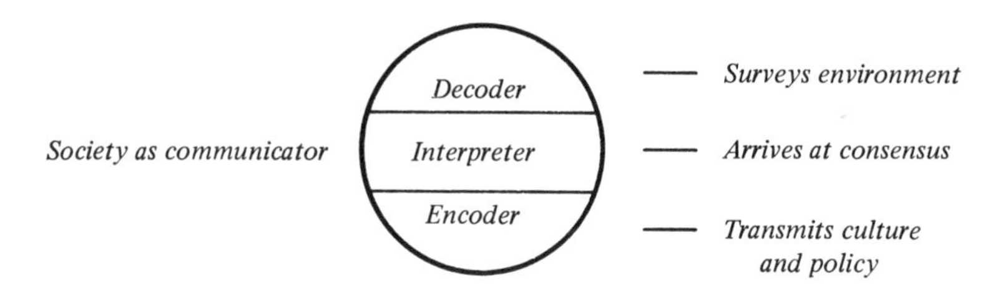


It also encodes messages to maintain our relations with other societies in the world, and messages to transmit our culture to its new members. Mass communication, which has the power to extend our eyes and ears almost indefinite distances, and to multiply our voices and written words as far as we can find listeners or readers, has taken over a large share of the responsibility for this social communication. Newspapers, radio, television watch the horizon for us. By telling us what our leaders and experts think, by conducting a discussion of public issues, these media, and magazines and films as well, help us to interpret what is seen on the horizon and decide what to do about it. The textbook and educational films have led all the other media in encoding our culture so that the young persons coming into our society may learn as quickly and easily as possible the history, standards, roles, and skills they must know in order to be good members of society. This is not to say that all the media do not contribute in some degree to all these functions. For example, a book like *1984* may be as much a report of the horizon as the most current news story. And on the other hand, it is certainly true that a great deal of our culture is transmitted currently through television, radio, newspapers, and magazines. But the faster media are better equipped to be watchmen, and are more often so used. The slower, longer lasting media are better equipped to be teaching aids and are so used. The important thing is that *all* the mass media have important uses in providing the network of understandings without which the modern large community could not exist.

So much for the basic effect, which we see every day in the kind of customs around us, the people and problems talked about, and the language we speak. This is the slow, imperceptible effect. This is like building the stalagmite. But how about the specific effect of a given message transmitted by mass communication? How can we predict what the effect will be on the mass audience?

We can't predict the effect on the mass audience. We can only predict the effect on individuals. Communication organizations have developed group encoding, but there is only individual decoding. Therefore, we can predict the effect of mass communication only in the way we try to predict the effect of other communication—that is, in terms of the interaction of message, situation, personality, and group.

The first thing which becomes obvious, therefore, is that inasmuch as there are many different combinations of personality, situation, and group in any mass audience, there are likely to be many different kinds of effects. It is equally obvious that since mass communication doesn't know much about the individuals in its audience, predicting effects is going to be extremely difficult.

Nevertheless, there are certain things to be said. The problem of attention constantly faces mass communication. The average American (whoever he is) probably gives four or five hours a day to mass communication. If he lives in a big city, he gets a paper that would itself take half that time to read. (He doesn't read all of it.) He is offered the equivalent of two weeks of radio and television every day from which he can choose. He is offered a bewildering array of magazines and books and films. From these also he must choose. Other attractive ways to spend leisure compete with communication. He sometimes combines them—listening to music while he reads, playing cards or eating while he hears a newscast, playing with the baby while he watches television. Therefore, we can predict at least that any individual will have a fairly small chance of selecting any given item in mass communication, and that if he does select it, his level of attention may be rather low. This is responsible for many cases of "mis-hearing" radio. We know also that readership of the average newspaper story falls off sharply after the first few paragraphs, so that a member of the mass audience is likely not to see at all the latter part of a long newspaper story.

There are of course many cases in which markedly high attention is aroused by mass communication, and plentiful instances of listeners identifying closely with radio characters and adopting the mannerisms and language of movie heroes. It has been said that the mass media have brought Hollywood, Broadway, and Washington nearer than the next town, and there is a great deal of truth in this. There are also some cases in which very spectacular overt results have been accomplished by mass communication.

Let us recall one of them. Can you remember when CBS broadcast Orson Welles' performance of H. G. Wells' "War of the Worlds"? The script featured the invasion of the United States by armies from outer space. Perhaps you were one of the people who ran screaming for the hills, or armed yourself to wait for the invaders, or tried to call your loved ones long distance for a farewell talk. Or perhaps you were not. Perhaps you were one of those who heard the CBS announcers explain carefully that it was a play made from a book of fiction. Those who didn't hear those announcements were engaged in proving what we have just said about the low level of attention to some parts of mass communication.

But that doesn't entirely explain why people became hysterical and did things they were rather ashamed of the next day. And in truth, this is one of the really spectacular examples of mass communication effect. This happened without any specific reference to groups; it happened spontaneously in thousands of homes near the supposed scene of invasion. Why did it happen? Research men have studied the incident, and think they have put together the puzzle. For one thing, it was a tense time. People were full of anxiety, which could have been triggered off in many ways. In the second place, people trusted—still trust—radio news; the play was in the form of newscasts and commentaries. Therefore, the communication as it was interpreted really represented a spectacular change in the situation: the Martians were invading! Apparently the group element played no large part in this event, but the other three did. The message was accepted (minus the important identification as fiction). The listeners had a good deal of anxiety ready to be used. The message convinced them that the situation had indeed changed for the worse. Each according to his own personality and situation then took action.

As we have said, that was, fortunately, one of the few really spectacular examples of mass behavior. Another one was the Gold Rush that resulted in the 1890s when the newspapers brought word of gold in Alaska. Some people might say that what the Communists have been able to accomplish is a spectacular advertisement for the power of mass communication, and that subject is worth looking at because it shows us not only some of the differences between the ways we use the mass media and the way dictators use them, but also some of the principles of communication effect.

It is true that one of the first acts of the Communists, when they take over a country, is to seize the mass communication system. (That was also one of Hitler's first acts.) They also seize the police power and the control of productive resources, and they organize an intricate system of Party groups and meetings. I don't know of any case in which the Communists have put the whole burden of convincing people and gaining members on mass communications alone. They always provide a group structure where a convert can get reinforcement, and meetings to which a potential convert can be drawn. They use mass communication almost as an adjunct to these groups. In Korea and China, the mass media actually become texts for the groups. And the Communists do one thing more. If at all possible, they secure a monopoly on the mass communication reaching the people whom they are taking over. When they took Seoul, Korea, in 1950, they confiscated radio receivers wherever they found receivers despite the fact that they had captured Radio Seoul, intact, the most powerful transmitter in that part of Asia. They were willing to give up the use of Radio Seoul, if by so doing they could keep their subjects from foreign radio.

Now obviously, a state monopoly on communication, as well as control of resources and organization of a police state, is a long way from our system. And as long as our mass media are permitted free criticism and reporting, and as long as they represent more than one political point of view, we have little to worry about in a political way from them. But even though we may look with revulsion at the Communist way of using mass communication, still we can study it. And let us refer back to the four elements which we said were instrumental in bringing about communication effects–message, situation, personality, and group. The Communists control the messages. By their police power, control of resources (and hence of food and pay), they can structure the situation as they see fit. Their group organization is most careful, and offers a place–in fact compels a place–for every person. Thus they control three of the four elements, and can use those three to work on the fourth–the personalities of their receivers.

The Communists, who have now had thirty-five years' practice in the intensive use of mass communication for accomplishing specified effects, are apparently unwilling to predict the results of their communication unless they can control three of the four chief elements which enter into the effect.

Let us take one final example. There is a great deal of violence in mass communication content today. Violence is interesting to children. Yet only a few children actually engage in acts of criminal violence. Most children do no such things. They sample the violent material, and decide they would rather play football. Or they attend faithfully to the violent material, use it to clear out vicariously some of the aggressions they have been building up, and emerge none the worse for the experience. Or they adopt some of the patterns in a mild and inoffensive way when they play cops and robbers. Only a few children learn, from the mass media, techniques of crime and violence which they and their pals actually try out. Now what is it that determines which of those children will be affected harmfully by those messages of violence, and which will not?

We can attempt to answer this question from cases we have studied. And the answer is simply that the other three elements–personality, situation, and group influence–will probably determine the use made of the message. If the child is busy with athletics, Scouts, church, or other wholesome activities, he is not likely to feel the need of violent and antisocial actions. On the other hand, if he is bored and frustrated, he may experiment with dangerous excitement. If he has a healthy personality, if he has learned a desirable set of values from his family group, he is less likely to give in to motivation toward violence. On the other hand, if his value standards are less certain, if he has lost some of his sense of belonging and being loved (possibly because of a broken home), he may entertain more hospitably the invitation to violence. If the group he admires has a wholesome set of standards, he is not likely to try an undesirable response, because the group will not reinforce it. On the other hand, if he belongs to a "gang" there is every reason to expect that he will try some of the violence, because in so doing he will win admiration and status in the group. Therefore, what he does will depend on the delicate balancing of these influences at a given time. Certainly no one could predict—except possibly on an actuarial basis—from merely seeing such a message exactly what the response to it would be. And it is entirely probable in the case we have mentioned that the community, the home, and the school—because they influence so greatly the other three elements—would have much more to do with the young person's response than would the message itself.

The all-pervasive effect of mass communication, the ground swell of learning that derives from mass communication acting as *society communicating*—this we can be sure of, and over a long period we can identify its results in our lives and beliefs. The more specific effects, however, we must predict only with caution, and never from the message alone without knowing a great deal about the situation, the personality, and the group relationship where the message is to be acted upon.

# 55. DEFINING ADVERTISING GOALS

*Russell H. Colley*

*One basic problem in the measurement of advertising effects is that too frequently the advertising objectives or goals were not made explicit and, therefore, were not understood.*

*The author of the present article presents several useful concepts dealing with the purposes of advertising under a variety of conditions.*

## UNDERSTANDING ADVERTISING'S PURPOSE

It is a fact of modern business life that many different people are involved in the creation and approval of advertising. . . . For a small advertiser, there may be a half-dozen different people concerned, while a larger advertiser may have dozens of people involved in the advertising of a single product, hundreds of people concerned with the entire product line.

Do all of these people have a common understanding of the purpose of advertising?

We have already indicated what would be the result if you were to conduct a little survey among these individuals asking: "What are we trying to accomplish with this campaign or ad for this product at this time?" The same diversity of opinion would undoubtedly result if the survey asked the more general question: "What is advertising's purpose in our company?"

Source: From Russell H. Colley (ed.), *Defining Advertising Goals for Measured Advertising Results,* New York: Association of National Advertisers, Inc., 1961, pp. 49–60. Russell H. Colley: Management Consultant, Darien, Conn.

The President may be strongly minded toward building a "corporate image." The Sales Manager may regard advertising as a means of getting larger orders from retailers. Financial people may regard advertising as an expense, chargeable to a given fiscal period. The Advertising Manager or the agency account executive may regard advertising as an investment, directed toward building a brand image and increasing share of market.

The job of gaining a common understanding of advertising's contribution is highly important. Few of those who influence and approve key advertising decisions have had any direct advertising experience. But the final decision-makers in American industry are reaching out for a better understanding of advertising and how it can be employed most profitably in the business.

Robert F. Elder, President of the Plax Corporation, expressed the feeling voiced by many other chief executives, in these words: "Most management men want to understand advertising and are eager to listen attentively when you talk to them about it in simple, realistic, down-to-earth terms—and what it means to corporate sales and profits."

Discussions of the advertising process, what it is, and how it operates may be helpful in gaining a general understanding of advertising's function and contribution in various kinds of business situations.

## WHAT IS ADVERTISING?

Those who have spent their lives in advertising may, on first consideration, feel it is naive to pose the question, "What is advertising?" Such a question, they may say, is appropriate only for students and trainees, but not for experienced and sophisticated marketing and sales executives.

However, different meanings are frequently attached to the terms "advertising," "sales promotion,"[1] "publicity," "selling," and "marketing." Terminology differs from industry to industry and within an industry. Differences of opinion on "what is

[1] There is no universally accepted distinction between "advertising" and "sales promotion." In some companies "advertising" includes all forms of mass paid communication directed toward influencing the *end consumer,* whereas "sales promotion" includes those forms of mass communication directed toward informing and influencing the *channels of distribution:* salesmen, distributors, dealers. In other companies, "sales promotion" includes mass communication materials (literature, catalogs, displays, films) which are used *by* the channels of distribution (salesmen, retailers) as selling aids. Hence, a piece of product literature mailed directly to a customer is advertising; literature distributed by the salesman or dealer is sales promotion. Still another (and perhaps the most traditional) distinction between advertising and sales promotion is that advertising consists of time, space and preparatory costs in *commissionable media.* All other mass commercial communications are regarded as "sales promotion." In some industries and channels of distribution the term "sales promotion" is used to refer to any and all activities used to promote sales including: premium offers and other special inducements to consumers, special price offers, sales drives and contests, as well as advertising. Under such usage the term "sales promotion" becomes almost synonymous with "merchandising" and even "marketing." The first important consideration is that some agreed-upon definition be arrived at, as a basis for common understanding within the company and between company and agency. Resolving industry-wide semantic differences is a longer-range effort.

advertising?" are clearly demonstrated when a budget is prepared. In some companies the advertising budget includes only paid space and time. In others it includes practically all forms of the printed word including sales literature, price sheets, publicity releases, house organs, employee communications, etc. (One advertising manager thought it was going a little too far to charge his budget for repair and maintenance of the clock over the branch office building.) It is important that those within a given company have a common understanding of terminology.

We start with the obvious fact that advertising is a form of communication. So is a letter or a personal call by a salesman on a customer. The difference is that advertising is *mass* communication. So is a story in a newspaper or magazine, or a play on television. So is a sermon or a political speech. As a matter of fact, all of the fine arts–music, poetry, painting, drama–are forms of communication. They convey a frame of mind. By whatever the means, somehow these forms of art make contact and thereby transmit a mood or "message" from one human mind to another.

We begin to separate advertising from the many other forms of communication when we add the term "commercial" or "paid." It is paid for by a sponsor who expects to induce some kind of action on the part of the reader or listener that will be beneficial to the advertiser. To sum up in a definition: *Advertising is mass, paid communication, the ultimate purpose of which is to impart information, develop attitude and induce action beneficial to the advertiser (generally the sale of a product or service).*

Paid political announcements, recruitment ads, even the "lost dog" ad in the classified columns of the newspaper are all advertising. They are mass communications, paid for by a sponsor who wishes to achieve some end: the election of a candidate, the hiring of personnel, or the recovery of the family pet. But the bulk of all advertising aims toward the ultimate sale of a product or service. It is this area of advertising as a marketing force with which we are primarily concerned.

## HOW THE ADVERTISING PROCESS WORKS

The ultimate purpose of most advertising is to help bring about the sale of a product or service.

To come to grips with this question of the purpose of advertising we ask two very simple and obvious questions:

1. *When? (Speed of reaction)*
2. *How much of the sales-making load is to be carried by advertising?*

Answers to the question *"When is advertising expected to bring about a sale?"* will run the complete gamut. A department store runs an ad in the evening paper announcing a sensational sale of an item. Next morning, people are lined up waiting for the doors to open. An hour later clerks are saying, "Sorry, we're sold out."

A corporation runs a "corporate image" ad aimed at prospective employees at the student level. Ten years later a man who read the ad may apply for a job, or he may specify the company's products on a purchase order, or he may buy some of the company's stock.

Of course, the time objective of most advertising falls somewhere in between these two extremes. The advertiser of automobiles, insurance, farm equipment or machine tools does not expect people to rush out and buy his product. But he does expect to move the prospect a little closer to the purchase of his product. Advertising's job is to increase *propensity* to buy—to move the prospect, inch-by-inch, closer to a purchase. If one out of ten or even one out of a hundred of the people who are exposed to the ads take *near-term buying action* we may have a huge success on our hands.

Let's examine the second question: *"How much of the selling load is advertising expected to carry?"*

At one extreme we have a mail-order advertiser who would say, "100 per cent," because advertising is the only commercial communication force. At the other extreme is the industrial company in which personal selling is the key sales-making force. Advertising assists by carrying part of the communicating work load. One corporation, having a line of both consumer and industrial products, figured the advertising-to-sales ratio varied from a high of 25 per cent to a low of 0.25 per cent.

Between these extremes we have the wide range of products where advertising is blended with packaging, promotion, price and personal selling; all of these forces contributing to the consummation of a sale.

To repeat, we have two variables:

1. The speed of reaction to advertising,
2. The share of the communicating work load to be carried by advertising.

*The Communications Spectrum.* The concept of the "Marketing Communications Spectrum" . . . offers a starting approach to the solution of our problem. This concept is applied common sense. It breaks the subject up into logical and comprehensible steps. It begins with the obvious assumption that advertising is a communication force. Advertising does not physically impel the consumer toward the purchase of goods; its purpose is to create a state of mind conducive to purchase. Advertising, therefore, is one of several communication forces which, acting singly or in combination, move the consumer through successive levels of what we have termed the communications spectrum. These levels as shown in Figure 1 are Unawareness, Awareness, Comprehension, Conviction and Action.

The lowest level of this communications spectrum is Unawareness. At this level are the people who have never heard of our product or company. The messages about the product have not penetrated to the point where the consumer recognizes or recalls the brand or company name. Now it is conceivable that people buy products or vote

**Figure 1. Marketing Communications Spectrum**

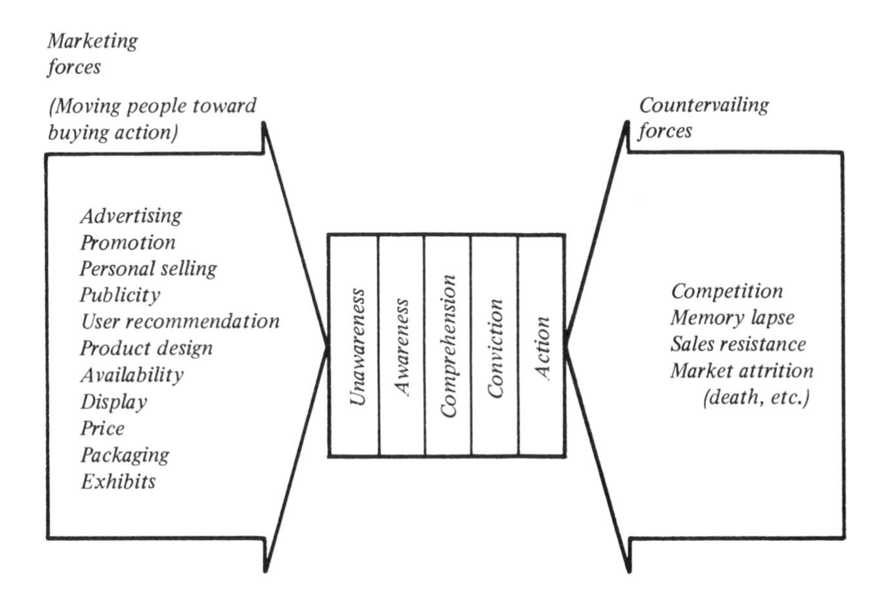


for candidates whose names are unknown to them. The chances are, however, that such a product makes few sales and such a candidate gets few votes. As a bare minimum, we strive for achieving consumer Awareness.

The next level above Awareness in the communications spectrum is that of Comprehension. In this state the consumer not only is aware of the product or service, but knows the brand name and recognizes the package or trademark and, in addition, possesses some degree of comprehension of what the product is and does. He may say, "Brand A is a headache remedy which the maker claims will give fast relief and will not upset the stomach," or "The B company is a manufacturer of earth-moving equipment that will scoop up twenty tons in one bite."

The next level of the spectrum, Conviction, can be illustrated by a consumer who says, "Brand B is a name for a polyester fiber made by the X Company. Garments made of this fiber dry faster, wear longer and hold their shape better. I intend to buy this product in the future." It may also be illustrated by a woman who prefers a particular brand of lipstick or a man who prefers a particular brand of beer on an emotional rather than a strictly rational basis.

Finally, there is Action, in which the consumer has made some overt move toward the purchase of the product. He may have visited a dealer's showroom and asked for a demonstration. He may have asked for literature or for a salesman to call. He may have asked for or reached for the brand at the retail store. Consummation of the sale may have been beyond the power of advertising: the dealer did not have the brand in stock, the salesman failed to follow up the lead, the price was considered too high, or the product lacked appeal when physically examined. However, the advertising induced action.

Advertising performs its role when it contributes to moving the consumer through one or more levels in the spectrum: awareness of the existence of the product, comprehension of the features and advantages, rational or emotional conviction of the benefits and, finally, action leading to a sale.

*The Marketing Communications Mix.* Advertising is one of several forces contributing to awareness, comprehension, conviction and action. Other forces will vary, depending upon whether this is a "consumer" or "industrial" product or service. They may include: person-to-person selling, recommendation of user or retailer, publicity and various other forms of mass communication such as displays, exhibits, films, literature, etc.

Rarely does a single communication force move a prospect through the entire cycle. The exceptions prove the rule. Mail-order type advertising can move a reader through the entire spectrum from unawareness to a cash-in-advance sale in a few hundred words. Door-to-door salesmen and street-corner demonstrators can sell kitchen utensils, cosmetics, brushes, etc., to consumers in a few minutes of persuasive selling.

But the use of advertising or personal selling to achieve the wrapped-up, one-shot sale is but a tiny fraction of total advertising and selling effort. All of the forces of marketing communication are brought together in a "mix" or "blend" to move the prospect step by step, even inch by inch, toward the ultimate goal of a satisfied customer.

The purpose of advertising is to perform certain parts of the communicating job with greater economy, speed and volume than can be accomplished through other means.

In some instances–notably consumer package goods–advertising may be called upon to carry the major part of the marketing communicating work load: from awareness, through comprehension, conviction and right through to action. Consider a product sold through self-service grocery and drug outlets. Advertising is the major communicative force between manufacturer and consumer. The function today of the package goods retailer is mainly to make the goods conveniently available at a price and to provide facilities for the physical exchange between goods and money.

In other product lines, notably industrial goods, advertising is a complementary communicative force. The typical company salesman calling on industrial accounts may make only three or four calls a day. If we subtract the time he spends behind a steering wheel, in reception rooms, in handling various service duties and in building friendly relations, the actual face-to-face time spent in *presenting the merits of his product* to the customer is small. The cost per sales call and per selling minute is high; the rate of penetration of sales messages to the many thousands of buying influences is slow. *Advertising's job is to increase the productivity of the salesman by relieving him of a substantial part of his communication work load.*

Falling somewhere in between these two extremes are consumer durables and semi-durables (autos, appliances, home furnishings, jewelry, clothing, etc.). Advertising's job is to deliver people who are informed and emotionally favorable to a brand, across the retailer's threshold (and, of course, advertising informs and influences the retailer, too). Consummation of a sale hinges upon product appearance, price, availability in desired size and color and a dozen other factors.

Advertising's job may vary with the season or the stage of a product's development. It may be to introduce a new product or a new use of an old product. It may be to hammer away at product benefits or to create a favorable emotional disposition toward a company or brand. In some cases the primary function of advertising is to remind people to buy or to stimulate impulse purchases.

*In every case the function of advertising is to perform a commercial communication task more economically than by some alternate means.*

*Advertising Is Automated Marketing Communications.* We tend to regard automation as a relatively recent development in American industry, and so it is when applied to the factory or office. We tend to overlook the fact that advertising is "automated marketing communication." Automation can be a powerful force for increased productivity *if* it is applied selectively. It would be foolish to propose that every operation in a factory or office should be automated. The process of boring cylinders in an engine block may lend itself to automation, whereas the assembly of carburetors may not. It may be economical to put factory payroll or finished goods inventory on an electronic computer in one company and not feasible in another company.

In a similar manner, we approach marketing communications on a "task basis":

- What are the communicating tasks to be done?
- What parts of the total communicating job is advertising uniquely and economically qualified to perform?
- What is the ideal "mix" of these communication forces for *each* product at this particular stage in its marketing development?

## MARKETING MIX IN ACTION

If we refer again to Figure 1, we see that advertising is one of several marketing forces acting upon potential customers and moving them toward buying action. Seldom does a single force, such as advertising or personal selling, perform the entire task alone. And rarely is a single force powerful enough to move a prospect through the entire spectrum, from unawareness to action, through a single message. Advertising's function is to move the consumer, step by step, closer to buying conviction and finally, to buying action.

In some situations, advertising may be designed to work at all levels at the same time. Let's assume that the market is equally divided into the five levels. (See Figure 2).

Let's assume that, as a result of an advertising campaign, half of those at each level move up one rung on the ladder. Then we would have Figure 3.

**Figure 2.**

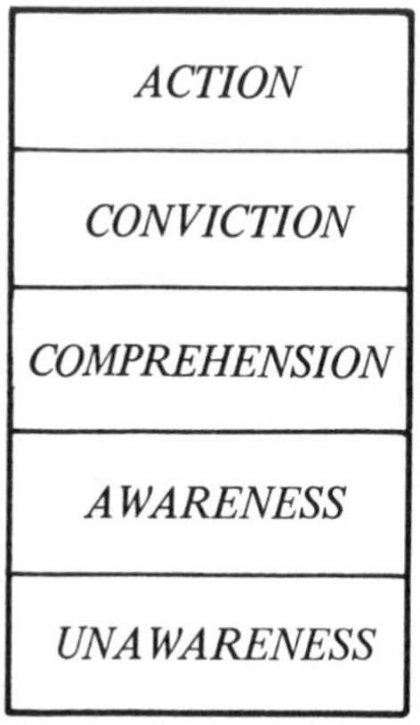

| | |
|---|---|
| *ACTION* | *20% are presented users of the product (ACTION)* |
| *CONVICTION* | *20% are convinced but haven't gotten around to buying* |
| *COMPREHENSION* | *20% comprehend the product but are not convinced* |
| *AWARENESS* | *20% are aware of the product but don't know its advantages* |
| *UNAWARENESS* | *20% never heard of it* |

Advertising in this instance has worked "across the board," moving some people from unawareness to awareness, others to comprehension, conviction and action.

Under certain market conditions (such as intense competition), advertising may perform a valuable economic function if it succeeds in *holding its present share of the consumer mind.* In addition to replacing customers lost to competition, the advertising has succeeded in counteracting such opposing forces as memory lapse and the losses that occur through death and through customers "outgrowing" the need for the product (example: baby food).

Consider some entirely different situations. The force of advertising may be directed at one particular level in the spectrum, rather than "across the board." Some situations call for advertising that is entirely *action*-oriented. (See Figure 4).

**Figure 3.**

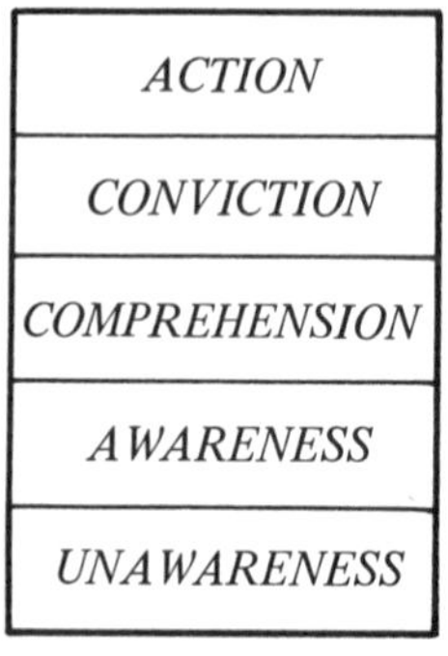

| | |
|---|---|
| *ACTION* | *30% present users (ACTION)* |
| *CONVICTION* | *20% conviction* |
| *COMPREHENSION* | *20% comprehension* |
| *AWARENESS* | *20% awareness* |
| *UNAWARENESS* | *10% unawareness* |

For example, consider a leading brand of razor blades. Everyone is acquainted with the product. And while not 100 per cent of the people are convinced, the brand's high share of industry indicates that this is not the key problem. What is advertising's job? It may be well to *remind* people to buy: men forget to buy blades, use old blades beyond their normal length of life. Similarly, advertising of such impulse items as soft drinks is strongly action-oriented.

A leading established brand in a highly competitive situation—let's say a headache remedy—may channel the bulk of its advertising efforts toward the *conviction* level of the spectrum. Advertising's job is to demonstrate product superiority and create a brand preference. Action occurs when a consumer with high-buying propensity is confronted with the need and is exposed to the product at the point of purchase. (See Figure 5.)

In a similar way we have situations in which the major advertising emphasis is placed at the comprehension or awareness level. Then there are other situations in which the emphasis changes from one season to another: announcement advertising to introduce a product or feature; demonstration advertising to build comprehension and conviction; image advertising to build emotional preference; and finally, "buy now" advertising to get action.

**Figure 4.**

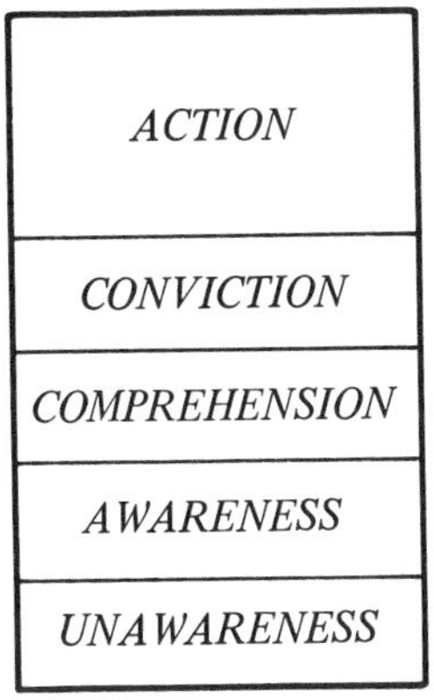

*ACTION*

*CONVICTION*

*COMPREHENSION*

*AWARENESS*

*UNAWARENESS*

**Figure 5.**

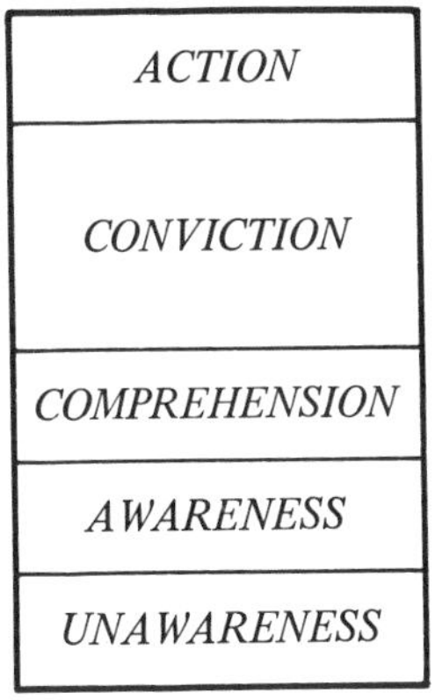

*ACTION*

*CONVICTION*

*COMPREHENSION*

*AWARENESS*

*UNAWARENESS*

# 56. THE PLANNING OF ADVERTISING MEASUREMENT

*Darrell Blaine Lucas and Steuart Henderson Britt*

*Marketing managers and advertising managers long have been interested in attempts to measure the effectiveness of the dollars spent on advertising; and over the years a variety of measures have been developed and used.*

*In the following selection the authors evaluate alternative approaches to the problem of measurement.*

What an advertiser usually wants to know is what kind of impression is being built for his product or service; what he is really concerned about is whether one advertisement or one advertising campaign will produce more sales—or fewer sales—than another advertisement or another campaign.

His basic question usually is, "Will my cash registers ring more often if I run this advertisement?" This search for certainty is quite natural.

Unfortunately, there is no advertising test which will guarantee that the cash registers will ring if a certain advertisement is run. Some of our brightest minds have addressed themselves to this subject, and a wide variety of techniques has been worked out. But the "magic formula" to answer this question has not been found.

What can be found, of course, is whether certain themes and layouts are more effective than others as to memorability, interest, importance, attractiveness, understandability,

Source: From Darrell Blaine Lucas and Steuart Henderson Britt, *Measuring Advertising Effectiveness,* New York: McGraw-Hill Book Company, copyright © 1963, pp. 5–11. Used by permission of McGraw-Hill Book Company. Darell Blaine Lucas: Professor of Marketing in the School of Business, New York University. Steuart Henderson Britt: Professor of Marketing, Graduate School of Business, and Professor of Advertising, Medill School of Journalism, Northwestern University.

etc. From this kind of information, we can assume that themes that are found to be more memorable, interesting, important, attractive, understandable, etc., are more likely than others to produce sales.

Perhaps it would be more accurate to say that such advertising themes are more likely than others to produce *predispositions to buy* the advertised product or service. After all, a great deal of advertising is not designed to make sales, but rather to predispose people to buy.

Although it is a shock to many a business executive to face the bitter truth—there is *no* method of advertising research which can *guarantee* that his cash registers will ring if certain advertising is run—nevertheless, almost every business executive wants more and more information as to what his company's dollars spent in advertising produce for his company. And he usually wants this information in advance of running the advertising.

But to come by such information is not easy. In fact, it is a slow, laborious process, and it is going to take years and years of research to establish general principles which may not even be applicable to *all kinds* of advertising.

One of the main problems is that so much advertising research has to be particularistic rather than generalistic. As Norman Heller of MarPlan says:

> This is due, of course, to the predominant requirement in advertising that each research project must pay off, that research be conducted to answer a specific problem for a specific client. Rarely is an attempt made . . . to extend the data beyond the immediate problem, to interrelate it with other studies, to theory-build, or to understand beyond the immediate boundaries of the study. Our copy tests tell us which of two or three specific ads looks most promising; our motivation studies tell us which themes to develop for brand X—but when the next research request comes through, the only benefit derived from these previous studies is perhaps an improvement or refinement in some research technique. To put it another way, our studies, for the most part, provide us with islands of isolated data, which live short lives.[1]

And too many advertisers inflate their own egos by having the kinds of "research" done for them which will produce nice, pleasant score cards—like the report cards that they hope their offspring will bring home from school.

True, most advertisers give lip service and even hearty "Amens!" to the statement that more money should be invested in advertising research. But most stop short with the "Amens." They have been agreeing with each other, especially in public addresses for the past thirty years or more that advertising research is desirable, but very few really carry out advertising research on any significant scale. Too many prefer to rely entirely on their own personal judgment as to advertising effectiveness, while at the same time they may pay many thousands of dollars a year for rating services which are circulation figures rather than measures of advertising impact.

Yet advertisements are business investments; truly effective advertisements may be two, three, or four times better than weak ones.

[1] Norman Heller, "The New Development in Copy Research," speech before the Copy Research Council, New York, March 19, 1958.

What needs to be determined with respect to any advertising that is to be tested is: *What was its real objective?* Was the purpose to close an immediate sale? Did it aim at some specific step leading to a sale? Was the objective to impart information? Was the purpose one of building good will? Was the building of imagery the main idea; if so, what imagery? Was the advertising designed to build a long-range consumer franchise?

These are the sorts of questions that need to be asked (and there are many more) and to which answers need to be given *before* research is undertaken as to the effectiveness of an advertising message.

> Advertising attempts to move consumers from *unawareness* of a product or service . . . to *awareness* . . . to *comprehension* . . . to *conviction* . . . to *action.*[2]
>
> A variation is that advertising should move people from *awareness* . . . to *knowledge* . . . to *liking* . . . to *preference* . . . to *conviction* . . . to *purchase.*[3]

So we must start with the fact that every successful advertisement must make contacts with enough people, must hold contacts long enough to make an impression, and must make useful, lasting impressions.

## NEED FOR ADVERTISING RESEARCH

The purpose of an advertisement is to produce for the advertiser a profit in terms of money, reputation, good will, or understanding—or all of these.

However, the problem has become increasingly complicated.

> As advertising becomes national, as the time lapse between advertising and sales increases, as products become more alike, as the variety of advertised products increases, as we begin to talk about corporate images, brand images, product images, unconscious motivation, discretionary spending, and the soft sell—as all these factors become more numerous and more salient, we get more and more uncertain about how advertising really does work, or at least, how any one particular ad ought to work.[4]

What is a good advertisement for one set of conditions is not necessarily a good advertisement for another. As the product or service, the market, and the situation vary, the advertisement varies also. Not only may different kinds of advertising campaigns be needed for different products or services, but there may be need for variations within the campaign itself.

[2] Russell H. Colley (ed.), *Defining Advertising Goals for Measured Advertising Results,* Association of National Advertisers, Inc., New York, 1961, especially p. 55.

[3] Robert J. Lavidge and Gary A. Steiner, "A Model for Predictive Measurements of Advertising Effectiveness," *Journal of Marketing,* vol. 25, October, 1961, pp. 59–62.

[4] Clark Leavitt (Leo Burnett Company, Inc.), "The Application of Perception Psychology to Marketing." speech before Forty-fifth National Conference of American Marketing Association, Cincinnati, June 20, 1962.

What this means is that the specific purpose of the advertising campaign and of the particular advertisement needs to be clearly understood in advance. In far too many instances, this simply is not the case. This leaves the researcher in a most difficult situation, with his tail wagging between his legs but not knowing which way to jump—he wants to be helpful, but does not know how to because the objectives of the advertising have not been clearly defined.

Based on reports from more than three hundred companies, a study carried out for the National Industrial Conference Board observed that "when they were pressed for a statement of the precise goals of their advertising, many companies were able to furnish reasonable objectives, but in the majority of cases these were admittedly thought out after the advertising had been run."[5]

Without clear-cut objectives for the advertising, there can be no clear-cut objectives for the advertising research. The research can be done in dozens of different ways, and there is no single *best* way to test advertising effectiveness. But the choice of methods can be narrowed down effectively if the research practitioner can get a statement of advertising objectives more specific (and thus less whimsical) than "Which of these campaigns will sell the most goods?" or "Which ad will do the best job?"

Is the aim of the advertisement primarily to get the brand name recalled? Or are there certain specific sales points that are to be put across; if so what are they? Or is the purpose just to create a favorable mood about the product or service? Just what are the objectives, anyhow? They need to be defined in as specific terms as possible.

Advertising research is like the six blind men and the elephant. The question for the advertising researcher is "What part of the elephant am I being exposed to?" And "Is it all right for me to feel other parts of the elephant?"

None of this is intended as criticism of advertisers or of advertising. The job of the advertising man—whether advertiser or agency man—is difficult because even the seemingly simple advertisement actually is quite complex.

> Neither the man creating it nor the public seeing it can appreciate the maze of individual decisions it can represent. From the walls of caves to the color television screen, the choices and decisions that can form each advertisement have increased. . . .
>
> Larger budgets, increased competition, narrowing profit margins demand greater accuracy in recognizing and making each decision in this complex maze of possibilities. . . .
>
> If the creation of an advertisement is complex, the measurement of its effectiveness is still more complex. Such measures must not only tell what happened, but why. They must provide guides through the maze of decisions that can create the next advertisement.[6]

This emphasizes once more the fact that there is no *one* research method that will provide *the* answers. But it also indicates once more the need for both advertiser and researcher to agree on the specific questions that are to be answered.

[5]Harry Deane Wolfe, James K. Brown, and G. Clark Thompson, *Measuring Advertising Results,* Business Policy Study, 102, National Industrial Conference Board, Inc., New York, 1962, p. 6.

[6]Special brochure of The Television Bureau of Advertising, Inc., New York, 1961, p. 1.

Too many businessmen think that comparative sales results are the only check on advertising effectiveness. If sales during and after a campaign are higher than before, it is easy to assume that the advertising had an effect on the increase in sales—and vice versa. But this does not distinguish between the success of advertising in different media or of different approaches used in a campaign or of other variables affecting sales.

Actually, *copy research* may be defined as the analysis and evaluation of the advertising message—both print and broadcast—and includes both pretesting and posttesting. The word "copy" is used here . . . to refer to *all features* of an advertisement, whether print or broadcast, that distinguish it from all others.

All of the top advertising agencies carry on extensive copy research, and a survey of the fifteen largest agencies by one author (Britt) reveals that most of them locate the copy-research function in the research department—although two of the agencies have copy research assigned to the copy department, and one agency decentralizes copy research according to client assignments.

*Four Basic Questions.* No matter what the advertisement, four basic questions always need to be answered:

1. What do we know about the product or service?
2. What shall we say?
3. How shall we say it?
4. How well did we do?

The first question—"What do we know?"—is a problem for the copywriters and art and design people *before* the advertising is prepared, before even rough sketches are made. In this prewriting stage, research can be helpful in fact gathering in the search for copy ideas. Another way of stating this is to say that research may help the copywriter in learning what consumers' attitudes are. Since we are concentrating on what might be said, this means that a number of different ideas might be tried out in a preliminary way as to their relative strength even before they are developed into advertisements.

The second question—"What shall we say?"—is answered at the time the preliminary writing and layouts are being prepared. Here is where advertising testing can become even more useful because the basic advertising themes can be compared and tested against each other as to importance, exclusiveness, pleasantness, legibility, understandability, imagery, or whatever.

Similarly, the third question—"How shall we say it?"—may be answered as the layouts or the story boards are being prepared. Here again is an opportunity for more theme testing to determine how effective one theme seems as compared with another.

The fourth question—"How well did we do?"—is a matter of posttesting. Since the advertising has already run, there is nothing that copy research can now contribute to these advertisements. What can be learned, though, involves readership information or "Proved Name Registration" or other kinds of data which, it is hoped, will serve as guides to creative people as they prepare the next advertising.

*Four Stages in Copy Research.* These four questions thus become the basis for a four-step research program:

1. Research prior to the development of the advertising,
2. Research during the development of the advertising,
3. Pretesting of advertisements,
4. Posttesting of advertisements.

Research may be applied at any or all of the four stages in the building and testing of specific advertisements.

*First,* the research prior to the development of the advertising has to do with both the development of the advertising ideas and the evaluation of these ideas. There is continuous analysis of past experience by most advertising people in the search for guiding principles. Advertising people usually supplement these principles with more specific rules or observations accumulated through what they believe to be their own successes and failures. Ratings of the noting and reading of past advertisements furnish guides to ensure more favorable attention to future advertising messages. These ratings and other evidences of past success help the creative man to accumulate his own rules for creating superior copy.

*Second,* the research during the development of the advertising essentially is the evaluation of the advertising ideas in rough form. When the writer approaches the problem of preparing new advertisements, he may seek guides from exploratory studies and consumer surveys. Almost all creative writers seek some contact with the consumers for whom their advertisements are written. Scientifically planned consumer surveys make it possible to obtain advertising guidance through consumer contacts.

*Third,* the pretesting of the advertising consists of research on a print advertisement or a commercial before it is run. This includes measurement of various consumer responses after new advertisements are prepared, but before money has been spent to circulate them. Since most of the cost of advertising is the cost of circulation in media, it is important to discover if there are any weaknesses and to make revisions in advance.

*Fourth,* the posttesting of advertising is research on the effectiveness of the advertisement or commercial—or campaign—after it has run. Various techniques are used to check up on the effectiveness of current advertisements and to enlarge the "rules" to be applied to similar future advertising situations.

# 57. CLUES FOR ADVERTISING STRATEGISTS: PART 1

*Donald F. Cox*

*Writers of advertising texts and advertising strategists often rely on widely accepted "rules" for effective advertising. Occasionally, however, the rules are either oversimplifications or erroneous statements of how consumers respond to certain types of advertising.*

*Donald F. Cox studied the findings of mass communications research, and discovered various studies that help to explain how consumers respond to advertising. As an interesting example, contrary to the widely-held belief that constant repetition increases the effectiveness of an advertising campaign, mass communications research indicates that constant repetition may sometimes create negative responses among audience members.*

Can continued repetition of the same advertising appeal boomerang and cause *fewer* rather than more people to want your product? "Never," or, "almost never," say many advertising strategists and advertising textbook writers. Assuming that, except in unusual circumstances, repetition cannot be overdone, they advocate its continued use as an important advertising strategy. However, recent research findings from advertising and mass communications research studies support an opposite conclusion: i.e. that repetition can be, and often is, overdone. In effect, more and more advertising dollars can be spent to drive people away from wanting a product.

Source: From *Harvard Business Review,* vol. 39, September-October, 1961, pp. 160–176. Donald F. Cox: Doctoral candidate, Harvard University Graduate School of Business Administration.

I would like to review and to report on some findings of advertising and mass communications research which are relevant to the basic problems faced by the advertising strategist. There are two points to keep in mind throughout:

1. Important advertising decisions are based on, and to a large extent determined by, certain basic assumptions as to how advertising and the underlying process of mass communications operate.
2. These basic assumptions are not necessarily in agreement with recent research findings in the area of advertising and mass communications research.

If I seem to be critical of the advertising strategist's thoughts or actions, it is not because I am unsympathetic to the difficulties under which he works. It is because I share his interest in getting the job done better.

One note of warning is in order. The conditions faced by a particular advertiser may be quite different from the conditions on which research findings are based. For example, the subjects used in some of the experimental studies which will be reported were college students who are not entirely representative of the audience to which most advertisers address their appeals.

It would therefore be unwise to accept the findings of any one research study at face value without first determining whether the conditions on which the research is based do apply to the advertiser's particular situation.

It would be equally unwise to reject the research findings unless one is quite confident that the conditions on which the findings are based are quite irrelevant and that if the advertiser's unique conditions *were* substituted, the findings would be different. It is all too easy to reject, out of hand, information which does not agree with our own preconceptions.

A number of recent reports testify to a concern among advertising men that consumers often have less than complete faith in the credibility of advertising. It is a sign of the times that *Printers' Ink* is currently engaged in a "continuing study" of "truth and taste in advertising."[1]

The "credibility" problem confronts not only the obviously dishonest advertiser, but also advertisers who maintain high ethical standards. Some people tend to be suspicious of anyone who is trying to sell something. One way of showing this suspicion is to express disbelief in a company's advertising. But what is the effect of this suspicion? How does an audience react when it perceives a communicator as being high in credibility (i.e. impartial and honest) as opposed to one low in credibility (i.e. biased)?

Carl I. Hovland and Walter Weiss conducted an experiment in which two groups listened to the same persuasive material and were later measured for changes in

[1] *Printers' Ink,* July 22, 1960, p. 11.

their opinions.[2] The variable tested was the degree of credibility of the communicator. The communicator presented to one group was introduced in such a way as to appear to be high in credibility (e.g. Dr. Oppenheimer writing about atomic submarines) and the communicator to the second group was made to appear biased and low in credibility (e.g. *Pravda*). As might be expected, when the groups were tested after listening to the communication, there was less changing of opinion in the group which had listened to the low-credibility source.

The most interesting finding of the study resulted when the subjects were tested four weeks later. At this time the percentage of those exposed to the high-credibility source who had changed their opinions decreased. On the other hand, of those exposed to the low-credibility source, the percentage who changed their opinions actually *increased*—what the authors termed the "sleeper effect." In other words, both the positive and negative prestige effects of the source of the communication tended to disappear after several weeks. (The results are portrayed graphically in Figure 1.)

These findings were confirmed and extended by the results of a later experiment by Herbert C. Kelman and Carl I. Hovland.[3] Groups of high-school students were exposed to communications arguing for lenient treatment of juvenile delinquents. Each group was exposed to the same message, but in one case the communicator was introduced as

**Figure 1. Reactions to high- and low-credibility sources**

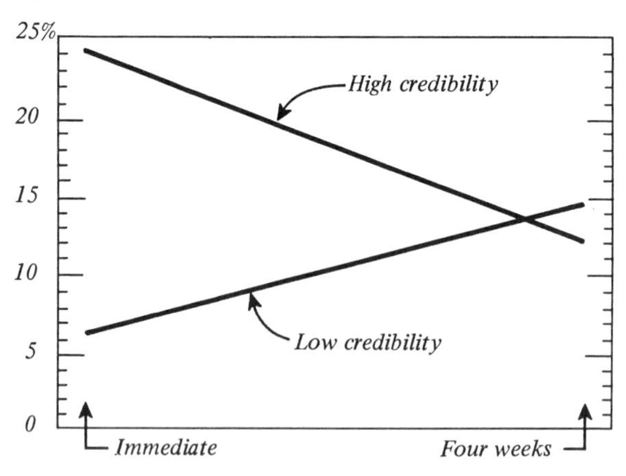


*Source: Carl I. Hovland, Irving L. Janis, and Harold H. Kelley,* Communication and Persuasion, *Yale University Press, New Haven, 1953, p. 225.*

[2] Carl I. Hovland and Walter Weiss, "The Influence of Source Credibility on Communication Effectiveness," *Public Opinion Quarterly,* Winter, 1951–1952, pp. 635–650. This information is also reported by Carl I. Hovland, Irving L. Janis, and Harold H. Kelley in *Communication and Persuasion,* Yale University Press, New Haven, 1953.

[3] Herbert C. Kelman and Carl I. Hovland, "Reinstatement of the Communication in Delayed Measurement of Opinion Change," *Journal of Abnormal and Social Psychology,* vol. 48, 1953, pp. 327–335.

an impartial and sincere expert (a judge) whereas the other speaker was introduced as a suspicious character who might well benefit from leniency toward young criminals. Attitudes were measured after the communication, and it was again found that initially the "positive" communicator was more influential in changing attitudes.

However, three weeks later the researchers remeasured the attitudes of half of the subjects and found that the effect on attitudes was now about the same for both speakers. Although the listeners had not forgotten the source, apparently they had dissociated the content from the source of the communication. For the remaining half of the subjects, the introductory remarks of the speakers were replayed just prior to the delayed testing (which also took place three weeks after the original communication). It was found that this "reinstatement" of the sources had an effect almost equal to that of the initial communication. In other words, after a period of three weeks the subjects apparently no longer associated the negative or biased speaker with the *content* of the communication and therefore were more likely to agree with the content of his remarks. However, when they were reminded of the biased source, they again discounted his remarks and were thus much less likely to follow his suggestions.

These findings related to the "sleeper effect" suggest several interesting possibilities in the way of advertising strategy. For example, a coffee growers' trade association which has been trying, by advertising every four weeks or so, to educate housewives in the art of making good coffee might consider the use of concentrated advertising; that is, it might concentrate all advertising which might ordinarily run through a six-month period in one or two weeks. Presumably one of the problems to be faced is source credibility; the housewife's reaction to an ad might be, "They just want me to use more coffee." Yet according to the association's present strategy, advertising is timed to reinstate the communicator every four weeks. This may not be helping the situation! The findings I have reported suggest that in certain situations it might be better for the advertiser to dissociate himself as the source of the message. (Let me emphasize, however, that just because a company is advertising does not mean it will automatically be considered to be low in credibility. Some will be; some will not be. Also keep in mind that advertisers of branded products probably do not want their names to be dissociated from the content of the communication.)

A recurring issue in advertising strategy concerns the use of appeals which are primarily "rational" as opposed to appeals which are primarily "emotional." As well as I can determine, the emotional advertising appeal is definitely considered more effective by advertising strategists, except in certain situations such as advertising of expensive appliances. This enthusiasm for emotional appeals is definitely not shared by communications researchers who have been unable to demonstrate in any clear-cut fashion that the emotional appeal is more effective than the rational appeal. In fact, recent thinking and research have led to the belief that the most effective appeal may be one which is both highly emotional *and* highly rational.

This belief, however, was not suggested at first. One of the earliest studies on the topic was an experiment by George W. Hartmann which compared the effectiveness of "rational" and "emotional" appeals in obtaining votes for the Socialist party.[4] Voters in one set of wards received leaflets emphasizing rational appeals (i.e. outlining the goals of the party and urging those who agreed with the goals to vote for the party); in another group of wards voters received leaflets stressing emotional appeals (i.e. how the Socialist program would handle the threats of war and depression). The control wards received no leaflets. Election returns showed a 50 per cent increase in the Socialist vote in the wards subjected to the emotional appeal as compared with a 35 per cent increase in the wards receiving the rational appeal, and a 24 per cent increase in the control wards. In this case the "emotional" appeal was more effective than the "rational."

Hovland, Janis, and Kelley cite several other studies which support the contention that emotional appeals are superior to rational appeals. However, they also note that other experimental findings "fail to confirm the superiority of 'emotional' appeals and even suggest that such appeals can be less effective than 'rational' ones."[5]

There are several possible explanations for these conflicting results. It is conceivable that some of the conditions of the experiments varied with a consequent variation in results. Also, it is extremely difficult to equate appeals on dimensions such as the amount of copywriting skill involved. The same man may, for example, write much more effective emotional copy than he does rational copy.

The basic cause of the discrepancy in results, however, is probably conceptual rather than situational. How are we to distinguish between emotional and rational appeals? If we use the term "rational" to define an individual's attempt to maximize his satisfactions (whether they be economic or *other* psychological satisfactions) or to minimize his dissatisfactions, then all behavior must be viewed as being rational. On the other hand, if we use the term "emotional" to denote behavior that is in any way connected with feelings, attitudes, or emotions, then all behavior must be viewed as being emotional. In short, the terms are not very useful in describing human behavior—especially when they are used in contrast with one another.

A more useful type of distinction would involve varying *kinds* and varying *levels* or *degrees* of rational or emotional behavior or appeals, as the case may be. Thus, all appeals must in some sense be emotional in that they must be directed at some existing attitude or motive. However, they may vary in

1. the strength of the appeal to that motive (more or less emotional), and
2. the explicitness with which a given course of action is related to the satisfaction of that motive (more or less rational).

It may well be, as Raymond A. Bauer has suggested to me, that in many situations an appeal which is both highly emotional *and* highly rational would, to a significant degree,

[4]George W. Hartmann, "A Field Experiment on the Comparative Effectiveness of 'Emotional' and 'Rational' Political Leaflets in Determining Election Results," *Journal of Abnormal and Social Psychology,* vol. 31, 1936, pp. 99–114.

[5]Hovland, Janis, and Kelley, *op. cit.,* p. 57.

increase the prospect's need to satisfy a motive and, at the same time, point out an explicit course of action which would lead to satisfaction of the aroused need. The rational element of the communication would have to be strong enough to allow the recipient of the communication to assure himself that he could satisfy the motive by following the suggested course of action. For example:

A recent advertisement for nylon cord automobile tires contained photographs of two stones. On the left side of the page a small stone was pictured lying on a highway. The photograph on the right was of a gravestone. The caption read, "One stone leads to another." This is an example of a negative or fear-arousing appeal.

My own reaction to this ad was that it was extremely effective in arousing the emotions. I could almost picture the scene of a grisly highway accident caused by a speeding, stone-ruptured tire. However, I found the rational element of the ad utterly unconvincing. While I had become uncomfortably aware of the fact that a stone meeting a speeding tire could cause death on the highway, the rational part of the ad simply did not provide me with enough of the right kind of information to convince me that nylon tires could prevent such a disaster—or even that nylon is superior to a good rayon cord tire. As far as I am concerned, the ad did not achieve its purpose because its rational element did not convince me that my aroused emotions could be relieved by purchasing nylon tires.

As I say, this was my own reaction to one advertisement. More satisfactory (though not conclusive) evidence on this point comes from a study by Irving L. Janis and Seymour Feshbach.[6] They conducted an experiment in which groups of students heard one of three versions of a fifteen minute talk on dental hygiene. Each version contained the same general information and made similar recommendations, but differed in the strength of the fear appeal used. For example:

- The "strong" fear appeal emphasized the pain caused by tooth decay and was illustrated with slides showing diseased gums.
- In the "moderate" appeal the threats appeared less often and in a milder form.
- In the "minimal" fear-appeal version the more severe threats were replaced by fairly neutral information.
- In addition, the strong appeal emphasized the personal consequences of improper dental hygiene (i.e. "This can happen to you"); the moderate and minimal appeals described the consequences in impersonal language.

The main results of the experiment indicate that the minimal fear appeal was more effective. The net change toward conformity with the recommended hygienic behavior (as reported by the subjects) in the group exposed to the minimal appeal was 36 per cent; in the group exposed to the moderate appeal the net change was 24 per cent; in the audience for the strong appeal the net change was only 8 per cent. These results support the hypothesis that in certain situations appeals which build up a minimal level of emotional tension are more likely to be effective than those which lead to higher levels of tension. Janis and Feshbach suggest that one of the apparent reasons

[6] Irving L. Janis and Seymour Feshbach, "Effects of Fear-Arousing Communications," *Journal of Abnormal and Social Psychology,* vol. 48, 1953, pp. 78–92.

is that subjects exposed to the strong fear appeal showed more resentment toward the communicator and consequently were more likely to reject the communication.

Hovland, Janis, and Kelley suggest also the possibility of a mechanism which they call "defensive avoidance." Their hypothesis states that, "When fear is strongly aroused but not adequately relieved by the reassurances contained in a persuasive communication, the audience will become motivated to ignore or to minimize the importance of the threat."[7] While the experimental evidence for this hypothesis is slim, at least none of the data contradict the contention. Furthermore, the hypothesis is consistent with other psychological evidence in the operation of defensive mechanisms.

What is the significance for business? Earlier, I suggested that an emotional appeal tends to become less effective as the strength of the aroused motive increases *relative* to the individual's own feelings of certainty that the motive will be satisfied. The role of the rational element in the communication is to spell out, in a believable way, how the advocated course of action can lead to the satisfaction of the aroused motive, and thereby increase the individual's own feeling of certainty of the motive being satisfied.

If this contention is realistic, the implications for advertising strategy seem clear. Not only must the advertiser be honest and promise no more than his product can deliver; he also must promise no more than a potential consumer thinks his product *should* deliver. To illustrate again:

> I have heard of a product which, on the basis of tests, performs exceptionally well. The advertiser, naturally, feels justified in promoting the remarkable achievements of his product. The only problem is that the test results are so remarkable that very few people believe them enough to try his product. While his claims are able to *arouse* emotions (e.g. the feeling that "it would be a great product–if it worked"), he is unable to provide potential customers with adequate assurance that the product will satisfy the emotions which have been aroused. Since he is unable to convince consumers of the exceptional performance of his product, it is conceivable that he might do better if he claimed less for the product.

It is often said that there are two sides to every story, but only rarely do we see or hear both sides of an advertising story. There are occasional advertisers who say, "Other products are good, but ours is better," or, "Other brands cost less, but you get more quality if you buy our brand"; however, in the general run of advertisements these are exceptions rather than the rule. Are there any advantages to presenting both sides of the story? Several interesting experiments have been devoted to answering the question, "Which is more effective, a one-sided or two-sided argument?"

Carl I. Hovland, Arthur A. Lumsdaine, and Fred D. Sheffield presented to groups of soldiers one of two versions of a talk which argued that the war with Japan (after Germany's surrender) would last for at least two years.[8] One version stressed Japan's strength; the other also stressed Japan's strength but gave some opposing arguments

[7] Hovland, Janis, and Kelley, *op. cit.*, pp. 87–88.

[8] Carl I. Hovland, Arthur A. Lumsdaine, and Fred D. Scheffield, *Experiments on Mass Communications,* Princeton University Press, Princeton, 1949.

dealing with that nation's weaknesses. The soldiers were asked to estimate the probable length of the war before and immediately after listening to the communication.

One of the noteworthy features of this experiment is that the investigators recognized the importance of specifying the conditions under which a variation in appeals is or is not effective. Had they considered their audience to be an undifferentiated mass, and had they tallied their results accordingly, they would have concluded that a one-sided argument was just as effective as a two-sided argument. However, in analyzing the results they split the soldiers into two groups—those initially opposed to the communicator's position and those initially in favor (but able to become more extreme in their view). Their findings are summarized in Table 1.

In other words, presenting both sides of the argument is more effective if the individual addressed is initially opposed to the issue, but the one-sided argument is more effective with those initially favoring the communicator's position. The implications are clear for advertising strategy, although it needs to be emphasized that before acting on them the advertiser should first find out whether and to what extent his audience is opposed or in agreement with his message.

Hovland, Lumsdaine, and Sheffield also considered the soldier's education as a variable and found that the communication giving both sides of the argument was more effective with the better-educated group regardless of initial position, whereas the one-sided presentation was primarily effective among the less well-educated soldiers who were already in favor of the communicator's position. Here, too, there are implications for advertising strategy—although it is again important to study the advertiser's situation first (e.g. the education level of potential buyers).

In listening to some advertising men, and in reading some of their writings, I am struck by the metaphors they use to describe their advertising strategy. There seems to be a great deal of reference to weaponry and other symbols of aggression and hostility. They often talk, for example, of "hitting" people, "taking pot shots," "turning on the heat," "banging away," "blasting away," and so on. An agency vice-president has said,

**Table 1. Net per cent of individuals changing opinion in direction of position advocated by communicator**

| | *Exposed to one-sided argument* | *Exposed to both sides* |
|---|---|---|
| Initially opposed to communicator's position | 36% | 48% |
| Initially in favor of communicator's position | 52 | 23 |

Source: Carl I. Hovland, "Effects of the Mass Media of Communication," in Gardner Zindzey (ed.), *Handbook of Social Psychology,* Addison-Wesley Publishing Company, Inc., Reading, Massachusetts, 1954, p. 1079.

"I would consider the use of several different media for short periods of time too much like using a shotgun when you need the heavy and sustained firepower of a battalion artillery."

Could it be that some members of the audience (the "enemy"?) want to run for cover when this artillery begins to blast away at them in the form of monotonous, irritating, unending repetition of the same jingle, slogan, or whatever other ammunition has been fired at them for the past three to ten years? Can repetition be overdone?

Not according to the textbook writers. Their answer to this question is a qualified, "No." Rosser Reeves, the leading exponent of continued repetition of a single successful appeal, maintains that "unless a product becomes outmoded a great campaign will not wear out."[9] Melvin S. Hattwick says that you probably cannot overdo repetition, but if repetition were overdone, it would only lead to " 'overlearning' which . . . is certainly no hindrance to selling merchandise. In fact it is a real aid."[10] Darrell B. Lucas and Steuart Henderson Britt contend that "the surest way for an advertiser to maintain a competitive advantage is to repeat his messages so often that they are always fresh in the minds of the consumers." But they suggest that "repetition of a central theme with variations is more effective than repetition without variation."[11]

The textbook writers offer little directly relevant evidence to support their conclusions. Nevertheless, their counsel does lend unamious and even vigorous encouragement to the advertiser who would pursue a strategy of continued repetition of the same advertising appeal.

By contrast, communications research offers little evidence which would support the use of excessive repetition of the same appeal to the same audience. For example, Hovland, Janis, and Kelley, after reviewing several experiments, say:

> Repetition does not influence the retention of the information content of a communication in any simple manner. While the usual effect is to increase retention under some circumstances, too frequent repetition without any reward leads to loss of attention, boredom, and disregard of the communication.[12]

One study they cite found "improvement in retention with increasing repetition up to three or four times. Thereafter, the effect of additional repetition is slight."[13]

[9] Rosser Reeves, *Reality in Advertising,* Alfred A. Knopf, Inc., New York, 1961, p. 32.

[10] Melvin S. Hattwick, *How to Use Psychology for Better Advertising,* Prentice-Hall, Inc., Englewood Cliffs, N.J., 1950, p. 244.

[11] Darrell B. Lucas and Steuart Henderson Britt, *Advertising Psychology and Research,* McGraw-Hill Book Company, New York, 1950, pp. 80–81.

[12] Hovland, Janis, and Kelley, *op. cit.,* p. 247

[13] *Ibid.,* p. 249.

A three-step study carried out by the Schwerin Research Corporation combines both laboratory and real-life exposure to commercials (see Table 2):

1. An audience was invited to view a television program in a theater. During the program break the audience viewed a commercial for a drug product. Immediately after the program the audience was subjected to several tests of recall of the commercial.
2. The commercial which had been thus tested was then exposed on regular television for a period of two weeks. At that time, another audience (42 per cent of whom said that they had seen the commercial on regular television) was invited to the theater. Like the first audience, these people were exposed to a television program which included this commercial and were then tested for recall.
3. The commerical then continued to be exposed on regular television for another two weeks, bringing the total period of regular television exposure to one month. At the end of this period, the commerical was again tested with a new audience in the same way as before. Of this third audience 59 per cent reported that they had seen the commercial on regular television.

The entire procedure was repeated for two more one-month periods, with two different commercials for the same product and two different audiences (ranging in size from 250 to 730).

Let us call the first commercial "A," the second "B," and the third "C." We see, from the results of one of the measures of recall (shown in Table 2), that Commericals A and C were less effective after four weeks of exposure than after two weeks. It would appear that these commericals had been overexposed. Commercial B is the only one which shows steadily increasing recall. However, this may have happened because Commercial B received only one-third as much exposure on regular television as the other two did.

**Table 2. Share of audience recalling brand name and at least one sales point**

| | *Test* | | |
|---|---|---|---|
| *Commercial* | *#1 First exposure* | *#2 After 2 weeks* | *#3 After 4 weeks* |
| A | 55% | 46% | 36% |
| B | 23 | 25 | 50 |
| C | 32 | 54 | 44 |

Source: "When Should the Effects of Television Advertising Be Measured? Part I: Recall," *Technical and Analytical Review,* Spring, 1960, p. 9.

In another series of studies the Schwerin research group showed commercials for thirty-one different products to thirty-one different audiences.[14] After each commercial was shown, the audience was questioned to determine its "competitive preference," i.e. the share of people who want the advertised product. These competitive preference scores were recorded and were compared with the competitive preference scores which were obtained by the same thirty-one commercials in a second test. The second test (which used different audiences but otherwise was conducted like the first) took place after the commericials had been shown on regular television for periods of from three to thirty months.

These results, too, are not encouraging to the repetitive advertiser. In the case of 77 per cent of the products tested, significantly fewer people wanted the product after the second test (i.e. after three to thirty months of exposure on television) than after the first. Because the amount of exposure on regular television was not controlled, these results cannot be considered conclusive. However, they hardly lend support to the strategy of continued repetition of the same advertising appeal. Rather, they buttress the contention of Hovland, Janis, and Kelley that too frequent repetition of a communication can lead to disregard of that communication. The effect is not merely a matter of diminishing returns, but of *negative* returns. That is to say, excessive repetition can boomerang and cause an actual loss in learning or a negative opinion change.

Although I am unable to relate the results of the measures used by the Schwerin people with sales results, there is some reason to believe that there might well be a positive relationship. If there were such a relationship, then the advertiser who repeats the same commercial to the same audience too often may actually be counteracting the effect on sales of his earlier advertising. Even though his total sales might be holding steady for the time being, sales to that segment of the market which has heard or seen the commercial too often could be sharply reduced.

Media selection is one of the thorniest problems of advertising strategy. Ideally, the strategist should develop the most economical media plan which will best fit the many facets of a company's advertising situation and objectives. Unfortunately he is often in the position of having to consider too many factors and to decide among too many alternative media plans—all the while having to base his decision on far too little reliable information. What help does the present state of communications research offer the befuddled media man?

Very little, I'm afraid. There are two basic reasons for this. First, while many media research studies are in fact available, the research methodology employed in many of them is simply not adequate in view of the immense difficulty of media research—especially research on the comparative effectiveness of media. Secondly, some of the

[14] "When Should the Effects of Television Advertising Be Measured? Part II: Changes in Attitude and Behavior," *Technical and Analytical Review*, Summer, 1960, p. 1.

very studies which might *eventually* prove to be helpful can compound existing difficulties because they seriously challenge some commonly accepted assumptions about media strategy.

There is considerable evidence which would support the contention that a medium may have persuasive power in its own right. If, for example, we were to present the same commercial on color and on black-and-white television, we might find, as did the Burke Marketing Research organization in 1960, that one-and-a-half times as many color-TV viewers recalled the commercial as did those who viewed it in black and white.[15] We might then conclude that color TV is a more effective medium than black-and-white TV. But we could be wrong.

After reviewing over fifty studies of the comparative effectiveness of various media, the Division of Academic Research Services of the Pennsylvania State University concluded that "the great majority of the studies reviewed (practically all of those made before 1950) suffer from serious defects in design which tend to vitiate their conclusions."[16] Among the defects in study design which were listed in the report was the failure to randomize subjects among treatments.

This particular shortcoming is present in the TV study just mentioned. Although the researchers tried to match viewers of color TV with viewers of black-and-white TV by picking pairs of neighbors—one of whom owned a color set, the other a black-and-white set—there is no guarantee that the neighbors were identical with respect to such characteristics as personality type, education, and intelligence which might account for differential recall. It is possible, for instance, that color-TV owners tend to be more intelligent, or more interested in the programs and products which were televised, and hence more likely to recall seeing the commercial.

Unless a study carefully controls for important variables, either by precise matching of respondents or by assigning respondents to an experimental treatment (e.g. watching a program on color TV) at random, the results cannot be considered conclusive.

Even when the methodological problems are solved, a difficult problem of comparison remains. The powers of persuasion of any one medium depend not only on the medium *per se*, but on the type of product advertised, the nature of the message, and the types of people to whom you are advertising. While it may be practically possible to detail some of the specific conditions under which one medium is more effective than another, I have encountered little up-to-date, published research which would permit useful generalization.

If the findings of recent studies that challenge basic assumptions about advertising media are realistic, some rethinking of the problems of media utilization may be in order.

[15] "The Effectiveness of Color vs. Black-and-White Television Advertising" (mimeographed), Burke Marketing Research, Inc., 2374 Kemper Lane, Cincinnati.

[16] "Studies of the Comparative Effectiveness of Various Media of Communication" (mimeographed), 1959, p. 5.

The medium is often said to be instrumental in "delivering" or "selecting" the audience. But it is more likely, I think, that "audience selection" is the result of the interaction between media characteristics and audience predispositions and that in the final analysis the audience selects the medium rather than vice versa. Available research evidence would seem to support two closely related generalizations about media:

1. The process of audience selection of media is not random. Any particular medium will have more appeal for some groups than for others.
2. Within the larger group which is attracted to a particular medium some subgroups will be more attracted than others.

For example, in support of the first generalization, we would expect that doctors would be the primary readers of medical journals. But we must not stop here. Herbert Menzel and Elihu Katz found that the most influential doctors in a medical community "were more likely to be readers of a large number of professional journals and valued them more highly than did doctors of lesser influence."[17] By way of contrast, the least influential doctors were more likely to learn of new drugs through detail men, direct mail promotion, and periodicals from drug houses.

Similarly, while we would expect most women to be somewhat exposed to mass media, Elihu Katz and Paul F. Lazarsfeld report that opinion leaders are more likely to be exposed to certain mass media (because they read more magazines) than are the women they influence.[18] This study also finds that an opinion leader's sphere of influence is likely to be limited to a specific area such as marketing, fashions, or moviegoing. Interestingly enough, there is a tendency for opinion leaders to be more exposed to media that are appropriate to their own sphere of influence.

In addition to opinion leadership, there are many other bases of differential exposure to mass media. For example, Katz and Lazarsfeld have found highest exposure to "popular fiction" (such as movie and "true story" type magazines and daytime radio and TV serials) among women–

- Who are lower in social status.
- Who are less "gregarious" (regardless of social status).
- Who are higher in "anxiety"–i.e. who "sometimes feel blue and depressed," independently of gregariousness.

The foregoing studies support two important implications which may conflict with the assumptions held by some advertising strategists. One concerns competition among media; the other concerns the use of the same advertising appeals in media which attract different audiences.

[17]Herbert Menzel and Elihu Katz, "Social Relations and Innovation in the Medical Profession," *Public Opinion Quarterly,* Winter, 1955-1956, pp. 337–352.

[18]Elihu Katz and Paul F. Lazarsfeld, *Personal Influence,* The Free Press of Glencoe, New York, 1955, pp. 309–320.

*Competition Among Media.* It is fashionable these days to criticize the "rating game" by which television programs prosper or perish according to their ratings (in cost-per-thousand viewers). I cannot resist joining the critics, and will even go them a step further and criticize the equivalent of the rating game in other media—the use of figures on cost-per-thousand readers, listeners, or passersby as the primary basis for media decisions.

However, the basis of my criticism is different from that of the popular critics. Furthermore, my criticism applies only to those advertising strategists who use cost-per-thousand figures as the primary basis for making either/or decisions among certain "competing" media. It may be that the media attract different audiences or otherwise perform different functions for the advertiser, in which case a decision to buy either Medium X or Medium Y made solely or primarily on the basis of cost-per-thousand readers may be unwise.

It is doubtful whether any media man would admit to using cost-per-thousand figures as the only important basis for marketing media decisions. However, it has been my experience that when "hard" figures (such as cost-per-thousand numbers) are available, they tend to drive out or displace "soft" or less tangible data. Thus, while we may feel that we are weighing *all* of the important factors the "hard" dollars-and-cents figures may actually influence a media decision more than we realize they do.

The figures on cost-per-thousand viewers may be a useful starting point in deciding among competing media. Alone, however, they are far from an adequate measure. There are at least two reasons for this:

1. I have noted that a particular medium may have more appeal for some groups (and subgroups) than others. To the extent that different media aid in attracting specific and relatively different audiences, they do not "compete" so long as those audiences represent potential purchasers of a product. For example, if we are marketing a household product which is purchased by both lower- and middle-class housewives, it might be unwise to make a choice between advertising in either the *Ladies' Home Journal* (presumably middle class) or *True Story* (presumably lower class). The product should probably be advertised in both magazines because their audiences are different.

2. To varying degrees, media may effectively reinforce one another either through the process of what might be called mutual reinforcement or through complementary reinforcement. By *mutual* reinforcement I refer to the added effectiveness which results when the same appeal is transmitted to the same audience via several different media. For example, we might predict that if the same audience were exposed to the same appeal on TV, on radio, and in magazines, the effect would be greater than that of triple exposure to any one of the media. Unfortunately, there is little published evidence which would either support or contradict this contention.

   *Complementary* reinforcement may occur when two or more media transmit different appeals or otherwise perform different functions for the same product in communications directed toward the same audience. For example, in a review of a study of the adoption by doctors of a new drug, Elihu Katz reports that commercial media play an "informing" role (i.e. tell the doctors about the drug and its availability) whereas the professional media play a "legitimizing" role (i.e. the prestige of the journal and medical society are associated with the drug).[19] Accordingly, if the advertiser believes that both roles are important to his campaign, he would be unwise to view the commercial media as competing with the professional media.

*Different Appeals in Different Media.* Typical procedure in developing an advertising campaign seems to be to

1. set advertising objectives,
2. determine a basic advertising appeal which will induce people to take the desired action, and
3. develop a media plan which will most effectively deliver the campaign to the right people at the lowest cost-per-thousand.

In effect, a medium is considered as little more than a vehicle which delivers a standard message to a desired audience. The media plan is tailored to fit the advertising message. Except for the way in which it is presented, the message varies little from one medium to another.

It seems plausible to predict, however, that the same factors which make a person more attracted to one medium than to another are also likely to be operative in making him or her more susceptible to specific kinds of appeals which are transmitted in that medium. In other words, not only should advertisers utilize different media to reach specific audiences, they also should consider the possibility of using different appeals in each of the media. For example:

> We would expect that the advertiser of the household product previously mentioned might get more "mileage" out of his advertising if he used one kind of appeal in *True Story* and a different kind of appeal in the *Ladies' Home Journal.* Let us assume that he is considering the use of a "fear-arousing" appeal. While this appeal might be effective in the *Ladies' Home Journal,* he probably should not use it in *True Story.* Why? Because we know from the Katz and Lazarsfeld study that readers of *True Story* are more likely to be high in anxiety. Further, we know from the study by Janis and Feshbach that people who are high in anxiety are less likely to be influenced by fear-arousing communications. Putting these two findings together would suggest that our advertiser had better use some other appeal than "fear-arousing" in the *True Story* ad.
>
> Also, the advertiser should probably avoid the use of two-sided arguments with *True Story* readers whereas he might find two-sided arguments very effective with the presumably better-educated readers of the *Ladies' Home Journal.*

I must admit that for purposes of emphasis I have greatly oversimplified these observations on media strategy. The topic is a challenging one, and I can only urge the reader

[19] Elihu Katz, "The Two-Step Flow of Communication," *Public Opinion Quarterly,* Spring, 1957, pp. 67–68.

with unanswered questions to look further into some of the publications that I have mentioned.

In Part II of this article[20] I will present a number of studies which support the notion that an advertising audience should not be considered as one large and undifferentiated mass—especially if optimum advertising effectiveness is desired. I shall also review research studies that have important implications for measuring advertising effectiveness.

[20]Chapter 58, which follows.

# 58. CLUES FOR ADVERTISING STRATEGISTS: PART 2

*Donald F. Cox*

*Here is a review of some of the major research findings and theories, attempting to explain the nature of advertising audiences. The key phase in communication lies in the nature of the audience, a vastly heterogeneous mass whose attitudes cannot usually be changed just by advertising.*

*The following article–a continuation of the selection immediately preceding–indicates the wide range of behavior in response to a message stimulus.*

Basically there are two ways of viewing the audience–what I call the "egotistical" and the "realistic" views. Of these two, the most satisfying to the mass communicator is the first, which enables him to think of the audience as a relatively inert and undifferentiated mass that he can often persuade or influence. It is "egotistical" because it attributes great powers to the communicator and regards the audience as a swayable mass. Proponents of this view would probably hold that if you "hit them hard enough" (or "loud enough, long enough, and often enough"), sooner or later they will buy your product.

Perhaps the "realistic" view is more valid. With it, the audience is regarded as a body of individuals who may respond to a communication or commercial in a variety of ways, depending on their individual predispositions. This view also holds that while the communicator, the communication, and the medium play important roles in the communications process, in the final analysis it is the audience which decides whether

Source: From *Harvard Business Review,* vol. 39, November-December, 1961, pp. 160–182. Donald F. Cox: Doctoral candidate, Harvard University Graduate School of Business Administration.

(and to what extent) it will be influenced. Further, this view acknowledges the importance of the audience in its own right, through the process of social and personal influence.

Let us examine some evidence which should demonstrate that the "realistic" view *is* realistic, and the "egotistical" view *is* egotistical.

In order for an audience to be influenced in the desired manner by a communication, several conditions must be met:

- The audience must, somehow, be *exposed* to the communication.
- Members of the audience must interpret or *perceive* correctly what action or attitude is desired of them by the communicator.
- The audience must remember or *retain* the gist of the message that the communicator is trying to get across.
- Members of the audience must *decide* whether or not they will be influenced by the communication.

We might consider these four conditions—exposure, perception, retention, and decision—as the gateways to effective communication and persuasion.

Communications research has established beyond much doubt that the processes of exposure, perception, retention, and decision do not often occur in a random fashion among the population. To varying degrees, people are predisposed to expose themselves to certain kinds of communications and media and not to others. Different people tend to get different meanings from the same communication and to remember or forget different aspects of a communication. Finally, different people make different decisions as to whether or not they will be influenced.

Since each of these processes involves a selection or choice by individual members of the audience, we may refer to them as *selective exposure, selective perception, selective retention,* and *selective decision.* Let us first examine some studies which illustrate the operation of the selective processes, and later discuss the implications of these studies in the area of advertising strategy.

*Selective Exposure.* The conditions under which people engage in selective exposure and the extent to which this process is operative have not been fully specified or documented by communications research. However, the general conclusion seems to be that most people tend to expose themselves to communications in which they are interested or which they find congenial to their existing attitudes and to avoid communications that might be irritating, or uninteresting, or incompatible with their own opinions. The following studies are illustrative:

- Danuta Ehrlich, Isaiah Guttman, Peter Schönbach, and Judson Mills found that new car owners were much more likely to read advertisements for the car they had just purchased than were owners of the same make but an earlier model.[1] The new car owners were also much more likely to read ads about their own car than they were to read about other makes. The hypothesis is that the new car owners were seeking reassurance by exposing themselves to what were, no doubt, very "congenial" communications.

- Charles F. Cannell and James C. MacDonald found that only 32 per cent of a sample of male smokers were consistent readers of articles on health (including articles dealing with the relationship between smoking and lung cancer), whereas 60 per cent of nonsmoking males read such articles.[2]

*Selective Perception.* Even when people are accidentally or involuntarily exposed to a communication, they sometimes misinterpret or distort the intended meaning of the communication. For example, Patricia L. Kendall and Katherine M. Wolf report a study in which cartoons which were intended to ridicule prejudice were misinterpreted in some way by 64 per cent of the people who saw them.[3] Misinterpretation was most frequent among prejudiced respondents who either saw no satire in the cartoons or interpreted them as supporting their own attitudes. One respondent felt that the purpose of a cartoon intended to ridicule anti-semitism was "to show that there are some people against the Jews and to let other people feel freer to say they're against 'em too, I guess."

Carl I. Hovland, O. J. Harvey, and Muzafer Sherif presented communications arguing the desirability of prohibition to three types of people—"Drys," "Wets," and those "Moderately Wet."[4] They found that the greater the difference between the attitude of the recipient and the position advocated by the communication, the more likely the recipient was to regard the communication as propagandistic and unfair, and even to perceive the stand advocated by the communication as further removed from his own position than it actually was. Conversley, when the distance was small between the recipient's own stand and the position advocated by the communication, the recipient was likely to view the communication as being fair and factual and to perceive it as being even closer to his own stand than it actually was.

Habits also can cause distortion of a communication because people often see or hear that which, on the basis of past experience, they expect to see or hear. Gordon Allport and Leo Postman report that a picture in which a Red Cross truck was shown loaded with explosives was ordinarily perceived by subjects as a Red Cross truck carrying medical supplies (because that is the way it "ought" to be).[5]

[1] Danuta Ehrlich *et. al.*, "Postdecision Exposure to Relevant Information," *Journal of Abnormal and Social Psychology,* vol. 54, 1957, pp. 98–102.

[2] C. F. Cannell and J. C. MacDonald, "The Impact of Health News on Attitudes and Behavior," *Journalism Quarterly,* vol. 33, 1956, pp. 315–323.

[3] P. L. Kendall and K. M. Wolf, "The Analysis of Deviant Cases in Communications Research," in Paul F. Lazarsfeld and Frank N. Stanton (eds.), *Communications Research,* Harper & Brothers, New York, 1949, pp. 152–179.

[4] C. I. Hovland *et. al.,* "Assimilation and Contrast Effects in Reactions and Attitude Change," *Journal of Abnormal and Social Psychology,* vol. 55, 1957, pp. 244–252.

[5] G. Allport and L. Postman, "The Basic Psychology of Rumor," *Transactions of the New York Academy of Sciences,* ser. II, vol. 8, 1945, pp. 61–68. Reprinted in E. E. Maccoby, T. M. Newcombe, and E. L. Hartley (eds.), *Readings in Social Psychology,* Henry Holt & Company, New York, 1958, pp. 54–64.

In summary, the research cited indicates that under certain conditions people misinterpret or distort a communication so that it will be more compatible with their own attitudes, habits, or opinions.

*Selective Retention.* There is another way a person can reduce the dissonance or lack of internal harmony resulting when there is a discrepancy between his attitudes and those expressed by a communication with which he is faced. He can simply forget rather quickly the content of the communication! If this process is operative, we should also expect that a person would learn more quickly, and remember for a longer period, communications which *are* compatible with his own attitudes.

A study by Jerome M. Levine and Gardner Murphy supports these contentions.[6] Here it was found that procommunist material was better learned and better remembered by procommunists than by anticommunists; and the reverse was true for anticommunist material. Another example of selective retention occurred in an experiment by Claire Zimmerman and Raymond A. Bauer.[7] Given some material which was to be used in preparing a speech, subjects remembered fewer of the arguments which might have been received unfavorably by the audience they were slated to address.

*Selective Decision.* Even when a person has been exposed to a message, correctly perceives its intent, and remembers the main content, he still must decide whether or not to be influenced in the manner intended by the communicator. Because of individual predispositions, different people make different decisions as to whether or not (and to what extent) they will be influenced.

For example, in not one of the studies which I have reported has there been an instance in which every member of the audience made the same decision. In every case, some people decided to be persuaded; others did not. We can only assume that just as certain people are predisposed to expose themselves selectively to certain kinds of communications and to avoid others, they are also predisposed (i.e. more susceptible) to being influenced by some types of communications and appeals and not by others. In the Hovland, Harvey, and Sherif experiment, those whose attitudes strongly favored prohibition were predisposed *not* to be influenced by arguments against prohibition, and vice versa. Persuasion occurred most often when the individuals' attitudes toward prohibition were only slightly different from those advocated by the communication.

The evidence which I have thus far introduced seems to indicate quite clearly that people are very capable of resisting attempts to *change* their attitudes and behavior. If a persuasive communication seems incompatible with their own attitudes, they may avoid it, distort its meaning, forget it, or otherwise decide not to be influenced.

[6] J. M. Levine and G. Murphy, "The Learning and Forgetting of Controversial Material," *Journal of Abnormal and Social Psychology,* vol. 38, 1943, pp. 507–517.

[7] C. Zimmerman and R. A. Bauer, "The Influence of an Audience on What is Remembered," *Public Opinion Quarterly,* vol. 20, 1956, pp. 238–248.

If these conclusions are valid (as they seem to be), what are the implications for advertising? Although I am unable to offer much in the way of direct evidence, I can put forth two suggestions:

- A great deal of advertising must function either to *reinforce* existing attitudes and behavior (e.g. maintenance of brand loyalty), or to *stimulate* or activate people who are already predisposed to act in the desired manner (e.g. people who enjoy reading murder mysteries are most likely to be on the lookout for, and to be influenced by, advertising of murder mysteries).
- A related implication is that advertising is not, in itself, a cause of audience effects, but rather works with and through various mediating factors such as audience predispositions and personal influence (e.g. word-of-mouth advertising).[8]

It would be a mistake to contend that predispositions are so highly developed and so rigid that attitudes and behavior patterns never change. They do. However, I would argue that *changing* a person's attitudes or behavior (as opposed to *reinforcing* present attitudes or *activating* those already predisposed) is beyond the scope of most advertising, *except* where:

1. The attitude or behavior involved is of little importance to the individual. People to whom it makes little difference which brand of toothpaste they use are more likely to be influenced to switch brands by toothpaste advertising. Even here, however, some activation of predispositions is involved; people with false teeth are less likely to use any toothpaste.
2. The mediating factors (predispositions and personal influence) are inoperative. People may be influenced directly by the advertising for a new product because they have not been able to form attitudes which would predispose them against the product.
3. The mediating factors, which normally favor reinforcement, themselves favor change. If for some reason our friends begin buying color television sets, we are more likely to be influenced by advertising for color TV sets.[9]

If these contentions are realistic, it would then appear that a major function of effective advertising is to "select" people who are already predisposed to buy a product and present them with appeals (appropriate to the types of potential customers) which would hopefully trigger the desired response. *In those instances where change of important attitudes or behavior is the advertising objective, failure is more likely than success unless the advertiser can somehow work with or through the mediating factors.*

Now let me offer two generalizations that may shed more light on the predisposition factor:

- Some people or groups are more predisposed than others to be influenced by advertising for a particular product or brand.

[8] See Joseph T. Klapper, "What We Know About the Effects of Mass Communications: The Brink of Hope," *Public Opinion Quarterly,* vol. 21, 1957–1958, pp. 453–474.

[9] Points (2) and (3) are taken from Klapper, *op cit.*

- Within that group which is more predisposed toward a particular product, some individuals or subgroups will be more predisposed to be influenced by certain kinds of appeals, while others will be predisposed by different kinds of appeals.

In order to indicate the bases of these predispositions, I will discuss the three groups of factors which interact to make an individual more (or less) predisposed to be influenced by any particular communication:

1. the physical and economic reality which an individual experiences,
2. his personality, and
3. the social environment in which he lives.

*Physical and Economic Reality as a Basis of Predisposition.* This is the most obvious of the predisposing factors. It is well recognized that a person's income, age, sex, and so on, will predispose him or her to buy certain products and to refrain from buying others. Similarly, products he has owned or now owns may be partial determinants of his future susceptibility to advertising. For some products it is relatively easy to predict, on the basis of physical and economic predispositions, which large group within the population will be most likely to buy.

Within this large group, however, it is sometimes possible to distinguish several subgroups, each of which—though predisposed to buy the product—could best be reached by different communications or different appeals. Taking new owners and old owners of automobiles, for instance, and assuming that both groups were predisposed to buy the same make of auto within the following two or three years, I wonder if an auto manufacturer's advertising would not be more effective if different appeals were made to each group.

Maybe present advertising could be retained to reach both groups and be as effective as could be expected for old owners, but in addition specific appeals could be directed to new owners (by direct mail). This might be effective in giving them greater reassurance at a time when they most need it and thus increase the probability that their next car will be of the same make.

*Personality as a Basis of Predisposition.* Various studies (such as that by Irving L. Janis *et al.*[10]) have attempted to show that some personality types are more susceptible to influence than others are. There may be some truth in this supposition, but it is rather difficult to prove that *in general* one person is more persuasible than another. More likely, people are predisposed (on the basis of their habits, attitudes, and motives) to be more susceptible to persuasion on certain issues or by certain kinds of appeals. For example, the study by Irving L. Janis and Seymour Feshbach of fear-arousing appeals aimed at changing dental hygiene practices found that people who were high in anxiety were

[10] I. L. Janis et. al., see *Personality and Persuasibility,* Yale University Press, New Haven, 1959.

least likely to be influenced by strong fear appeals.[11] Other examples of personality as a basis of predisposition can be found in the preceding discussion of selective exposure, perception, retention, and decision. One further example is the finding of Elihu Katz and Paul F. Lazarsfeld that women who are low in "gregariousness," or who report that they "worry more than others," or who are "sometimes blue and depressed" are more likely to have higher exposure to "popular fiction" (such as movie and "true story" type magazines and daytime serials).[12]

These findings can hardly be considered exhaustive, but they represent an interesting beginning. As the study of personality advances, we should expect to see a great many more relationships revealed between personality variables and predispositions to being influenced by certain specific kinds of appeals. The real difficulty at the present time seems to be the lack of reliable and useful tests for measuring individual personality differences. However, just because the effect of personality is not well documented in the research on communications does not mean that it is not important. It may turn out to be *the* most important determinant of predispositions.

*The Social Environment as a Basis of Predisposition.* In this age of the "organization" man and the "other-directed" man it is well known, and even accepted, that to varying degrees our behavior is influenced by other people and groups. What is not so well known is the *extent* to which our social environment shapes our behavior and attitudes in subtle ways we may not even be aware of. When I speak of the social environment as a basis of predisposition, I do not refer to direct, overt attempts by one person to influence another (which is called personal influence); instead I refer to indirect, often barely noticeable social influences.

A classic experiment by Solomon A. Asch offers a striking example of the effect of unmentioned group "norms" on individual behavior.[13] Subjects in groups of eight were asked to match the length of a given line with one of three unequal lines. The correct answer was quite obvious, but seven of the eight subjects had been previously instructed to give the same *wrong* answers. In one third of the cases the person who was not let in on the experiment agreed with the unanimous (though visibly incorrect) majority—even though he "knew" what the correct answer was, and even though no overt attempt at influence was made.

Another example of social influence is reported by Francis S. Bourne.[14] He found that women who made negative statements about a food product, but who said the product was popular with their friends, used more of the product than did women who made positive statements about the product, but who said it was unpopular with their friends.

[11] I. L. Janis and S. Feshbach, "Effects of Fear-Arousing Communication," *Journal of Abnormal and Social Psychology,* vol 48, 1953, pp. 78–92.

[12] E. Katz and P. F. Lazarsfeld, *Personal Influence,* The Free Press of Glencoe, New York, 1955, p. 378.

[13] S. A. Asch, "Effects of Group Pressure upon the Modification and Distortion of Judgements," in *Readings in Social Psychology,* see footnote 5.

[14] F. S. Bourne, "Group Influence in Marketing Decisions," in Rensis Likert and Samuel P. Hayes, Jr. (eds.), *Some Applications of Behavioural Research,* UNESCO, Paris, 1957.

In other words, if you know your friends favor a particular brand or product you may be more predisposed to use it yourself.

Bourne offers some evidence which suggests that social influence of this sort is operative chiefly among products which are conspicuous (i.e. both visible and unique). This remains to be seen, but it is fairly clear that in some situations group norms or sentiments play a considerable part in predisposing us to act in certain ways—probably much more so than most of us realize. Since different people belong to different reference groups which may hold varying attitudes toward a particular brand or product, it follows that some groups will be more, or less, predisposed to be influenced by advertising for a product than will others.

And within these groups some people may be more susceptible to advertising (or certain appeals) than others. For example, Harold H. Kelley and Edmund H. Volkart found that individuals who least valued their membership in a group were not so likely to resist attempts at influence which were counter to the values of the group.[15]

The effect of group norms and other social pressures raises many interesting questions and problems for advertising strategy—questions which I cannot now explore. Let me try, however, to offer two generalizations for advertisers to consider:

1. The fact that the economic and physical reality, the personality, and the social environment act to predispose certain groups to be more or less susceptible to influence than others is well recognized by marketing and advertising strategists. Most successful marketing programs begin with an appraisal of "Who buys (or is most likely to buy) the product?" or "To whom will (or does) the product appeal?" In addition, we see a good deal of the practice of selective marketing or market segmentation; that is, producing and marketing products which have a particular appeal for a limited and specific segment of the market.
2. But only rarely do we notice an advertiser making use of *selective advertising*; that is, the use of different appeals to sell the *same* product to different segments of the market. The research to date clearly suggests that the possibility of making greater use of selective advertising is, for many companies, well worth investigating (and I shall discuss it in more detail later).

Earlier I excluded personal influence from our discussion of predisposing factors. But personal influence, of course, cannot be long excluded. Not only are members of the audience themselves influenced by mass communications; they also are stimulated at times through personal communication.

Many of the studies of personal influence were stimulated by an earlier study of voting behavior which had suggested a hypothesis called the "two-step flow of

[15] H. H. Kelley and E. H. Volkart, "The Resistance to Change of Group-Anchored Attitudes," *American Sociological Review,* vol. 17, 1952, pp. 453–465. The findings are summarized by Carl I. Hovland, Irving L. Janis, and Harold H. Kelley, *Communication and Persuasion,* Yale University Press, New Haven, 1953, chap. 5.

communication." According to this theory, ideas "flow from radio and print to opinion leaders and from them to less active sections of the population."[16]

Two pioneering studies which are of particular significance in studying the process of personal influence have been conducted. One is by Elihu Katz and Paul F. Lazarsfeld on the flow of influence among housewives in Decatur in the areas of marketing (food and household products primarily), fashions, public affairs, and movie-going.[17] The other is by Herbert Menzel and Elihu Katz on the spread of a new drug among doctors.[18]

Based on respondents' own assessments (the accuracy of which may be questioned), the Decatur study concluded that in marketing, personal influence has greater impact than has advertising because respondents reported "more exposure to personal advice than to advertisements; and second, among those exposed to each source, 'most important influence' is more often attributed to people than to formal advertisements." The drug study did not attempt to evaluate relative impact, but did conclude that interpersonal communication and social support are important factors in encouraging doctors to face the risks of medical innovation.

The two studies suggest that influence is related "to the personification of certain values (who one is); . . . to competence (what one knows); and . . . to strategic social location (whom one knows)."[19]

For example, the Decatur study suggests that:

- There is little overlap in opinion leadership—a person tends to specialize in one sphere—e.g. marketing *or* fashion *or* movies.
- In marketing, there is a concentration of opinion leadership among "large family wives" (older women with two or more children).
- Influence flows among people of the same social status and usually among the same age group.
- Women who are "gregarious" are more likely to be opinion leaders.

The Decatur study also shows that opinion leaders are more likely to be exposed to the mass media than are the people whom they influence, and also that they are particularly likely to be exposed to the media appropriate to their own sphere of influence. In the case of fashion, it even appears that the opinion leaders are "not only more exposed to the mass media but are also more affected by them in their own decisions."[20] The drug study also showed that "influential doctors were more likely to be readers of a large number of professional journals and valued them more highly than did doctors of lesser influence."[21]

[16] Paul F. Lazarsfeld, Bernard Berelson, and Hazel Gaudet, *The People's Choice,* Duell, Sloan & Pearce, New York, 1944, p. 151.

[17] Katz and Lazarsfeld, *op. cit.*

[18] H. Menzel and E. Katz, "Social Relations and Innovation in the Medical Profession," *Public Opinion Quarterly,* vol. 19, 1955–1956, pp. 337–352.

[19] Elihu Katz, "The Two-Step Flow of Communication," *Public Opinion Quarterly,* vol. 21, 1957, p. 73.

[20] *Ibid.,* p. 75.

[21] *Ibid.,* p. 76.

The obvious implication is to advertise to opinion leaders and let them carry the ball from there. Opinion leaders are very interested in a specific sphere, are more exposed to media, and hence are probably more likely to notice and read advertisements appropriate to their sphere of influence. However, just because they are exposed to the advertising does not necessarily mean that they will be influenced by it. (In the Decatur study, only the fashion leaders were.)

Actually, a good case can be made for the proposition that as far as *change* is concerned, opinion leaders are more likely to show high resistance than are their followers in many cases. This point was not brought out in the Decatur study, but the drug study noted that it was not the influential doctors who *first* began using the new drugs, but rather doctors who were relatively isolated from the rest of the medical community. If these innovators were isolated because they were not too highly regarded by the influential doctors, it is not likely that they had a great deal of direct personal influence over the influential doctors.

In studying the process of personal influence (rather than looking at "opinion leaders" as such) we would probably be more realistic if we distinguished between two kinds of leaders–the *innovators* and the *"influentials."* Influentials may have considerable personal influence over others in the group, but they may enjoy this influence because they recognizably hold the norms and values of the group.

If, as is often the case, the norms of the group favor the *status quo,* the influentials have an investment in this *status quo,* hence are more likely to be resistant to change. Unless the norms of the group favor innovation (as in fashion or in some areas of the medical profession), the innovators are very likely to be the deviant or isolated members of the group, none too popular with the rest of the group, and with little direct personal influence over anyone in the group. However, the innovators may affect the behavior of others (including the influentials) through a process of "social influence by example." For example, in a study of the adoption of hybrid seed corn, Bryce Ryan and Neal Gross discovered that the influential farmers took their cue from innovating farmers after seeing the good results they had obtained.[22] Adoption by most of the others in the community followed adoption by the influentials.

In sum, unless the norms of the group favor innovation, innovating and influencing are two separate processes which are carried out by two different types of people. It is therefore necessary to redefine the simpler notion of opinion leadership in order to take into account two types of opinion leaders–the innovators and the influentials.

The implications of these findings for advertising strategy are not clear. The process of personal influence is undoubtedly of major importance in the marketing of goods and services; yet, at the present time only a handful of relevant studies on this important topic are available. It is fairly clear, though, that it is beneficial to have the right people talking about your product, provided they are saying the right things. What should be done in order to encourage this is not self-evident. As a start, though, I would suggest

[22]B. Ryan and N. Gross, "The Diffusion of Hybrid Seed Corn in Iowa Communities," *Rural Sociology,* vol. 8, 1943, pp. 15–24.

that word-of-mouth activity be used as one measure of advertising effectiveness. In this way, a campaign could be judged partly on the basis of the amount of word-of-mouth activity it stimulated. It may well be that having one person talk about your product to his friends is worth more than having the friends exposed to a commercial or advertisement for the product.

What implications does research on mass communications have for testing advertising effectiveness? This is a problem which has always been of concern to advertisers. The research supports two propositions (which, incidentally, conform what most advertising researchers already know—that measuring advertising effects is a delicate and difficult operation). However, the following propositions, and the research and theory underlying them, do more than confirm the obvious; they may help establish a useful basis for measuring ad effectiveness.

In general, the essence of the two propositions is that the connection between a person's factual knowledge and his attitudes or opinions and between the latter and his behavior is not necessarily a direct, one-to-one relationship. More specifically:

1. *It is possible for a person to change his factual knowledge without changing his attitudes or his behavior.*

   One illustration of this proposition is found in the Janis and Feshbach study of the effect of fear-arousing appeals on changing attitudes and behavior regarding dental hygiene practices.[23] Similarly, a study by Carl I. Hovland, Arthur A. Lumsdaine, and Fred D. Sheffield found that the film *The Battle of Britain* was considerably more effective in changing factual information than it was in changing opinions—based on tests before and five days after the film showing.[24]

   Does this mean that measures of advertising effectiveness such as the Starch Readership Service and the Gallup-Robinson IMPACT technique are of dubious value? Both services measure name association and recall (e.g. factual information), and research has shown it is possible to effect changes in information without eliciting corresponding changes in attitudes or behavior—or, in other words, without achieving the goals of most advertising. Let us reserve judgment on these measures until we consider the next proposition. At that time they may appear potentially more useful than they do here.

2. *It is possible for a person to change his behavior without first changing his attitudes (i.e. attitude change may follow behavior change).*

   It is often impractical to attempt to relate advertising effects to sales. The closest substitute would seem to be a measure of changes in attitudes produced by an advertisement. The assumption would be that advertising works by first causing changes in attitude that in turn produce changes in behavior. Therefore, since we cannot measure

[23] Janis and Feshback, *op. cit.* See also the discussion of the study in *Harvard Business Review*, September–October, 1961, pp. 164–166.

[24] C. I. Hovland et al., *Experiments on Mass Communications*, Princeton University Press, Princeton, 1949.

the behavior, the next best thing is to measure that which immediately precedes the behavior—attitudes.

This procedure sound logical, but, unfortunately, it so happens that attitude changes may *follow* rather than precede behavior changes. For example, it is possible that a person will see an advertisement, buy the product, and then change his attitude toward the product in the direction advocated by the ad. Raymond A. and Alice H. Bauer suspect "that one of the major ways in which mass media influence public attitudes is via the second-order effect of having first elicited behavior based on other existing attitudes."[25] If this contention is realistic, measurement of changes in attitudes may not be a valid criterion for evaluating the effectiveness of an ad. For example:

> Let us imagine that a number of consumers bought a particular brand of shoe polish after having seen some advertising for that brand, but without exhibiting any measurable change in their attitudes toward the brand. Assume that the advertising was influential, not because it changed their basic attitudes, but because it reminded them, at the point of purchase, that the brand existed, and they therefore decided to try it.
>
> Suppose the manufacturer was trying to evaluate the effectiveness of his campaign so that he could better focus his advertising efforts. If he had measured the consumers' attitudes before and after advertising (but before they had bought the product), he would have found no change in their attitude toward his brand. He probably would have concluded that the advertising had no effect whatever.
>
> But advertising had, in fact, triggered the purchase by reminding consumers of the brand's existence. The manufacturer would have thus erred in evaluating the effects of his advertising. On the other hand, if he had measured consumers' attitudes before advertising, and again after they had made the purchases (and had changed their attitudes), he would have concluded that advertising had caused consumers to change their attitudes and thus buy his product.
>
> This, too, would have been a mistake and might have led him to the wrong conclusions about how he should advertise his product. If, as we have assumed, the real reason why his advertising was effective was because it reminded people to buy the product, a campaign of "reminder" advertising would be indicated. The manufacturer, however, after studying the results of either type of attitude survey, would probably have concluded that (a) the advertising *was not* effective, or (b) the advertising *was* effective because it changed consumers' attitudes. This might have led him to the erroneous conclusion that (a) he did not have to advertise, or (b) that he should launch a campaign which would change people's attitudes.

Unfortunately, it is difficult to find direct evidence in support of the proposition that behavior change can take place without being preceded by attitude change. When Jack W. Brehm asked young women first to rate the desirability of eight products (mostly appliances), then offered them their choice between two of these products, and again asked them to rate the products, he found that after making their choice, the subjects showed a marked increase in preference for the product chosen.[26] They also showed a marked *decrease* in their preference for the product *not* chosen. The extent of this decrease in post-decision preference was considerably greater if the subject had initially

[25] R. A. and A. H. Bauer, "America, Mass Society and Mass Media," *Journal of Social Issues,* vol. 16, no. 3, 1961, pp. 3–66.

[26] J. W. Brehm, "Post-Decision Changes in the Desirability of Alternatives," *Journal of Abnormal and Social Psychology,* vol. 52, 1956, pp. 384–389.

given both products about the same rating. In other words, the more difficult the choice she had to make, the more likely she was (after the decision) to prefer the chosen product more and the rejected product less.

Similarly, Judson Mills tested students' attitudes toward cheating, then created a situation where some of them were able to cheat during a test.[27] He remeasured their attitudes, and found that those who had cheated became more lenient in their attitudes toward cheating, while those who had not cheated became more severe.

The theory which predicts these kinds of behavior is called the *theory of cognitive dissonance.* This theory was developed by Leon Festinger,[28] and holds that when a person chooses between two or more alternatives, discomfort or dissonance will almost inevitably arise because of the person's knowledge that while the decision he has made has certain advantages, it also has some disadvantages. The girl who chose a toaster in the Brehm experiment did so because she liked it, but she would have liked the iron, too. Also, the cheaters knew there was an advantage to cheating, but they recognized that it was not the right thing to do, hence a disadvantage.

The theory holds that dissonance arises after almost every decision, and further that the individual will invariably take steps to reduce this dissonance. There are several ways in which this can be done, but the most likely way is to create as many advantages as you can in favor of the alternative you have chosen and to think of as many disadvantages as possible relating to the other alternatives. Thus the girl who chose the toaster decided that she really liked it much more than the iron, and so on. The same explanation accounts for the new car owners reading more ads about their cars than old car owners.

It is important to remind you: I am not suggesting that attitude changes may not also precede changes in behavior. Undoubtedly they do. However, while the evidence I have offered is only suggestive, there are some grounds for believing that behavior change can take place without being preceded by attitude change. This, combined with the fact that some attitude change almost always follows any important decision or behavior change, makes any attempt at using attitude change to measure advertising effects a delicate and potentially misleading operation.

Having built up a little background on dissonance theory, we can now return to the other possible indirect measures of advertising effectiveness–recognition and recall. The theory of cognitive dissonance would hold that when a person faces the chance of being exposed (or is exposed) to knowledge or opinions (i.e. cognitions) which are related to, but in conflict with, some of his own cognitions, dissonance arises. For example, if I own a Ford but suddenly hear an announcer extolling the wonders of a Chevrolet, the cognition that I own a

[27] J. Mills, "Changes in Moral Attitudes Following Temptation," *Journal of Personality,* vol. 26, 1959, pp. 517–531.

[28] L. Festinger, *A Theory of Cognitive Dissonance,* Row, Peterson & Company, Evanston, Ill., 1957.

Ford will be dissonant with the cognition that the Chevrolet is a wonderful car. As we know, the theory suggests that I will take steps to reduce this dissonance. But how? I have several alternatives:

- To buy or consider buying a Chevrolet *(selective decision).*
- To turn off the set or otherwise ignore the commercial *(selective exposure).*
- To distort the communication—"Sure, Chevrolet is good, but that model is probably very expensive to operate compared with my Ford" *(selective perception).*
- To forget the entire communication very quickly or forget parts of the communication that produce the most dissonance *(selective retention).*

If I am somewhat predisposed to buy a Chevrolet, and if the commercial has been effective in acting on my predisposition, I may take the first alternative—even if it is only so far as to say I will certainly consider a Chevrolet next time. In this case, the advertising has been effective and I am less likely to engage in the alternative defenses. If, however, I am not so predisposed and the commercial has not been effective, then I will certainly try to reduce the dissonance by avoiding the commercial, distorting it, and/or forgetting some or all of it rather quickly.

If I am somewhat predisposed to certain information, is it not possible that measures of exposure and recall can be very useful in evaluating the effectiveness of an advertisement? As I have argued earlier, advertising seems to work by selecting and acting on those people who are already predisposed to buy the product. Therefore, a good measure of exposure and recall should offer valid testimony to the ad's ability to select and act on those so predisposed. The ones who are not predisposed, or who were not acted on, will already have taken steps either to avoid exposing themselves, or to distort or not recall properly all or part of the message.

What criteria then should be met by a good indirect measure of advertising effectiveness? In addition to meeting acceptable standards of research methodology, an indirect measure should:

- *Measure exposure under natural conditions (or allow for the effects of forced exposure).* Any artificial medium must be suspect because it reduces the opportunity for selective exposure.
- *Measure respondents some time (at least a week—preferably two weeks) after they have been exposed to the communication.* This is to allow the process of selective retention to operate.
- *Measure a verbatim playback of the message.* That is, respondents' unaided recollections of the contents of an ad should be recorded *in toto.* It is important to know not only *how much* has been remembered, but also what portions of the message have been forgotten or remembered—what portions are dissonant or consonant, and *with whom.* Respondents can also be identified on the basis of relevant characteristics in order to determine how different types of people react to the advertisement.
- *Measure distortion of the message.* It is important to know what parts of the message are distorted and the nature of these distortions. This would be partially handled by the verbatim playback, but might also require one or two probing questions.

Unhappily, neither the Starch system nor the Gallup-Robinson IMPACT technique meets *all* of these criteria. But the IMPACT technique does come very close, and with a few slight modifications would meet the suggested criteria. The needed modifications would include delaying the measure of recall for several weeks where practicable, measuring distortion more systematically, and classifying responses by types of respondents.

For those who want high readership or viewership scores we should note that by measuring recall immediately after exposure, under forced exposure conditions, by probing deeply, and so on, it is possible to achieve inflated results. However, all the evidence indicates that people tend to set up barriers against communications which are incompatible with their own attitudes or which do not interest them. I feel, therefore, that an indirect measure of advertising effectiveness which determines whether or not, and to what extent, a consumer has engaged in the process of selective exposure, perception, and retention will be more realistic and hence more valuable to a company in evaluating its advertising efforts.

I would like to close by putting forward an advertising strategy which seems to be supported by much of the research evidence which has been presented—*the strategy of selective advertising.* This strategy is based on two key assumptions:

- Advertising works primarily by reinforcing or otherwise acting upon people already predisposed to act.
- The closer the match between the appeals used and the individual's predispositions, the more likely he is to expose himself to the advertisement, and to act as desired.

Ideally, since we consider people to be different from one another, every individual should be approached with slightly different appeals in order to come closest to matching his predispositions. Obviously, this is quite impractical. What has happened instead is that most advertisers operate at the other end of the continuum; that is, they assume that for practical purposes everyone is more or less alike, and that an appeal which is good for one is good for all.

This approach also may be quite impractical—if we think in terms of opportunity cost. It seems that an ideal strategy would involve a compromise somewhere between these two extremes. The advertiser cannot advertise selectively to everyone, but neither should he think that "for all practical purposes" everyone is alike. People are not all alike. However, some segments of the population do have many common characteristics. We would expect much more similarity among people in the same social class than we would among people of different classes. We would also expect more similarity among young people than between people of two age groups, and so on. There are many ways in which the population might be segmented into groups reasonably homogeneous in their predispositions toward any particular product.

If this is the case, then the task of selective advertising is to select those groups and subgroups which are relevant to the particular product and to match appeals with group predispositions. In other words, a selective advertising campaign would not usually rely on only one appeal or one type of media but would run as many different appeals in as many different media as were necessary to match particular groups which make up the potential market for a product—up to the point where this increased number of appeals maximized the return on advertising investment. Just where the optimum point is located is rather beyond the scope of this article. It seems likely, however, that in most cases the optimum strategy would be to use more than one appeal.

There is still another argument for the use of a variety of appeals. Not only do people differ from one another, but any one individual has many needs which might be satisfied by a product. Dorwin Cartwright suggests that the "more goals which are seen as attainable by a single path, the more likely it is that a person will take that path."[29] In other words, the product is the path by which the person may attain certain goals. Use of a variety of appeals increases the number of goals or needs which the product might be seen as satisfying, and hence increases the probability of triggering off one or more predisposing factors.

In addition, the use of a variety of relevant appeals allows the advertiser to repeat his product story several times in several ways without arousing the wrath of the listener who might be irritated by constant repetition of the same appeal.

Robert K. Merton's analysis of Kate Smith's marathon effort in selling war bonds offers testimony to the power of selective advertising.[30] Merton identified some sixty different appeals used and found that "each new entreaty sought out a new vulnerability in some listeners." As I have suggested, Miss Smith's use of a variety of appeals was effective in two ways:

1. it offered one person more reasons to buy, and
2. it touched some predisposition in a wide variety of people.

An appeal which was not relevant to the predispositions of some would likely trigger off responses in others, and so on.

To conclude, the strategy of selective advertising would strongly reject the notions that there is but *one* market for a product and that this market can best be reached by *one* appeal which has universal selling power. The strategy of selective advertising would hold that such contentions are myths which have little basis in reality.

Perhaps the day will come when advertisers will abandon their belief in the undifferentiated market and the universal appeal. This day should mark a considerable step forward in the art of advertising strategy.

[29] D. Cartwright "Some Principles of Mass Persuasion," *Human Relations,* vol. 2, 1949, pp. 253–267.
[30] R. K. Merton, *Mass Persuasion,* Harper & Brothers, New York, 1946.

# 59. DOES ADVERTISING BELONG IN THE CAPITAL BUDGET?

*Joel Dean*

*Whether advertising is an investment and so should be treated like other parts of the capital budget is a question of moment to marketing managers. Viewing promotion as an investment could bring dramatic changes in decision-making, market-testing, measurements of effectiveness, and value judgments that are required in determining how much to spend on promotion.*

*The economic case for an investment approach to the advertising budget is the theme of this article by a distinguished economist.*

*Should advertising be budgeted as an expense or as an investment?*

Advertising is now book-kept and budgeted as though its benefits were used up immediately, like purchased electricity. Management thinks about advertising as it is book-kept, as a current expense. The decision as to how much a corporation should spend on persuasion is made by the same criteria as for materials used up in the factory—impact upon the current P&L. The advertising budget is part of the *operating* budget.

Source: From *Journal of Marketing,* vol. 30, October, 1966, pp. 15–21. Joel Dean: President of Joel Dean Associates, New York, and Professor of Business Economics, Columbia University.

So far as is known, no corporation puts advertising in its capital budget. But maybe it belongs there. Several disinterested parties say so:

The stock market says it belongs there. It says the benefits derived from promotional outlays are just as capitalizable as the tangible assets that the bookkeeper does capitalize. It says this when Bristol Myers sells at ten times its book value.

Corporation presidents occasionally say it belongs there, especially when they evoke *investment* in advertising to justify poor current profits.

New entrants into any industry say advertising belongs in the capital budget. They say it by including the promotional outlays required to build brand-acceptance as an integral part of the total investment required to break into the business.

Antitrust economists say advertising belongs in the capital budget. They say it by viewing brand-acceptance, which is built up by promotion, as just as substantial a barrier to entry as the investment required in buildings and machinery.

It is just possible that the bookkeeper's guide to top-management thinking about advertising is wrong.

## THE APPROACH

The plan of this article is, first, to find whether promotion is an investment; second, to consider how to optimize it if it is an investment, and third, to speculate on the probabilities that this novel approach, even if theoretically valid, will do any good.

The approach here to the problem of how much to invest in advertising is formal and objective, rather than intuitive. The premise is that the overriding goal of the corporation is to maximize profits. The viewpoint is that of an economist concerned with managerial finance.

This article is confined to the conceptual framework for deciding how much to invest in promotion. Measurement problems are not examined, nor are the mechanics of application. The analysis is presented in terms of advertising, but is equally applicable to all forms of persuasion. Advertising is used as an example simply because it is the purest and most indisputable form of selling cost, and for many firms also the largest.

My thesis is as follows. Most advertising is, in economic essence, an investment. How much to spend on advertising is, therefore, a problem of investment economics. A new approach is required—economic and financial analysis of futurities. This approach focuses on future after-tax cash flows and centers on the profit-productivity of capital.

## IS PROMOTION AN INVESTMENT?

To determine whether, as a matter of economics, outlays for advertising and other forms of promotion constitute an investment, rather than a current expense, is our first task.

So we must bravely face three basic questions concerning the economics of investment in corporate persuasion:

1. Precisely what is a business investment; how is it distinguished from a current expense?
2. Just what are promotional costs; how should they be distinguished from production costs?
3. What are the distinctive characteristics of promotional outlays; do they disqualify promotion for investment treatment?

*Concept of Investment.* What distinguishes a business investment from a current expense?

An investment is an outlay made today to achieve benefits in the future. A current expense is an outlay whose benefits are immediate. The question is not how the outlay is treated in conventional accounting, how it is taxed, or whether the asset is tangible or intangible. The hallmark of an investment is futurity.

*Concept of Promotional Costs.* Precisely what are promotional costs? How do they differ from production costs?

Promotional costs are outlays to augment the demand for the product—that is, to shift its price-quantity demand schedule upward, so that more will be sold at a given price. In contrast, production costs are all outlays required to meet this demand.

This different dividing line means that some costs which are conventionally classified as marketing costs, for example, physical distribution, are here viewed as part of production costs. It means also that some costs usually viewed as production costs, for example, inspection, are here viewed as promotional costs, even though they are incurred in the factory.

This is the cost dichotomy needed for clear thinking about promotional investments. A clear idea of the purpose of an outlay is indispensable for a useful estimate of its effectiveness. Moreover, the criterion for optimization is quite different for production costs than for promotional costs. For production, it is sheer cost minimization; for promotion, it is not cost minimization but something much more intricate, as we shall see.

*Distinctive Traits of Promotional Outlays.* Do promotional investments differ from unimpeachable corporate investments in ways that make it impractical to manage them like true investments?

Promotional investments *are* different from traditional corporate investments—for example, capital tied up in machinery. The question is whether these differences call for a different intellectual apparatus for measuring productivity and rationing the firm's capital.

Promotional investments *are book-kept differently.* They are not capitalized and not depreciated. But this does not keep them from being investments. They tie up capital with equal inflexibility and do so with similar expectation of future benefits.

Promotional investments *are taxed differently.* Unlike acknowledged investments, they are deductible against income fully at the time of outlay, regardless of the delay of benefits. The fact that the tax collector is oblivious to promotional investments increases their productivity. Immediate tax writeoff of the entire outlay halves the investment after tax and steps up its true rate of return.

Promotional investments *are generally spread out over time* and usually can be adjusted in amount in relatively small steps. However, this is irrelevant in determining whether or not they are true investments.

Most promotional investments *have an indeterminate economic life.* Brand-acceptance "planted in the head" of a teenager by television may influence his purchases for fifty minutes or fifty years. But uncertainty of duration of the benefits does not make the promotional outlay any less an investment. The obsolescence-life of a computer is also quite uncertain.

Promotional investments *have multiple benefits* which can be reaped in optional ways. The profitability of augmented demand may be taken out either in higher prices or in larger volume. But this is not unique to promotional investments. Usually, factory modernization not only saves labor, but also increases capacity and improves product-quality and employee morale.

Promotional investments *usually have irregular and diverse time-shapes in their benefit streams.* But this is a common characteristic of many tangible investments. Some oil wells, for example, come in as gushers, have an unexpected midlife rejuvenation from repressuring, and live out a tranquil old age as pumpers.

Promotional investments *have a benefit-stream which is difficult to measure and to predict.* But they share this characteristic with many forms of outlay conventionally classified as capital expenditures. Obsolescence of chemical-processing equipment, for example, is hard to predict, yet vitally affects its rate of return.

Promotional investments are *provocative;* they may induce rivals to retaliate. This adds to the difficulty of measuring and predicting benefits. Tangible investments, however, can also provoke competitors' reactions in ways that erode their profitability (for example, retail store modernization).

All this adds up to the fact that promotional investments *do* have unusual characteristics, different from many other investments that now fight for funds in the capital budget. However, these traits either are not distinctive, or if they are, do not destroy the essential investment-character of the promotional outlays.

All promotional outlays are now conventionally viewed exclusively as current expenses. Some are, if the time lag of benefits is sufficiently short; but others are instead true investments, because the delay in their benefits is substantial. Most promotion is a *mixture,* and the richness of the investment-mix varies over a wide range.

## HOW TO OPTIMIZE INVESTMENT IN PROMOTION

Granted that much advertising is largely an investment in economic reality, how should a corporation determine how much it should invest in promotion? To solve this problem, we need answers to the following questions:

1. Does a satisfactory solution for the problem already exist?
2. Why has such an important problem remained unsolved?
3. To what corporate goal should the solution be geared?

4. How does promotion tie into other ways of getting business?
5. What are the determinants of the productivity of capital invested in promotion?
6. What concepts of measurement are needed to calibrate productivity of capital?
7. What is the most appropriate yardstick of capital productivity for promotional investments?
8. How would rate-of-return rationing work for investments in corporate persuasion?

*Problem Unsolved.* Has the problem of how much a corporation should spend on advertising and other forms of persuasion been already satisfactorily solved?

The problem is important. The answer is crucial to the competitive success of many firms, and may involve vast expenditures.

In the future, it is likely to be even more vital. Depersonalized distribution, increased urbanization, rising consumer affluence, revolutionary advances in technology, and bigger economies of scale in some promotional media are dynamic forces which will make the decision as to how much to invest in promotion a jugular issue for many corporations in the next decade.

Surprisingly, this crucial problem is not yet solved. Despite yards of computer printouts and millions of dollars spent on advertising research, most corporations do not really know whether their promotional outlays should be half or twice as large as they now are.

*Reasons for Failure.* Why has such an important problem remained unsolved? There are three main causes.

The first cause is *failure to acknowledge the importance of futurity.* The full impact of most promotional outlays upon demand is delayed with associated uncertainty. Hence, the conceptual framework of analysis that management needs for solving this problem is the kind that is used in modern, sophisticated management of conventional corporate capital appropriations.

A second cause is *lack of a conceptual apparatus whose orientation is economic.* The problem of optimizing promotional investment is basically a matter of managerial economics, that is, balancing incremental promotional investment against predicted benefits, so as to augment sales most profitably.

The third cause of failure is *the difficulty of measuring the effectiveness of promotional outlays.* Their impacts on demand are diffused, delayed, and intricately interwoven with other forces. To make the kind of investment approach needed to produce practical benefits will require an open mind, fresh concepts, substantial research spending, and great patience.

*Overriding Corporate Goal.* What is the corporate goal to which the solution of optimum investment in promotion should be geared?

Promotional outlays, like other expenditures, should be judged in terms of their contribution to attainment of the corporation's objectives. Most companies have several goals, some of which conflict; but the solution for the problem of how much to invest in promotion should be geared primarily to the goal of profitability.

The master goal of the modern corporation should be maximum profits in the long run. More explicitly, it should be to maximize the present worth at the corporation's cost of capital of the future stream of benefits to the stockholder.

All other objectives–such as growth or market-share or eternal life–should be either intermediate or subsidiary to this overriding corporate objective.

*Business-Getters.* How does promotion relate to other ways of getting business?

A company has three ways to augment its sales: by cutting price, by spending more on promotion, and by bettering its product. The three members of the business-getting threesome pull together. But being alternatives, they are at the margin rivalrous substitutes.

The three reinforce each other in a complex symbiotic relationship. For a product that is superior to rivals in wanted ways, promotional outlays will be more effective than for an inferior product. A given amount and quality of promotion will produce more sales of a product priced in correct economic relationship to buyers' alternatives than for an overpriced product.

Each of the three business-getters can have delayed impacts and hence be a business investment. Their delayed and intertwining effects on sales, now and in the future, increase the problem of measuring the effects of promotional investment.

*Determinants of Capital Productivity.* What are the determinants of the productivity of capital invested in promotion?

These need to be identified to find out whether capital tied up in advertising will yield enough profits to earn its keep. Its yield must pay for the cost of this capital in the marketplace, or its opportunity costs in benefits passed up by not investing the money somewhere else.

The productivity of an investment in promotion is the relation of its earnings to the amount of capital tied up. This relationship requires explicit recognition of four economic determinants to be measured: (1) the amount and timing of *added investment;* (2) the amount and timing of *added earnings;* (3) the *duration of the earnings;* and (4) the *risks and imponderable benefits* associated with the project.

1. *Added investment.* The appropriate investment base for calculating rate of return is the added outlay which will be occasioned by the adoption of a promotion project as opposed to its rejection.

   The investment should include the entire amount of the original added outlay, regardless of how it is classified on the accounts. Any additional outlay for point-of-purchase displays or for distribution of samples to consumers should be included in the investment amount, as should future research expenses caused by the proposal.

The timing of these added investments has an important effect upon true profitability and should, therefore, be reflected in the rate-of-return computation.

2. *Added earnings.* Concern with capital productivity implies, of course, that the company's goal is profits.

   The productivity of the capital tied up is determined by the increase in earnings or savings, that is, net cash receipts, caused by making the investment as opposed to not making it. These earnings should be measured in terms of their after-tax cash or cash equivalents.

   Only costs and revenues that will be different as a result of the adoption of the proposal should be included. The concept of earnings should be broad enough to encompass intangible and often unquantifiable benefits. When these have to be omitted from the formal earnings-estimates, they should be noted for subsequent appraisal of the project.

3. *Durability of earnings.* The duration of the benefits from a promotional investment has a vital effect on its rate of return.

   Economic life of promotion depends (a) on frequency of purchase; (b) on loyalty-life-expectancy, that is, longevity of customers; (c) on gestation period of the purchase decision; and (d) on erosion by the promotional efforts of rivals.

   For advertising investments, durability is often the most difficult dimension of project value to quantify. But the problem cannot be avoided. Some estimate is better than none; and estimates can be improved by well-directed research.

4. *Risks and imponderable benefits.* Appraising the risks and uncertainties associated with a project requires a high order of judgment. It is only disparities in risk among projects which need to be allowed for, since the company's cost of capital reflects the overall risks. Although measurement of this sort of dispersion is difficult, some headway can sometimes be made by a necessarily arbitrary risk-ranking of candidate projects or categories of projects.

   Most projects have some added benefits over and above the measurable ones. If excessive weight is given to these imponderables, then there is danger that rate-of-return rationing will occur. When a low rate-of-return project is preferred to a high one on the grounds of imponderable benefits, the burden of proof clearly should rest on the imponderables.

*Concepts of Measurement.* For calibrating these four determinants of return on investment, what concepts of measurement are needed? Four are particularly useful:

1. *Alternatives.* The proper benchmark for measuring added investment and the corresponding added earnings is the best alternative way to do it.
2. *Futurity.* Future earnings and future outlays of the project are all that matter.

3. *Increments.* Added earnings and added investment of the project alone are material.
4. *Cash flows.* After-tax cash flows (or their equivalents) alone are significant for measuring capital productivity.

1. *Alternatives.* There is always an alternative to the proposed capital expenditure.

   The alternative may be so catastrophic that refined measurement is unnecessary to reject it; but in any case, the proper benchmark for the proposal is the next profitable alternative way of doing it.

2. *Futurity.* The value of a proposed capital project depends on its future earnings.

   The past is irrelevant, except as a benchmark for forecasting the future. Consequently, earnings estimates need to be based on the best available projections. The outlays and earnings need to be estimated year by year over the economic life of the proposed promotion, and their time shape needs to be taken into account explicitly.

3. *Increments.* A correct estimate of both earnings and investment must be based on the simple principle that the earnings from the promotional proposal are measured by the total *added* earnings by making the investment, as opposed to *not* making it . . . and that the same is true for the investment amount.

   Project costs should be unaffected by allocation of existing overheads, but should reflect the changes in total overhead and other costs likely to result from the project. No costs or revenues which will be the same, regardless of whether the proposal is accepted or rejected, should be included and the same goes for investment.

4. *Cash flows.* To be economically realistic, attention should be directed exclusively at the after-tax flows of cash or cash equivalents which will result from making the promotional investment.

   Book costs are confusing and immaterial. But taxes do matter, because advertising investments are favored over depreciable investments in after-tax rate of return.

*Yardstick of Financial Worth.* The productivity of capital in a business investment is the relationship between its earnings and the amount of capital tied up. To measure this productivity for promotional investments, we not only must have a correct conceptual framework of measurements, but also must choose the most appropriate yardstick of investment worth.

The concept of advertising as an investment already has some limited acceptance in new-product introduction. The measure of productivity of capital often used is the payout period–a crude yardstick. The cutoff criterion is also set rather arbitrarily to get the original outlay back in two years or three years. Such standards have no objective justification as compared with corporate cost of capital.

What is the best yardstick of economic worth for investments in persuasion? Clearly, the yardstick that is economically appropriate for investments in promotion is true profitability as measured by discounted-cash-flow analysis.

1. *Discounted-cash-flow analysis.* The discounted-cash-flow (DCF) method is a new approach to measuring the productivity of capital and measuring the cost of capital.

   The application is new, not the principle. Discounting has long been used in the financial community, where precision and realism are indispensable. The essential contributions of discounted-cash-flow analysis to management thinking about investment in promotion are three:

- An explicit recognition that time has economic value—and hence, that near money is more valuable than distant money.
- A recognition that cash flows are what matter—and hence, that book costs are irrelevant for capital-decisions except as they affect taxes.
- A recognition that income taxes have such an important effect upon cash flows that they must be explicitly figured into project worth.

   The discounted-cash-flow method has two computational variants.

   The first is a rate-of-return computation, which consists essentially of finding the interest rate that discounts gross future after-tax cash earnings of a project down to a present value equal to the project cost. This interest rate is the rate of return on that particular investment.

   The second variant is a present-value computation which discounts gross future after-tax cash earnings of all projects at the same rate of interest. This rate of interest is the company's minimum acceptable rate of return. This should be based on the company's cost of capital. Special risk should be reflected either by deflating project earnings or by adjusting the cutoff rate for projects of different categories of risk. The resulting present-value is then compared with the project cost investment. If the present value exceeds it, the project is acceptable. If it falls below, it is rejected.

   In addition, projects can by this variant be ranked by various kinds of profitability indexes which reflect the amount or ratios of excess of present value over project cost.

   Both variants of the discounted-cash-flow approach require a timetable of after-tax cash flows of investment and of gross earnings which cover the entire economic life of the project.

   In practice, the timetable can be simplified by grouping years in blocks. For projects for which investment is substantially instantaneous and gross earnings are level, simple computational charts and tables can be used to estimate the discounted-cash-flow rate of return directly from estimated economic life and after-tax payback. For projects with rising or declining earnings streams, this conversion is more complex.

2. *Superiorities of DCF.* The discounted-cash-flow method of analysis is particularly needed for measuring the profitability of promotional investments, for two reasons.

   First, the outlays are usually spread out. Second, benefits, mainly incremental profits from added sales in the future, are always spread out and usually have a non-level time-shape.

The superiorities of discounted-cash-flow analysis over rival yardsticks for measuring the productivity of capital in promotional investments are imposing:

- It is economically realistic in confining the analysis to cash-flows and forgetting about book-allocations.
- It forces guided thinking about the whole life of the project, and concentration on the life-time earnings.
- It weights the time-pattern of the investment outlay and the cash earnings, so as to reflect real and important differences in the value of near and distant cash-flows.
- It reflects accurately and without ambiguity the timing of tax-savings.
- It permits simple allowances for risks and uncertainties, and can be adapted readily to increasing the risk allowance over time.
- It is strictly comparable to cost-of-capital, correctly measured, so that decisions can be made quickly and safely by comparing rate of return and the value of money to the firm.

*Rate-of-Return Rationing.* How should rationing of capital work for persuasion-investments?

Rate-of-return "battling" among capital proposals is the essence of capital rationing. The standard of minimum acceptable profitability should (after proper allowance for special risks and for imponderables) be the same for all, namely, the company's market cost-of-capital or its opportunity cost-of-capital, whichever is higher.

Market cost-of-capital is what the company probably will pay for equity and debt funds, on the average, over the future. For a large publicly-held company, this cost can be measured with adequate precision for rationing purposes. There is no better cutoff criterion.

Opportunity cost-of-capital is the sacrificed profit-yield from alternative investments. Only when a company refuses to go to market for funds can its opportunity costs stay long above market cost-of-capital.

## PRACTICAL VALUES

Will putting advertising in the capital budget do any good?

Granted that as a matter of economic principle much advertising and other forms of promotional spending are investments . . . and granted also that conceptually correct and pragmatically proved techniques for optimizing investment outlays are available for promotional investment . . . the question is whether this sophisticated and powerful mechanism, applied to promotional investments, will have any practical value.

Most business investments are not made in ignorance of their probable impacts, whereas, many of the outlays for persuasion now are. Characteristically, the amount and timing of the effects of advertising are unknown. The duration of their impact on economic life is unknown, and the probabilities of effectiveness are also unknown. Quite possibly, attempting to estimate these unknowns cannot improve overall results.

The problem of how much to invest in promotion can be solved either by intuitive and perhaps artistic processes, or through a more formal and more systematic study of objective evidence. Quite possibly men of experience and good judgment can determine how much the corporation should invest in promotion by subjective judgment, regardless of whether advertising is formally put in the capital budget. This article is nevertheless confined to a consideration of ways in which sophisticated economic models and systematic quantitative study can help to find the appropriate size of the appropriation for corporate persuasion.

## IN SUMMARY

1. Much advertising (and other corporate persuasion) is in economic reality partly an investment. The investment-mix varies over a wide spectrum.
2. Investments in promotion are different from conventional capital expenditures; but these distinctive characteristics do not disqualify promotion for investment treatment.
3. Profitability must be the basic measurement of the productivity of capital invested in promotion. Despite the multiplicity of conflicting corporate goals, the overriding objective for decisions or investment of corporate capital should be to make money.
4. The main determinants of profitability of an advertising investment that need to be estimated are the amount and timing of added investment and of added earnings, the duration of advertising effects and risks.
5. The measurement concepts of capital productivity that must be estimated are future, time-spotted, incremental, after-tax cash flows of investment outlays and of added profits from added sales.
6. Discounted-cash-flow (DCF) analysis supplies the financial yardstick most appropriate for promotional investments. By comparison, payback period, although widely used, has no merit.
7. Advertising belongs in the capital budget. Promotional investments should be made to compete for funds on the basis of profitability, that is, DCF rate of return.
8. The criterion for rationing scarce capital among competing investment proposals should be DCF rate of return. The criterion of the minimum acceptable return should be the corporation's cost of capital—outside market-cost or internal opportunity-cost, whichever is higher.
9. Putting advertising into the capital budget will not perform a miracle. Judgment cannot be displaced by DCF analysis and computers. But judgment can be economized and improved. The most that it can do is to open the way for a research approach which is oriented to the kind of estimates that are relevant and that will permit advertising investment in promotion to fight for funds on the basis of financial merit rather than on the basis of personal persuasiveness of their sponsor.
10. An investment approach to produce practical benefits will require fresh concepts, substantial research-spending, and great patience.

# VI

## *Appraising and Controlling the Marketing Program*

*The last steps in the administrative process—control and reappraisal of the marketing program—provide the link for commencing the administrative process anew, so that in a sense it is a "never-ending circle."*

*However, control procedures cannot be set up and reappraisals made of the marketing function without adoption of certain objectives for a comparison of results. Thus, the concern of a business firm should be control of objectives, plans, and organization, for far too often the notion of controls is thought of as applying to individuals only.*

*Both control and reappraisal in marketing have always provided extremely difficult problems, because so much of what is done in marketing can be viewed only as a combination of activities. Unlike the situation in the physical sciences it is difficult to "break out" the effects of a single variable (for example, advertising). But over the past few years some progress has been made in evaluating the effects of certain marketing actions, as the readings in the present section show.*

*A precise statement of objectives and the development of a written plan of action are extremely important in the control of marketing activities, even if the* exact *contributions of each element in the plan cannot be made.*

*The marketing concept places great emphasis on profits. The mounting costs of marketing and the use of computers have encouraged an increased flow of information about profitability with respect to such subjects as individual accounts, types of accounts, products, product lines, salesmen, and sales districts, thereby enabling corrective action to be taken quickly. This means, of course, that distribution cost accounting will most certainly assume greater importance in the future.*

# 60. MEASURING THE COST AND VALUE OF MARKETING

*Stanley C. Hollander*

*One important aspect of control is the measurement of inputs and outputs over a given time period. This has always been difficult to accomplish with respect to most marketing activities.*

*This article discusses the complexities and frustrations of evaluating the cost and value of marketing.*

When did marketing begin? When were the first criticisms of marketing voiced? We do not know the answer to either question, but we can be certain of two things. One is that the function of marketing, that is, trade and exchange, has been part of the human economic system for many thousands of years. The other is that criticisms and defenses of trading activities are almost as old as trade itself. In 1776, these criticisms provoked a thundering answer from Adam Smith:

> The statute of Edward VI, therefore, by prohibiting as much as possible any middleman from coming in between the grower and the consumer, endeavoured to annihilate a trade, of which the

AUTHOR'S NOTE: The author wishes to acknowledge his debt to a former teacher, Professor Reavis Cox of the University of Pennsylvania, whose work and lectures have shaped many of the thoughts expressed herein.

Source: From *Business Topics,* vol. 9. Summer, 1961, pp. 17–27. Stanley C. Hollander: Professor of Marketing, Graduate School of Business Administration, Michigan State University.

free exercise is not only the best palliative of the inconveniences of a dearth, but the best preventative of that calamity: after the trade of the farmer, *no trade contributing so much to the growing of corn as that of the corn merchant.*[1]

Smith declared: "The popular fear of engrossing and forestalling [buying for resale] may be compared to the popular terrors and suspicions of witchcraft."[2] Today the fear of witchcraft seems to have abated; it has been many years since books attacking witches made the best seller lists. But the persistent popularity of books attacking marketing suggests that the fear of engrossers and forestallers has not vanished. The attacks have, of course, aroused a ready response, and the marketing journals have been filled with criticisms of the critics, interspersed with a modicum of self-criticism.

As is true of most such debates, the discussions have tended to generate considerably more heat than light. Only in fairly recent years have we had any really serious attempts to measure both the costs and the benefits of marketing in our society. The dearth of such studies is not the fault of the many serious and well-intentioned people who have debated the value of marketing. It is simply an indication of the complexity and magnitude of the problem.

## A PRODUCTIVITY ANALOGY

The difficulty of measuring marketing productivity may be illustrated by attacking a comparable problem: attempting to measure the productivity of a magazine article. An examination of the silent postmortem in which you will indulge after finishing this or any other article will suggest some of the difficulties we face when we try to evaluate the marketing system.

In either case we are trying to determine a ratio. On the one hand, we have the inputs into the system, the social and individual contributions of the product or process; and on the other hand, we have the outputs—the social and individual benefits. If the benefits are high in proportion to the inputs, we describe the article, the product, or the system in question as *highly productive.* But if the ratio is low, then the system is not very productive. The concept is simple to state; the real problems arise when we attempt to apply it.

*Types of Input.* The reading experiences that provide the final tests of a magazine article's value result from two major categories of inputs. One group consists of those supplied by the publisher and the people and firms associated with him. These include the work of paper and ink manufacturers, printers and production craftsmen, the postal service and the newsdealers, editorial employees, illustrators, and even authors. Supposedly the value of their services is measured by the prices and wages these contributors receive during the process of assembling and distributing the magazine. But this

[1] Adam Smith, *The Wealth of Nations,* Modern Library edition, Random House, New York, 1937, p. 499. Emphasis supplied.
[2] *Ibid.,* p. 500.

supposition involves a number of assumptions to which we will want to return shortly. Magazines, like every other product and service, present a number of unique problems in social cost measurement. For example, publications that derive much of their revenue from advertising may incur heavy production and promotional expenses so as to attract the readership that will attract advertising, which in turn, may, in various ways, affect the prices and sales of the commodities advertised. Under such circumstances it is often difficult to determine the exact inputs provided by each participant. A similar quandary arises out of the eternal debate between the publishers and the postmasters-general over the relationship of postal charges to the costs of furnishing postal services.

Another group of inputs is extremely important and many of these are often overlooked. These are provided by the readers, and include their time and effort as well as whatever they may pay, directly or indirectly, for the publication. These inputs are analogous to the time, effort and money expended by consumers in both the shopping and the consumption process. And, from the standpoint of the individual consumer, these are the personal costs that must be balanced against the personal benefits.

*Simple Evaluation.* Let us start with the simplest version of this problem; the individual judgment each one of you will make after finishing this article. Undoubtedly, you will ask yourself whether it has been worth reading or not. Not *how* worthwhile, or *how* it compares with other things you might have read instead, but simply, "Am I pleased or not that I decided to take the time to read this article?" This is the sort of judgment that we all make frequently. Yet notice how often our reactions are ambivalent. We say of some experience or book or lecture, "I guess it was worthwhile," or "I don't know–it wasn't too bad," or "I'm rather glad I read it, and yet maybe I could have used the time more profitably."

Now it is no wonder that our judgments are sometimes vague. To decide that reading a particular article, or engaging in any other activity, is worthwhile involves a very complex accounting process. Very few of us have enough time to do all the things we would like to do, or to read all the things that we would like to read. The segments of time that we invest in reading a particular article may be especially precious segments, on a busy day or when there are many alternative activities clamoring for our attention. Then again, the time may consist of minutes spent in the dentist's anteroom, when there is little else that we can do and when we really only want a little intellectual anaesthesia before climbing into the chair. The article may demand considerable attention and intellectual effort, which we may consider as output, as a source of enjoyment (witness the pleasure many people derive from solving puzzles) or, under other circumstances and at other times, we may consider as input, as an unwarranted drain on our energies. The benefits of our reading are elusive and subtle. We may obtain intellectual exercise, new insight, stimulation and entertainment. Or our reading may prove stultifying, boring, or misleading. All of this we have to balance in some rough and ready fashion before we can say whether the magazine was, or was not, worthwhile.

*Complexities of Evaluation.* However, this is still at the kindergarten level in productivity evaluation. Let us look at two more problems of greater complexity. One arises out of the fact that such rough balance sheets are really inadequate for comparative purposes or for social appraisals. Suppose, in the course of a year, that each of us reads two hundred magazine issues. Each issue consumes its own combination of time, money and energy; each yields its own patterns of information, insight and entertainment. How can we compare these two hundred; can we rank them in an ordinal line, and will our judgments be consistent each time that we express them? How can we add these two hundred patterns into a composite figure if we want to compare this year's reading with last year's, or with the magazines we read ten years ago? How can we make comparisons between, say, the magazines published in the U.S. and those published in other countries, or between publications issued under various auspices? What measures can we use to quantify either the inputs or the outputs, and how do we relate them to each other? It is perfectly apparent that these considerations are frivolous and frustrating, yet this is exactly the sort of problem we face when we try to make comparative judgments about the productivity of marketing.

But the problem is still more complex. Magazine articles are written in the hope of reaching large audiences. Each member of that audience is an individual. Each has his own standards, each has his own alternative ways of spending his time, each seeks his own particular satisfactions and ends. None is a replica of the others. In evaluating the effectiveness of an article, how can we add all of their tastes, inclinations, and judgments into a single composite whole? Shall we regard one person's intense pleasure as the equivalent of several people's mild displeasure? Shall we allow extra, or reduced, weight in our calculus to the connoisseurs, to those who are the most sensitive to small differences, or to those whose swings on the manic-depressive axis are the widest?

## WEIGHING THE COSTS

Conceptualizing and evaluating are equally difficult in any attempt to aggregate all of the inputs and outputs of a complex economic system. Given certain assumptions and conditions, it is relatively easy to measure the physical results of highly specific, small operations. For example, it is not too hard to determine which of two machines is more efficient at punching out sardine cans. This may involve some judgments about the relative cost of labor, capital and raw materials in the future. For example, one machine may be more efficient at low levels of output and the other at high levels, so some judgments have to be made about the nature of future demand for sardine cans. But practical, workable estimates can be made, and some of these judgments work out fairly well. Similarly, we can compare two different methods of putting those sardine cans on the supermarket shelves, subject to some assumptions as to the total number of cans to be stacked, the cost of labor, and the alternative uses for the stockmen's time in the store. But the only available measure, aside from miscellaneous hunches, guesses and opinions, of whether the whole operation is worthwhile is whether enough people buy those sardines to warrant allocating the social energies necessary to produce canned sardines instead of something else.

There seem to be only two measures by which we can evaluate the total inputs into the total marketing system. One is hours of labor, the other is monetary costs. Both have their limitations.

*Labor as a Measure.* Labor hours are not all homogeneous, and hence we have a problem if we try to use number of hours worked in marketing as the measure of marketing cost. How can we properly equate an hour of time worked by an unskilled laborer with an hour of time spent by a highly trained engineer or architect? They are both human beings. Moreover, the job that is assigned to the laborer may be far more burdensome than the work performed by the professional. But each hour of the skilled man's time represents an expenditure of the human capital invested in training, and so, in a sense, constitutes a higher cost than does an hour of common labor. The problem can be resolved through evaluating each hour of labor at its actual wage or salary rate, but this approach leads into the monetary problems we will face in a moment. Another difficulty, of somewhat less significance, bothers the statisticians who try to compute labor productivity figures. They argue whether it is more accurate to use actual hours worked as the labor investment, or whether paid vacations, holidays and sick leaves should be added. The issue is often described as the question of hours worked versus hours paid for. (Although it would drive the statisticians crazy, conceptually one might be justified in including some portion of the future hours to be spent in paid retirement as part of this year's "labor paid for.")

Another problem is more difficult. The number of hours invested in marketing measures, at any one moment, only a portion of the total cost of the system. Our economy also draws upon natural resources and upon the capital that the past has produced. We can only equate units of capital and units of labor by converting them to a common factor—their monetary value. This again leads us to the problems inherent in applying monetary measures to marketing input.

*Money as a Measure.* Some of these problems are technical in nature. For example, should we evaluate the capital equipment used in any one year on the basis of its original cost, original cost minus depreciation (and if so, at what rate), cost to reproduce, or cost to replace with modern equipment? How shall we measure the labor of unpaid family workers? What shall we do about deferred compensation? More basic problems center around two major assumptions that underlie the use of monetary costs as a measure of input. When we use monetary costs expended in the private sector as our measure, we are, in effect, assuming that the government's contribution to marketing, which is considerable, is roughly equal to the net tax burden (also considerable), that is levied upon marketing. If the contribution and the taxes are unequal, then one party is, in a sense, contributing more to the bargain than it derives from the other. Our other assumption is that the costs represent free market values, that each dollar earned represents equal sacrifices, that each dollar spent obtains equal pleasure, and that there has been no exploitation of any of the participants in the system.

But there is an even more fundamental problem. The U.S. Census uses a monetary concept, "the value added by manufacturing," to measure the output of the manufacturing industry. The value-added figure is obtained by subtracting the total cost of the materials (and some services) that manufacturing industry purchases from the total amount of its sales. Many writers now advocate using a similar concept in marketing. A moment's reflection, however, shows that this concept of output is roughly equivalent to a monetary cost measure of input. Profits are usually a relatively small portion of the total figure and certainly are, at least in part, the price of certain managerial and enterpreneurial services. So, under this accounting, input and output will always be roughly equal.

*Consumer Satisfaction.* The most difficult part of the whole business is to measure the real output of marketing. In spite of all talk about motivation research, hidden persuaders and the like, we really seem to know very little about what people want from the marketing system. An example from retail distribution may help to illustrate this point.

One school of thought holds that most people look upon stores very largely as places in which they can obtain merchandise. According to this point of view, people consider shopping as a nuisance, and are most satisfied when they can obtain their purchases with minimum expenditures of time, money, and effort. Some interesting experiments with shopping games and with records of consumer behavior tend to substantiate this view, although the results are by no means conclusive.[3] On the other hand, there is the view advanced by many motivational researchers and by some very successful merchants, that people like to shop. The advocates of this position maintain that shopping is an end in itself, apart from the goods that are purchased, and that the retail system should be designed to maximize the pleasures of shopping.[4] Now, of course, no hard and fast election can be made between these two approaches. Much depends upon the customer, the products being purchased, the place and the time. Some people seem to react to shopping differently than others.[5] Most people will display one attitude when buying antiques, and another when purchasing a tube of toothpaste. Some people, who normally try to rush in and out of the supermarket, will be willing, when traveling, to spend hours in the quaint native marketplace, probably much to the annoyance of the natives. If we have only ten minutes in which to catch a plane, we want the airport newsstand to have our favorite magazine readily accessible; if we have two hours to kill between planes we like the airport bookstore that permits uninterrupted browsing. But even after allowing for all of these differences, we find that a fundamental question for both managerial strategy and social evaluation in retailing has been answered only indifferently and on an *ad hoc* basis.

[3] Wroe Alderson, *Marketing Behavior and Executive Action,* Richard D. Irwin, Inc., Homewood, Ill., 1957, p. 183.

[4] See, for example, Pierre Martineau, *Motivation in Advertising,* chap. XV, "A Store Is More Than a Store," McGraw-Hill Book Company, New York, 1957, pp. 173–85.

[5] An interesting classification of shoppers appears in Gregory P. Stone, "City Shoppers and Urban Identification," *American Journal of Sociology,* July, 1954, pp. 36–45.

The devices for identifying and measuring consumer satisfaction in any general sense are limited to votes in the marketplace, which is probably the most significant single argument for a free marketplace.

## COST RESEARCH

A few unusually dedicated analysts have attempted to measure the costs of marketing in our society, in the face of all the difficulties we have noted and in spite of a number of technical obstacles we have not considered. In general, these people have been well aware of the problems and limitations inherent in their work. But they have felt that even a rough approximation of the actual figures would be ample reward for the herculean labors involved in such a task.

*Stewart and Dewhurst.* By far the best known single study of this sort is *Does Distribution Cost Too Much?* (New York: Twentieth Century Fund, 1938), a study conducted by Professors Paul W. Stewart and J. Frederic Dewhurst under the sponsorship of the Fund. Stewart and Dewhurst worked with census figures on purchases and sales, and other data, to trace the 1929 flow of commodities in this country from original sources (agriculture, importation, and extractive industries) to final buyers (consumers, institutions, public utilities, and export) via such intermediate levels as manufacturing and trade. Increases in value resulting from transportation and from wholesale and retail trade were assigned as costs of marketing; increases at the manufacturing level were apportioned between marketing and processing. Stewart and Dewhurst estimated that, in 1929, final buyers absorbed $65.6 billion worth of finished tangible goods, of which three-fourths, or $19 billion, went to individual ultimate family consumers. These figures do not include the consumption of services, such as hircuts, medical attention or personal transportation. Total marketing costs for this $65 billion worth of goods were estimated at $38.5 billion.

In other words, according to this analysis, retailing, wholesaling, transportation, advertising, selling and other marketing activities took 59 cents out of every consumption dollar spent on goods or tangible commodities. This figure, which as we shall see has been subjected to some very serious criticism, included marketing and transportation expenses at all levels. Thus, it embraced practically all of the selling and distribution expenses involved in transferring cotton to the yarn spinner, in transferring cotton yarn to the fabric weaver, and in transferring fabric to the shirt manufacturer, as well as the marketing costs involved in moving finished shirts to the consumer. Stewart and Dewhurst were careful to point out that their figure, 59 cents, was meaningless unless it was compared with what distribution did in return for its compensation. They also were careful to point out that a more efficient manufacturing system, turning out large quantities and obtaining economies of scale, would necessitate a more complex marketing system. Nevertheless, in reading their report one can sense a sort of physiocratic bias, a feeling that changes in form utility ought to be relatively more costly than changes in time, place and posession utility.

*Barger Study.* In 1955, Harold Barger, relying on the vast data collections assembled by the National Bureau of Economic Research, published his study *Distribution's Place in the American Economy since 1869* (Princeton: Princeton University Press, 1955). This is generally regarded as the most authoritative work yet published on the subject. Barger limited his analysis to wholesale and retail trade, and did not include manufacturers' marketing costs, as did Stewart and Dewhurst.

Barger was not overly impressed with distribution's performance in some respects. He concluded, for example, that labor productivity per man hour increased in commodity production at an annual rate of 2.6 per cent per year from 1869 to 1949. Contrasted with this, he found that productivity in distribution went up only 1 per cent per year. The analysis is somewhat limited, since the measure used, total volume handled, does not allow for changes in functions performed. However, probably most of the difference is due to the greater relative application of machinery and other forms of capital in manufacturing than in trade.

However, he did find that wholesaling and retailing accounted for only about 35 to 36 cents out of the consumer's dollar in 1929. Since he was working with only a portion of the total distributive activity for that year, rather than with the whole, we should expect his figure to be smaller than the Stewart and Dewhurst 59 cents. However, most analysts, including Barger, believe that part of the discrepancy is really a correction of the old figure, that would reduce it by an indeterminate amount, perhaps 8 or 9 cents.

*Cox Study.* For the last several years Reavis Cox and some of his associates at the University of Pennsylvania have been conducting an investigation of marketing costs to serve as a companion to, or as a revision of, the Stewart and Dewhurst study. Their work has not yet been published, although it should be released in the near future. Cox gave an advance presentation of some of their findings at the 1960 meeting of the American Statistical Association. There he disclosed that an analysis of the Bureau of Labor Statistics' massive input-output table for the U.S. economy in 1947 revealed that ultimate consumers that year took $96 billion worth of goods, of which $41 billion, or about 43 per cent, went for distribution *activities.* This figure included the marketing expenses incurred by manufacturing firms, as well as the marketing activities of the distributive industries, i.e. wholesalers, retailers, transportation agencies and advertising agencies. The distributive industries themselves accounted for about 31.1 per cent of the final value of all consumption goods, and a considerably smaller portion of the total final value of consumer services.[6]

*Department of Agriculture.* In addition to these three studies and many smaller scale attempts there has been the massive work of the U.S. Department of Agriculture in measuring what it calls "marketing margins" for agricultural products. Unfortunately for our purposes, the Department uses the word "marketing" to embrace almost

[6] 1960 *Proceedings of the Business and Economics Section, ASA,* American Statistical Association, Washington, D. C., 1961, pp. 319–22.

everything that can happen to agricultural products once they leave the farm. It determines its so-called marketing margin for consumer food products by subtracting the farm value of raw foodstuffs and by-products from tne final retail value of agricultural foods. This margin thus includes, for example, both the cost of grinding wheat into flour and the cost of baking bread. The procedure is somewhat analogous to saying that the cost of manufacturing Ford cars is part of the cost of marketing iron ore.[7]

The economists who prepare the USDA marketing margin reports are always extremely careful in explicitly stating just what is included in their figures, although the same cannot always be said for the people who use those figures in political debate. But the agricultural definition yields results which simply are not comparable to the marketing cost studies we have examined, however useful the Department's work may be for other purposes. In 1939, for example, the Department said that 63 per cent of the consumer's farm food dollar was absorbed by marketing costs, a slightly higher figure than has been reported for the last several years. Professors Beckman and Buzzell of Ohio State University reanalyzed the 1939 figures and found that just about one-third of the total 63 per cent was the cost of processing prepared and semi-manufactured foods. The true marketing cost was about 41 per cent, a figure much closer to those reported in the Barger and Cox studies for consumer goods in general.[8]

## THE ACTUAL OUTPUT

But even the most accurate marketing cost figure is relatively meaningless until it is compared with the work performed by marketing. Much of that work, as we have noted, consists of intangibles that resist quantification, and so we do not have an output figure to set against the cost percentage. But it is an inescapable fact that a dynamic, high level economy involves a very considerable amount of marketing work. Even the Soviets, who have not been outspoken admirers of our marketing system, are beginning to pay us the compliment of imitation as their own economies emerge from the subsistence level. The western world is just beginning to notice such communist developments as a conference on advertising methods held in Prague in 1958, and attended by delegates from the Soviet Union, East

[7]The Department does usually make one reasonable but inconsistent adjustment in these figures. Consumer expenditures for restaurant meals are adjusted down to the retail store value of equivalent foodstuffs. The work of a restaurant chef is not treated as marketing, but the work of a cook in a frozen food plant is. In this connection though, it is only fair to say that increases in the sales of prepared food, the so-called "built-in maid services," fall short of explaining all of the recent changes in farm marketing and processing margins. Finally, we may note that in a recent unofficial study, two leading USDA economists added farmers' costs for machinery and purchased supplies into the total marketing margin reported for farm food products. Frederick V. Waugh and Kenneth E. Ogren, "An Interpretation of Changes in Agricultural Marketing Costs," *American Economic Review,* May, 1961, pp. 213–27.

[8]T. N. Beckman and R. D. Buzzell, "What Is the Marketing Margin for Agricultural Products?" *Journal of Marketing,* October, 1955, pp. 166–68.

Germany, Albania, Bulgaria, Poland, Czechoslovakia, Hungary, Rumania, Yugoslavia, China, Mongolia, North Korea and Vietnam.[9]

Dr. E. D. McGarry, of the University of Buffalo, has provided the best statement of what constitutes the actual output of marketing.[10] He lists six major functions of marketing which may be summarized as follows.

## Six Functions of Marketing

*The contactual function:* the searching out of buyers and sellers. This is a not inconsiderable task. A typical supermarket may carry five to six thousand items produced by hundreds of different processors.[11] One study of twelve representative drug stores found that each carried an average of 1,300 proprietary items (minerals, vitamins, patent medicines, etc.) alone, out of a selection of perhaps 20,000 or 30,000 such items produced for distribution through drug stores.[12] The American consumer draws upon a selection of literally tens, perhaps hundreds, of thousands of items. An elaborate and often unnoticed mechanism is needed to maintain contact between all of the people who use and produce both these items and their components, supplies and equipment.

*The pricing function:* in our society, the principal device for allocating our supply of scarce resources.

*The merchandising function:* the work of gathering information about consumer desires and translating it into practicable product designs.

*The propaganda function:* "the conditioning of the buyers or of the sellers to a favorable attitude toward the product or its sponsor." This is the most criticized of all the marketing functions. But probably few will dispute the need for some activity of this sort to support an economy in which consumption rises above subsistence and in which the advantages of scale are obtained through mass production in advance of sale.

*Physical distribution:* the brute job of transporting and storing goods to create time and place utility.

*The termination function:* something of a catch-all category, that includes both the process of reaching agreement in the case of fully negotiated transactions, and all of the contingent liabilities that remain with the seller after delivery takes place.

[9] Lazlo Sonkodi, "Advertising in a Socialist Economy," *Cartel,* July, 1959, pp. 78–79. Sonkodi's source is, interestingly enough, a publication called *Magyer Reklum*, i.e. *Hungarian Advertising.* For a discussion of other Russian Marketing developments, see Marshall Goldman, "Marketing–A Lesson for Marx," *Harvard Business Review,* January–February, 1960, pp. 79–86.

[10] "Some Functions of Marketing Reconsidered," in Reavis Cox and Wroe Alderson (eds.), *Theory in Marketing,* Richard D. Irwin, Inc., Homewood, Ill., 1950, pp. 263–79.

[11] "The Dillion Study," *Progressive Grocer,* May, 1960, p. D18.

[12] Burley, Fisher and Cox, *Drug Store Operating Costs and Profits,* McGraw-Hill Book Company, New York, 1956, p. 263.

Since many of these functions are concerned with intangibles, facile evaluation of marketing performance seems unlikely, and perhaps impossible, even for the future. Probably room will always exist for debate concerning both the objectives of marketing and the means used to achieve these objectives. We may be certain that our present methods are not perfect. We may well anticipate the development of new and better techniques for the performance of many marketing tasks. Nevertheless, even though their work resists quantification, marketers need not apologize for their share of the consumer's dollar.

# 61. THE MARKETING EXECUTIVE AND MANAGEMENT INFORMATION SYSTEMS

*Arnold E. Amstutz*

*This is a discussion of the characteristics of successful management information systems in use by operating and policy managers concerned with the marketing function.*

*A four-part framework for evaluating information systems is suggested and representative systems are examined within its context. Finally, the management implications of on-line, real-time, and micro-analytic, simulation-based, system structures are also discussed.*

This paper is concerned with the present state of the art in market-oriented management information and control systems and the impact of these systems on policy and operating management. As such, this discussion will be narrowly focused. Normative questions of what management should or should not expect or obtain from an information system will not be considered.

*Objectives.* The two major objectives of this paper may be simply stated as:

1. To identify relevant characteristics of successfully implemented management information and control systems.

Source: Raymond M. Haas (ed.), *Science, Technology, and Marketing,* Chicago: American Marketing Association, 1966, pp. 69–88. Arnold E. Amstutz: Assistant Professor of Management at the Sloan School of Management, Massachusetts Institute of Technology.

2. To evaluate the impact of representative systems on the managements they were designed to serve.

*The Process of System Evolution.* It is seldom possible to impose a pre-packaged information system on a management group. There are no generalized management information systems. Each company's management has unique information requirements; a unique perspective on the environment within and outside of their firm; unique priorities; and a style of management which is the unique product of the particular personalities making up the management group. Successful system development is a matter of evolution. Effective management systems will evolve over time as management and system specialists learn to communicate, structure problems, and achieve a joint focus on increasingly broad information needs.

The process of designing and developing a management information system to meet the requirements of a particular management's decision style makes significant demands on management time and thought. If the resulting product is to be compatible with management's perspective, priorities, and systems of measures, management's models of the decision environment must be made explicit and used as the basis of system design. In addition, management must evaluate the implications of alternative system structures in terms of criteria which only they can supply. Intelligent choice between alternatives must be based on management's understanding of the implications of available structures. In order to achieve understanding the manager must take the time necessary to become familiar with the management implication of basic system design concepts.

## DIMENSIONS OF EVALUATION

No two managements have the same information needs. As indicated earlier, the characteristics of systems developed for different managements are as different as the managers' personalities, the problems they face, and their approach to the complex art of management. Despite these differences it is possible to identify sets of dimensions for use in evaluating specific systems and isolating similarities and differences between systems. Figures 1 and 2 illustrate four such dimensions.

*Information Recency.* The first dimension, information recency, refers to the time lapse between occurrence of an event in the environment and inclusion of data describing that event in the system. This may range from several weeks in the case of certain market developments to a few hours or minutes for automated inventory control.

*Information Aggregation.* The second dimension, information aggregation, describes the detail with which information is maintained in system data files. Inventory control systems in which information regarding product components or sub-assemblies is maintained at the item level are representative of relatively disaggregated (micro) data maintenance while industry market share statistics of the type developed through trade associations are representative of highly aggregate (macro) measures.

As illustrated in Figure 1, there is normally a relationship between level of aggregation and the time delay involved in incorporating associated data in the system.

*Analytical Sophistication.* The third dimension, analytical sophistication, refers to the sophistication of models or structure encompassed by the system. As illustrated in Figure 2, the lowest level of analytical sophistication is that required to identify a particular file and record. At this level it is only necessary for the computer to retrieve the specified record and display the information which it contains. The second level of analytic sophistication involves aggregation–gathering together numbers from within one or more records to produce a total or subtotal. At the third level the computer may be programed to perform arithmetic averaging or to compute differences. The fourth level, logical analysis, introduces the use of classification schemes through which various types of data are aggregated within sub-sets or conditionally segmented.

At the fifth level of analytical sophistication statistical analyses may be employed to develop extrapolations from historic data, statistical best estimates, analyses of variance, or trend estimates.

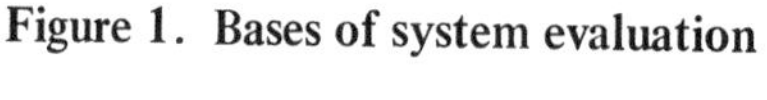

**Figure 1. Bases of system evaluation**

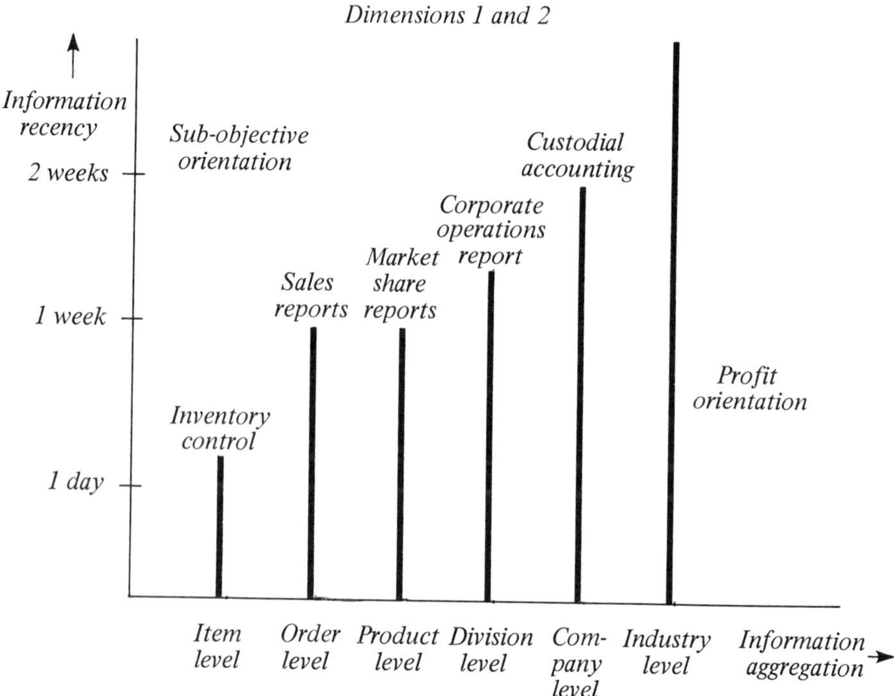

**Figure 2. Bases of system evaluation**

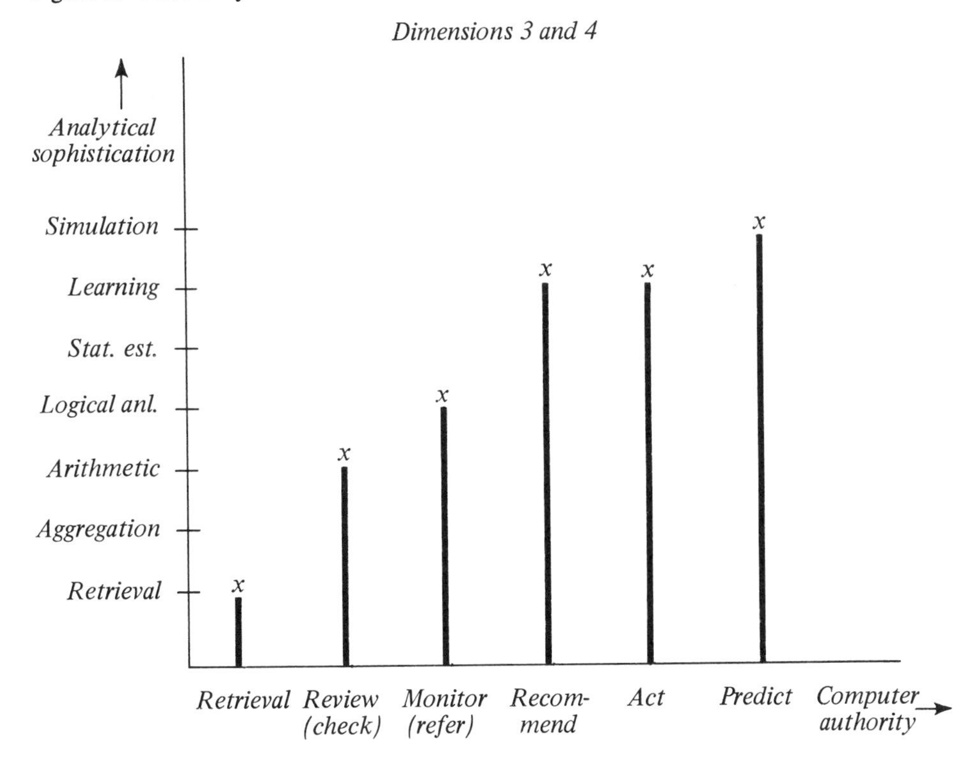


The term "learning" is used in Figure 2 to indicate adaptive system processes through which the computer is programed to modify parameter values or model structures on the basis of experience (data inputs received) over time.

At the most advanced level of analytic sophistication, simulation models on which the system is based constitute an artificial environment paralleling real world markets referenced by the information systems. The manager's perception of the environment has been explicitly modeled to a sufficient extent and detail to justify the assumption that the models making up the simulated environment duplicate in all relevant aspects the response pattern of the real world environment monitored through the information system. Inputs to the information system are directly related to process variables in the simulation models. At this stage in development the system provides management with the capability of testing proposed policy and strategies in the simulated environment; choosing between alternatives on the basis of resulting output; implementing the policies in the real world environment; and evaluating the effectiveness of implemented plans through the information system. The manager references the simulated environment to ask "What if?" and the information system monitoring the real world environment to determine "What is?".

*Computer Authority.* The final dimensions of system evaluation, authority delegated to the computer, is closely associated with the system's analytic sophistication. Management is more willing to delegate authority to sophisticated systems and, conversely, as management places greater demands on an information system, a greater level of analytic sophistication must be embodied in the system structure.

At the lowest level, management may delegate to the computer authority to retrieve information from specified records and files–entrust to the computer system processes associated with identification and retrieval. Once a retrieval capability has been established it is usually a short step to the next level of computer authority. Recognizing that the computer has access to all records in the file, management concludes that while the computer is "looking at" the contents of each record it might as well check the reasonableness of record content to insure against gross clerical errors. At this stage the computer is delegated a supervisory function checking on human personnel responsible for input.

As management comes to accept computer review for purposes of error detection, they normally begin to think in terms of other functions which the computer could perform "while looking at all those records." It follows quite naturally to have the computer perform additional analyses on records already being reviewed and to refer for further review and action situations meeting criteria established by management.

Management frequently finds that certain classes of monitor output are consistently subjected to additional analyses to determine whether or not action is warranted. In such situations it is natural to suggest that the computer be programed to perform the additional calculations in order to add a recommendation for action to the monitor report.

As management gains experience with computer-based recommendations they may find that in most situations they are able to implement computer recommendations without further investigation. Criteria may be modified to isolate non-typical cases requiring additional review. The computer is then given authority to take action on the remaining cases in which its recommendations are a valid basis for action.

The hierarchy of Figure 2 suggests that delegation of authority to predict involves a higher level of management dependence on the computer than authority to act. While the models on which the computer bases its action normally involve prediction, the potential impact of computer-based prediction is often greater than computer action. Computer-originated actions may adversely affect the firm's position at a point in time. However, actions relate to the operating sphere while predictions are the basis for planning. Thus, inaccurate prediction may have a damaging effect on the firm's activities for months or years while erroneous actions can be corrected in days or weeks.

The chance for successful computer-based prediction is ironically reduced by the very nature of management-computer interaction. Since predictions are often based on relatively sophisticated models, management is frequently hesitant to accept the computer's prognostication until they have gained experience with the system and had an opportunity to "see how well it does." With the passage of time management's satisfaction with predictions which are verified by subsequent experience increases. However, as time passes the modeled environment may change—the original models may become less and less applicable. Finally at that point when management is ready to take action based on the computer's predictions, the models may be completely outdated and no longer accurately represent the decision environment. When this happens the stage is set for disillusionment or worse. It is considerations such as these which argue strongly for management involvement in the system design process, familiarity with system structure, and understanding of models on which system decisions and predictions are based.

## CHARACTERISTICS OF SUCCESSFUL SYSTEMS

While specific functions performed by successful systems are as varied as the managements to which they contribute, four common characteristics of successful systems, or perhaps more correctly the environment in which successful systems operate, can be noted.

1. The system is founded on management's conception of the decision environment.
2. The user-manager understands the system structure.
3. The system is based on disaggregated data files.
4. System development has proceeded to increasing levels of sophistication through a process of gradual evolution.

*Management's Conception of the Environment.* If a system is to provide meaningful information to a particular management it must reflect that management's priorities and provide information of a type and in a form which is assimilable in the context of existing management decision processes. In most situations this requirement specifies that the information must be selectively generated—management is simply incapable of assimilating reams of paper—and must be based on accepted measures—output must relate directly to management conceptions of processes occurring in the monitored environment.

In order to meet this requirement an information system must be based on explicit models of the environment provided by management. In most instances management's initial system definition is stated in qualitative "business terms." Before meaningful specifications can be established, this frequently vague and ambiguous initial statement must be refined and restated in explicit terms. Factors considered relevant in the decision environment must be defined and differentiated from those to be excluded.

*Management Understanding.* Management must be involved in this quantitative specification of system boundaries. They must understand and accept the conceptual structuring of system requirements in terms sufficiently explicit to define the measures and analytical procedures to be encompassed by the system. If this level of communication is not achieved, it may be impossible for those concerned with system formulation to develop a system which will be used.

But, it may be argued, this means involving management in wholly unacceptable detail. "Management is appropriately concerned with the big picture. It is unrealistic to expect them to become involved in questions of measurement." The response to this objection is to reiterate the area of eventual system application—matters of company policy. It is difficult to conceive of a point in the decision-making process at which involvement is more warranted than in insuring precise description of the decision structure—unambiguous system specification.

The process of explication often uncovers the not altogether surprising fact that various members of management have different implicit conceptual models of the decision environment. Making these models explicit removes the ambiguities which permit vague words to mean different things to different people. Alternative representations are proposed and necessitate the creation and validation (or rejection) of more than one model.

As with any other specialized tool the information system must be carefully designed to meet the specific requirements of the craftsman who will use it and the user must understand its function and capabilities. There is no such thing as a generalized information system. It is difficult to conceive of a more specialized and highly segmented market than that for management information. The products which have gained acceptance in this market have been one of a kind special orders produced with careful attention to the needs and preferences of the ultimate user.

*The Disaggregated Data File.* At the heart of every successful information system is a disaggregated data file—a file in which information is maintained in detailed time sequence as it is generated. As new inputs are received they are maintained along with existing data rather than replacing or being combined with existing information. As a result, structural biasing through aggregation which destroys much information value is avoided.

The disaggregated customer file contains the name, address, demographic, and financial experience records for particular consumers. Each transaction is recorded in chronological order in the file so that at any point in time it is possible to recreate the company's interactions with each consumer over time. In a similar manner the product file is organized to reference a detailed chronological sales record.

The importance of a disaggregated file rests in part on the evolutionary process through which successful information systems develop. Although an information system may initially be designed to perform strict limited functions, as management gains experience, these functions change. If data are initially structured (aggregated) to meet first stage requirements, later modification of the system's functions necessitates costly file reorganization.

The existence of a disaggregated file facilitates system evolution. Given access to detailed chronological data, the manager is able to test new concepts and ideas against historical data asking the question, "What would have happened if we had used these criteria in our monitor system—performed this analysis to isolate actionable situations?" In the first stages of system development it is simply impossible to anticipate the direction of later advancement. Aggregate data files may preclude highly profitable system modification. The disaggregated data file provides the flexibility which is the prerequisite of intelligent system evolution.

*Design for Evolution.* Successful information systems are designed to permit expansion and change. As indicated above, the disaggregated data file is a key element in system flexibility. In addition, data files must be designed to permit expansion. Variable, rather than fixed record length file structures and self-expanding file constructs are basic to the well planned system.

As management gains experience in working with well organized and accessible data they become increasingly interested in and prepared to use more advanced analytical procedures. The system's analytical structure must not preclude this advancement. Programs must be organized to permit experimental use of new techniques as well as the permanent incorporation of additional capabilities as part of the standard system configuration.

## EXAMPLES ILLUSTRATING BASIC CONCEPTS

The remainder of this discussion will be devoted to examples illustrating system concepts associated with the management impact of information systems. On a previous occasion, the author presented a paper to the American Marketing Association describing a basic marketing information system developed for use by a small electronics company introducing a new product to a difficult-to-define market.[1] A relatively simple retrieval system that performed basically repetitive clerical operations and data organization was reviewed. Building upon this earlier work, consideration in the balance of this paper will be given to the impact of system conversion to on-line operations and the introduction of monitor, advisory, and decision-making functions. The impact of real time information acquisition and micro-analytic simulation will also be considered.

*An On-Line Management Information System.* The term "on-line" relates to systems in which direct man-machine communication is made possible by the use of remote access consoles through which management may interrogate or, given appropriate programs, interact with the computer. The point-of-origin device is generally a teletype or comparable typewriter-based machine; however, in some more recent systems, video display consoles utilizing a television-like display unit in lieu of paper output

[1] "A Basic Marketing Information System—A Case Study in the Economical Use of Computerized Management Information Systems," a talk presented to the American Marketing Association Meeting in Dallas, Texas, June 16, 1964.

have been employed. The use of television displays facilitates the rapid presentation of extensive displays. In most instances the manager using a display unit of this type has the option of obtaining hard copy through ancillary printers.

The on-line system may directly parallel the off-line or batch process system with the remote access console serving the same function as the card reader or input tape unit in the batch system—communicating to the computer the desired report format and source references. With the introduction of direct access the problem of communication language must be considered. The language problem is obviated in batch processing since clerical personnel code requests for card input. It is, of course, possible to continue using the card code structure on-line. The manager requesting information must then type onto his console the same information punched in the batch process request card. Since card codes are designed to be economically communicated and directly read by the machine, this coding procedure requires that the manager work in terms of numeric code structures. While not an impossible requirement, this type of communication can be very frustrating.

Simpler communication is frequently achieved through the use of control words or function keys. In this case the manager uses a function specifier such as CHART, DISPLAY, or CALCULATE to indicate the action to be taken by the machine or presses a "function" key which generates the desired process code. The function specifier is then followed, usually in relatively strict format, by a series of nouns and adjectives indicating the data source on which the desired report is to be based. The statement "DISPLAY BRAND X SALES, 6/1/61–12/31/61, DOLLARS, UNITS, MONTHLY" is representative of this type of request.

From the executive's point of view, the easiest form of communication is achieved when the machine can be programmed to accept "free form English language requests." The language is never totally free form in that the machine has a limited vocabulary—it is assumed that the person communicating with it will limit himself to a pre-determined set of topics. In the absence of strict formatting, there is a danger of ambiguity leading to misunderstandings between manager and computer. However, proper preparation of report formats insures that the manager is made aware of that which the computer thought he wanted. If the report content indicates that the computer is "confused," the manager restates his request using a different word order or a more explicit statement. With experience, the manager learns to avoid ambiguous expressions. In the interest of efficiency, he is apt to develop the habit of communicating with the machine in relatively strict format despite the "free form" capability.

The output illustrated in Table 1 was obtained via an on-line console (in this case a teletype machine) interrogating the retrieval system. In this instance the manager has typed the request, "REPORT DISTRIBUTOR ACTIVITY FROM SEPTEMBER 1965 THROUGH OCTOBER 1965." The computer has interpreted the word "ACTIVITY" to mean "sales and estimated profit." This definition is consistent with management's emphasis on providing profit computations whenever sales figures are given.

**Table 1. On-line output – example 1**

*Report distributor activity from Sept. 1965 thru October 1965*

*Sales and estimated profit*

| | | |
|---|---|---|
| *SEP* | | |
| Distributor 1 | 1170.53 | 399.95 |
| Distributor 2 | 649.63 | 238.77 |
| Distributor 3 | 755.08 | 284.51 |
| Distributor 4 | 1066.97 | 348.56 |
| Distributor 5 | 541.01 | 197.43 |
| *OCT* | | |
| Distributor 1 | 990.63 | 327.04 |
| Distributor 2 | 567.18 | 186.53 |
| Distributor 3 | 707.95 | 218.86 |
| Distributor 4 | 850.51 | 297.83 |
| Distributor 5 | 520.11 | 189.10 |
| Ready | | |

Table 2 illustrates a second request and the corresponding computer response which demonstrates another aspect of system design. Although not evident to the reader unfamiliar with file content the interrogation requesting "company" information in fact provided data applicable to only one region of the firm's operations and a limited portion of the product line. Through the use of a password convention the system had previously established the identity of the inquiring individual. The information displayed in response to the word "COMPANY" was at the highest level of aggregation to which this individual had access on the basis of pre-determined priorities. In this instance the figures relate to the regional level for those product lines which are the legitimate concern of the individual originating the inquiry. This type of security control insures that each individual using the system will have access only to data which is relevant to him. Through the use of aggregation structures which interpret limiting words such as "company" in context of a need-to-know hierarchy the system designer may insure that, once correctly identified by the computer, the president making a request for "value of company inventory" will receive actual balance sheet figures while

**Table 2. On-line output – example 2**

*Ready*
*Report company quarterly sales, profit from first 1965 thru third 1965*

| | *Sales* | *Gross profit* |
|---|---|---|
| Quarter 1 | 149660.55 | 34184.92 |
| Quarter 2 | 114589.05 | 28875.66 |
| Quarter 3 | 73799.81 | 21130.12 |

Ready

the custodian making a similar inquiry will be given the value of janitorial supplies on stock.

*A Monitor System.* Without expanding the system's capability measured in terms of the first three dimensions of evaluation, management may elect to grant additional authority to the computer by developing programs which enable it to monitor the content of all accessed files. In taking this step, management is delegating to the computer authority for review and referral. The information system is used to implement a policy of management by exception with the computer directed to review all relevant data and refer to management only those situations which meet previously established criteria.

Installation of a monitor system introduces a new class of management problems. Policies must be formulated for computer implementation. Vague descriptions of "the sort of situation we are looking for" must be reduced to explicit definitions of that which will constitute an exception appropriate for referral. These specifications must indicate the data to be reviewed, frequency of review, and criteria of selection.

Table 3 illustrates one type of monitor report obtained by adding those capabilities to the retrieval system. This report indicates that the computer has encountered a situation in which a statistically significant, adverse sales trend has been established in one outlet of a particular distribution channel class while other outlets in that same class are showing a favorable trend.

*The Advisor Function.* If management is willing to go beyond the specification of criteria for referral and establish procedures to be followed when specific situations are encountered (e.g. write a letter, schedule a salesman call) the computer may be programed to recommend an appropriate course of action. System expansion to encompass this function implies movement along two of the previously specified dimensions. Additional authority must be delegated to the computer system and, in most instances, more complex analytical programs must be developed and tested. The implications of alternative policies are frequently examined by using historical data to establish the recommendations which would have been generated had each policy been implemented during a past time period.

**Table 3. Sample monitor output**

*Monitor report*

Product –

Basis – dollar sales trend

Dates covered – 01/01/64–0/08/64

Channel – electronic supply.

Outlet –

| | | | |
|---|---|---|---|
| Avg. channel sales | 800. profit | 250. trend | +46. |
| This outlet | 210. | 62. | -34. |

*The Decision Function–Direct Computer Action.* Once management gains sufficient confidence in the quality of computer-based recommendations they may extend the authority granted the computer one step further along the delegation dimension illustrated in Figure 2. The computer may be permitted to take the recommended action (e.g. write the letter or send the order) subject to intermittent review by supervisory personnel.

From a systems standpoint, differences between the advisory and decision-making functions are small–it is as easy to program the computer to write a letter as to generate a report indicating that a letter should be written. However, from management's point of view, the relative impact of the computer is greatly increased once it is given the authority to act on behalf of the company. There is great solace in knowing that someone with whom we share human sensitivities is going to determine whether or not action should be taken. Management has an at-times justified fear of what an unattended computer might do if left to its own resources.

Successful implementation of decision systems is a result of management understanding of the procedures controlling the computer's action and careful specification of the precise level of authority granted the computer–the specific situations in which it is permitted to take particular actions. In some situations management requires approval by supervisory personnel of computer-based actions involving a commitment of resources above a certain level or the generation of communication beyond a specified point. In all instances, management establishes orderly review procedures to be followed as part of a continuing assessment of computer-based actions. Just as policies implemented by human subordinates are reviewed to determine their continuing applicability, it is necessary to insure that models governing computer actions continue to be applicable to changing market conditions.

*Learning Through Simulated Experience.* Given access to a detailed disaggregated data file and a flexible program structure, management is able to test the effect of alternative analytical approaches under historical conditions–to determine what would have happened if a particular decision procedure had been employed during the period of simulation.

In simulating past conditions, the computer at the point of decision, has no more information than it would have had were it making its decision at that moment in the then existing environment. Data following the point of decision are totally unavailable and the system must function on the basis of analyses of conditions existing at the decision time and historical records of conditions which prevailed prior to that time. As the computer moves through simulated time, information becomes available only when it enters the simulated time period when the information was generated. Through this process, years of hypothetical operating experience may be simulated in a few months of research. Following extensive testing of alternative criteria, the decision procedures which yield the highest performance in terms of previously defined measures are implemented in the operating system.

*Real Time Data Acquisition.* The concept of real time process control is not new. It normally involves a situation in which some aspect of the production process is to be monitored to determine whether or not specified conditions are being met; evaluated to determine whether corrective action is required; and, when required, modified to establish the desired conditions. The basic elements of a real time system are:

1. A means of sensing the environment.
2. A conditional referral procedure.
3. A feed-back mechanism permitting the environment to be changed.

The development of real time information systems has not been simple. Although the basic concepts of real time process control are, at first blush, applicable to information system design, conditions motivating real time management information acquisition are not always clear.

At the present time, managers are faced with hardware capabilities which greatly simplify real time access. Rapid data acquisition has improved the quality of airline reservation services, inventory control, and environmental surveillance systems. There is, however, a natural temptation, aggravated by the pressures of computer salesmen, to apply the real time capability in situations where there is no need for real time data acquisition. Movement in the direction of real time processing is along the information recency dimension of Figure 1 in the direction of shorter time lags between event occurrence and system notification of the event. More rapid file updating is not necessarily harmful. However, the emphasis on recency created by the real time capability can cause management to give undue attention to recent events while ignoring more significant long-term trends. It is ridiculous for a management to be concerned, for example, if sales in a particular region between 10 o'clock this morning and 2 o'clock this afternoon are off by 5 per cent from sales during the same period last week.

*Simulation-Based Information Systems.* Systems discussed in the preceding sections have, for the most part, been based on relatively simple arithmetic or statistical models relating limited data from the marketplace to a single, dependent, performance measure. Since the planning and implementation of marketing programs involves the coordination of many types of management activity, information systems have been designed to make use of micro-analytic behavioral simulations of the market environment. Two characteristics of the marketing decision structure strongly motivate the use of simulation-based systems.

1. Controlling conditions in the market are a function of complex human behavior and responses.
2. Management must influence actions and responses in the market through persuasion since they are unable to exert direct control.

Management information systems based on micro-analytic market simulation generally focus on the processes through which management attempts to influence behavior in the market. The models on which such systems are based encompass detailed representations of retailer, distributor, salesmen, and consumer and industrial purchaser behavior as well as competitive interactions in the environment external to the firm.

The data files associated with these information systems encompass measures of the extent and nature of inputs to the market environment generated by the company and its competitors. The objectives in developing a simulation-based information system are to achieve an artificial (model-based) environment structured to accept inputs of the type monitored by the information system, and to generate outputs comparable to those obtained from the real world environment.

Figure 3 illustrates the structure of a simulation-based information system. Inputs from the market environment are reviewed and formatted by a pre-processor system before being transferred to the master data file. The data file serves as the reference source for the information system and provides the historical data base for simulation model initialization.

Management has the ability to interrogate the data file directly and obtain responses following procedures comparable to those associated with the basic retrieval system discussed earlier. This set of interactions is noted by A in Figure 3. Management's use of the simulation model as a basis for testing proposed programs is illustrated by the interaction set indicated by B. Proposed plans are inputted to the information system which establishes hypothetical conditions for runs of the simulation model. Results obtained in the simulated environment are transferred to the information system which formats them for presentation to management. Following this process, management is able to evaluate the conditional results of proposed programs using the same procedures and equipment employed to assess the current state of the market through traditional interrogation.

Once a program has been finalized, the proposed plan is established as a reference, and simulated measures based on the plan are generated for use by the monitor sector of the information system. As the plans are implemented in the market environment, actual measures of market performance are compared with simulated measures indicating the expected results of planned implementation. Significant deviation from plans becomes the criterion for monitor referral to management as indicated by C in Figure 3. The information system may be used to evaluate the results of research activities as well as operating plans, as indicated by D.

Development of a micro-analytic simulation involves procedures comparable to those followed when developing less complex models. However, due to the structural detail, the extent of management involvement required in order to achieve the pre-conditions of successful system implementation are greatly increased. Model development begins with management's definition of system scope and the objectives to be achieved through system use. Initial specifications establish boundary definitions for the simulated environment. As the development process continues, increasingly detailed descriptions of

Figure 3. Simulation-based system structure

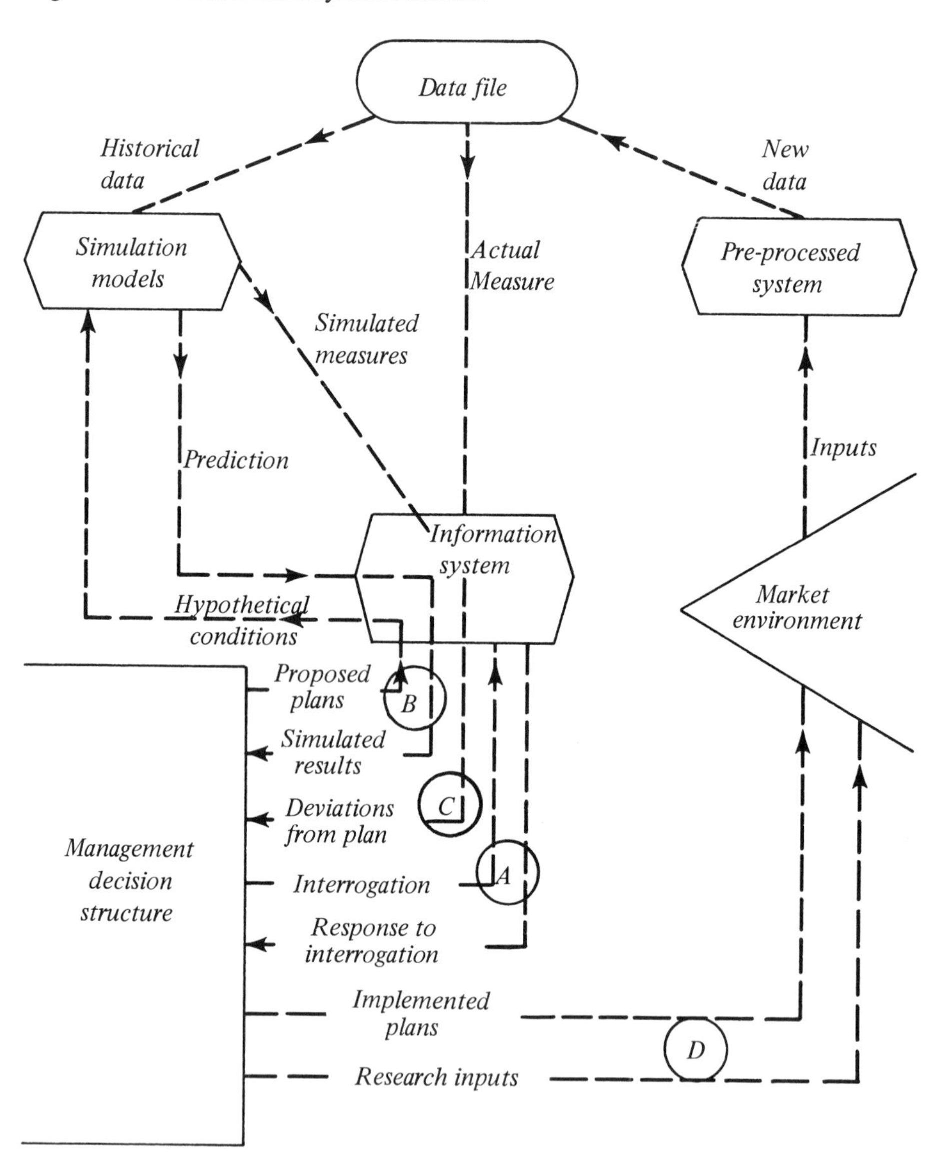


behavior within key sectors of the environment and interactions between sectors are established. Models are designed to facilitate the simulated generation of measures referencing key backlogs, delays, and transfer points at which the rate of product, information, or value flow may be monitored. Key decision and response elements are identified and factors influencing these processes are delineated. Hypothesized relationships between inputs and observable behavior are formulated in terms of measurements which permit validation of the model against data from the real world. Once validated at the function level, decision and response formulations are combined in a simulation structure encompassing artificial populations exhibiting actions and responses covered by these formulations.

The behavior of population groups within each simulation sector is described by accumulating simulated individual behavior. Population behavior may be summarized in terms of the proportion of purchases allotted to each brand (brand shares), changes in population attitude distributions towards brands, or any other measures encompassed by the real-world information system. Once the simulation models have been validated to management's satisfaction the simulation structure may be used to produce outputs over time comparable to those received as input from the real-world market environment.

## SUMMARY

This paper has examined characteristics of successful management information systems in use by operating and policy managers concerned with the marketing function. It has focused on the attributes and impact of representative systems. Four dimensions of information systems evaluation have been suggested: (1) information recency, (2) level of information aggregation, (3) analytic sophistication, and (4) degree of computer authority. Representative systems performing retrieval, monitor, advisory, and decision functions have been examined in the context of this dimensional framework. Management implication of on-line, real-time, and micro-analytic, simulation-based, system structures have also been discussed.

# 62. BETTER MANAGEMENT OF MARKET INFORMATION

*Kenneth P. Uhl*

*If one studies the organization charts of all but the most astute marketing-oriented firms, it would be found that the marketing information department is "dangling" at the edge of the chart, well-removed from the rest of the firm's service departments. In fact, most business firms do not have a centralized information department at all, but rely on each function of the business to conduct its own fact-finding in its own way.*

*Following is a statement of the case for the centralized information office, whose director "has the obligation to be authoritarian when more than advice is needed" regarding information. Production and finance data, as well as marketing data, could be collected by the information office, thus ensuring a free flow of information throughout the organization.*

Many executives have been dismayed to discover that corporate excellence in production and finance alone has not led to success. Excellence in marketing is also needed. As a result, the marketing function has been elevated to the vice-presidential level, and many firms have begun to orient their activities to their customers' needs. It has been hoped that this increased emphasis on marketing, popularly called the marketing concept, would promote the needed marketing excellence—but all too frequently

Source: From *Business Horizons,* vol. 9, Spring, 1966, pp. 75–82. Kenneth P. Uhl: Associate Professor of Marketing, University of Iowa.

it has not. Instead, marketing problems have continued to grow larger and become more difficult.

Attempts at solutions have been many, and successes have been few. A common response has been to restructure marketing organizations. Older and simpler line-and-staff structures have been strengthened with more staff specialization and changes in titles and authority bases. Multiproduct firms have created merchandising offices and have experimented with brand managers or product managers. Multimarket firms have experimented with varying degrees of geographical decentralization and have installed various territorial marketing managers who have been charged with profit responsibility.

But success has been spotty, at best, and improvement is still needed. This author's contention is that the handling of marketing information must be better managed—and the focus is on how to do it.

To begin, extensive rethinking is required about both the use and the management of marketing information in the firm. In terms of use, management must insist on planning, organizing, directing, and controlling the marketing function through information as a replacement for "management" by intuition. This means that necessary information must be both available and used.

In terms of management, the old separate segments of intradepartmental information programs are largely unmanageable as composite programs. Instead, new facilities and new organizational structures must be envisioned and installed. The need for such correction has been overwhelmingly obvious to executives who have gained control over production, finance, and other areas through the development and use of information programs.

Similar, if not greater, gain can be accomplished in marketing. Enough has been learned by some firms to indicate that marketing fat can be converted to muscle through the development and use of adequate marketing information programs. The need for marketing information improvements is obvious; the emphasis here will be on plans and programs to bring about such improvements.

## MARKETING INFORMATION ENTITY

The basic structural weakness in virtually every ill-informed firm has been the absence of one entity for processing marketing information. Such firms have been typified by the presence of uncoordinated bits and pieces of the information function scattered here and there. Marketing information as an activity has seemed to be everywhere; it has belonged to no one and has received little development and use by these firms. As a result, they do not consider marketing information an activity that is manageable or even worthy of management. The marketing concept has not been developed sufficiently to make management see the need for composite marketing information systems.

A fundamental requisite for better managed marketing is that the scattered information activities be both perceived and managed as an entity. That is, these activity components must be (1) identified throughout the organization, (2) thought of as being parts of a whole, and (3) managed as an information unit.

These components, furthermore, must be managed through a single, separate, and centralized office. One director must be responsible for the entire marketing information program in all of its scattered locations. Through such an arrangement all marketing information activities can be managed as a system—a system which by its very nature must circulate and function internally and wherever the firm wishes to market its offerings.

There is no single precise description of the activities, responsibilities, and authorities of marketing information offices, nor is there one organizational arrangement that is patently superior to all others. Some broad guidelines, however, can be applied to a multitude of specific situations.

## ESTABLISHING AN INFORMATION OFFICE

The office of marketing information must assume broad and pervasive responsibilities. Specifically, it must be responsible as consultant, coordinator, and controller for each of the basic marketing information components—searching/securing, analyzing, transmitting, storing, and using. Some difficulties do result, particularly because of the traditional treatment of the marketing information function.

The last component, the *using* function, is the most demanding and the least aided by recent technological advances in information handling. Basically, to manage the using function, the director's office must know who needs what information, when, and why. Knowing "why" is essential if the office is to serve as both manager and consultant. The office must make known to users the firm's information resources, including their costs,[1] it must be able to evaluate information requirements and requests and to moderate and temper those which appear unreasonable. To do this the office must have the capacity to discern which offices should have what information. It must also be able to consult with using units relative to what information they should be using and how they should use it. In other words, to information users, the office should be synonomous with both marketing information and its effective use. The director serves as a consultant to the organization, though, like the company attorney, he has the obligation to be authoritarian when more than advice is needed. Finally, the using component dominates and dictates to the information system. The system exists solely to facilitate better management—better management through more and better information availability and use.

The components of *searching/securing, transmitting, analyzing,* and *storing* must be completely under the guidance of the marketing information office. These four

[1] Some of the problems of cost and benefit estimating are discussed in R. S. Alexander, "Let's Have a Marketing Research Done," *Journal of Business,* Seton Hall University, December, 1963; David W. Ewing (ed.), *Effective Marketing Action,* Harper & Brothers, New York, 1958, pp. 219–23; and Wroe Alderson and Paul Green, *Planning and Problem Solving in Marketing,* Richard D. Irwin, Inc., Homewood, Ill., 1964.

components, while different in form, are similar in how they should be managed. The overall task of the office is to see that each component is present in correct capacity, properly allocated in the organization, and performed with necessary efficiency—all relative to the needs of the using units. In other words, the office must see that there is not too little or too much searching/securing, transmitting, analyzing, and/or storing capacity relative to the using needs of the organization, and that capacity is properly allocated and efficient. Continuing audits of the information components relative to users' information requirements provide the information office with the guidance it needs for the management of the marketing information function.

This is not to suggest that all four of these activities should be performed by the information office. Clearly, it would be a most unusual organization and situation in which these four components could be centralized within an information office or any other single office. Their management must be centralized, but the actual operations are likely to be located in many different departments. Each activity should be located where it can be performed most efficiently, relative to the needs of the using units.

Some of the activities must be largely centralized in the information office, while others can be performed far more efficiently in a number of locations. For example, at a minimum, the information office must serve as a central information index and know rather precisely what information is available and where. In this case, information may be stored in various locations throughout the firm. However, random access memory storage units, computers, and electronic transmission facilities have opened up new possibilities for massive centralization of information storage.[2]

About the same statements can be made about information analysis. Simple analysis encourages performance in securing and using units. However, more complex, more difficult, or more burdensome numerical problems suggest the advantages of centralized analysis and use of specialists and computer facilities. Also, more complex, non-numerical analysis calls for use of specialists. A case in point is the type of analysis and synthesis performed by brand managers in developing advertising proposals. And a not-to-be-forgotten objective of the information manager is to get each necessary information component performed efficiently. This goal requires, among other things, seeing that each is performed by the correct unit.

The searching/securing and transmitting components must be carefully controlled because of their diverse and widespread nature. Gerald Albaum, an information research expert at the University of Arizona, has clarified the diverse nature of information by classifying it into two categories: planned and unsolicited.[3] The planned type can be assigned to various offices based on source contacts and searching/securing capacity. Where these do not permit use of noninformation offices, these supply components

[2]While numerous articles and books are available, a single publication containing views of both academicians and businesmen is: George P. Shultz and Thomas L. Whisler (eds.), *Management Organization and the Computer,* The Free Press of Glencoe, New York, 1960.

[3]Gerald Albaum, "The Hidden Crisis in Information Transmission," *Pittsburgh Business Review,* July, 1963, p. 1.

can be assigned to the marketing information office. For example, a sales group may have both the capacity and the source contacts to actively search/secure and transmit information on competitive pricing patterns. In contrast, the same sales group would not have the capacity to search/secure customer segment profiles or to gage product images. These tasks, therefore, would normally accrue to a special marketing information group.

Unsolicited (that is, incidental) information, in contrast to planned information, cannot be anticipated relative to specific kind, source, timing, or availability. For example, a competitive firm may be planning to lower the price on its entire product line by 20 per cent. Receipt of this information prior to initiation of the action certainly would be useful, but is not normally available. Much marketing information cannot be anticipated.

Searching/securing and transmitting incidental information calls for (1) information sensitivity by all members of the organization, (2) transmission channels direct enough that small scattered facets have a chance for meaning and survival by reaching a central assembly point while they are still alive, and (3) in general, an organizational environment that encourages incidental information sensitivity, receptiveness, and transmission. The eyes, ears, and other senses of the organization obviously cannot be centralized. But to create the necessary environment and facilities requires centralized management of the information function.

It has been shown that a single, separate marketing information office must exist to make one person responsible for all marketing information within the company. And because both the information-using units and the supplying components are scattered, the emphasis of information management must be on coordination and consultation, but with the element of control vested in the office. The office must oversee the entire area of marketing information. The director must be concerned with company-wide management of all of the marketing information components. Parts of these components may be largely centralized and therefore under the immediate control of the information director. Others, because of their locations, must be managed somewhat less directly through numerous overlays. In this latter and more difficult control situation, the success of the information office will be largely dependent on its ability to gain recognition as the marketing information specialist.

## ADAPTING THE ORGANIZATION

Information requirements and environments of firms are somewhat diverse; no one information system or information organizational structure is able to fit the needs of all. Development of detailed and specific organizational frameworks for information offices is beyond the scope of this article, but some observations can be made about the placement of the office in the organization.

First of all, the major purpose of the organizational structure is to provide a framework that will facilitate efficient management of the firm's information function. And this problem concerns not only the marketing director and his staff, but all top corporation policy makers. Because the information function must undergo sweeping changes, extensive and penetrating rethinking is called for about frameworks that will encourage development and use of information for marketing control. This focus must not be exclusively on the marketing area, for solutions may require company-wide attention.

Three possible locations for the marketing information office merit serious consideration. Two of these, the marketing research office and the merchandising office, are within the marketing division. The third location is outside marketing in a company-wide information office. The most favorable location is determined largely by (1) the prevailing information climate (that is, the extent of development and the use and respect for marketing information) and (2) the existing marketing organizational structure. These influences will become more explicit as the location alternatives are explored.

*Marketing Research Office.* The first and the most obvious location to consider as headquarters for the marketing information function is the existing company-wide marketing research office. After all, its manager typically reports directly to the marketing vice-president, and the sole concern of such an office is with marketing information. In addition, there may be no other recognized marketing information specialist. However, these points require further examination because they hold the basic insights as to the information climate in a firm.

The company-wide research office appears, on many organizational charts, to be on a common plane with the advertising and selling functions. In practice, however, it may be deeply shrouded in the marketing organization with few people, little funds, and even less influence. In such situations, the office is probably concerned with but a small portion of the total marketing information needs of the organization. In fact, it probably is limited to problem-focused research—and only problems it can manage.[4] Also, the advertising and sales groups in such situations dominate and provide most of what little information they believe they need—and the marketing research office, if not held in contempt, is suspect, and perhaps rightly so. When this situation prevails, the company-wide marketing research office cannot be changed to the far broader marketing information office. At best, under proper nuturing, it might become a useful part of it.

On the other hand, the marketing research office may regularly provide continuing information for control and planning through sales or distribution cost analysis or both, measures of market opportunity and sales forecasts, as well as special fire-fighting help. In such cases it probably is a respected and helpful ally to the advertising and sales groups, and it may be perceived by the organization as being on at least equal footing with these groups. Unfortunately for marketing research, this sort of pattern is

[4]This point is well expressed by Lee Adler in "Phasing Research Into the Marketing Plan," *Harvard Business Review,* May-June, 1960, p. 113: "But the problems that are defined for investigation by researchers are so delimited that the findings made either deal with too small a piece of the total problem or cannot be easily related to other aspects of the total problem."

uncommon. In firms where this favorable kind of situation prevails, however, the company-wide marketing research office can be a good base for the company-wide marketing information office.

As such, the office remains an integral but expanded part of the marketing structure and reports to and draws its authority directly from the marketing vice-president. This arrangement does not gain formal company-wide integration of *all* information activities. However, such a favorable organizational orientation can foster informal and, perhaps, sufficient common and integrated use of information facilities and information.

*Merchandising Office.* The other existing location within the marketing area that can contain the orientation and capacity to develop into the marketing information office is the company-wide merchandising office. This office is normally responsible for the coordination and control of the activities of product or brand managers. These have been successful where they have been able to remedy otherwise inept marketing information programs; this they have done by determining marketing information needs, fulfilling the recognized needs, and using the marketing information in planning activities. The managers have had to become information scavengers. In light of their planning needs, they have scrambled among the existing structures and functions seeking and assembling advice and information. In brief, they have pulled the scattered information function together in behalf of each product.[5] (Their achievement of this function has been somewhat inadvertent, in that primary emphasis has been on preparation of merchandising and advertising plans and proposals.)

This shows that the successful merchandising office has had considerable exposure and experience in management of marketing information activities. For this reason firms with successful brand and product management structures can transform the merchandising office into the even broader information office. Such an information office continues to report directly to and draw its authority from the marketing vice-president. However, it is broadened to include such activities as marketing research and continuous information flows.

Not all firms containing a merchandising office should try to convert it into their marketing information office. There are two obvious blocks. *First,* many merchandising offices and their activities are too overlayed with existing structures and activities. As a result, conflicts, duplications, and ambiguities could persist and lessen the effectiveness and efficiency of the office as well as of the entire marketing organization. *Second,* the major emphasis may have been on preparation of plans and proposals—not on information as such. In such cases, the office has too little information know-how to be able to serve as the base for the company-wide marketing information office.

[5] For more extensive views of brand and product manager activities see Gordon H. Evans, *The Product Manager's Job,* AMA Research Study 69, American Management Association, 1964; B. Charles Ames, "Payoff from Product Management," *Harvard Business Review,* November-December, 1963. p. 142; and Harold Sekiguchi, "The Product Manager Concept and Its Role in Product Administration," unpublished Ph.D. disertation, University Library, University of Iowa, 1964.

In such situations, the merchandising office must be carefully examined as to its functions and capacity relative to the firm's proposed marketing information system. The needed activities must be moved into an information office and the old merchandising office removed from the structure.

*Outside the Marketing Structure.* In many firms the marketing area does not provide a suitable climate for the development or use of a marketing information office. In such firms marketing and its management simply are not far enough removed from the old sales management concepts. That is, they are not sufficiently information-oriented. This may not be obvious; organizational charts and titles may give little hint of the condition which may be marked by the following characteristics. Marketing has been granted vice-presidential status, the accompanying responsibilities of forecasting, budgeting, and planning have been grudgingly accepted and poorly performed. In addition, broad marketing research has been discouraged, and new attempts at managing marketing information consistently fail. In such cases only rudimentary marketing information is available—and the marketing managers are largely to blame. Because of their lack of ability or unwillingness to investigate new methods, managers have continued to try to guide the marketing division by instinct, intuition, or formula, even when the firm's size and pressure of competition have called for use of new tools and information. In such an environment, marketing information does not serve as a management aid.

Top management should listen no longer to excuses for this shoddy style of "management." In these situations, where intuition has run wild, appropriate marketing information programs cannot be developed solely within and by the old line sales and marketing types. Top management must cause marketing information offices to be both *developed* and effectively *used.*

A primary purpose of placing the marketing information office outside of a marketing division is to get it into a more favorable climate. The office, therefore, must be in an environment that encourages marketing information development and use; conducive to this goal is a location with other information activities. It is also true that the office must work through and have a close relationship with marketing operating units. It must have the proper base of authority, but even more important, marketing units must perceive the arrangement as being reasonable and proper. This situation is facilitated by the creation of a company-wide information office containing not just marketing information, but also information relative to production, finance, and other areas.

*Central Information Office.* To this point, poor information climates have been considered as the impetus for establishment of separate, central, company-wide information offices. In addition, however, such an arrangement offers inherent advantages that should be considered by managers whose firms already enjoy favorable information climates. Basically, the central information office offers (1) opportunities for increased efficiency, (2) greater perspective, and (3) more effective use of information—all of which contribute to better management.

Brief elaboration may provide more meaningful insight. Such a company-wide information office, reporting directly to the president, on a vice-presidential level at least, gives increased and dramatic sanction to the information function, its operation, and information use. In addition, it raises the authority base, which, while hardly replacing the need for diplomacy, aids it and improves information management.

Such an office provides greatly improved information perspective that is required to see all facets and to detect and eliminate duplication and misallocations of information components. Also, the director, with more perspective than would be possible were the office located in the marketing structure, can be a better judge of information needs, among nonmarketing units in particular. In general, increased perspective facilitates fulfillment of the responsibilities of the office.

Finally, centralization of information *management* facilitates centralization of appropriate facets of information components, which leads to increased opportunity for specialization, and increases the ability and the capacity of the information function. Basically, computer, storage, transmitter, and human facilities and know-how become more jointly available to the marketing task, as well as to all others. No one activity is isolated, but instead, advances in one, more readily become available to others through this closer integration. For example, cost accountants cannot remain concerned only with production, and computers cannot be purchased solely for financial and production needs. Both machines and men can be selected primarily because of their abilities to render the largest information payoffs; this is the purpose of company-wide information offices.

The fundamental requisite for better managed marketing is that the marketing information function be both perceived and managed as an entity. In terms of the information components, there must be a single, separate, and centralized management of the marketing information program. That is, the entire program—all of its components, all of its facets, all of its scattered locations—must be the responsibility of one director. His responsibilities must be broad and pervasive, for this control stiuation is not an ordinary one. The information director must be responsible as consultant, coordinator, and controller of each of the information components. Some of these components may be largely centralized and consequently under the direct control of the director. Others must be managed somewhat less directly through numerous overlays. In this latter and more difficult control situation, the office must gain recognition as the ultimate source of information know-how.

Three locations can be considered for the information office. Firms with strong, well-received, well-respected company-wide marketing research offices may be able to broaden them into marketing information offices. Another suitable location is the merchandising office. This office will have the best chance for success where it has had considerable exposure and experience in management of information activities. Finally, in some firms the information office simply cannot be located in the marketing structure because the prevailing information climate is just too suppressive. In such situations creation of company-wide information offices, including the marketing information office, seems to be the best way to cope with a very difficult, but all too common problem. And even firms with favorable information climates may be better able to develop and use information systems that are managed from company-wide information offices.

In the past few years much has been written about the impact that computers and other improved information handling facilities will have on organizational structures and on management. Some have viewed the advances and concluded that they will result in massive centralization with almost no middle management, while others have said that the advances will encourage the use of more decentralized forms of organization.[6]

A relevant focal point that has been implicit in this study is that the new technology—particularly information analysis, storage, and transmission—will be an immense aid to information management and, in turn, to information use. Random access memory storage units and computers and accompanying accessories and know-how will both permit and encourage (if not dictate) increased recognition of information systems, per se, as well as increased centralization of information functions. But clearly, total centralization of the system would be most unusual because of the nature of its basic components. Finally, neither massive organizational centralization nor decentralization is likely to be dictated by (1) increased use of the new technology, (2) management of the information system as an entity, or (3) increased centralization of the information system. Instead, improved information systems will facilitate many organizational forms—forms that will take their shapes based on market needs and problems, not on information restraints.

Top management's success in remedying its marketing malady through a central information office depends largely on the extent to which it is able to:

1. Locate and develop the marketing information office outside the influence of the old line marketing group,
2. Locate within the office as much of the marketing planning and control activity as is necessary to ensure effective use of the office,
3. Restrict information duplication and back-up activities in the marketing division once they are assigned to the information office (that is, allow marketing management no alternative information aid),
4. Establish a company-wide information office and structure to contain the marketing information office.

[6] For example see Edward McCreary, "Counter-trend to Decentralization: Top Management Tightens Controls," *Dun's Review and Modern Industry,* July, 1959, pp. 32–34; and Harold F. Smiddy, "Managerial Decision-Making," *Advanced Management,* November, 1958, p. 10.

# Index